Strategies for Teaching Learners with Special Needs

Seventh Edition

EDWARD A. POLLOWAY
Lynchburg College

JAMES R. PATTON
Pro-Ed, Austin, TX

LORETTA SERNA
University of New Mexico

Merrill
Prentice Hall

Upper Saddle River, New Jersey
Columbus, Ohio

Library of Congress Cataloging-in-Publication Data

Polloway, Edward A.

   Strategies for teaching learners with special needs / Edward A. Polloway, James R. Patton, Loretta Serna;—7th ed.

      p. cm.

   Includes bibliographical references and index.

   ISBN 0-13-027430-5

   1. Mentally handicapped children—Education—United States. 2. Mentally handicapped children—Education—United States—Curricula. 3. Learning disabled children—Education—United States. 4. Individualized instruction—United States. 5. Remedial teaching—United States. I. Patton, James R. II. Serna, Loretta. III. Davis, Ann Castel. IV. Title.

LC4631 .P65 2001
371.9′0973—dc21

00-028365

Vice President and Publisher: Jeffery W. Johnston
Executive Editor: Ann Castel Davis
Editorial Assistant: Pat Grogg
Production Editor: Sheryl Glicker Langner
Production Management: Holly Henjum, Clarinda Publication Services
Photo Coordinator: Anthony Magnacca
Design Coordinator: Diane C. Lorenzo
Cover Art: Laura DeSantis/Artville
Cover Designer: Ceri Fitzgerald
Production Manager: Laura Messerly
Director of Marketing: Kevin Flanagan
Marketing Manager: Amy June
Marketing Services Manager: Krista Groshong

This book was set in Garamond Book by The Clarinda Company and was printed and bound by R. R. Donnelley & Sons Company. The cover was printed by Phoenix Color Corp.

Photo Credits: pp. 2, 422, 453 by Anne Vega/Merrill: pp. 18, 289, 510 by Scott Cunningham/Merrill; pp. 62, 94, 331, 484 by Barbara Schwartz/Merrill; pp. 125, 163, 231, 263, 383 by Anthony Magnacca/Merrill; p. 189 by Tom Watson/Merrill.

Merrill
Prentice Hall

BK
$28.00

10 9 8 7 6 5 4 3
ISBN 0-13-027430-5

Dedicated
to
Dorothy K. Patton
For your love, encouragement, and strength.
You were what most strive to be.

And to the memory of
Ruth Ann Payne
For her contributions to the early editions of this text
as well as for her warmth, spirit, and generosity.

Fe
s
teach
sonal
orgai
teach
have
   As
Lear
and
tiona
relev
ory, r
teach
sente
to ac
vide
exter
and
tives
sity f
in th
prese
mate
evan
   Tl
numl
in su
the c
popt
ter ii
legisl
liver
are c
is giv
teach
next
ers'
last s
effec
the t

**TAF
ANI**

The
teach

Discover the Companion Website Accompanying This Book

THE PRENTICE HALL COMPANION WEBSITE: A VIRTUAL LEARNING ENVIRONMENT

Technology is a constantly growing and changing aspect of our field that is creating a need for content and resources. To address this emerging need, Prentice Hall has developed an online learning environment for students and professors alike—Companion Website—to support our textbooks.

In creating a Companion Website, our goal is to build on and enhance what the textbook already offers. For this reason, the content for each user-friendly website is organized by chapter and provides the professor and student with a variety of meaningful resources. Common features of a Companion Website include:

FOR THE PROFESSOR—

- Every Companion Website integrates **Syllabus Manager**™, an online syllabus creation and management utility.
- **Syllabus Manager**™, provides you, the instructor, with an easy, step-by-step process to create and revise syllabi, with direct links into Companion Website and other online content without having to learn HTML.
- Students may log onto your syllabus during any study session. All they need to know is the web address for the Companion Website and the password you've assigned to your syllabus.
- After you have created a syllabus using **Syllabus Manager**™, students may enter the syllabus for their course section from any point in the Companion Website.
- Class dates are highlighted in white and assignment due dates appear in blue. Clicking on a date, the student is shown the list of activities for the assignment. The activities for each assignment are linked directly to actual content, saving time for students.
- Adding assignments consists of clicking on the desired due date, then filling in the details of the assignment—name of the assignment, instructions, and whether or not it is a one-time or repeating assignment.
- In addition, links to other activities can be created easily. If the activity is online, a URL can be entered in the space provided, and it will be linked automatically in the final syllabus.
- Your completed syllabus is hosted on our servers, allowing convenient updates from any computer on the Internet. Changes you make to your syllabus are immediately available to your students at their next logon.

For the Student—

- **Chapter Objectives**—outline key concepts from the text

a coordinated set of activities for a student, designed within an outcome-oriented process, which promotes movement from school to postschool activities including postsecondary education, vocational training, integrated employment (including supported employment), continuing and adult education, adult services, independent living, or community participation. The coordinated set of activities shall be based upon the individual student's needs, taking into account the student's preferences and interests, and shall include instruction, community experiences, the development of employment and other postschool adult living objectives, and when appropriate, acquisition of daily living skills and functional vocational evaluation.

The amendments added two significant elements to the transition mandate. First, by age 14, and updated annually thereafter, a statement of transition service needs must be in place. Second, "beginning a least one year before the child reaches the age of majority under State law," a statement that the student has been informed of his or her rights that will transfer to the student on the age of reaching majority must be completed.

Least Restrictive Environment. Schools must educate children with disabilities—to as great an extent as possible—in general education settings with their nondisabled peers. The least restrictive environment principle provides an opportunity for students to attend school in the most inclusive setting possible, which is often defined as the general education setting (i.e., in a regular classroom). Legal trends indicate that the courts have been increasingly supportive of more inclusive placements (Osborne & Dimattia, 1994).

Parent and Student Participation in Decision Making. Parents have always been encouraged, at least legally, to participate in the special education process. Parental consent must accompany every decision that affects a disabled child. Specifically, parents must consent to the evaluation of a student's educational abilities and needs, the determination of necessary services, and the actual placement of a child in any type of special program. Parents have the right to obtain an independent educational evaluation (IEE) of their child. Parents are considered participants in the development of their child's IEP. Lastly, parents have had the right to challenge or appeal any decision related to any aspect of the special education process.

The 1997 amendments make it clear that parents are key members of the IEP team, with the same status as anyone else on the team. The amendments also strengthen efforts to increase student involvement in the decision-making processes related to their education, especially as this relates to transition planning.

Procedural Safeguards. Safeguard was included to protect both the rights of parents and their children. Parents have the right to educational records, the right to obtain an IEE, the right to request a due process hearing, the right to appeal decisions, and the right to initiate civil action when appealing a final hearing decision. New disciplinary language, particularly in relation to change of placement due to violation of school rules or code of conduct, weapons, and illegal drugs was added to the amendments.

Section 504 of the Vocational Rehabilitation Act

This section of the Rehabilitation Act has had profound effects on access for students with characteristics that have a limiting effect on their ability to learn and has greatly decreased discriminatory practices. Specifically, any students who has a physical or mental impairment that substantially limits one or more major life activities can qualify for special services under Section 504.

Perhaps of greatest importance in the 1990s has been the use of this law to provide services to students who may not be categorized under IDEA (i.e., those who require special education services per se) but who nevertheless need certain accommodations and are entitled to protection under law. Students with attention deficit hyperactivity disorder (ADHD) are most notable in this regard (Dowdy, Patton, Smith, & Polloway, 1998).

Americans with Disabilities Act (ADA)

Although the ADA implications for educational programs are virtually the same as those under Section 504, this 1990 landmark legislation is critical because it represents broad civil rights coverage for individuals who are disabled. Although the specific elements of the legislation are too numerous to list, teachers who serve as advocates for persons with disabilities should be aware that this law establishes guidelines in the following areas: employment, public accommodations, transportation, state and local governmental operations, and telecommunications systems.

EDUCATION REFORM AND SPECIAL EDUCATION

Although public education has experienced a long history of criticism, perhaps at no time did the American education system come under closer scrutiny than during the mid-1980s and the 1990s. Professionals, business leaders, politicians, parents, and other laypersons increasingly called for literate graduates, offering varying directions for change. The common factor has been that these people have been united in their demand for accountability and system reform.

A series of national commissions and reports in the 1980s was particularly strident in its support of major changes in the system (e.g., National Coalition of Advocates for Students, 1985; National Commission on Excellence in Education, 1983). A central focus of this criticism, particularly in the mid-1980s, was an increased commitment to educational rigor. Specifically, this period of educational reform called for action to raise standards and increase accountability (Michaels, 1988).

Surprisingly absent from the early calls for reform was attention to students with disabilities and to the role of special education. For example, *A Nation at Risk* (National Commission on Excellence, 1983) only indirectly addressed special education in a single brief passage:

> We must emphasize that the variety of student aspirations, abilities, and preparation requires that appropriate content be available to satisfy diverse needs. Attention must be directed to both the nature of the content available and to the needs of particular learners. The most gifted students, for example, may need a curriculum enriched and accelerated beyond even the needs of other students of high ability. Similarly, educationally disadvantaged students may require special curriculum materials, smaller classes, or individual tutoring to help them master the material presented. Nevertheless, there remains a common expectation: We must demand the best effort and performance from all students, whether they are gifted or less able, affluent or disadvantaged, whether destined for college, the farm, or industry.
>
> Our recommendations are based on the beliefs that everyone can learn, that everyone is born with an urge to learn which can be nurtured, that a high school education is within the reach of virtually all, and that life-long learning will equip people with the skills required for new careers and for citizenship. (p. 24)

While this statement may have sounded an implicit challenge to special education, there was little immediate research and programmatic attention to the effects of the reform movement on students with disabilities. This lack of attention was particularly inopportune because this time period corresponded chronologically with increasingly urgent calls for the integration of students with disabilities into general education classrooms. The reform movement led to calls for restructuring schools in various ways that are beyond the scope of this chapter. Nevertheless, the key reform element upon which special education teachers must focus is the trend toward the inclusion of students who are disabled into general education classrooms and the related implications that derive from this movement.

Inclusion

The most constant theme of reform in special education has been the continuing commitment to giving students with disabilities the opportunity to have a place in society. Figure 1–1 schematically outlines this trend, reflecting the move from relative isolation toward true inclusion. Clearly

FIGURE 1–1

Historic changes in education for students with disabilities

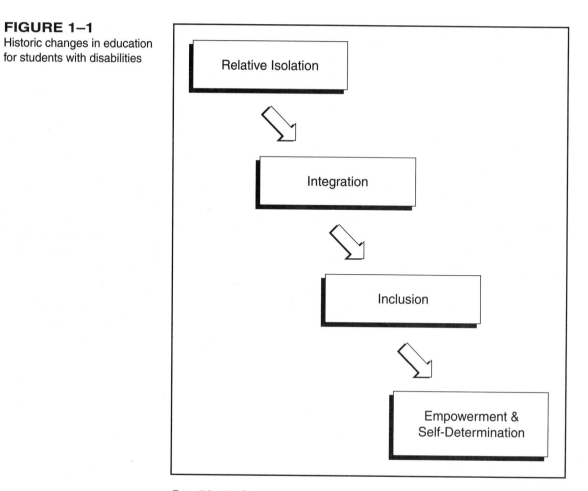

From "Historic Changes in Mental Retardation and Developmental Disabilities," by E. A. Polloway, J. D. Smith, J. R. Patton, and T. E. C. Smith, 1996, *Education and Training in Mental Retardation and Developmental Disabilities, 31,* p. 9.

the late 1980s and 1990s have represented an active period of educational history in terms of calls for increased integration of students with disabilities. Specifically, the advent of the Regular Education Initiative (REI) (e.g., Reynolds, Wang, & Walberg, 1987; Wang, Reynolds, & Walberg, 1986; Will, 1986) and the calls for full inclusion (e.g., Thousand & Villa, 1990a & b) have increased the likelihood that many students with disabilities will receive a significant portion of their instruction in the regular classroom. For example, according to *The Twentieth Annual Report to Congress,* 45.4% of all students with dis-

abilities (ages 6–21) were served in regular classes for at least 80% of the day and 28.7% in resource rooms during the academic year of 1995–96 (U.S. Department of Education, 1998).

While there may be virtually universal agreement on the importance of community integration for students with disabilities, there continues to be relatively widespread disagreement concerning the trend toward full inclusion for a given student in the schools (see Jenkins, Pious, & Jewell, 1990; Fuchs & Fuchs, 1994; Kauffman & Hallahan, 1994; Thousand & Villa, 1991; Willis, 1994). This disagreement is apparent among professional and advocacy groups (see Table 1-1). However, there remains little doubt that the role of the special education professional has changed in recent years, and dramatically so in some cases.

Teachers are encouraged to carefully consider their role in the process of facilitating the inclusion of students with disabilities in general education and in evaluating the efficacy of these efforts. The authors prefer the use of the term *supported education* (Hamre-Nietupski, Mac-Donald, & Nietupski, 1992) to the term *inclusion*. Supported education emphasizes the fact that successful inclusion hinges on the provision of appropriate supports in the general education classroom and ultimately the development of circles of support (Smull, 1994) to facilitate the success of the individual beyond the school environment.

Empowerment and Self-Determination

An outgrowth of the movement toward inclusion has been the focus on the empowerment and self-determination of individuals with disabilities. Moreover, the recent amendments to IDEA and the emphasis on the rights of students transferring to them when they reach the age of majority underscore the importance of empowering students with disabilities.

Empowerment is a multifaceted concept that embraces many essential aspects of what it truly means to be respected and given dignity. Figure 1-2 (adapted from Geller, 1991, 1994a, 1994b) provides a model to illustrate this concept.

For teachers, a commitment to empowerment as a goal involves the need to give more attention to assessing how well students are developing the ability to make choices, to become advocates for themselves, and to exercise control over their lives. The central feature is self-determination. As Wehmeyer (1992) noted:

> Self-determination refers to the attitudes and abilities necessary to act as the primary causal agent in one's life, and to make choices and decisions regarding one's quality of life free from undue external influence or interference. (p. 16)

Self-determination is a developmental process that is lifelong and one that is more difficult for people with disabilities because of stereotypes "which imply that they cannot, or perhaps should

TABLE 1-1
Inclusion positions of disability advocacy groups

Organization	Continuum of Services	Full Inclusion
The Arc (formerly Association for Retarded Citizens)	not encouraged	strongly support
Division on Mental Retardation and Developmental Disabilities (MRDD, CEC)	maintain	based strictly on individual needs
Learning Disabilities Association (LDA)	maintain	based strictly on individual needs
National Joint Committee on Learning Disabilities (NJCLD)	maintain	based strictly on individual needs
The Association for Persons with Severe Handicaps (TASH)	not encouraged	strongly support

Note. From "Mental Retardation and Learning Disabilities: Complementary Concepts or Mutually Exclusive Categories," by E. A. Polloway, J. R. Patton, T. E. C. Smith, and G. H. Buck, 1999, *Journal of Learning Disabilities.* Copyright 1995 by PRO-ED, Inc. Reprinted with permission.

FIGURE 1–2
Model of empowerment

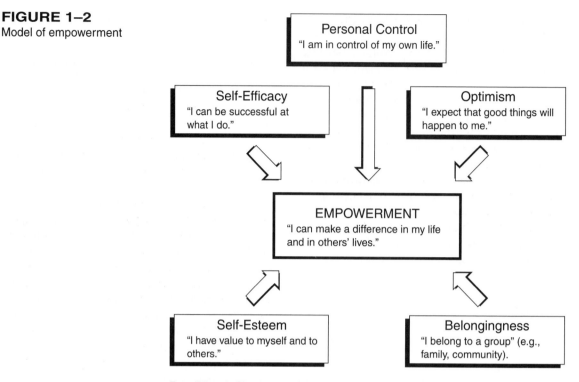

From "Historic Changes in Mental Retardation and Developmental Disabilities," by
E. A. Polloway, J. D. Smith, J. R. Patton, and T. E. C. Smith, 1996, *Education and
Training in Mental Retardation and Developmental Disabilities, 31*, p. 10.

not, practice self-determination" (Ward, 1988, p. 2).The attitudes required relate closely to those highlighted in Figure 1–2 and focus on personal perceptions and beliefs about oneself and one's interactions with others.The abilities required to achieve self-determination clearly relate to decision-making and problem solving. It is increasingly clear that these concerns need to be part of the responsibilities of teachers and that such foci should be included within the curriculum.

TEACHING AND TEACHERS

A book devoted to instructional methods should first address the nature of teaching and teachers' appropriate role in education. However, describing what teaching is and precisely what role special educators should play is no easy task. Practicing teachers could provide endless descriptions; teaching is a real joy for some, a job for others, and a nightmare for a few. For most, teaching consists of both good and bad days, and it is everyone's continuing desire to ensure that the former far outnumber the latter.

Effective Teaching

On a fundamental level an effective teacher is someone with requisite skills for teaching that successfully promotes learning. Teacher effectiveness is basically a function of the two dimensions of the amount of learning the child masters and the nature of the teaching behaviors associated with this learning (e.g., time and effort). Brophy and Good (1986) suggest that learning also include socialization and personal/affective development, in addition to gains in the typical academic curricular areas.

Obviously, the more a student learns, the more effective is the teacher and/or the learning climate. If students learn more quickly from one teacher than from another, the more efficient teacher will also logically be judged as the more effective. In other words, the effective teacher not only helps students to learn more but also may accelerate learning. Thus, teacher effectiveness depends on the amount learned and the time in which learning takes place.

Use of this concept leads to consideration of competencies that produce a specifiable degree of effectiveness. Included, for example, in Oliva and Henson's 1980 descriptions of the effective teacher are experiential, training, and personality attributes of the teacher:

- has a broad general education
- holds an adequate self-concept
- possesses personal characteristics conducive to classroom success
- displays fairness
- explains things thoroughly
- is humorous and open-minded
- is knowledgeable and interested in the subject to be taught
- understands basic principles of the learning process
- demonstrates effective techniques of instruction and classroom management

Effectiveness is most frequently viewed from a more instructional orientation as suggested by the last two items on the list. Rosenshine and Stevens (1986) developed a general model of effective instruction from the research literature, highlighting six specific teaching activities associated with student achievement and assumed to be exhibited by the effective teacher:

- a review or check of the previous day's work (reteaching, if necessary)
- presentation of new content/skills
- guided student practice (with a check for understanding)
- feedback and correction (reteaching, if necessary)

- independent student practice
- weekly and monthly reviews

Englert (1983) reinforced the significance of the attributes of effective teaching. She identified four teacher behaviors that are linked to achievement: maintaining a high level of content coverage, providing successful practice activities for students, providing feedback to signal the beginning and the conclusion of individual learning trials, and maintaining a high level of student task involvement.

More recently, the concept of effective instruction has been further expanded by the emerging research on social constructivism. For example, Englert, Tarrant, and Mariage (1992) have identified four areas of importance: embedding instruction in meaningful activities; promoting dialogue for self-regulated learning; demonstrating instructional responsiveness; and establishing classroom learning communities. These principles are further discussed in the next chapter.

While the concept of effective instruction has expanded, it is still not the sole criterion of good teaching. Good teaching includes effective teaching but also considers a student's attitude toward instruction. If learning situations are distasteful, then teachers clearly are doing a disservice to students, the content, and themselves. Professionals must therefore strive to consider both the effective and affective sides of teaching.

The Teacher as Professional

Beyond the instructional demands of a teacher's role, special educators must also display a high degree of personal determination to positively influence the education, adjustment, and acceptance of persons with special needs. Bateman's (1971) historical challenge still has merit. Teachers must have a personal philosophy of education, have a willingness to be agents of social change, be accountable for services provided, possess and continue to develop personal competencies and knowledge base, and care deeply about all human beings, including themselves. These professional attributes serve as the foundation for advocacy crucial to the welfare of students. However, they may also present special problems to the professional.

Although teachers, particularly beginning teachers, probably would not be well advised to upset the structure of education, the role of special educators as change agents requires them to question whether their own and others' actions best benefit students. Accepting minimal levels of professional conduct or acquiescing to administrative practices contrary to students' and parents' basic interests threatens those aspects of special education that originally attracted committed individuals.

To illustrate potential dilemmas, Bateman (1982) discusses several situations in which teachers must decide between what is best for the child and what is consistent with local policy. She notes the following dilemmas that teachers may face: informing parents of their legal rights, knowing that such information will give parents a basis for demanding more extensive services for their child; testifying at due process hearings when the employer is believed to be at fault; and instructing in controversial topics, such as sex education, which the teacher deems crucial to the curriculum but which often conflict with parental concerns or administrative guidelines. These examples present ethical dilemmas that challenge special educators and for which no easy solutions exist (Howe & Miramentes, 1991). Assuming a professional role thus requires the commitment of an advocate as much as it demands competence in instruction.

Finally, a last professional concern for teachers within the domain of ethics concerns the continuing dilemma of making decisions about the value of specific educational interventions. What may be one person's belief system vis-à-vis an intervention or treatment may be perceived by others as poor practice, quackery, or even fraud.

In order to insulate one from possibly ineffective or even harmful interventions, teachers must commit themselves to continuing professional development. This may involve credit and non-credit workshops, conferences, and regular reviews of professional journals. In a field historically beset with new, exciting yet often unproven

ideas it is wise to be cautious in adopting treatments which, at a minimum, threaten the availability of precious instructional time and/or financial resources. For example, Worrall (1990) warned of the potential dangers of readily embracing a new intervention that lacks reasonable research support, claims to be suppressed by some vaguely unidentified agency, is surrounded by mystery and myths, or is promoted by individuals with questionable credentials. In addition, Worrall (1990) provided a series of helpful suggestions based on Food and Drug Administration (FDA) guidelines that have utility beyond the areas of medical and health treatments. The suggestions include:

1. If it sounds too good to be true, it probably is.
2. Be suspicious of any product or therapy that claims to treat a large number of illnesses.
3. Be wary of any treatment or product offering a "cure." In legitimate medicine, cures are actually few and far between.
4. Don't rely only on testimonials from satisfied users. They rarely can be confirmed.
5. Be cautious when "complete," "immediate," "effortless," "safe," or "guaranteed" results are promised.
6. Legitimate . . . researchers do not use words such as "amazing," "secret," "exclusive," "miracle," and "special" in describing treatments.
7. Be skeptical if a "doctor" claims that a treatment is being suppressed by the medical establishment or the FDA. (p. 212)

This discussion merely introduces the special education professional to the complex but important domain of professional ethics within the field.

A Personal Perspective

Evaluating our personal views of teaching has reminded us of certain observations from our own teaching careers that are worthy of sharing. They concern approaches that reflect the variant ways in which some teachers respond to the pressures of teaching.

Some teachers are so actively preparing and keeping up with the necessities for daily survival that they do not have the time to look up from their content and see students. Until such an awakening occurs, they may teach only isolated facts or concepts, rather than students. Curriculum may consist primarily of assigned work seemingly better designed to keep students busy than to promote learning. The central point to be learned is that teachers must first teach students rather than content.

Other teachers appear to place their primary concern on making students well adjusted and content. This attitude may lead to an overemphasis on affective, inappropriately operationalized concerns or an unbalanced focus on instructional diversions. However, such a curriculum may result in discontent and will hinder students' emotional and academic growth. For example, a heavy emphasis on accommodations, as is sometimes made by secondary special education teachers, underscores the problems that can result from efforts that focus attention away from serious academic and/or functional curricula or, even worse, create dependency. Therefore, the teacher must keep in mind the need to place a priority on practical, beneficial, and functional content along with a vision of what the realities of life after high school are for their charges.

Finally, other teachers may view themselves as managers, modifiers of behavior, and, in extreme cases, practitioners whose calling is to cure those with problems. Such individuals may be skilful and talented and may set out to teach effectively in the true sense of the word. However, the efforts of these teachers may inadvertently be devoid of affective concerns. Occasionally these overdiligent taskmasters unintentionally alienate their students or perhaps their own co-workers and consequently create some uncomfortable situations. Teachers must remember that all individuals have feelings and need to maintain a sense of self-worth.

The teacher stereotypes outlined here represent possible responses, albeit somewhat simplified, to the realities of instructional demands and pose a significant challenge to professionals. The goal of this book is to provide positive assistance to the teacher in focusing on students, effectively teaching important content, and providing instruction within a supportive environment.

FRAMEWORK FOR CONCEPTUALIZING THE DELIVERY OF EFFECTIVE INSTRUCTION

Much time is spent discussing the effectiveness of programs, materials, and people. But what does *effective* mean? On a general level, responding to the query "What is effective instruction?" is relatively easy. An answer to the question would probably imply that some type of learning takes place. In this book, effective instruction is considered to be the most facile acquisition of a wide range of knowledge or skills in a psychologically healthy, appropriately structured, student-centered learning environment.

Model of Effective Instruction

There is a growing amount of information, much of it data-based, indicating what elements of teaching constitute effective instructional practice. Figure 1–3 represents our model of effective instructional practice that captures the key elements. It is predicated on a division of all phases of the instructional process, with a focus on three major time-related aspects: (a) activities and events that precede teaching; (b) various activities associated with the actual instructional process; and (c) actions that are performed subsequent to instruction. Furthermore, the model reflects interactivity across the three areas. For instance, various evaluative activities will have an effect on management dimensions or instructional practices. The comprehensive nature of delivering effective instruction is evident from examination of all of the entries on the model.

Pursuant to the purposes of this book, the elements of this model will be covered throughout the book. The first column of the model, "Management Considerations," is addressed in Chap-

FIGURE 1–3
Dimensions of effective practice

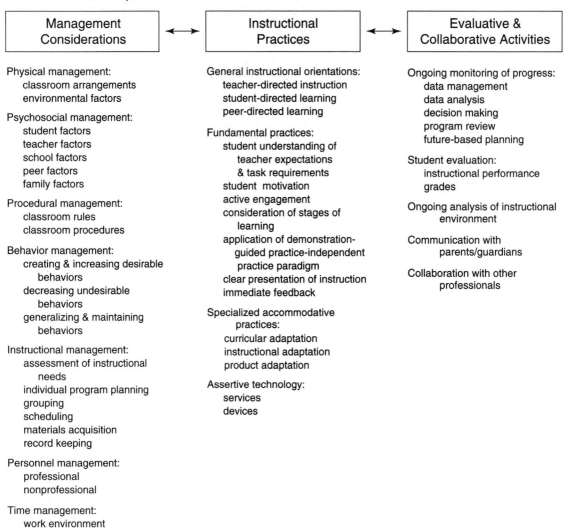

ters 2 and 3. The second column, focusing on "Instructional Practices," is covered thoroughly in
Chapter 4. The topics highlighted in the last column in the model, "Evaluative & Collaborative Activities," are discussed in Chapters 2 and 5. It is fit-
ting to present this graphic representation of the
key elements of effective practice in this first
chapter of the book, thus serving as a reference
for the discussions that follow in subsequent
chapters.

Organization of the Book

As just described, the chapters in this book relate
to the model presented above and deal with the
broad range of management issues, instructional
practices, and curricular concerns associated
with teaching students with learning and behavior problems.

Chapters 2 and 3 cover topics associated with
the entries in the first column of Figure 1-3. The

organization and management of a classroom is initially discussed in Chapter 2. Topics include various classroom arrangements, grouping, scheduling, homework materials selection, grading, and record keeping. Chapter 3 includes further management strategies to facilitate behavior change. General goals, prerequisites to successful management, and specific techniques for promoting appropriate and discouraging inappropriate behavior are discussed.

Chapter 4 provides a detailed discussion of effective instructional practices, as depicted in the second column of Figure 1–3. The chapter is fundamental to understanding how to deliver and adapt the content discussed in the curricular chapters (i.e., Chapters 7–12), which come later in the book.

Chapter 5 focuses on the important issue of collaboration with general education teachers and paraeducators. This is element is crucial to providing appropriate education to students with learning and behavioral difficulties who are placed in inclusive settings.

Chapter 6 provides an overview of curriculum development and program design. Attention to the nature of curriculum precedes an analysis of various curricular orientations found in schools and a discussion of program design.

Chapters 7 to 12 present strategies for instruction within six important curricular areas: spoken language, reading, written language, mathematics, science, and social studies. Each chapter includes information on assessing learners within a particular curricular area, general and specific approaches to instruction, and suggested teaching activities.

Four critical topical areas for students with special learning needs are covered in Chapters 13 to 16. Chapter 13 discusses study skills. Chapter 14 covers the areas of social competence and self-determination. Chapter 15 addresses issues related to teaching the creative arts—areas too often overlooked—yet subjects that students need to have. Chapter 16 provides information about life skills instruction, career development, and transition planning.

This text provides concepts and information with which to develop good teaching techniques. Good teachers are, above all, effective; they nurture learning, are confident, constantly evaluate their teaching programs, and make learning enjoyable. Most teachers gain additional skill with experience; in time they accumulate a variety of motivating methods and materials. Although it seems that nothing takes the place of experience, enthusiasm can prove to be a productive substitute. A teacher who remains enthusiastic, continues to work hard, masters good teaching competencies, and develops a broad repertoire of skills, ideas, and instructional activities can achieve teaching excellence. Our hope is that this text will help you get there.

TEACHER TIPS

With the implementation of IDEA many teachers, administrators, academics, and parents are debating about the regulations. IEP myths, battles, and truths must be demystified in order to provide children with disabilities with the best education available. One myth that must be demystified is "what is meant by Free Appropriate Public Education." Barbara Bateman addresses this issue.

"Nothing is more fundamental of the IDEA than the principle that every child with a qualifying disability is entitled to a free appropriate public education (FAPE). The meanings of free and public are reasonably clear, but the meaning of appropriateness frequently causes confusion. How does one know what is appropriate?

CONTINUED

Appropriate does not necessarily mean ideal. Though schools may wish to afford every child an opportunity to maximize his or her potential, the IDEA does not require this. The U.S., Supreme Court has held:

> . . . Insofar as a State is required to provide a handicapped child with a "free appropriate public education," we hold that it satisfies this requirement by providing personalized instruction with sufficient support services to permit the child to benefit educationally from that instruction. Such instruction and services must be provided at public expense, must meet the State's educational standards, must approximate the grade levels used in the State's regular education, and must comport with the child's IEP. In addition, the IEP, and therefore, the personalized instruction., should be formulated in accordance with the requirements of the Act and, if the child is being educated in the regular classrooms of the public education system, should be reasonably calculated to enable the child to achieve passing marks and advance from grade to grade (Board of Education v. Rowley, 458 U.S. 176 (1982))."

Based on the ruling, Dr. Bateman goes on to note that what constitutes educational benefit lies at the center of numerous court cases. Additionally, how much progress is sufficient to indicate a child is receiving educational benefit is also questionable. What may be clear is that neither social promotion nor slight achievement indicate sufficient progress and determining the progress of the goals set forth in the IEP is of primary importance.

Bateman, B. & Linden, M.A. (1998). *Better IEP's: How to develop legally correct and educationally useful programs.* Longmont, CO: Sopris West.

TEACHER TIPS

During the signing ceremony of the IDEA Amendments, President Clinton made the following remarks about the impact this legislation has had on the education of students with disabilities:

> Since the passage of the IDEA, 90% fewer developmentally disabled children are living in institutions—hundreds of thousands of children with disabilities attend public schools and regular classrooms; three times as many disabled young people are enrolled in colleges and universities; twice as many young Americans with disabilities in their twenties are in the American workplace . . . We have to continue to push these trends, to do everything we can to encourage our children with disabilities. . . . To the millions of families (with children with disabilities) . . . we are saying, we are proud of you for your devotion to your children, for your belief in them, for your love for them, and we are going to do everything we can do to help you succeed in preparing them. To the teachers and administrators who make all the difference, we are saying, we are depending on you and we are going to do what we can to support you. . . . To the American people we are saying that we do not intend to rest until we have conquered the ignorance and prejudice against disabilities that disable us all. ("Remarks of President Clinton," 1997, p. 24)

Yell, M. L., Rogers, D., & Rogers, E. L. (1999). The legal history of special education: What a long, strange trip it's been. *Remedial and Special Education, 19* (4), 219–228.

TEACHER TIPS

Technology

According to Dr. Diane Golden, Director of the Missouri Assistive Technology Project, the reauthorization of IDEA has raised the awareness of assistive technology for students with disabilities. That is, IEP teams are now required to provide evidence that assistive technology was considered as part of a student's program.

IEP teams should consider the types of educational needs of students in the areas of academic subjects, study skills, daily living skills, leisure or recreation skills, and program accessibility. Dr. Golden goes on to recognize that certain disabilities may require 100% expected use of assistive technology. These disability areas include: (a) deaf and hard of hearing; (b) blind and visually impaired; (c) physical disability; (d) deaf/blind; and (e) multiple disabilities. Other disabilities requiring a high percentage of assistive technology are students with traumatic brain injury and autism.

Dr. Golden offers some guidelines that IEP teams may wish to consider:

- Assistive technology may be specified in any part of the IEP.
- IEP teams must consider assistive technology for each student in Special Education.
- Schools must assume maintenance or replacement responsibilities for family-owned assistive technology that is written in the IEP.
- Families cannot be held legally liable for assistive technology that is damaged during home use that is specified in the IEP.
- Try-out of assistive technology, in the school environment, is the best assessment of how a device will work for a student.

Special Education Technology and Practice (January, 1999). Assistive Technology Policy and Practice: What is the right thing to do? What is the responsible thing to do? What is required and must be done? A conversation with Dr. Diane Golden. Knowledge by Design, Inc., Whitefish Bay, WI.

CHAPTER 2

Strategies for Classroom Management: Organization and Planning

This chapter focuses on physical and instructional dimensions of management that are intricately associated with effective teaching. These topics include those activities that teachers need to perform to operate their classrooms efficiently—functions like the physical arrangement of the classroom, student grouping, instructional planning, selecting and adapting curricular materials, assigning and monitoring homework, record keeping, and grading. Chapter 3 then examines management further in terms of classroom rules and procedures and behavior change.

Although a strong case can be made for the value of flexibility in instruction and thus in classroom organization, it remains a reality that students with special needs profit from classrooms and instructional programs that are well-organized, orderly, and predictable (Abrams & Segal, 1998; Montague & Warger, 1997). The discussions that follow in this chapter should provide a basis for developing classrooms and programs that promote learning through structure and organization and yet promote interest and involvement through flexibility, variety, and responsiveness.

MANAGING THE PHYSICAL ENVIRONMENT

The classroom environment is a crucial determinant of successful teaching and learning, yet discussions of teacher competencies frequently overlook it. Christenson, Ysseldyke, and Thurlow's 1989 review of critical instructional factors noted the importance of a positive climate in the classroom, partly related to an orderly school environment. The issue of environmental planning takes on new meaning with the inclusive education movement. Needed accommodations might include seating arrangements that stimulate responding and discourage distractibility, technology that assists in highlighting important points, charts that provide reminders of specific rules, and classroom areas that encourage cooperative interaction and sharing. Although physically a prosthetic environment (i.e., a classroom designated to facilitate learning; Lindsley, 1964) is separate from the teacher-student dyad, conceptually it is an extension of the teaching-learning paradigm. Antecedents and consequences emerge from any environment. The effectiveness and efficiency with which they are managed are enhanced in a well-planned environment. The discussion of various environmental aspects in this chapter should assist teachers in planning an effective environment and should provoke further thinking about environmental options.

Environmental Design

Historically, U.S. education has recorded dramatic changes with regards to what the school environment should be and how it should appear. The one-room school of the turn of the twentieth century eventually led to graded, self-contained classes. Later, the emphasis shifted to open classrooms, which were esthetically pleasing with carpeted floors, nondistracting illumination, brightly colored walls and furnishings, and ample space in which to create. However, many schools became disenchanted with this concept and returned to more traditional, structured situations. Today, emphasis is being given to the advantages of cooperative learning situations and more cooperative teaching arrangements between special and general education (Bauwens & Hourcade, 1994). Currently multi-grade classrooms are again being considered in many schools.

While a significant number of students with special needs still receives special education in resource or self-contained settings, the trend to place these students in more inclusive settings will continue to build. However, two basic points must be considered: (1) most students with special needs will need supports to ensure that their experiences in general education settings are successful; and (2) not all students benefit from the same type of educational setting. For these reasons it is essential that educators remain vigilant about how students with special needs are progressing regardless of setting.

Students who are disabled may initially require more structure and guidance than their nondisabled peers. However, one of a teacher's major goals must be to help students learn how to handle and control their own behavior in less structured situations. This fact is particularly significant in light of the movement toward inclusion. Therefore, classroom arrangements should provide structure, organization, and regimentation when needed as well as freedom, exploration, and choice. To achieve these seemingly conflicting goals, teachers should conceptualize the degree of structure along a continuum from highly structured to less structured arrangements and determine which best suits the needs of particular learning tasks. Educational environments must be flexible and adaptable to individual needs, must allow for differing levels of need within a given group of students, and must change as students grow.

Several noteworthy considerations related to designing and organizing an educational environment (adapted in part from Reeves, 1989) include:

- *Sense of community*: Students need to feel welcome in a classroom as an important member of this community—this is especially important in inclusive settings. The teacher plays a crucial role in creating an accepting and nurturing classroom environment.
- *Personal territory*: Students and teachers alike need a sense of their own turf. This may include a place to keep personal possessions as well as a place to be alone to think and to be separate from the group.
- *Authentic motivation*: A classroom setting in which students are motivated to participate in the learning process has three fundamental factors: collaboration (learning together in teams); content (relevant and meaningful); and choice (opportunities to make a decision about what is learned) (Kohn, 1993).
- *Classroom flexibility*: Patterns of use within a classroom need not be fixed or predetermined. The environment must allow itself to be manipulated by its users so that spaces can be changed.
- *Environmental acknowledgment*: A school facility must allow its occupants to stamp their presence on it. It must be ready to accept the graphic presentation of student activities and interests so that the building reflects who the students are and how they are doing.
- *Flexible seating and work areas*: Classrooms should acknowledge that people work in a variety of natural postures (e.g., sitting up straight, lounging, leaning, and standing). It should offer a variety of seating and work-surface heights to accommodate individual styles.
- *Work aesthetic*: The look of learning in action is a busy one, with things out and in use. An engaging, relevant environment becomes attractive to its users.
- *Barrier-free*: The environment must be able to accommodate students whose disabilities demand special attention (e.g., physical or vision needs).

Classroom Arrangement

Each classroom teacher must operate within certain administrative guidelines and physical limitations. Nevertheless, the teacher must provide for large and small group instruction, individual work, and a nonseated area where students can become involved in interesting independent activities. Whether the room is a small resource room or a large general education setting, these dimensions are essential for developing a prosthetic, effective environment.

The starting point for classroom arrangement is the same as that for all other instructional strategies: the assessment of students' strengths and needs in core curricular areas and in their response to various environmental demands. After this initial assessment, teachers may begin to develop a prosthetic environment. As more is learned about the students and as they learn and develop, the classroom should be adaptable and flexible.

When students are in inclusive settings, their needs will be addressed as a result of the collaborative efforts of the general and special educators. Even though special educators do not have sole responsibility for the inclusive classroom design, they can make reasonable suggestions for accommodating specific students. In general, recommendations for special settings are frequently applicable for the general education classroom as well.

In determining possible ways of organizing a setting, the teacher can begin by drawing a rough sketch of the floor plan of the room or, if programming is available, a computer diagram can be developed. Basic equipment, such as desks, chairs, tables, is then added. Space should be allotted for areas for large and small group instruction, seat work, carrels, and places where learners can work away from their desks, such as interest centers. Recreation and technology areas are also useful to designate as space allows.

There are multiple strategies available for desk arrangements in the classroom. Dowdy, Patton, Smith, and Polloway (1998, pp. 80–81) described the advantages and disadvantages of three approaches. Advantages of vertical rows are that they create an orderly environment and create opportunities for students to physically interact with each other. A disadvantage is that vertical rows make it difficult for students in the back to see or hear the teacher. A large group circle allows the teacher and students to see each other easily, facilitates discussion, and provides an alternative to traditional row-by-row seating, but it also limits opportunities for physical interaction among students. Small clusters facilitate student interactions and provide an alternative to traditional row-by-row seating, but they require teachers to move about the room, make it difficult for teachers to see all of the students at all times, and can restrict total group discussion.

One valuable concept to consider is the division of the classroom into high- and low-probability areas. Based on the *Premack principle* (i.e., making highly desirable activities contingent on those rated lower), this concept operates by allowing students to spend time in favored high-probability areas through successful work completion in the low-probability areas. Classroom design based on the Premack principle offers an opportunity to combine primary instructional areas with sections devoted to reinforcement activities.

For resource settings, physical environmental issues are also important, albeit less often discussed. A key concern is for space, which then ultimately governs what can be accomplished in terms of curriculum in the resource room. Harris and Schultz (1993) note that size needs can be determined only after considering the following:

- the predominant activities that will take place (e.g., instruction, assessment, consultation)
- the nature of resource room activities and whether they will occur simultaneously (e.g., social skills training that would interfere with teaching reading comprehension)
- the number of students and adults who will be in the room at the same time
- the needs of teachers for storage of equipment and materials and for materials preparation
- the needs of students with physical conditions that require special equipment

Figures 2-1 and 2-2 show the floor plans for two different types of resource room settings. Figure 2-1 depicts a possible arrangement if a large classroom is available for housing the program. Figure 2-2 illustrates how a room with a smaller square footage could be arranged. These are only suggestions and teachers are encouraged to arrange their space in ways that address student needs and maximize engagement.

Complements to the Instructional Environment

Several common adjuncts can assist the teacher in designing an effective environment. These include study carrels, interest centers, and other aesthetic features. Additionally, microcomputers and related technology have unquestioned potential for making significant contributions to instruction.

Study Carrel. Classrooms can benefit from having at least one study carrel for use with students who have learning-related difficulties. Carrels or cubicles have the two main purposes of limiting outside stimuli and providing a specific place for concentrated study.

FIGURE 2–1

Sample floor plan for a large classroom

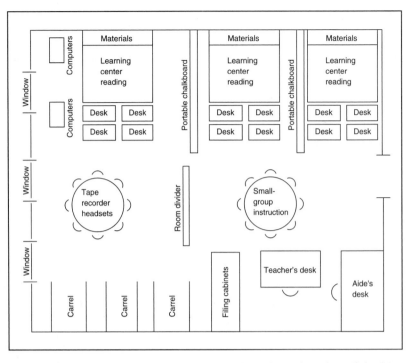

From *The Resource Teacher: A Guide to Effective Practices,* 2nd. ed. (p. 123), by J. L. Wiederholt, D. D. Hammill, and V. L. Brown, 1993. Austin, TX: PRO-ED. Copyright 1993 by PRO-ED, Inc. Reprinted with permission.

A study carrel should be designed to minimize the distraction of various other classroom activities and thus it should be placed in a quiet area. Cubicles come in many shapes and forms. Some are commercially produced; others are cardboard refrigerator cartons; still others are little more than a small table and chair placed in the back corner of the classroom, where the student sits facing the corner. The carrel becomes a work area for the student who uses it as a special place for concentrated study. The teacher may suggest that students go to their "office" to study, or students may ask for permission to do so. Use of carrels should emphasize the positive features they afford (i.e., a quiet place to work) rather than their association as a location where one is sent for inappropriate behavior.

Interest Centers. Interest centers are an outgrowth of independent seat work activities. They are attempts to add variety into classroom instruction and to enrich the curriculum. Interest centers can be used for instruction in which a student works at the center to review something previously learned or apply something learned in a new way, the promotion of social interaction for two or more students who are working together, and the development of independent work skills and self-direction.

Teachers should consider several key components of interest centers: (a) the characteristics of the user, (b) objectives that the activities are designed to meet, (c) interest value to students, (d) procedures and directions, and (e) materials or equipment needed. Because centers are intended for students, the user is the most important element. In developing ideas for effective interest centers, teachers should keep in mind the user's characteristics (e.g., behavior, language). In effect, an interest center becomes a well-planned lesson presented primarily without the teacher's direct assistance.

FIGURE 2–2

Sample floor plan for a smaller classroom

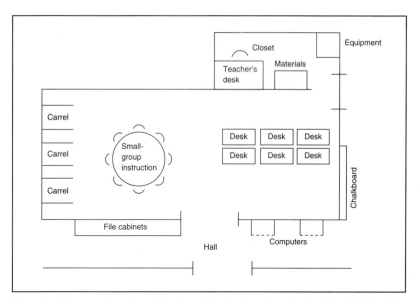

From *The Resource Teacher: A Guide to Effective Practices,* 2nd ed., (p. 124), by J. L. Wiederholt, D. D. Hammill, and V. L. Brown, 1993. Austin. TX: PRO-ED. Copyright 1993 by Pro-Ed, Inc. Reprinted with permission.

Another important component is to determine the objectives of the particular center. Without clear objectives, the results of the center will always be in question. Did the student learn something beneficial? An interest center can be an attractive creation, but without clear objectives it is of limited educational value.

For centers to be effective, they must be engaging. Students must find the activities as well as the materials used in the centers stimulating. Teachers should not overlook the importance of matching the activities of the learning center, which are related to the overriding instructional objectives, to the particular interests of students in the class.

Procedures and directions go hand in hand in promoting effective use. They provide students with parameters, so that they will understand what is expected and how they can accomplish the objectives of the center. Procedures are general guidelines telling students how to use the center; directions tell them how to perform the specific activities.

The last concern in developing a center is securing the materials and equipment. The best advice to follow is to keep it simple. Making centers complicated increases the probability that students will not be able to use them effectively without the teacher's help, thus defeating the purpose of providing independent study. Keeping component parts of an interest center to the minimum increases the probability of the students working efficiently.

Because teaching students to work in an interest center is important it must be done directly and precisely. In the same way that students can be taught how to study independently or how to stay on task in a working situation, they can also be taught how to appropriately use a center.

Bulletin Boards. Bulletin boards can facilitate the development of a prosthetic environment by making the classroom attractive and by promoting both incidental and directed learning. Regardless of the goal, bulletin boards should be integrated into the curriculum and thus planned for and prepared accordingly.

One of the most popular uses of boards is to display students' work. In addition to featuring art, the displays can also include students' academic work samples and thus provide social recognition for their respective products.

Bulletin boards also foster creativity by giving students an opportunity to choose topics or themes and develop their own material to be displayed. Local customs and special events can provide further ideas for themes. Teachers should also recognize the value of bulletin boards with middle and high school students. Allowing students to design, create, and produce their own displays is simultaneously an excellent learning tool and a motivational device.

DESIGNING INDIVIDUALIZED EDUCATION PROGRAMS

The passage of PL 94-142 incorporated the individualized education program into routine pedagogical practice. Changes to IDEA in 1990 (PL 101–476) added the requirement that plans for transition services be part of the IEP for all students no later than age 16. The 1997 changes to IDEA (PL 105–17) added other features to this document.

The IEP is the primary document that outlines specific plans for services, placement, transitional planning, and now other assurances. Ideally, data gathered for the eligibility process and any further information collected by multidisciplinary specialists and by both special and regular teachers can assist with the development of the IEP. Realistically, special education teachers will have to conduct further curriculum-related assessments to gather the type of instructionally useful data to be able to develop appropriate goals and objectives and to know where to begin instruction.

Although IEPs can be used for a number of purposes, three stand out from the rest. First, IEPs should provide instructional direction. Effective written goal setting can help to remedy the "cookbook approach" (i.e., pulling together isolated or marginally related instructional exercises in the name of good teaching). Second, IEPs function as the basis for evaluation. Formally established learning objectives for students help determine the effectiveness and efficiency of instruction, although this form of accountability is not intended

to become the basis for evaluating teacher effectiveness per se. A third use of IEPs is improved communication. Individual education programs can facilitate contact among staff members, teachers, and parents, and ideally between teachers and students. Parental involvement, in particular, has resulted in increased mutual support and cooperation between home and school.

IEP Team

The identified members of the IEP team, as specified in the most recent reauthorization of IDEA, reflect key emphases of the new law: parent involvement, coordination with the general education curriculum, and involvement in the general education settings. The members include: parents of the student; special education teacher; regular education teacher; local education agency representative (i.e., a person with authority to commit necessary resources); person who can interpret the evaluation results; the student, when appropriate; and other knowledgeable persons whom the parents or school may choose to invite.

IEP Components

Individualized education programs are intended to serve as the guiding document for the provision of an appropriate education. Moreover, IEPs function as an integral link between assessment and instruction; thus, the development of the IEP follows the collection of assessment data. The individual education program then details the least restrictive, most appropriate placement and outlines the instructional program. The IEP must be evaluated and then rewritten annually as long as services are still necessary.

The major components of the IEP, as of 1997, included some new features. The general content of an IEP is:

- statement of the child's present level of educational performance;
- statement of measurable annual goals, including benchmarks, or short-term objectives;
- statement of the special education and related services and supplementary aids and services to be provided to the child;

- statement of the program modifications or supports for school personnel that will be provided to the child;
- explanation of the extent, if any, to which the child will not participate with nondisabled children in the regular class;
- statement of any individual modifications in the administration of state or district-wide assessments of student achievement;
- projected date for the beginning of the services and modifications;
- anticipated frequency, location, and duration of those services and modifications;
- statement of how the child's progress toward the annual goals will be measured;
- statement of how the child's parents will be regularly informed of their child's progress toward the annual goals.

Two other components of the IEP will be necessary for older students.

- Transition services: By age 14, a statement of transition service needs must be in place (focus on student's course of study) and, by age 16, a statement of needed transition services is required; and
- Transfer of rights: Beginning at least one year before a student reaches the age of majority under state law, the IEP must include a statement that the student has been informed of his or her rights that will transfer upon reaching the age of majority.

The remainder of this section focuses primarily on the first two general components, listed above. Measurable annual goals and benchmarks/short-term objectives evolve from descriptive statements of a student's present levels of educational performance. The regulations for IDEA '97 that were published in March of 1999 specify, to some extent, elements that should be part of these components.

Present Levels of Educational Performance. A summary of a student's current functioning provides a basis for subsequent goal setting. Performance levels should be determined for all areas needing special instruction. Depending on the individual, relevant information could be gathered for academic skills, behaviorial patterns, self-help skills, vocational talents, or communication abilities.

Performance levels should be viewed as summaries of an individual's strengths and weaknesses. We suggest that these statements emphasize the positive aspects of the student (i.e., what the student can do), while clearly indicating what needs to be addressed.

Although performance statements can take a variety of forms, including formal test scores, informal test results, behavioral descriptions, a listing of specific abilities relative to a sequence of skills in a given area, and self-report data obtained from the student, descriptions that are instructionally relevant are warranted. Gibb and Dyches (2000) recommend that present levels of educational performance include the following three elements.

- Statement of how the disability affects the student's involvement and progress in the general curriculum.
- Description of the student's performance levels in the skill areas affected by the disability.
- Logical cues for writing the accompanying goals for improvement. (p. 6)

Annual Goals. The next key component of an IEP is listing measurable annual goals. As the name implies, these goals predict long-term gains that can be evaluated clearly during the school year. The annual goals should reflect the educator's (and the parents') best guess of what the student can reasonably achieve within the school year. The following features can help determine realistic expectations: (a) chronological age, (b) past learning profile, and (c) recent learning history and response to instruction. Teachers can conceptualize annual goals, which may range from outcomes that might be considered the most optimistic to the most pessimistic. Against these parameters, reasonable estimates can be derived.

Annual goals should include four major elements. IDEA of 1997 list four characteristics of an annual goal.

- It must be measurable.
- It must tell what the student can reasonably accomplish in a year.
- It must relate to helping the student be successful in the general education curriculum and/or address other educational needs resulting from the disability.
- It must be accompanied by benchmarks or short-term objectives. (Gibb & Dyches, 2000, p. 12)

Measurable goals provide a basis for evaluation. Statements should use precise, behavioral terms that denote action and can therefore be operationally defined (e.g., pronounce, write, or identify motorically) rather than vague, general language that confounds evaluation and observer agreement (e.g., know, understand, or appreciate). "Will correctly identify all initial consonant sounds" is more appropriate than the unmeasurable "will learn to read."

Positive goals provide an appropriate direction for instruction. Avoiding negative goals creates an atmosphere that is helpful in communcation with parents as well as in charting student progress. The goal "will learn to respond at appropriate times" gives the student something to strive for, as opposed to "will learn to keep mouth closed," which negatively emphasizes something to avoid.

Goals should also be oriented to the student. Developing students' skills is the intent, and the only measure of effectiveness should be what is learned, not what is taught. Thus, "will verbally respond to questions with two-word phrases" is preferable to "will be given oral language readiness materials."

Finally, goals must be relevant to the individual student's current and future needs across a range of academic, personal/social, and daily living domains. Unfortunately, research indicates that IEPs frequently do not meet this criterion. For example, goals for students with mild disabilities have often been found to overemphasize academic areas to the relative exclusion of other areas such as social-emotional (Epstein, Polloway, Patton, & Foley, 1989), and career-vocational or socio-behavioral (McBride & Forgnone, 1985).

Benchmarks/Short-Term Objectives (STOs). STOs are intended to serve as major stepping-stones toward annual goals. The objectives should therefore illustrate the path that the teacher will follow to reach the goals. Generally, short-term objectives have been conceptualized and developed as more specific respresentations of the skills to be learned. Although IDEA '97 does not specify how to write short-term objectives, they should be specific, observable, measurable, student-oriented, and positive. They should also include a stated criterion of task success, and consideration that annual goals may not have addressed explicitly.

One of the most important tasks in developing IEPs is establishing objectives that are consistent with the student's annual goals. Because the objectives are viewed as sequential steps to those goals, the STOs should reflect major instructional achievements between the current performance level and the ultimate goal. Typically, three to eight objectives per goal are sufficient, with each objective representing a skill that might reasonably be acquired in 1 to 3 months. Table 2–1 provides some sample goal/short-term objective clusters. This understanding of objectives should set them apart from the process of daily or weekly lesson planning (as discussed later in this chapter).

Numerous software packages containing sequenced goal-objective clusters have been developed in recent years. Most school districts now have instructional objective data banks that teachers can access to generate IEPs. Although the benefit of reduced paperwork and possible time savings by utilizing computer databases may be significant, there remains the issue of whether a student's program is truly consistent with individual needs.

One recent development in the effort to make IEPs more functional and more closely tied to actual learning activities of students is the use of

TABLE 2–1
Sample goal-objective clusters

Goal 1: Identify and write numerals 0–100 with 95% accuracy as measured by teacher-made test.
1. Recognize the numerals 0–100 with 95% accuracy.
2. Write and say in sequence the numerals from 0–100 with 95% accuracy.
3. Write and say in isolation the numerals from 0–100 with 95% accuracy.
4. Write from memory the numerals from 0–100 with 95% accuracy.

Goal 2: Divide shapes and set into halves, quarters, and thirds with 95% accuracy.
1. Divide shapes into halves with 95% accuracy.
2. Divide sets into halves with 95% accuracy.
3. Divide shapes into fourths with 95% accuracy.
4. Divide sets into fourths with 95% accuracy.
5. Divide shapes into thirds with 95% accuracy.
6. Divide sets into thirds with 95% accuracy.

Goal 3: Multiply a three-digit number by another three-digit number using regrouping.
1. Give the answer to each fact with 95% accuracy when multiplication facts with a multiplier of 12 or less are presented, one at a time, visually and auditorily.
2. Multiply a two-digit number by another two-digit number without regrouping with 95% accuracy.
3. Multiply a two-digit number by another two-digit number with regrouping with 95% accuracy.
4. Multiply a three-digit number by another three-digit number without regrouping with 95% accuracy.
5. Multiply a three-digit number by another three-digit number with regrouping with 95% accuracy.

portfolios in IEP development. Fitzgerald, Kay, Tefft and Colburn (1994) found in their qualitative research that students indicated that traditional IEPs tended to be "unfriendly documents" that use school-specific terminology, while portfolios are more friendly, use "real life" language, and thus are more likely to involve the students themselves. Swicegood (1994) offered some suggestions for linking the IEP with portfolio assessment. These included:

- List student objectives. They should be observable and measurable (via informal assessment means such as work samples, observations, and so forth).
- With the student and team members, generate portfolio components. Include work products that show growth on the objectives.
- Attempt to give the student as much ownership as possible over building the portfolio.

- Use periodic conferences to hold the student accountable for growth and to evaluate and refine the objectives.
- Periodically complete a summary sheet . . . to synthesize data from the portfolio. This brief summary serves as a tool for teacher reflection on instructional effectiveness as well as a vehicle for communication with parents and the student. (p. 13)

ORGANIZING AND PLANNING FOR INSTRUCTION

With the physical environment set, teachers are next faced with the management of the instructional day. Although this area is broad-based and all-inclusive, this section focuses on four key topics: grouping for instruction, scheduling, lesson planning, and unit teaching.

Grouping for Instruction[1]

A major organizational concern is instructional grouping. A discussion of how best to group for instruction must first address a concern for individualization. Among the foremost principles on which the field of special education was founded is the importance of individualization in instruction. In many cases the primary justification for the provision of special services has been the assumption that instruction must be geared to the individual's specific needs.

Nonetheless, a distinction should be made between the concepts of individualization and one-to-one instruction. Individualization refers to instruction appropriate to the individual, whether or not it is accomplished on a one-to-one basis. By this definition, individualization can be accomplished through one-to-one or one-to-two ratios, in small groups, or even occasionally in large groups. In elaborating on this concept, Stevens and Rosenshine (1981) stated that "individualization is considered a characteristic of effective instruction if the term implies helping each student to succeed, to achieve a high percentage of correct responses, and to become confident of his or her competence" (p. 3). Thus, even though individualization presumes that instruction is geared to the needs of the individual student, it does not mean that it is provided on a one-to-one basis. The following discussion focuses on the issue of one-to-one versus group instruction.

Instructional Concerns. There are three predominant concerns—instructional effectiveness, efficiency, and social benefits—which are each important in the context of inclusive-education.

Effectiveness is a measure of whether the skills taught have been learned by students. Research on the effectiveness of grouping alternatives has been equivocal. In several studies advantages for

one-to-one instruction have been reported (Matson, DiLorenzo, & Esveldt-Dawson, 1981; Westling, Ferrell, & Swenson, 1982); in other instances group procedures have been found more effective (Oliver, 1983; Orelove, 1982; Rincover & Koegel, 1977). More commonly, comparable results have been reported (e.g., Handleman & Harris, 1983; Ranieri, Ford, Vincent, & Brown, 1984).

Although most research on effectiveness has been primarily concerned with the acquisition of new skills, several studies have also considered maintenance and generalization. In these cases some interesting results were reported. For example, generalization advantages were reported for group instructional efforts by Fink and Sandall (1980), and Oliver and Scott (1981). Elium and McCarver (1980) reported that group training and one-to-one instruction produced comparable response maintenance when evaluated after a 1-year follow-up.

Although few studies directly compared group and one-to-one training models used with children with mild disabilities, there has been substantial support for instructional strategies in which group arrangements are an essential element. In particular, direct instruction programs, characterized by small group work, have demonstrated effectiveness for students identified as mildly disabled, disadvantaged, and slow learners (e.g., Becker & Carnine, 1980; Gregory, Hackney, & Gregory, 1982; Stevens & Rosenshine, 1981).

Efficiency refers to the amount of time required for something to be learned. Most research in this area has favored the use of group instruction (e.g., Elium & McCarver, 1980; Kazdin & Erickson, 1975; Orelove, 1982), thus reaffirming what many professionals in the field of special education have known for years.

An undeniable benefit of group instruction is an increase in the number of students who can be served. Even more urgent is the reality that more students receive their education in general education settings where group instruction is very much the core of the instructional routine.

A third consideration relative to the efficacy of group or one-to-one instruction is that of *social outcomes*—whether there are benefits or

---

[1] Portions of this discussion are adapted from "The Efficacy of Group Instruction v. One-to-One Instruction: A Review" by E.A. Polloway, M. E. Cronin, & J. R. Patton, 1986, *Remedial and Special Education* 7(1), 22–30. Copyright 1986 by PRO-ED. Adapted by permission.

detriments. One social benefit of group instruction is simply the opportunity for learning to participate with others. Fink and Sandall (1980) posit that the introduction of small-group work with preschoolers results in an increased ability to function in common school situations. Handleman and Harris (1983) state that group work provides more normalizing experiences, which can promote successful inclusion. On the other hand, a predominant focus on one-to-one instruction can result in greater difficulty for students once they are more fully integrated into the general education classroom (Bryan, 1983).

A potential solution to the problem of isolation or rejection and one that further enhances learning is *cooperative learning* (Slavin, 1983; Slavin, Madden, & Leavey, 1984). Cooperative learning approaches structure goals and tasks for groups of students, both disabled and nondisabled, to facilitate successful learning and socialization. Cooperative learning can be defined simply as classroom techniques that involve students in group learning activities with recognition and reinforcement based on group performance (Slavin, 1980).

A variety of cooperative learning strategies can be used. Smith, Polloway, Patton, and Dowdy (1998) summarized them as follows:

- *Peer tutoring*: An opportunity for peer instruction that benefits both the tutor and the student being tutored. Examples include reviewing directions, drill and practice activities, recording material dictated by a peer, and providing pre-test practice (e.g., spelling).
- *Classwide peer tutoring*: This approach divides classes into two teams for competition of several weeks' duration. Students work in pairs and are tutored and provide tutoring on the same material. Students accumulate points for their team by giving correct answers and using correct procedures and individual scores on master tests are then added to the team's total.
- *Group projects*: This cooperative learning alternative allows students to pool their skills and knowledge in order to complete a specific assignment. Group projects are uniquely appropriate for inclusive settings where the talents of

high, average, and low achievers can be blended together into specific aspects of the task.
- *Jigsaw*: This format gives each student in a group an individual task (i.e., "a piece of the puzzle") to be completed before the group can reach its goal.
- *Student-team achievement divisions*: This concept involves the assignment of students' diversely constituted teams that convene to review specific lessons. The teams work together to achieve mastery of the content, comparison of answers reached, answers developed, discussion of differences, and internal group questioning (Slavin, 1987).

Implications. Research on grouping arrangements encourages the consideration of group experiences for students who are disabled. A variety of positive benefits can accrue from the use of group methodology, including the promotion of observational learning, facilitation of overlearning and generalization, the teaching of turn-taking, increased and better use of instructional time, more efficient student management, and increased peer interaction. What seems to be the most critical variable favoring group instruction is increased contact with the teacher. In Stevens and Rosenshine's (1981) classic review of best practices, the importance of "academic engaged time" and its relationship to higher achievement levels was clearly demonstrated. The opportunities for teacher demonstration and corrective feedback are strong arguments in favor of group instruction.

Special Grouping Considerations

Grouping for Acquisition. Meeting students' diverse needs across different stages of learning requires organization. The teacher's goal is to maximize teaching to ensure optimal acquisition of skills and abilities. For the teacher to work daily with each child, the problem becomes one of ensuring the highest degree of learning efficiency.

The initial option is to work with each student on a one-to-one basis. This approach has the advantage of providing the learners with instruction specifically tailored to their needs and abilities. Individual teaching appears to be ideal for the acquisition stage of learning. However, as noted earlier, an one-to-one arrangement has a number of drawbacks.

Teaching lessons to the entire class provides another alternative, which can increase instructional time for each child. Teachers can thus supervise each student throughout entire periods and can provide constant instruction of a large group nature. However, because large groups may not properly accommodate individual needs, such instruction may drastically reduce the acquisition of skills, knowledge, and concepts.

The obvious alternative to one-to-one and large-group models is to provide instruction in small groups. Unfortunately, grouping evokes images of educational or recreational rank-ordering (e.g., reading groups of sparrows, redbirds, and crows). However, use of grouping should not dictate rigid adherence to a standardized grouping arrangement across all subjects. To assist students in acquisition learning, the group can organize around a specific skill the members need to acquire. Groups should be flexible and fluid; they should neither restrict a student's improvement beyond the group mean nor force the child to work too fast.

Bickel and Bickel (1986) noted that grouping for instructional purposes has positive benefits under the following conditions.

1. Number and size of groups are dependent on student characteristics and content taught.
2. Different groupings are used for different subjects.
3. Frequent shifts among groups occur during the school year as well as between years.
4. Groups are based on current levels of skills.
5. Groups are established as a result of instruction.
6. There is a combination of small group and whole class instruction.
7. Groupings are responsive to instruction (p. 494).

How do large-group and one-to-one models fit into this grouping picture? Large-group instruction never quite accommodates the acquisition stage of learning, but it can provide the class with general introductions, serve as a forum for class-wide discussions, and allow more advanced students a chance to review what other students are seeing for the first time. On the other hand, individual attention will continue to demand some class time. It may be essential for students who are unable to learn in the small group setting, who are working on a skill different from the focus of the rest of the class, or who are receiving assistance with specific aspects of work assignments. One-to-one instruction suggests the need for supports such as a paraeducator, cooperative teaching, or resource services.

Ideally, grouping can afford the teacher some organizational flexibility while providing a vehicle to give individuals what they need. For example, a class divided into three groups during a 1-hour academic period could provide several advantages: each child would receive 15 or 20 minutes of teacher-directed, small-group instruction; the teacher would need to plan for only a limited number of children outside the group at any one time; and the teacher could still supervise individual students occasionally and briefly. Thus, this flexible system would allow maximum efficiency at each learning stage.

If acquisition of a skill or concept is important, then its learning cannot be left to chance. Instruction through flexible grouping arrangements is essential to sound teaching that maximizes the probability of learning.

Enhancing Proficiency and Maintenance. A system for ensuring proficiency and maintenance must accompany acquisition learning strategies. Small-group instruction provides a regular opportunity for students who are not working directly with the teacher to pursue educational activities that further develop and maintain what was acquired through teacher-directed instruction. Some simple techniques and activities to assist in fluency building and overlearning of skills previously taught include the following:

■ tutoring by a peer
■ board work

- group projects
- individual seat work folders
- instructional games
- software programs
- working cooperatively with partners
- writing a short composition
- silent reading assignments
- tutoring other students

In addition, several guidelines may help teachers keep these activities going smoothly. These include:

1. Ensure that students display acceptable independent working and interpersonal relationship skills.
2. Choose assignments that can be accomplished independently to avoid constant interruptions by students.
3. Be sure directions for completing each task are clear.
4. Build in self-correction methods so that students will receive immediate feedback.
5. Vary the activities, allowing each student to experience several different activities during a period.
6. Allow students some freedom to choose their activities.
7. Allow time to provide feedback or reinforcement for independent work.

One strategy that can significantly enhance proficiency and maintenance learning is the use of peer tutoring, a cooperative learning strategy with proven effectiveness (Cooke, Heron, & Heward, 1983). To ensure that peer tutoring is effective, however, teachers need to monitor the program carefully. Salend (1990, p. 252) offered the following suggestions.

1. Establish specific goals for the sessions.
2. Plan particular learning activities to meet the identified goals.
3. Select tutors who have demonstrated proficiency in the content to be taught.
4. Train students to function as successful tutors.
5. Match tutors and tutees.

6. Schedule sessions for no longer than 30 minutes and no more than three times per week.
7. Periodically monitor the tutoring process and provide feedback to both members of the dyad.
8. Allay potential parental concerns by explaining to parents the role and the value of peer tutoring.

Finally, it should be noted again that after acquisition, proficiency, and maintenance the fourth component of learning that should be planned for is generalization. Instruction in the classroom should provide the basis for generalizing from the resource room to the inclusive setting, learning in the community, learning new content by building on previously learned material, and working with different instructors.

SCHEDULING

The importance of a carefully planned schedule within the context of an organized classroom cannot be overemphasized. By planning interesting, creative, and exciting activities throughout the day, the teacher can develop an enjoyable, educationally profitable program, with the additional benefit that students are intrinsically motivated to participate in ongoing lessons. Additionally, an effective schedule maximizes the appropriate use of time.

Scheduling involves the temporal arrangement for each day, supplemented by a series of specific lesson plans. The daily schedule ensures sufficient activities for the day and, conversely, sufficient time to complete them. A carefully planned schedule intersperses more relaxed learning activities with those more challenging to students. Because schedules for students with special needs often call for changes from inclusion to pull-out, these general considerations should be reflected in the student's IEP. The following discussion initially focuses on elementary classes with subsequent attention to secondary school classes. The section continues with attention to block and resource schedules.

A key element of any effective schedule is the smooth transition between instructional activities. Therefore, an overriding concern for the teacher once the schedule has been built is to strive for the efficient use of time. The following guidelines can assist in enhancing classroom transitions.

1. Teach appropriate transition behaviors.
2. Let students practice appropriate behavior.
3. Provide reminders for students during the class period so they know how much time is available.
4. Give students a prompt that an activity or class period is nearing an end.
5. Use special transition activities (short and quick) that can facilitate the smooth movement from one activity to another.
6. Remediate transition problems such as slowness and disruptiveness.
7. Acknowledge quick, smooth transitions.

The following discussion highlights elements of the school day including primary and closing activities and major academic foci.

Opening and Closing Activities

Regardless of whether education personnel are in self-contained classes, have a general education classroom, or are working cooperatively with a general educator, it will be important to consider ways to begin and end the school day. A teacher interested in establishing a sense of community, acceptance, and mutual concern wants to plan activities that can become regular routines that accomplish these ends.

The day might begin by allocating approximately 15 minutes to a number of activities—for example, collection of lunch money, recognition of birthdays, and discussion of planned events for the day. Openings should be conducted to establish the sense of community referred to earlier as well as a learning set for beginning the day's activities. Although the suggestions described here are most appropriate for elementary students, they can be easily adapted for adolescents.

The discussion of the date is commonly conducted using a large calendar visible to all students. Students can place or write numerals indicating the day, the month, and the year. Effort should be made to ensure success and decrease the probability of guessing, which can hamper rather than facilitate learning. One approach allows a student to choose the correct number from a pair of numbers instead of having to select from a large number of possibilities. For secondary level students, it would be appropriate to discuss events—international, national, regional, and local—that happened on the particular day.

One of the most important activities conducted during openings is a discussion of the plan for the school day. Preparing students for daily activities brings together the classroom routine and student expectations. In inclusive settings, the key is to involve these students with special needs in the process. For more limited students, pictures might be drawn; for more advanced individuals, words depicting the activity might be written, or the responses could be written in phrases or complete sentences. After completing discussion of what has already happened, the teacher may focus on what activities will follow.

Closing exercises should review daily occurrences, end the day, and set the stage for orderly dismissal. First, the teacher might review the daily activities by going over the schedule presented in the opening exercises. This is a good time for the teacher to ask various students what they enjoyed most and least.

Next, the teacher may get the students involved in activities by giving specific end-of-the-day assignments. These can be accomplished individually, in pairs, or by small groups. Typical assignments involve emptying the wastebasket; sweeping the floor; straightening the desks; and making sure pets have water, food, and their habitats secured. Toward the end of this period, the teacher may wish to play music that is age-appropriate and of interest to the students.

Scheduling Academic Periods

After opening and closings are accounted for, approximately $4\frac{1}{2}$ to 5 hours remain in the school day. The teacher's primary concern should now be scheduling the content areas deemed most important within the overall curriculum. Reading and math are two curricular areas that require intensive, individualized instruction. The following discussion gives examples of ways to schedule a 60-minute period of instruction in each of those areas.

Reading. In this example a class of 18 students, as might be common in any programmatic setting where students will spend the entire period, is used for illustration; grouping is the basic instructional format. The class is broken into three groups of six students each, labeled Groups A, B, and C. Each group meets with the teacher for 20 minutes of direct instruction during the 70-minute period. Group A illustrates the components of a typical reading session.

During the initial 20-minute block, Group A meets with the teacher for instruction on initial consonants. A series of activities allows presentation of the concepts involved in a variety of ways. Charts are used to help students associate sounds and symbols with the beginnings of familiar words. Next, the teacher reads a group of words aloud, with the students noting what sound or letter is heard at the beginning of each word. Students are then asked to complete riddles using words beginning with prescribed consonants. Twenty minutes of direct instruction are thus presented with three related activities sandwiched between brief introductory and closure activities.

For the next 40 minutes the teacher assigns proficiency activities to complement the direct teaching activity. Interesting and diverse activities that allow for student choice can ensure attention—for example, worksheets with pictures to be labeled by the initial consonant sound of the item portrayed; silent reading of a story appropriate for these specific skills and for the child's independent reading level; a visit to a learning center that develops skills in writing consonants. Each assignment should reflect previously acquired skills.

The remaining 10 minutes in the period are kept flexible for a variety of instructional purposes, including individual mini-lessons for students experiencing difficulties with specific skills, time to check over seat work, an opportunity to reinforce appropriate behavior exhibited during the period, and time to gather evaluative information for future planning.

Mathematics. A second intensive period of instruction is mathematics. Grouping again lends itself well to direct instruction, with individual assignments providing proficiency and maintenance activities. Based on the same class size used in the previous example, three groups have been established for direct teaching periods. Obviously, the groups must be reorganized around specific skills that particular children need. They must also be flexible enough to allow a student to move out of a group after mastery. The structure discussed here reduces the group teaching lesson to 10 minutes per group, thus increasing the time that the teacher spends in individual instruction and assistance.

During the initial 10-minute period, Group A receives seat work to help maintain arithmetic skills previously acquired—a short worksheet covering two-digit subtraction without regrouping. At the end of the 10 minutes, the teacher circulates throughout the class for 5 minutes, checking seat work and helping the students in the group who have just left the direct-teaching experience begin their assignments.

During the next 10 minutes, Group A meets with the teacher for a lesson in regrouping. The time is divided between the teacher's illustrating the process and the students' practicing either at the board or on paper. At the end of their 10 minutes, the students in Group A have an opportunity to work independently on problems they have mastered during the group instruction. Individual work folders are useful in organizing assignments for each student. Approximately 15 minutes of exercises are provided for Group A students at this time. For the initial 5 minutes, when they are beginning their work, and again after the next group's 10-minute instructional period, the teacher is available for consultation and assistance.

During the final 15 minutes of the period, no groups are meeting with the teacher, and a variety of additional activities can be made available to students who have completed their seat work. In this final period of time, the teacher is able to check work, teach specific skills to individual students, and evaluate the day's lessons for future plans and prepare for transition to the next period.

The scheduling examples discussed in this section reflect several purposes to which any effective schedule should respond: to meet prescribed individual learning goals and objectives, to facilitate the planning process for the teacher, to ensure varied teaching activities, and to provide a well-ordered day of learning. A well-designed schedule is valuable because it assists the teacher in planning a series of different activities and events that make coming to school interesting and stimulating enough for students and structured enough for efficient teaching.

Scheduling at the Secondary Level.
The majority of high school programs encourage students with special needs to participate in general classes that are relevant to their needs and in which they can succeed. Thus, each student's needs should be carefully evaluated as a basis for maximum, appropriate inclusion. Whether in inclusive settings or in special education classes, scheduling remains an important concern.

Secondary schools traditionally have used a daily schedule composed of six to eight time periods 50 minutes in duration. Typically, about three fourths of each student's daily schedule consists of academic classes, with the remaining portion devoted to other activities as well as lunch or study halls. Often, students in programs such as vocational education follow a general schedule slightly different from that of the majority of students and may attend school for a half-day session for academic work and spend the other half-day receiving other types of training.

In the overall secondary school schedule, the individual period is the pivotal unit during which daily instruction takes place. An individual period may contain several components, such as daily activities, weekly activities, and activities requiring more than 1 or 2 weeks to accomplish.

High school teachers may seem to have little need to develop a daily schedule because they all have a fixed schedule. However, because the events typically fit neatly into approximately 50-minute blocks, effective planning at the high school level may be more difficult. The teacher must develop a series of mini-schedules—one for each class—which should contain brief opening and closing exercises as well as predetermined procedures for transition. Depending on the teacher's particular objectives, daily instructional activities usually begin by introducing daily, weekly, or unit concerns to be addressed on that specific day. Activities aimed at fostering various stages of learning follow the introduction. For example, new activities are probably aimed at acquisition learning, whereas review activities might be geared to proficiency, maintenance, or generalization learning. Closing activities then represent an attempt to relate the different things that have taken place during the period.

Often, a specific objective cannot be accomplished in a single day or period. Thus, weekly (or monthly) activities focus on coordinating ongoing activities. Also, because the objectives of weekly activities are somewhat broader, weekly objectives can be integrated more easily with similar concerns elsewhere in the school.

The key element in scheduling is teacher flexibility. A teacher who seldom deviates from a fixed schedule invites student boredom, apathy, and resistance. A variable schedule can renew student interest and active participation. Flexibility in the daily schedule can be enhanced in a variety of ways. One way is to vary the class format from day to day, such as by using lectures, class discussions (led by teacher or students), and cooperative learning activities during several individual periods. If varied activities are used, the teacher must organize each individual period differently.

A teacher who uses a lecture method might set up a daily schedule such as:

Class: American History
Topic: The Causes of the Civil War
Activity: Introduction   9:00
    Lecture   9:05
    Conclusion   9:45
    Dismissal   9:50

During this class session the most time would be spent acquainting students with various Civil War concepts (e.g., key battles of the war). In this situation, instructor output is high and student output is relatively low.

For a class session focused more on discussion, a typical schedule might be as follows:

Class: American History
Topic: The Causes of the Civil War
Activity: Introduction   9:00
    Discussion—Topic I (slavery)   9:05
    Discussion—Topic II
      (other economic issues)   9:25
    Summary of discussion   9:45
    Dismissal   9:50

This type of arrangement allows much more input and output by class members.

A period devoted to student projects might resemble Schedule 3.

Class: American History
Topic: The Causes of the Civil War
Activity: Introduction   9:00
    Presentation of Project I
      (the Battle of Gettysburg)   9:05
    Presentation of Project II
      (the Emancipation Proclamation)   9:20
    Presentation of Project III
      (Appomattox)   9:35
    General discussion   9:50
    Dismissal   9:50

Of the three scheduling arrangements mentioned, this last one obviously allows the greatest amount of student responsibility.

Another way to achieve flexibility is to include a variety of presentation modes within one period. This approach is appropriate because many students find it difficult to learn when they are expected to listen to a lecture, read from a text, or discuss a topic for the entire class session. One such 50-minute period might be scheduled as follows.

Class: Life Skills I
Topic: Criminal Justice
    8:35 Opening exercises
    8:40 Brief introductory lecture on rights and
          responsibilities
    8:50 Reading from "Law and Justice" text
    9:00 Discussion of what happens when a
          person is arrested and introduction of
          Miranda rules
    9:20 Closure
    9:25 Class dismissal

An anticipatory set might be achieved through an opening statement about what is to be covered (e.g., "Today we are going to look at what law and justice mean to us. We will be interested in answering questions such as What is law? Why should we have laws? Who enforces the law?"). The discussion session might probe what happens when a high school student is arrested. Closure might involve a forward look (e.g., "Tomorrow we are going to discuss where we get our attitudes toward law and determine differences between shoplifting, income tax evasion, and other offenses. What other issues do you think we need to be concerned with?").

Block Scheduling

One increasingly popular option to traditional daily scheduling is scheduling by blocks; this method typically extends the class instructional period. For example, at the high school level, periods may increase in length from 50 minutes to 90 to 100 minutes. Figure 2–3 provides a sample elementary schedule and Figure 2–4 depicts a sample secondary schedule. In general, block schedules are purported to enhance school climate, provide for fewer disruptions in the day, facilitate inclusion programs, and focus attention

FIGURE 2–3

A parallel block elementary school schedule

Teachers	50 mins	50 mins	50 mins	50 mins
Teacher A	Language Arts & Social Studies (Reading-Writing Groups 1 & 2)		Reading-Writing Group 1	Reading-Writing Group 2
Teacher B	Language Arts & Social Studies (Reading-Writing Groups 3 & 4)		Reading-Writing Group 3	Reading-Writing Group 4
Teacher C	Reading-Writing Group 5	Reading-Writing Group 6	Language Arts & Social Studies (Reading-Writing Groups 5 & 6)	
Teacher D	Reading-Writing Group 7	Reading-Writing Group 8	Language Arts & Social Studies (Reading-Writing Groups 7 & 8)	
Extension Center	Reading-Writing Groups 6 & 8	Reading-Writing Groups 5 & 7	Reading-Writing Groups 2 & 4	Reading-Writing Groups 1 & 3

Source: CEC (1996). Block scheduling gaining steam. *CEC Today, 2*(10), p. 1.

(especially at the secondary level) on fewer classes at a time, which can be taught in more creative ways with more time available for varying classroom activities (Buckman, King, & Ryan, 1995; Council for Exceptional Children, 1996). A comprehensive discussion on block scheduling is available in Canody and Rettig (1995).

Resource Teaching

Basic scheduling principles can also be applied to resource programs. These concerns are briefly outlined here as an adjunct to the general principles of scheduling discussed earlier. For further information, the reader is encouraged to review Wiederholt, Hammill, and Brown (1993) and Harris and Schultz (1993).

1. Regular, frequent instruction in the resource room (four to five periods per week) is preferable to only one or two periods per week.
2. To the maximum degree possible, students should be grouped with same-age peers for instruction.
3. Instructional periods should be set up to allow for consistency across curricular needs for a given group of students, with attention given concurrently to individual differences.
4. Resource teachers should determine the extent of their responsibilities for school-wide

assessment activities and committee work (e.g., child study committees) and should allow sufficient planning time.

5. Resource teachers' schedules should avoid the appearance of preferential treatment (e.g., absence of bus duty or lunch duty).
6. Individual determination should be made as to whether students will be best served by having their resource instruction in a particular area (e.g., reading) scheduled in lieu of or in addition to regular class instruction in that area.
7. When scheduling results in a student's missing instruction in a given curricular area, resource teachers should investigate ways to help the student compensate for this gap.
8. Individual periods should provide students with an appropriate sequence of instructional activities that incorporates previously mentioned principles of opening exercises, acquisition instruction, proficiency/maintenance and generalization activities (as appropriate), and closure.
9. Program management often dictates the development of appropriate contingencies for students in terms of moving directly to and from the regular classroom and adhering to scheduled times for instruction.
10. Resource teachers should serve as advocates to avoid instructional abuses that stem from incorrect administrative practices relative to

FIGURE 2–4

A 4/4 secondary school semester block for 8 courses

Blocks and Times	Fall	Spring	Fall	Spring	Fall	Spring
	1/3 of School Follows This Schedule		1/3 of School Follows This Schedule		1/3 of School Follows This Schedule	
Block I & HR 8:00-9:35 am	Course 1	Course 5	Course 1	Course 5	Course 1	Course 5
Block II 9:40-11:10 am	Course 2	Course 6	Course 2	Course 6	Course 2	Course 6
Lunch and Block III 11:15-1:25 pm	Lunch 11:15-11:50		Course 3 11:15-12:00		Course 3 11:15-12:45	Course 7 11:15-12:45
	Course 3 11:55-1:25	Course 7 11:55-1:25	Lunch 12:05-12:35			
			Course 7 12:40-1:25		Lunch 12:50-1:25	
Block IV 1:30-3:00 pm	Course 4	Course 8	Course 4	Course 8	Course 4	Course 8

Source: CEC (1996). Block scheduling gaining steam. CEC Today, 2(10), p. 1.

the resource model (e.g., haphazard blending of resource and self-contained models, significant variance in groups within a given period in terms of curricular needs and age levels).

Although these principles may reflect the ideal rather than the real, they are intended to serve as the direction in which programs should move. These scheduling principles can provide a basis for improved effectiveness and accountability.

INSTRUCTIONAL PLANNING

Instructional planning builds on effective schedules. Two key topics are lesson plans and unit teaching.

Lesson Planning

Lesson plans should focus directly on the teaching objectives derived from the students' IEPs. Thus, plans should be consistent with prior assessment of students' specific learning needs. Certainly IEPs do not provide a blueprint for daily instructional planning. However, as Langone (1990) aptly noted, the key is translation, that is, "the ability of the teacher to translate the short-term objectives of the IEP to smaller, more workable components called instructional objectives" (p. 407). Without such translation, IEPs lose func-

tionality and become merely means of maintaining compliance with federal law and state regulations (Smith, 1990a, b).

Lesson plans force teachers to identify what they will teach and how. The important aspect for the teacher is not the format of the lesson plan but rather the careful consideration of what will be taught and how. In fact, a survey of over 200 special educators indicated that more than half (58.5%) reported that they did not write out plans for each lesson they taught although the teachers did indicate the key role of conscious (i.e., mental) planning for preparation (Searcy & Maroney, 1996a). The essential concern is whether the system used by the teacher results in sufficient preparation for teaching.

Figure 2–5 illustrates a typical lesson plan format. Because teachers present varied types of material to many students, experienced teachers may not regularly write such detailed lesson plans; however, many do and they are particularly valuable to beginning teachers (Maroney & Searcy, 1996b) because constructing detailed plans assists in focusing precisely on the instructional process.

Regardless of format and specificity, all plans should attend to the questions of why, what, and how. An assessment of needs determines why. The what is expressed as objectives stated in terms of observable student performance, which can be evaluated to determine whether the student has

FIGURE 2–5
Sample lesson plan

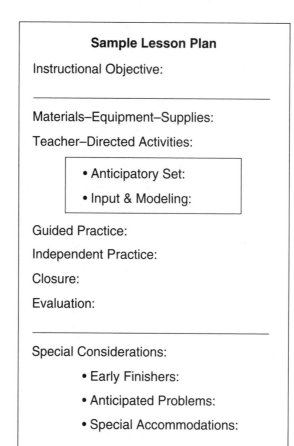

attained the objective. For illustration purposes, Table 2-2 provides data on the patterns of special education teachers using five planning methods for each of 14 potential lesson plan components.

The *how* of the lesson plan is the method of presentation; it describes the teaching process and any materials or programs to be used. All plans should also provide for evaluation of teaching efficiency and effectiveness.

Some specific suggestions on developing lesson plans include:

1. Create interest in and clarify the purpose of lessons. This is particularly important for students with special needs.
2. Provide direct instruction on key topics to help students acquire an initial grasp of new material.

3. Assign independent practice, some of which can be accomplished in class and some of which should be done as homework.
4. Plan activities for students who finish early.
5. Anticipate problems that might arise during the course of the lesson and identify techniques for dealing with them (Smith, Polloway, Patton, & Dowdy, 1998).

Unit Teaching

Curricular planning need not focus entirely on specific, insular areas such as math, spelling, or reading. Rather, a teacher can incorporate a range of content into instructional units. For instance, a capable teacher might spend a significant portion of a school day on a specific project (e.g., a class play or mock TV show) and in so doing integrate

TABLE 2–2
Lesson planning methods used by special educators

Lesson Plan Component	Planning Method									
	Written Out		Habit or Instinct		Conscious Planning		Student Choice		Other	
	%	n	%	n	%	n	%	n	%	n
Student objectives	26.6	55	4.8	10	55.1	114	—	0	13.5	28
Materials required	37.7	78	15.9	33	35.3	73	1.0	2	10.1	21
Time required	14.5	30	23.7	49	40.6	84	7.2	15	14.0	29
Prerequisite skills	2.9	6	29.0	60	57.0	118	0.5	1	10.6	22
Seating arrangement	9.2	19	24.6	51	16.4	34	30.9	64	18.9	39
Anticipatory set	9.7	20	33.3	69	42.5	88	1.0	2	13.5	28
Instructional steps	28.0	58	24.2	50	35.3	73	—	0	12.5	26
Check Understanding	15.5	32	34.8	72	38.2	79	1.0	2	10.6	22
Guided practice	28.5	59	28.0	58	32.9	68	1.0	2	9.6	20
Independent practice	41.1	85	16.4	34	27.5	57	4.3	9	10.6	22
Closing	7.2	15	42.5	88	37.7	78	0.5	1	12.1	25
Evaluation	34.8	72	17.9	37	32.9	68	1.0	11	14.5	19
Follow-up activity	23.2	48	22.7	47	36.2	75	3.9	8	14.0	29
Self-evaluation	1.9	4	47.8	99	31.4	65	1.4	3	17.4	36

Note. All percentages were calculated based on $N = 207$.
Source: Searcy, S., & Maroney, S. A. (1996). Lesson planning practices of special education teachers. *Exceptionality, 6,* p. 179.

writing (preparing the script), reading (reading the script for tryouts and rehearsal), and math (selling tickets, anticipating the number in the audience). Other curricular areas, such as science and social studies, can also be integrated into the play. Skilled teachers who are familiar with their pupils can individualize such a project by assigning responsibilities according to each pupil's needs and abilities. Other opportunities are also available; for example, a cooking/baking project provides opportunities for reading skills (e.g., reading recipes) and math skills (e.g., determining proportions of ingredients, counting ingredients, monitoring baking time).

By definition, unit teaching involves integrating material from several content areas that focus on one theme. It is similar in conceptualization to the concept of integrated curriculum. The instructional objectives, incorporated from the multiple content areas, should be stated in clear, concise, observable terms as in any lesson plan. Unit teaching presents material in an engaging, relevant format that can enhance transfer of learning. In general, unit teaching is most appropriate for maintenance and generalization learning. The following list outlines the specific aspects to consider in constructing an instructional unit.

1. Unit theme and general objectives
   a. Clearly identify the theme.
   b. State the rationale as related to students' needs.
   c. Pre-test students' abilities relative to them.
   d. Establish relevant general objectives.
2. Specific learning objectives
   a. Establish specific objectives for thematic factors.

  b. Establish specific objectives for skills ac-
     quisition, maintenance/proficiency, and
     generalization.
3. Integrated content areas
  a. Identify curricular areas included.
  b. Outline how each area will be incorpo-
     rated.
4. Unit activities outline
  a. Identify daily sequence of activities (for ap-
     proximately 10 to 20 sessions).
  b. Ensure that activities relate to unit objec-
     tives.
5. Evaluation
  a. Outline overall plan for evaluation of unit.
  b. Specify in terms of learner performance
     and instructional effectiveness.
6. Resources and References
  a. Identify resources available for student use
     and instructor preparation.
  b. Consider books, articles, audiovisual mate-
     rials, and speakers.

Unit teaching can be an excellent organizational teaching strategy for adding instructional
variety while addressing proficiency, maintenance, and generalization. Units provide meaningful contexts for instruction and opportunities
to include functional life skills as well as direct,
concrete experiences. Teachers should select unit
themes based on students' interests and ability
levels. Table 2–3 lists possible topics for instructional units across four broad curricular areas.

PLANNING HOMEWORK STRATEGIES

An important element of the educational reform
movement has been an increased call for collaborative efforts between the school and families.
As the U.S. Department of Education's report indicated, "parents are the earliest, and can be the
most consistent and proximal, influence in establishing and supporting lifelong learning" (1991,
p. B-20).

Although a number of areas of educational
practices may affect home-school interactions, a
key aspect is homework. While numerous dis-

TABLE 2–3
Sample instructional units

Science	Social Studies
solar energy	family history
neighborhood fauna	ethnic studies
pond life	map and globe skills
magnetism	backyard history
appliances	local geography
kitchen physics/chemistry	supply and demand
electricity	community resources
grocery store science	voting and elections
rocketry	citizen rights
weather	citizen rights
Career Development	**Health and Safety**
career clusters	dental care
job searching	foreign travel
interviewing techniques	treatment of maladies
résumé writing	first aid
occupational interest	smoking
hobbies and leisure	diet and health
activities	driving
postsecondary options	AIDS
using community	exercise
transportation	drug abuse
community helpers	household hazards
occupations of family	medical insurance
members	alcohol

agreements abound, the literature generally favors homework as having a desirable effect on
school achievement (Cooper & Nye, 1995).
When this conclusion is combined with the reform literature supporting increased use to enhance quality, it is apparent that students with
special needs will need to be able to respond effectively, especially as they spend more time in
inclusive settings. The increased awareness of
this reality led to the US Department of Education funding three major research projects in the
1990s with significant effects on the literature in
this area. While less than a dozen articles and
only a handful of papers were published previously on the topic, since then at least three
special journal issues one book, and over 50
manuscripts have been published (Polloway, Bursuck, & Epstein, 1999).

Two conclusions are clear. First, several difficulties are likely to be experienced by students with special needs. Second, it appears reasonable to conclude that while homework presents special problems for students with disabilities and their families, intervention efforts can result in beneficial outcomes. The following suggestions provide direction for developing and implementing homework practices.

Management Considerations[2]

Management recommendations refer to school-initiated procedures associated with the homework process. These are activities over which teachers have direct control and can be associated with various dimensions of classroom management.

Assess Student Homework Skills. Identifying potential problems associated with homework can assist in preventing them from occurring or keep them from becoming serious. Both standardized instruments, such as the Homework Problem Checklist (Anesko, Schoiock, Ramirez, & Levine, 1987), and nonstandardized instruments are useful. It is a good idea to have parents assess the skills of their children too.

Assign Homework from the Beginning of the Year. Getting students accustomed to the routine of having homework is best accomplished by assigning it early in the school year and continuing with it on a regular basis. The purpose of the assigned homework can vary and does not have to be tied intricately to academics. For example, an early homework assignment could ask students to complete an interest inventory, which would give the teacher valuable background information.

Establish a Class Routine for Homework. If the homework process is to run efficiently, adequate time must be allocated to as-

sign, collect, and evaluate homework. Teachers need to have a reasonable amount of time to inform students of their homework assignment. If sufficient time is not available, a predictable amount of confusion ensues when, for example, assignments are given to students as they are exiting the room after the bell rings. Similarly, time must also be dedicated to collecting and evaluating homework on the next day.

Communicate Consequences. Students need to know the rules of the game regarding homework. Students certainly need to know the procedures that are expected of them as well as the consequences of violating these procedures. Logical consequences for noncompletion of assignments should be determined before students arrive for the first day of classes.

Minimize the Demands on Teacher Time. Homework is only one of many duties that teachers must manage during the instructional day. Therefore, any mechanism created to handle homework must demonstrate efficiency. If individualized assignments are indicated, they can be provided by adapting the general assignment rather than developing completely different activities.

Present Instructions Clearly. The results of not understanding a homework assignment have both short- and long-term implications. In the short term, some students stop paying attention if they are not able to follow what is being said; others may not get off task but may comprehend little of what is said. In the long term, they simply are not able to complete the assigned work. A thorough explanation of a homework assignment should include the following components: (a) state the purpose, (b) give directions for completing the assignment, (c) provide an estimate of how long the assignment should take, (d) note when it is due, (e) clarify the format to be used, (f) identify the materials needed to successfully complete the assignment, and (g) indicate how it will be evaluated.

To complement clearly presented instructions, teachers should query students to deter-

[2]This section is adapted from "Practical Recommendations for Using Homework with Students with Learning Disabilities," by J. R. Patton, 1994, *Journal of Learning Disabilities, 27*, p. 570–578. Reprinted with permission.

mine whether they understand what is assigned. If students are required to write their homework, this can be visually checked. Another technique to ensure that students understand and are prepared to complete an assignment is to let them begin working on it in class.

Use Assignment Books. For many students with disabilities, tasks that require organizational ability and memory skills can be troublesome. Homework assignment books—either commercially produced or teacher-generated—can help compensate for these difficulties. Typically, the students will write their assignments in these books and the teachers can initial the books before the students leave the class, confirming that the correct assignment has been recorded.

Folders also can be used to collect homework when students enter class. This provides a quick and simple way for the teacher to evaluate completion of the assignment, thus underscoring the importance of turning assignments in on time.

Implement Classroom-Based Incentive Programs. Systems can be designed to reinforce the completion and the accuracy of homework. Although the ultimate goal is to develop responsibility and internal controls, teachers may want to consider using various types of incentive systems to assist those students who struggle to deal with the demands of school. Points systems and daily reports cards are examples of these types of techniques.

Have Parents Sign Homework. If a home-school homework program includes nothing else, it should at the very least have parents sign the homework that is assigned. Research has found that the regularity of this action has the strongest relationship to time spent on homework (Holmes & Croll, 1989). Recognizing Salend and Schliff's 1989 finding that only 10% of the special education teachers who work with learning-disabled students indicate that they often require parents to sign homework, it behooves us to implement this simple suggestion.

Evaluate Assignments. Homework that is collected, evaluated, and used to determine a grade is more meaningful to students and has a positive effect on achievement. A substantial number of teachers who work with students who are disabled do not regularly follow these guidelines (Salend & Schliff, 1989). The challenge is to find ways to manage this aspect of the homework process efficiently. Some suggestions have already been given; other ideas include assignments that can be evaluated through peer grading or self-correction techniques. Other suggestions include the use of paraeducators (e.g., educational assistants) to evaluate the homework.

Assignment Considerations

Suggestions in this area relate to the assignment itself. They include the purpose for the assignment, its demands on the student, various adaptations that are possible, and selected cautions.

Recognize the Purpose of the Assignment. The major reasons why teachers assign homework vary; however, the most frequently cited ones are practice opportunities, completion of unfinished work, preparation for future course activities or upcoming tests, and extension. Teachers of students with learning disabilities use practice and completion type of homework activities most frequently (Salend & Schliff, 1989). Guided by a clear purpose for giving homework, teachers should also identify specific objectives for each assignment. As noted above, teachers should inform students of these objectives when a homework assignment is introduced.

Establish Relevance. Related to the instructional purpose for assigning homework is the perceived importance of it from the student's perspective. As Check and Ziebell (1980) point out, "with a reasonable amount of assigned homework [the student] will have little objection to doing his lesson if he or she can see the value of this work to his class work and to future career demands" (p. 440). Teachers are advised to show students how a particular assignment relates to their scholastic or nonacademic lives.

Use Appropriate Learning Stage. One way to look at the value of homework is to examine its use as a function of the different stages of learning. Homework is best used for proficiency, generalization, or maintenance types of learning activities Rosenberg's 1989 research with students who were learning disabled led to the recommendation that it is unwise to have students work on assignments if they do not "demonstrate at least moderate acquisition of instructional material" (p. 323). Keeping assignments at students' independent level may be the single most critical principle in the area of homework. Similarly, if the assignment is complicated or differs significantly from what the student knows, the likelihood of problems arising increases dramatically. Assigning interesting and motivating homework is not jeopardized by this recommendation and therefore should still be encouraged. There is also evidence that homework is effective with students who have learning disabilities when the rates of completion were at least 70%, the percentage of correct responses to assigned activities averaged 70% or better, and, as discussed earlier, students demonstrated at least moderate acquisition of the material (Rosenberg, 1989). These findings suggest that teachers consider ways to provide incentives for completing assignments if internal systems are nonoperative and carefully plan the types of homework given so that students' chances of responding correctly are maximized.

Select Appropriate Type of Activity.

The type of homework assigned will depend on the reason for giving it. The probability that students will complete an assignment successfully will depend on, among other factors, whether they understand how to use homework materials. Teachers who are trying to move students into inclusive settings should identify the types of assignments given in these classes and create assignments of a similar nature.

Adapt Assignments.

As more students face the challenges of completing homework assignments in general education classes, it is imperative that practical ways to adapt assignments be identified. Adaptive techniques that should be considered include shorter assignments, extended time-

line, alternative evaluation techniques (i.e., based on effort, not accuracy), fewer assignments, extra credit opportunities, alternative response formats, and group assignments. Polloway, Epstein, Bursuck, Jayanthi, & Cumblad (1994) found that general education teachers favored adaptations that give extra assistance over those that seemingly give an advantage to students with disabilities, such as adjusting due dates.

Student Considerations

The recommendations in this section focus on requisite skills and information that students need to be proficient at various homework tasks as well as certain skills that can be developed through the process.

Demonstrate Minimum Levels of Competence.

To complete homework assignments successfully, students must possess acceptable levels of content knowledge and skill competency. Further, to work as independently as they can on homework requires proficiency in using academic support skills, otherwise known as study skills. If students are deficient in areas such as using a dictionary, skimming, scanning, or time management, they should be taught these skills.

Promote Interdependent Learning.

We talk about making students independent learners when we really want to make them interdependent learners. Students benefit not only from being able to direct their own learning activities but also from knowing how to seek assistance when needed. Examples include asking for clarification when they are confused and contacting resource persons when information is needed. A homework hotline is an example of a support system based on the idea of interdependence that is often available to students and their families.

Develop Self-Management Skills.

Allied to the goal of making students more involved in directing their own learning is the development of self-management behaviors. To be self-directed learners, students must demonstrate the ability to manage their study behaviors. Teaching self-management skills or creating systems that require these skills can prove beneficial for students who are having difficulty completing assignments. Consistent with this focus, a significant outcome of a successful homework system is the students' taking responsibility for outside class aspects of their own learning. Teachers should help students understand that the effort they put forth can lead to academic success.

Consider Student Preferences. When developing a comprehensive homework program, it is beneficial to consider students' views on homework practices. A number of recent studies address the issue of student preferences. A particularly good illustration is the research by Nelson, Epstein, Bursuck, Jayanthi, and Sawyer (1998). They surveyed the preferences of middle school students for homework adaptations made in the general education classroom. After reporting data on homework preferences for students with high-incidence disabilities and variant levels of achievement, they also reported the students' choices of adaptations most liked and least liked and also the frequency of typical rationales provided by students. This information is presented in Tables 2–4 and 2–5; these data provide a rich portrait of students' views on homework.

Parent Involvement

Parents are a critical part of the homework process and so it is essential to involve them in appropriate ways. A key area that is problematic is home-school communication about homework (Jayanthi, Sawyer, Nelson, Bursuck, & Epstein, 1995). These general recommendations suggest how parents can best participate in the homework process.

Serve in a Supportive Role. The primary role of parents regarding homework should be to support and reinforce what is taught at school. If homework is properly designed by the teacher, the nature of the assignments will lend themselves to this type of involvement.

Create an Environment Conducive to Homework. This recommendation involves five major components. First, parents need to set a specific time for doing homework and see to it that their children respond. Second, a distraction-free setting for doing homework must be arranged. Students who are disabled can benefit from having their home learning environments structured so they can attend to their assignments better. Third, parents should help their child to obtain all necessary materials and equipment needed to complete homework assignments. It is the responsibility of the student to bring home any school material needed. Fourth, parents can play important roles while the homework is being done and after it is completed. Letting their child know how much they appreciate the effort being made and providing positive feedback when the homework is done are motivating to students. Finally, for parents to be effective contributors to the homework process, they need to stay involved over time. Without long-term interest in and interaction with their child's homework, parents will notice problems in many instances.

Communicate Views to School Personnel. If a smooth school-home communication system is operating, this suggestion is moot because many ongoing opportunities to share views on homework exist. Nevertheless, parents should be contacted regarding homework to request their views and to be informed of their child's school-based performance. In addition to these general recommendations, Table 2–6 lists some specific strategies that can assist in enhancing home-school collaboration.

DEVELOPING RECORD-KEEPING PROCEDURES

Record keeping consists of collecting, maintaining, and utilizing student information and data for instructional and/or administrative purposes. Many teachers find managing a data/information system difficult, and the pressures of an already demanding amount of paperwork discourage some from establishing record-keeping systems.

TABLE 2–4
Frequency of students' choices of adaptation as most liked and frequency of typical rationales

Item/Rationales	Frequency[3]
Give assignments that are finished at school	53 (25.1%)
Allows times for other activities	35
Reduces homework or makes it easier	20
Makes help available (from teacher or other students)	9
Allow a small group of students to work together to complete an assignment	28 (13.3%)
Makes help available (from other students)	11
Makes homework more enjoyable	10
Allows discussion and sharing of ideas with others	8
Allow extra credit	27 (12.8%)
Improves performance	22
Begin assignments in class and check for understanding	24 (11.4%)
Makes help available	15
Improves performance	8
Facilitates understanding of content of homework assignment	6
Grade assignments according to effort	23 (10.9%)
Positively affects emotions and self-concept (student wouldn't feel as pressured/worried)	8
Is more equitable (different students have different abilities)	10
Give more reminders about due dates	15 (7.1%)
Facilitates organization (would remember to complete and submit assignments)	14
Give shorter, more frequent assignments	12 (5.7%)
Facilitates organization (would remember to complete, avoid procrastination)	7
Reduces homework or makes it easier (would have time for, seems like less)	3

Note. Frequencies given for choice of adaptation do not sum to 211 because adaptations chosen by fewer than 10 students are not included in the table. Frequencies given for rationales do not equal the frequency of students choosing that adaptation because students may have expressed more than one rationale for their choice and atypical rationales (expressed by fewer than 5 students) are not included in the table.
[3]$N = 211$.
Source: Nelson, J. S., Epstein, M. H., Bursuck, W. D., Jayanthi, M., & Sawyer, V. (1998). The preferences of middle school students for homework adaptations made by general education teachers. *Learning Disabilities Research & Practice, 13,* p. 114.

Although initiating such a system requires effort, it need not continue to consume inordinate amounts of time. A properly designed, efficient record-keeping system should reduce the time needed to prepare for teaching.

Two types of record-keeping systems are discussed here. The first type assists the teacher in the daily management of the instructional pro-gram while the second involves evaluating student performance.

Daily Assignment

Teachers face two problems in the smooth delivery of instruction: keeping track of assignments and activities that students are to do and inform-

TABLE 2–5
Frequency of students' choices of adaptation as most liked and frequency of typical rationales

Item/Rationales	Frequency[3]
Give fewer assignments than given to other students	52 (24.6%)
Is inequitable (is unfair, everyone should be treated the same)	34
Negatively affects emotions and self-concept (student would be perceived as different from others or as less capable)	17
Interferes with learning and understanding content of assignment	8
Give different assignments than given to other students	37 (17.5%)
Is inequitable (is unfair, everyone should be treated the same way)	12
Makes help unavailable (from peers because they wouldn't have the same assignment)	9
Negatively affects emotions and self-concept (student would be perceived as different from others or as less capable)	6
Require use of an assignment notebook	30 (14.2%)
Interferes with individual choice and accountability (want to use own way of keeping track)	19
Interferes with organization (using a notebook is inconvenient and a waste of time)	14
Give shorter assignments than given to other students	26 (12.3%)
Is inequitable (is unfair, everyone should be treated the same)	21
Negatively affects emotions and self-concept (student would) be perceived as different from others or as less capable	7
Give shorter, more frequent assignments	14 (6.6%)
Interferes with organization (can't be flexible in scheduling when to complete)	8
Allow oral rather than written answers	12 (5.7%)
Interferes with learning and understanding of content of assignment (written answers are easier to understand and remember)	8

Note. Frequencies given for choice of adaptations do not sum to 211 because adaptations chosen by fewer than 10 students are not included in the table. Frequencies given for rationales do not equal the frequency of students choosing that adaptation because students may have expressed more than one rationale for their choice and atypical rationales (expressed by fewer than 5 students) are not included in the table.
[3]$N = 211$.
Source: Nelson, J. S., Epstein, M. H., Bursuck, W. D., Jayanthi, M., & Sawyer, V. (1998). The preferences of middle school students for homework adaptations made by general education teachers. *Learning Disabilities Research & Practice, 13,* p. 114.

ing students of what they are to do, especially seat work activities. Once again, developing appropriate systems requires some effort but can eliminate two classroom administrative hassles.

Figures 2-6 through 2-9 are examples of assignment sheets. These samples are provided as guides only; the best method for any given teacher is custom-made. Regardless of the system chosen, however, students must understand how it works; to accomplish this, any system must be demonstrated and practiced. Figure 2-6 is a simple daily activity sheet for one subject area. It

TABLE 2–6
Strategies for home-school collaboration on homework

- Provide computer-generated progress reports on homework performance to parents. These reports should include descriptive comments about performance.
- Communicate using written modes of communication (e.g., progress reports, notes, letters, forms). Use brightly colored paper to grab attention and prevent misplacement.
- At the beginning of the year/semester, give parents information regarding assignments, homework adaptations available in the classroom, and policy on missed assignments and extra credit homework.
- Communicate with other teachers to avoid overloading the student with homework (and to) prevent homework completion problems at home.
- Have face-to-face communication with other teachers and parents.
- Reflect understanding that homework may be a lower priority for families when compared with other issues (e.g., school attendance, family illness) and respond accordingly by addressing these other issues first.
- Help students in completing and submitting homework on time (e.g., remind students of assignments due dates periodically, assign homework in small units, write assignments on the board).

Source: Adapted from Jayanthi, M., Bursuck, W., Epstein, M. H., & Polloway, E. A. (1997). Strategies for successful homework. *Teaching Exceptional Children, 29,* p. 4–7.

contains the date of the assigned activity, a description of the assignment, some type of evaluative information (e.g., points, checkmarks), and any necessary comments. Glisan (1984) developed a daily sheet that is a variation of the one presented in Figure 2-6. She includes columns for the points earned for the assignment, the points applied to a contract system, and a subjec-tive evaluation of behavior indicated by one of three symbols. A sample sheet following this format is given in Figure 2-7.

Figures 2–8 through 2-10 illustrate other samples of daily assignment sheets. The specific procedures for using these particular forms are provided in the figures. Even though Figure 2-9 represents a more complicated system, even ele-

FIGURE 2–6
Basic Daily Activity Sheet

| Name _____ |
| Subject _____ |

Date	Assignment	Evaluation	Comments

FIGURE 2–7
Daily Assignment Sheet

DAILY SHEET

Allen Sheppy

Subject __English__

Year __92-93__

Period __5th__

DATE	ACTIVITY	COMMENTS	FINAL POINTS	CONTRACT POINTS	+/–/o
Monday Sept. 14	As the Year Passes Card 6	Fin ———————	12/14		+
Tuesday Sept. 15	Card 7	Inc — refused to work- upset about girl			—
Wednesday Sept. 16	Card 7 absent	ex			

From Record Keeping for Individualized Junior-Senior High School Special Education Programs (p. 28), by E. M. Glisan, 1984. Freeport, IL: Peekan Publications. Copyright 1984 by Peekan Publications, Inc. Reprinted with permission.

FIGURE 2–8
Student's Daily Assignment Sheet

	Monday 3/10	Tuesday 3/11	Wednesday 3/12	Thursday 3/13	Friday 3/14
Phonics Workbook A	21	22		23	24
Phonics Cards	6		7		

Code:	Each cell with a number	=	specific page in the instructional material.
	Date above the column	=	dates assigned.
	Diagonal line (╱)	=	student indication that assignment has been completed.
	Diagonal line (╲)	=	teacher indication that work has been corrected.

FIGURE 2–9
Record sheet for second grade mathematics

Math

Student:	Ronnie Smith
Teacher:	Ms. Jones
Testing Modifications:	Extended Time

Skill Area	Objective	Progress					Comments
2M1	Read numbers to 12 with 100% accuracy.	9/10 9/13 9/26 10/1 10/2 11/4 1/20 2/8					10/1-Back after chicken pox 2/8-Writes 5 backwards
2M2	Write numbers to 12 with 100% accuracy.	10/1 10/18 10/23 11/1 11/6 12/4 1/13 3/18					11/1-Provide model of numbers
2M3	Recall with addition facts through sums to 5 with 90% accuracy.	10/12 11/2 11/30 12/18 2/7 3/2 4/18 6/1 6/23					4/8-Use of flashcards with peer
2M4	Recall with addition facts where 1 addend is 0, 1, 2, 3, with 90% accuracy.	12/6 12/21 1/6 1/18 2/1 3/2 3/18 3/26 4/18 4/27					3/18-Had fight with classmate
2M5	Recall subtraction facts related to sums of 5 with 80% accuracy.	1/22 2/3 2/17 2/28 3/7 4/22 5/19					
2M6	Recall subtraction facts for which subtrahend is 0, 1, 2, 3, with 80% accuracy.	3/4 3/12 3/30 4/7 4/12 5/1 5/17 5/22 5/30 6/3					
2M7	Read and write 2-digit numbers for objects grouped by 10s and 1s with 80% accuracy.	4/2 4/17 4/28 5/6 6/13					
2M8	Read, write, and count numbers through 100 with 100% accuracy.	N					
2M9	Skip count by 2, 3, 5, 10 with 80% accuracy.	N					

Key to symbols:　□ - objective introduced　　P - partially mastered

○ - unsuccessful attempt　　N - not introduced

9/26 - successful probe

mentary-aged students with special needs are capable of learning and using it efficiently. Figure 2-10 shows how a record-keeping system allows for individual differences (i.e., testing modifications), can be tied closely to the scope and sequence of a particular program (i.e., skill area code and specific objective), provides usable information regarding the current status and ongoing progress of an individual student (i.e., progress column), and includes other qualitative information (i.e., comments column). As the developers of the form suggest, forms can be created on a computer ahead of time.

If designed and introduced properly, some systems enable students to pick up their individual folders, turn to the assignment sheet, and begin seat work without any teacher direction. Some teacher assistance may still be needed but a well-established system generally releases a teacher from using valuable class time on a daily basis to direct students to assignments.

Monitoring Student Performance and Progress

Obtaining information about a student's progress in a given program or about an instructional technique's effectiveness is essential to effective teaching and has been strongly advocated by proponents of curriculum-based assessment. Such an assessment regularly requires instructionally related decisions. Although a certain amount of "clinical" judgment, acquired with experience, can be quite accurate, most evaluation specialists suggest collecting observable, measurable data. Record keeping becomes particularly important as teachers and school systems are subject to accountability measures.

A variety of techniques for keeping track of data have been developed (Table 2-7). Sometimes referred to as formative evaluation, recording techniques may include narrative/anecdotal logs, charts, or matrices. All of these forms involve recording quantifiable data, usually in terms of a correct number or percentage. Another useful procedure is precision teaching, which focuses on accuracy as well as rate and can predict a student's progress based on previously collected data. Above all, the system chosen should provide important information about student learning without being burdensome to the teacher.

Keeping records of student progress emphasizes the accurate, systematic collection of data. It assumes that one can observe and measure the student performance being monitored. If developed prior to the beginning of a school year, such a system can be implemented immediately.

A number of suggestions developed by Guerin and Maier (1983) may help in designing a data-based system for monitoring student progress.

1. Use recording procedures that are as simple and efficient as possible.
2. Have students or teaching assistants, when appropriate, participate in the recording process.
3. Record information so that it represents the critical elements of the event accurately.
4. Use a recording format that does not require transfer of the raw data to another form. (pp. 57-58)

Another suggestion is to graph the data collected. Although this idea is recommended because of the ease in interpreting the data contained in a graphic representation, one caution must be noted. Often, teachers post performance statistics (e.g., students' performance charts) on the wall for all to see. This display reinforces students who are progressing, does not motivate students who are not, and is based on an external motivation orientation. If such graphing of student performance is needed, it should be done in folders that students can inspect privately.

IMPLEMENTING EFFECTIVE GRADING PRACTICES

Grading is a required form of student evaluation and record keeping and an integral part of our educational system. As Hess, Miller, Reese, and Robinson (1987) indicate, "grading is an important aspect of documenting the educational experience of students [and thus] assignment of grades has created and will continue to create debate within the educational community" (p. 1). Thus, grading practices recently have been subjected to frequent deliberation and review (see Bursuck et al. 1996; Bursuck, Munk & Olsen, 1999; Polloway, Bursuck, Jayanthi, & Epstein, 1996).

Grades serve a variety of crucial purposes including administrative, student, teacher, guidance, and parent (Table 2-8). However, while serving these functions, grading practices have clearly not been without criticism. For example,

TABLE 2–7
Systems for evaluating student progress

Technique	Data	Possible Interpretation
Narrative Log	Marie did better today in math and reading. Her acting-out behavior was under more control.	Marie actually 1. did better, or 2. did more work The teacher was 1. less hassled, or 2. in a better mood
Arithmetic chart		Child's percentage correct has increased.
Learning Matrices		Child has mastered first and second tasks but not third or fourth.
Precision Teaching		Child initially had many errors. Errors were isolated and worked on separately. Learning is now occurring. Child should master task within 3 to 4 days.

Note: From *Evaluating Exceptional Children: A Task Analysis Approach* (p. 139), by K. W. Howell, J. S. Kaplan, and C. Y. O'Connell, 1979, Upper Saddle River, NJ: Merrill/Prentice Hall. Copyright 1979 by Merrill/Prentice Hall. Adapted by permission.

Terwilliger (1977) identified the following concerns: grading is simplistic in nature, it overlooks intangible outcomes of learning, it is an ineffective motivator, it is not sufficiently concerned with mastery, it leads to failure, it subjects all to universal standards, and it promotes competition rather than cooperation. Although each of these represents more bias than validation, all suggest some problematic areas that a fair, equitable, and effective grading system needs to consider.

TABLE 2–8
Functions of grades

Administrative Functions
to indicate whether a student has passed or failed
to indicate whether a student should be promoted or not
to be used by employers in evaluating prospective employees
to transmit information from one school district to another
to provide the public with a guarantee of competence

Student Functions
to give students a reward and a sense of achievement
to give students feedback on progress
to motivate students
to give students experience of real-life situations
to test performance in real life

Teacher Functions
to evaluate students' progress during the course
to assess amount of effort put in by the student
to give feedback on teaching
to grade in relation to other students
to grade in relation to criteria of excellence
to maintain standards

Guidance Functions
to assist personal development of students
to predict future performance
to provide for screening of candidates for occupations and schools
to stimulate students to greater efforts
to determine the number of courses in which a student should enroll
to decide on the advisability for enrolling in other courses
to permit participation in school activities, play on teams, and win scholarships

Parent Functions
to give parents feedback on student progress
to provide parents with information about appropriateness of course placement
to provide parents with a means of evaluating the success of the IEP

Note: Adapted from Grading-Credit-Diploma: Accommodation Practices for Students with Mild Disabilities, by R. Hess, A. Miller, J. Reese, and G. A. Robinson, 1987, Des Moines, IA: Department of Education.

Grading issues are particularly significant for students with disabilities, given increased school inclusion. The data that are available paint a negative picture of grading patterns. Zigmond and her colleagues (Donahue & Zigmond, 1990; Zigmond, Levin, & Laurie, 1985) examined the performance of students with learning disabilities in regular classes in high school. Collectively they found that approximately 60 to 75% of the students who were learning disabled passed their mainstream classes. However, Donahue and Zigmond found that the students were clearly receiving below-average grades with an overall grade point average of 0.99 (i.e., "D" work). Thus, although these students were passing, grading

patterns confirmed a lack of academic success. Similar patterns of grades were also reported by Valdes, Williamson, and Wagner (1990) in the National Longitudinal Transition Study.

Solutions to the problem of grading probably can best be found through student advocacy and tactful interpersonal relationships. The special education teacher generally needs to provide a clear description of an individual student's strengths, weaknesses, capabilities, and needs, thus giving the classroom teacher additional data on which to base a letter grade evaluation. The solution that emphasizes cooperative efforts is the one most likely to succeed. As a model of collaboration, Figure 2-10 presents a schematic of such a process be-

FIGURE 2–10

Making grading decisions in inclusive classrooms

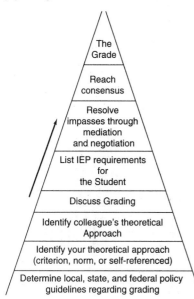

Source: Kroegel, M. (1999). *Making the grade: A case study of assessment and grading practices in an elementary inclusive classroom.* Unpublished doctoral dissertation, Virginia Tech.

tween a special and general education teacher. It was developed by Kroegel (1999) based on the discussion of such a process by Christianson (1998).

To facilitate this process, teachers should jointly consider possible adaptations that will be effective and also be deemed acceptable by general education teachers (Polloway et al., 1996). Table 2-9 provides data on the evaluation of the effectiveness and use of ten adaptations as rated by elementary general education teachers while Table 2-10 provides data from secondary teachers. A more extensive list of grading adaptations is presented in Table 2-11. Finally, an important consideration that must be weighed is the perceived fairness of specific adaptations as viewed by both teachers and peers (Bursuck et al., 1996; Bursuck et al., 1999).

The following general suggestions also may prove helpful to collaborative grading efforts:

1. Keep the lines of communication open at all times, meeting on a regular basis to discuss student progress.
2. Ensure that all teachers are aware of a student's level of functioning by sharing assessment data and including them in IEP meetings.

TABLE 2–9

Elementary teachers' ratings of grading adaptations[a,b]

---

1. Grades are based on the amount of improvement an individual makes. (#1)
2. Separate grades are given for process (e.g., effort) and product (e.g., tests). (#3)
3. Grades are based on meeting IEP objectives. (#9)
4. Grades are adjusted according to student ability. (#2)
5. Grading weights are adjusted (e.g., efforts on projects count more than tests). (#4)
6. Grades are based on meeting the requirements of academic or behavioral contracts. (#5)
7. Grades are based on less content than the rest of the class. (#7)
8. Students are passed if they make an effort to pass. (#6)
9. Grades are based on a modified grading scale (e.g., from 93–100=A, 90–100=A). (#8)
10. Students are passed no matter what. (#10)

---

[a] Ranked from most to least *helpful* for students with disabilities as rated by general educators.
[b] Numbers in parentheses refer to general educator's rankings of adaptations from most to least likely to be *used* with nondisabled students.
Source: Adapted from Bursuck, W., Polloway, E., Plante, L., Epstein, M. H., Jayanthi, M., & McConeghy, J. (1996). Report card grading practices and adaptations. *Exceptional Children, 62,* 301–318. (Permission not required).

TABLE 2–10
Secondary teachers' ratings of grading adaptations[a]

---

1. Separate grades are given for process (e.g., effort) and product (e.g., tests).
2. Grades are based on the amount of improvement an individual makes.
3. Grading weights are adjusted (e.g., effort or projects count more than tests).
4. Grades are based on meeting the requirements of academic or behavioral contracts.
5. Grades are based on meeting IEP objectives.
6. Grades are adjusted according to student ability.
7. Grades are based on a modified grading scale (e.g., from 93–100=A, to 90–100=A).
8. Grades are based on less content than the rest of the class.
9. Students are passed if they make an effort to pass.
10. Students are passed no matter what.

---

[a] Ranked from most to least helpful.
Source: Struyk, L. R., Epstein, M. H., Bursuck, W., Polloway, E. A., McConeghy, J., & Cole, K. B. (1995). Homework, grading, and testing practices used by teachers with students with and without disabilities. *The Clearing House, 69,* p. 53.

3. Stress effort as a criterion central to grade assignment.
4. Emphasize the acquisition of new skills as a basis for grades assigned, thus providing a perspective on the student's relative gains. Charting progress may help illustrate gains.
5. Investigate alternative procedures for evaluating content taught (e.g., oral examinations for poor readers in a science class).
6. Advocate school-wide use of narrative reports as a major portion of the report card, especially for younger children. Salend (1990) identified a series of alternative grading systems that should also be considered. Briefly, these include the following:

   - *individualized education program*: The grade awarded depends on the number and level of competencies of the individual program objectives mastered.
   - *student self-comparison*: Students come to agreement with teachers on instructional goals. Students then measure their progress according to goals achieved. The teacher then records achievements on the students' report cards.
   - *contract grading*: The teacher and student agree on the quality and quantity of work required for specific grades.
   - *pass/fail systems*: Minimum requirements are set and the student who does not meet the standard has failed while the one who satisfies the requirement receives a pass.
   - *multiple grading*: In each subject, the student is graded in three different areas: ability, effort, and achievement. A report card may show three grades or an average.
   - *level grading*: The teacher uses a subscript to determine the level at which the student is performing as compared to the average student of his or her grade.

ORGANIZING MATERIAL SELECTION AND USE

Instructional materials are a key element in the teaching process. Although there is little documentation as to how teachers select instructional materials, it is likely that many do not thoroughly investigate what they are acquiring. In some cases, as with major program adoptions, teachers may actually have limited input into the final decision of a selection committee. Nevertheless, there is a sequence of stages that should guide the selection and use of instructional materials.

TABLE 2–11
Common grading adaptations

Adaptation	Description	Example
Changing grading criteria		
A. Vary grading weights.	A. Vary how much certain criteria (activities or products) count toward a grade.	A. Increase credit for participation in in-class group activities and decrease credit for essay exams.
B. Modify curricular expectations.	B. Identify individualized curriculum upon which to base grade.	B. Write on student's IEP that she will be graded on work on addition while rest of class works on fractions.
C. Use contracts and modified course syllabi.	C. Teacher and student agree on quality, quantity, and time lines for specified work.	C. Written contract states that student will receive an A- for completing all assignments at 80% accuracy, attending all classes, and completing one extra-credit report.
D. Grade on basis of improvement.	D. Assign extra points for improvement over previous performance.	D. Change a C to a B if student's total points were significantly higher than in previous marking period.
Changes to letter and number grades		
E. Add written comments.	E. Add comments to clarify details on criteria used to determine the letter grade.	E. Write on report card that student's grade reflects performance on IEP objectives and not on regular classroom curriculum.
F. Add information from student activity log.	F. Keep written anecdotal notes indicating student performance in specific areas over time.	F. State on student's report card that although student's grade was the same this quarter, daily records indicate student completed math assignments with less teacher assistance.
G. Add information from portfolios and/or performance-based assessment.	G. Collect student work that measures effort, progress, and achievement.	G. State on student's report card that student's written language showed an increase in word variety, sentence length, and quality of ideas.
Alternatives to letter and number grades		
H. Use pass/fail grades.	H. Give student a "pass" if she meets the minimum requirements for the class.	H. Give student a pass for completing 80% of daily work with at least 65% accuracy and attending at least 90% of classes.
I. Use competency checklists.	I. Construct a list of goals and objectives for the quarter.	I. Attach a checklist to report card indicating that during last quarter student mastered addition facts, two-digit addition with regrouping, and counting change to $1.00.

Note. Adapted from "Can Grades Be Helpful and Fair?" by D. Munk and W. Bursuck, 1998. *Educational Leadership, 55*(4), Figure 1, p. 46. Used by permission of the Association for Supervision and Curriculum Development. Copyright © 1998 by ASCD. All rights reserved.
Source: Munk, D. D., & Bursuck, W. D. (1998). Report card grading adaptations for students with disabilities: Types and acceptability. *Intervention in School and Clinic, 33*, p. 307.

Hammill and Bartel (1990) suggest that materials selection should be considered through an analysis of the curriculum-student-teacher triad. They suggest that it is

> analogous to that of the building-occupant-builder triad. The specifications for the building most certainly affect the types of materials to be used, but the selection of materials is also affected by the needs of the occupants, the desires of the builder, and what he or she knows to be effective and available. (p. 537)

During the selection process, it is useful to keep in mind key variables stemming from each aspect of the triad.

Need and Availability

Teachers regularly find it important to obtain new instructional materials. New teachers may find it helpful to keep with their training programs a prepared "wish list" of materials (categorized by subject area) that they would like to have in their classrooms. Their new classrooms may be well stocked, or new materials may have to be selected and obtained quickly—a difficult task. Continuing teachers should also keep an updated wish list. The need to obtain materials may arise for any number of reasons: a new area/topic/unit may need to be presented, the particular needs of students may require specialized intervention, or a program may need variety. Staying aware of what is available can be accomplished by consulting catalogs, attending conferences and in-service opportunities, taking courses, and visiting other classrooms. To order any desired material, it is essential that a current catalog be consulted, because an outdated price list will significantly delay final acquisition. Teachers may want to put their names on the mailing lists of major educational publishers. It is also important to note that specific materials can change from one publisher to another quite quickly. Finally, in instances where special services are organized regionally, an intermediate unit may have resources available for loan or to assist with purchases.

Evaluation

The most important stage in selecting materials is thorough and systematic examination. Gall (1981) suggests three major strategies: examine the actual materials, read any evaluative data that are available, and field test the materials with the targeted student groups. Checklists, rating scales, and inventories can provide a framework for inspection of materials. Gall has developed a comprehensive set of criteria to help with the process (Table 2–12).

It is also advisable to obtain evaluative information about the instructional materials being considered. Of particular interest are critical reviews that have appeared in journals and technical reports that accompany the materials. In addition, a publisher often provides evaluative data collected during the development of a particular material. Unfortunately, most instructional materials are published without formal field testing, so teachers will most often need to validate the usefulness and effectiveness of materials on their own.

To conduct a field test, one must obtain the desired materials for a set amount of time, either by requesting an examination copy from the publisher or by borrowing the materials. Publishers are reluctant to send out major programs on an examination basis; however, such materials may sometimes be available at a school district's resource/materials center.

In reality, most teachers may be unable to accomplish all these suggestions because of logistical limitations. Nevertheless, such an approach is strongly recommended; the ultimate goal is to acquire instructional materials that are appropriate and useful.

Ordering Materials

When it is time to actually order materials, a few ideas are worth considering. In addition to current pricing information, teachers should be aware of budget, time line, and procedures.

In general, teachers need to be aware of how much money they can spend on acquisition of materials and whether the available funds are re-

TABLE 2–12
Materials evaluation criteria

Publication and Cost
1. Is the cost of the materials reasonable relative to other comparable materials?
2. Were the materials adequately field tested and revised prior to publication?
3. Is this edition to be in publication for several years, or is a new edition to be released shortly?
4. Does the publisher of these materials have a good reputation among educators?
5. Are there likely to be difficulties in obtaining sufficient quantities of the materials for each student who will be using them?
6. Are there special resources required to use the materials?
7. Does the use of the materials require special skills or training?

Physical Properties
8. Are the materials likely to appeal to the user's aesthetic sense?
9. Does the product make unnecessary use of consumable materials?
10. Do the materials have components that are especially vulnerable to wear?
11. Are there possible hazards to students or teachers using the materials?

Content
12. Does the developer use an approach consistent with the curriculum being followed?
13. Are the objectives of the materials compatible with the curriculum?
14. Are the materials free of biases that are misleading or unacceptable to teachers, students, and the community?
15. Do the materials reflect the contributions and perspectives of various ethnic and cultural groups?
16. Are the scope and sequence of the materials compatible with the curriculum?
17. Is the content of the materials free of sex stereotypes?
18. Does the content of the materials reflect current knowledge and culture?

Instructional Properties
19. Do the materials contain helpful assessment devices?
20. Are the materials compatible with other materials currently being used?
21. Does the design of the materials allow teachers to use them differently, according to student needs?
22. Does the publisher provide any data on the effectiveness of the materials in actual use?
23. Are the materials appropriate for the students who will be using them?
24. Is use of the materials easily managed by the teacher?
25. Are students likely to have the prerequisite knowledge or skills necessary for learning the content of the materials?
26. Are the materials written at an appropriate reading level for the students who will be using them?
27. Do the materials include activities that students are capable of doing and they will enjoy doing?
28. Do the materials include activities that teachers will find interesting and rewarding?

Note: Adapted from *Handbook for Evaluating and Selecting Curriculum Materials* (pp. 118–120), by M. D. Gall, 1981, Boston: Allyn & Bacon.

stricted to certain types of purchases (e.g., textbooks, equipment, consumable items). They also need to know what materials are regularly supplied by the school district (e.g., art supplies, workbooks, etc), recognizing that this policy varies among school districts and sometimes from school to school. Additional funds for instructional materials acquisition are sometimes available within school districts and possibly through professional organizations. These monies may be distributed as small grants to support innovative projects, for example, and may require a proposal.

Actual procedures for ordering materials must also be clearly understood. Teachers must know whether there is a time line or, more precisely, a deadline for ordering instructional materials. In many situations orders for the coming school year must be submitted well in advance. Individual requests usually require a sequence of approvals before final authorization is granted. The value of being organized, current, and prepared is obvious. Finally, with the advent of increased use of inclusive classrooms for students with special needs, the need for collaborative materials selection and ordering becomes crucial.

Material Use

Although many curricular materials can be used in the form in which they are provided by the publisher, it is important to evaluate whether they might be more effective with modification. The diverse learning needs of students with disabilities suggest that specific materials may require individualization. This concern is particularly apt with materials designed primarily for use in the regular classroom with nondisabled students.

Lambie (1980) identified a series of questions that can be posed to determine a basis for modification. Areas of concern include the number of items on a page, speed of the program, sufficiency of repetition, presence/absence of feedback, presentation of directions, language level of the material, inherent interest of the material, durability of the material, and sequence of skills or concepts. She also provided basic guidelines to assist with planning and implementing changes in

materials. Teachers need to become familiar with the strengths and weaknesses of the material and the characteristics of the learner(s) to determine whether a mismatch is likely to occur; they should consider changes only when a mismatch has been established; they should focus on the simplest changes possible that will enhance the effectiveness of the material; they should evaluate the effectiveness of the changes; and they should be sure that any supplements are compatible with the material being used (e.g., requiring similar reading skills).

SUMMARY

The implementation of successful strategies for classroom organization and management can clearly differentiate between effective and ineffective educational programs. The various topics addressed within this chapter represent important concerns that should be addressed as precursors or follow-ups to the process of teaching.

An effective environment facilitates student learning. To be esthetically pleasant, a classroom should look lived in, show graceful wear, and contain signs of renewal. One way that teachers can plan the classroom environment is to develop a floor plan of the room and add necessary equipment to it. Environmental designs should include areas in which to conduct a variety of instructional activities as well as a place for social interaction and reinforcement.

An important consideration for teachers is the grouping of students. Particular concerns relate to the effectiveness and efficiency of small-group, large-group, and one-to-one arrangements. Effective practices for acquisition and proficiency/maintenance learning also have implications for grouping.

Planning a daily schedule can be deceptively simple, yet very important in setting the stage for each instructional day. Lesson plans are an integral part of scheduling and should attend to the why, what, and how of teaching. A daily schedule may begin with opening exercises and end with closing exercises, with varied activities occurring throughout the day. Although a high school schedule differs significantly from an elementary schedule, both follow the same principles and procedures. Resource programs require other specific considerations vis-a-vis scheduling. An alternative to daily lessons is unit plans, which have the advantage of placing the material to be learned in a relevant context to facilitate the smooth transfer of learning.

Homework is increasingly becoming a key concern for teachers. Teachers should develop consistent procedures for assigning it, involving parents, and evaluating assignments.

Record keeping must be an integral part of all educational programs. Data collection on student progress and teaching activities provides the basis for evaluating student performance and program effectiveness, and thus determines the modifications that are necessary.

Special attention should be given to the unique problems associated with the grading process. Grading patterns indicate low success rates for students with special needs in inclusive settings so adaptations are warranted.

Instructional materials are an important adjunct to the instructional process. Teachers should carefully determine need, be aware of materials' availability, evaluate the materials and select on adapt them to meet students' learning needs.

TEACHER TIPS

Elementary Level

EARLY FINISHERS:
HELPING THEM FIND SOMETHING TO DO

For young children who are very bright, school can get boring. Unless teachers plan ahead, some students may finish their assignments, then be left with long periods of time with nothing to do. You can help students learn to structure their time so that they use it wisely. Designing enrichment activities can teach students to avoid distracting behaviors and engage in more challenging learning activities. Here are some suggestions.

- Create a "menu" of enrichment activities, so students have choices when they complete required work.
- Design an independent study contract form that is simple to follow and use.
- Have students complete an interest survey early in the year, so you know what they enjoy and what motivates them.
- Get them moving and doing. Focus on learning activities that involve action, not just pencil and paper tasks.
- Plan thematic units that have options. With long-term units, students can work on projects that are open-ended and will keep them engaged for more than one class period.
- Keep them reading. Make reading more fun by using reading charts that focus on word origins or graphs that describe topics of interest.
- Write, write, write. Let students use computers and encourage them to become independent writers.
- Play games. Have large-group games, small-group games, two-person games, and individual games available in your class, so students can always be participating.

TEACHER TIPS

MORE HOMEWORK DOESN'T HAVE TO MEAN MORE HEADACHES: STRUCTURING SUCCESS FOR STUDENTS WITH BEHAVIOR DISORDERS

Increasing demands for more rigorous standards in education have meant some changes in teaching practices. Reforms have included lengthening the school day, implementing minimum competency testing, and modifying grading practices. In addition to these changes, teachers have also been encouraged to revise their practices regarding homework.

There is a strong body of research that indicates the positive effects of homework on academic achievement. Consequently, many school districts have implemented policies requiring teachers. especially those in secondary schools, to increase the amount of homework they assign. Of course, when teachers give homework, some students will have problems completing it. A recent study comparing the homework problems of nondisabled students with students who have behavior disorders suggests some strategies that may help these students be more successful. The interventions should focus on three important areas:

- providing teacher training in effective homework practices
- teaching students effective organization and learning strategies
- improving home-school communication

In addition, teachers who follow some key guidelines will find that their students are more successful at completing their homework assignments. Here are a few tips:

1. When assigning homework, give clear directions.
2. Make sure that homework assignments are relevant.
3. Don't give assignments that are too long or too complex for students to complete on their own.
4. Monitor, evaluate, and consequate homework performance consistently.
5. Work with parents to identify students' difficulties and plan interventions.

Soderlund, Bursuck, Polloway, & Foley (1995).

TEACHER TIPS   Technology

MANAGING STUDENTS' COMPUTER USE

Gardner and Edyburn (1993) have stressed the need for time-management strategies for accessing computers, whether the classroom has one computer or access to a school-wide lab. Phillips (1983) suggested four strategies for classrooms with only one computer.

The first of these suggestions is to use a rejection system that permits all students to see the results of class responses to questions in the lesson that the teacher or a student enters into the classroom computer. This allows students to compare their responses to those of their classmates.

Phillips (1983) also suggested the use of a timer to indicate when a student is to quit a program and allow another student to reset both the program and the timer. Setting a time frame in advance may make students more willing to move on to another activity at the end of their sessions. In addition, using timers that students can read may make them more inclined to use their computer time efficiently.

Another time-management method is block time. One variant allows for a preset schedule for each student in the classroom. In another, nonscheduled format, students sign up to use the computer in predetermined blocks of time. It is important for the instructor to be aware of student use patterns and make changes when necessary.

A second set of management issues surrounds a school-wide computer lab. Most computer labs serve both regular and special education students, so software adjustments such as rate of response may not remain consistent from lab visit to visit. Gardner and Edyburn (1993) suggest that teachers schedule access to the lab to coincide with the end of planning periods. That way, they can determine that software is appropriately set up for student use. Another suggestion is to use computer assignment sheets that detail the instructions for the day's lesson. These sheets can be kept in a lab notebook that students can return to if they need guidance. Computer cue sheets can also be developed that illustrate the "how to" of a program and guide students through it step-by-step. Educators can also teach students to set program features such as type and amount of feedback by themselves and then monitor the settings to determine their appropriateness.

The most essential element of successful computer-related classroom management is proximity control. Students need the teacher's physical presence for advice and aid, and the teacher needs to spend some time prior to instruction learning the features of the programs being used. Getting help from volunteers such as parents or student aides can increase the success of the computer lab experience for students and teachers alike.

Strategies for Classroom Management: Behavior Change Strategies

A major factor in successful teaching is the ability to implement educational strategies that increase a student's motivation to perform while assisting in the development of appropriate classroom behavior. The teacher's role is as a change agent whose primary goal is designing and implementing effective interventions. Given that research consistently indicates "high marks" for the effectiveness of behavioral techniques for promoting learning in students with special needs (see Lloyd, Forness, & Kavale, 1998), it is clear that such interventions should be key components of a teacher's repertoire. Therefore, this chapter focuses on strategies for changing behavior with an emphasis on those approaches that have been found particularly effective with students who have special needs.

In considering the various techniques to assist in behavior change, the primary focus is on effectiveness. To facilitate this, the teacher should reflect on two key concerns. The first is the need to be systematic. Haphazard modification is misleading in the interpretation of results. It can also be confusing and possibly detrimental to the student who needs structure and predictability. The need for a systematic policy of record keeping to accompany teaching techniques cannot be overstated, particularly for children with more serious learning difficulties.

The second important concern is creativity. Countless approaches may be effective for a given instructional problem. A teacher should be creative in devising alternatives and should become both proficient in the appropriate use of these alternatives and experienced in deciding when a given technique should be applied. In his classic article, Payne (1972) stressed the importance of being systematic and creative, noting the unlikely but nevertheless valid similarities between teaching and mind reading. As he noted:

> We know that in a mind reading act it is highly probable that the types of questions asked at the 6 P.M. performance will differ from those asked at 8 P.M., 10 P.M., or midnight. In education we know that it is highly probable that when children play on a playground of gravel, someone someday is going to throw rocks. We know this as experienced educators, but what teacher has ever been instructed to anticipate this situation, let alone know the alternatives in handling it? The lesson we can learn from the mind reading profession is the value of keeping records of children's behavior; the next step is to develop creative and effective alternatives for dealing with specific behavior. (p. 375)

This chapter is divided into six major sections. The initial section focuses on prerequisites to successful classroom management with particular attention paid to antecedent variables. The second section introduces the concept of functional behavioral assessment. The succeeding two sections deal with increasing appropriate behavior and reducing inappropriate behavior. Next, there is a discussion of several special considerations in programming. Finally, the chapter concludes with a discussion of behavioral intervention plans (BIP), as required under IDEA. Throughout the chapter a variety of specific strategies for behavior change are presented. The key to effectiveness is to use these strategies within a comprehensive plan that is responsive to the needs of the individual student.

PREREQUISITES TO SUCCESSFUL MANAGEMENT

Despite the abundance of alternative methods for behavior management, some discrepancy remains between a teacher's acquisition of a repertoire of empirically validated tools and subsequent success in managing the class. This discrepancy is particularly problematic because it is difficult to tease from research the precise variables that ensure subsequent success in management. Successful management is frequently not due to learning and exercising a series of high-powered behavior change strategies but rather to employing effective procedures in the classroom that frequently have a preventive effect. Certainly a teacher's ability to structure the environment and to present organized instruction is crucial to overall management success.

As Berliner (1988) stressed, higher achievement in classes and schools is associated with "an orderly, safe environment [and] a businesslike manner among the teachers" (p. 21). Thus, the key prerequisites to successful classroom management discussed here are outgrowths of the information presented in the previous chapter. Establishing a prosthetic, positive learning environment is an effective way to prevent problems (see Table 3–1).

Classroom Procedures

Antecedents to learning can be traced back to teachers' initial planning in setting up their instructional days. As Christenson, Ysseldyke, and Thurlow (1989) concluded in their review of critical instructional factors, proactive management—structuring the classroom as a basis for management—is the key element in avoiding disruptions and increasing instructional time. In addition to concern for the physical and temporal environment, a number of procedural aspects of teaching are important. Evertson, Emmer, Clements, Sanford, and Worsham (1984) focused on the specific elements involved in planning classroom procedures that "form the mosaic of the management system" (p. 24). Table 3–2 illustrates the five major areas that Evertson et al. have identified as keys to procedural planning at the elementary level. Specific concerns are listed for each major area. The column to the right then provides space for identification of particular procedures to be followed or expectations to be held.

A similar format to that of Evertson et al., a procedural planning sheet for secondary level classes, is presented in Table 3–3.

Classroom Rules

Most children and adolescents function best when they know what is expected of them. Students need to be aware of what a teacher expects and will accept. Explaining classroom rules and then posting them are sound practices to aid in preventing problem behaviors; students should not have to test the limits if the teacher has clearly explained the distinction between acceptable and unacceptable behaviors. Classroom rules should be few in number and essential to classroom functioning (Christenson et al., 1989), clearly defined, and linked to specific consequences when violated. Teachers should encourage students to discuss the rules and assist in their formulation and development. Later, students can also assist in the addition, deletion, or modification of the rules. Students frequently benefit from learning the give-and-take process of developing and modifying classroom rules.

The following example illustrates how rules can help upper elementary level children learn self-control. A teacher and students initially agreed on two rules.

TABLE 3–1
Elements of positive classroom climate

- Order, structure, and consistency.
- Well-organized and predictable environment.
- Clear and realistic expectations.
- Students experience success, academically and socially.
- Curriculum stresses student interests and talents.
- Teacher able to interpret communicative intent of students.
- Students given choices and input into classroom decisions.
- Students encouraged to express feelings.
- Students able to socially interact with others.
- Students' psychological needs (belonging, safety, competence, and self-esteem) met.
- Positive teacher-student relationship.

Source: Abrams, B. J., & Segal, A. (1998). How to prevent aggressive behavior. *Teaching Exceptional Children, 30* (4), p. 12.

TABLE 3-2

Planning classroom procedures at the elementary level

Subject	Procedures or Expectations
I. Room use	(Note: To be filled in for an individual classroom.)
A. Teacher's desk and storage areas	
B. Student desks and storage areas	
C. Storage for common materials	
D. Drinking fountains, sink, pencil sharpener	
E. Bathrooms	
F. Center, station, or equipment areas	
II. Seat work and teacher-led instruction	
A. Student attention during presentations	
B. Student participation	
C. Talk among students	
D. Obtaining help	
E. Out-of-seat procedures during seat work	
F. When seat work has been completed	
III. Transitions into and out of the room	
A. Beginning the school day	
B. Leaving the room	
C. Returning to the room	
D. Ending the day	
IV. Procedures during reading or other groups	
A. Getting the class ready	
B. Student movement	
C. Expected behavior in the group	
D. Expected behavior of students out of group	
V. General procedures	
A. Distributing materials	
B. Interruptions	
C. Bathrooms	
D. Library, resource room, school office	
E. Cafeteria	
F. Playground	
G. Fire and disaster drills	
H. Classroom helpers	

Note. From *Classroom Management for Elementary Teachers* (p. 32), by C. M. Evertson, E. T. Emmer, B. S. Clements. J. P. Sanford, and M. E. Worsham, 1984, Upper Saddle River, NJ: Prentice Hall. Copyright 1984 by Prentice Hall, Inc. Adapted with permission.

TABLE 3–3

Planning classroom procedures at the secondary level

Subject	Procedures or Expectations
I. General procedures	
A. Beginning-of-period procedures	(Note: To be filled in for an individual classroom.)
1. Attendance check	
2. Students absent the previous day	
3. Tardy students	
4. Behavior expected of all students	
5. Leaving the room	
B. Use of materials and equipment	
1. Equipment and materials for students	
2. Teacher materials and equipment	
C. Ending the period	
1. Readiness for leaving	
2. Dismissal	
II. Procedures during seat work and teacher-led instruction	
A. Student attention during presentations	
B. Student participation	
C. Procedures for seat work	
1. Talk among students	
2. Obtaining help	
3. Out-of-seat procedures	
4. When seat work has been completed	
III. Procedure for student group work	
A. Use of materials and supplies	
B. Assignment of students to groups	
C. Students goals and participation	
IV. Miscellaneous procedures	
A. Signals	
B. Public address (PA) announcements and other interruptions	
C. Special equipment and materials	
D. Fire and disaster drills	
E. Split lunch period	

Note. From *Classroom Management for Elementary Teachers* (p. 34), by C. M. Evertson, E. T. Emmer, B. S. Clements, J. P. Sanford, and M. E. Worsham, 1984, Upper Saddle River, NJ: Prentice Hall. Copyright 1984 by Prentice Hall, Inc. Adapted with permission.

1. Students must receive permission for a hall pass.
2. Students are to talk only while in certain designated areas ("blue areas").

The rules were discussed on the first day of school; the teacher then printed them on a poster board and fastened it to the wall. During the hall pass discussion, the teacher displayed the pass. The blue areas were designated by blue tape attached to the floor. If a student situated outside of the blue study area talked during a study period, the teacher merely turned and pointed to the individual violating the rule and indicated the rule. After the first week, the students knew these two rules and seldom violated them. Success was achieved because the class did not want to violate reasonable rules and responded appropriately when they were consistently applied. Subsequently, other rules were then introduced as needed.

Establishing rules is a crucial aspect of the prevention of specific management problems. Thereafter, regular review, immediate notification of infractions, and frequent praise for compliance facilitate adherence.

Group Management

A classic contribution to classroom management is Kounin's (1970) research on which teacher variables predicted compliance and appropriate behavior in students. Berliner (1988) notes that Kounin's work was "enormously influential . . . and has given us a set of concepts that help us understand the process of monitoring a workplace free from deviance and in which students attend to their assignments" (p. 32). As Kounin reports, previous efforts to determine the efficacy of "desists"—that is, traditional statements that teachers make so that students will desist from inappropriate behaviors—had proven less than fruitful. According to Kounin, the following variables are among those related to successful classroom management.

1. *With-it-ness,* essentially awareness, refers to the teacher's ability to follow classroom ac-
tion, be aware of possible deviance, communicate awareness to the class, and intervene at the initiation of the problem. Christenson et al. (1989) refer to a similar concept of having an "ongoing surveillance system" (p. 22).
2. *Overlapping* indicates an ability to deal with two events simultaneously and thus to respond to target behaviors promptly.
3. *Movement management* refers to smooth transition between activities. When the teacher can maintain momentum between instructional periods, the degree of behavioral compliance is likely to increase. Table 3–4 illustrates transition cues to facilitate this process.
4. *Group alerting* consists of specific skills for maintaining attention throughout various teaching lessons, as with a specific signal or procedure that involves all students.
5. *Accountability and format* include the methods that teachers develop to ensure a group focus by actively involving all students in appropriate activities.
6. *Avoiding satiation* on instructional activities refers to the ability to vary activities to prevent inappropriate behaviors.

These principles will minimize the time needed for problem management, thus leading to an increase in the time available for individualized instruction. They provide for classroom management that is based on prevention.

School-Wide Management Systems

Any discussion of prerequisites to successful classroom behavioral management would be incomplete without mention of school-wide management systems. Such approaches are attractive because they reach all students in general and also provide a foundation for interventions with individual students (Nelson, Crabtree, Marchand-Martella, & Martella, 1998). They put in place consistent rules, procedures, and support systems that enhance the likelihood that students with disabilities will be successful and at the same time provide a preventive focus that may de-escalate the occurrence of challenging behaviors.

TABLE 3–4
Varieties of transition cues: elementary level

1. Teacher gives verbal cues to group or individuals.
2. An appointed child gives verbal cues to group or individuals.
3. Teacher touches children to dismiss.
4. Lights blink, a bell rings, a piano sounds, or a buzzer buzzes to signal dismissal.
5. Teacher begins a song that routinely tells children to move.
6. Teacher makes a routine gesture or stands in a routine place to signal dismissal.
7. Teacher distributes cards with symbols for the students' intended destination printed on them.
8. Teacher gives each child an object that will be needed in the next activity.
9. Teacher tells children to go and find their names at the destination.
10. Teacher dismisses children by gender or physical characteristics (e.g., brown eyes, red hair).
11. Teacher dismisses students by letters in name.
12. Teacher shows a letter, number, or word and asks for volunteers to identify it; correct answers earn dismissal.
13. Teacher dismisses students by tables or rows.
14. Children look at a picture list on the chalkboard or cue card to learn where to go next after finishing an assigned activity.

Note. Adapted from "Teaching mainstreamed children to manage daily transitions." by S. E. Rosenkoetter and S. A. Fowler, 1986, in *Teaching Exceptional Children. 19*(1), p. 22.

While models differ significantly between schools, the common features of such programs are as follows:

- Total staff commitment to managing behavior, whatever approach is taken.
- Clearly defined and communicated expectations and rules.
- Consequences and clearly stated procedures for correcting rule-breaking behaviors.
- An instructional component for teaching students self-control and/or social skill strategies.
- A support plan to address the needs of students with chronic, challenging behaviors (ERIC/OSEP, 1997, p. 2).

One key issue for all teachers concerning school-wide discipline programs is the equity of the rules and procedures for students (Butera, Klein, McMullen, & Wilson, 1998). The discussion later in the chapter on behavioral intervention plans reflects these concerns.

FUNCTIONAL BEHAVIORAL ASSESSMENT

Prior to the discussion of individual intervention strategies, it is appropriate to briefly consider the importance of assessment data. Of particular value is the use of a functional behavioral assessment (FBA) to provide an understanding of the nature of individual behavioral patterns of students with special needs. As Wheeler (1998) noted, "challenging behaviors serve a function or purpose. It is important that teachers . . . realize the dynamics of the interrelationships between the limited skill repertoire of the learner, insensitivity of the environment to the needs of the learner, and subsequent demands and expectations placed on the learner by the teacher" (p. 264).

The purpose of an FBA is to provide a contextual view of the nature of specific behaviors and behavioral patterns (Fad, Patton, & Polloway, 2000). In doing so, teachers can determine the cause(s) of a given behavior and thus provide a basis for intervention (McConnell, Hilvitz, & Cox, 1998). Using an FBA approach requires professionals to understand and evaluate a behavior within the broad context of the student's home and school environment. A typical functional behavioral assessment format provides a structured way to analyze the contextual aspects of a behavior by asking for an exact description of the specific behavior in question along with information regarding precipitating conditions, consequences that follow the behavior, and hypotheses about the purpose the behavior serves. In Figure 3-1, a sample, completed FBA is shown. It provides a link to specific assessment techniques that can be used to analyze behaviors (see Table 3-5). This form also allows professionals to add other qualitative information (e.g., academic, social/peer, family) that might play a factor in the demonstration of a behavior.

A functional behavioral assessment provides a valuable approach to more fully understand a behavioral pattern as a basis for selecting intervention strategies. Further, it provides a basis for the development of a behavioral intervention plan (discussed at the end of the chapter). The information obtained from the FBA can then be used as a critical aspect of the steps of successful behavioral change programs (i.e., definition and measurement of a target behavior, identification of the nature of behavioral occurrences, identification of factors causing the behavior, and determination of appropriate procedures for intervention) (Simpson, 1998). It also is an essential

FIGURE 3–1

Sample functional behavioral assessment

Behavior # 1 Defies teacher's authority/refuses to follow directions

Precipitating Conditions (Setting, time, or other situations typically occurring *before* the behavior)	**Specific Behavior** (*Exactly* what the student does or does not do)	**Consequences** (Events that typically *follow* the behavior)	**Function of the Behavior** (*Hypothesized purpose(s)* the behavior serves)
☐ unstructured time in ☒ academic instruction in language arts/social studies ☒ when given a directive to read aloud/write papers ☐ when close to ☐ when provoked by ☒ when unable to complete assignments ☐ other ☐ none observed	When given a directive to read aloud or to complete independent written assignments, Michael yells at his teachers and refuses to follow instructions.	☒ teacher attention ☒ peer attention ☐ verbal warning/reprimand ☐ loss of privilege (what kind?) ☒ time out (where/how long?) office — 10 minutes ☐ detention (how long?) ☒ removal from class ☐ in-school suspension (how long?) ☐ other	☒ escape/avoidance ☐ gaining attention ☐ expression of anger ☒ frustration w/written or independent work ☐ vengeance ☐ seeking of power/control ☐ intimidation ☐ sensory stimulation ☐ relief of fear/anxiety ☐ other

Specific Assessment Techniques Used To Analyze This Behavior

☒ Observation	☒ Student Interview	☒ Administrator Interview	☒ Parent Interview
☒ Behavior Checklist/Rating Scale	☐ Video/Audio Taping	☒ Teacher Interview	☐ Other ______

Related Information/Considerations

Academic: Poor organizational skills; low skills in reading & writing; problems working independently

Social/Peer: Has lots of friends; seems to get embarrassed

Family: Michael has also been defiant at home (refuses to follow directions). Michael acknowledges his frustration with independent tasks.

Other: Can be very friendly; good at basketball; enjoys socializing with friends.

The FBA addresses the relationship among precipitating conditions, the behavior, its consequences, and the function of the behavior. The FBA also reflects a consideration of all relevant data gathered, both as background information and by using specific assessment techniques.

Source: Fad, K., Patton, J.R., & Polloway, E.A. (1998). *Behavioral intervention planning* (p. 18). Austin, TX: Pro-Ed.

TABLE 3–5
Representative behavioral assessment methods

1. Behavior monitoring forms e.g., contracts, point sheets): Forms that can be used for managing behavior include behavioral contracts that are negotiated between the student and teacher and sheets that are used for indicating the points students receive for demonstrating appropriate behaviors.

2. Grades on assignments recorded in grade book: Grades on class assignments or activities are typically recorded in a location (i.e., grade book) that can be consulted for ongoing performance information.

3. Anecdotal notes: This technique represents any type of note-taking that is developed to describe ongoing behaviors. Anecdotal formats vary greatly, representing the specific needs of the situation or the person taking the notes. Anecdotal notes are sometimes referred to as narrative reports or continuous recording.

4. Tally sheets or hand-held counter of the frequency of target behavior(s): One of the most regularly used systems for recording the number of times a certain behavior or set of behaviors are observed to occur. Different formats of forms are available. Some predeveloped forms for collecting frequency data are available.

5. Tape recordings (audio or video): Taping provides a permanent record of any situation. From such recordings, one can generate anecdotal records or frequency counts. These recordings can also be shared with students to assist them in understanding their behaviors.

6. Progress reports/interim notices: Progress reports provide an ongoing appraisal of the progress associated with behaviors and intervention programs. They are typically issued on a more regular basis than grades.

7. Portfolios/work samples: Any variety of a collection of student products. Sometimes portfolios represent a student's best work; other times they include a sampling of all work that has been generated.

8. Student self-assessments or ratings: Any system whereby students evaluate their own behavior and record their beliefs about their behaviors according to the criteria established by the technique (e.g., checklist, rating scale) can be used.

9. Teacher/parent rating scales: Such scales typically include a list of statements about various behaviors or conditions along with a range of choices completed by teachers and parents. Rating scales that are given to parents must be written in a manner that is easily understood.

10. Parent feedback forms: Home-school communication is a system that requests information from parents on target behavior(s). A format that helps structure the feedback increases the chances that communication between parents and teachers is clear, thus preventing misunderstandings.

11. Time totals on stopwatches: The determination of how long a behavior exists or how long it takes for a student to begin to demonstrate a desired behavior requires a time measurement. All variations of how this is collected (i.e., live versus taping) require some type of timing system, the most likely of which is a stopwatch.

12. Graphing behavioral performance: Because of its visual format, graphing represents one of the best methods for displaying ongoing behavioral performance. Computer software now simplifies this task significantly and provides attractive displays. Students can be involved in the graphing of their own progress.

Source: Adapted from Fad, K., Patton, J.R., & Polloway, E.A. (1998). *Behavioral intervention planning* (pp. 34–35). Austin, TX: Pro-Ed.

element in the development of positive behavioral supports in which interventions are focused on changing the system or setting within which a behavior occurs and/or the skills of an individual as a basis for changing challenging behaviors (Ruef, Higgins, Glaeser, & Patrode, 1998).

INCREASING APPROPRIATE BEHAVIOR

The majority of intervention efforts undertaken to produce behavior change are oriented toward increasing appropriate, desirable behaviors. For students with special needs, this orientation includes a variety of adaptive behaviors, most notably academic, social, and daily living skills. The most pedagogically sound method of providing consequences to increase appropriate behavior is through positive reinforcement.

Principles of Positive Reinforcement

Reduced to its simplest terms, positive reinforcement refers to the supplying of a desirable consequence after appropriate behavior. In more precise terms, it refers to those consequent environmental events that increase a specific desired behavior by presenting a positive reinforcer. Positive reinforcement can be simply a smile or a wave extended to a courteous driver, a weekly paycheck, or a thank you from someone receiving a gift. The classroom presents constant opportunities for the use of positive reinforcers. The key is to select the "least intrusive" reinforcer that will produce the desired results.

Positive tools can be used in three basic ways. First and most common, reinforcement can be made contingent on appropriate target responses selected to be increased. This approach provides motivation for building new skills. Second, positive events can be used to reinforce a behavior incompatible with one to be decreased. An example might be reinforcing on-task time to decrease out-of-seat behavior. Third, teachers can positively reinforce peers to demonstrate to a given student that certain actions will receive reinforcement. For example, the teacher might praise several students

for raising their hands in class as an alternative to reprimanding another pupil for talking out of turn.

Successful use of positive reinforcement initially involves determining reinforcer preferences. With a wide variety of alternatives available, a teacher can establish a menu of reinforcers most effective for an individual student. A menu could include a list inclusive of free time, use of a software game, or some tangible prize.

The following techniques can be used to develop a menu:

- direct questioning of the student
- indirect questioning of parents, friends, or past teachers
- observation of the student within the natural environment
- structured observation (i.e., arranging specific reinforcement alternatives for selection)
- trial and error of a variety of reinforcers (i.e., reinforcer sampling)

Generally, teachers can construct a reinforcement menu by selecting from a pool of three types of reinforcers: social, tangible, or activity reinforcers. In considering these options, it is important to remember that the measure of a positive reinforcer is its effects on an individual's behavior.

Social Reinforcers. Praise is the positive reinforcer most readily available to teachers. Praise, and all reinforcement, is most effective if used appropriately—that is, if it is meaningful, specific, and immediate. The following examples illustrate the importance of these three attributes.

Maria has just completed her arithmetic assignment. If her teacher checks the work and then informs her that she is wonderful, praise has been provided, but it is not meaningful. If, instead, the teacher tells her that she is doing well in her work, some meaning is involved in the praise, but specificity is lacking. The best manner of praising is to state exactly how well Maria has done (e.g., "I like the way you arranged the problems on your paper. You have numbers 1, 2, and 3 correct"). For an older student the teacher might say, "Tom, the quality of your work has improved dramatically—you made no errors on today's spelling assignment."

The third criterion of appropriate reinforcement is immediacy. During acquisition learning, praise needs to follow each desired response immediately. For example, if intensive efforts to teach Carly to go directly to her seat after entering the room are to succeed, then she should receive praise as soon as she does so. The immediate, systematic application of praise is used to assist her in learning this behavior. After acquiring the behavior, she may be placed on a maintenance schedule of periodic praise. Even during maintenance, however, the praise should come immediately after the desired response.

A second social reinforcer that can be used in combination with praise is physical contact. Characteristics of the teacher and the student must determine how much touching is used and how effective it is. Careful consideration of its appropriateness is particularly important given the possibility of some contact being seen as inappropriate by students, their parents, or others. Physical contact can take several forms. Shaking hands, a pat on the back, and a high- or low-five can all serve as positive consequences depending on the situation. Certainly, some instances are not as acceptable as others (e.g., it would be better for a senior high teacher to shake a student's hand rather than give a pat on the back), but the teacher usually has some options to use contact in supplementing praise.

Tangible Reinforcers. The addition of tangible reinforcement to an instructional program may enhance the value of the social reinforcers with which they should be paired. Tangible reinforcers can be a powerful component of the reinforcer hierarchy for many students.

The tangible item with primary reinforcing value is usually food because it is desired instinctively. For some students, food can be very effective. However, because highly desirable edible items, such as sweets, are often nutritionally unsound, the volume of food intake should be considered. One efficient method of using food as a consequence is to break it down into small pieces that can be earned for specific steps in an instructional task. An example is the use of a soft drink, which can be dispensed in small quantities, such as by sips through a straw and by refills of a creamer cup. Each sip can be awarded on correct completion of an academic task or performance of a specific desired behavior. For adolescents, obtaining a soft drink at the end of the day can become the focus of points earned throughout earlier instructional periods.

Other paired reinforcers might be considered to promote delaying gratification. Pairing allows certain items to serve as symbols of reinforcers and to be exchanged later for other reinforcers. In our society money serves this purpose; in the classroom this same principle can be applied through the use of points or tokens. Both represent items that learners desire; they will work to earn those tokens because they have learned that they are paired with the actual reinforcers. On a basic level tokens can be used in an individual instructional session to reinforce appropriate behavior and then can be exchanged immediately upon task completion. On a grander scale tokens can become the exchange medium for a classroom-based economy, which is discussed later.

Activities. Activities can also be highly reinforcing positive consequences. As an incentive, an activity should be an event in which a child earns the right to participate because of appropriate behavior. The teacher must distinguish between positive activities that the child normally has been accustomed to, such as lunch and recess, and those that are contingent on certain behavior. This concept requires that the activity be desirable for the student as well as extra. The following example illustrates the concept.

Joan has completed her math worksheet and is allowed to go to recess. If this period is the regular recess available to her, it is not a reward and thus may not serve as an effective consequence. If she does not complete her worksheet and still gets recess, she has not earned anything by doing her work. And if she does not complete her math and consequently does not get to go, then recess actually has been taken away, and a form of punishment has been applied. To make recess a positive reinforcer requires that it be made extra by allowing more time or by providing an additional period. In this way Joan can earn extra time rather than earning time that is rightfully hers anyway. If recess is used contingently, Joan is not punished if she fails to complete her math assignment; she simply does not earn extra time.

In addition to activities like recess, many other alternatives are available to the teacher. Depending on the student, free time, being first in line, taking the lunch money to the office, or assisting with school maintenance can become positive consequences. Table 3–6 contains other activities that might be reinforcing to individual students.

Reinforcement Schedules. An important consideration after the selection of a particular consequence is the schedule according to which it is presented to the learner. In general, schedules can be defined as either continuous or intermittent. A continuous schedule indicates that reinforcement is given with each occurrence of a given behavior; it is most useful for teaching and learning at the acquisition stage.

Intermittent schedules provide reinforcement less frequently and are more advantageous for maintenance/proficiency and generalization learning. Six intermittent schedules are fixed ratio, fixed interval, fixed response duration, variable ratio, variable interval, and variable response duration. A *fixed ratio* schedule specifies a particular relationship between occurrences and reinforcement (e.g., 5:1) and can be illustrated by piecework (e.g., stacking bricks) or rewards given according to the number of worksheets completed (e.g., a token given for every worksheet completed with 90% accuracy). *Fixed interval* reinforcement specifies the amount of time that will elapse before reinforcement—for example, using classroom timers and awarding points to all students working when the buzzer sounds at regular 5-minute intervals. A *fixed duration* schedule differs from a fixed interval schedule in that the target behavior must have occurred for the duration of the entire interval in order for the individual to earn the reinforcement. *Variable ratio, variable*

interval, and *variable duration* schedules allow planned alterations in the frequency, elapsed time, or duration of time, respectively, between reinforcers.

Reinforcement schedules should be selected according to specific instructional objectives. For certain goals, such as completing worksheets or establishing quiet time during reading, fixed schedules may be most appropriate. In many situations, however, variable schedules are more effective, because students are unable to predict receipt of reinforcement as precisely; thus, programming tends to produce behaviors most resistant to extinction. The variable ratio schedules inherent in slot machines illustrate how effective these contingencies can be in maintaining desired responses. Variable interval or duration schedules are most appropriate for nondiscrete behaviors such as on-task or in-seat.

Gradual Change Processes. The basic principles of positive reinforcement can create a false picture that learning, as defined by behavior change, is simply a matter of selecting the correct reinforcer and scheduling it effectively. For most educational objectives, learning is best characterized as a gradual process of behavior change. The purpose of shaping is to reach an academic or behavioral goal through the gradual achievement and mastery of subgoals. The process involves establishing a shifting performance criterion to reinforce gradual increments in performance. As it is most precisely defined, it refers to the gradual change in performance that is tied to a single behavior, to distinguish it from chaining, which generally refers to multiple, related behaviors such as in dressing.

A shaping program includes four component steps (Martin & Pear, 1992): specification of a final desired behavior, selection of the starting behavior, choosing of the specific shaping steps, and movement through the steps at an appropriate pace, with reinforcement provided accordingly. Because shaping is based on a series of small, more easily achieved subgoals, it provides the teacher with a valuable strategy for building responses that are well beyond a child's present functioning.

TABLE 3–6
Activity reinforcers

Selecting topic for group discussion	Helping the custodian
Selecting game or activity for recess	Helping the principal
Reading to a friend	Getting an extra recess
Tutoring a classmate	Passing out milk at lunch
Going to the office	Cleaning the lunchroom
Erasing chalkboards	Sitting in the front row
Emptying trash or pencil sharpener	Sitting in the back row
Using the tape recorder	Reading comics, magazines
Listening to the radio with earplugs	Having a class break for soft drinks
Having extra time in favorite subject	Making visual aids
Doing community projects	Playing games of all kinds
Going out first to recess	Doing arts and crafts
Taking attendance	Keeping behavioral point records
Collecting lunch money	Acting as "bank" teller
Handing out papers	Being an usher
Helping to correct papers	Sitting next to the window
Being team captain	Sitting next to the door
Passing out books	Cleaning erasers
Passing out scissors or crayons	Displaying a bulletin board
Collecting scissors or crayons	Taking down a bulletin board
Helping put up a bulletin board	

A brief case example illustrates the shaping process. Tommy is learning to print the "T" in his name. Initially the teacher may accept and reinforce a somewhat scribbled approximation of the letter but, eventually his writing is shaped as the "T" more closely approximates a legible letter.

Shaping behavior through successive approximations to the desired goal is one of the basic uses of reinforcement. When combined with both task analysis and prompting, it can be the basis for teaching precise, manageable skills to students. Such an approach provides the foundation for chaining, the linking of skills to complete a complex behavioral task. Forward chaining can be used to teach sequential steps in consecutive order, as with self-help skills such as shaving; backward chaining can effectively teach skills such as dressing by beginning just short of the completed task and gradually requiring the student to complete more steps within the task hierarchy.

Positive Reinforcement Programs

Effective teaching often requires the use of systems for implementing reinforcement strategies. This section describes several reinforcement programs that have been successfully used in classroom situations, as well as the Premack principle, which conceptually underlies the various programs.

Premack Principle. The most basic concept for dealing with consequences is the Premack principle (Premack, 1959). It is often called "grandma's law" because it is reminiscent of the traditional dinner table remark, "If you eat your vegetables, then you can have your dessert." The principle asserts that a low-probability activity can be increased in frequency when paired with a high-probability activity. For example, a student who finishes a spelling lesson (a low-probability behavior) will be allowed to go out and play volleyball for 5 minutes (a high-probability behavior). Because volleyball is a desirable activity, the student has increased incentive to finish the lesson.

The Premack principle provides the basis for the use of management contingencies. Teachers can make activities or tokens contingent on completion of an academic task or performance of a specific appropriate behavior. As noted in Chapter 2, the Premack principle also can be used to arrange the physical and temporal environment in the classroom.

Contingency Contracting. Contracting represents a potentially effective, versatile management system. Contracts can be oral or written; they state the work assignment the learner has contracted to complete and the consequences that the instructor will provide on completion. Contracts should be perceived as binding agreements between student and teacher; signatures on written contracts emphasize this perception. In his classic work, Homme (1969) identified ten fundamental rules of contracting.

1. The contract reward should be immediate.
2. Initial contracts should call for and reward small approximations.
3. Small rewards should be given frequently.
4. The contract should call for and reward accomplishment rather than obedience.
5. The performance should be rewarded after it occurs.
6. The contract must be fair.
7. The terms of the contract must be clear.
8. The contract must be honest.
9. The contract must be positive.
10. Contracting as a method must be used systematically.

Although contracts are usually associated with individuals, within a large class setting contingency contracting can also be handled efficiently and effectively. For example, a teacher responsible for a 1-hour arithmetic period can make assignments that a student will need approximately 50 minutes to complete.

The remaining 10 minutes can then be given to students to play games, explore the Internet, or work at an interest center, contingent on the completion of specific academic tasks. Although the instructional time has been decreased by one sixth, the students' motivation to complete their work and gain their free-choice time will probably compensate for the reduced time.

Figure 3–2 illustrates a simple form for an individual contract. Changes and elaborations depend on the instructional goals of the specific situation. Contracts can be an extremely useful technique in a classroom situation. They can be age-appropriate, can provide initial training in understanding formal contracts, can facilitate home-school coordination, and can serve as an appropriate step toward self-management.

Group Contingencies. Group contingencies are another possible source of effective intervention strategies. They represent peer-mediated interventions and can include independent contingencies (i.e., all members of the group work individually toward reinforcement provided on an individual basis); dependent contingencies (i.e., reinforcement is contingent upon performance of a designated student); and interdependent contingencies (i.e., reinforcement is contingent on the performance of a group of students).

Token Economies. Another systematic method for programming reinforcement is through the establishment of a token economy. In general, a token system is based on items symbolizing actual reinforcers, much like the use of monetary rewards. Just as adults receive money for their performance, students can earn tokens for appropriate behavior and completion of tasks. Just as adults can exchange their money for food, clothes, shelter, and entertainment, students can redeem their tokens for items they desire.

Token systems afford the teacher a number of distinct advantages over other forms of contingency management. Tokens can help bridge the gap between a specific behavior and the actual reinforcer with a minimal disruption in instruc-

FIGURE 3–2
Sample contingency contract

tion. In addition, the interest generated by obtaining tokens may actually increase the value of the reinforcer for which they are exchanged. Tokens can be constructed to ensure portability and availability and can allow for a flexible reinforcement menu without incorporating a variety of reinforcers into the instructional class activities. Finally, token economies can have positive effects on teachers by emphasizing the need to reinforce students frequently and consistently.

Tokens can also be beneficial in enhancing skill training and academic learning. Amounts to be paid when work is completed can be established for specific assignments. For example, a math sheet might be worth 10 tokens when completed with 90% accuracy. With this added incentive for work completion, teachers frequently find that a student's quantity of work and rate of learning improve dramatically.

Token systems can be used in a variety of ways. Outgrowths may include banking and checking, stores, and classroom governments. Tokens can also become integral parts of inclusion efforts, home-school relations, and interdisciplinary arrangements in residential facilities. Token economies can have direct educational benefits beyond providing an organized program of consequences. Currency-based economies are particularly helpful in meeting career education

goals. Such a system's ultimate goal of reducing a learner's reliance on external reinforcers also has direct implications for the possible success of self-regulatory forms of behavioral intervention (discussed later).

Although token economies have been criticized for stifling the spontaneity of both the teacher and the instructional program, in practice such programs can be tailored to facilitate a creative atmosphere. One technique that can assist in increasing the interest and excitement of existing token economies is auctions.

Auctions can enhance the functioning of a token economy by helping to maintain student motivation at a high level through the addition of variety to the token economy, by giving students an opportunity to learn to appreciate the intricacies of saving and spending currency, and by broadening the scope of available reinforcers. Their function is to supplement the classroom store (i.e., the redemption center for tokens or currency). As an adjunct to a visit to the store, an auction can occur on a periodic basis. Consistent with the traditional conception of this type of arrangement, students should bring their earnings and receive a chance to bid on specific items on the auction block.

Successful auctions use unique and different items with particular appeal to a specific age group. Some successful items include used athletic equipment, old books, jewelry, perfume and cologne, wallets, trophies, software programs and a variety of games. Abandoned or recycled items may be as attractive as new ones.

BEHAVIOR REDUCTION TECHNIQUES

Successful teaching requires the ability to resolve problem behaviors successfully (see Box 3-1). The use of reductive strategies requires an initial consideration of the techniques most natural to the classroom and school environment and thus the least restrictive yet effective options (Nelson & Rutherford, 1983). The following list provides a sequence from least to most restrictive classroom management alternatives.

1. natural and logical consequences
2. differential reinforcement
3. extinction
4. verbal reprimand
5. response cost
6. time out from positive reinforcement

Natural and Logical Consequences

Before teachers consider high-powered consequences for inappropriate behavior—and before punishment strategies are implemented—attention should be given to consequences that are natural and/or logical relative to a given behavior. Although in some instances these may be behaviorally defined as punishment, their cognitive relationship to the behavior itself makes them more attractive alternatives. As West (1986) notes, the use of natural and logical consequences can result in children and adolescents learning responsibility.

Natural consequences occur when a parent or a teacher "does not intervene in a situation but allows the situation to teach the child. The technique is based on this adage: Every generation must learn that the stove is hot" (West, 1986, p. 121). Two examples illustrate how this process can operate in a classroom setting. A student may refuse to do classwork or homework. The natural

consequence is that he receives no credit for the work. The teacher need not say or do anything. In another situation a child may habitually forget her permission slip to attend a class function away from school. The natural consequence is that she has to stay behind when the class goes on a trip. Natural consequences are an effective means to teach common sense and responsibility (West, 1994).

With certain behaviors, natural consequences could result in severe eventualities, such as injury. For example, depending on the natural consequences of walking into the street without looking would clearly be inappropriate. In these instances consideration should be given to alternatives that are logical consequences of the behavior. Logical consequences attempt to tie the disciplinary response directly to the inappropriate behavior (West, 1994).

West (1986) aptly describes the role of logical consequences:

> The secret of good consequences is the logic between the misbehavior and the consequences. For example, it is not logical for a parent to drive consistently to school to give a child a forgotten lunch box. In this instance, the parent takes the consequence for the child. What is logical is that the child . . . borrows money from the principal. In this way, the child learns from the error. Often it is difficult to think of perfect consequences, but with practice, such techniques become easy to master. (p. 123)

Several examples of logical consequences in the classroom were provided by Dreikurs, Grunwald, and Pepper (1982). When a student pushes another child in the hall, the teacher may give the child the choice of not pushing or of going back to the classroom, waiting until the group has reached its destination, and then starting out alone. A student who is late from recess might be given the choice of returning with the others or standing by the teacher during recess until it is time to return to class. Dreikurs et al. provide the following summation of logical consequences.

> There is no pat formula for applying logical consequences. What will work in one situation may not

BOX 3.1

The Invention of the School Discipline Lists

For years, one of the most frequent observations is that public schools have experienced a profound change in the types of problems with which teachers reported having to deal. O'Neill (1994, p. 8–11) reveals the mythology of this "research":

> [Recently] the results of a national teacher survey appeared on our bulletin board. First in 1940 and again in 1990, teachers recorded their main problems working in the public schools. The top seven offenses 50 years ago were talking, chewing gum, running in the halls, making noise, getting out of line, violating the dress code, and littering. This was innocent fun, but the modern list read like a police blotter—drugs, alcohol, pregnancy, suicide, rape, robbery.
>
> As a social scientist, I felt a mix of skepticism and jealousy that anyone got such clean results out of real people. I decided to look for the source of the lists, to find out who did the questionnaire and just what they had asked. . . .
>
> Despite hundreds of articles I found quoting the lists, for months their origin stayed a mystery . . . Eventually I found the source. In fact, no surveys ever were done. One individual made them up. . . . Their creator put them forward solely as his opinion. Later experts portrayed them as scientific surveys, often altering the items, streamlining them, or including a source to make them sound more genuine. . . . The lists became true folklore.
>
> The author of the school "surveys" was T. Cullen Davis of Fort Worth, Texas. One of the wealthiest men in Texas . . . [he became active] lobbying against sex education and the teaching of evolution in the schools. Around 1981, as part of this campaign, Davis assembled the lists and passed them to fellow evangelicals. "They weren't done from a scientific survey," Davis told me. "How did I know what the offenses in the schools were in 1940? I was there. How did I know what they are now? I read the newspapers. . . ."
>
> Although many teachers have fine intentions in quoting the lists, I believe that spreading them is, on the whole, harmful to public schools. They are wrong about teachers' true concerns and they distort the daily reality of the profession.
>
> A 1991 National Center for Education Statistics survey focused on discipline, safety, and crime, asking high school principals to rate each item as a "serious" problem in their schools, "moderate," "minor," or "not a problem." The big three turned out to be tardiness, absenteeism, and fights. Only 3% rated weapons as even a moderate problem. Drugs were well below alcohol and tobacco, and crimes came at the bottom . . .
>
> These bogus school surveys may not last for centuries, but they probably will be with us for years into the future. They give educators one more reason to get the message out that schools are on the whole safe and are performing their role of education.

Excerpted from O'Neill, B. (Dec., 1994). The invention of the school discipline lists: A concocted story of myths about public education passed down. *The School Administrator, 51* (11), 8–11.

work in another. The child who likes to go outdoors, for example, will be differently affected by being kept in during recess than a child who hates to go out. Therefore, by treating these two children in different ways, similar results can be obtained. And since they have participated in setting up the logical consequences, they do not feel that they are punished by the teacher. It must be remembered that the use of logical consequences requires an understanding of the child and of the situation. When to do what and to whom requires judgment about many imponderables because every situation is unique. (p. 127)

In considering the use of behavior reduction strategies, the teacher is encouraged to continuously evaluate how natural and logical consequences can enhance a management program.

Differential Reinforcement Strategies

A number of strategies are available to reduce inappropriate behaviors through positive reinforcement strategies. As outlined by Webber and Scheuerman (1991), these include differential reinforcement of a low rate of responding (DRL), differential reinforcement of the omission of behavior (or of other behavior) (DRO), and differential reinforcement of incompatible (DRI) or alternative behaviors (DRA).

A DRL strategy employs reinforcement based on the successive reduction of behavioral occurrences; it can thus be used, for example, to gradually decrease talking out of turn during an instructional period. DRL is an underused yet effective tool for changing behavior.

As a classroom example, consider a program for students in sixth grade. An initial average problem level of 10 examples of profanity per day is determined. An initial criterion standard of 5 is set. Reinforcement (e.g., an agreed-upon group activity) is then based on staying below this level in a given period. Subsequently, the standard can be lowered to 3, to 1, and to 0, thus essentially shaping down the behavior as the rate of behavior is successively reduced.

DRO procedures call for reinforcement based on the omission of a given behavior or the occurrence of other behavior. Repp, Felce, and Barton (1991) describe two types of DRO schedules. With momentary DRO, reinforcement is delivered if the target behavior is not occurring at the end of an interval (e.g., when the bell rings). It is best used to "catch" students who are or are not behaving appropriately. For example, it could be used to decrease the occurrence of out-of-seat behavior. With whole interval DRO, students are reinforced if the target behavior does not occur for the entire time period. To return to the previous example, reinforcement in this case could be tied to a student's remaining seated for a period of 10 minutes. Subsequently, with a DRO schedule sequence, the time could be increased to the entire instructional period; the inappropriate behavior is effectively omitted during these successively longer periods.

DRI/DRA approaches can be used to strengthen behaviors that are not compatible with or that represent an alternative to the targeted inappropriate behavior. Thus, the reinforcement of hand raising could be used to decrease the occurrence of calling out in class. When using a DRI approach, it is important to select an incompatible behavior that requires "doing something" so that the student is not reinforced for simply "sitting quietly" (Demchak & Koury, 1990). A traditional measure of whether the behavior selected is appropriate is to ask, "Can a dead person do it?" The following example underscores the importance of this consideration.

Van frequently leaves his seat during work periods. Dealing directly with this behavior would involve negative alternatives (e.g., a reprimand from the teacher, 5 minutes in time-out). In the interest of promoting a positive atmosphere in the classroom, another option is to positively reinforce a target behavior that is incompatible with Van's being out of his seat. Staying seated might be a likely choice, but it would not pass the "dead person test." Thus, options such as being on task and completing work assignments would be more appropriate. With this plan Van would receive positive consequences in the form of praise, a pat on the back, or tokens whenever he stayed in his seat. Ignoring him if he got out of his seat would prevent his obtaining any positive teacher response to his disruptiveness.

Positive methods, in this case via differential reinforcement, are not the panacea for all behavior problems, but they do represent a valuable option and should be considered before more restrictive means are selected. Thus, they offer an attractive alternative to reliance on aversive techniques.

Good-Behavior Game. One example of the use of differential reinforcement (especially DRL) is the good-behavior game. This technique, originally reported by Barrish, Saunders, and Wolf (1969), divides a class into teams or groups. Each person has specific standards for meriting free time. Teams that remain below the maximum number of occurrences of inappropriate behavior receive the designated reinforcement. The technique, which relies on an interdependent group contingency (defined earlier), is easy to implement and has been used successfully in general education as well as in special education settings.

Although group contingencies such as those in the good-behavior game may seem unfair to individual students who are penalized for the actions of others, teachers may want to use them if, in the long run, all students will profit. Because well-behaved students already suffer in a disruptive environment, any technique that effectively enhances classroom management serves their best interests. Naturally, the teacher must modify the structure of the game if one student consistently misbehaves for attention-seeking purposes and thus penalizes the team.

Extinction Procedures

As behaviorally defined, extinction refers to the withholding of reinforcement that previously maintained a specific behavior or behaviors. Analysis of antecedents, behaviors, and consequences relative to a particular situation may indicate that change can be effected by removing the reinforcer maintaining the behavior, thus extinguishing the response. The most typical use of extinction in the classroom occurs when teacher attention has inadvertently been tied to students' inappropriate behavior. For example, the teacher may originally have spoken to students only when they were disruptive. An extinction procedure would then involve withholding attention at these times so that only appropriate behavior elicits reinforcement. For other behaviors, peers may need to be involved in the intervention plan if their attention has been maintaining the inappropriate behavior. For example, if a child is using infantile language to receive others' attention (e.g., laughter), then peers will need to be trained to withhold their laughter in response to this behavior.

Several cautions are needed concerning the use of extinction. First, extinction should be used only for a behavior for which it is apt to be effective. Thus, for example, its utility is likely to be greater for talking out in class than for self-stimulatory behavior (e.g., twirling a pencil). Sec-

ond, the initial withholding of attention or other forms of reinforcement may prompt a dramatic rise in the target behavior as students increase their efforts to receive attention. The efficacy of the procedure thus cannot be truly evaluated until several hours or perhaps days have passed. Third, extinction occasionally produces an initial aggressive response. A fourth concern is consistency of application. Without a commitment to consistency, the teacher may accidentally reinforce the undesirable behavior on an irregular basis and thus inadvertently maintain it at a higher rate of occurrence. Finally, other students may begin to imitate the behavior being ignored, thus exacerbating the situation. Alberto and Troutman (1995) aptly comment on the use of extinction:

> "Just ignore it and it will go away. He's only doing it for attention." This statement is one of the most common suggestions given to teachers. In truth, extinction is much easier to discuss than to implement. It will go away, all right, but not necessarily rapidly or smoothly. (p. 308)

Punishment

Although positive consequences should underlie intervention efforts, circumstances may require occasional use of some form of punishment. We use the term punishment in this chapter even though we are aware of the variant ways it has been interpreted and misinterpreted. Our general definition of punishment stresses its meanings as related to decelerative or reductive effects on behavior.

Punishment is distinct from, although often confused with, negative reinforcement. It is worth noting simply that punishment is associated with a decrease in inappropriate behavior whereas negative reinforcement frequently functions as a threat to be avoided and thus is associated with increases in avoidance behaviors. For example, although punishment in the form of verbal reprimands may lead to a decrease in classroom talkouts, the environment of the class may become so unpleasant that increases in behavior such as truancy to avoid the class may occur through negative reinforcement. Thus, these are different but related learning principles.

There are two general types of punishment. The first involves the removal or withdrawal of positive reinforcement, for example, restricting privileges or instituting a system of fines. The second includes the presentation of a negative event, such as corporal punishment or a verbal reprimand. Two examples of the first form, time out and response cost, are discussed initially, followed by a look at the presentation of negative events.

Time Out. Punishment through withdrawal of positive reinforcement is best typified by time out, which generally entails preventing a student from receiving the positive reinforcement that otherwise would be available (hence its full name, "time out from positive reinforcement"). Time out can include planned ignoring, contingent observation (i.e., the student is removed from but can still observe the group), exclusion from the time-in environment, and seclusion in an isolated room or cubicle (Nelson & Rutherford, 1983). The discussion here focuses primarily on the last of these forms.

Teachers should observe several cautions in using time out. First, the effectiveness of time out depends on the presence of positive reinforcement in the classroom and its absence in the time-out area. Without both of these elements, the procedure can be of only limited assistance to the teacher. For example, if Susan dislikes the classroom situation (e.g., there is a substantial amount of yelling by the teacher and difficult work assignments) and she is sent to the hall for time out, where friends wander by and chat, she has been rewarded for her behavior, not punished. This approach in the long run could increase her misbehavior.

A second caution about time out pertains to the other end of the spectrum. Making the time-out area an uncomfortable room is neither necessary nor acceptable. The time-out area should be bland and unstimulating but not a dungeon. Time out may occur in a corner of the room or in a small room adjacent to the classroom. It should be used sparingly for short periods (i.e., 5 to 10 minutes. If it needs to be used frequently, the teacher should carefully consider alternatives.

Research reported by Skiba and Raison (1990) illustrates both appropriate and inappropriate use of time out. Reviewing data on use with students who were behaviorally disordered, they found that on the average students made less than two trips to time out per week and that these averaged 9.6 minutes. At this rate, the researchers found an absence of negative implications for access to instruction. However, two students had spent more than 6000 minutes in time out in a year (the equivalent of 20 instructional days) at 20 minutes per visit. Clearly, it must be questioned in these cases both whether the procedure was effective and whether absence to this degree from the instructional program could ever be justified.

Use of time out naturally varies according to the space available, the type of students, and the teacher. Regardless of the circumstances, however, time out should be (Gast & Nelson, 1977):

- selected only after trying alternative solutions
- preceded by an explicit statement about when it will be used
- accompanied by a brief explanation of why it is being used
- kept brief
- documented through record-keeping procedures (see Figure 3–3)
- terminated contingent on appropriate behavior
- combined with reinforcement for incompatible behavior

Consistency in structure helps time out to proceed more smoothly. For example, a timer can be given to students when they go to time out so that they know when they can return. The time-out room should be removed from the rest of the classroom and not be used for academic purposes. For younger children, gradual introduction of time out may be wise, perhaps progressing from their sitting next to the time-out room, to being placed inside it with the door open, and eventually to being placed inside it with the door closed if the deviant behavior continues. Even with these steps, it may not be appropriate for some children.

Time out must be used carefully. The student must know in advance that the teacher will not accept a particular behavior. Classroom rules must

FIGURE 3–3
Record of time out

Student name: _____ Teacher name: _____

School: _____ Inclusive dates: _____

Policy and procedures for use of time out in this classroom: _____

_____

_____

Date Used	Precipitating Behavior	Time Placed	Time Removed	Response to Time Out

clearly indicate which specific behaviors merit time out, and the teacher must enforce the rules consistently. The teacher should also consider any legal aspects that may apply in a given school district.

Response Cost. A second example of punishment based on withdrawing positive reinforcement is the use of response cost (RC). Such procedures include, in particular, subtracting points or tokens within established reinforcement systems. Response cost procedures can be used concurrently with positive reinforcement in the classroom, producing a reasonably rapid decrease in behavior, and they can be combined with other procedures to yield a comprehensive behavior program (Heron, 1987).

Walker (1983, p. 52) supported the potential benefits of RC but identified some cautions. Response cost is likely to have maximum effect when the teacher has clearly explained the system to the students, has closely tied it to a reinforcement system, and has developed an appropriate feedback and delivery system. In addition, Walker suggests seven rules for implementation:

1. RC should be implemented immediately after the target response or behavior occurs.

2. RC should be applied each time a target behavior occurs.

3. The student should never be allowed to accumulate negative points.

4. The ratio of points earned to those lost should be controlled.

5. The teacher should never be intimidated by the target child using RC.

6. Subtraction of points should never be punitive or personalized.

7. A student's positive, appropriate behavior should be praised as frequently as opportunities permit.

Corporal Punishment. For years one of the most pervasive forms of school discipline has been corporal punishment. Although its use waned in the late twentieth century, and has been banned in 26 states, there is ample evidence of its continued consideration as a disciplinary option (Evans & Richardson, 1995; Johnston, 1994).

The legal right to use corporal punishment originally stemmed from the concept of in loco parentis, whereby parents ceded their rights to the school as a condition for the education of their children. Additional rationales that proponents have used include a legal basis in the

Supreme Court's decision in *Ingraham v. Wright* in 1977, apparent biblical support, and alleged practical benefits of quickness and effectiveness (Evans & Richardson, 1994; Smith, Polloway & West, 1979). Rose (1989) indicated that corporal punishment is applied most frequently in response to fighting, classroom disruptions, disrespect, disobedience, and truancy.

Opposition to corporal punishment has included arguments on moral (e.g., linked to an era when "might makes right" dominated) and physical (e.g., a serious threat to health when carried to excess) grounds. Psychologically, corporal punishment has been viewed as a causative factor in anxiety, hostility, lack of self-direction, and immaturity. A further critical concern is that it functions primarily as a suppressor and thus represents a direct challenge to the active learning process that is crucial for development. By emphasizing what to avoid rather than what to strive for, it stifles growth and blocks an opportunity for teachers to model skills that would promote adaptation both within and outside school. In addition, it has become a convenient crutch at times for ineffective or incompetent teaching; it provides a response to problems that might have been prevented by good teaching. Evans and Richardson (1994) argue that teachers should professionally commit to not using corporal punishment and develop effective alternatives. Despite its common use in some schools, virtually no empirical evidence supports its effectiveness.

Punishment in Perspective. Punishment continues to be a technique commonly used in the classroom. Teachers would be naive to assume that they will never rely on any form of punishment, especially given the fact that discipline problems are regularly rated as a serious problem in the public schools.

In considering possible procedures, the teacher should make selections based on the least restrictive option; that is, interventions chosen should curtail an individual's freedom no more than necessary to yield the desired behavior change (Barton, Brulle, & Repp, 1983).

If punishment in some form is to be used, the following guidelines should be considered (Heron, 1978; MacMillan, Forness, & Trumbull, 1973; Rose, 1988).

1. State the contingencies in advance so that students will know what the expectations are and what the consequences will be.
2. Be specific in identifying behaviors associated with punishment.
3. Initially select the less intrusive forms (e.g., soft reprimand).
4. Time the punishment so that it is presented early in the occurrence of the behavior.
5. Make it intense enough to result in suppression of the behavior while avoiding embarrassment.
6. Combine it with a clear rationale.
7. Be consistent.
8. Use it sparingly.
9. Reinforce behavior incompatible with the inappropriate behavior.
10. Evaluate spillover effects such as changes in the behavior of other children as a function of the punishment of target children.
11. Avoid physical punishment.
12. Evaluate the effectiveness of the approach used.

SPECIAL CONSIDERATIONS

Strategies for Adolescents

Although many of the tools previously discussed in this chapter have been used effectively with older students, special circumstances should be considered in selecting a strategy to implement with adolescents. In light of the inherent difficulties in motivating students with long histories of school failure and chronic patterns of inappropriate behavior, intervention programs must be carefully evaluated to determine their likely outcome. First, natural and logical consequences relative to the outcome of the behavior should be emphasized (e.g., being late results in detention). Second, careful attention should be given to the reinforcers controlled by a student's peer group. The use of peer-mediated strategies should be carefully considered as possible interventions. As noted earlier these strategies can be dependent (e.g., students are reinforced based on the behavior of the child), interdependent (e.g., reinforcement is given to a group working together), and independent (e.g., all students work on similar tasks for similar reinforcement but the reinforcement is contingent on only the individual's performance).

For use with adolescents, reinforcers that require a minimum of teacher intervention should be sought; this concern is particularly important with response cost procedures that can be associated with confrontational outcomes. A point system, for instance, would be easier to use than a token system if something must be removed from a student's total.

Most important, teachers must carefully choose strategies based on their anticipated reception by adolescents. In the case of positive reinforcement programs, the system must be designed in an age-appropriate fashion; for example, token programs using Daffy Dollars or the like are obviously high-risk approaches at the secondary level. Furthermore, backup reinforcers for any systematic positive reinforcement program must reflect students' interests and must be varied. For behavior reduction strategies, teachers should obviously avoid interventions with potential for exacerbating current situations.

Maintenance and Generalization

A key element of any intervention program is its relationship to the maintenance of acquired behaviors and skills over time and ultimately to their generalization to other settings and other behaviors. The goal of all change programs should be the development of the ability in students to retain and apply what they have learned. Efforts toward this end have evident implications for long-term consequences for students with disabilities in various key areas such as problem-solving skills, job skills, and related social skills.

A key component of maintenance and generalization can be achieved via the development of student-regulated strategies, including self-management.

Student-regulated strategies can be defined as interventions which, though initially taught by the teacher, are intended to be implemented independently by the student. The concept is an outgrowth of cognitive behavior modification which has been a popular and exciting option for educational intervention for students with disabilities since the early 1980s. (Dowdy et al., 1998, p. 137).

The key is focusing on the promotion of independence in the student.

Self-Management. The goal of self-management programs is to "try and make children more consciously aware of their other thinking processes and task approach strategies, and to give them responsibility for their own reinforcement" (Reeve, 1990, p. 76). Self-management thus represents a shift from extrinsic to intrinsic control. This transition can be facilitated by considering these procedures: (a) gradually reducing the frequency and amount of extrinsic reinforcement provided, (b) gradually delaying access to extrinsic reinforcement through the use of feedback to students, (c) gradually fading from the application of artificial reinforcers to reliance on natural occurring reinforcing events, and (d) teaching self-control through an emphasis on the cognitive aspects of behavior change." (Wallace & Kauffman, 1986).

Teachers can provide instruction in a number of ways that will promote a shift to self-regulation through the use of cognitive interventions. Initially having their roots in the field of mental retardation, cognitive interventions have been more widely researched and advocated for students with learning disabilities (Polloway, Patton, Smith, & Buck, 1997). The concept of cognitive behavior modification (CBM) can be described as follows:

[CBM] generally refers to the use of behavior modification methods (frequently direct measurement of behavior and manipulation of antecedents and consequences) to alter cognition (thoughts and feeling states) as well as overt behavior. The idea behind CBM is that cognition partially controls behavior and that altering thought processes might therefore be an effective way of modifying overt behavior. Moreover, cognition is accessible (to others through language and to oneself through conscious awareness and introspection) and can be modified in much the same ways that overt behavior can be controlled. Thus, CBM includes cognitive strategy training-teaching skills in thinking and self-control. (Wallace & Kauffman, 1986, p. 100)

A substantial literature base on self-management has developed and continues to be subject to review, refinement, and varied interpretation (e.g., Gerber, 1988; Harris, Graham, Reid, McElroy, & Hamby, 1994; Meichenbaum, 1983; Nelson, Smith, Young, & Dodd, 1991). A number of specific aspects of self-management can be utilized. Self-instruction includes a cognitive approach to management, using self-cuing to inhibit certain inappropriate behaviors and to direct appropriate ones. Pfiffner and Barkley (1990) described self-instructional approaches as follows:

Self-instructions include defining and understanding the task or problem, planning a general strategy to approach the problem, focusing attention on the task, selecting an answer or solution, and evaluating performance. In the case of a successful performance, self-reinforcement (usually in the form of a positive self-statement, such as "I really did a good job") is provided. In the case of an unsuccessful performance, a coping statement is made (e.g., "Next time I'll do better if I slow down") and errors are corrected. At first, an adult trainer typically models the self-instructions while performing a task. The child then performs the same task while the trainer provides the self-instructions. Next, the child performs the task while self-instructing aloud. These overt verbalizations are then faded to covert self-instructions (p. 525).

Self-determination of reinforcement places on the student the primary responsibility for selecting reinforcers so that they can be self-administered, contingent on performance of the specified appropriate behavior (Dowdy et al., 1998). Self-evaluation or self-assessment involves the learner in determining the need for change in behavior and then measuring (in some form) the change. Young, West, Li, and Peterson (1997, p. 92) highlight components of self-evaluation, done in consultation with the teacher:

■ determining the expectations or standards for acceptable behavior for each of the settings in which behavior is monitored;

■ comparing the counts or ratings of behavior (based on self-monitoring) to the standards; and

■ determining whether or not the behavior is acceptable or should be changed in either quantity or quality.

The most researched self-management strategy is the technique of self-monitoring, or recording, of behavior (Harris, et al., 1994). Self-monitoring, particularly of on-task behavior, is a relatively simple technique that has been validated with children of average ability who have learning disabilities (e.g., DiGangi, Maag, & Rutherford, 1991; Dunlap, Dunlap, Koegel, & Koegel, 1991; Prater, Joy, Chilman, Temple, & Miller, 1991), below-average intellectual levels (Rooney, Polloway, & Hallahan, 1985), mental retardation (Nelson, Lipinski, & Boykin, 1978) and behavioral disorders (Dunlap et al., 1991; McLaughlin, Krappman, & Welsh, 1985).

One common approach to self-monitoring involves an easily implemented series of techniques that can be used in both general and special education classrooms (Hallahan, Lloyd, & Stoller, 1982). It consists of the use of a tape-recorded tone that sounds at random intervals, averaging every 45 seconds, and a self-recording sheet. Children are instructed to ask themselves, each time the tone sounds, whether they were paying attention and then to mark the *yes* or *no* box on the self-recording sheet (see Figure 3-4). Although this strategy has been used with accompanying reinforcement for correct use of the self-recording sheet, in most instances it has been successful simply with appropriate training in the techniques.

The mechanisms described here have been effectively utilized, primarily with students who are in the 8- to 11-year-old age bracket and those of around average IQ. Modifications may be needed for other students—for example, more intensive training for students with lower IQs (Rooney et al., 1985). Self-monitoring studies with students identified as mentally retarded have included such aids as pictorial cues and videotape practice, as well as backup reinforcers to improve self-recording ability (e.g., Howell,

Rueda, & Rutherford, 1983). An example of a helpful pictorial cue from Prater et al. (1991) is in Figure 3-5. Dunlap et al. (1991) outlined the key steps in a successful self-monitoring program as follows: define target behavior, identify functional reinforcers, design the self-monitoring method or device, teach the child to use the device, and fade the use of the device (pp. 17–18). Figure 3-6 illustrates a sample self-monitoring device.

FIGURE 3–4
Self-monitoring sheet

From *Improving Attention with Self-Monitoring: A Manual for Teachers* [Appendix B], by D. P. Hallahan, J. W. Lloyd, and L. Stoller, 1982, Charlottesville, VA: University of Virginia Learning Disabilities Research Institute. Copyright 1982 by University of Virginia Learning Disabilities Research Institute. Reprinted with permission.

FIGURE 3–5
Self-monitoring pictorial cue

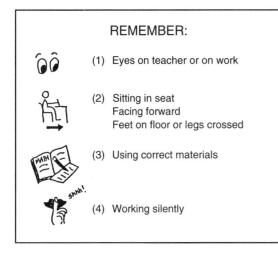

From "Self-Monitoring of On-Task Behavior by Adolescents with Disabilities," by M. A. Prater, R. Joy, B. Chilman, J. Temple, and S. R. Miller, 1991, *Learning Disability Quarterly, 14* (3), p. 169. Copyright 1991 by the Council for Learning Disabilities. Reprinted by permission.

Home-School Coordination

A third consideration is the coordination of home and school practices. Several specific techniques are discussed here to assist in the process of coordination concerning problem behavior.

An effective approach for enhancing collaboration is home-school contingencies. These arrangements tie behavior in school to reinforcement at home. They can be very effective as well as cost efficient (Pfiffner & Barkley, 1990).

A *daily report card* and a passport are two similar concepts that can be operationalized to enhance communication and consistency within a home-school management program. Daily report cards provide a system for home-based reinforcement tied to feedback on classroom performance. Such a package can be used for feedback on schoolwork, homework, and behavior. Further, it can range in complexity from simple rating-scale responses to precise behavioral definitions, and can be tied to nonspecific consequences or to specific short- and long-term reinforcement. Finally, daily report cards can be individually designed. Figure 3–7 provides an example of a daily report card.

The passport is another communication tool between home and school. It can take the form of a notebook brought to each class and then taken home on a daily basis. Teachers and parents and, possibly, bus drivers and administrators can make regular notations. Reinforcement is based on having the passport as well as on the specific behaviors indicated in it (Walker & Shea, 1988). Passports provide an opportunity for parents and teachers that is similar to that of daily report cards. These aids can help ensure consistency in behavioral standards and management procedures and can assist in the generalization of specific target behaviors.

FIGURE 3-6
Self-monitoring device

Katy's Self-Monitoring Checklist

Step	Problem Number									
	1	2	3	4	5	6	7	8	9	10
1. I copied the problem correctly.										
2. I regrouped when I needed to.										
3. I borrowed correctly. (The number crossed out is 1 bigger.)										
4. I subtracted all of the number.										
5. I subtracted correctly.										

From "Using Self-Monitoring to Increase Independence," by L. K. Dunlap, G. Dunlap, L. K. Koegel, and R. L. Koegel, 1991, *Teaching Exceptional Children, 23*(3), p. 21. Copyright 1991 by The Council for Exceptional Children. Reprinted with permission.

FIGURE 3–7
Daily report card

DAILY STUDENT RATING CARD

NAME _____ DATE _____

Please rate this child in each of the areas listed below as to how he performed in school today using ratings of 1 to 5. 1=excellent, 2=good, 3=fair 4=poor, 5=terrible or did not work.

AREA	CLASS PERIODS/SUBJECTS 1	2	3	4	5	6
participation						
class work						
handed in homework						
interaction with other children						
teacher's initials						

Place comments on back if needed.

From "Educational Placement and Classroom Management," by L. Pfiffner and R. Barkley, 1990. In *Attention Deficit Hyperactivity Disorder: A Handbook for Diagnosis and Treatment* (p. 522), ed. by R. Barkley, New York: Guilford. Copyright 1990 by Guilford Publications. Reprinted with permission.

BEHAVIORAL INTERVENTION PLANS

Under the Individuals with Disabilities Education Act (IDEA), students with disabilities are protected from arbitrary suspension or expulsion from school in instances in which their behavioral difficulty was determined to be related to their disability (i.e., the behavior was determined to be a *manifestation of the disability*) (note: see Figure 3-8 for a sample guide for this purpose). This provision clearly has decreased the likelihood that such students could be denied a free, appropriate public education. The unforeseen result was that the protection of the rights of an individual became perceived as a potential threat to school discipline in general and to the safety and security of other students, teachers, and staff (Fad et al., 1998). Teachers—both general and special education—are concerned with the problem of balancing individual rights with equitable school discipline policies (Butera et al., 1998). This need for balance led to the development of the 1997 IDEA discipline amendments (Zurkowski, Kelly, & Griswold, 1998).

The extent of serious behavioral problems associated with students with disabilities has been controversial. Nevertheless, clearly a distinct minority of such students does present troublesome behaviors that challenge a school's ability to educate all students effectively. As a result, it is not surprising that when regulations for the amendments to the IDEA were developed in 1999, a key issue was determining the appropriate balance between the rights of students with disabilities and the need for an orderly learning environment (Fad et al., 2000).

FIGURE 3–8

Manifestation determination

The information on this sheet can be used by the committee when considering a change of placement resulting from the student's behavior and to structure the committee discussion. Minutes of the meeting may reflect these specific concerns and how they will be addressed in the BIP.

Yes No

☐ ☐   1. Does the student have a disability?

             If *yes*, is the disability characterized or defined by differences in any of the following?

                ☐ behavior

                ☐ communication skills

                ☐ self-control

                ☐ cognitive functioning (i.e., understanding of rules, etc.)

☐ ☐   2. Does the student know the difference between right and wrong?

☐ ☐   3. Does the disability cause any of the following behaviors?

                ☐ impulsive, spontaneous misbehavior

                ☐ violent behavior

                ☐ defiance of authority

☐ ☐   4. Is the misbehavior in question an example of the type of behavioral concerns caused by the disability?

☐ ☐   5. Does the disability cause the student to have limited tolerance for stress?

             If *yes*, did this play a role in the misbehavior?   ☐ Yes ☐ No

☐ ☐   6. Does the disability make it difficult for the student to build or maintain satisfactory relationships with peers and/or teachers?

             If *yes*, did this play a role in the misbehavior?   ☐ Yes ☐ No

☐ ☐   7. Does the disability impair the student's ability to express feelings in an appropriate manner?

             If *yes*, did this play a role in the misbehavior?   ☐ Yes ☐ No

☐ ☐   8. Has the student been able to follow the rules in the past?

☐ ☐   9. Is the evaluation data current enough to use as the basis for decisions?

☐ ☐ 10. After reviewing previous disciplinary records, is it possible to determine whether there is a pattern of misbehavior?

☐ ☐ 11. Has the student's placement been reviewed?

☐ ☐ 12. Has the information in the Functional Behavioral Assessment (FBA) been reviewed?

☐ ☐ 13. Are the current IEP goals and objectives appropriate?

☐ ☐ 14. Have all appropriate special education services, including supplementary aids and supports, been provided?

☐ ☐ 15. Is the student making educational progress?

Source: Fad, K., Patton, J.R., & Polloway, E.A. (1998). *Behavioral intervention planning* (p. 11). Austin, TX: Pro-Ed.

FIGURE 3–9

Sample behavioral intervention plan

Specific Goal(s)	Proposed Intervention(s)	Person(s) Responsible	Evaluation		Methods
			Progress Codes: / = ongoing X = mastered D = discontinued		
			Schedule		
			Date	Code	
When Michael is given directions to read aloud or to complete written work independently, he will: 1. say "okay" 2. begin the assignment 3. ask for help if he needs it.	—Reduce number of teacher directives —Provide advance organizers —Model correct response —Positive verbal praise when he demonstrates the appropriate behaviors —Home-school contract for privileges (basketball games, time with friends) —Cool off in office	} Teacher Parents-Teacher-Student Principal-Student	4/30/98 5/15/98		—Tally sheets —Contract forms —Discipline referrals

These goals were developed with consideration of the following information:

☒ Parent concerns regarding special circumstances:
   Prefers positive approaches

☒ Teacher/administrator concerns regarding special
   circumstances: Would like parent &
   student to agree to a contract

☐ Outside agency/professional concerns regarding
   special circumstances:

Source: Fad, K., Patton, J. R., & Polloway, E.A. (1998). *Behavioral intervention planning* (p. 20). Austin, TX: Pro-Ed.

The legal resolution of this debate was the incorporation of a requirement for specific practices in the 1997 amendments to IDEA. Foremost among these were the establishment of clearer guidelines for the removal of students with disabilities from the regular school setting, the need for functional behavioral assessment (FBA; discussed earlier), and the establishment of a requirement for the development of a behavioral intervention plan (BIP) for individual students who present challenging behaviors within the school setting.

The 1999 federal regulations provided limited direction regarding the form of a BIP. Given this latitude, appropriate practice suggests that BIPs should include the following components: the overall goals to be achieved, attention to planned

activities, the persons responsible for implementing the proposed activities, timelines to be followed, and plans for intervention. Outlining these elements, Figure 3–9 illustrates a sample BIP completed in case study format.

Comprehensive plans include attention both to behavior change in the individual as well as changes in the system or setting that may play a causative or contributory role.

SUMMARY

Behavior change strategies afford teachers a wide variety of options for motivating and managing students with disabilities. The techniques discussed in this chapter focus on the importance of understanding behavior and on antecedent and consequent events in successful teaching and learning.

Systematic use of positive reinforcement can increase appropriate behavior. Teachers can program positive consequences to shape desired behaviors through contingency contracting and token economies, both of which are based on the Premack principle.

Behavior reduction strategies can include the use of a variety of differential reinforcement strategies. Although teachers should emphasize positive intervention, they may need to select techniques from among the various forms of punishment to successfully decrease targeted inappropriate behaviors.

Several critical concerns should be considered by teachers that relate to strategies for use with adolescents, self-management approaches, and home-school collaboration. The techniques discussed in this chapter can be powerful tools.

Teachers should use them carefully, constantly evaluating whether the changes are sought and achieved in their students' best interests. Federal law (i.e., IDEA) requires the development of a behavioral intervention plan in specific instances of challenging behaviors.

TEACHER TIPS

Elementary Level

Many special education teachers may be required to use several types of behavior management programs with students who are confrontational in a verbally or physically aggressive manner. In order to do so they may consider the use of three basic approaches to this type of behavior: prevention, defusion, and follow-up. The prevention stage of the behavior management approach is a period of time when a teacher places a strong focus on teaching desirable behaviors. These behaviors include proactive behaviors such as social skills, rule-following, self-management skills, and problem-solving skills. During this period, rules are established and consequences for rule infractions are enforced.

In many scenarios, teachers react to confrontational or inappropriate behaviors by presenting an ultimatum. The student usually reacts by not complying and may display additional oppositional behavior. When this situation arises, the teacher will find it best to use methods found in the defusion stage of a behavior management program. During the defusion period teachers use strategies designed to address the confrontational behaviors after the behavior has begun. The goal here is to stop the behavior before it escalates into a dangerous situation. Some of these strategies include:

1. Focus on the task and ignore the noncompliant behavior. Redirect the student and if necessary present a small negative consequence for the behavior.
2. Present options privately. A teacher should state the rule of desired behavior, request that the student "take care of the problem," and present options for the student on how to take care of the problem.
3. Disengage and delay responding in the presence of serious threatening behavior.

Colvin, G., Ainge, D., & Nelson, R. (1999-2000). How to defuse confrontation. In K. L. Freiberg (Ed.). *Educating exceptional children* (pp. 126-129). Gillford, CT: Dushkin/McGraw Hill.

In his "Children's Mental Health Bulletin," Alexander (1999) states that at least 80% of middle school-aged children reported engaging in bullying behavior. This behavior ranged from excessive taunting and spreading rumors about another student to destruction of property and physical aggression toward others. Alexander also states that most children will have to deal with a bully at some point in their school lives. He believes that bullying is worst in the middle school years, as students make transitions to new schools. Most often this bullying peaks during the first few months of school, when students vie for power among their peers.

Although many teachers recognize that power struggles are a part of life and that children must learn to deal with difficult individuals, bullying can destroy a child's well-being and confidence. This lack of confidence and a preoccupation with bullying events can affect the way a student approaches school and his classroom experience.

What can teachers, parents and children do? Alexander recommends three strategies.

1. Teachers can help children learn to avoid being a victim. Teach children to act with confidence since many bullies go after people who appear anxious, sensitive, quiet, or cautious. Bullies are drawn to people who are somewhat shy.
2. Children can also engage in certain behaviors:
   a. Run. If you see a bully coming, run home, to the principle's office, teacher, or to another adult;
   b. Stay near other people, especially friends. Bullies can't stand groups of happy, smiling, friendly people;
   c. In a loud and firm voice, tell the bully, 'Don't do that. I don't like it.' 'Leave me alone,' 'Take your hands off me';
   d. Don't be afraid to tell an adult. You are not a tattletale if you report someone who's hurting you;
   e. Walk around with confidence! You may not be lucky enough to have an older sibling who protects you in the hallway, but you should walk around as *if* you did."
3. Parents can help by believing their child when he/she reports being bullied.
   a. Contact the child's teacher and ask about supervision during recess and between classes;
   b. Know the signs of being bullied:
      1. child wants to skip school or is too sick for school;
      2. child has unexplained bruises;
      3. child has experienced a slip in grades;
      4. child is reluctant to talk about school;
      5. child frequently requests lunch money to replace "lost money";
      6. child comes home in dirty clothes (from fights).

Alexander, C. J. (1999). *The Children's Mental Health Bulletin*. Santa Fe, NM.

TEACHER TIPS

Technology

Teachers can now find many websites that focus on behavior management issues and suggestions. One such site is called *Athena*. Some examples from this site include suggestions for teachers on how to manage computer time for their students to developing a classroom management profile for your class. The latter of the two suggestion hold particular interest in that it gives teachers some insight to their managerial styles.

The authors of this information are Kris Bosworth, Kevin McCracken, Paul Haakenson, Marsha Ritter Jones, Anne Grey, Laura Versaci, Julia James, and Ronen Hammer. These teachers adapted a questionnaire by John T. Santrock that asks an individual about his/her parenting styles. The questionnaire has 12 questions that are responded to through the use of a one to five point scale, with the response of one indicating the teacher strongly disagrees and a response of five indicating the teacher strongly agrees with the statement. Some of the statements are as follows:

1. If a student is disruptive during class, I assign him/her to detention, without further discussion.
2. I don't want to impose any rules on my students.
3. The classroom must be quiet in order for students to learn.
4. I am concerned about both what my students learn and how they learn.

After responding to each statement, the teacher follows a score guide and applies the final score to one of four behavior management styles. These styles include: (a) authoritarian style; (b) authoritative style; (c) laissez-faire style; and (d) indifferent style. The authors do not advocate any one style as being most appropriate, but suggest that successful teachers may need to evaluate a situation and then apply the appropriate style. The intent of the exercise is to inform the participant and arouse curiosity regarding classroom management styles.

Note: The interesting aspect of this site is that the authors give a short description of each behavior management style and then quote students' thoughts about each style. For example, a student's response to an authoritative style was as follows: "I like this teacher. She is fair and understands that students can't be perfect. She is the kind of teacher you can talk to without being put down or feeling embarrassed."

Source: Center for Adolescent Studies. K. Bosworth, Director. table.htmltable.html

CHAPTER 4

Effective Instructional and Accommodative Practices

Since the 1950s researchers have worked to demonstrate that certain teacher behaviors have a significant impact on student learning. Although teachers and researchers continuously work toward the success of students, the concern over teacher effectiveness became pronounced during the early 1950s when the "Sputnik" era forced the people of the United States to admit that other nations were becoming more technologically advanced in math and science. As a result of this concern, researchers focused on math and science by concentrating on the development of content and curriculum (e.g., new math). Little consideration was given to the role of the teacher and how teacher behaviors could influence learning of these content areas.

By the 1960s the people of the United States were consumed with political, economic, and social issues. Civil rights issues as well as the Vietnam War influenced the concerns of effective teaching. Researchers became interested in the role of schools and the ecological dimensions of socially and economically depressed areas as having an impact on student success. Student-teacher relationships and behaviors were given little attention except by behavioral theorists, who were developing a technology to observe and understand human behaviors in different environments.

As the researchers in applied behavioral analysis gained momentum in the 1970s, the focus on teacher behaviors that promote student learning became evident. This research became increasingly important as the implementation of PL 94-142 went into effect. All students were of concern, and students with learning and behavior problems were of particular concern because it was evident that they were not benefiting from traditional teaching methods.

With the onset of the teacher effectiveness research in the 1970s and 1980s, the fields of education and psychology demonstrated that what teachers and students do in the classroom is incredibly important. For example, researchers found that teachers who use teacher-directed instruction are able to show greater student achievement among students with mild disabilities (Englert, 1983, 1984; Sindelar, Smith, Harriman, Hall, & Wilson, 1986). Teacher effectiveness variables such as time on task (e.g., the amount of time students spend on a particular task—both allocated and engaged time) (Haynes & Jenkins, 1986), content covered (e.g., amount of information presented to students in a given time period), teacher delivery of content, feedback, and formative evaluation are crucial if student learning is to take place (Mastropieri & Scruggs, 1994). See Figure 4-1 for a display of general teacher-effectiveness variables.

Over the years much of this research proved to be experimentally effective when student learning issues surfaced. Much of what has been developed, however, has been done without addressing several new and recent classroom issues. For example, today's classrooms are much more diverse and complicated than in past decades. Students who are (a) from different cultural backgrounds, (b) bilingual, (c) in inclusive classrooms where special education services are provided, (d) involved in any number of outside of school issues (e.g., gangs), and (e) at different academic levels are now being served by one teacher. Teachers must take all these students into consideration when teaching. Trying to maximize time-on-task behaviors or direct instruction is of little use if the classroom atmosphere is hostile, confrontational, or apathetic. Teacher variables such as praising, caring, negotiating, and helping students feel important also contribute to the learning process. Stressing effective teacher behaviors, therefore, can make a difference in the impact on students' learning.

This chapter is intended to describe some of the effective teaching approaches outlined in today's literature and highlighted in the middle column of Figure 1-3. Many of the approaches presented have been thoroughly experimentally evaluated for students with and without disabilities. Others are being experimentally evaluated at present and show great promise in meeting the needs of today's youth. The chapter is divided into three major sections. The first part is devoted to examining some of the realities of teaching in

FIGURE 4–1

General teacher-effectiveness variables

EXAMPLES OF GENERAL EFFECTIVE TEACHING BEHAVIORS	RESULTING IN DESIRED STUDENT BEHAVIORS

1. Classroom management skills
  a. Rules established and enforced
  b. Clear instruction given
  c. Consistent reinforcement or desired behavior
  d. Environment is structured so children can predict behavior in each classroom area
  e. Transition periods are structured
	1. Desired classroom behaviors
	  a-e. On-task behavior without disruptions, or no unnecessary behaviors occurring during academic time

2. Systematic instruction is used
  a. Introduction of content
  b. Explanation of procedures/materials
  c. Questioning student understanding
  d. Modeling and demonstrating
  e. Guided practice
  f. Descriptive feedback
  g. Independent practice
  h. Pacing
	2. Students demonstrate mastery over skills and content
	Students meet IEP objectives

3. Assessment of learner progress	3. Students understand goals and objectives and are able to monitor their own progress
4. Modification of content when children are having difficulties	4. Student frustration is diminished
5. Self-reflection/evaluation of teaching and student-teacher interactions	5. Students learn respect, fairness, self-evaluation skills, and problem solving
6. Good communication skills	6. Students learn communication skills and parents are always informed

schools today that teachers must consider before stepping into classrooms. The second part of this chapter presents an overview and description of the following effective teaching practices: (a) self-reflection and knowledge of students; (b) teacher-directed instruction; (c) self-directed learning; and (d) peer-directed learning. The third part of the chapter discusses a range of accommodative practices involving curriculum, materials, instruction, and products/assignments.

SELF-REFLECTION AND KNOWLEDGE OF STUDENTS

Teaching a number of diverse students in one classroom has become an issue of concern for many educators. Students from various cultures, languages, and socioeconomic backgrounds as well as students with learning problems, physical and medical disabilities, and emotional/behavioral problems, are challenging teachers to find ways to be more effective facilitators of learning. To compound this issue, many teachers take positions in schools that differ from their own cultures, past experiences, and expectations. Teachers may find that these differences are sources of frustration and that they can result in a lack of empathy and understanding for these children.

As a part of the reform in education, teacher education, and pedagogy, researchers recognize the issues of diversity and are devoting their efforts to investigating the interactions among teachers, students, schools, and community. Based on the preliminary data beginning to surface, investigators believe that teachers must "know themselves" (e.g., their beliefs, values, and expectations) and their students (e.g., culture, neighborhood, family, disability) in order to best instruct and meet the needs of these children. In response to these preliminary data and beliefs, researchers in general education (e.g., Cochran-Smith, 1995) and special education (Institute of Research in Learning, 1995) are investigating the utility of the critical self-reflection of teachers as well as the need to learn about students' functioning in and outside the classroom. The idea behind these investigations is that self-reflection and personal knowledge of students will result in an effective, responsive curriculum in the classroom.

This knowledge is gained through specific methods of inquiry that require a classroom teacher to become a teacher-researcher. Cochran-Smith, (1995) states that the teacher-researcher treats the classroom, schools, and community as research sites "by raising questions and collecting data as a vehicle for discovering meaning in variations of children's behaviors and interpreting classroom events and interactions" (p. 498). The

knowledge gleaned from these inquiries can change teachers' practices in their classrooms. Cochran-Smith goes on to explain that teaching through systematic and "self-critical inquiry" allows teachers to engage the following behaviors:

- changing teaching approaches
- identifying contextual variables in the classroom, home, and community
- analyzing children's learning opportunities
- understanding how children understand their academic and social environment
- reconsidering the curriculum or pedagogy taking place in the classroom

The following discussion will briefly explain each perspective and describe its value with regard to teacher effectiveness.

Changing Teaching Approaches

Self-critical reflection is a kind of self-examination that begins when teachers look at their own histories as people and as educators. They examine their lives in regard to race, class, and disabilities, and through the perspective of being a child, parent, and teacher. This reflection also examines the overt or covert assumptions we make about the motivations and behaviors of students, their parents, and other teachers, and the most appropriate methods we use to teach.

The desired outcome of the reflective evaluation process is to uncover the teacher's beliefs, assumptions, and biases toward education, schools, and children and youth as well as themselves. With this knowledge, teachers can begin to realize their own understanding of empirical and conceptual research. This understanding enables teachers to learn how to confront and deal with diversity in the classrooms and to teach more effectively. Researchers suggest that once understanding of self takes place, teachers are able to make the necessary changes in their teaching behaviors.

Identifying Contextual Variables Within the Classroom, Home, and Community

Contextual variables, as they pertain to self-reflection skill, may be thought of as those historical and social experiences that contribute to the way children learn and the manner in which teachers instruct their students. These variables can include cultural contexts of the classroom (e.g., rules, social and academic structure), school, family, and community. In addition, difficult-to-identify variables such as attitudes, values, beliefs, and language contribute to the learning of children and youth as well as the teaching behaviors of teachers.

For example, students who come from families that do not abide by rules or do not value the need for scheduled time (e.g., coming to school on time) will find themselves negotiating a different environment at school. Understanding these differences and taking into consideration all the environmental variables can allow teachers and students to come to a mutual agreement regarding the behaviors and expectations of the child. In this way, the teacher and student function as a productive team/community in the classroom.

Analyzing Students' Learning Opportunities

As teachers engage in self-reflection and research on student learning, they begin to ask questions about their (a) teaching, (b) curriculum construction, (c) analysis of student work (e.g., written work), and (d) social behavior. This examination allows teachers to analyze the learning opportunities that are or are not available to students during an academic lesson or social interaction. By asking questions about their teaching and curriculum, teachers learn that management issues are artifacts of the structure of the lesson. Self-questioning allows teachers to recognize whether students are given opportunities to learn effectively. Teachers begin to recognize how particular materials, instructional practices, and participation influence learning. Teachers learn that these factors can (a) structure, (b) limit, (c) support, and (d) enhance all aspects of children's academic gains and social interactions.

Understanding How Children Understand Their Academic and Social Environment

Self-reflection and forming research questions allow teachers to observe students and how they may best learn. Especially when teachers are dealing with diversity issues in the classroom, observing children allows them to understand their charges by considering their backgrounds, behaviors, and interactions with others. By observing and interviewing children, teachers can compile questions regarding the child's learning and development during academic or social situations. For example, a teacher may observe that a child does not interact well with peers in the classroom. A resulting question such as "How can we engage the child in our activities?" may be the source of attempting new and different approaches with the child. Teachers then analyze classroom data to determine the success of their interventions.

Reconsidering the Curriculum

When working with diverse students in a classroom, teachers discover the importance of developing curriculum that is relevant and meaningful to students with regard to their daily lives. Topics such as ethnicity, poverty, family life, jobs, and how they impact student's lives can be infused into the curriculum. Subjects such as social studies, math, literature, and language provide contextual frameworks to teach concepts needed for adulthood (Chapter 16 examines this idea in more depth). When the curriculum relates to students' lives and has meaning to them, the learning environment is enriched. Student participation is greater, motivation is higher, and the learning of content with regard to self and community occurs.

EFFECTIVE TEACHING PRACTICES

This section of the chapter focuses on three general instructional orientations available to teachers (refer to the first entry in the middle column of Figure 1–3) when working with students with special needs. It describes the basic elements of teacher-directed, student-directed, and peer-directed learning.

Teacher-Directed Instruction

Teacher-directed instruction implies that the teacher plays an active role in the teaching process. This role varies depending on the objectives of the lesson or subject area. For instance, spelling instruction typically differs from laboratory activities in science. Blosser (1986) affirms the importance of this component: "instructional techniques which help students focus on learning (preinstructional strategies, increased structure in the verbal content of materials, use of concrete objects or realism) are effective in promoting student achievement" (p. 169). Good (1983) argues persuasively that teachers engaged in active instruction do make a difference in student learning. Students with mild learning problems often require special services because they are not dealing well with traditional methods and materials. It is essential that these students be provided with lessons in which teachers pace instruction briskly, question students appropriately, and involve them actively.

Since the early 1960s teacher-directed instruction has been proven to be an effective teaching model for students with diverse needs (e.g., Phillips, Phillips, Fixsen & Wolf, 1974). This method of teaching involves a systematic approach that includes well-sequenced, highly focused lessons that are presented in a fast-paced manner (Gersten, Woodward, & Darsch, 1987). Teachers who engage in direct instruction present lessons that provide students with opportunities to respond and receive feedback on what they think about the lesson being presented. They are shown how a skill is performed and are then given ample time to perform the new skill in a guided practice situation. Teachers enthusiastically engage all students by providing positive as well as constructive feedback while they are practicing, the ultimate goal being mastery over the skill. Typically, such lessons follow a particular pattern so that students can predict the structure of the lesson and the learning environment.

One of the most widely used instructional methods is the use of direct instruction. Although there are many versions of direct instruction, each approach typically includes the essential elements of explaining the skill, teaching the skill, modeling the skill, practicing the skill, and giving feedback on the skill performance. The following description of direct instruction is a systematic instructional approach that was developed by Serna and Lau-Smith (1995). This direct-instruction approach was constructed to provide new teachers with an easy way to remember the direct-instruction procedure as well as to employ generalization procedures so the student can perform the skill outside the classroom environment.

The procedure is divided into seven steps. These steps were put into an acronym, PURPOSE, so teachers could easily remember what they should be doing (Fig. 4–2). The PURPOSE format (or any direct-instruction format) is the foundation upon which lesson plans are built. The following discussion and figures are included to exemplify how the teaching format should be implemented during instructional periods.

Prepare the Student to Learn the Skill. The letter **P** in the acronym PURPOSE requires the teacher to prepare the students to learn the skill. During this step, the teacher is required to gain the students' attention and direct their learning toward the skill. This requires that the teacher prepare the students to learn the skill and know why it is important to learn (i.e., a rationale for needing the skill). To do this, the teacher asks the students to: (a) define the skill to be learned, (b) state why it is an important skill to learn, and (c) explain where they can use this skill once they have learned it. This series of questions and answers is employed to check for the students' understanding of the skill and to describe the skill as it is to be learned. It is important that the teacher incorporate an interactive dialogue with the students and listen to their answers.

Understand the Skill Steps. The letter U represents the second instructional step in the

FIGURE 4–2
The Learning with PURPOSE structured teaching model

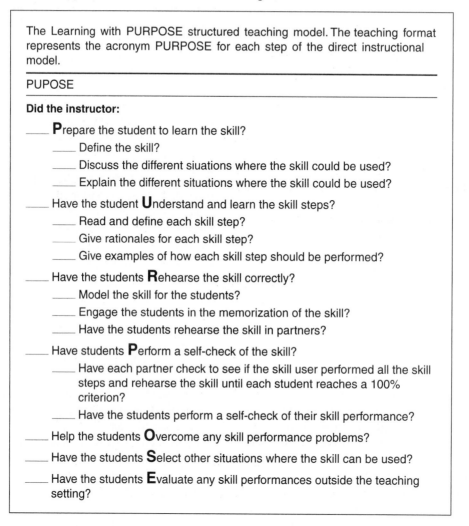

The Learning with PURPOSE structured teaching model. The teaching format represents the acronym PURPOSE for each step of the direct instructional model.

PUPOSE

Did the instructor:

____ **P**repare the student to learn the skill?

   ____ Define the skill?

   ____ Discuss the different siuations where the skill could be used?

   ____ Explain the different situations where the skill could be used?

____ Have the student **U**nderstand and learn the skill steps?

   ____ Read and define each skill step?

   ____ Give rationales for each skill step?

   ____ Give examples of how each skill step should be performed?

____ Have the students **R**ehearse the skill correctly?

   ____ Model the skill for the students?

   ____ Engage the students in the memorization of the skill?

   ____ Have the students rehearse the skill in partners?

____ Have students **P**erform a self-check of the skill?

   ____ Have each partner check to see if the skill user performed all the skill steps and rehearse the skill until each student reaches a 100% criterion?

   ____ Have the students perform a self-check of their skill performance?

____ Help the students **O**vercome any skill performance problems?

____ Have the students **S**elect other situations where the skill can be used?

____ Have the students **E**valuate any skill performances outside the teaching setting?

---

acronym PURPOSE and requires the teacher to help the student understand the skill components to be learned. In this step, the teacher reviews each component of the skill's task analysis. This is done by presenting each skill component individually, asking students to state what it is and why it is needed to execute the skill. If the students are unable to do this, the teacher should explain the skill component, give an example of it, and state why it is an essential component of the skill. Again, the teacher should involve the students in the discussion of the skill steps. This instructional

step also requires that the teacher have a good understanding of the skill steps and be able to explain each one clearly and succinctly.

This step also implies that some preliminary work has been done before the skill is taught through a direct instructional approach. This work involves the task analysis of the skill so that each step is easy to grasp. The task analysis of the skill allows the teacher to determine if the skill is too difficult for a student. It allows the teacher to determine at what point the student is having trouble. By analyzing the steps associated with each skill, teachers are able to modify the skill to best meet the needs of the students.

Rehearse the Skill. After the students have a clear understanding of each skill component, the **R** step in the acronym PURPOSE requires teachers to rehearse the skill for and with the students. This means that the teacher first models how to perform the skill and then allows the student to practice the skill until mastery is achieved. The teacher begins by modeling the skill exactly as it should be performed. If the skill that is being modeled is an interactive skill, the teacher models the skill through a role-play situation. This interactive modeling requires that the teacher seek out another person to help with the role play. It is always useful if the teacher has rehearsed the skill before presenting it to the class. Usually in interactive modeling, the students will perform the skill exactly as the teacher models it; the importance of accurately modeling the skill cannot be emphasized enough.

If the skill is a cognitive skill, the teacher must model the skill by using tools such as a chalk board or an overhead projector and "talk through" each step of the skill. This modeling can be difficult as the teacher does not want to leave out any skill step that may be required to complete the entire skill. The importance of having the students hear and see what the teacher is thinking is also underscored. Students will see and hear how a person thinks through a cognitive problem and can perform the skill according to this example.

After the modeling, the teacher should ask the students for feedback to see if they were able to identify each skill component that was performed in the entire skill. This is done by asking the students about each skill step and requiring them to provide some details about the skill component that was just modeled. The teacher should praise the students for their correct answers and refresh their memories when they cannot remember what happened during the performance of a skill step.

Once the feedback from the students is accomplished, the teacher should require the students to learn each of the skill components before they are asked to perform the skill. This task can be accomplished through some sort of learning strategy. The type of strategy will depend on the age and cognitive ability of the student. Some of the strategies available include: (a) memorization of the skill steps through verbal rehearsal, (b) utilization of a mnemonic as is seen in the following example, and/or (c) use of flash cards or pictures. When the students are able to verbally state each step of the skills, they should try to perform the skill under guided practice. Mastery of the skill should be achieved during this step.

Perform a Self-Check. After a mastery rehearsal, the teacher and student must perform a self-check of the skill performance. This step is represented by the second **P** in the acronym PURPOSE. This self-check involves an evaluation of each skill component. When the student thinks that mastery of the skill has been accomplished, he or she should ask the teacher to evaluate the performance for accuracy. This outside check will confirm the students' perceptions of their own performance.

Overcome Any Performance Barrier. As with the acquisition of any skill, there may be difficulties in obtaining performance at levels that are targeted. If the student is having difficulty achieving mastery over the skill, the **O** in the acronym PURPOSE is used to help students to overcome any performance problems. This is usually done by employing a specific technique that enhances the student's learning of the skill.

When these situations occur, the teacher must pinpoint where the student's problem lies (through the task analysis) in order to help the student overcome the performance problem, and develop an appropriate instructional intervention. The teacher may need to develop supplemental materials such as flash cards, use techniques such as mapping or webbing, or provide extra practice to accomplish the desired goal of learning the skill to the level of mastery that is desired.

Select Other Situations Where the Skill Can Be Performed. As the student achieves mastery over the skill, the teacher and student must select other situations where the skill can be used. This activity refers to the **S** step in the acronym PURPOSE. During this step of instruction, the teacher focuses on generalizing a skill mastered in the classroom to other situations. Together, the student and teacher decide where or with whom the skill can be used and determine when the student will use the skill. The student and teacher might talk about how the skill will be performed and the importance of using the skill in the selected situation. Once a specific situation is selected, the student and teacher agree that the student will perform the skill as soon as the occasion arises and that the student will report the outcome of the performance as soon as possible. Other situations may include homework or various social situations where a skill can be employed outside the classroom environment. This generalization step requires students to use the skill in situations where it is most meaningful to them.

Evaluate the Situation. Finally, the last instructional piece of the lesson that is recommended is the **E** step in the acronym PURPOSE. This step requires the teacher and student to evaluate the skill performance in the generalized situation. Once the situation has occurred, students must evaluate the effectiveness of their performance and determine the outcome resulting from the performance. If possible, students should be encouraged to use a checklist to evaluate how well each skill component was executed. If all the skill components were executed successfully, the student must then determine whether the performance of the skill accomplished the desired goal. If the desired goal was obtained, the performance of a skill was a success.

If the student did not perform the skill correctly, the teacher and the student should determine why it was not performed correctly and develop a procedure that would help the student the next time the performance of the skill is necessary. The student should continue to practice the skill so that maintenance of the skill is not a factor in the poor performance of the skill the next time it is needed. Peers or teachers can assist in this maintenance phase.

If the student performed the skill correctly but the desired goal was not obtained, the student and the teacher should analyze the situation to determine why the use of the skill did not aid in the acquisition of the goal. It is important to identify other factors in the environment, including other people, that may have played a role in the outcome of the situation. Based on the student's report, the student and teacher should decide how the situation could have been handled differently or what other techniques could have been used. If problems persist, the teacher engages in additional practice of the skill with the student or problem-solves with the child to ensure that a similar situation outside the classroom might be met with more favorable results in the future.

Some Final Thoughts on Teacher-Directed Instruction. As the process just described shows, teacher-directed instruction is characterized by a series of activities in which the teacher must engage. In addition to the major steps highlighted in the PURPOSE acronym, several preliminary activities are also necessary. These preparatory steps involve setting the purpose of the lesson, identifying the ultimate goals students are to achieve, and determining whether students demonstrate all prerequisite skills needed to perform the skill that will be taught. If students do not exhibit these prerequisite skills, they will need to be taught before or in conjunction with the targeted skill.

Self-Directed Learning

Ultimately, students should become independent learners, able to direct their own behavior in ways that assist in maximizing the amount of time engaged in learning (i.e., student-directed learning). Many students with special needs have significant difficulty in this area, which can limit their chances of successful inclusion in general education where self-regulated behaviors are expected. Cohen and deBettencourt (1983) suggest that it is the teacher's responsibility to help students to become independent learners and to structure the classroom environment to help them achieve this goal.

Since the early 1980s a movement emphasizing students' self-direction of their academic learning and performance has been present in education (e.g., Corno, 1989; Harris, 1990; McCombs & Marzano, 1990; Paris & Newman, 1990). Researchers in the area of self-direction are concerned with students' learning, motivation, and behaviorally proactive regulation of their own learning and environment (Zimmerman, 1986). This concern has materialized into teaching students how to teach themselves.

For example, Bandura's (1986, 1989, 1991) research indicates that self-directed learners determine their learning processes and attainments by setting goals for themselves, applying strategies to achieve the goals, and managing the behaviors with reinforcers that motivate and guide their efforts toward reaching their goals. Self-directed learners typically demonstrate a variety of metacognitive skills as well as self-regulation skills resulting in motivation, negotiation skills needed to navigate their learning environment, and the social interaction skills needed to support their self-directed behaviors.

The need to teach self-direction skills to students with disabilities has become even more important as the recent amendments to IDEA have stressed that students be more actively involved in their programs. For example, active and meaningful participation in a student's own IEP meeting suggests that the student direct the meeting and be able to articulate long- and short-term goals as well as a plan to reach these goals. Because many students receiving special education services have never participated in their IEP meetings to this extent, they lack the skills needed to (a) make choices, (b) construct goals, and (c) plan strategies to achieve desired outcomes. The following discussion consists of two types of teaching that will foster self-direction skill in students with disabilities: skill building and problem-based learning.

Self-Direction Taught Through Skill Building. The first type of teaching focuses on skill building through direct instructional procedures and includes the components necessary to teach the self-direction skills of:

- action planning
- goal setting
- goal planning
- self-management

Action planning is a procedure used to develop a long-term strategy to accomplish desired goals. The strategy involves the identification of many goals and tasks that might be needed to accomplish a desired life achievement (e.g., going to college, getting a job, moving to a different state, attaining financial stability). This long-term strategy will include (a) identifying steps that will lead to attaining the life achievement, and (b) analyzing each step and breaking it down into the tasks/goals needed to accomplish that specific step (Serna & Lau-Smith, 1995).

Action planning is an important skill to teach students because it gives an individual a purpose for engaging in certain activities. Purposeful activities give meaning to our lives and to who we are as individuals. When the lives of successful people are studied, it is found that most of them develop an action plan when seeking to accomplish different life achievements. Without a specific plan, these people would not have a direction toward their dreams. It is important therefore that we allow students to dream and then teach them how they might successfully make those dreams come true.

Through the use of direct instruction, students are able to develop their own action plans and determine a strategy that will allow them to accomplish their dreams. Seeing each step that is required to accomplish that dream can give purpose to the many tasks that must be completed. An action plan can give purpose to education and to each content subject area that applies to the attainment of the dream.

Goal setting can be defined as a skill that allows an individual to determine the tasks or events that need to be accomplished so certain outcomes can be obtained. A person who engages in a goal-setting skill will develop a clear statement that outlines the specific terms of a task or event (what is to be accomplished, who will accomplish the task, where the task will be accomplished, and when the outcome task or event will be completed) (Serna & Lau-Smith, 1995).

Teachers might introduce this skill to a student by stating that many people complain about not having or getting the things they want. Often, they do not know specifically what they want so they have a difficult time working toward getting something. The skill of goal setting is important because it will help the student to clarify the goal (Serna & Lau-Smith, 1995).

A student might set a goal by identifying what is wanted or what needs to be accomplished (e.g., getting a good grade in math class). Then the student must put this task into a proactive "I will" statement (e.g., "I will get a good grade in math"). After the proactive statement is written, the student must determine if this is an ongoing goal, a short-term goal, or a long-term goal. Clarification of the goal statement must occur by determining what exactly the task is, with whom it will be accomplished, where it will be accomplished, and by when it will be accomplished. Once these questions are asked, a well-developed, clarified goal statement must be written (e.g., "I will get an A in my math class by the end of fall semester"). Again, this skill can be taught through a direct instructional format and can be used in all content-oriented classes as well as behavior-related endeavors.

Goal planning is a skill that allows an individual to develop the steps needed to achieve a particular goal. A goal or goal statement does not mean very much unless the student has developed a plan to accomplish it. The skill of goal planning is important because it will help a student clarify, in behavioral terms, what he or she needs to do to accomplish the goal (Serna & Lau-Smith, 1994–1995). A student could begin the goal-planning process by reviewing the goal statement just outlined. Next, the student would think of at least five different activities or steps (behaviors) that would help in the accomplishment of the goal. Figure 4–3 provides an example of this process.

Once a list of activities has been generated, the student must prioritize which activity must be done first. The student then clarifies each one by answering the *what, with whom, where,* and *when* (deadline) questions. Using this information, the student should develop a plan that outlines how the goal is to be accomplished.

Self-management to accomplish goals is a complex set of procedures used to regulate or guide a person's behavior so that a goal can be accomplished. It is a procedure that has been used by many researchers and educators to manage behavior problems in the classroom. Under the umbrella of self-directed learning, however, teachers must instruct students in how they can learn to manage their own behavior by determining what rewards they will use for reinforcement after a task/activity has been accomplished, developing a self-monitoring system (e.g., a checklist) that will help them account for their behavior, recording whether they accomplished an activity under the set guidelines, and actually monitoring their behavior toward meeting their goals (Watson & Tharp, 1993). The following set of self-management skills accompanies a set of self-direction skills used to instruct students to become more independent and self-directed learners (Serna & Lau-Smith, 1994–1995). (See also Chapter 3.)

The following set of procedures is used to regulate or guide a person's behavior so that a goal can be accomplished. To manage behavior, an individual must have already identified a task, behavior, or goal that needs to be accomplished. (This is usually done through the use of a goal-setting and goal-planning skill.) Once the goal has been established and planned, an individual must determine what consequences (rewards) will need to be established in order that each goal step of the goal is rewarded after it is accomplished. After the rewards are established, a monitoring system must be developed so the individual can determine whether the goal steps are being accomplished in a timely manner. Once all these elements are in place, the individual is ready to implement the entire plan and monitor his or her progress toward meeting the

FIGURE 4–3
Goal planning Skill

GOAL PLANNING

⇨ **YOUR SKILL**

Skill Steps	Examples
1 Write down at least 5 different activities, steps, or behaviors that you can do to meet your goal. *Use your goal Setting Worksheet to organize your steps for each goal.* *If you are having trouble identifying a list of activities, ask for help or use your Seeking Information skill in the Formal Networking domain.*	If your goal statement is: "I will get an 'A' in my English class by the end of Fall semester," you may need to perform these steps to achieve it: 1. Take notes during class. 2. Complete homework assignments on time. 3. Participate in class discussions. 4. Do daily reading assignments on time. 5. Pay attention in class.
2 **Prioritize** your list of goal steps by deciding which one is the most important to achieve. Next, decide which goal step is the last step you need to achieve. Fill in the other steps based on your most and least important goal steps.	1. Top Priority Goal Step—Pay attention in class. 2. _____ 3. _____ 4. _____ 5. Low Priority Goal Step—Participate in class discussions.

3 **Clarify** each goal step so the following questions are answered:
What is the action or behavior?
With whom will it take place?
Where will it take place?
When (deadline) will it be accomplished?
	Goal Step needing clarification: Pay attention in class
	
	  What — pay attention by listening and following directions
	
	  With whom — to the teacher
	
	  Where — in English class
	
	  When — every day

4 **Use** the information in Step 3 to develop a descriptive sentence for each goal step. The group of clarified statements makes up your **Plan** to accomplish your goal,.	"I will pay attention in my English class every day by listening to the teacher and following directions."

(continued)

FIGURE 4–3   *(Continued)*

Skill Steps (continued)	Examples (continued)
5 **Review** your goal step deadlines and see if you think they are reasonable for you to achieve. If your deadlines are not reasonable, change the deadline so that you will be successful.	If your goal statement is: "I will participate in English class discussions every day," this may not be reasonable to do **every day** if you find it difficult to talk in class. Additionally, your teacher might not have class discussions every day. You may need to change your goal step to say "I will participate in English class discussions 2 times a 3 week."

⇨ **CHECK YOURSELF**

Ask yourself the following questions:

Are my goal steps specific and clear enough so I know exactly what I need to do to accomplish each goal step? If not, did I rewrite it or find some person to help me?

Do I have the required skills to accomplish the goal steps and eventually my goal plan? If not, did I seek out a peer or trusted adult who can help me acquire these skills.

Will my goal plan allow me to meet my goal deadline?

⇨ **OUTCOME OR PRODUCT**

A clearly written goal plan that specifies the behaviors you need to do to obtain your goal.

From *Teaching with PURPOSE: Lesson Plans for Teaching Self-Determination Skills to Students Who Are At-Risk for Failure,* by L. A. Serna and J. A. Lau-Smith, 1994, Unpublished manual.

goal. Thus, the skill of self-management has three subskills:

- developing a reward system
- developing a self-monitoring system
- monitoring the behavior

The first subskill in the skill of self-management is *developing the reward system.* This skill involves simple yet distinct steps. The first step requires that the teacher and students identify the items, activities, or people that are rewarding to them. This requires some brainstorming or some preliminary work on the part of the teacher (i.e., developing a list of possible rewards to choose from). From the identified list of rewards, choose four ways that students can positively reinforce themselves daily and weekly. Also, students should choose four ways they can give themselves bonus rewards for accomplishing their goals by the predetermined deadline.

The second subskill in the skill of self-management involves the *developing of a self-monitoring system.* This skill requires that students have in place: (a) a goal, (b) a goal plan, and (c) a reward system. Once these three components are in place, the students begin by reviewing their goal and goal steps. Using the rewards (identified in the subskill on developing a reward system) and the goal steps (developed in the goal planning skill), the students must fill out a self-contract by (a) deciding when the self-contract will begin, end, or be reviewed; (b) specifying the goal steps to be accomplished; (c) determining the reward to be received upon the completion of the goal steps; (d) asking someone else to witness the signing of the contract; (e) deciding on the bonus and when it will be obtained once the goal is reached; (f) stating what penalty will be enforced if the goal steps are not performed; and (g) scheduling a review of the contract to determine if it is working or if it needs to be changed. After these terms are delineated, the students create a system to monitor their progress, as this will assist them in their self-management process.

The final subskill in the self-management skill is the task of *monitoring the desired behavior.* Students begin this skill by locating their self-contract and reviewing the goal steps, rewards, penalties, and signature commitment. The subskill then begins by developing rules or criteria that must be followed for each goal step. The rules should be specific actions on behaviors that the students must do in order to accomplish the goal step. Once the criteria are developed, the students must follow through with their plan, outlined in their self-contract. This is done by setting a start-up date and then starting. After the students begin to perform their goal steps, they must monitor their behaviors by using a self-monitoring sheet (created in the subskill on developing a monitoring system). This step is accomplished by appropriately marking a plus (+) or minus (−) sign to indicate whether they completed the goal step according to the rules or criteria established. Following the completion of the each goal step and according to the criterion established, the students reward themselves.

Self-Direction Skills Taught Through Problem-Based Learning. Problem-based learning consists of activities in which the students become actual investigators of a real problem or topic. As Reis and Cellerino (1983) noted, the original problem-based model stemmed from work with gifted and talented students. This model required that students use appropriate methods of inquiry to solve problems. Their activities were intensive and long range so that final products included a walking robot, the production of a dramatic marionette show that outlined the development of clowns from the thirteenth century to the present, a continuation of Tolkien's *Lord of the Rings* in the form of a novel, creating the illustration of a children's Christmas book, and many others.

Although these examples are quite elaborate, the same methods are now being advocated for use in classrooms with diverse learners (Renzulli, 1994). Such methods of teaching require that students engage in several activities. First, students are guided, through different activities, to explore many topics, issues, and areas into which they may delve more deeply. To do so, teachers must assess the interests of the students. This may require that the teacher explore several avenues as students may not know what they would like to learn about.

The second activity a student must explore is choosing a topic and determining certain goals and objectives that are to be accomplished in order to develop the content into an interesting project. Teachers can help students determine these goals and objectives by working with them to decide what is to be accomplished. It is very important that teachers listen to students so that the project is the students' idea and not the teacher's.

The third activity or step in this process is developing a management plan. This plan includes timelines, getting the student started, and finalizing product ideas. After the plan of management is outlined, the student begins to research the ideas and produce the products based on research and guidance from the teacher. The final step of this process is guiding students through the process of independent or small-group study to help them evaluate what they have accomplished. Although Renzulli and his colleagues have developed a specific Student Product Assessment Form (Renzulli & Reis, 1985), students and teachers can develop evaluations plans that best suit their needs.

Peer-Directed Learning

The main goal in using peer-related strategies is so that learning can occur as a function of a joint operation. Whereas this orientation does have a teacher connection, the focus is on activities in which students with learning-related problems engage along with their fellow students.

Since the early 1970s, teachers have been implementing peer tutoring and collaborative learning programs in their classrooms. These programs contribute to the enhancement of students' learning to improve behavior patterns and academic performances (e.g., Franca, Kerr, Reitz, & Lambert, 1990) and function as a supplemental tool to the direct teaching procedures just described. The following discussions will describe how to set up a peer tutoring system in a classroom and outline several collaborative learning procedures that can be part of a general education and special education classroom.

Peer Tutoring. Peer tutoring is a process that involves the pairing of a competent student with a student who is less competent in a particular behavioral or academic area. Peer tutoring procedures have been used for the purposes of (a) teaching academic skills, and (b) developing social behaviors with regard to classroom discipline, peer relations, and appropriate interaction behaviors. The term "peer" is used to indicate that students of similar age, grade, or academic status are working with one another.

The effectiveness of peer tutoring has been demonstrated across ages, settings, and types of students. Content areas such as reading, arithmetic, spelling, and social skills are a few of the subjects that facilitate the use of peer tutoring. It has been applied across grade levels, including elementary, middle school, and high school with positive gains received by both the tutor and the tutee (e.g., Franca et al., 1990; Polirstok, 1986).

Utilizing peer tutoring through structured classroom lessons has several advantages. Cooke, Heron, and Heward (1983) summarize the advantages as follows: (a) Children can effectively teach each other skills when tutors emphasize repetition, mastery, and a review system; (b) tutors are able to learn from teaching other students; (c) tutors can individualize content material to meet the needs of each student; (d) students can engage in one-to-one instruction without requiring a full class lesson; (e) one-to-one teaching greatly increases the opportunity for correct responses by the tutee; and (f) students—both tutor and tutee—gain in their self-esteem, self-respect, and ability to interact with each other on a constructive and appropriate basis.

Teachers wanting to set up a peer tutoring system must begin by identifying potential peers who would be willing to be tutors. When selecting tutors, teachers must consider that the students should be individuals who can help in the teaching process. They can be fast or slow, yet competent in the area of content that will be taught. These students should be enthusiastic about being peer tutors and willing to learn the procedures necessary to work with another student. Once the students are selected, a direct instructional method can be used to teach them how to tutor in a particular content area. Figure 4–4 outlines a direct instructional procedure, using the PURPOSE format described earlier, that a teacher might use when preparing potential students to become peer tutors.

Cooperative Learning. Cooperative learning is a method of instruction that teachers can employ in addition to peer tutoring to enlist the support of their students while simultaneously promoting the academic and behavioral skills of the desired lesson. According to Schniedewind and Salend (1987), teachers can structure their class lessons so that students work together to achieve a shared academic goal. These authors state that:

> Cooperative learning is especially worthwhile for a heterogeneous student population, because it encourages liking and learning among students of various academic abilities, handicapping conditions, and racial and ethnic backgrounds. (p.22)

When planning a cooperative learning lesson, teachers should consider four basic elements of cooperative learning: (a) positive interdependence, (b) individual accountability, (c) collaborative skills, and (d) processing. Within a lesson, *positive interdependence* is structured by having each student group agree on (a) the answer to the task and (b) the process for solving each problem. In this way, students work toward a common goal or outcome (Johnson, Johnson, & Holubec, 1986).

FIGURE 4–4
Teaching peers how
to be tutors

A Systematic Procedure for Teaching Peers to be Tutors

• **Prepare the students to learn about peer tutoring:**

   _ Ask the students if they know the *definition* of a "tutor."

   _ Ask the students why it is *important* to be a tutor to a peer.

   _ Ask the students for *examples* of what subjects they might tutor.

• Help the student to **Understand an learn the steps to being a tutor.**

   _ *Outline* the steps the tutors must exhibit in order to tutor a peer in a designated subject area (e.g., a spelling lesson)

   _ *Explain* each step to the tutors and ask them to tell you why that step is important to exhibit when tutoring the subject.

   _ *Require* that the tutors learn the steps needed to teach the lesson

• **Rehearse** the skill by watching a model and then practicing the lesson with someone else

   _ *Show or model* how you would like the tutors to execute the lesson when tutoring another student in a particular subject area (e.g., go over each step they must engage in if they are tutoring someone in the area of spelling or math).

   _ Have the students *Rehearse* the lesson the lesson with you role-playing the role of the tutee.

   _ *Give feedback* to the tutors after each role-play situation — making sure that they are able to teach the lesson to your criteria.

• **Perform a self-check** to ensure that the lesson was performed correctly.

   _ Once the tutors have role-played the lesson to criteria, have them *Evaluate* whether they performed each step needed to teach the lesson.

• **Overcome any performance problems** to produce the desired outcomes or products.

   _ If a tutor is not exhibiting all of the steps needed to correctly teach the lesson, *work with the tutor* until he/she is able to execute the lesson appropriately.

• **Select** or recognize other situations where the skill can be performed.

   _ Pair the tutors with other students and have them *begin tutoring* the students on the lesson.

• **Evaluate the performances** of the tutor and the tutee during the lesson.

   _ *Evaluate* whether the tutor executed the lesson appropriately and if the tutee's skill level improved because of the tutoring lesson.

The element of *individual accountability* is structured by having the teacher randomly score a group's work and determine whether the correct answer has been written on their answer sheet. If the answer is correct, the teacher then asks a random student to explain how to solve each problem. Individual account-ability is determined if individual group members have mastered the process of solving the problem or demonstrate the skills necessary for accomplishing the task.

Collaborative skills are also fostered by cooperative learning. These skills emphasize student support for one another (e.g., praising and offering help), enthusiasm for group work, and contributions to the group's efforts. These collaborative skills are necessary for the appropriate behaviors to occur within a group.

Finally, the teacher must include the element of processing the lesson. *Processing* requires that the group evaluate how well they worked together and what they could do in the future to be an even more effective group member or group. This type of evaluation requires that the group function as a whole as well as that individual group members engage in self-evaluation for personal improvement in the classwork.

Although much of the research and literature regarding cooperative learning groups focuses on students in general education classrooms, some investigators have begun to adapt these procedures for special education teachers. Guidelines for designing and implementing cooperative learning strategies for classrooms providing special education services include: (a) selecting a format for cooperative learning, (b) establishing guidelines for working in groups, (c) forming cooperative learning groups, (d) arranging the classroom, (e) developing cooperative learning skills, (f) evaluating cooperative learning, and (g) confronting problems (Schniedewind & Salend, 1987). Figure 4–5 presents these guidelines, along with an explanation and examples of how each guideline is used by teachers who provide special education services.

ACCOMMODATIVE PRACTICES

In today's classrooms, teachers wanting to meet the diverse needs of their students are faced with many challenges. One of the predominant challenges is meeting the curricular needs of these children. This challenge becomes more complex when teachers are also asked to teach the wide volume of information that is necessary to prepare today's children for a competitive world. They must not only teach the information that many of us learned as children, they must add the new and ever-expanding information that has emerged in since the 1980s.

A second challenge faced by teachers in today's classrooms is that much of the information they must teach is quite complex and abstract. The dawn of computers and technology in general has opened a wide world for students. This expanding world requires that they learn new and different material. New vocabulary is necessary and how this new information is applicable to everyday life must be understood if the new knowledge is to be appreciated.

Unfortunately, many students have little interest in learning things that they do not understand or that seem irrelevant to their immediate future. A third challenge, the lack of motivation among students, is a formidable barrier that teachers encounter on a daily basis. If teachers are unable to introduce new information in an

FIGURE 4–5

Guidelines for cooperative learning groups for students with disabilities

Guidelines for Working in Groups

- *Each group* will produce one product.

- *Each group member* will assist other group members to understand the materials.

- *Each group* will seek assistance from his or her peers.

- **No** g*roup member* will change his or her ideas unless logically persuaded to do so.

- *Each group member* will indicate acceptance of the group's product by signing his or her name.

From "Cooperative Learning Works," by N. Schniedewind and S. J. Salend, 1987, *Teaching Exceptional Children,* 19 (2), pp. 22–25.

understandable manner, students will become easily frustrated and will not persist on their own to learn the material. If teachers are unable to teach students how to acquire new concepts and to have them relate these concepts in a meaningful way, the students will not pursue the new content areas presented to them in their classes.

Finally, a fourth challenge that teachers must meet is the expectation for improving on local, state, and national competency exams. This expectation is placing more and more pressure on increasing the scores of children in their classrooms. Test-taking skills, knowledge-based skills, and overall aptitude skills are of the utmost concern to administrators. When students are unable to score well on these exams, the schools and the academic curricula are pressured to improve performances.

The question of how we can best meet the overall curricular needs of our students is therefore being asked on a more frequent basis. Attention must be given to the curriculum itself (i.e., what is covered) along with a focus on the acquisition of knowledge or concepts that students need in order to understand the content being covered.

Accommodative practices, which may go under different names (e.g., accommodation, adaptation, modification), require that teachers make decisions about what content to teach, translate content into easy-to-understand formats, and present the information in memorable ways. Popular content enhancement strategies students (Bulgren, Schumaker, & Deshler, 1993) include lesson organizers or advanced organizers, chapter survey procedures, and unit organizers. These strategies have been documented to aid students in the acquisition of more information presented in written form. What these strategies do not do, however, is teach students to understand the information they glean from textbooks or lectures. Of concern is how teachers prepare lessons so that students will learn concepts and not memorize or rote learn the material presented.

The accommodative practices discussed next are organized into four categories (see Fig. 4–6). This system is an adaptation of a model for cur-

riculum development developed by Maker and Nielson (1996). The content domain refers to changes in curricular areas relating to the knowledge and skills students learn. Materials accommodations relate to selection, use, and development of specific print and nonprint materials used in classrooms. The instruction domain includes a variety of teacher-directed, student-directed, and peer-directed variables related to the effective delivery of instruction. The last domain involves accommodations associated with assignments given to students and the products they are asked to generate as a part of the learning experience.

Curricular Content Accommodations

Curriculum can be defined as the planned and guided learning experiences under the direction of the school. It relates significantly to the content that is covered and that leads to knowledge acquisition and skills development. This topic is discussed in more detail in Chapter 6.

Students can be motivated by curricula that they find relevant and meaningful with regard to their daily lives. Kohn (1993) notes that a key condition for developing authentic motivation is the content of the tasks—learning that is contextualized where there is a connection to student's lives and interests. Interestingly, many of the content areas discussed in this section relate well to this notion.

For the most part, the skills discussed in this section are skills that are never taught directly to students because they are presumed to learn these skills incidentally. The following discussion highlights a number of skill areas that may be excluded from the curriculum to which students with special needs are exposed. However, each of these may be essential curricular accommodations for students.

Study Skills. Without question, one of the most important areas in which learners with special needs must achieve competence is study skills. This topic is so important that we dedicated an entire chapter to it (see Chapter 13). Study skills are

FIGURE 4–6
Accommodative practices

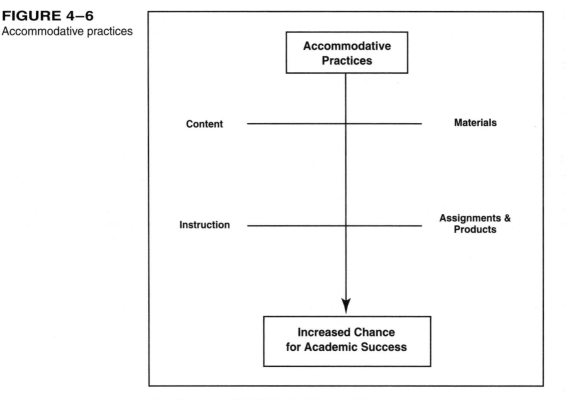

From Dowdy et al. (1998). Reprinted by permission.

tools for learning and can be described as the specific skills that individuals employ to acquire, record, remember, and use information efficiently. These skills are useful not only in school but in everyday living as well (Hoover & Patton, 1995).

Learning Strategies. Learning strategies are another set of skills that can be extremely valuable to students. Learning strategies are "task-specific techniques that students use in responding to classroom tasks" (Archer & Gleason, 1995, p. 236). Utilizing a cognitive orientation to learning, these types of strategies provide students with a method for using their own abilities and knowledge to acquire, organize, and integrate new information. Ultimately, successful demonstration of learning strategy competence leads to more self-regulated, independent learning as these strategies are generalizable to other situations where a specific task is required. Learning strategy

instruction can be particularly helpful to students with ADHD who can benefit from tactics that help them focus on the task at hand.

Many different learning strategies exist and, accordingly, various systems for organizing learning strategies can be found as well (Archer & Gleason, 1989; Deshler, Ellis, & Lenz, 1996; Hoover & Patton, 1995). Table 4-1 shows general types of learning strategies according to the function the strategy serves, as presented in certain resource materials.

Many of the learning strategies just described are accompanied by a "remembering device" (Archer & Gleason, 1995); this can consist of a word or acronym that relates to the steps one must follow to implement the strategy. Other mnemonic techniques are available for organizing and retrieving information and these can be taught to students with special needs. One technique is the use of reconstructive elaborations

(Scruggs & Mastropieri, 1989). This technique uses acoustically similar keywords and a graphic representation to link two concepts. For example, in assisting the student to remember the capital of the state of New York, the teacher could associate New York with "new pork" and Albany with "all baloney" and then use the statement: "A person asks a butcher, 'Is this new pork?' and the butcher replies 'It's all baloney.'" This statement is coupled with the illustration depicted in Figure 4–7. Therefore, to retrieve the capital of New York, the student thinks of the keyword phrase and relates this to the graphic scene and the link to the other keyword phrase.

Social Skills. Appropriate social skills are essential for success in school, on the job, and in the community. Social skills refer to the ability to demonstrate behaviors that are socially desirable and the ability to refrain from displaying behaviors that elicit negative responses within the context of two or more persons interacting. Social skills should be proactive, prosocial, and recipocal in nature so that participants of the interaction share in a mutually rewarding experience. Comprehensive coverage of this subject is provided in Chapter 14.

When social skills problems exist, they tend to be one of following four types: total skill deficit—

TABLE 4–1

Types of learning strategies as a function of primary operation

Acquiring Information	Organizing Information	Demonstrating Competence
Deshler et al. (1996)		
■ word-identification strategy	■ first-letter mnemonic strategy	■ sentence-writing strategy
■ paraphrasing strategy	■ paired-associates strategy	■ paragraph-writing strategy
■ self-questioning strategy	■ listening and note-taking strategy	■ error-monitoring strategy
■ visual-imagery strategy		■ theme-writing strategy
■ interpreting-visuals strategy		■ assignment-completion strategy
■ multipass strategy		■ test-taking strategy
Archer and Gleason (1989)		
■ reading expository material	■ gaining information from verbal presentations (lectures, demonstrations)	■ completing daily assignments
■ reading narrative material		■ answering written questions
		■ writing narrative and expository products
Hoover and Patton (1997)		
■ active processing		■ preparing for and taking tests
■ analogy		
■ coping	■ organization	■ rehearsal
■ evaluation		

Note. Developed from *Teaching Students with Learning Problems to Use Study Skills: A Teacher's Guide,* by J. J. Hoover and J. R. Patton, 1997, Austin, TX: PRO-ED; *Skills for School Success,* by A. Archer and M. Gleason, 1989, North Billerica, MA: Curriculum Associates; and *Teaching Adolescents with Learning Disabilities: Strategies and Methods,* by D. D. Deshler, E. S. Ellis, and B. K. Lenz, 1996, Denver: Love Publishing.

FIGURE 4–7

Mnemonic illustration for teaching the capital of New York.

Note. From "Applications of Mnemonic Strategies with Students with Mild Mental Disabilities," by M. A. Mastropieri, T. E. Scruggs, M. E. S. Whittaker, and J. P. Bakken, 1994, *Remedial and Special Education,* p. 37. Copyright 1994 by PRO-ED, Inc. Reprinted with permission.

all components of skill are absent; partial skill deficit—some critical elements of the skill are absent; and performance deficits—the person can demonstrate skill but does not use it or does not use it with sufficient frequency; or control deficits—undesirable social behaviors (i.e., obtrusive or excessive) are present (Sargent, 1991). Each of these situations requires a more formal approach to social skills development.

All too often, social skills development is not addressed directly within the school curriculum. Social skills training should be part of the explicit curriculum for many students with special needs. In reality, such training is part of the hidden curriculum in many schools because of the ultimate importance of competence in this area.

Related Life Skills. Another area of curricular attention that might be absent from the educational programs of many learners with special needs is that of life skills instruction. The inclusion of life skills topics can be extremely useful to students both in the present and in the future.

Life skills can be thought of as specific competencies (i.e., knowledge and skills) of local and cultural relevance that are needed to perform the events and activities typically encountered by most adults in everyday life. Without question, life skills competence is needed to deal successfully with the many challenges and demands of adulthood.

The conceptualization of life skills provided here is broad and includes skills previously discussed in areas such as study skills and social skills. Life skills include a range of other important knowledge and skill areas that are discussed in Chapter 16.

Instructional Materials Accommodations

Many different types of materials are used in school settings. These include a wide variety of print materials that students must be able to read and information to be used at a later time. Other nonprint materials such as maps, globes, models, photographs, videos, and computer-based images are also available in school settings. All these materials can pose problems for students with ADHD.

The key concerns that precipitate the need to make accommodations to instructional materials for the most part cut across the different types of materials. These concerns are presented below.

- The student does not display the skills necessary to handle the material.
- The conceptual complexity of the material exceeds the level at which the student understands. Often the student does not have sufficient background knowledge and experience to make sense of the information being presented.
- The linguistic complexity of the material is such that the student is unable to extract meaning from it. Primary sources of problems are vocabulary and syntactic factors.
- The amount of information presented to students is overwhelming. Typically emphasis has been placed on breadth of coverage rather than depth of coverage. In reference to textual

materials, Deshler, Ellis, and Lenz (1996) note that "even when textbooks are written in ways that 'invite' learning, the sheer volume of information included in textbooks can be overwhelming for teachers and students alike" (p. 417). Students can be overwhelmed by nonprint sources of information as well.

- Far too often the design/format features of materials (e.g., advanced organizers, layout, organization, graphics, cueing, clarity, use of examples, practice opportunities) are lacking or insufficient, thus making them difficult to use, especially for students who are encountering learning-related problems. In other words, the "considerateness" (Armbruster & Anderson, 1988) or user-friendliness of materials is frequently in question.

Textual Materials. For the purpose of this chapter, text-based materials refer to any type of material that requires reading as the primary means of obtaining information. Text-based materials typically used in classrooms include basal textbooks, workbooks, worksheets, literature, weekly periodicals, handouts, and other reproduced materials. The general cautions and content enhancement considerations previously mentioned are true for these types of materials.

Two general approaches can be implemented to address problems that arise with text-based materials: (1) substitution of an alternative material in place of the existing textual material; and (2) content enhancement techniques, which include strategies to increase comprehension and tactics for retaining information over time. The first technique aims to avoid the problems associated with existing textual material. The other option primarily supports the student in using existing material, particularly when the student is in a general education setting. The following discussion of the various techniques for dealing with textual material is based on the recommendations of Schumm and Strickler (1991).

Using an alternative method for conveying existing textual content can be helpful to certain students. Tactics for doing this range from the complete substitution of existing text to the modification of the existing text. Some of the following suggestions are more likely to be implemented than othes due to time, effort, and availability factors.

- Audio-tape textual material: Ideally, the material being used is already available through Recordings for the Blind and Dyslexic and the student can qualify for this service. Otherwise, unless volunteers or other students are available to do the taping, taping may be difficult to do. Lovitt and Horton (1991) do not recommend taping on the basis that "many texts are 'inconsiderate'. . . . It seems apparent that if a passage is disorganized and incoherent, it will continue to be disorganized and incoherent when taped" (p. 443).

- Read the material aloud: This suggestion has the same advantages and limitations as the taping recommendation.

- Pair students to master textual material: This technique has short-term and targeted usefulness and requires the availability of such supports whenever the textual material is being used.

- Use other ways to deliver the material (e.g., direct experiences, media): Other vehicles for delivering information are extremely useful for presenting content-laden topics. The drawback to this idea is the availability of appropriate alternatives and the time to do them.

- Work with students individually or in small groups: This works when students can understand the textual material to some extent and time is available on a regular basis for performing this activity.

- Use a multilevel, multimaterial approach: Textbooks that are written at lower readability levels are available in a number of content areas. Other supplementary reading materials, also written at a lower reading level, can be introduced too. This approach allows students to remain in a specific course and gain the information they need through the use of materials they can handle. This technique is enhanced by the use of some of the other suggestions previously discussed.

- Develop abridged versions of textual content: The merit of this suggestion is that students are able to use condensed textual material that is suited to their reading levels. The fact that this type of material almost always needs to be written by the teacher or other personnel is a drawback because of the time and energy involved. It is for this reason that Lovitt and Horton (1991) do not recommend this technique.
- Simplify existing textual material: Vocabulary, terminology, and expressions that are difficult for students to understand can be simplified by the teacher. In place of rewriting complete textual passages, one can place a transparency over a page of written material and, with a marker, cross out the more difficult words and write a more understandable equivalent in the margin (Hoover & Patton, 1997).

A variety of ways exist for enhancing existing content so students are better able to understand what they read. The following recommendations focus on tactics for improving comprehension of textual material, particularly grade-level material.

- Provide students with purposes for the reading they are being asked to do: this simply helps students appreciate what the goal of the reading assignment is.
- Preview the reading assignment: this very important activity, which too often is omitted, prepares the student for some of the specifics of what they will encounter. This prereading activity should introduce the student to new vocabulary and concepts that that may pose problems. The use of a diagram or story frame may be helpful.
- Teach students how to use format features: an extremely useful set of skills includes the ability to use headings, bold-face type, visual aids (e.g., figures, tables, exhibits, photographs), opening sections, and summaries of textual material to gain an organization and additional meaning from the textual material.
- Engage the student prior to reading: stimulating thinking about what is to be read is extremely helpful. The use of an anticipation guide that asks students certain questions that will be answered during the course of their reading is one such tactic.
- Use a study guide: some commercial textbooks provide these supplementary aids; other texts do not. The primary objective of using this type of aid is to guide the student through the reading material by having them respond to questions or statements related to the passages they are reading or have read. Study guides are a way of organizing and guiding the comprehension of textual material.
- Utilize graphic organizers: these techniques use visual formats or structures to help students organize information for better comprehension. Many examples of these techniques such as central story problem, story frames or story maps, and semantic mapping are provided in Chapter 9.
- Modify the nature of the reading assignment: it might be necessary to reduce the length of the assigned reading or to slow the pace at which content is being covered.
- Highlight the textual material: if it is possible to highlight the actual textual material prior to a student using the material, a teacher can focus the reader on important points in the passage. Highlighting can also be used prior to reading by having the student go through the text and highlight all headings, thus introducing the reader to what will be encountered.
- Teach comprehension-monitoring strategies: various strategies have been developed to help students think about how well they are understanding what they are reading and how they can address any problems they are having. Examples of this type of accommodation are also addressed in Chapter 9.
- Adapt text-based activities: Reorganizing and rewriting the "end of chapter" questions that are often included with textbooks may be needed. For students experiencing reading problems, these types of questions can be very frustrating.

The immediate comprehension of what has been read must be paired with the longer-term retention of information acquired through reading textual material. As Schumm and Strickler (1991) note, "some students can read the words and can comprehend material during ongoing reading . . . nonetheless, some students do not perform well on tests due to difficulty with long-term memory" (p. 83). Whether the need is test-related (and this is an important reality in general education settings) or whether the need is for general knowledge, ways to assist students to retain what they have read are needed.

- Utilize graphic aids: various types of visually based formats can be used in the postreading phase.
- Incorporate formal learning strategies: some specific strategies that include a retention component can be taught to students. Table 4–1 lists some of these strategies. Most techniques ask the student to write a short description of the main points or summary of what they read.
- Teach test-preparation skills: an assortment of skills that are needed to prepare for tests work in conjunction with material that has been read. In most secondary and postsecondary settings, it is assumed that students can handle the reading material and use what has been read to respond successfully to questions that are asked on tests.
- Teach class discussion-preparation skills: much like successful test performance, contributing to class discussions can require preparation as well, especially for students who struggle with reading the textual material on which the discussions will be based. Structured ways of organizing information may be needed.

Adapting Other Instructional Materials. Textual material is not the only type of instructional material that may need to be adapted. Other types of curricular materials may pose problems for learners with special needs.

Often, accommodations may need to be made with the math materials, typically basal math series, that are used in most schools. Key factors that teachers must consider when using math texts with students who are experiencing problems focus on both student materials as well as the teacher's guide. A complete discussion of

these issues is presented in Chapter 11. If the challenges associated with using this approach to teaching math are recognized, solutions can be implemented.

Attention also needs to be given to any type of learning aid (e.g., outside readings, realia, games, learning centers, in-class projects) that might be part of the ongoing instructional program. Caution must be exercised to ensure that students know how to use these materials. If textual material (e.g., lab manuals) is part of the learning aid, the preceding specific suggestions may need to be implemented. In regard to the use of instructional games, students need to possess appropriate game-playing skills and behaviors—this is extremely crucial if students play games in cooperative situations without constant teacher involvement or supervision.

Instructional Accommodations

This section extends the discussion on effective teaching practices presented in the first part of the chapter. The purpose of this section is to remind us of certain elements of effective teaching that may need to be adjusted and adapted in order to optimize the learning environment for learners with special needs.

Learning Considerations. A critical learning-related issue that teachers must understand is that there are different types of learning. The reason why this is important is because certain instructional conditions and adaptations are required for each type of learning, as they are used with students with special needs. Mastropieri and Scruggs (1994) identify the different types of learning as discrimination learning, factual learning, rule learning, procedural learning, and conceptual learning. Each type of learning is used in school and home. Academic and social examples of each type of learning are presented in Table 4–2.

The discussion provided earlier in the chapter applies to all of the types of learning. However, since conceptual learning can pose such significant problems for many students, a more thorough coverage of it is provided. Fundamentally, careful planning and instructional delivery are

TABLE 4–2
Types of learning

Learning Type	Reading	Arithmetic	Social
Discrimination	*p* vs. *q*	+ vs. −	cooperate vs. compete
Factual			
Associative	*l* = *ell*	5 + 2 = 7	Laughing at other people is rude.
Serial list	a, b, c, d, e . . .	2, 4, 6, 8, 10, 12 . . .	School song or motto.
Rule	If two vowels appear together, say the long sound of the first vowel.	To divide fractions, invert and multiply.	Do unto others as you would have others do unto you.
Concept	vowel	prime number	courtesy
Procedure	1. Read title 2. Self-question 3. Skim passage 4. Self-question 5. Read carefully 6. Answer questions	1. Count decimal places in division. 2. Move decimal point in divisor that many places to the right, insert caret. 3. Place decimal point directly above caret in quotient.	1. Walk quietly in line. 2. Take tray, utensils, and napkins. 3. Put lunch on tray. 4. Take carton of milk. 5. Walk quietly to lunch table.

Note. From *Effective Instruction for Special Education* (2nd ed., p. 42), by M. A. Mastropieri and T. E. Scruggs, 1994, Austin, TX: PRO-ED. Copyright 1994 by PRO-ED, Inc. Reprinted with permission.

required to help students understand the vast array of concepts presented to them in school.

Concept formation is the act by which new categories are formed. It is the first step toward developing concept attainment. Concept formation involves three steps: (a) identifying and enumerating the information that is relevant to a problem, (b) grouping items according to some basis of similarity, and (3) developing categories and labels for the groups (Joyce & Weis, 1980). When engaging students in the task of identifying and grouping items or developing categories, teachers might ask open-ended questions that are matched to particular types of activities. For example, the question, "What did you see?" might cue students to list all that they were able to see or identify. The question, "What belongs together?" may initiate the categorization of items of information.

When teaching concept attainment the teacher must recognize that activities involve searching for and listing attributes that can be used to distinguish the exemplars from the nonexemplars of various categories. Looking at "alike and different" between exemplars is one method of concept attainment. A sorting process of "yes" and "no" instances is a concept attainment game that can be used to distinguish common attributes. For example, a teacher may wish to introduce the concept that words with "at" sound the same. The teacher might present the students with a list of words. As she reads the words, the students are to answer "yes" or "no" in relation to the "at" concept (Joyce & Weis, 1980).

The ability to work through the elements of the concept is the difference between a guessing game and conceptual learning—the difference between understanding the content and rote memorization. When presenting a lesson, teachers will find it important to help students focus on a discussion of attributes and on right answers as well. What makes one concept different from another is the combination of attributes. The distinguishing of attributes and their unique value range is called *criteria attributes*. If any one criteria attribute is missing from the object, that object is an example of a different concept. When teachers prepare their lessons by analyzing concepts in terms of their elements, they are likely to incorporate conceptual learning into their lessons.

In working with learners with special needs, attention should also be given to the stages of learning. Many problems arise when these basic stages of learning are ignored or misapplied. The primary stages or levels of learning are acquisition, proficiency, maintenance, and generalization. It is crucial to recognize the aim of each stage and to apply it appropriately in instructional contexts.

Delivery of Effective Instruction. When teaching students who have a variety of learning-related challenges, teachers should implement the effective teaching practices, as examined previously. In addition, other related instructional elements should be reviewed.

- Capitalize on location: Proximity to students who are experiencing learning-related problems can assist students to attend to the important dimensions of what is occurring in the classroom, give them easier access to support, and minimize behavioral problems that might arise.
- Take great care in presenting new information: Mastropieri and Scruggs (1993) have identified six factors that are crucial for teaching new information to students. They refer to them as the SCREAM variables: *s*tructure, *cl*arity, *r*edundancy, *e*nthusiasm, *a*ppropriate pace, and *m*aximize engagement.

- Use multisensory experiences: that multisensory activities can have a drastic impact on learning, as some people claim, should not deter from the fact that such activities can be instructionally useful.
- Make needed lecture-related accommodations: much attention has been given already to text-based issues. Just as important is the need to attend to adaptations that might be needed in lecture-type settings. Teacher-controlled adaptations include scheduling the session so more breaks are possible, organizing the lecture so that a variety of instructional methods (e.g., discussion, media) are utilized, moving around the room, being responsive to the audience and to specific students, highlighting important points, and providing advanced organizers. The use of preparatory activities like those used in enhancing comprehension of text are applicable here as well. In addition, note-taking skills and listening strategies may need to be taught. If the lecture format allows for discussion, then the student may also need to develop better question-asking skills.
- Use assistive technology: familiarity with the range of assistive technology (AT) options is warranted (see Lindsey, 2000). AT options range from low-tech applications (e.g., tape player) to high-tech ones (e.g., FM systems for helping students concentrate on what is being said). Without question, the use of AT with students with special learning needs may make a substantial difference in their academic progress. It is essential that teachers know what devices are available, how students can be evaluated, and, if AT devices are used, how they work.

Instructional Planning. Three elements need to be discussed in relation to planning. First, lesson plans should include a section on accommodating students who have learning-related needs. One suggestion is to include a section on special needs as part of the lesson-planning form. The second issue is the use of different input and output modes in teaching. The benefits of doing this are twofold: (1) it allows the teacher to address the needs of students; and (2) it introduces variety. A model, based on the work of Cawley, Miller, & Carr (1989), for considering the individual instructional needs of students and for planning instructional variety is presented in Figure 4–8. As can be seen for most subject areas for which planning is needed, 24 options exist for developing instructional activities/experiences.

The third issue related to planning is grouping. In peer-directed learning situations such as a cooperative learning arrangement, students with special needs will have to display a host of skills in order to be successful in this type of situation. When planning instruction and deciding on grouping arrangements, teachers need to consider a number of factors: purpose for the grouping, group size, physical conditions, student characteristics, and, as mentioned, the requisite academic and social (e.g., cooperative) skills.

Product and Assignment Accommodations

This final component of the model of accommodative practices (Fig. 4-6) involves recommendations that relate to the types of student-generated products that are required, various aspects associated with the assignments that are given, and the way student knowledge and skill acquisition are evaluated and ultimately reported.

Alternative Products. For some time professionals in the field of gifted education have promoted the idea of a variety of product options. Such thinking can easily apply to the instructional programs of students who have special learning needs as well. To give students options and some choice about those options is desirable practice and supported by the emerg-

FIGURE 4–8
Student input/output options.

Student Input /Output Options						
Output: **Input:**	**Writes**	**Talks**	**Makes**	**Performs**	**Solves**	**Identifies**
Reads						
Listens						
Views						
Does						

Note. Adapted from *Mathematics for the Mildly Handicapped: A Guide to Curriculum and Instruction,* by J. F. Cawley, A. M. Fitzmaurice-Hayes, and R. A. Shaw, 1988, Boston: Allyn & Bacon, and from *Facilitator Manual, Teacher Training Program: Mainstreaming Mildly Handicapped Students in the Regular Classroom,* by P. B. Smith and G. Bentley, 1975, Austin, TX: Education Service Center, Region XII.

ing emphasis on self-determination. All too often teachers tend to make the same assignments. For students with special needs and who have strengths in areas in which they are seldom allowed to show their ability, having alternative products might be just what they need. The notion of having different outcomes for students fits with the previously discussed suggestion of varying input and output modes. An exhaustive list of examples of various alternative products that could be used can be found in Dowdy, Patton, Smith, and Polloway (1998).

Assignment Adaptations. Frequently, it will become necessary to modify in-class and out-of-class assignments given to learners with special needs so that they can handle what is assigned. Teachers can alter assignments in the following ways: shorten assignments (i.e., break them into smaller versions), change the criterion that has been established that designates successful completion of the assignment, allow more time to complete the assignment, reduce the difficulty of the content, and change the output mode (Table 2–3).

Each of these adaptations can be beneficial to students. The important point is that none of these adaptations should be made if they are not needed and, if they are needed, the least amount of change as is necessary should be made. A good example of assignment adaptation is a page from a math workbook of 16 subtraction algorithms involving money values. For a student who is experiencing difficulty with this type of activity but who is capable of doing the math, some type of adaptation might be indicated.

Homework. A staple of the education diet is homework. Most of the literature supports the use of homework as having a desirable effect on school learning. Whereas homework may present special problems for learners with special needs and their families, certain homework-related suggestions can result in beneficial outcomes. A thorough discussion of such recommendations is provided in Chapter 2 and also discussed elsewhere (Patton, 2000).

Testing Options/Modifications. Another area that is of great interest to teachers and parents is testing. Although there may be no obvious solution on how to test students with special needs appropriately and with fairness to them and to their peers, some adaptive practices can be given. Polloway, Bursuck, Jayanthi, Epstein, and Nelson (1996) have conducted a series of studies related to homework, grading, and testing. In the course of their research, they identified the testing adaptations that teachers thought were the most helpful to students. This ranking, presented in Table 4–3, is a useful resource for making testing adaptations.

Grading Considerations. Along with testing and homework, grading is one of the most discussed topics related to students with special needs who are in a general education classroom. Specific suggestions related to this critical issue have been offered by Polloway and colleagues (1996) and are discussed in Chapter 2.

SUMMARY

Today's teachers face many diverse circumstances and challenges in their classrooms. One such circumstance is the growing number of students from diverse backgrounds and cultures. These children have experienced the world from a different knowledge base and come to the classroom with different ways of conceptualizing information. A second circumstance is the amount of information that teachers must be prepared to teach so that students can function on a daily basis. A third circumstance involves the complexity of today's society and the fast-changing knowledge that must be learned. Technology has opened up a new way of learning as well as a number of complex issues. Students no longer learn compact packages of information obtained from textbooks but must use a vast number of different tools. As they deal with these circumstances, teachers face educational and professional challenges. One way to meet these challenges is to use self-reflection skills that constantly evaluate the teacher's performance and effectiveness in the classroom.

A second solution may be the implementation of empirically based instructional procedures. Teacher-directed, student-directed, and

TABLE 4–3
Teachers' Ratings of Helpfulness of Testing Adaptations

Rank[a]	Adaptation
1	Give individual help with directions during tests.
2	Read test questions to students.
3	Simplify wording of test questions.
4	Give practice questions as a study guide.
5	Give extra help preparing for tests.
6	Give extended time to finish tests.
7	Use black-and-white copies.
8	Give feedback to individual student during test.
9	Highlight key words in questions.
10	Allow use of learning aids during tests (e.g., calculators).
11	Give frequent quizzes rather than only exams.
12	Allow students to answer fewer questions.
13	Allow oral instead of written answers (e.g., via tape recorders).
14	Give the actual test as a study guide.
15	Change question type (e.g., essay to multiple choice).
16	Teach students test-taking skills.
17	Use tests with enlarged print.
18	Test individual on less content than rest of class.
19	Provide extra space on tests for answering.
20	Give tests in small groups.
21	Give open-book/notes tests.
22	Allow word processors.
23	Allow answers in outline format.
24	Give take-home tests.

Note. From "Treatment Acceptability: Determining Appropriate Interventions Within Inclusive Classrooms," by E. A. Polloway, W. D. Bursuck, M. Jayanthi, M. H. Epstein, and J. S. Nelson, 1996, *Intervention in School and Clinic,* 31, p. 140. Copyright 1996 by PRO-ED, Inc. Reprinted with permission.
[a] Ranked from most helpful to least helpful by general education teachers.

peer-directed learning, as discussed in the second part of this chapter, provide vehicles for addressing the instructional needs of students. Teaching students how to think for themselves and work with others will enhance their ability to succeed in their world and should be one of the primary foci of any student's educational program.

Finally, a fourth solution may lie in the implementation of a variety of accommodative practices that are based on a particular student's needs and immediate instructional demands. Operating with the philosophy of only making accommodations when absolutely necessary helps students become more capable of dealing with a real world that is not always accommodating.

TEACHER TIPS   **Elementary Level**

"TWO-STUDENT" IDEAS TO BEGIN COOPERATIVE LEARNING

Cooperative learning arrangements can be challenging if your students have not mastered critical social skills or if they have little experience working with others. It may be best to begin cooperative learning with pairs or partners, so students can learn to work together in less complicated and demanding situations. In *Putting It All Together for Student Success,* the authors suggest some simple ways to structure cooperative learning with groups of two:

Study Buddies: one student reads, the other follows along and asks questions; then they switch roles.

Partners: students are assigned to a two-person team; one partner will repeat the teacher's directions, the other will ask questions and clarify; before asking the teacher for help, they ask each other.

Reading Pairs: two students read the same material; both write an answer to the comprehension questions; then they compare and produce their best response.

Math Pairs: pairs of students work the problems independently; they check each other's work, compare, and decide on the correct answer.

Radio Readers: students choose a selection, then read together orally; this allows them to build their fluency and rhythm, as well as model accurate reading for each other.

Spell Checkers: pairs of students check each other's writing for correct spelling.

Peer Editors: students edit each other's writing, checking punctuation, grammar, usage, and organization; students sign off after completing their editing; students edit with a blue pen and the teacher uses red.

Lab Partners: in the science lab, students work together to complete the laboratory assignment, handing in one completed lab with both students' names.

Fad & Gilliam (1996).

TEACHER TIPS   **Secondary Level**

Many teachers struggle with the concept of "motivation" and how to motivate their students to want to learn and engage in academic endeavors. Miller (1998) instructs teachers that motivation is a complex concept and there are many different ways of approaching this classroom issue. From 1954 we see Maslow introducing a hierarchy of needs that, when met, a student is motivated to learn. On the other hand behaviorists approach motivation as a behavior that must be externally regulated and that students will become motivated if they experience the reward of benefit for their efforts. Humanistic psychologists and cognitive psychologist believe in a more intrinsic approach to motivation. Students must see the value of their behavior and in some cases talk themselves

(continued)

through the action in order to complete a task. Some of these theories, however, do not give teachers much in the way of practical application to the classroom.

Miller (1998) indicates that there are certain criteria for increasing student motivation. These include: (a) arouse interest in your students—build their curiosity and include novel features in your teaching; (b) give purpose and direction to learning—that is, be organized and clear in your expectations, (c) encourage persistence or provide rewards (social and concrete) for your students' efforts; and (d) empower students with choice and decisions—allow your students to direct their activities and give them opportunities to provide input into their learning.

Instruction also increases motivation and learning. For example, Miller (1998) indicates direct instruction can serve as a motivator if the instruction is delivered: (1) in small groups of five or less students; (b) as exciting and fast paced; (c) with an overview of both past and current learning; (d) that include an explanation of the purpose of the lesson; (e) with ample feedback given throughout the lesson; and (f) in less than 40 minute periods.

Miller, D. (1998). *Enhancing adolescent competence: Strategies for classroom management.* Belmont, CA: West/Wadsworth.

TEACHER TIPS   Secondary Level

As the research on resiliency or protective factors increases, we find that the identification of teachable skills may influence significantly the lives of children with special needs. Werner (1999) has conducted two longitudinal follow-up studies that identify several protective factors within children with high-incidence disabilities. These protective factors seem to contribute to the success in the lives of these children. Some of these factors can be fostered in the classroom. They include:

- self-help skills
- practical problem-solving skills
- special talents
- positive self-concept
- impulse control
- planning, foresight (goal setting)
- persistence
- self-management

Werner, E. E. (1999). Risk and protective factors in the lives of children with high-incidence disabilities. In R. Gillmore, L. P. Bernheimer, D. L. MacMillan, D. L. Speece, & S. Vaughn (Eds.). *Developmental perspectives on children with high-incidence disabilities.* Hillsdale, NJ: Lawrence Erlbaum Associates.

Strategies for Collaboration

Ginger Blalock

Special education has witnessed significant changes since the passage of Public Law 94-142 in 1975, reauthorized in 1990 as PL 101-476, the Individuals with Disabilities Education Act (IDEA), and reauthorized again in 1997. Perhaps the most profound change for special educators has occurred in the redefining of professional and partner roles in response to federal, state, and local legislative and regulatory action. The special education arena now places a variety of demands upon the educator in the classroom, center, or community. Teachers are expected to be effective in instruction and management as well as in their interactions with many others in diverse roles and often from backgrounds very different than their own. This expectation is particularly evident in most interviews for educators' positions as well as those for professional preparation programs where teamwork is a major component. Today special educators must operate as part of a team in many aspects of their role, including screening, assessment, individual program planning, developing placement options, and monitoring success. In addition, teachers regularly feel the effects of external forces (reform efforts in state/local systems and in content disciplines, the inclusive education movement, Goals 2000, site-based restructuring, board-mandated curricula), whether or not they have had a part in influencing those forces. They must work with many others to operationalize the important aspects of those initiatives or changes within the instructional program.

Although teaming skills are recognized as learned behaviors that typically require direct instruction, many personnel preparation programs fail to adequately prepare their participants to collaborate with the range of likely partners (O'Shea, Williams, & Sattler, 1999; Villa, Thousand, Nevin, & Malgeri, 1996). This chapter focuses on issues and strategies for developing partnerships with four key groups of significant others with whom special educators should and must work: (a) families (the consumers), (b) general educators, (c) paraeducators, and (d) related services personnel. Most of the chapter describes approaches to create and support successful collaboration with these partners, based within the key issues surrounding those partnerships. Since many of the central principles of collaboration apply to all types of partnerships, the general features of consultation and collaboration are presented first as a foundation for the subsequent, more specialized sections.

CONSULTATION AND COLLABORATION: MODELS AND SKILLS

Definitions of Collaboration

At the heart of working with essential partners are aspects of the concepts of consultation and collaboration. According to Idol, Nevin, and Paolucci-Whitcomb (1994), *consultation* generally involves an expert who works with one or more consultee(s) to create a positive change for the target learner or issue. Thus, consultation implies expertise, which may inadvertently lead to unequal status. The consultant-consultee relationship places the consultant (often the special educator) in a position of authority (whether warranted or not) on a variety of learning, behavioral, or even legal/administrative matters. This stance seems to propel the myth that special educators have the "secrets" to working with students with exceptionalities, perpetuate the mystique the field has acquired, and relegate "ownership" of this group of students to special education personnel. A more equitable arrangement might be to have each participant serve as consultant in her or his particular area of expertise (the concept of a multi- or interdisciplinary team), so that all key parties (general educator, special educator, student, parent or caregiver, therapist, medical professional, adult provider, and employer, among others) have the opportunity to share their knowledge and skills. Thus, the term *collaborative consultation* is defined as "an interactive process that enables groups of people with diverse expertise to generate creative solutions to mutually defined problems" (Idol, Nevin, & Paolucci-Whitcomb, 1994, p. 1).

Five basic elements make up collaborative consultation, according to Nevin, Thousand, Paolucci-

Whitcomb, and Villa (1990): (a) an agreement by all group or team members to view all partners (including novices) as having unique and needed expertise, (b) frequent face-to-face interactions, (c) shared leadership responsibilities and accountability for one's commitments, (d) orientations that acknowledge reciprocity's role and that weigh task or relationship actions in terms of their contribution to the group goal, and (e) a commitment to use consensus building in a conscious effort to improve interaction and/or task achievement abilities. In this configuration, collaborative consultation essentially equals collaboration, which better conveys the cooperative role essential to successful inclusion of diverse learners in general education.

On a broader, school-based level, collaborative consultation is useful in various situations, including student assistance or school screening teams (Chalfant & Pysh, 1989), teaching teams (Thousand & Villa, 1990a), consulting teacher programs (Idol, 1993), and self-governance procedures such as curriculum or school restructuring committees (Idol & West, 1991). Collaboration models that more specifically involve family members, placement of diverse learners in general education programs, and related services personnel are described in their respective sections.

Stages of Collaborative Consultation

This section addresses the stages through which collaboration progresses, according to Idol et al. (1994). Six stages comprise the collaborative consultation process; readers are encouraged to consult their work for a comprehensive background and for specific implementation strategies. The six problem-solving stages include:

Stage 1. Gaining entry and establishing team goals: The consultant and consultee(s) work together to identify the broad problem and plan accordingly.
Stage 2. Problem identification: Both parties gather data as needed, identify the specific problem(s) and set specific goal(s) to address identified challenges.

Stage 3. Intervention recommendations: Both parties suggest ideas for activities to address the challenges.
Stage 4. Implementation of recommendations: The consultee(s) and consultant may each implement recommended interventions.
Stage 5. Evaluation: Both parties may be involved in selecting an evaluation model and in monitoring success.
Stage 6. Follow-up: Both parties are continuously engaged in ongoing follow-up or follow-along so that interventions can be changed as needed.

Collaborative consultation and collaboration imply that both parties are in parallel positions to share ideas, talents, professional development experiences, materials, and energy as the team or partnership evolves. To take advantage of these opportunities, partners need certain qualifications or abilities, described in the following section.

Skills Required for Collaboration

Idol et al. (1994) assert that use of the collaborative consultation process requires that group members have three areas of expertise: "(a) an appropriate underlying knowledge base, (b) interpersonal communicative, interactive, problem-solving skills, and (c) intrapersonal attitudes" (p. 2). The underlying knowledge base incorporates all that the profession now knows and strives to know about what does and does not work in serving diverse learners within the range of service delivery models. A systems orientation that aims at strategic learning environments and a problem-solving perspective drive the professional's approach to the most effective use of the knowledge base. The other two components are described in the following sections.

Interpersonal Skills for Collaboration. Bos and Vaughn (1998) and Idol et al. (1994) have outlined several major areas of interpersonal skills that Idol and colleagues referred to as "generic principles of collaborative consultation." These areas incorporate attitudes or perspectives in addition to behaviors or skills, summarized next.

- Team ownership of the identified problem: equitable access to information, participation in decision making, and interactions across multiple disciplines—a working alliance.
- Recognition of individual differences in the effort's developmental progress: understanding and acceptance of where one is and where the group is along the continuum of team stages and changes.
- Situational leadership to guide the practice of collaborative consultation: strategically employing skills such as flexible presentation, flexible implementation, and leadership styles (e.g., telling, selling or encouragement, participating, and delegating) to accomplish tasks.
- Cooperative conflict resolution processes: moving from categorizing, organizing, and concluding, to presenting opposing viewpoints, to seeking new information and experiences, to reasoning to revised conclusions.
- Appropriate interviewing skills: assuming responsibility for, adapting for diversity within, and directing the progress of the conversation so that data required to enhance the learner's outcomes is obtained. Stages to accomplish this include (a) ask open questions, (b) obtain specificity, (c) identify the problem, (d) problem solve, and (e) summarize and give feedback.
- Active listening behaviors: receiving information without judgment, questioning to clarify messages, restating, paraphrasing, summarizing, and responsive body language.
- Oral and written communication using common (nonjargon) terms and positive nonverbal language: assumption of "mutually interdependent roles as senders and receivers," including ongoing feedback and positive use of the elements of nonverbal language to improve one's perceptions about messages.

Intrapersonal Attitudes Related to Collaboration. Idol et al. (1994, pp. 33–37) delineate a set of intrapersonal beliefs, values, and experiences that significantly shape one's approach to the collaborative consultation process. The "attitudes" are actually practices that can enhance one's personal and professional growth and greatly promote the group's interactions and task accomplishments.

- Face fear.
- Share a sense of humor.
- Behave with integrity.
- Live with joy.
- Take risks.
- Use self-determination.
- Think longitudinally.
- Create new norms.
- Respond proactively.
- Adapt upward (not regress to poorer functioning).
- Use self-differentiation (separate self from surrounding systems and pressures, as well as take responsibility for one's own outcomes and well-being).

These practices appear useful as guides to all professional endeavors because of their orientation toward positive outcomes and responsible decision making.

Personnel Preparation Strategies

Cates, McGill, Brian, Wilder, and Androes (1990) describe the roles of all parties involved in developing and enhancing full inclusion programs, with particular emphasis on universities' preparation of teachers to embrace those roles. The implications for teacher preparation are clear. General education students must learn methods and curricular modifications that respond to the diverse learning needs of all students in the classroom. A single course in exceptionalities and/or mainstreaming is insufficient to create the attitude change, mindset, and skills needed to individualize for each learner. Innovative colleges of education now are integrating diversity training within their teacher preparation programs to address all learners' challenges and in the process are modeling collaboration across disciplines for their students and colleagues in the field.

Induction Support and Advanced Professional Development. Districts and universities have learned how important mentoring, professional development, and other forms of support are for teachers in their first few years of teaching, just to keep them in the profession. In addition, experienced teachers require regular opportunities to acquire new competencies and for renewal, which is appropriate within such a demanding career. This section describes strategies for ensuring the relevance and capacity-building impact of a school's, district's, or agency's professional development program.

Needs Assessment. Professional development activities, whether formal training or technical assistance, should always be based on the results of a formal or informal needs assessment, that is, linked to a real need. Duncan, Schofer, and Veberle (1982) offer a useful perspective about assessing needs:

> It is essential to differentiate between what is needed and what is wanted. . . . Personnel may request a topic that is currently of high interest or may be a popular "fad" or may be related to a real issue in education; however, the topic may or may not be related to real or immediate needs. We like to think of an inservice need as something which, if corrected, would improve delivery of educational services. (p. 11)

Needs assessment is the collecting and analyzing of information that will assist in decision making. Given the job and life demands faced by many adults, this assessment process needs to be precise, timely, and relevant.

Often, needs assessments can best be conducted while simultaneously developing skills in formal training sessions. Blalock, Bassett, and Donisthorpe (1989) found that the following steps in cross-training sessions helped potential collaborators move closer to collaborating while also assessing needs for further support.

- Anonymously sharing perceptions about the other discipline, to "vent" frustrations developed over time and help all share humor about stereotypes

- Self-assessing one's attitudes and goals about the collaborative process
- Self-assessing one's feelings about the other professional(s), the student(s), and the agency, and describing how those perceptions might impact the collaborative process
- Self-reporting the five highest skills learned throughout their lives that would support collaboration (e.g., goal planning, organization, communication)
- Small group problem-solving of a case situation, drawing on each other's strengths and backgrounds
- Brainstorming ways to support collaboration immediately, 6 months in the future, and 2 years in the future

Thus, at every point through the experience, information about professional development needs became available to aid in planning for follow-up.

In-service Training Workshop and Technical Assistance. Three broad formats can be identified for in-service workshops and related training activities in general: (a) awareness, (b) instructional or procedural information, and (c) hands-on learning (skill-building). Awareness workshops simply seek to expose participants to a body of information or to foster a particular attitude (often so that additional, more in-depth instruction or development is welcome). This format is probably most common for numerous one-shot in-school workshops, such as presentations during orientation sessions at the start of a year. Sample topics include:

- needs and possible strategies for self-determination instruction
- breadth and scope of special education and related services
- characteristics of and instructional supports for students with specific exceptionalities
- roles of the consulting teacher, transition specialist, or related services provider

The *instructional or procedural information* format aims to share useful guidelines for developing instruction or other interventions. Even though the presentation may at least partially appear like an awareness workshop (i.e., lecture type, large-group arrangement), the goal is quite different. Representative topics include the following:

- procedures relative to student support teams, referral procedures, or IEPs/ITPs
- descriptions of formal tests used in the assessment process
- discussion of appropriate behavioral support strategies

Both the awareness and the instructional format are typically isolated events without opportunity for active involvement or follow-up, so generalization to the classroom may be questionable. Two alternatives are the active training format and the technical assistance, individualized problem-solving format, both of which emphasize much more learner participation. Examples of appropriate topics for *active training* formats follow.

- literacy instruction models and their implementation steps
- administering, scoring, and interpreting a formal test
- viewing specific behaviors on a videotape, recording data, and writing plans
- reviewing student strengths and weaknesses and cooperatively writing IEPs
- engaging in a multidisciplinary transition planning meeting

Several programs have been developed to follow the ongoing active training format and to promote a *cooperative problem-solving approach* to instructional issues and cases. *Collaboration in the schools* (West, Idol, & Cannon, 1989) teaches all school personnel to communicate, interact, and problem-solve in an effort to meet all students' needs. This program uses a six-stage process to incorporate therapists, teachers, and administrators in cooperative procedures that produce systemic change on behalf of diverse learners. *The collaborative problem solving guide* (part of the *Teaming Techniques Series*) developed by colleagues at the University of Kansas (Knackendoffel, Robinson, Deshler, & Schumaker, 1992) promotes role responsibilities and forward-focused action plan-

ning to assist in individual student cases. The Strategic Intervention Model (SIM) Trainers Network that has emerged from the University of Kansas Center for Research on Learning follows this type of format in both the trainers' initial and updated learning experiences as well as in experiences provided by the trainers to others.

Technical Assistance. Ongoing collaboration can take the form of general instructional "advice" and assistance (such as informal mentoring) as well as training or demonstrations related to an identified need. Advising might include suggestions for management strategies, approaches to assessment, curricular development or changes, and specific methodological issues. Teachers may find very useful the format of problem-centered collaboration, such as developing a plan to solve an isolated problem. For example, a student may miss science in order to receive special services (a pull-out model) and thus miss out on important information about the environment. In this format, the team could generate a workable alternative together. Another format for techical assistance may involve developmental consultation, a long-range process of sequenced objectives (Heron & Harris, 1982), such as those leading to restructuring of schoolwide grading practices. Regardless of the process employed, collaborative consultants need to remember that the role of listener is more important initially than the role of advisor; it is necessary to determine what really is needed before providing assistance. In addition, a teacher's classroom should not be "invaded" (e.g., for the purpose of analyzing a program prior to placing a student with a disability in the program); it is hoped that the consultant can arrange to be invited into the classroom to observe and discuss the program.

Collaboration with Families

The most essential partners in the educational process are those most affected: the individuals with special needs themselves and their family members. Our educational institutions as a whole are just recently working to keep that belief foremost in their agencies' thinking and actions. Families of students with special needs are not only faced with the typical challenges of child rearing but also must deal with additional demands associated with a family member with special needs. Additionally, the extent of family involvement in the child's program may depend on events affecting the family at a given time. Wehmeyer, Morningstar, and Husted (1999) also summarize the changing characteristics of families that present new sets of challenges (family composition, employment patterns, widening income gaps, ethnic/cultural identities). Teachers must be sensitive to these responsibilities and issues. The concerns of families are particularly noteworthy in a time of increased inclusion, when needs for support and increased communication are likely to be significantly increased. This section offers several suggestions for inviting and supporting families to be real partners in the educational experience, while Chapter 14 describes how self-determination instruction can increase students' participation in their educational experiences.

Changing Paradigms to More Family-Centeredness

Increasingly the fields of special education and rehabilitation view families as "systems" with their own set of unique dynamics, their own unique cultures, and their status as a "system" to be regarded with respect equal to that given to agencies. Schoeller (1995, p. 5) asserts that to "walk the walk" and "find the story in the stranger" (i.e., to listen well to what they have to say) are the best ways to identify what youth and families want and need. One major role of professionals in this relationship is to inform families and individuals with exceptionalities what their options are, as well as what the likely outcomes will be, and then to empower the family to make the decisions about best options. Some parental needs that teachers can help to meet include (a) clear and accurate information concerning their child, (b) the opportunity for frequent communication, (c) assistance with academic and behavioral supports strategies, and perhaps (d) help with linking with other parents for mutual support.

Families' overriding need from teachers and other school professionals may quite likely be the belief that a partnership exists, that is, that meeting the student's needs is truly a shared concern and that input from family members will be genuinely sought and respected (Dowdy et al., 1995). Granting families agency status helps bureaucratic systems (which schools are) more systematically treat families with the respect they merit. Systems deal with each other by giving sufficient advance notice of joint meetings such that attendance by all desired parties is maximized, holding meetings at times and locations agreeable to other parties, monitoring meeting exchanges to support all voices being heard, and ensuring that copies of all pertinent information are distributed in a timely fashion. Families should (and with this paradigm, will) receive equal consideration. A number of specific indicators of a collaborative partnership were summarized by Wehmeyer, Morningstar, and Husted (1999), including:

■ Prompt, honest, open sharing of information, impressions, and judgments
■ Two-way sharing of information without fear of being judged negatively
■ Mutual respect for each other's expertise and sensitivity to new areas of learning
■ Shared goals, planning, and decision-making.

It is crucial that teachers accept and impress upon parents their vital role in the assessment, IEP planning, and instructional process. The impact of parent participation on struggling students' academic performance has been clearly documented (Callahan, Rademacher, & Hildreth, 1998). To achieve their cooperation, sharing with them the variety of ways in which they can be involved will be beneficial. Table 5–1 summarizes possible roles that parents can play.

Conferences

Communication is the key to positive relationships. A key element of home-school communication is the meeting or conference. Conferences provide teachers with the opportunity to demonstrate understanding of family situations and good

TABLE 5–1
Parents' role in the assessment process to identify disabilities

Before the evaluation, parents:

- May initiate the evaluation process by requesting that the school system evaluate their child.
- May be notified by the school, and give their consent, before any intial evaluation of the child may be conducted.
- May wish to talk with the person responsible for conducting the evaluation.
- May find it useful to become informed about assessment issues in general and any specific issues relevant to their child.
- May need to advocate for a comprehensive evaluation.
- May suggest specific questions they would like to see addressed through the evaluation.
- Should inform the school of any accommodations the student will need.
- Should inform the school if they need an interpreter, translator, or other accommodations during their discussions with the school.
- May prepare their child for the evaluation process, explaining what will happen and, where necessary, reducing the child's anxiety.

During the evaluation process, parents:

- Need to share with the school their insights into the child's background and past and present school performance.
- May wish to share with the school any prior school records, reports, tests, or evaluation information on their child.
- May need to share information about cultural differences that can illuminate the educational team's understanding of the student.
- Need to make every effort to attend interviews the school may set up with them and provide information about their child.

After the evaluation, parents:

- Need to carefully consider the results that emerge from their child's evaluation, in light of their own observations and knowledge of the child.
- May share their insights and concerns about the evaluation results with the school and suggest areas where additional information may be needed. Schools may or may not act upon parents' suggestions, and parents have certain resources under law, should they feel strongly about pursuing the matter.
- Participate fully in the development of their child's Individualized Education Program (IEP).

Note. From "Assessing children for the presence of disability," by B.B. Waterman, 1994, *NICHCY News Digest, 4*(1), p. 12. Copyright 1994 by NICHCY. Adapted with permission.

communication skills. Some specific suggestions can be helpful with family conferences and program planning meetings.

1. Be honest and direct with families.
2. Avoid technical terms.
3. Be clear and concise.

4. Do not speculate about issues for which you have no information. Discuss only what you know and what you can document.
5. Prepare for the meeting by discussing the meeting with parents well in advance, agreeing mutually on a time and location for the meeting, organizing your notes, reviewing pertinent

information, and planning an agenda (preferably with input from the family and student).

6. Create a positive atmosphere, agree on the purpose of the meeting, employ good communication skills, take notes on what is being discussed, and end the meeting with a positive statement of appreciation to the family members for coming.

7. After the meeting, organize your notes for future reference, initiate action on any items requiring attention, and determine when a follow-up meeting is needed.

8. If you are scheduling a conference that may be a hostile one, have someone else sit in to help verify what transpires and to assist with redirecting awkward interactions. Encourage family members to do the same.

Informal Communication

Other forms of communication may be less formal than conferences but equally important and productive. These include telephone contacts, which are often a key way of monitoring positive communicaiton lines, and written communication.

Telephone conversations provide an excellent vehicle for sharing information, usually of a more immediate nature. Some teachers encourage families to call them at home whereas others discourage this practice. A teacher's job can be enriched by open lines of communication with families, which sometimes requires being available beyond the school day. Teachers should take notes on every phone conversation with families that relate to a student, school, or home issue. Research indicates definite benefits from telephone communication, even if primarily through voicemail (Jayanthi, Nelson, Sawyer, Bursuck, & Epstein, 1994).

Written communication is another ongoing vehicle for home-school collaboration. The most common form of written communication is the note, intended to convey information in a variety of formats. Teachers with written language or spelling challenges should have someone else proofread their notes. Progress reports to parents are also common. Although they typically occur only at the end of a grading period, more regular correspondence about progress is encouraged— daily for some students, less often for others. Whatever the schedule, teachers need to develop systems for sharing progress information with parents in a form they can use. One approach uses student assignment books with space for homework assignments and for teacher and parent comments as well. This type of interchange can easily occur on a daily basis. In research on home communication, general educators at elementary and middle school levels indicated that assignments sheets and parent signatures on assignments were helpful (Polloway, Epstein, Bursuck, Jayanthi, & Cumblad, 1994).

Some teachers find newsletters an interesting way to convey to families what occurs in their classrooms. Obviously, this technique does not address individual student concerns, but it helps to share overall program information, upcoming events, and general topics. Even though the quality of newsletters varies greatly according to the equipment and technical expertise available, we believe that newsletters should look attractive and be error-free. Teachers who want to produce newsletters should be alert to what may be the biggest obstacle—keeping to a regular schedule.

Teachers and families may be creative in identifying other methods for ongoing communication and regular planning. It is the responsibility of educators to search for a mutually agreeable set of means by which to accomplish that collaborative work, so that students have the opportunity to do their best work.

COLLABORATION WITH GENERAL EDUCATORS

General education personnel at all of K-12 levels are the second most important partner group for special educators. The particular configuration of the special/general education interaction may vary, depending on which student and/or program situations exist. This section describes the barriers to effective partnerships as well as a variety of possible arrangements.

Barriers to Collaboration

Several issues may impede the success of students with exceptionalities who are partially or fully served in general settings and of the teachers attempting to serve them:

- students' reluctance or limited ability to own decisions about placement and program
- the teacher's focus on the class as a whole rather than on individual learning needs
- required coverage of content standards overlaid with needs for curricular accommodations
- insufficient preparation or confidence to individualize for diverse learners, especially those with extreme behavioral problems
- lack of funds needed to directly support all students who need individualized help (e.g., adaptive equipment, extra personnel)
- lack of real assistance because of the caseloads among special educators and delays with referrals
- intensification of teachers' daily challenges when students with exceptionalities are included on top of a full class load
- overreferral of students for special education assessment and placement and the subsequent phenomenon of several who do not qualify, creating greater frustration (Bos & Vaughn, 1998; Elliott & McKenney, 1998; Jones & Carlier, 1995).

Changing Relations, Changing Options

The ongoing relationships between general and special education have been transformed regularly since the passage of Public Law 94-142 in 1975, at least on paper. The early Education of All Handicapped Children Act required that students with special education needs be educated in the least restrictive environment (LRE) possible that still maintained optimal learning and development by the individual. During the 1970s this mandate led to *mainstreaming,* wherein students were placed in general education settings, with or without support, depending upon their needs. Often students' physical presence in general instruction was on a part-time or very part-

time basis. Support toward success in that setting often included the initial support of a paraeducator (e.g., educational assistant) to "smooth over" the transition, some materials modifications by the special educator prior to instruction, or associated skills development or tutoring in the special education setting.

The term used for similar arrangements in the 1980s was *integration,* a label that also extended to participation in community activities. The process of movement from special education back to general settings required transitions and was far more complex than a simple physical relocation. Successful integration was predicated on systematic preparation of both the receiving teacher and the student on what to expect (both academically and sociobehaviorally). In many cases the advance preparation should have extended beyond those groups to include other students, parents of all students, and administrators. Some key questions for the team in this process were:

1. How best can the teachers contribute to successful integration or inclusion of the student?
2. What role should the teachers serve in developing collaborative relationships with other teachers, therapists, family members, and agency staff?
3. What levels of planning are necessary to ensure that smooth transitions occur?

The 1990s witnessed the emergence of a somewhat different model of serving all students in the general class; this model first focused on students with severe disability levels because of their often widespread exclusion from experiences with age-level peers. The concept of *inclusive education* conveys a more connected (and hopefully more supported) participation by the student with an exceptionality in general education and, thus, greater collaborative efforts among key professionals serving the student. When implemented well, this concept may reflect fairly on highly sophisticated collaboration, as the general and special educators (including all professionals and paraeducators) team in any of a variety of "flavors" to plan, deliver, and evaluate instruction for all the students in the class. Preservice preparation, professional development activities, and technical assistance, combined with the team's shared experiences, allow all parties to expand their skills and expertise as they work with students other than those for whom they were originally prepared. A number of recent texts, such as the one by Smith, Polloway, Patton, and Dowdy (1999), provide rationales and strategies for unifying learners with a broad range of diverse learning needs, including needs linked to cultural and language differences as well as specific exceptionality categories.

However, inclusive education must be approached with careful planning and an individualized learner perspective, or its potential pitfalls quickly become apparent. Many advocacy and professional organizations (Council for Learning Disabilities, Learning Disabilities Association of America, CHADD, Council for Exceptional Children, National Education Association, etc.) have issued position statements or papers that (a) affirm inclusion as an important goal when appropriate, and (b) caution against wholesale placement policies that ignore specific learners' special support needs. A number of philosophical and practical issues about inclusive education, the widely differing models of implementing it, and some research findings that challenge its efficacy all have helped to sustain widespread and often emotional debate in the field about this viewpoint. In some instances these debates create the impression that only radically opposed positions exist, perhaps because some schools and districts have elected to implement this theory to the fullest extent. York, Doyle, and Kronberg (1992, p. 2) reason that "inclusion does not mean that students must spend every minute of the school day in general education classes . . ., that students never receive small-group or individualized instruction, or that students are in general education classes to learn the core curriculum only." Their sample planning tool (shown in Figure 5–1 in adapted form) offers an easy-to-follow procedure for maximizing the possibility of successful placements.

Collaboration Models Linking General and Special Education

Since the inception of special education programs, the relationship between general and special educators has been essential to eliminate inappropriate referrals for testing or placement in special education and to pursue appropriate general education arrangements for individual students. Reducing or eliminating unsuitable referrals for testing for special education placement is an important goal for all school personnel. Certainly, eliminating any misdiagnoses (false positives) is the ultimate aim of any assessment program within general and special education. Several collaborative models have been found very effective in accomplishing that purpose. One of the first was the Mainstreamed Assistance Team (MAT) project, which used a multidisciplinary preventive prereferral and intervention process to serve large numbers of students with mild disability levels as well as nondisabled at-risk students (Fuchs & Fuchs, 1987). The Student Assistance team (SAT) described by McKay and Sullivan (1990) involved collaboration within a team of general and special educators, to serve both mainstreamed and unidentified at-risk students in the general program. The five-step process led to interventions that could be aimed at the entire class or individual students. Use of the SAT approach was found to decrease the referrals for special education services as well as the number of "no exceptionality" classifications.

Similar to the MAT and SAT has been the Teacher Assistance Team (TAT) model (Chalfant & Pysh, 1989), defined by Bos and Vaughn (1998, p. 472) as "a within-building problem-solving model designed to provide a teacher support system for classroom teachers." The TAT model is built around a set of assumptions that recognize the knowledge, experience, and power that teachers bring to the learning experience and that encourage teachers to rely on each other to seek their own solutions (Chalfant & Pysh, 1989). TATs follow a basic set of procedures: a core team of three members is elected by their

FIGURE 5–1

Sample planning tool for movement from elementary to middle school inclusive education services

WHAT	WHO	BY WHEN
Step 1: Initial information received from sending school		
General and special elementary educators complete "Student General Information Sheet" and copy log notes.		
Both sending and receiving teachers share general information about student.		
Middle school team member follows up if forms not received by (spring date).		
Step 2: Middle school class placement done		
New students are assigned to classes, teachers, homerooms, and advisors through input by all key team members.		
Individual support needs and student combinations within each classroom and family or grade are considered.		
Middle school principal is contacted about new student placements for inclusion in computerized scheduling.		
Letter informs parents of assignments and of upcoming transition meeting. Short parent questionnaire accompanies the letter.		
Step 3: Teachers and students contact each other across settings		
Middle school teachers visit elementary sites to observe.		
Students are assigned middle school buddies and visit middle school, meeting with buddies in advisory group and lunch.		
Staff assume welcoming roles for students in transition.		
Step 4: Student-centered transition team meetings held		
Individual student teams meet in May to: • review information on student related to move • develop initial transition plan using existing tools • identify IEP meeting or periodic review for fall		
Step 5: Grade-level team meetings held or further planning		
Step 6: Dates for IEP and periodic reviews		

From "A Curriculum Development Process for Inclusive Classrooms," by J. York, M.B. Doyle, and R. Kronberg, 1992, *Focus on Exceptional Children, 25*, p. 7. Copyright 1992 by Love Publishing, Inc. Reprinted with permission.

peers (most should not be specialists), and those who are asking for help join the team for their respective concerns; others are asked to join as needed. Referring teachers complete a request for help that includes the following information:

1. What do you want the student to be able to do differently?
2. What are the student's strengths and weaknesses?

3. What strategies have been used to help the student resolve the issues?
4. What other background information and/or test data are relevant?

The team member assigned to the "case" examines the case information, gathers additional data if needed, creates (and shares) a visual representation of the problem, and arranges a problem-solving meeting. At the meeting, recommendations for the teacher(s) to use in the classroom are generated, or referral to another program might be suggested. Finally, the team's success in resolving issues brought to them is evaluated. This approach's numerous benefits for students, families, and professionals have been documented (Bos & Vaughn, 1998; Chalfant & Pysh, 1989).

Lawton (1999) recently described the burgeoning movement of co-teaching by general and special educators, sharing the enthusiastic reports of two co-teachers who state they would never return to teaching by themselves. Benefits to students were said to be the critical factor, citing one student's dramatic progress as an example:

> . . . one 10-year-old mentally retarded boy she has taught for three years in an inclusion class at the school. When he started in the multiage class, the boy had poor social skills and couldn't stay on task. Now the boy can "tell you what he did over the weekend. He can tell you two or three things in a row, on a topic, and then switch to something else. That's a goal we had for his IEP. . . ." (p. 1)

Cook and Friend (1995) listed a range of options for co-teaching:

1. One Teacher, One Assistant: One teaches the large group; the other circulates, particularly helping students with special needs.
2. Parallel Teaching: Each teaches the same information to half the class.
3. Alternative Teaching: One offers remedial support to those who need it (whether or not they have a label); the other teaches the remainder.
4. Team Teaching: Both teach the entire group together (e.g., one models while the other describes or elaborates; both role-play or present information).
5. Station Teaching: Teachers divide content into two or more parts and present those parts at different locations around the room.

Cook and Friend offered suggestions for successful co-teaching that could make or break such a partnership, including a series of questions for creating a collaborative working relationship in co-teaching.

The essential elements for establishing collaborative programming seem similar to those employed for specific problem-solving. Nowacek (1991) gleaned several stages in the process from her extensive interviews with teachers about their teaming. These stages are summarized in Table 5–2.

1. Taking the First Steps. Deciding to collaborate and selecting the collaborators were the first steps experienced by Nowacek's interviewees. The choices were the teachers', although having a supportive administration was very helpful. In one case the speech/language therapist approached a special educator and general educator about co-teaching and introduced them to a multisensory program that gave them a focus with which to begin working together. In another case professional development on a collaborative model inspired a group of special educators to implement the model. They carefully reviewed and planned students' schedules and caseloads before identifying content area teachers with whom they needed (and secondarily also wanted) to collaborate. In the third situation, the high school principal introduced the special educators to successful team teaching through a visit to another city, then he recruited general educators to participate. In all situations, educators' choice and empowerment to act were key.

2. Planning Roles and Responsibilities. General and special educators often find that new or modified skills and activities are needed as a next step to make inclusive programming successful for individual students and for themselves. Each group may need to self-teach or learn formally better ways to work collaboratively. Langone (1998) describes competencies needed for inclusive settings, including management of personnel, management of time, materials, technology, and environment, and management of communication needs and conflict. Nowacek's 1991 interviewees all described an

evolution of their roles as the needs became clear over time. In addition, the roles varied across situations and were flexible and dynamic within each sit-

TABLE 5–2
Stages, features, and examples of the process to establish collaborative programs

Steps	Features	Examples
1. Deciding to collaborate and selecting the collaborators	Teachers have choices. Supportive administration is very helpful. Many varied role groups are potential partners. Needs assessments can help direct decisions.	Professional development activity inspired a group of special educators to try it, and they selected potential partners based on students' needs.
2. Planning roles and responsibilities	Often staff find they need new or modified skills and activities, including how to collaborate. They may need to self-teach or learn formally how to do that. Partners may need to define just what roles they are willing to play. Those roles will change each year as kids' needs change and teachers' growth evolves.	"I did a lot of grading the first year . . . . I just felt it was real important that I understood the kids' work . . ." "You have to be willing to look and see what the needs are and then fit yourself into those . . ."
3. Discussing implementation problems	Structured processes help teams tackle barriers to student or collaboration success. Problem-centered, team-oriented approach is required due to ongoing systemic challenges. Students are part of the solution.	Problem-solving worksheet, teacher work groups, and circles of friends help generate good solutions to barriers.
4. Planning the curriculum	Options for participation and team support exist all along the spectrum. Systematic processes for planning allow strategic up-front curricular development that can build in easy access/participation for all.	Students may do the same things, totally different things, or anywhere in between. Curricula can be designed flexibly to allow varied modes for getting info, responding, and engaging.
5. Making modifications	Teams plan specific changes in content, delivery, materials, etc. that students require to succeed. Strategic organization and delivery of content can enhance all learners' achievement.	Adding or highlighting pictures for nonreaders during oral reading time. Graphic organizers can "unlock" stories, chapters, lessons, units, and courses.

uation. For instance, the speech/language therapist reported:

In the special education classroom, sometimes I taught the whole lesson and monitored the cooperative learning groups by myself. Other times, while I was teaching, the other teacher would see something different from a different perspective and would move in and out of the lesson. Other times, we both taught part of the lesson and both moved around to monitor the groups.

In the regular education classroom, I generally introduced the concepts using the multichannel approach, and then Susan and I worked together with the groups. Susan incorporated the ideas and techniques into other subjects which reinforced these concepts. (Nowacek, 1991, pp. 267–268)

At the high school level, the special education teacher reported her roles:

. . . the aide role at times . . . In one class I ended up retyping the tests in a less crowded format for the LD students, which was not really the best use of my time in some ways, but it was a way of getting the point across that this is another way of formatting tests. And after a while she [the regular educator] saw what I was doing and she started doing it for all tests . . .

I helped plan lessons, even those I didn't teach. . . . We'd talk about a lesson that was coming up and I'd find out what the teacher's expectations were. Often she had the ideas and I was able to help her implement them. We'd discuss students' needs within that class; what kind of activities would be done . . . alternative ways of teaching a lesson or dividing groups up . . . I felt much more able to teach World History . . . so I did more co-teaching in that class.

In one class, the kids were having difficulty taking notes . . . so sometimes I would take notes on the board or an overhead . . . and then sometimes I would make copies of my notes. . . . When we had tests, I would do study guides. (Nowacek, 1991, p. 269)

This teacher made conscious decisions about the roles she was willing to play in the second year and discussed those with her partner. For example, she wanted to avoid the "good cop, bad cop" phenomenon and asked her partner to deal with discipline problems equally. Both general and special educators must know and use a variety of strategies to ensure that all students have an opportunity to learn. The special educator must not be relegated to a "glorified assistant" role because that is likely to end the collaboration (Lawton, 1999; Nowacek, 1991).

Shared decision making at some point is critical (in this case, during or prior to the IEP process, given the expanded role of general educators in that activity). A number of tools or graphic organizers exist to help teams identify key issues and reach agreement on directions to take. First, preparing all parties for the inclusion of the target student(s) is essential. Welch and Link (1991) proposed a NEED (Need Evaluation Examination Data) form for the team "to identify and prioritize the strategic skills that must be taught to students so they can successfully meet the demands of classroom environments" (p. 93). Wong, Kauffman and Lloyd (1991) suggested a set of important questions to ask when choosing programs for inclusion of students with emotional or behavioral disorders. They also promoted use of a mainstream classroom observation (MCO) form that outlines classroom practices and demands, followed by a student-teacher match (STM) form that compares instructional practices to student performance.

Welch and Link (1991) used a TASK (teacher, administrator, strategist, kid) planner to help those parties "collaboratively list specific roles and responsibilities to be implemented throughout the strategic intervention" (p. 94). This step must involve sharing essential instructional information about the student (as in Fig. 5-2) as well as joint decisions about appropriate modifications (see Fig. 5-3) and grading techniques (see Fig. 5-4). Donaldson and Christiansen (1990) created a collaborative decision-making model that also involves joint planning at two stages of the student's involvement in general education, entry (identification of problems) and instruction/resource analysis (identification of supports needed for success). Finally, Langone (1998) listed a number of technology solutions of great support for collaborative inclusive programming, including data bases for monitoring and evaluation of student performance, word processing for ease of communication, and data storage useful for IEPs, testing and scoring, student tracking systems, and report generation, among others.

3. Discussing Implementation Issues. Logistical issues become very important in this collaborative process for inclusive schooling. First and foremost, the *schedules* of students and teachers become paramount in making it work. The specialist may be the only one of her kind in the group, grade level, or "family" with whom she is teaching and thus must spread herself rather

FIGURE 5–2

Form for sharing instructional information about students with special needs

---

SPECIAL EDUCATION TO VOCATIONAL/OCCUPATIONAL EDUCATION

Student _____ School _____
          Last   First   MI

Date ___/___ 19___   D.O.B. ___/___/ 19___

Reason for Placement: _____

Present Levels of Performance (based on prior performance and baseline data):
_____
_____

Key Medical Information (including seizures, medications, etc.): _____

Behavioral Considerations and Supports: _____

Interest Area(s): _____

Prior Work Experience(s): _____

General Strengths & Weaknesses: _____

Adaptations/Modifications Recommended for Student Success in:
__Classroom __Lab/Shop __Community Site __Other: _____
A. Physical/Motor:

B. Communication:

C. Cognitive/Academic:

D. Work-Related Behaviors:

Supports to be Provided by Special Education Teacher:

Please put additional comments on the back.

Developed by the members and faculty of the SPC ED 593/Topics-Team Strategies in Occupational Education of Special Populations class. University of New Mexico, Fall 1987. Reprinted with permission.

---

thin. For instance, at the middle school level, she may be teaming in the core classes (language arts, mathematics, social studies), have 1 or 2 pull-out sections for study skills instruction and extra support for staying caught up in content classes, and have a shared planning period with her teammates. The shared planning period is difficult to come by but is critical for successful teaming and problem-solving. Figure 5-5 depicts a continuum of options for teaming that may occur as students' needs for support drive the time and intensity of the collaboration experience.

Another logistical issue pertains to the particular *grade level* of the student(s). Elementary programs generally tend to be geared more to addressing diverse learning needs. As a result, scheduling, adaptations, teaming, and other arrangements are likely to be flexible and focused on student success. High school programs have a tendency to be much more content-oriented than learner-oriented, with the focus on having students acquire large amounts of information in target areas rather than on learning about learning. Thus, the focus on acquiring Carnegie credits

FIGURE 5–3
Classroom modifications

Classroom Modifications

On a classroom or building basis, make a list of all modifications currently used to promote learning. What additional modifications should be added to the list? On an individual basis, ask the student what accommodations would support his/her learning. Describe to the student examples or modifications and give specific examples of available alternatives. Obtaining a "match" in student learning and classroom expectations will foster an acceptance of the individual student and his/her uniqueness in the classroom.

Instructional Level
Let student work at success rate level of about 80%
Break down task into sequential steps; list, colorcode.
Sequence the work with easiest problems first.
Base instruction on cognitive need (concrete, abstract).

Instructional Materials
Fold or line paper to help student w/spatial problems.
Use graph paper or lined paper turned vertically.
Draw arrows on test/worksheet to show related ideas.
Highlight/color-code on worksheets, texts, tests.
Mark the material that must be mastered.
Reduce the amount of material on a page.
Use a word processor for writing and editing.
Provide a calculator or computer to check work.
Tape reference materials to student's work area.
Have student read text while listening to audiotape
    of the text.

Format of Directions and Assignments
Introduce multiple long-term assignments in phases.
Read written directions or assignments aloud.
Leave directions on chalkboard during study time.
Write cues at top of work page (noun = _____).
Ask student to restate or paraphrase directions.
Have student complete first example with teacher
    prompt.
Provide folders for unfinished work and finished work.

Instructional Strategies
Use concrete objects to demonstrate concepts.
Provide outlines, semantic or graphic organizers,
    or webbings.
Use voice changes to stress points.

Point out relationships between ideas, concepts,
    and/or vocabulary.
Repeat important information often.

Teacher Input Mode
Use multisensory approach for presenting materials,
Provide written copy of information on chalkboard.
Demonstrate skills before student does seatwork.

Student Response Mode
Accept alternate forms of information sharing.
Allow taped or written report instead of oral.
Allow students to dictate info to each other.
Allow oral report instead of written report.
Have student practice speaking first to self and then
    small groups.

Test Administration
Allow students to have sample test to practice.
Teach test-taking skills.
Test orally.
Supply recognition items and not just total recall.
Allow take-home tests.
Ask questions requiring short (not all rote) answers.

Grading Policies
Grade some items, tests, assignments on pass/fail basis.
Grade on individual progress or effort.
Change the percentage required to pass.
Do not penalize for handwriting or spelling on a test.

Modifications of Classroom Environment
Seat students according to attention or sensory need.
Remove student from distractions.
Keep extra supplies on hand.

From "Regular Education Teacher Modifications for Mainstreamed Mildly Handicapped Students," by S.M. Munson, 1987, *Journal of Special Education, 20*, pp. 48–49. Copyright 1987 by PRO-ED, Inc. Reprinted with permission.

FIGURE 5–4

Tips for grading and evaluating students with special needs

Guidelines: Avoid penalizing students for having disabilities. Base grades on students' ability levels, not on direct competition with students with whom they cannot compete academically.

1. If possible, plan grading system jointly.
2. Share grading.
3. Include the student, if feasible, in all decision-making about evaluation.
4. Use contracts (predetermined criteria).
5. Use IEP criteria (based on mastery of objectives).
6. Give pass-fail or credit/no credit (minimum criteria).
7. Use multilevel testing (short, concrete answers to abstract essays, with "best" level most heavily weighted).
8. Use variant grading system or multiple grades (e.g., personal growth, effort, variety of tasks assessed differently, comparison to others).
9. Use checklists (subtasks).
10. Use student self-comparison (based on improvement).
11. Grade on mastery of competency-based learning (set objectives).
12. Use point system (deemphasizes test scores).
13. Grade on percentage of items attempted.
14. Give narrative or written, descriptive evaluations.

and passing competency exams often generates a resistance to creative scheduling, content arrangement, and teaming options. Exceptions exist, of course, as in the specialized, team-oriented academies around which many high schools now pattern their curricula, or the block scheduling that many high schools now offer. Middle school programs tend to share characteristics of both, and many middle school personnel are rethinking their roles and approaches because of their recognition of that stage as such a critical turning point for youth.

Problem-solving sessions become an integral part of initial and ongoing planning for all parties involved. Bishop and Jubala (1994) describe how a special educator and general educator met regularly at the beginning of a student's sixth grade year to identify his needs and adapt his program as necessary. They examined the sixth-grade schedule, addressing times when the student required more support or curricular adaptations and ways to meet those needs. Knackendoffel et al. (1992)

found a worksheet format particularly useful for resolving a range of dilemmas (see Fig. 5–6).

Student-Driven   Solutions. Numerous examples exist of creative answers to inclusive education issues that peers readily work out. The MAPS and Circle of Friends strategies (Forest & Lusthaus, 1989) necessarily include the target student's friends in brainstorming activities and have proved very helpful in solving problems. Bishop and Jubala (1994) describe how a meeting of one student's circle of friends addressed the student's refusal to wear his hearing aids. The friends' demonstration of orthodontic retainers, glasses, and protective sports equipment helped the student see that everybody uses special equipment, and he began wearing his aids.

Teacher-Generated Solutions. Teacher work or study groups are "simply two or more teachers who get together on a regular basis to help each other understand and solve the problems they encounter as they try to improve educational outcomes for students" (Ferguson, 1994, p. 43). The original groups began in Oregon from a

FIGURE 5–5

Continuum of teacher collaboration options aimed at maximum general education opportunities for students with disabilities

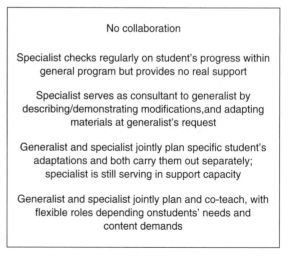

No collaboration

Specialist checks regularly on student's progress within general program but provides no real support

Specialist serves as consultant to generalist by describing/demonstrating modifications, and adapting materials at generalist's request

Generalist and specialist jointly plan specific student's adaptations and both carry them out separately; specialist is still serving in support capacity

Generalist and specialist jointly plan and co-teach, with flexible roles depending on students' needs and content demands

FIGURE 5–6
Problem-solving worksheet

PROBLEM-SOLVING WORKSHEET

Team Members: Role:

_____   _____
_____   _____
_____   _____

Student: _____   Date: _____

Problem:

Details: _____
_____
_____

Alternative Solutions Brainstormed: Ratings:

_____ — — —
_____ — — —
_____ — — —
_____ — — —
_____ — — —

Solution(s) To Be Tried First:

_____
_____

Implementation Steps: When?   Who?

_____ _____   _____
_____ _____   _____
_____ _____   _____
_____ _____   _____
_____ _____   _____
_____ _____   _____

How Will the Plan Be Monitored?

_____
_____

What Are the Criteria for Success?

_____
_____

Date and Time of Next Appointment: _____

---

need to identify or develop innovative interventions for students with severe disabilities, resulting in the Elementary/Secondary System (ESS) used in several states. Teacher work or study groups often collaborate with area universities to support themselves in proactively addressing the changes and problems that occur systemically. Three critical features drive the groups: (a) teacher directedness, (b) outcomes orientation, and (c) a focus on continuous evaluation and improvement. Ferguson describes three common rules (be positive, be fair, and keep focused), gives a series of "tricks" (e.g., do not interrupt) and guidelines, and exemplifies the most effective teacher work groups. In many schools or districts, solutions are collaboratively created by curriculum committees, school restructuring councils, site-based management teams, grade-level families, or other ongoing teams.

4. Planning the Curriculum. This section first discusses processes for curricular planning and then the content that appears most promising. York, et al. (1992) presents a curriculum development process for inclusive classrooms that incorporates four "rounds."

1. Teams initially plan and prepare for a smooth transition to the new arrangement. This stage may include initial dialogues about inclusion, identifying potential barriers, and planning strategies to maximize a sense of community.
2. During the first weeks team members encourage cohesiveness and identify the needs and performance of the target student(s).
3. Later, the entire class collectively envisions their desired future of inclusiveness. (What do they want to happen in their classroom among learners with special needs? All learners?)
4. Given what they now know, the team decides how to optimize current options; individual student priorities are carried out within the schedule and attention is given to specific learning outcomes.

Giangreco, Cloninger, and Iverson (1993) specified four major levels for student participation in the general curriculum. Determining the appropriate level for each student is a critical prerequisite to planning the content and delivery of the curriculum.

- same as others: same activities, same curricular focus and objectives
- multilevel: same activities but different level (e.g., fewer items, lower grade level demands of items)
- curriculum overlapping: same activities but different objectives (e.g., a health objective within a science class or a functional math objective within a vocational class)
- alternative: different activities, different objectives

Donaldson and Christiansen (1990) identify five options or supports along their *continuum of decision points about students' performance:*

behavior management → part-time assistance → instructional options → instructional options plus part-time help → full-time assistance

These levels correspond somewhat with those sequenced in Figure 5–5. Fad and Ryser (1993) find that emphasis on social/behavioral factors is just as important as academic competencies when supporting students' success in general education. Langone (1998) reminds readers of the benefits of community-based (contextualized or situated) learning for students with disabilities, an option that should be considered during curricular planning.

The field has focused recently on principles of curriculum design as a key to student success. Simmons and Kameenui (1996) elaborate on six major principles of curriculum design to prevent academic failure across the curriculum:

Big Idea: Concepts, principles, or heuristics that facilitate the most efficient and broad acquisition of knowledge (focus on essential learning outcomes)

Conspicuous Strategies: Explicit, planned, and purposeful steps for accomplishing a goal or task (most important in initial teaching)

Mediated Scaffolding: Instructional guidance provided by teachers, peers, materials, or tasks (varied according to learner need and experiences)

Strategic Integration: Integrating knowledge as a means of promoting higher-level cognition (results in a new and more complex knowledge structure)

Primed Background Knowledge: Pre-existing information that affects new learning (readies learner for successful performance)

Judicious Review: Structured opportunities to recall or apply information previously taught (varied, distributed, cumulative, judicious)

Orkwis and McLane (1998) summarize the key principles of *universal design in curriculum development,* intended to maximize access to the curriculum for all students from widely differing backgrounds and strengths. The "big idea" is that designing curricula initially with (a) lots of flexibility for differing modes and (b) supportive, strategic organization of content sets everyone up for success. An analogy is the architectural plans for a new building, where access to all rooms, pathways, and entries/exits is built in from the beginning. The result is that the building is accessible to all, at little or no additional cost whereas having to remodel an existing building to provide access would be extremely expensive. The three major components of universal design are described below.

1. *Curriculum Provides Flexible Means of Representation* (presentation of information by the teacher takes multiple formats):
   ■ *Alternatives that Reduce Perceptual Barriers:* text, audio, image/graphic
   ■ *Alternatives that Reduce Cognitive Barriers:* big ideas (summaries of key concepts) and background knowledge (making sure they have the basics)
2. *Curriculum Provides Flexible Means of Expression* (so students can respond with their preferred means of communication)
   ■ *Alternatives that Reduce Motor Barriers to Expression:* writing, speaking, drawing/illustrating

   ■ *Alternatives that Reduce Cognitive Barriers to Expression:* explicit (conspicuous) strategies (pointing them out as you go) and scaffolding (giving the underlying support that students need with gradual, rapid fading)
3. *Curriculum Provides Flexible Means of Engagement* (includes both balanced options for engagement as well as motivational variables):
   ■ *Support and Challenge*
   ■ *Novelty and Familiarity*
   ■ *Developmental and Cultural Interest*
   ■ *Flexible Curricular Materials* ("half full" curricula that allow for direct input from and participation by all students)

A number of classroom routines have been published that provide structure for building curriculum in ways that maximize low achievers' success in general or special education programs by strategically organizing the introduction of ideas and experiences. A representative sample of these is listed below.

Classroom Routine	Description
Concept Anchoring (Bulgren, Schumaker, & Deshler, 1994)	Strategic introduction of new, hard-to-grasp concepts
Lesson Organizer (Lenz, Marrs, Schumaker, & Deshler, 1993)	Visually guided process that links prior to current and future learning, organizes lesson for maximum understanding
Unit Organizer (Lenz, Bulgren, Schumaker, Deshler, & Boudah, 1994)	Visually guided process that invites student participation, links prior/current/future learning, and raises conceptual understanding
Course Organizer (Lenz, Schumaker, Deshler & Bulgren, 1998)	Same principles, but at course level

According to Scruggs and Mastropieri (1993), curricular modifications should also be based upon the type of skills or experiences taught by the curriculum, as well as on the teacher's specific beliefs about or strengths in implementing the curriculum (including level of enthusiasm). For example, their research on science instructional approaches suggests that hands-on activities may produce more favorable academic and affective outcomes among students with exceptionalities than more traditional content-oriented approaches. Learner engagement is a powerful element of effective instruction.

5. Modifications. Students with exceptionalities will invariably require some personalized package of modifications of instructional content, delivery, materials, environment, response options, and/or evaluation methods within the general setting. Smith, Polloway, Patton, and Dowdy (1999) offer specific curricular modifications distinguished by elementary and secondary levels. Most of the available lists of modifications cross grade levels, as does the example shown in Figure 5–3. Increasing resources in ready-to-use formats (e.g., workbooks or notebooks) are available, including items such as graphic organizers, test adaptation recommendations, alternative assessment strategies, communication tools, organizational strategies, and other supports. The bottom line is that modifications must be tailored to individual students' needs, such as adding or highlighting pictures to allow a nonreader to follow along with a novel the class is reading, or providing speech therapy within a student's small science group (where they are learning technical vocabulary) rather than pulling the student out of class (Bishop & Jubala, 1994). Many modifications are simple and beneficial to all learners whereas some require more preparation.

Several ways exist of making textbooks come alive for struggling readers. For example, Bassett (n.d.) developed a "Content Area Reading Teaching Packet" that takes students through the following components:

Pre-reading activities: brainstorming concepts, narrowing down key vocabulary, direct vocabulary instruction (if needed), categorization exercise

Reading the chapter with a selective study guide: (eliminates nonessential content, personalizes and strategizes the reader's engagement with the text)

Post-reading activities: troika (trio) review, cinquain creation, and kinesthetic activities

Schumm and Magnum (1991) have created a framework for textbook thinking around four themes: Friendliness (How friendly is my reading assignment based on several features?), Language (difficulty level), Interest (boring to very interesting), and Prior Knowledge (What do I bring to the material?). Schumm and Strickler (1991) share guidelines for adapting content area textbooks, with specific techniques organized by four major categories:

- Substitute the textbook for those with severe word-recognition problems
- Simplify the textbook for those whose reading levels fall far below the text level
- Highlight key concepts for those with comprehension difficulties
- Increase idea retention for students with long-term memory challenges.

Nolet and Tindal (1993) found that certain procedural approaches maximized the success of students with special needs in science classes. They urged content area teachers to (a) specify the concepts and principles they deemed critical (the "big ideas"), and (b) model problem-solving formats within a rich context. Special educators were encouraged to help format the content for effective learning by low achievers in either content or specialized settings. Finally, alternative assessment approaches were recommended, including modalities such as sketches, oral responses, and think-aloud work samples.

COLLABORATION WITH PARAEDUCATORS

Paraeducators comprise a significant portion of the work force serving individuals with exceptionalities and their roles continue to evolve as those of teachers and other staff change as well, including becoming an important part of the collaborative process as students are increasingly served in the general classroom (Villa, Thousand, Nevin, & Malgeri, 1996). Their strategic participation can make or break a program or a single student's success. Unfortunately, few teacher and administrator preparation programs work on how to select, train, lead, and collaborate on a long-term basis with these staff members (Langone, 1998; Villa, Thousand, Nevin, & Malgeri, 1996).

Definitions

Anna Lou Pickett, Director of the National Resource Center for Paraprofessionals in Education and Related Services, and her colleagues Faison and Formanek (1993) defined paraeducators as

employees: (1) whose positions are either instructional in nature or who deliver other direct services to students and/or their parents; (2) who work under the supervision of teachers or other professional staff who have the ultimate responsibility for the design, implementation and evaluation of instructional programs and student progress. (p. 11)

This definition clearly refers to those whose job titles include teacher or educational assistants, human service technicians, therapy assistants, job coaches, and many others. These personnel work in settings that range from preschool to adult services and from total integration to almost total segregation.

Rationales and Framework

Reasons to include paraeducators as team members and to prepare to utilize their services fully are apparent. Even model programs may be damaged if interpersonal or values conflicts between two or more adults or failure to embrace job responsibilities interfere with students' learning. Students or consumers ultimately pay the price. These problems typically result from inadequate communication and lack of planning. This section provides suggestions for improving and monitoring collaboration between professionals and paraeducators in educational or re-

lated services programs. The ideas offered are based on the notion that effective teamwork is the desired outcome; the ultimate goal is high quality of life for persons with exceptionalities (resulting from effective, efficient instructional and support programs).

Teamwork in the classroom or center involves distinct, complementary roles that sometimes overlap but that serve separate, unique purposes. The professional who wants to fully utilize the paraprofessional's potential contributions should use a democratic style of leadership, with most responsibilities shared. Since the only real justification for hiring another adult in a program is to improve teaching and learning, paraprofessionals should actively participate in almost every aspect of the teaching process and classroom management. The teacher should ask, "Is this a task that I would readily do, but because of time or student factors I cannot or should not do it right now?" If the answer is "yes," and the paraeducator understands that perspective, most problems of role expectations can be dispelled. The ideas that follow are based on this flexible team approach and are designed to fully integrate the paraprofessional into the program as a true partner.

Taking the First Steps: Recruitment and Employment of Paraeducators

The New Careers Movement, a major force in employing paraeducators in education and social services, emerged in the 1960s in response to teacher shortages, the War on Poverty, and cries for social and educational reform. One of the movement's outstanding elements was the enlistment of local residents, many of them previously unemployed, underemployed, or eager for career changes, for training and employment in the helping professions. The advantages of targeting community residents for these jobs are numerous: their understanding of the backgrounds, languages, and major issues of students and families; familiarity with local expectations and resources; ability to communicate with community agency or business personnel; and, often, somewhat easier access to rapport with reluctant learners. In many communities paraeducators have long filled in as critical translators with parents whose native language is other than English. Employment of paraeducators also has generated an excellent recruitment pool for teaching and therapist positions.

Employed paraeducators can be a primary resource for publicity in their home communities about job openings and should be encouraged to inform likely candidates about job opportunities. Each applicant will present a different profile of experiences, abilities, interests, educational philosophies, and goals. The task for the professional is to develop a specific job description for the paraeducator and to match applicants to the particular job's demands. Administrators desiring quality team collaboration should require professionals to help interview their prospective team members so the best matches are made. Conversely, experienced paraprofessionals should help to interview applicants who may later become their supervisors.

Defining Roles and Responsibilities

The instructional team model begins with a definition of roles and responsibilities for each team member. The biggest area of frustration between educators and paraeducators appears to be their spoken or more often unspoken expectations about respective roles and duties. Professionals have the ultimate responsibility for their students' assessment and intervention programs and therefore are closely engaged with preparation of IEPs or other individualized plans. Devleopment and implementation of a beneficial program for a student, however, necessarily involves many other personnel, such as ancillary or related services providers, the paraeducator, parents, the student, and possibly others. The paraeducator role is one of support and assistance, whether in general or specialized settings, teaming with various people, supervising small groups, tutoring students, supporting socioemotional adjustment, or coordinating with other professionals and parents (Blalock, 1991). Figure 5–7 suggests a breakdown of some major responsibilities delegated to both the teacher and the paraprofessional, as a way to ensure that both are clear about role expectations.

More detail about tasks frequently found in special education or related programs could be developed into lengthier checklists for discussion and possible demonstration.

A number of roles have evolved over the years that deserve discussion as well as careful planning, preparation, and selection if they are applied. Many paraprofessionals serve as translators and interpreters for students and families from diverse backgrounds, so Medina (1982) provided guidelines about acceptable duties and important training and utilization recommendations for these two roles. Their support of students included in general education has been widespread and seriously appreciated for at least 20 years, but few have been prepared and truly supported in that role. "The inclusion team should establish that the instructional assistants are a significant part of the educational team, with the stipulation that they must not take independent action and make decisions without the teachers' knowledge" (Langone, 1998, p. 9). Langone also cautions that the team needs to specify the role of paraeducators in order to protect them from being assigned inappropriately or being overused.

Paraprofessionals have been increasingly hired to implement community-based instruction (CBI), work-study, transition, and supported employment programs in schools, colleges, adult agencies, and the community. A growing number of programs for students of 18 to 22 years of age to learn adult life skills in the community exist across the United States, employing paraeducators as community support assistants. While these paraeducators work under the ultimate supervision of professionals (e.g., transition teachers), they typically are very independent in the community once trained, providing critical instruction or support in natural settings to individuals or small groups so that students with moderate or significant support needs can apply classroom learning in meaningful ways.

Identifying Strengths, Weaknesses, and Work Styles

During interviews and initial employment, the supervising professional has the opportunity to

FIGURE 5–7

Complementary duties of teachers and paraeducators

Teacher	Paraeducator
Program/Classroom Management	
Plans weekly schedule with team, if applicable	Helps with planning and carrying out of lessons/activities
Plans lessons/activities for class and individuals, with team	Makes teaching aids, helps gather or copy teaching materials
Plans learning centers	
Is responsible for all students at all times	Provides emergency classroom supervision
Participates in teacher's duty schedule	Participates in paras' duty schedule
Arranges schedules for each student's related services	Accompanies students to other locations in the school
Assessment	
Assesses all students as needed on an ongoing basis	Assists with giving, monitoring, and scoring tests, other assignments
Administers formal tests	Helps with observing/charting student behaviors/progress
Is responsible for collection and recording of all student data	Assists in grading assignments or tests and recording grades
Teaching	
Introduces new material	Assists with follow-up instruction for small groups or individuals
Teaches entire class, small groups, or individuals	Helps support large group instruction as needed
Behavior Management	
Plans strategies for behavioral supports program for entire class or individuals	Assists in implementing the teacher's behavioral supports program, using same emphasis/techniques
Parent Collaboration	
Meets with parents	Helps with parent contacts, such as phone calls or notes
Initiates conferences	Contributes to parent conferences and
Schedules IEP meetings	IEP meetings when appropriate and feasible

assess, at least informally, the applicant's experiences, abilities, interests, educational philosophy, and goals in an effort to match the position and the person effectively. Brizzi (1982) suggests a variety of questions that could provide insights into the assignment of academic and general responsibilities:

- Why do you want to work with students?
- Tell me what you think makes the best learning environment.
- What do you think you can offer the students in this class?
- What are your talents? Skills? What do you do in your leisure time?

- Do you type? Speak another language? Participate in sports, recreation, games? Like math? Do artistic activities?
- Are you comfortable communicating with students? Staff? Parents?
- What work have you done before? What did you like and dislike about your previous job(s)?
- What is your goal beyond this job?
- What subjects did you like and dislike in school?
- Who was your favorite teacher and why? What kind of teacher did you dislike and why?
- What could students learn from you that would help them develop independence? What do you think an independent person is? (p. 4)

The supervising professional can enhance the paraprofessional's willingness to respond by sharing some personal experiences in some of the areas mentioned. Patience and a little coaxing are recommended because few paraprofessionals (especially potential ones) are used to discussing their strengths and talents.

Individual work styles are also important to understand for a teamwork relationship. They are best explored when team members first begin to work together, to avoid or minimize mistaken assumptions and disappointments. Figures 5–8 and 5–9, based on Houk and McKenzie's 1985 scale, delineate a limited number of work style behaviors for supervisors and paraeducators. The parallel structure of the two forms aids discussion about areas in which the pair's ratings significantly differ, so that solutions can be planned before potential problems arise.

For those who prefer a more informal assessment of work style differences, Brizzi (1982) proposes several questions that might be asked:

- How do you like to work? Do you prefer to initiate activities or be directed toward most tasks?
- How do you want to be corrected if a mistake occurs?
- Are you likely to ask for help or let your supervisor know when something is unpleasant, or are you likely to avoid talking about it? (p. 4)

These questions can be modified to meet both parties' work style tendencies.

Team Planning Strategies

If teachers and paraeducators want a very successful program operation, they need to seek mutually satisfying ways to accommodate the differences in their work styles. Differences in most of life's major indices (e.g., education, income, religion, culture or language) are practically guaranteed between teachers and paraeducators (Blalock, 1991). For example, if a supervisor values a paraprofessional's instructional and management abilities but the paraprofessional's need to stick to the duty-day hours prevents planning time, numerous options may be possible depend-

ing upon agency policies about flex time. For example, if some flexibility exists, the paraprofessional might stay longer one day per week to participate in planning and take that time off within the week; the teacher and the paraeducator might plan independent activities for the students for one period twice weekly so that they could do some planning; or another teacher or paraeducator in the grade-level team may be able to fill in to allow planning once weekly. Figure 5–10 shows one format combining regularly scheduled feedback and planning sessions with specific assignments and tasks for both team members. Creativity and humor in problem-solving will go far in addressing the inevitable roadblocks to effective programming.

Supervisors can significantly enhance the confidence and sense of belonging of paraeducators by consistently including them, when appropriate, in decision-making regarding students' programs, unit plans, activities, and collaboration with other professionals and parents. IEP and annual review meetings are another important arena in which experienced paraprofessionals contribute critical information about the students with whom they work. Even if they do not attend IEP meetings, paraprofessionals should be familiar with each student's IEP goals and objectives. In addition, they may be key participants in some parent conferences, providing valuable information, language translation, or clarification of school policies or cultural practices. Such meetings as well as other events throughout the year provide the opportunity to highlight the important contributions made by paraeducators. Administrators and supervising teachers often have to set the stage for recognition of the role of paraeducators in instructional programs; their advocacy efforts communicate that the participation of paraprofessionals as team members is truly valued.

Paraeducator Professional Development Activities

Inadequate attention to training needs is reported to be a significant factor in burnout among special education paraeducators (Blalock, Rivera,

FIGURE 5–8
Inventory of supervisor's work style

Supervisor's Work Style

Please indicate the manner in which you tend to manage your work site by placing a check mark on each continuum wherever you believe your style is represented. Your answers will help you and your paraprofessional(s) decide how best to work together.

1. Will you identify specific materials and methods to be used, or will the paraprofessional have freedom to choose?

    Structured / . . . . / . . . . / . . . . / . . . . / Unstructured

2. Will specific duties be assigned for exact periods of time, or will the para have a flexible schedule?

    Firm / . . . . / . . . . / . . . . / . . . . / Flexible

3. Will the para's job require specific training and/or abilities, or will the duties be fairly simple or easy?

    Complex / . . . . / . . . . / . . . . / . . . . / Simple

4. Will you provide close supervision, or will you expect the paraprofessional to work independently?

    Supervision / . . . . / . . . . / . . . . / . . . . / Independence

5. I like to be very punctual.

    Most like me / . . . . / . . . . / . . . . / . . . . / Least like me

6. I am a very flexible person

    Most like me / . . . . / . . . . / . . . . / . . . . / Least like me

7. I have some very firm beliefs about educational interventions.

    Most like me / . . . . / . . . . / . . . . / . . . . / Least like me

8. I like to take on challenging tasks.

    Most like me / . . . . / . . . . / . . . . / . . . . / Least like me

9. I like to let the para know exactly what I expect.

    Most like me / . . . . / . . . . / . . . . / . . . . / Least like me

10. I like to give frequent feedback about the para's work.

    Most like me / . . . . / . . . . / . . . . / . . . . / Least like me

11. I encourage others to think for themselves.

    Most like me / . . . . / . . . . / . . . . / . . . . / Least like me

12. I regularly let the para know how s/he can improve.

    Most like me / . . . . / . . . . / . . . . / . . . . / Least like me

13. I like taking care of details.

    Most like me / . . . . / . . . . / . . . . / . . . . / Least like me

14. I like to bring problems at work out in the open.

    Most like me / . . . . / . . . . / . . . . / . . . . / Least like me

15. I try to ensure the para's inclusion as a team member.

    Most like me / . . . . / . . . . / . . . . / . . . . / Least like me

FIGURE 5–9
Inventory of paraprofessional's work style

Paraprofessional's Work Style

Please place a check mark on each continuum to indicate which job features you believe bring out your best efforts. Your answers will help you and your supervisor decide how best to work together.

1. Should the materials and methods you use with students be specifically identified, or do you prefer choosing them?
   Structured / . . . . / . . . . / . . . . / . . . . / Unstructured

2. Do you like to know exactly when to start and stop a task, or do you like to have a flexible schedule at work?
   Firm / . . . . / . . . . / . . . . / . . . . / Flexible

3. Would you prefer duties that require specific training and/or skills or tasks that are fairly simple or easy?
   Complex / . . . . / . . . . / . . . . / . . . . / Simple

4. Do you prefer close supervision, or do you like to work independently?
   Supervision / . . . . / . . . . / . . . . / . . . . / Independence

5. I like to be very punctual.
   Most like me / . . . . / . . . . / . . . . / . . . . / Least like me

6. I am a very flexible person
   Most like me / . . . . / . . . . / . . . . / . . . . / Least like me

7. I have some very firm beliefs about educational interventions.
   Most like me / . . . . / . . . . / . . . . / . . . . / Least like me

8. I like to take on challenging tasks.
   Most like me / . . . . / . . . . / . . . . / . . . . / Least like me

9. I like to know exactly what is expected of me.
   Most like me / . . . . / . . . . / . . . . / . . . . / Least like me

10. I need to have frequent feedback about my performance.
    Most like me / . . . . / . . . . / . . . . / . . . . / Least like me

11. I like to be encouraged to think for myself.
    Most like me / . . . . / . . . . / . . . . / . . . . / Least like me

12. I need to know how I can improve, on a regular basis.
    Most like me / . . . . / . . . . / . . . . / . . . . / Least like me

13. I like taking care of details.
    Most like me / . . . . / . . . . / . . . . / . . . . / Least like me

14. I like to bring problems at work out in the open.
    Most like me / . . . . / . . . . / . . . . / . . . . / Least like me

15. I want to be included as part of the instructional team.
    Most like me / . . . . / . . . . / . . . . / . . . . / Least like me

FIGURE 5–10

Sample schedule of responsibilities and interactions

Time	Teacher Activity	Paraprofessional Activity
8:00	Planning for the instructional day	Open windows, adjust blinds Check work box and find spelling words Grade, record, make list of common spelling errors
8:30	Conference with para: change approach to managing two children's behavior: select new strategy and plan how to evaluate success	
9:00	Welcome children	Assist teacher
9:30	Opening Begin reading, working with groups or using selective reading	Take attendance Work with two groups in reading, using flash cards and word games
10:00	Spelling: present new lesson	Prepare spelling tape for two students to use at listening center
10:20	Recess	Recess
10:30	Math: present lesson to group 1 (group 2 finishing assignment from previous day) Present lesson to group 2 Give individual help	Listen to lesson presentation Help individuals as needed in group 2 Give individual help to students in group 1 Give individual help and correct math papers
11:30	Students to lunch Evaluation with paraprofessional	
11:30	Lunch	Finish math papers

Anderson, & Kottler, 1992). These poorly paid positions typically require only a high school diploma or equivalency and 18 years of age, and the supervisor necessarily becomes the primary trainer (or training arranger) for the paraeducator. Initial discussions of expected duties are important means of identifying training needs. The most common topics of college or commercial courses or training packages include:

- human growth and development
- overview of exceptionalities and their effects on development
- basic special education or rehabilitation principles and approaches
- paraeducator roles and interactions

- positive behavioral supports and systems
- health and safety
- specialty core(s) (e.g., severe/low incidence issues, psychiatric disorders)
- supervised field experiences

After areas of needed training are determined, the most feasible scheduling and vehicles to achieve the training must be explored and arranged—for example, scheduling specific demonstrations of procedures when they are actually needed by students in order to maximize relevance. Options for securing specific training vary from location to location, potentially involving specialists in clerical, media, technologies, administrative, ancillary, therapeutic, community resources, and content areas. Formal training programs for paraeducators in special education, rehabilitation, human services, or child development often are the richest sources of intense, connected educational experiences. Community colleges are the primary settings for certificate or associate degree programs in these areas; a few 4-year colleges and universities also offer such programs. Conversely, several colleges of education offer coursework for supervisors on training and utilization of paraeducators.

One of the most important resources for field-tested training materials for or about paraeducators is the National Resource Center for Paraprofessionals in Special Education and Related Fields, located at the Graduate Center of the City University of New York. Its director, Anna Lou Pickett, also shares information about training materials and programs around the United States in the Center's quarterly newsletter, *New Directions.*

Langone (1998) describes a series of activities that could support the paraeducator in effective support of inclusively served students: brief training programs, periodic review sessions (e.g., on observation and recording techniques), developing a training manual (possibly with photographs of methods in progress), and including them in regular planning.

A number of programs have been developed for preparing CBI or work-study assistants, job coaches, and community support assistants (Blalock, Mahoney, & Dalia, 1992; Center for Rehabilitative Studies, University of North Texas, 1990; Leitner & Bishop, 1989).

Several important considerations relate to how teaching adults is different from teaching children. Because adults' needs to learn are based on actual life demands, their learning activities should target tasks perceived as part of their lives. Adults are also more task-oriented than theory-based, preferring to do rather than to listen. Thus, role-playing and problem-based learning are important strategies. In addition, training personnel need to validate the adults' lives and work experiences and use them as foundations on which to build new learning—for example, by using commonly shared situations as examples (a local sports event, the opening of a new mall, growing up in the same town). Adults must be involved in any decisions about desired learning outcomes (i.e., goal setting), as well as assessment strategies and the steps to achieving those goals.

Monitoring and Feedback Techniques

Regularly scheduled meetings provide a forum for supervisors to give ongoing feedback (especially positive) about paraeducators' performance. The 1-minute praisings and 1-minute reprimands promoted by Blanchard and Johnson (1982) have proved to be quick, powerful management tools that leave no room for doubt or surprises. Another feedback device for teachers and assistants was produced by Krueger and Fox (1984) and is easily modified or used in oral rather than written form (Fig. 5–11).

Many performance rating instruments have been developed for paraeducators in special education and related fields (Blalock, 1984; Pickett, 1989; Vasa, Steckelberg, & Sundermeier, 1989). However, the most important guideline is that feedback should be based directly on the current job description(s) provided to the paraprofessional. To carry meaning, performance feedback also should relate to future goals for both student and paraeducator growth.

Finally, career ladders provide a *long-term incentive* for improving competence and exhibiting professionalism that short-term supports cannot sustain for very long (e.g., time off for courses, payment for training costs). Career ladders typically involve a sequence of three or four levels, each distinct from the other in terms of required competencies and salary levels; these levels are usually implemented by an employing agency and/or the state education department, sometimes in partnership with area colleges or universities. Professionals who extend themselves to improve paraeducators' working conditions and expertise through avenues such as a career ladder will experience enhanced teamwork and watch their students reap the rewards many times over.

FIGURE 5–11
Paraeducator feedback form

In order for us to work more effectively with students, it is important that we assess our activities on a regular basis. Please complete this form and return it to your supervising teacher.

1. List the activities that you most enjoyed this week.

_____
_____
_____

2. List the activities that you least enjoyed this week.

_____
_____
_____

3. Comment on activities that you might like to do next week.

_____
_____
_____

4. How can we work together more effectively?

_____
_____
_____

COLLABORATION WITH OTHER PERSONNEL

A whole spectrum of other partners, beyond the general and special education teachers, are critical to ensure that school, center, and community programs accomplish their missions well. Some of these potential team members include administrators and related therapists in the schools or centers, community and state agency personnel, community members such as employers and government officials, and many others. Traditionally, related services personnel have included IDEA-identified professionals in this category— those who provide the related services required by students to benefit from their educational programs and which are identified in their IEPs. The primary partners in this category include assistive technology specialists, speech/language therapists, occupational therapists, and physical therapists. IDEA's recent reauthorizations also included rehabilitation services specialists if needed. However, other partners' services may also be required for a particular student's program or to meet the family's needs. Therefore, this section offers ideas to support collaboration with local agency staff, employers, and other community support personnel.

The same basic principles and practices of collaboration that have been explored throughout this chapter apply to team members from other areas. A few additional considerations are shared next.

Working with administrators is essential to implementing innovative programs and also can open doors for better programming for students with exceptionalities. However, administrators often must be convinced of the benefits of new directions and are constantly besieged with competing requests to exhaust their school's limited resources. One strategy is to go in numbers (as a team) with your requests for planning and consulting time, reconfigured student assistance teams, or other priorities, and to be prepared for rejection the first time. Often one's initiative in developing a request is acknowledged without being granted, but repeated requests by a team, based on data and student-centered goals, can often achieve the desired ends.

Hunt (1995) detailed the qualities of exemplary collaborations that would characterize the best joint efforts of multidisciplinary teams or

FIGURE 5–12
Qualities of an exemplary collaboration

Qualities of an exemplary collaboration

- Unconditional support: Based on a shared goal, team members may agree to disagree.
- High morale: Positive attitudes pervade interactions, strengthened by team members respect for each other.
- Shared responsibility: Leadership crosses membership of the team.
- Removal of barriers: Working together to solve problems tends to wreak havoc on barriers.
- Team spirit: Equity about who each is underlies the group's mentality.
- Team member development: Support for each other's growth and effectiveness is pervasive.
- Community support: Ongoing favorable interactions with the community generate, in turn, community support for the team's work.

From "What Does It Take?" by P. Hunt, 1995. *What's Working: Transition in Minnesota* (p. 1), Minneapolis, MN: University of Minnesota Institute on Community Integration. Copyright 1995 by the University of Minnesota Institute on Community Integration. Reprinted and adapted with permission.

community teams. Hunt's list is adapted for Figure 5–12. At the community level, Goetz, Lee, Johnston, and Gaylord-Ross (1991) offer several strategies for collaborating with employers and co-workers to promote job-site inclusion of persons with disabilities, including emphasizing the natural supports that can be instrumental in their success (e.g., co-workers' prompts, supervisors' praise).

EVALUATING THE COLLABORATIVE EXPERIENCE

Participants, and perhaps overseers, of the collaborative activities need regular opportunities to step back, check on the progress of both team and target students, and change the interventions as needed in order to enhance students' performance and to give the process a chance for sustainability. Evaluation serves as the final component of a collaborative program so that feedback on current efforts can influence future activities. Within a school, evaluation may be handled in an informal fashion, such as partners asking each other about their perceptions of the process and its outcomes. However, in some instances a more structured approach is beneficial, particularly if district-wide or school-wide collaborative training has been implemented. Saver and Downes (1991) developed a Peer Intervention Team model, or PIT Crew, that followed seven progressive, interrelated consultation stages, the last two of which were monitoring/evaluation and follow-up. They offered excellent examples of both formative and summative evaluation tools for their elementary education model. Knackendoffel et al. (1992) created a Self-Evaluation Checklist (Fig. 5–13) for team members to reflect on their own use of good communication skills and problem-solving steps.

SUMMARY

This chapter first lays the foundational concepts and skills needed for collaboration with individuals or groups. Four key stakeholder groups with whom special educators need to collaborate are discussed: families, general educators, paraeducators, and associated personnel both within and outside the school. The imperative to connect with the full range of partners becomes increasingly evident as greater attention is paid to the assets and needs of the whole person in educational systems with increasingly diminished resources (e.g., teacher shortages, government budget cuts, and greater competition).

FIGURE 5–13
Self-evaluation checklist

Self-Evaluation Checklist

Did you use the following skills:	Yes	No
Assume a posture of involvement?	☐	☐
Lean torso slightly forward	☐	☐
Directly face the other person	☐	☐
Maintain eye contact	☐	☐
Use appropriate facial expressions	☐	☐
Minimize distractions	☐	☐
Use nonverbal encouragers?		
Nod your head	☐	☐
Smile	☐	☐
Take notes	☐	☐
Provide brief verbal encouragers?	☐	☐
Make reflecting statements?		
Paraphrase	☐	☐
Reflect emotions	☐	☐
Pause after making the statement	☐	☐
Ask good questions?		
Open-ended questions	☐	☐
Close-ended questions	☐	☐
Indirect questions	☐	☐
Clarifying questions	☐	☐
Summarize information periodically?		
Use partnership-building skills?		
Accepting statements	☐	☐
Compliments or appreciation statements	☐	☐
Empathic statements	☐	☐
Focusing statements	☐	☐
Agreement statements	☐	☐
Productive solution statements	☐	☐

Did you complete all the problem-solving steps:	Yes	No
Define the problem?	☐	☐
Gather specific information about the problem?	☐	☐
Explain the problem-solving process?	☐	☐
Identify alternative solutions?	☐	☐
Ask other person to suggest ideas first.	☐	☐
Introduce your ideas in an open-minded manner.	☐	☐
Summarize solutions mentioned?	☐	☐
Analyze consequences of each solution?	☐	☐
Rate each solution?	☐	☐
Select the best solution?	☐	☐
Determine satisfaction with chosen solution?	☐	☐
State your support for the decision?	☐	☐
Develop a plan of action?	☐	☐
Specify implementation steps	☐	☐
Indicate who is responsible for each step	☐	☐
Indicate when each step will be completed	☐	☐
Develop a monitoring system?	☐	☐
Specify criteria for success?	☐	☐
Schedule the next appointment?	☐	☐

Notes and comments about use of skills:

Notes and comments about use of problem-solving steps:

From *Collaborative Problem Solving: A Step-by-Step Guide to Creating Educational Solutions* (pp. 69–70), by E. A. Knack-endoffel, S. M. Robinson, D. D. Deshler, and J. B. Schumaker, 1992, Lawrence, KS: Edge Enterprises. Copyright 1992 by Edge Enterprises, Inc. Reprinted with permission.

TEACHER TIPS

The success of a collaborative effort does not happen automatically. Members of the collaborative team must possess certain skills and attitudes. One such attitude is the idea of working together as a team rather than just a group of people coming together. Maddus (1992) makes a clear distinction between groups and teams of people working together. The following are a few of his distinctions:

<table>
<tr><th>Groups</th><th>Teams</th></tr>
<tr>
<td>

■ Members think they are grouped together for administrative purposes only. Individuals work independently; sometimes at cross purposes with others.

</td>
<td>

■ Members recognize their interdependence and understand both personal and team goals are best accomplished with mutual support. Time is not wasted struggling over 'turf' or attempting personal gain at the expense of others.

</td>
</tr>
<tr>
<td>

■ Members tend to focus on themselves because they are not sufficiently involved in planning and the unit's objectives. They approach their job simply as hired hands.

</td>
<td>

■ Members feel a sense of ownership for their jobs and unit because they are committed to goals they helped establish.

</td>
</tr>
<tr>
<td>

■ Members distrust the motives of colleagues because they do not understand the role of other members. Expressions of opinion or disagreement are considered divisive or non-supportive.

</td>
<td>

■ Members work in a climate of trust and are encouraged to openly express ideas, opinions, disagreements, and feelings. Questions are welcomed.

</td>
</tr>
<tr>
<td>

■ Members are so cautious about what they say that real understanding is not possible. Game playing may occur and communication traps set to catch the unwary.

</td>
<td>

■ Members practice open and honest communications. They make an effort to understand each other's point of view.

</td>
</tr>
</table>

Maddux, R.B. (1992). *Team building: An exercise in leadership.* Menlo Park, CA: Crisp Publishing, p 5.

TEACHER TIPS

Collaboration among educational professionals is a skill and an activity that is becoming increasingly important. In particular, collaboration is important when educators must participate in the designing and delivery of school and community-based services for students needing an array of support. The degree in which educators collaborate and the quality of their collaboration skills has not been widely investigated. One group of researchers (Foley & Lewis, 1999), however, has explored the idea that collaboration and collaborative-based educational delivery systems may depend on the self-perceived competence of the secondary school principals.

Foley and Lewis' (1999) goal was to describe the self-perceived competence of secondary school principals to function as leaders in collaborative-based systems and to identify factors contributing to their leadership skills. This goal was based on the assumption that secondary schools and their personnel characteristically include a number of challenges to the development and implementation of collaborative-based structures. For example, one challenge concerns the environmental aspects of secondary schools. Typically, a teacher is isolated in his/her classroom and does not have the opportunity to enter into a dialogue or collaborative effort with teachers within and outside his/her academic field. A second challenge that Foley and Lewis identified was the fact that secondary school special and general education teachers do not regularly interact with each other or with community service providers. Finally, Foley and Lewis state that the typical managerial role of administrators in secondary schools may be a challenge. Most administrators take on the role of primary decision maker concerning the operation and function of the school. This administrative style does not lend itself to the principles of collegiality, parity, and shared decision making that are the structure for collaborative-based interactions.

In their study of 500 principals, Foley and Lewis asked administrators to rate their level of competence to serve as leaders of collaborative-based programs. Their results indicated principals rated themselves as "average" in the area of guiding collaborative-based programs. Perceived competence in this area seemed to be linked to the number of clock hours of non-credit-generating professional-development activities, academic degrees, and the number of years teaching in general education.

Foley, R.M. & Lewis, J. A. (1999). Self-perceived competence of secondary school principals to serve as school leaders in collaborative-based educational delivery systems. *Remedial and Special Education*, 20, pp. 233–243.

TEACHER TIPS

Although collaboration among educators may be difficult due to time constraints and other barriers, one option that many teachers are investigating is collaborative efforts on the Internet. For example, a collaboration effort "About the K-12 Collaborative" (http://www.k12connection.org/http://www.k12connection.org/) introduces educators and others to the Internet technology dealing with collaboration. The site is designed to help K-12 teachers develop content for their classrooms on the Internet. When a teacher joins this effort, s/he can work alone or with others to develop Internet content for the classroom. The goal is to enrich the students' knowledge of different subjects. It is hoped that the students will be introduced to many different subject areas available to them on the Internet. Here are some of the activities available to teachers:

■ Collaboration Projects
These are projects intended to be started for teachers, by teachers. A teacher can join a group, start a group of his/her own, or just take advantage of the information (projects) available for teachers.

■ The K-12 Collaborative Toolkit
This activity is a type of storage unit. A teacher may store: (a) sites in a personal web Site Tracker; (b) lesson plans; (c) schedules and to-do lists; and (d) address books. Note: all lesson plans are intended to be created by teachers for private use or to be shared with others.

■ The K-12 Mailing List
This activity is a public mailing list. Teachers can send or receive e-mail to or from anyone on the common mailing list.

■ Discussion Forums
This activity is an on-line discussion or chat room.

Other sites available [from Okolo (2000)]:
■ Resource Village: A Place for Teachers: www.mmhschool.com
■ Education Place: http://www.eduplace.com
■ EdWeb: http://edweb.gsn.org

Source: http://www.k12connection.org/http://www.k12connection.org/

PART II

Curriculum

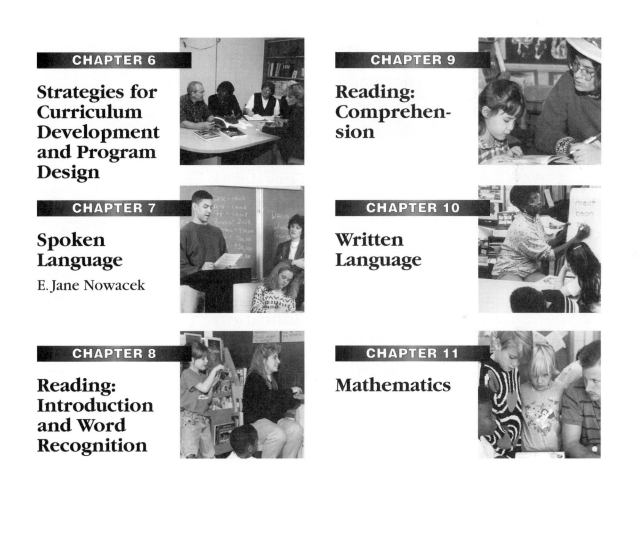

Strategies for Curriculum Development and Program Design

The most critical programming component for individuals with disabilities is the curriculum. Ultimately, regardless of teaching effectiveness and efficiency, questions related to the value of education must properly address the issue of what has been taught. This chapter presents an overview of the content of educational programs for learners with special needs.

It is helpful to begin by considering the various applications of the term *curriculum*. It can refer strictly to the courses taught in school or to a document that includes a design that others have developed and that a teacher implements in the classroom. Hoover and Patton (1997) refer to curriculum as planned and guided learning experiences under the direction of the school with intended educational outcomes. Armstrong (1990) defines it as a "master plan for selecting content and organizing learning experiences for the purpose of changing and developing learners' behaviors and insights" (p. 4).

The primary concern of the curriculum should be its functionality in meeting the needs of the individual student. For our purposes, curriculum functionality is defined as the degree to which the curriculum prepares students for the environments in which they will live and learn. At the same time, it is critical that careful attention be given to how a student's needs can be met within inclusive settings.

This chapter is based on the assumption that curriculum develops from basic considerations of program design and gains its value from the ways in which teachers apply these considerations. The chapter begins by discussing several major curricular considerations. Major program orientations are identified and evaluated for benefit to students with disabilities. The advantages and drawbacks of specific orientations are discussed both as background for subsequent chapters dealing with various content areas and to further delineate elements of program design. The last section of the chapter focuses on key factors that influence the decisions that are made regarding to curricular orientation.

BASIC CURRICULAR CONSIDERATIONS

This section focuses on important concepts that are helpful to understanding the curricular needs of students. The three topics covered include the various types of curricula that exist in schools, the impact that IDEA has had on curricular issues, and the need for providing curricula that are comprehensive in nature.

Curriculum Types

Hoover and Patton (1997) point out that fundamentally curriculum needs to be conceptualized on the basis of what is taught and what is not taught but should be. The three types of curricula that are frequently mentioned are explicit, hidden, and absent (Eisner, 1985; Schubert, 1993). These are defined below.

- *Explicit curriculum* refers to the formal and stated curriculum that teachers and students are expected to follow.
- *Hidden curriculum* refers to the actual curriculum implemented in the classroom.
- *Absent curriculum* refers to the curriculum that, for whatever reason, is not included in school.

The explicit curriculum can be found in a state's standards or in a school district's curriculum guides. This type of curriculum includes the specific goals and objectives for different subject areas across grade levels. With the increased attention to and pressure of state standards and school accountability, a heightened interest in ensuring that this content is covered pervades classroom instruction today.

The hidden curriculum is what students are exposed to on a daily basis. It is likely to include much of the explicit curriculum as well as lessons on topics other than those that are stated in curriculum guides. The hidden curriculum includes interpretations of the explicit curricula related to implementation procedures and the emphasis different explicit curriculum aspects receive. It also includes the insertion of content that the teacher chooses to cover, either by necessity based on student needs or by personal interest.

The absent curriculum represents content that is not covered. Sometimes this is because certain content is not part of the explicit curriculum. Other times, it is a choice made by teachers. Eisner (1985) noted that what teachers choose to exclude or not to teach may be just as important as what they elect to teach in their classrooms.

As Hoover and Patton (1997) stress, elements from all three types of curricula operate continually in classrooms, sometimes in complementary ways and other times in conflicting fashion.

Relationship to General Education Curriculum

The 1997 amendments to the Individuals with Disabilities Education Act (IDEA) provided a number of changes to the way that special education is conducted. One of the most notable changes was the emphasis that students with special needs must have access to the general education curriculum. This is reflected in the many instances on the IEP where the "access to the general education curriculum" issue arises.

It is safe to say that the general education curriculum is the explicit curriculum for the majority of students in the school. Thus, the thrust of special education is to ensure that students gain those skills and acquire the knowledge that will allow them to gain access to the curriculum afforded to general education students.

The curricular dilemma facing professionals in special education is finding the balance between providing the general education curriculum to students with special needs and providing a curriculum that meets their current and future needs. The next section and the remainder of this chapter explore this issue.

Comprehensive Curriculum

When educational programs are designed for students who are disabled, the importance of a comprehensive curriculum should be apparent because the primary goal is to develop an outcomes focus that is consistent with the diverse needs of these students. A comprehensive curriculum refers to a program of study that is guided by the reality that each student is in school on a time-limited basis; the real test of the value of the curriculum is how students fare once they exit the program. As a consequence, educators must consider what lies ahead for their students; this requires a perspective that is sensitive to the environments in which students will need to adapt and function in the future. Hence, curriculum design must foremost be governed by a "subsequent environments as an attitude" approach (Polloway, Patton, Smith, & Roderique, 1992). The central attributes of a comprehensive curriculum include

- responding to the needs of an individual student at the current time,
- accommodating the concurrent needs for maximum interaction with nondisabled peers, access to the general education curriculum, and attention to crucial curricular needs that are absent from the general education curriculum,
- developing from a realistic appraisal of potential adult outcomes of individual students,
- ensuring consistency with each individual's transitional needs across level of schooling and life span,
- remaining sensitive to graduation goals and specific diploma track requirements.

The importance of comprehensive curriculum at the secondary level is a common theme in special education in particular as well as in education in general. It has been articulated by many teachers in anecdotal reports and identified through studies of secondary special education settings (e.g., Halpern & Benz, 1987). It can also be inferred from discouraging national statistics on graduation, dropout, and employment rates and involvement in postsecondary programs for students with disabilities (e.g., Affleck, Edgar, Levine, & Kortering, 1990; U.S. Department of Education, 1994; Edgar, 1987; Edgar & Polloway, 1994; Neel, Meadows, Levine, & Edgar, 1988). The data that have been reported from follow-up and follow-along studies present the following picture.

- Many individuals who spend time in special education are not being prepared for the complex demands of adulthood.
- A large percentage of the students who have special needs do not find the school experience valuable and are dropping out.
- The educational programs of many students in special education do not meet their current academic, social, and emotional needs.
- The provision of continuing educational options for adults with special needs, including recruitment, ongoing support, specialized training, and follow-up services is warranted.

The recurring need that such statistics underscore is for relevant curricula that address the concerns and features listed above. However, although a careful analysis of secondary programs is essential, consideration of curricular design must begin at the elementary level in order to overcome the problems that otherwise may be recognized at the secondary or postsecondary level.

PROGRAM ORIENTATIONS

Curricular or program orientations have been defined differently by various professionals (Polloway et al, 1989; Vergason, 1983; Zigmond & Sansone, 1986). Most discussions have highlighted three general orientations: remedial, focusing on basic academic skills and social adjustment; maintenance, including tutorial approaches and training in the use of learning strategies and study skills; and functional, emphasizing vocational training and an adult outcomes orientation. However, because of the confusion that often arises from the use of these terms, a different organization, based on a model proposed by Bigge and Stump (1999), is emphasized in this chapter.

The program orientations discussed in this section include four general types:

- general education curriculum without supports/accommodations;
- general education curriculum with supports/ accommodations;

- specialized curriculum with a focus on academic/social skills development or remediation; and
- specialized curriculum with a focus on adult outcomes.

This organization is consistent with the distinctions made by Edgar and Polloway (1994) between support and content models. The former refer to models that seek to maintain students in the general education curriculum, with the most common intended outcome being preparation for postsecondary education whereas the latter provide differentiated curriculum to prepare for successful citizenship those individuals who are not planning to go to college.

General Education Curriculum without Supports/Accommodations

As Bigge and Stump note, this orientation simply refers to the curriculum that students with and without specific learning needs experience. It is the primary curriculum provided. It will be the curricular option of choice when students exit special education or, while still eligible for special education and related services, do not need any accommodations or supports while in general education settings.

A common concern is that with the trend toward increased school inclusion certain limited instructional support might be needed but will not be available for students. As a consequence, students may flounder, receive poor grades, and be at risk of dropping out. Nevertheless, having students functioning successfully in general education settings is clearly the goal for many students who receive special education services.

General Education Curriculum with Supports/Accommodations

This program orientation suggests that students with special needs are in general education classrooms where various accommodations are made and/or certain supports are provided. In reference to the former point, Bigge and Stump (1999) note that "attention is given to adapting or modifying the curriculum in ways that allow certain students with disabilities and special education needs to gain knowledge, skills, and understandings from it" (p. 57). In relation to the latter point, the concept of supported education is a vital one here.

Supported education is based on Hamre-Nietupski, McDonald, and Nietupski's 1992 suggestion that embedded in the concept of inclusion is the assumption that appropriate supports are being provided in the general education classroom.

Edgar and Polloway (1994) defined general education support models for secondary level students in the following way:

> Support models are most appropriate for adolescents who have a reasonable opportunity of attending and being successful in postsecondary academic and training settings. These are the students who have the interest and aptitude necessary for success at that level. . . . [They] generally are students with reading and writing skills above the sixth- or seventh-grade level, reasonable study skills, appropriate social skills to function in regular classrooms, and the desire to go on to higher education. Development of an appropriate preparatory curriculum for these students should become a primary focus during high school. Curricular foci should include maximum participation in regular high school programs, not only for generation of units toward a regular diploma, but also for attention to content necessary for college success. In general, because of the academic demands associated with college preparatory classes, regular class support such as cooperative teaching or other forms of collaboration is preferable to special education content instruction. For success in academic postsecondary programs, attention should also be given to transitional needs relevant to these settings, including intensive writing instruction, study, and college survival skills training skills (e.g., time management organizational skills and selection of major). (pp. 445–446)

Support models presume that students will profit from the curriculum offered in the general education classroom. Their goal is thus to enhance success in such classes. Whereas tutorial instruction has often been the most common means of providing support to students who experience difficulties, other program orientations offer more attractive alternatives to this challenge.

Cooperative Teaching. Cooperative teaching represents a very viable system of general education class support for students with disabilities as well as for other students who experience learning difficulties. Although cooperative teaching is certainly not content as such, the approach is clearly becoming increasingly popular. The principles of teacher collaboration on which it is based are discussed at some length in Chapter 5. It is sufficient to note here that cooperative teaching involves a team approach to supporting students within the inclusive classroom. It serves as an important alternative to the academic content model provided in special education settings (discussed later) by combining the content expertise of the classroom/subject teacher with certain pedagogical skills of the special education teachers.

Whereas the structure of a cooperative teaching model can be implemented in a variety of forms, it essentially involves special education teachers joining their students in general education classes for at least a portion of the instructional day. Wiedmeyer and Lehman (1991, pp. 7–8) outline key features of a collaborative instructional model, which (as adapted) include the following functions.

1. Collaborative teaching
   a. sharing in planning, presenting, and checking assignments
   b. curricular adaptation
   c. incorporation of general education input into IEPs for shared students
   d. participation in parent conferences
2. Monitoring students
   a. checking for attending behaviors
   b. checking for note-taking and documentation of assignments
   c. possible pullout during in-class study time, either in general education room or resource room
   d. supplementary note-taking
   e. checking for appropriate use of in-class study time

3. Developing units for general education teachers in social skills, problem-solving skills, or study skills
4. Sharing materials and expertise in programming
5. Developing materials at a lower level
6. Providing generalization opportunities and activities
7. Pulling out groups within the general education classroom whenever needed for initial or review teaching
8. Demonstrating special techniques and strategies

Bauwens and Hourcade (1994) have clearly identified alternative forms that cooperative teaching can take. These include team teaching, complementary instruction, and supportive learning activities.

Team teaching involves having the general and special education teachers jointly plan one lesson and teach it to students with disabilities as well as to those without disabilities. Sometimes each teacher may be responsible for one aspect of the teaching.

With *supportive learning activities,* the general and special educators plan and teach the lesson to the whole class. However, the general educator's responsibility might be to deliver the main content and the special educator might plan and implement activities that reinforce the learning of the content material.

The third option is *complementary instruction,* which typically involves having the general education teacher teach the core content while the special education teacher focuses on related instruction in areas such as social skills or learning strategies. These roles could obviously be reversed depending on the expertise of the two professionals. Figure 6–1 illustrates a plan for a cooperatively taught lesson using all three strategies.

Tutorial Assistance. Traditionally, one of the most common models in special education, especially in programs for adolescents with learning disabilities, has been tutorial assistance. Most commonly used within a resource model,

such a program seeks to maintain the student within the regular class curriculum.

There are several apparent reasons that tutorial models have been and continue to be popular in some schools and school divisions. Foremost is the motivational aspect tied to such an approach. Quite simply, students are interested in the supportive services that come with this model and that enable them to be more successful in the regular classroom. Perhaps, as a byproduct, regular class teachers and parents may also be frequent supporters of such an orientation, although research has not confirmed this perception (McKenzie, 1991c). To the extent that such an orientation is effective, tutoring may have positive implications for grades and for diploma requirements.

In spite of the possible benefits of such an approach and although all special education teachers engage in some tutoring, this orientation has a short-term emphasis and may be of little lasting value. Among the main disadvantages of such an orientation are the following:

- valid concerns about whether the material taught and learned is relevant to the needs of the students
- concern about whether the instruction is responsive to an individual student's long-term needs
- possible undertraining of special education teachers, who are asked to provide tutorial assistance across a wide range of subjects
- possible overtraining because tutoring frequently requires little advanced training and can often be handled by a paraeducators

The tutorial orientation's heavy emphasis on short-term outcomes is responsible for its major advantages as well as its numerous disadvantages. Teachers working with students who require some tutorial support should investigate the possibilities of involving peers, paraeducators, and classroom volunteers in the process.

Paraeducators. An option for supporting students in inclusive settings used in schools today is the paraeduator support model. In this

FIGURE 6–1

Variations of cooperative
teaching in lesson plan

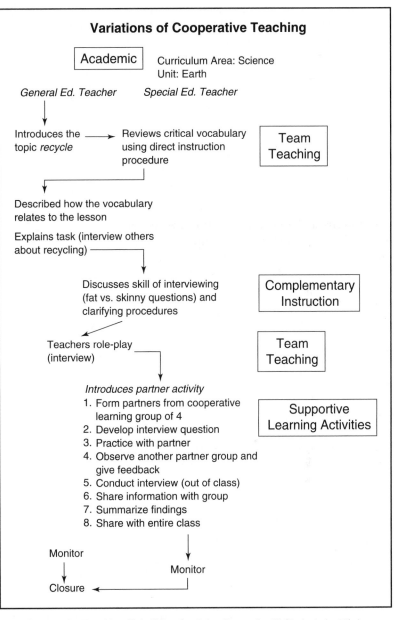

From *Cooperative Teaching: Rebuilding the Schoolhouse for All Students* (p. 66), by
J. C. Bauwens and J. J. Hourcade, 1994, Austin, TX: PRO-ED. Copyright 1994 by
PRO-ED, Inc. Reprinted with permission.

arrangement, paraeducators (educational aides, teaching assistants) accompany students with special needs into the general education settings where they may perform various duties, many of which are tutorial in nature. (See Ch.5.)

Pickett and Gerlach (1997) suggest that special education personnel learn how to work paraeducators. As the authors point out, the roles and responsibilities of teachers are changing such that they are increasingly becoming front-line managers responsible for supervising para-educators. They stress the notion that teachers and paraeducators are part of a team and both parties must learn how to function as team members in providing appropriate services to students in inclusive settings.

Natural Supports. Much emphasis in the transition/employment literature has been given to the role of natural supports in helping individuals be successful in the workplace. The concept of "natural supports" applies equally as well to the classroom setting. Bigge and Stump (1999) suggest that planning for the use of peers as natural supports provides a way of addressing student needs and IEP goals in inclusive settings.

Accommodations to Content, Materials, and Instruction. As discussed in Chapters 4 and 5, numerous accommodations can be made to better meet the needs of students with special needs. Most of the accommodations discussed previously have been designed for use in inclusive settings. This section will focus on three major accommodative practices that, when used, contribute to supporting students in general education.

Two of the practices (learning strategies, study skills) involve content modifications. For students to be successful, additional content (i.e., hidden curriculum) must be covered. The third practice (academic content mastery) primarily focuses on the use of alternative curricular materials to achieve access to the general education curriculum.

Learning Strategies. A learning strategies approach teaches students to learn how to learn rather than having them acquire specific skills. Thus it focuses on the development of independence. It utilizes a cognitive orientation, stressing ways that students can use their abilities and knowledge to acquire new information. As defined by Weinstein and Mayer (1986), learning strategies are "behaviors and thoughts that a learner engages in during learning and that are intended to influence the learner's encoding process" (p. 315). The learning strategies approach

goes beyond the special education environment and stresses maximum successful progress in the general education classroom. Specific strategies can be effective in enhancing, for example, reading comprehension, test taking, problem solving, word analysis, proofreading, and note-taking.

A learning strategies approach is particularly appropriate when a major instructional objective for a given student is generalization of skills to the general classroom or to a postsecondary environment. Within the schools, a major focus of the approach is thus necessarily the importance of cooperation between special and general education teachers. Alley and Deshler (1979) identify the characteristics of students who appear to benefit most from a learning strategies approach:

- reading achievement above a third-grade level,
- ability to deal with symbolic as well as concrete learning tasks,
- demonstration of at least average intellectual ability

However, they further note that these conditions are neither all necessary nor is this necessarily an exhaustive list. Clearly, components of a learning strategies approach can be effective for individuals beyond this defined population. It is sufficient to note that different programs can modify their target populations as they define their foci (Locke & Abbey, 1989).

A methodology for teaching learning strategies has been developed for this curricular model. As described by Deshler, Ellis, and Lenz (1996), the process includes eight steps.

1. Pretest the strategy to be taught and obtain a commitment from the student to learn.
2. Describe the particular strategy to be taught.
3. Model the use of the strategy.
4. Engage the student in the verbal elaboration and rehearsal of the strategy.
5. Provide practice in the application of the strategy in controlled materials (e.g., reading materials at the instructional level of the student).
6. Provide advanced practice in the application of the strategy in content materials (e.g., the regular science textbook) and provide feedback.

7. Confirm acquisition and obtain the student's commitment to generalize the strategy.
8. Achieve generalization through four phases:
   a. orientation as to where it can be applied
   b. activation of the strategy by moving from explicit to less explicit instructions and assignment
   c. adaptation through understanding the strategy and being able to make changes to meet different setting demands
   d. strategy maintenance over time

An illustrative example is the learning strategy for skimming assignments for study purposes called the *Multipass program* (Schumaker, Deshler, Alley, & Denton, 1982). It includes the following components:

■ *Survey*: look for main ideas, chapter organization (title, introductory paragraph(s), subtitles, summary paragraphs, etc.)
■ *Size up*: gain specific information (read questions, look for textual cues, self-question, skim, paraphrase, review)
■ *Sort out*: answer all chapter questions

Additional information on strategies and related cognitive interventions has been developed and/or summarized by Hoover and Patton (1995) and Rooney (1988). Figure 6–2 illustrates another strategy. Strategies specifically relevant to study skills are further discussed in Chapter 14.

The learning strategies approach is an effective way for students to use strategic behaviors in inclusive settings, especially for middle and high school students. However, there are certain considerations to attend to when evaluating the possible adoption of such an approach as a major part of the curriculum. First, if used exclusively, such a model can result in limited attention to other curricular needs, such as life skills. Second, careful attention should be given to the appeal of the particular strategy being taught. Motivating some students to learn a strategy that affords long-term benefits may be difficult. This approach's emphasis on transfer of learning, self-instruction, and independence recommends its use with students beyond the specific target population. Finally, the efficacy of various learning strategies must be judged in part by how well they can be generalized because a prime objective of this model is to foster transfer across content subjects and, to a lesser extent, to nonschool settings (Lovitt, Fister, & Kemp, 1988). This concern, however, could be voiced about virtually all other curricula as well. Thus, an emphasis on explicit training in the use of learning strategies seems to be very appropriate for students who have limited academic skills (Weinstein & Mayer, 1986).

Study Skills. Study skills are those skills that students employ to acquire, record, remember, and use information efficiently. Although a generally agreed upon list of study skills does not exist, a common set of skills can be identified. All students need to possess an array of study skills if they are to be successful in the general education curriculum. This topic is so important that an entire chapter is dedicated to discussion of study skills (see Chapter 13).

FIGURE 6–2
A strategy for attacking word problems

SAY the problem to yourself (repeat)
OMIT any unnecessary information from the problem
LISTEN for key vocabulary indicators
VOCABULARY Change vocabulary to math concepts
EQUATION Translate problem into a math equation

INDICATE the answer
TRANSLATE the answer back into the context of the word problem

The major study skills identified by Hoover and Patton (1995) include: reading rate, listening, notetaking/outlining, report writing, oral presentations, graphic aids, test taking, library usage, reference material usage, time management, and self-management. Although a subset of reference material usage, Internet usage should be elevated to a major category.

Study skills must be taught directly to many students who have special needs. A sequence for covering these important topics is depicted in Figure 6–3. As can be seen, these skills should be introduced at the elementary level and refined as the student moves through grade levels.

Academic Content Mastery. It is common at the secondary school level to rely on special education teachers to cover the general education curriculum (i.e., academic content model) within special education classrooms (McKenzie, 1991a,c). For example, McKenzie (1991a) reports that, in the 29 states that indicated the use of this model at the secondary level, 50% of academic content was taught by special education teachers, with an estimated 19% of students with disabilities receiving all their content instruction from these teachers. Two sample models can be identified within this orientation. The following discussion briefly outlines ways that these models have been put into practice.

The *replicated content* model refers to the teaching of the same subjects and skills in the special education setting as in the regular classroom. Further, these skills are taught using essentially the same instructional materials (e.g., content texts).

The *modified* model, on the other hand, more loosely follows the content, scope, and sequence of the general education curriculum. The curricular content typically includes selected topics that correspond to the general education curriculum. However, these topics are selected on the basis of some assumption of relevance to and potential success for learning by the students in the special education programs. Curricular materials may include high-interest-low-vocabulary texts and/or workbooks such as those published by companies that specialize in this area (e.g., Globe/Janus/Fearon). Depending on program design and intent,

FIGURE 6–3
Continuum of study skills as lifelong skills

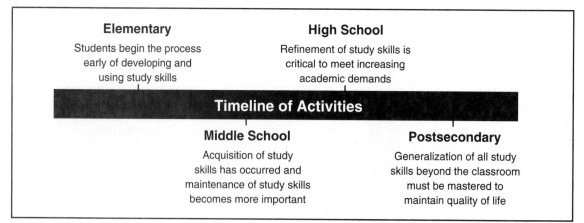

Source: Hoover, J. J., & Patton, J. R. (1995). *Teaching students with learning problems to use study skills: A teacher's guide.* Austin: Pro-Ed.

the classes may be provided either with or without graduation credits.

The rationale for the special-education-based approach to covering the general education curriculum lies in the fact that content instruction should be similar to that of their peers, as emphasized in the 1997 amendments of IDEA. When most successful, this model provides opportunities for students to eventually receive this instruction in inclusive settings. However, sometimes this program option results in a contemporary equivalent of the "watered-down curriculum."

Several key issues must be addressed when adoption of this orientation is being entertained. First and most critical is the functionality of the content for students' needs. Second, segregating students with special needs from their peers while giving them comparable content must be questioned, especially when this approach is compared to the general education support/ accommodation options described above. A third key concern is the competence of the special education teacher to deliver the academic content, particularly in the upper middle and secondary schools. The apparent lack of preservice and inservice preparation for special educators in science and social studies, for example (Patton, Polloway, & Cronin, 1987, 1994), emphasizes the absence of a strong training foundation for the provision of instruction. The teacher's competence to provide content area instructional strategies also must be considered (Putnam & Wesson, 1990).

McKenzie's (1991c) research suggests that (a) teachers associated with an academic content model (in contrast to those using a basic skills model, discussed in the next section) were perceived as less effective by parents and general education teachers; (b) general education teachers were less willing to include students who had been in this type of program; (c) students were less often accepted and less frequently involved in school activities. Finally, some accommodative features of such programs run the risk of causing a "serious lack of substance in the academic experiences . . . provided for students" (Zigmond & Miller, 1991, pp. 15).

Special Education Curriculum with a Focus on Academic and Social Skill Development and Remediation

The majority of students with special needs have historically received services in special education settings outside of general education classrooms. Since the 1980s, however, relatively few of these students have spent their entire instructional day in special education. Usually these students would be with special education teachers for specialized instruction in reading, language arts, and mathematics. In some instances instruction was targeted to social goals. This section describes two common curricular orientations found in special education classes.

Basic Skills. Unquestionably, the most common model for special education curricula has been and continues to be the remedial, basic skills orientation. Such a model presumes that the major attention of instruction should focus on developing academic skills. Therefore, intensive programming in reading, mathematics, and language provides the core of the instructional program. Clearly, a basic skills orientation addresses academic deficits and emphasizes apparent student needs.

A basic skills model is typically the focus of most elementary curricula for students with disabilities. Reviews of student IEPs suggest that middle school programs are also often primarily academic/remedial in focus (McBride & Forgnone, 1985), perhaps with the exception of programs for students with behavioral disorders (Smith, 1990a; Epstein, Patton, Polloway, & Foley, 1992). This orientation has a long-term outlook, based on the assumption that direct instruction of academic skills will ultimately increase academic achievement, may enable students to reach literacy level, and will allow them to spend more time in inclusive educational settings.

Few doubt that an academic focus is a necessary component of the curriculum for students who are mildly or moderately disabled or who have remedial needs; therefore, there is little reason to debate the merit of this orientation in the simple sense. The particular advantages of a remedial model are that it focuses on students' specific deficits, offers an intensive option to regular class programs, and can assist in increasing literacy, thus potentially benefiting the individual in both school and extra-school learning tasks (Alley & Deshler, 1979; Wiederholt & McNutt, 1979).

However, several notable difficulties are associated with a basic skills approach. First, such an orientation may neglect the specific strengths of students and may reinforce their sense of failure by continuing to focus on areas of difficulty. Second, although the special education setting may be able to provide intensive interventions such as in the area of reading (e.g., Slingerland, Wilson, Alphabetic Phonics), far too often the interventions that are offered are not intensive. Third, such an approach may fail to address issues of transfer, whether to the regular class setting or to postsecondary environments. Finally, there has been a relative lack of curricular programs appropriate for use with students at the secondary level. Therefore, continued reliance on a basic skills model with adolescent learners has been questioned (e.g., Deshler, Schumaker, Lenz, & Ellis, 1984).

Despite these difficulties, however, teachers should consider the proven effectiveness of individual programs. For instance, positive findings of the effectiveness of the *Corrective Reading Program* (CRP) (Gregory, Hackney, & Gregory, 1982; Polloway, Epstein, Polloway, Patton, & Ball, 1986; Thorne, 1978) with adolescents reinforce the observation made by Meyen and Lehr (1980) that a large number of adolescents can profit from academic remediation if exposed to intensive instructional programs. They characterized intensive instruction as possessing these attributes:

■ consistency and duration of time on task;
■ timing, frequency, and nature of feedback based on the student's immediate performance and cumulative progress;
■ regular and frequent communication by the teacher to the student of his or her expectation that this student will master the task and demonstrate continuous progress; and

■ pattern of pupil-teacher interaction in which the teacher responds to student initiatives and uses consequences appropriate to the responses of the student. (p. 23)

Careful consideration of the possible benefits and limitations of the basic skills model is important as the program design proceeds. Certainly, adoption of the academic remedial model alone requires caution. Because the underlying premise of remediation is cure, this model is unlikely to succeed totally with most students who have disabilities. At some point educators must shift the curriculum to achieve maximum independent functioning beyond the school setting.

Social Skills. The second model is characterized by an emphasis on social competence, typically recognized as critical to life adjustment (Epstein & Cullinan, 1987). It has been classified as a remedial model simply to indicate that it also represents a deficit view of the characteristics of individual students. A social adjustment orientation is rarely used as the sole focus of curricular efforts except in some instances in programs for students identified as emotionally and behaviorally disordered (Masters & Mori, 1986) where IEPs reflect such an emphasis (Epstein et al.,1992; Smith, 1990a,b). Three general, interrelated approaches may be associated with this model: social skills acquisition, behavior change, and an affective emphasis.

One potentially significant benefit of training in the social arena is its contribution to the successful inclusion of students with special needs into general education classrooms. Gresham's (1982, 1983) reviews of efforts in this area clearly present a strong case for requiring systematic social skills training as a key element of such efforts. In order to achieve successful inclusion via social adjustment, programs must respond to two major considerations. First, any program claiming a social adjustment orientation as a primary focus should be accountable for meaningful change. Too often, special education, especially in the form of affective education, has been neither special nor educational, showing little evidence of documented change in skills and/or behavior. As

Epstein and Cullinan (1987) note, the effectiveness of most commercial social skills curricula remains largely unknown. A second area of concern is the generalizability of the programs selected. To justify its use, a program must be able to demonstrate that it can contribute to a student's success in subsequent environments, a criterion that should be a central consideration in adoption decisions. Cognitive approaches to behavior change and social skills acquisition present a particularly beneficial option. Such self-management approaches were introduced in Chapter 3.

Emphasis on social facets of curriculum cuts across all functioning levels and age ranges. Teachers can safely assume that many children and adolescents who are mildly or moderately disabled need some instruction in this area. Chapter 3 discusses specific instructional approaches that can be used to teach social skills.

Specialized Curriculum with Focus on Adult Outcomes

The two "adult outcomes" models are interrelated but have been separated because some of their features are discrete. Both models are discussed briefly here and in significantly greater detail in Chapter 16. In addition, a third option, apprenticeship programs, is also discussed.

Life Skills. This adult outcomes orientation emphasizes a comprehensive life demands view of the postsecondary adjustment process. Although life skills curricula tend to include occupational/employment considerations, they focus less intensively on vocational training. These types of curricula are typically more responsive to varied concerns derived from the literature on adult adjustment and thus on the demands of adulthood (Cronin & Patton, 1993). As such, the model can never be seen as distinctly separate from social adjustment and vocational training. Although the concern for life skills instruction is here related to students with disabilities and not just for students with mental retardation, Clark, Field, Patton, Brolin, and Sitlington (1994) argue for its importance for all students. They note:

Students with disabilities are especially in need of life skills instruction in light of the predominance of evidence that indicates, for whatever reasons, a large percentage of them find adult living demands outside their skill range. The fact remains, there are other students within the educational system who find adult demands just as difficult when they leave school and have similar problems of adjustment—socially, vocationally, and in independent living. A life skills instruction approach should be a part of (i.e., included within existing coursework) or a recognized and approved option to (i.e., alternative coursework) every school curriculum for all students at all grade levels. Only then can all students and their families have the opportunity to make life-related decisions with regard to individual educational outcomes they view as important.

A life skills emphasis implies a top-down orientation to curricular development, that is, a focus looking down from the demands of adulthood. Bigge and Stump (1999) suggest that the major components of life skills curricula include: functional academics (e.g., money management); daily and community living skills (e.g., health, civic and social responsibilities, leisure skills, social skills, self-determination); and transition-related skills. Such a program is intended to be indexed against the realities of the community in which an individual will be living and thus clearly focuses on key transitional areas (Patton & Dunn, 1998).

A variety of approaches can be used to increase a life skills emphasis within the curriculum. As identified by Cronin and Patton (1993), these include (from least to most extensive) the infusion of life skills topics into existing course content, the dedication of portions of existing classes to real-life topics, and the creation of life skills coursework; these options are discussed further in Chapter 16.

Students who have been experiencing chronic difficulty in school may be inherently interested in a curriculum that radically shifts attention away from academic deficits and toward future learning and skill needs. Thus, an approach emphasizing life skills is frequently more attractive to adolescents and may have positive motivational consequences. For individuals with more significant cognitive disabilities, the importance of such a focus becomes even clearer.

A major caution relates to the nature of the program itself. Haphazard attention to life skills may provide little content of either immediate or long-term value; in addition, what constitutes community survival skills is subject to interpretation.

Both the vocational (discussed in the next section) and life skills orientations are consistent with the need to provide career education to students who are disabled. To appreciate the way that career education can be implemented across age levels, the reader is referred to Chapter 13.

Vocational Training. Vocational training, whether delivered through general vocational classes or through special vocational classes, has traditionally been associated with secondary programming for students with mild retardation. The classic work on this orientation is Kolstoe and Frey's 1965 work-study program for students identified as mildly retarded. More recently, a vocational emphasis has been considered for students identified as learning disabled or behaviorally disordered, as an alternative to the regular core curriculum at the high school level.

The obvious advantage of vocational training programs is that they are clearly related to transitional efforts undertaken to prepare adolescents for postsecondary environments. This relevance to adult settings is a major factor in the area of motivation. Enrollment in a vocational program may keep many students from dropping out of school—an important consideration, given recent data indicating that the dropout rate for students with special needs is significant.

When one considers vocational training programs, it is important to distinguish between general education programs in which students with special needs are included and separate vocational/special education programs. Edgar and Polloway (1994), based on the work of Gill and Edgar (1990), discuss an example of the former in the Pierce County Cooperative. This program includes students with disabilities in an inclusive vocational setting. Specifically:

Vocational and special education teachers form teams to develop collaborative programs for youth with definite occupational interests and with the academic and social skills necessary to function in a regular vocational program with reasonable accommodations. Special education provides support services to assist with reading technical manuals or acquiring the math skills to perform specific tasks or practice in a specific content area. The students must be able to compete with their nondisabled peers in order to participate in this program. The students must also take a sequence of courses that result in a set of skills valued by adult society [and] that lead directly to a postsecondary vocational training program. Students complete the regular high school credit requirements to graduate as well as the vocational courses, and graduates of this program have had a high rate of successfully attending and completing postsecondary education programs (p. 447).

Two recent trends are worthy of note. First, there is a significant need for community-based learning opportunities as an alternative or at least a complement to simulated vocational opportunities within a school setting. Community-based instruction moves education beyond the school so that specific skills can be taught *in situ*. The implications for generalization and realistic job training are obvious. Second, an encouraging trend in vocational training is the use of supported employment. Basically a job-coach approach, supported employment places individuals on the job and provides them with assistance that is gradually faded out over time. For example, an individual may be placed at a fast food outlet for a work opportunity, with support provided as necessary on the job.

The advantages of a vocational orientation are apparent. It provides specific training in skills for life beyond the school setting, adds relevance and motivation to the curriculum, and shifts the focus away from past failure in academic domains. The model clearly emphasizes training in skills relevant to adult outcomes and participation is associated with a significant decrease in school dropout rates.

Several possible concerns with vocational training also must be considered, however. These include students becoming locked into a vocational track early in their secondary school program with little chance of pursuing other options as they emerge. In some school settings, a limited number of vocational training options are available. Some vocational training programs focus on job skill development in areas that have limited community validity. Far too often, there is an absence of congruence between vocational assessment and instructional planning and instruction. Finally, exclusion of students with disabilities from general vocational education programs is a common problem. Although these possible concerns can be overcome, they nevertheless present significant issues to be addressed.

Apprenticeship. A third alternative[1] that has an adult outcomes emphasis focuses on an apprenticeship approach to training. It has an obvious relationship to the two models previously mentioned and is presented here as an additional alternative to consider. Figure 6–4 illustrates one such local program.

Edgar and Polloway (1994) emphasize three components in an apprenticeship and citizenship program. First, the curriculum option must be socially valued by the community (i.e., students, parents, teachers, administrative staff, peers, the community at large). These diverse constituencies must be included in planning and implementation.

Second, the curriculum must address outcomes that are valued by the larger community and that will provide the students with skills and attitudes that will enable them to be viewed as competent citizens. Desired outcomes include process skills (e.g., collecting and synthesizing information, making decisions, working in groups), knowledge of facts relevant to the community (e.g., cultural factors, geography, politics, local attitudes and values), possession of occupationally relevant information (e.g., the inner workings of a wide variety of jobs, employer-employee relationships, economic issues such as benefits, job security, and advancement), acceptable attitudes (e.g., on gender and multicultural issues, work ethic, honesty, de-

---

[1] This section is adapted from Edgar and Polloway (1994, p. 449-450) and used with permission.

FIGURE 6–4
Local apprenticeship program

To business and industry desperately seeking better qualified employees to fill what highly technical demands of modern industry, Campbell County Schools' Student Apprenticeship Training Program must look like a dream come true. Now in its third year, the program offers 14 apprenticeable occupations for students who qualify according to age, grades, recommendation by school officials, and an agreement to work hard at all competencies set by the employers.

Student apprentices earn high school credits and receive wages while learning on the job. They attend a half day schedule of classes at their home school as well as regular weekly instruction at the vocational technical center that integrates classwork with the job-related training.

The major objective of the program is to expand the skilled work force by providing students with career opportunities in skilled and technical trades while competing their high school education.

Industry seems willing to shoulder the extra responsibility involved in the apprenticeship program. "We can't have a program without employers to hire the students," Richard Edwards said. "When a company agrees to accept an apprentice, they are agreeing to a great deal of extra work." The employer must draw up a detailed plan for the student with required processes or a job description.

The apprenticeship program is a component of Tech Prep, which aims to improve high school technical instruction by integrating academic and occupational courses. Students completing the four-year apprenticeship receive a certificate of completion that is recognized by industries throughout the nation.

From *The Campbell Communicator, 9* (1), pp. 1, 3. Used/reprinted with permission.

pendability, volunteerism, being a responsible citizen, individual rights), and other skills (e.g., reading, math, writing, computer skills, independent living skills such as renting, using transportation, and healthy behaviors, specific job skills).

Third, the curriculum must address the instructional methods that will be used to achieve the desired outcomes. Examples of instructional methods include an integrated, activity-based learning model as the core; portfolio measurement to evaluate performance; and learning within a community context (i.e., learning that is directly related to the community). Student learning differences are recognized and celebrated. An emphasis is placed on cooperative learning activities (e.g., students work in groups, share in the work, process conflict and equity issues).

The issue of social acceptance in the school environment and the larger community can be addressed through systematic inclusion of the students in the social life of the school both through participation in extracurricular activities and through formal affiliation with local community-based social and/or recreational organizations. Interaction is addressed in relation to real events and activities that are of interest and importance to the individual.

Rather than being "second-choice options" to the academic program provided in general education, these alternative programs should be considered superior for certain students insofar as they develop citizenship values, attitudes, skills, and self-esteem and self-confidence. This model serves as an option for such students who may feel devalued by the current system and exit the system without the values and skills needed to improve our society.

PROGRAM DECISION MAKING

The alternative program models presented in this chapter do not represent mutually exclusive approaches. Rather, they reflect available general models that should be used based on the the best fit of student needs and program features. In reality, most educational programs include more than one of these models. A number of key issues related to program choice is noteworthy for determining the most desirable educational programs for students with special needs.

Program Orientation and Service Delivery

One initial concern is the correlation of program model and service delivery alternatives. Some

models (e.g., the learning strategies approach) work particularly well in general education, often with resource room support. Others (e.g., vocational training) demand more extensive curricular modification from the traditional academic focus of the general education classroom. Thus they would generally be associated with special education or alternative general education programs. Placement, however, should not dictate curricular needs. Instead, program decisions must be based on student needs and the needed knowledge acquisition and skill development should be part of whatever service delivery option that is chosen.

Clark et al. (1994) discuss this issue when they note in reference to life skills instruction that:

> the potential benefits of inclusive education are the stripping away of stigma, the building of self-esteem, and the developing of social skills and interpersonal relationships within an inclusive environment. Given this, the first consideration for where life skills should be taught should be general education settings and the community. Like any other instructional content area, it should be assumed that unless the student is unable to learn the needed life skills within an inclusive, general education setting, even with every provision of support and reasonable accommodations, no move to separate the student from his or her peers should be made. (p. 5).

At the same time, these authors also express caution:

> When the individual life skill needs of students with disabilities vary significantly from those of other students in general education, and after accommodations for their needs have been provided, meeting their needs in an alternative fashion becomes a critical responsibility and should not be compromised. A clear commitment to a life skills approach in both general and special education is an appropriate long-term goal for achieving both curriculum and inclusive education goals for students with special needs (p. 11).

Categorical versus Noncategorical Programming

A second issue relates to the question of categorical versus noncategorical programming. Matching a program model or models to traditional categories of exceptionality represents an inappropriate practice that reflects the problematic nature of common labeling systems (Hallahan & Kauffman, 1977; Smith, Price, & Marsh, 1986). For example, the simple presumption that students with mild retardation cannot profit from remediation may prove to be just as invalid as the presumption that students with learning disabilities need primarily remedial programming across age levels and should not be exposed to life skills topics.

Nevertheless, total disregard for area of exceptionality can cause problems, not so much because some cross-categorical differences have been empirically determined (e.g., Cullinan & Epstein, 1985; Edgar, 1987; Parmer, Cawley, & Miller, 1994; Polloway et al., 1986; Polloway & Smith, 1988) but rather more significantly, because the abolition of categorical groupings may give rise to an assumption that a differentiated curriculum is unnecessary. Curricular needs become most clear when attention is paid to subgroups identified by curricular needs across the respective areas of exceptionality. Focusing on identifiable subgroups can appropriately shift the emphasis from categorical labels to relevant programming. At the same time, a correction in course can be applied to categorically oriented programs that attempt to coincidentally meet students' diverse curricular needs. For example, it can be argued that the "homogeneous" grouping of all secondary students with learning disabilities in one program or one class is analogous to a "one-room school house" in terms of the challenge of meeting the students' variant curricular needs. The reason for this is because individuals may be planning quite divergent paths after high school (e.g., employment, trade/ technical school, 2-year or 4-year college).

Level of Schooling

A third factor in curricular decision making is level of schooling. Few question spending the majority of time in elementary programs on the development of basic skills and remediation of problematic areas through intensive instruction to maximize students' academic achievement. During the elementary years, social adjustment and early career preparation efforts, for example, can complement the academic core of the curriculum.

As students reach their middle and high school years, however, teachers must carefully rethink the focus of programmatic efforts. Academic instruction for those not bound for postsecondary education must be functional and thus must shift to a more practical, applied orientation. Halpern and Benz (1987) report that secondary teachers indicated the greatest need they have is for low-level, age-appropriate curricula in basic skills and for functional curricula in independent living and vocational areas. A shift in curricular focus is clearly important in light of the discouraging data on school dropouts and employment rates among students with disabilities (e.g., Affleck et al., 1990; Edgar, 1987; U.S. Department of Education, 1995) discussed earlier in the chapter.

With the new transition mandates of the 1997 amendments to IDEA, schools now must consider a student's course of study prior to the high school years. All students who qualify for special education must have a statement of transition needs as part of their IEP by age 14. The clear intent of this provision is to determine what type of programs will be best suited for the student during the transition years of school.

Transition Concerns

A fourth important curricular consideration is the inclusion of a transition focus across all levels of schooling. Although this emphasis is widely accepted vis-à-vis the transition from secondary school to the community, other transitions are also of significance. For example, transitions into and out of middle school receive far less attention and yet are vital to a student's development. Table 6–1 provides a set of illustrative activities for these two respective transitions.

TABLE 6–1

Elementary to middle and middle to high school transitions

More Common Activities	Transition to:	
	Middle Grades	**High School**
Elementary school **students** visit middle grades or middle grades students visit high school for an information session or assembly	53%	52%
Middle grades and elementary **administrators** or middle and high school administrators meet together on articulation and programs	46%	48%
Middle grades **counselors** meet with elementary or high school counselors or staff	44%	52%
Some practices that are more time-consuming, difficult to arrange, or costly are less frequently used. Fewer than 40% of the principals use these transitional practices:		

Less Common Activities	Transition to:	
	Middle Grades	**High School**
Parents visit middle grades school or high school for orientation in the fall after their children have entered	39%	31%
Middle grades and elementary **teachers** or middle and high school teachers meet together about courses and requirements	37%	35%
Parents visit middle grades school or high school while children are in the lower grade schools	34%	39%
Middle grades **students** present information at elementary schools or high school students present information at middle grades school	30%	36%
Elementary school **students** attend regular classes at middle grades school or middle grades students attend classes at high school	20%	16%
Summer meetings for **students** at the middle grades school or at high school	16%	13%
Buddy or big brother/big sister program pairs new **students** with older ones on entry	9%	4%

Note. From *Education in the Middle Grades: National Practices and Trends* (p. 49), by J. L. Epstein and D. J. MacIver, 1990, Washington, DC: National Middle School Association. Copyright 1990 by the National Middle School Association. Reprinted with permission.

Graduation Issues

A fifth concern is the question of diploma status at graduation. Particularly in states with minimum competency or other high-stakes testing, curriculum may need to provide students with the training necessary to succeed on competency tests and thus receive their diplomas. The 1997 amendments to IDEA require statements in students' IEPs indicating the participation in various high-stakes testing and what accommodations are warranted for students to participate (see Bryant, Patton, & Vaughn, 2000).

Students' incentive to receive a diploma and employers' positive response to it often make efforts to obtain it appear more important than acquisition of skills with more direct relevance to postschool adjustment (Cohen, Safran, & Polloway, 1980). Hence, schools are faced again with trying to achieve the balance between students' ultimate needs via appropriate programs and what may be required as policy.

Cross-Curricular Integration

Finally, it is important to consider ways that program design can accommodate cross-curricular integration. Since the previous discussion has tended to view content areas as discrete concerns, we shift our focus now to the development of integrated curricula. The principal idea of this type of programming is a closer relationship among different subject and skill areas (Kataoka & Patton, 1989). As Friedman (1994, p. 11) notes, integrated curricula "find common themes and then coordinate the teaching of related facts, concepts and skills."

Integrated curricula are particularly appropriate for students with disabilities. As Oyama (1986) points out, "Curricular integration appears appropriate for special learners since it provides numerous opportunities through related activities for basic skill reinforcement and extension" (p. 15). Integrated approaches to curriculum also provide a potentially effective vehicle for inclusive programs.

Although it is possible to design an entire curriculum around a broad-based theme, most integrative efforts are less extensive. Kataoka and Patton (1989) illustrate an integrated approach to a science theme (Table 6-2) and Oyama (1986) illustrates how integrative efforts can be worked into a basal reading series (Table 6-3). Cawley (1984) provides numerous examples of ways to integrate mathematics into a general curriculum. One suggestion is to adapt reading passages to include various quantifying statements that can then be used to generate sets of math-related questions. The advantage of this technique is that it capitalizes on material that the student has already read. Finally, one other important option is the infusion of life skills and transition education into integrated curricula.

In addition to these key issues, numerous more specific factors should be considered during the program decision-making process. Based on the initial work of Dangel (1981), as expanded upon by Vergason (1983), the critical variables listed in Table 6-4 should be considered in determining the correct curricular approach for an individual student or group of students. The final evaluation is simple: programs provided to students who are eligible for special education must be driven by student needs and not by what is available.

SUMMARY

In the mid-1900s, Richard Hungerford, an influential special educator, provided an appropriate perspective on programming for students who are disabled. He proposed the three Rs of a special education curriculum: relatedness, reality, and responsibility (Blatt, 1987). Each of these concepts has merit in our efforts to evaluate the needs of students, compare and contrast the curricular alternatives, and design an appropriate program that will prepare students who are disabled for success in subsequent environments. This chapter has focused on important curricular considerations, identifying alternative program options in general education and special education, and examining key issues related to program decision-making.

TABLE 6–2

Integrated curriculum matrix theme: interdependence and ants

Science Subtopics	Science Activities	Related Subject/Skill Areas					
		Math	Social Studies	Arts	Computer Application	Life Skills	Language Arts
Introductory Lesson	• Attraction of ants • Collection • Observation • Research ant anatomy	• Measurement of distance traveled as a function of time	• Relationship of population demographics for ants and humans	• Drawings of ant anatomy • Ant mobiles • Creative exploration	• Graphic drawings of ants	• Picnic planning • Food storage protection	• Oral sharing of observations
Ant Farms	• Individual setups • Daily observation • Development of collection procedures	• Linear measurement • Frequency counts	• Roles in the community • Relationship to human situations	• Diagram of farm • Diorama • Ant models • Role playing of ant behavior	• Spreadsheets for calculations • Graphing • Data-base storing observations	• Relate to engineers, architects, sociologists, geographers	• Library skills • Creative writing • Spelling • Research involving note taking, outlining, and reading
Food Preference Chart	• Research and predict • Construct apparatus for determining preference • Design data collection procedures • Collect/record data • Experiment with food substance positions	• Frequency counts • Graphs of daily results	• Discussion of human food preferences • Cultural differences	• Design data collection forms • Role-playing ant eating behavior		• Graphic designer • Food services • Researchers	• Vocabulary development • Oral reports
Ant Races	• Conduct races with and without food • Data collection • Predictive activities	• Temporal measurement • Averages	• History of racing • Sports and competition	• Film making • Rewrite lyrics to "The Ants Go Marching In" based on activities	• Graphic animation	• Athletics • Coaches	
Closing	• Analyze information	• Tabulate data		• Finalize visual aids	• Print out	• Guest speakers	• Presentation

Note. From "Teaching Exceptional Learners: An Integrated Approach," by J. C. Kataoka and J. R. Patton, 1989, September, *Science and Children, 16,* p. 54. Copyright 1989 by National Science Teachers Association. Reprinted with permission.

TABLE 6–3
Example of an integrated curriculum theme: friendship between people and animals

Reading Topic	Language Arts	Math	Science
Robing and the Sled Dog Race (A girl overcomes her desire to win an Alaskan dog race because of her concern for another racer.)	Discussion on value of friendship versus importance of winning Research on Alaska: various sources; note-taking; factual reporting	Read and record daily temperatures (graph) Compare and convert Fahrenheit to Celsius	Study weather components and weather patterns Set up a weather station: use various weather instruments; interpret and record data; make predictions
About Dogs (Probable history of the domestication of dogs)	Essay on dogs as helpers and/or friends	Bar graph of types and numbers of pets owned Graph of food intake and growth measurements of class pet	Collect data and report on history of breeding dogs for specific purposes Record observations of class pet
Arion (Greek folktale of a poet/singer who was saved by dolphins)	Creative writing: poems about dolphins		Identify endangered marine species (e.g., pink dolphin) List ways we can help that species

Social Studies	Creative Arts	Health	Career and Life Skills
Research Alaskan culture: people, climate, housing, food, employment Geography: map skills	Snowflake cutouts Paste on a friendship card	Discuss the effects of weather on health and safety	Consideration of weather forecasts for outings or travel Related careers: meteorologists, plotters, forecasters, TV weather announcers
Identify ways that dogs help us (e.g., guard, hunt, police, guide, herd, rescue) Visit or listen to a person from the humane society	Listen to stories (e.g., *Old Yeller, Sounder*)	Discuss and demonstrate responsibility in caring for class pet	Develop responsibility for caring for others Related careers: veterinarian, breeder, trainer
Obtain info on Save the Whales and Greenpeace organizations Research Greek culture	Listen to *Island of the Blue Dolphins* Dramatize dolphins movements Replicate a dolphin wall mural	Discuss water safety: safety rules, drownproofing	Environmental awareness Water safety Related careers: oceanographer, marine biologist, animal trainer, veterinarian, poet, writer

Note. From *Curricular Integration Through a Basal Reading Series,* by E. Oyama, 1986, Honolulu: University of Hawaii. Adapted with permission.

TABLE 6-4

Factors affecting curriculum and program decision making

Student Variables	Mainstream Environmental Variables	Special Education Variables
Cognitive-intellectual level	Teacher and nonhandicapped	Size of caseload
Academic achievement	student acceptance of	Access to curricular materials
Grade placement	diversity (classroom climate)	Focus of teacher's training
Motivation and responsibility	Administrative support	Support available to teacher
(in general)	Acceptability of variance	
Motivation	in curriculum	**Community Variables**
Behavioral pattern	Accommodative capacity	Access to postsecondary
Social skills	of the classroom	programs
	Flexibility and schedules	Economic climate
Parent Variables	Options for vocational education	Unemployment rates
Expectations		Evaluation of ecology of
Degree of support provided		community relative to
(e.g., financial, academic)		living climate
Parental values		Access to transitional services
Possible cultural influences		

TEACHER TIPS

Elementary Level

WHEN YOU'RE COLLABORATING, FOCUS ON THE MOST IMPORTANT SKILLS

Currently, general and special education teachers are working together more frequently. More and more instruction for students with disabilities is taking place in mainstream environments that include co-teaching arrangements, consultation models, and other cooperative situations. When working with a large group that includes students with disabilities as well as many students without disabilities, focus your instruction on skills that can help *all* students succeed.

Often, skills that we commonly call "school survival skills" are best taught to everyone at once, since everyone can benefit from them, including some of these in your daily instruction.

- For *Academic Survival,* teach skills like:
  note-taking
  time management
  test taking
  outlining
  reading for meaning
  skimming, scanning
  listening
  paraphrasing
  organization

- For *Social Survival,* teach skills like:
  giving and accepting compliments
  working together in a group
  giving and accepting criticism
  empathizing with others
  expressing appreciation
  dealing with frustration
  initiating and ending conversations
  compromising
  expressing appreciation

TEACHER TIPS

With the implementation of IDEA many teachers, administrators, and parents are debating the regulations. IEP myths, battles, and truths must be demystified in order to provide children with disabilities with the most appropriate education. One myth that must be demystified is "what is meant by free appropriate public education." Bateman and Linden (1998) address this issue.

> Nothing is more fundamental of the IDEA than the principle that every child with a qualifying disability is entitled to a free appropriate public education (FAPE). The meanings of free and public are reasonably clear, but the meaning of appropriateness frequently causes confusion. How does one know what is appropriate?
>
> Appropriate does not necessarily mean ideal. Though schools may wish to afford every child an opportunity to maximize his or her potential, the IDEA does not require this. The U.S. Supreme Court has held:
>
> . . .Insofar as a State is required to provide a handicapped child with a "free appropriate public education," we hold that it satisfies this requirement by providing personalized instruction with sufficient support services to permit the child to benefit educationally from that instruction. Such instruction and services must be provided at public expense, must meet the State's educational standards, must approximate the grade levels used in the State's regular education, must comport with the child's IEP. In addition, the IEP, and therefore the personalized instruction, should be formulated in accordance with the requirements of the Act and, if the child is being educated in the regular classrooms of the public education system, should be reasonably calculated to enable the child to achieve passing marks and advance from grade to grade (Board of Education v. Rowley, 458 U. S. 176 (1982))."

Based on this ruling Bateman and Linden go on to note that what constitutes educational benefit lie at the center of numerous court cases. Additionally, how much progress is sufficient to indicate a child is receiving educational benefit is also questionable. What may be clear is that neither social promotion nor slight achievement indicate sufficient progress; determining the progress of the goals set forth in the IEP is of primary importance.

Bateman, B. & Linden, M.A. (1998). *Better IEPs: How to develop legally correct and educationally useful programs.* Longmont, CO: Sopris West.

TEACHER TIPS

The World Wide Web is becoming a common tool for students in general and special education classrooms. Especially for older elementary and secondary children, the Web may be used to access many libraries, museums, websites, and research articles. The use of this technology can be expanded to serve students with disabilities in breaking down hurdles they encounter. Using technology in this fashion can:

1. Reduce barriers to full participation in society.
   Peters-Walters (1999-2000) states that students with multiple physical disabilities can use the web to complete a course in desktop publishing. The use of telecommunication and electronic mail can help student communicate with various people regardless of their disability.
2. Reduce communication barriers.
   Technology can help students with hearing impairments access information that may not have been accessible to them in the past. Students with hearing impairments can access electronic mail and communicate with other people on a regular basis without relying on the use of an interpreter.
3. Reduce barriers to the "basics" in an information society.
   For students with disabilities, the use of the computer and the World Wide Web to access information can be a door to learning about the world around them. When students get used to communicating electronically, they can access basic information that may not have been easily available to them in other forms.

There are some Web barriers to overcome, however, for students with disabilities. Peter-Walter outlines a few of these:

a. One barrier that people with visual disabilities face is not being able to access information because of its graphical format.
b. People with auditory problems cannot access the information in sound files.
c. People with attention deficit disorders can become easily distracted from the information by the use of continual animations.
d. People with physical disabilities may face the barrier of not being able to run the browser that would give them access to the information. (p. 177)

There are numerous devices to enable people with disabilities to access computers. Some of these are Web Tutorials, Dragon Dictate, Microsoft Access Pack, Word Prediction Software, switches, eyegaze, screen readers, refreshable Braille screen, and Touch Windows.

Source: Peters-Walters, S. (1999-2000). Accessible web site design. In K.L. Freiberg (Ed.). *Educating exceptional children* (pp. 176-180), Gillford, CT: Duchkin/McGraw Hill.

Spoken Language

E. Jane Nowacek

Spoken language is an important part of our lives outside and inside of school. Beyond the classroom doors language represents us in social and work interactions and helps shape others' impressions of our competence. For example, in a national survey personnel managers reported that corporate employers of new college graduates watch for excellent oral communication skills more than writing and technical expertise (Chaney & Burk, 1998). Behind the classroom doors, spoken language facilitates or inhibits the expression and understanding of ideas. As Donahue (1994) notes, difficulties with discourse may even prompt teachers to refer students for special education. The importance of spoken language in the school curriculum is highlighted further by Hoskins (1994):

> Disorders in oral language comprehension, auditory analysis, memory, and oral formulation interfere with performance in reading, spelling, and writing. As children move through the grades, written language disorders are often seen as the primary residual manifestations of what was initially an oral language disorder (p. 202).

This chapter focuses on instructional approaches teachers use to address specific problems that students experience in spoken language. It begins with a definition of terms and a conceptualization of language. This discussion serves as a reference point from which to define what are and are not language problems in students with disabilities. Given the variety of problems students experience, both formal and informal assessment procedures are discussed as well as the trend toward collaborative, or transdisciplinary, assessment and service delivery.

Three theoretically based instructional approaches (i.e., cognitive, behavioral, and social-cultural) provide the framework for a discussion of methods that address the spoken language problems of elementary and secondary students. The advantages and disadvantages of each theoretical perspective are examined so that teachers may select those methods that best meet their students' needs. Also to assist teachers, the special needs of adolescent learners and students from culturally and linguistically diverse backgrounds are discussed along with recommendations for modifications of classroom language and instructional environments.

DEFINITION OF TERMS

Many people use the words *communication, speech,* and *language* interchangeably. Each term, however, has a unique meaning. *Communication* is the process with which people convey information, ideas, needs, and emotions. Members of a teacher assistance team discussing modifications are communicating, as are babies crying and friends smiling. These examples point out that communication is a broad term that includes both verbal and nonverbal acts. It also encompasses paralinguistic cues, such as intonation, rate of speaking, and stress, that express emotions and attitudes (Bernstein & Tiegerman, 1997).

Speech is one of several forms of communication. Technically it involves the "sensorimotor process of producing orally sounds and sound sequences that comprise a linguistic code" (Reed, 1986, p. 336). People select speech or other types of communication such as writing and drawing depending on the context, the intent, the audience, and the message they want to convey (Bernstein & Tiegerman, 1997).

Speech is the most common expression of language, a "code whereby ideas about the world are expressed through a conventional system of arbitrary signals for communication" (Lahey, 1988, p. 2). This definition indicates that in language words represent persons, objects, actions, and events and are predictably arranged following specific grammatical rules so that people can understand and communicate ideas. Persons with disabilities who cannot hear and/or produce speech often use a manual language such as the American Sign Language (ASL). There are hundreds of languages, each having its own words and rules. Native speakers of a language do not learn all word combinations, but rather they learn the linguistic rules that enable each person to understand and to create an infinite variety of sentences (Shames, Wiig, & Secord, 1998). A language is a social tool that has meaning for a particular group of people who have the same knowledge of its words and rules.

COMPONENTS OF LANGUAGE

What people mean, the form of their message, and their intent and the context must be considered in order to define language completely. In other words, the content, form, and use of language all must be considered (Bloom & Lahey, 1978).

Content

The content of language, or semantics, refers to the meaning expressed and received. Much of learning in school requires students to master new vocabulary and to associate these words with the appropriate objects, concepts, and processes. For most students instruction will begin with individual, concrete words that are generally easier to master, then progress to abstract words and words that describe relationships (Wallace & McLoughlin, 1988). Understanding the relationships between concepts and the words that represent them is difficult for many special education students. For example, a student may have learned the meaning and spelling of a word such as *build* and yet may not be able to use it in an original sentence. This student has mastered the vocabulary word *build* but has not learned to associate the word with the concept and therefore cannot use it in his or her writing.

Form

Language includes not only word and sentence meaning (content), but also sounds and structure, or form. For the purposes of definition, language form can be divided into three subsystems: phonology, morphology, and syntax. *Phonology* refers to the sounds and sound combinations of a language and takes its name from the word *phonemes,* the smallest linguistic unit of speech that signals differences in meaning (Bernstein & Tiegerman, 1997). Phonemes, such as /m/ and /k/, have sound but by themselves do not have

meaning. However, when they are combined in systematic ways, they produce different words such as *man* and *can,* each of which has a distinct meaning. Students who have phonological difficulties are at risk for having problems decoding words using phonics, a sound-symbol approach to reading. In addition, they often may substitute one sound for another, such as *tar* for *car.*

The second subsystem of language form is called *morphology* and derives its name from *morpheme,* the smallest unit of speech that conveys meaning. Words (e.g., *bat, high, flies*) and prefixes (e.g., *re, bi*), suffixes (e.g., *est, able*), possessives (e.g., *Jane's*), and verb tense (e.g., *answering*) are examples of morphemes. Each morpheme indicates a unique meaning. Students with morphological problems frequently do not use verb tense correctly and may make statements such as "I goes to the movies."

Syntax, the third subsystem of form, refers to the sequence of words in sentences and the rules that govern this sequence. Some students do not understand that word order affects the meaning of sentences. For example, a student may omit words such as linking verbs and prepositions and assert, "I running trail" instead of "I am running on the trail."

Use

The final component of language is use or pragmatics. Linguists and educators have proposed several definitions for this term. Bates (1976) initially defined pragmatics as "rules governing the use of language in context" (p. 420). More recent definitions describe pragmatics or communicative competence as how well individuals adapt language to changing contexts, including the situation, setting, goals, and/or partner (Dudley-Marling, 1985). An example of this adaptation is apparent when a high school student yells across the school parking lot to a friend, "Hey, come here! I wanna talk to you," but says, "Excuse me, Miss Allison, may I please talk with you?" when addressing a teacher before class. This example illustrates the symbiotic relationship that exists between social and linguistic skills. Hymes (1971) explains this relationship in his definition of communicative competence as a language user's knowledge of sentences, not only as grammatical but also as appropriate. He or she acquires competence on when to speak, when not, and on what to talk about with whom, when, where, in what manner. (p. 21) Pragmatics involves not only knowledge of words (semantics) and grammar (syntax), but also knowledge of the social rules that govern interactions among speakers and listeners.

Today many professionals believe that the forms of languages are created, governed, acquired, and used in order to communicate (Bates, Thal, & MacWhinney, 1991). They conceptualize language and language interventions as pragmatically based and understand that "the social use of language gives rise to both the form (syntax) and meaning (content) expressed" (Snow, Midkiff-Borunda, Small, & Proctor, 1984, p. 78). From this functionalist perspective, language is viewed as a tool for communication between the speaker and listener.

To illustrate the importance of pragmatics, consider that many students with language and learning disabilities have difficulty understanding the subtle aspects of language, such as humor and slang, which in turn may affect their understanding and use of language. These students do not "get" the joke and miss the meaning of slang expressions. Over time their lack of understanding may have a negative influence on other's acceptance of them.

LANGUAGE DEVELOPMENT

The development of spoken language normally occurs without formal instruction; it develops as a result of exposure to spoken language (Learning Disabilities Association, 1999a). Although the process by which children acquire language is not fully understood, it is known that language as well as speech develop in identifiable stages beginning with the birth cry. Table 7-1 provides an overview of these developmental milestones.

LANGUAGE DISORDERS DEFINED

For a variety of biological and environmental reasons, not all children progress through these stages at the same rate or to the same degree. The resulting language problems range from mild to severe. The American Speech-Language-Hearing Association (ASHA) (1982) defines a language disorder as the impairment or deviant development of comprehension and/or use of a spoken, written, and/or other symbol system. The disorder may involve (1) the form of language (phonologic, morphologic, and syntactic systems), (2) the content of language (semantic system), and/or (3) the function of language in communication (pragmatic system) in any combination (p. 949). ASHA makes a clear distinction between language disorders and communicative variations that are not considered disorders. Communicative variations include communicative differences/dialects and augmentative communication. ASHA (1982 defines dialect in the following manner:

> Communicative difference/dialect is a variation of a symbol system used by a group of individuals which reflects and is determined by shared regional, social, or cultural/ethnic factors. Variations or alterations in the use of a symbol system may be indicative of primary language interference. A regional, social, or cultural/ethnic variation of a symbol system should not be considered a disorder of speech or language (p. 95).

This definition unequivocally states that no dialectical form of English (e.g., Appalachian English, Black English, New York dialect, southern English) is classified as disordered speech or language. Rather, ASHA maintains that each dialect is a functional form of English that permits speakers to communicate adequately while maintaining a "symbolic representation of the historical, social, and cultural background of the speakers" (ASHA, 1983, p. 24).

A second communicative variation is augmentative or alternative communication (AAC), which ASHA (1991a) defines as an integrated group of components, including the symbols, aids, strategies, and techniques used by individuals to enhance communication (p. 8). Consequently, AAC includes procedures and devices that supplement or replace communication through the typical means of speaking and writing. According to Lewis and Doorlag (1999) in schools two types of

TABLE 7–1
Speech and language milestone chart

By Age One
Says 2 to 3 words besides "Mama" and "Dada"

Imitates familiar words

Understands simple instructions

Recognizes words as symbols for objects

Between One and Two
Understands "no"

Uses 10 to 20 words, including names

Combines two words such as "Daddy bye-bye"

Makes the "sounds" of familiar animals

Gives a toy and brings objects from another room when asked

Uses words such as "more" to make wants known

Points to toes, eyes, and nose

Between Two and Three
Identifies body parts

Carries on a 'conversation' with self and toys

Asks questions such as "What's that?" "Where's my?"

Uses 2-word negative phrases such as "No want"

Forms some plurals by adding "s"

Has a 450-word vocabulary

Gives first name, holds up finger to tell age

Combines nouns and verbs as in "Mommy go"

Refers to self as "me" rather than by name

Tries to get adult attention as in "Watch me"

May say "No" when meaning "Yes"

Talks to other children as well as adults

Solves problems by talking instead of hitting or crying

Answers "where" questions

Names common pictures and things

Uses short sentences such as "Me want cookie"

Between Three and Four
Can tell a story

Has a sentence length of 4 to 5 words

Has a vocabulary of nearly 1000 words

Names at least one color

Begins to obey request as in "Put the book on the table"

Knows last name, name of street on which he or she lives, and several nursery rhymes

Between Four and Five
Uses past tense correctly

Has a vocabulary of nearly 1500 words

Points to colors read, blue, yellow, and green

Identifies triangles, circles, and squares

Can speak of imaginary conditions such as "I hope"

Asks many questions such as "who?" and "why?"

Between Five and Six
Has a sentence length of 5 to 6 words

Has a vocabulary of about 2000 words

Defines objects by their use and can tell what objects are made of

Knows spatial relations such as "on top," "behind," "far"

Knows address

Knows common opposites as in "big/little," "same/different"

Asks questions for information

Distinguishes left and right hand in self

Uses all types of sentences, as "Let's go to the store after we eat."

Between Six and Seven
Speaks in complex sentences that use adjectival and conditional clauses beginning with "if"

Begins to read and write

Understands concepts of time and seasons

Average sentence length is 7.5 words

Between Seven and Eight
Uses relative pronouns as objects in clauses as in "I have a cat that I feed every day."

Uses subordinate clauses beginning with "when," "if," and "because"

Average number of words per oral sentence is 7.6

Between Eight and Ten
Relates concepts to general ideas through use of connectors such as "meanwhile" and "unless."

Uses present participle active and perfect participle.

Average number of words in an oral sentence is 9.0.

Continued

TABLE 7–1 *(Continued)*

Between Ten and Twelve	
Uses complex sentences with subordinate clauses of concession introduced by "nevertheless" and "in spite of".	Has difficulty distinguishing among past, past perfect, and present perfect tenses of the verb
Uses auxiliary verbs "might," "could," and "should" frequently	The average number of words in an oral sentence is 9.5.

Adapted from Learning Disabilities Association of America (1999b). Speech & language milestone chart. [WWW document]. *URL http://www.ldonline.org indepth/speech-language/lda-milestones.html); (From Norton, D.C. (1985). The effective teaching of language arts* (2nd ed.). New York:Merrill/Prentice Hall).

AAC are frequently used: communication boards and electronic communication devices. Lewis and Doorlag point out that communication boards typically are considered to be "low tech" because they are constructed of paper or cardboard with photographs, drawings, or symbols that students can point to in order to communicate. In contrast, electronic communication devices are considered "high tech" because they "talk" using prerecorded speech (digitized speech), speech synthesizers, or a combination of both. In general, these aides require the "speaker" to make a movement that electronically activates the output (e.g., voice). For students with severe motor disabilities, neuroassisted modes are available that use brain wave activity or eye movements to activate the communication device. To address varied audiences, Kangas & Lloyd (1998) remind teachers that students who use AAC methods should use a variety of communication modes. For example, students who typically use manual signing to communicate at home may need another technique to communicate with school personnel who do not sign and students who typically use electronic communication devices may need a backup when the equipment malfunctions.

SIGNS OF LANGUAGE DISABILITIES

In addition to the students who receive special education services primarily because of language disorders, many students with disabilities receive related services to address secondary language problems. For example, Kavale and Forness (1987) report that 60% of students with learning disabilities exhibit some type of language difficulty. Key indicators of language disabilities are listed in the checklist in Table 7-2.

Upper elementary, middle and high school teachers may find signs of language disabilities in older students, reported in Table 7-3, helpful in identifying students who receive speech-language services in the past, but still have difficulty, and those students who have not received services for language and learning problems.

These difficulties illustrate that many students have language problems that adversely affect both their academic achievement and their social development. Therefore, it is crucial that teachers identify children with language problems as early as possible.

ASSESSMENT OF ORAL LANGUAGE

In order to learn whether a language disorder exists, to understand the exact dimensions of the disability, and to guide interventions, students' language must be evaluated. Teachers can play an important role in identifying language difficulties, initially by observing and recording students' atypical language and then by sharing these observations with the teacher assistance team in school. If classroom accommodations do

TABLE 7-2
Teacher referral of children with possible language impairment

The following behaviors may indicate that a child in your classroom has a language impairment that is in need of clinical intervention. Please check the appropriate items.

_____ Child mispronounces sounds and words.

_____ Child omits word endings, such as plural -s and past tense -ed.

_____ Child omits small unemphasized words, such as auxiliary verbs or prepositions.

_____ Child uses an immature vocabulary, overuses empty words, such as one and thing, or seems to have difficulty recalling or finding the right word.

_____ Child has difficulty comprehending new words and concepts.

_____ Child's sentence structure seems immature or overreliant on forms, such as subject-verb-object. It's unoriginal, dull.

_____ Child's question and/or negative sentence style is immature.

_____ Child has difficulty with one of the following:

_____ Verb tensing	_____ Articles	_____ Auxiliary verbs
_____ Pronouns	_____ Irregular verbs	_____ Prepositions
_____ Word order	_____ Irregular plurals	_____ Conjunctions

_____ Child has difficulty relating sequential events.

_____ Child has difficulty following directions.

_____ Child's questions often inaccurate or vague.

_____ Child's questions often poorly formed.

_____ Child has difficulty answering questions.

_____ Child's comments often off-topic or inappropriate for the conversation.

_____ There are long pauses between a remark and the child's reply or between successive remarks by the child. It's as if the child is searching for a response or is confused.

_____ Child appears to be attending to communication but remembers little of what is said.

_____ Child has difficulty using language socially for the following purposes:

_____ Request needs	_____ Pretend/imagine	_____ Protest
_____ Greet	_____ Request information	_____ Gain attention
_____ Respond/reply	_____ Share ideas, feelings	_____ Clarify
_____ Relate events	_____ Entertain	_____ Reason

_____ Child has difficulty interpreting the following:

_____ Figurative language	_____ Humor	_____ Gestures
_____ Emotions	_____ Body language	

_____ Child does not alter production for different audiences and locations.

_____ Child does not seem to consider the effect of language on the listener.

_____ Child often has verbal misunderstandings with others.

_____ Child has difficulty with reading and writing.

_____ Child's language skills seem to be much lower than other areas, such as mechanical, artistic, or social skills.

Reprinted with permission from Owens, R. E. (1999). _Teacher referral of children with possible language impairment._ (3rd ed.). Boston: Allyn & Bacon, p. 373.

TABLE 7–3
Common symptoms of language disorder in older students

Content

- has word finding/retrieval problems
- overuses limited vocabulary
- uses words inappropriately
- has difficulty defining words
- reduced comprehension of complex words
- fails to grasp double word meanings

Form

- uses grammatically incorrect sentence structures
- uses simple rather than complex sentences
- pauses for a prolonged period when constructing sentences
- uses placeholders such as "uh," "er," and "um"
- uses many stereotyped phrases that do not require much language skill
- uses "starters" such as "you know"

Usage

- uses redundant expression and information the listener has already heard
- uses nonspecific vocabulary such as "thing," and "stuff" whose referent is unclear
- lacks detail in giving explanations to a listener
- has difficulty introducing, maintaining, and changing topics in conversation (e.g., may get off track or introduce new topics awkwardly)
- uses clarification questions infrequently
- has difficulty shifting conversational style in different social situations (e.g., with friends vs. teacher, child vs. adult)
- has difficulty grasping the main idea
- has difficulty making references from materials not explicitly stated.

Cited in Haynes, W. O., Pindzola, R. H., & Emerick, L. L. (1992). *Diagnosis and evaluation in speech pathology.* Upper Saddle River, NJ: Prentice Hall. p. 129. Adapted from Haynes, W., Moran, M., & Pindzola, R. (1990). *Communication Disorders in the Classroom.* Dubuque, IA: Kendall-Hunt.

not result in improved language use, the team may recommend that the student be referred for a full evaluation to determine whether special education services are required. Traditionally, speech-language pathologists (SLPs) have had the sole responsibility for conducting these assessments and for providing interventions. The areas of language they assess in an evaluation include not only the components of content, form, and use, but also metalinguistics, the ability to use language to think about and analyze language on more than one level simultaneously (Reed, 1994). Evaluations of these areas typically include a combination of formal and informal assessment procedures.

Formal Language Assessment

Norm-referenced tests form the foundation of language evaluation for identification for special education. In general these instruments address the subsystems of speech and language (e.g., articulation, voice, fluency, and receptive and expressive

language) and the elements of language, including phonology, morphology, syntax, semantics, and pragmatics (Damico, 1991). They have the advantage of providing norms that allow professionals to compare the test scores of the student being evaluated with scores of other individuals of the same age or grade who were tested in the standardization sample to determine whether a difference in performance may indicate a language disability. Students who do not speak English have several options: translations of frequently used tests, tests that are norm-referenced in the student's primary language, culture-free and culture-specific tests, the use of bilingual evaluators, and assistance from speakers of the child's language (Winzer & Muzurek, 1998). Table 7–4 summarizes several of the norm-referenced instruments frequently used to assess student language.

Increasing numbers of educators (e.g., Notari-Syverson & Losardo, 1996) assert that the assessment process should not treat language as a collection of subsystems that can be tested and

TABLE 7–4
Formal assessment instruments

Test	Age/Grade Level	Description
Adolescent Language Screening Test (Morgan & Guilford, 1984)	11–17 years	Tests receptive and expressive vocabulary, concepts, sentence formation, morphology, phonology, and pragmatics
Bankson Language Test—2 (Bankson, 1990)	3–6 years	Tests syntax, semantics, and pragmatics
Bracken Basic Concept Scale (Bracken, 1984)	2–8 years	Tests concepts in 11 areas (e.g., quantity, comparison).
Clinical Evaluation of Language Fundamentals Revised (Semel, Wiig, & Secord, 1987)	5–16 yrs.	Contains 11 subtests for syntax and semantics
Communications Abilities Diagnostic Test (Johnston & Johnston, 1990)	3–9 yrs.	Tests syntax, semantics, pragmatics
Comprehensive Receptive and Expressive Vocabulary (CREVT) (Wallace & Hammill, 1994)	4–17 yrs.	Tests receptive and expressive vocabulary
Dos Amigos Verbal Language Scale (Critchlow, 1996)	5–13 yrs.	Tests cognitive levels of language in both English and Spanish
Language Processing Test (Richard & Hanner, 1985)	5–11 yrs.	Tests language-processing tasks of associations, categorization, multiple meanings, attributes
Language Proficiency Test (Garard & Weinstock, 1981)	Adolescent - adult	Range of language abilities—designed for students using ESL
Let's Talk Inventory for Adolescents (Wiig, 1982)	9 yrs – adult	Tests pragmatic skills in areas of ritualizing, informing, controlling, and feeling.
Let's Talk Inventory for Children (Bray & Wiig, 1987)	4–8 yrs.	Tests pragmatic skills
Multilevel Informal Language Inventory (Goldsworthy, 1982)	Grades K-6	Probes 3 levels of oral language. Tests semantics and syntax
Peabody Picture Vocabulary Test-Revised (Dunn & Dunn,1981, also available in a Spanish edition)	2–adult	Tests receptive ability in semantics
Prueba del Desarrollio Inicial del Lenguaje (Hresko, Reid, & Hammill,1982)	3–7 yrs.	Tests receptive and expressive language in semantic and syntactic tasks in Spanish

(continued)

TABLE 7–4 *(Continued)*

Test	Age/Grade Level	Description
Spotting Language Problems: Pragmatic Criteria for Language Screening (Damico & Oller, 1985)		Pragmatic-based language screening instrument. For English speaking, bilingual, and/or LEP students
Test of Adolescent Language-3 (Hammill, Brown, Larsen, & Wiederholt, 1994)	12–24 yrs.	Tests listening and speaking, spoken and written language, semantics and syntax, reading and writing
Test of Early Language Development-2 (Hreskso, Reid, & Hammill, 1991)	2–7 yrs.	Tests receptive and expressive syntax and semantics
Test of Language Development-2: Primary (Newcomer & Hammill, 1991)	4–8 yrs.	Contains subtests for expressive semantics, phonology, and syntax
Test of Language Development-2: Intermediate (Hammill & Newcomer, 1991)	8–12 yrs.	Tests syntax and semantics
Test of Pragmatic Skills-R (Shulman, 1986)	3–8 yrs.	Tests language usage
Test of Word Knowledge (Wiig & Secord, 1992)	Level 1: 5–8 yrs.	Level 1: Tests expressive vocabulary, synonyms, antonyms, definitions
	Level 2: 8–17 yrs.	Level 2: Definitions, synonyms, antonyms, multiple contexts, syntax, and receptive and expressive vocabulary
The Word Test - Adolescent (Zachman, Huisingh, Barrett, Orman, & Bragden, 1989)	12–17 yrs.	Tests semantics, brand names, signs of the times
Woodcock Language Proficiency Battery - Revised (Woodcock, 1991)	2 yrs.-adult	Tests oral language, vocabulary, synonyms, antonyms, reading, and writing.

analyzed in isolation. Instead, they argue that language must be treated holistically, as dynamic and contextual. In this view, assessment focuses on answering the question, "How competent is the student as a communicator?" (Damico, 1991, p. 179). Because competence changes depending on the situation, descriptive data must be collected in several contexts and, according to Simon (1987b), must focus on "the speaker, the listener, the instructional context, and the context in which communication occurs" (pp. 53–54).

Informal Language Assessment

Informal assessment procedures address some of these concerns because they parallel classroom conditions to a greater extent than norm-referenced measures and because they yield information not only about the student but also about the task and the setting (McLoughlin & Lewis, 1994). In addition, they compare a student's performance to specific tasks rather than to the performance of a norm group. This is an important consideration when assessing students who may not be represented in the norming sample. For example, when students from culturally/linguistically diverse (CLD) backgrounds are evaluated, informal procedures may be a preferable alternative to translations of standardized tests into other languages, which may be problematic (Damico, 1991; Winzer & Mazurek, 1998).

Using informal procedures, professionals can identify language disabilities, plan and modify instruction, and monitor student progress. However, as McLoughlin and Lewis (1994) point out, few informal measures provide reliability and validity data and therefore the quality of these measures is generally unknown.

Traditionally SLPs have had complete responsibility for conducting both formal and informal assessments. Recently, however, other individuals—teachers, paraprofessionals, and parents—have begun collaborating in informal assessment to sample a greater number of student language behaviors in real-life interactions and contexts (ASHA, 1991b). Although SLPs continue to have the major responsibilities for planning, interpreting, and communicating the evaluation results, in collaborative assessment all members of the team collect data. Because educators may be involved in this process, it is important that they be familiar with the following procedures often used in informal assessment.

Language Sampling. Language sampling has been the mainstay of informal spoken language assessment. Because the goal of this procedure is to collect a representative sample of the student's language, SLPs carefully plan the context, materials, and techniques that will be used and include a variety of familiar situations, persons, and tasks (Owens, 1999). Loeb (1997) describes the steps involved in eliciting a language sample:

- Typically SLPs collect language samples in naturalistic settings such as the classroom, cafeteria, or home when the student is engaged in "real" activities: such as play, everyday conversation, telling stories. The student's developmental level, physical and sensory abilities, interests, and past experiences are taken into account when selecting the toys, puzzles, books, and games that often are used to elicit the sample.

- During the sampling, the SLP audiotapes or transcribes on-line what the student says, notes the ongoing context, including nonverbal occurrences, and repeats what the student says when he or she is not understood. The size of the language sample will depend on the student's willingness and ability to interact. The larger the sample, the more representative it is.

- After the SLP has collected and transcribed the samples, he or she first identifies the language structures the student used; then compares the structures to those outlined in developmental norms to determine if the student's use of language is appropriate for the age level.

Although language sampling provides a rich source of information about students' expressive language, it does not provide information about the context in which students learn or about how students respond to instruction.

Ecological Assessment. In contrast, ecological assessment is based on the tenet that behavior cannot be understood apart from its context. As McCormick (1997a) indicates, ecological assessment examines the environments (e.g., math classroom, language arts classroom, gym) in which the student is expected to function. It permits comparisons of the student's performance to the demands of these settings to determine what needs to be taught and what adaptations should be made to promote success. There are a variety of ecological assessment instruments that vary in detail. For example, The Classroom Ecological Inventory (Fuchs, Fernstrom, Scott, Fuchs, & Vandermeer, 1994) examines several aspects of the classroom. It explores the physical environment, teacher-student interaction, posted classroom rules, and teacher behavior, including assignments in and out of class, tests, grades, and academic and social rewards. In addition, Owens (1995) provides a series of questions to help teachers determine where their students are failing in communicative interactions in the classroom.

1. Show a picture (e.g., of a girl jumping) and state, "The girl is jumping."
2. Tell the student to repeat a part of the target phrase (e.g., "Paul, 'say girl.'").
3. Reinforce the correct response.
4. Gradually increase the length of the target phrase the child is asked to imitate and reduce the frequency of reinforcement.
5. Present a variety of subject/verb combinations until the student consistently imitates them correctly.

Shaping. Shaping helps students develop new behaviors by systematically reinforcing responses that approximate the target response. For instance, if a behavioral objective targets producing a two-word phrase (e.g., "more juice"), the teacher would model using the phrase in context and reinforce the student's approximations (e.g., "more").

Generally, teachers and SLPs use imitation and shaping with students who are more severely limited in expression or who are beginning work on a specific language behavior. Imitation has the advantage of reducing the risk of speaking while allowing the student to participate in a conversational interaction (Bernstein & Tiegerman, 1993).

Cueing and Prompting. There are two types of prompts: (a) response prompts, including verbal directions, modeling, and physical guidance, and (b) stimulus prompts, cues that are used in association with task materials such as movement cues (e.g., pointing to the correct picture), position cues (e.g., the correct picture is placed closest to the student), and redundancy or exaggeration cues (e.g., highlighting with color, enlarging the size) (McCormick, 1997b). Teachers introduce these supports during the acquisition stage. They then fade the prompts as soon as the targeted behavior occurs with frequency to reduce the likelihood of prompt-dependence, or the student waiting for a prompt rather than trying a response. To avoid prompt-dependency McCormick suggests that teachers do the following:

1. develop and use a written plan to specify when and how they will use prompts and the correction procedures they will implement;

2. select prompts that minimize errors, but do not interfere with the instructional sequence;
3. have the student's attention before delivering the prompt;
4. pair natural prompts with instructional prompts and fade the instructional prompts as soon as possible; and
5. use prompts that focus the student's attention on the most relevant characteristics of the stimuli.

Educators and clinicians also use cues to support many types of students' responses. For example, when a student is unable to retrieve a word spontaneously, the teacher may use a cue to facilitate recall. These cues include the use of:

- phonetic cues, such as saying the beginning sound, or word fragment (e.g., saying umb . . . to elicit umbrella)
- rhyming words (e.g., saying bar, far . . . to elicit car)
- associative-semantic cues such as associated combinations (e.g., "bread and . . .")
- semantic categories (e.g., "it's a sweet-tasting food")
- serial cueing of well-established patterns (e.g., "January, February . . .")
- sentence completion (e.g., "I got a bike for my . . ." to elicit "birthday")
- nursery rhymes (e.g., "Jack and Jill went up the . . .")
- analogies such as metaphors, similes, proverbs, or idioms that may facilitate word retrieval (e.g., "dark as . . .")
- melodic and/or stress cueing (e.g., tapping the stress pattern in a multisyllable word, such as *dictionary,* or humming or singing a familiar tune or part of the alphabet to stimulate a letter or word cue).

Combination. Educators often combine teacher-directed approaches, especially when helping students to acquire the complex skills involved in social interactions. For example, McCormick (1997b) describes a typical instructional sequence that combines procedures and is designed to teach students to initiate interactions, take turns, and play (pp. 266–267):

TABLE 7–8
Discourse styles

	Directive	Interactive
Teacher role	Teacher initiates questions and evaluates student responses	Teacher elaborates students' thinking and comments on how the information relates to the students' knowledge, experiences, and feelings
Student role	Students answer questions	Students contribute relevant information, applications, and feelings
Teacher goal or expectation	Teacher expects enumeration of points associated with a topic: recall of events or details	Teacher desires integration, analysis, and connection and application of information
Organization	Information presented serially, sequentially, or linearly No shared understanding of the lesson intent or structure	Information presented in a more organized, hierarchical fashion Intentions and structural organization of the content/interaction are communicated (teacher comments/reminds students about how pieces relate)
Rules for participation	Rigid rules for participating Question-answer-evaluation sequence	Turn interruption permitted Student encouraged to relate and contribute information, experiences, and feelings
Functions of communicative acts	Teacher and students produce role-specific (unique) conversational acts with teacher asking questions and students responding	Student and teacher both comment, summarize, request information, predict, and ask for clarification; more varied functions by both teacher and students
Question asking	Emphasis on closed questions Specific answers/information sought Test or factual questions asked (recall of events or details) Predominance of question-answer-evaluation sequence	Emphasis on open-ended questions A number of relevant responses accepted Reflective, opinion-based application or evaluative questions (variety of question types) Balance between question asking and commenting
Topic maintenance and turn taking	Controlled exchange Few response alternatives for the student	Collaborative exchange Multiple opportunities for reciprocal interactions

(continued)

TABLE 7–8 *(Continued)*

	Directive	Interactive
	Teacher expects student to respond accurately and appropriately (maintains predictable routine)	Teacher permits and encourages students to make contributions and to relate the topic to other knowledge or information
	Topic controlled by the teacher	Topic guided/orchestrated by the teacher but with students permitted to develop or manipulate the topic; topic branching can occur
	Fewer turns per topic or subtopic	Greater number of topically related turn exchanges

Reprinted with permission from Merritt, D. D., & Culatta, B. (1998). *Language intervention in the classroom.* San Diego, CA: Singular Publishing (p. 151).

curricula. However, in order to facilitate communicative competence, teachers must develop parallel goals in language and academics and then monitor and provide feedback on members' communications as well as on their knowledge of content.

To ensure that all students contribute to the conversation and to promote interdependence, teachers often assign a specific role to each cooperative learning group member (e.g., a summarizer, an elaborator, an encourager) (Johnson, Johnson, & Holubec, 1994). Although these roles typically are defined in academic terms (e.g., summarize the important points of the group discussion), teachers can also define them to promote language learning. For example, elaborators might be directed to use the LINC strategy if vocabulary were a language goal for the student. In addition, teachers can promote student talk by using structured techniques in cooperative groups. For example, to increase information sharing, teachers may employ the three-step interview that pairs students within a team for the purpose of interviewing each other. After they alternate the roles of interviewer and interviewee, each person takes a turn sharing information learned from the interview with the other team members (Kagan, 1990). In comparing the three-step interview technique to typical group discussion, Kagan points out that the interview is "far

better for developing language and listening skills as well as promoting equal participation" (p. 13). See Kagan (1992) for a description of several other information-sharing and communication skills ideas.

Similarly, approaches based on the whole language philosophy provide frequent opportunities for students to engage in discussions and conversations with classmates about their reading and writing. Although specific definitions of whole language differ, there is general agreement that whole language is based on the following tenets (Goodman, 1991; Norris & Hoffman, 1993):

1. Language is whole.
2. Learning occurs whole to part. Learning should not be broken down into subskills that are taught in isolation.
3. Expression and comprehension strategies are built in meaningful, relevant language use.
4. Oral and written language develop reciprocally.

Given these principles, in classrooms characterized as "whole language," teachers typically do not schedule a specific time for language instruction; rather, they model appropriate language and provide feedback throughout the school day. They use the classroom activities (e.g., circle time, storytime, brainstorming before writing, class discussions about readings, partner and group projects involving science and social studies activities) to develop and promote the skills involved in listening to, understanding, and relaying information (Green, 1994). See Westby and Costlow (1994) for a description of a program that uses the whole language philosophy in order to promote the pragmatic, semantic, syntactic, and metacognitive abilities of students with language and learning disabilities.

Application of Instructional Approaches to Specific Language Problems

An understanding of the theoretical basis of instructional approaches helps teachers select methods appropriate for individual students. We know that for any given language problem there is more than one appropriate approach and that all models of instruction have strengths and weaknesses (Harris & Graham, 1992). Although the goal of all language interventions is to promote competent communication, some students with disabilities require instruction in foundational skills (Hoskins, 1994). This section offers teaching suggestions to address common language difficulties, using Larsen and McKinley's (1995) notion of language use serving as the umbrella under which content and form are taught.

Use

In a typical conversational exchange some responsibilities belong to the listener, some to the speaker, and some are shared by both the listener and speaker. Responsibility for maintaining the "flow" of conversation belongs specifically to the listener. This includes indicating the level of understanding and requesting clarification.

Indicating Level of Understanding and Giving Feedback. Because many students with disabilities, especially learning disabilities, are inactive listeners (Donahue, 1994), it is important for these students to learn to indicate whether or not they understand the speaker by using nonverbal cues (e.g., nodding or shaking the head) or verbal feedback (e.g., "Oh yeah!" or "I don't know what you mean."). The model-practice-feedback process is one of the most use-

ful means of promoting these behaviors. Also, teachers can structure small-group referential communication tasks (e.g., describing an object or giving explicit directions) so that listeners are required to inform the speaker of their level of understanding. Furthermore, cooperative learning group members can be instructed to require listeners to indicate their understanding, and in turn, to provide feedback during group discussions. Johnson and his colleagues (1994) caution, however, that students may have to be taught how to provide feedback.

Requesting Clarification. An extension of the responsibility of giving feedback is the need for listeners to inform speakers that the information they have given is not sufficient and to request repetition, clarification, or elaboration. The most successful intervention techniques for increasing requests for clarification involve two components (Fey, Warr-Leeper, Webber, & Disher, 1988). First, students must learn to detect whether the information the speaker has given is adequate to complete the required task. For example, a statement such as "Color the circle red" is not sufficient if more than one circle is present. Second, students must learn to produce requests for clarification (e.g., "Ask me which circle."). Modeling and the use of cues and prompts provides a structured format for this instruction.

Initiating Conversations. Just as listeners assume primary responsibilities in specific areas in order to maintain conversations, so a number of responsibilities fall primarily to the speaker. These include initiating conversation, giving and requesting information, and responding to the listener. During a conversation, whether at the beginning of an exchange or within an ongoing exchange, the speaker is responsible for organizing and producing an opening statement that informs the listener of his or her intent and that holds the listener's attention. Successful initiation of conversation:

■ getting the listener's attention in an acceptable manner, which may involve either an appropriate greeting at the beginning of an interaction or a transitional statement such as "Well, I was thinking . . ." during an interaction

- using paralinguistic skills (such as appropriate tone of voice) both at the initiation stage and throughout the interaction
- not interrupting, which requires the ability to perceive and make judgments about a social situation.

Teachers and peers model appropriate initiation techniques both during structured activities such as scripted role-playing and in ongoing activities such as asking for help or initiating play.

Giving Information and Making Requests. Another major responsibility of the speaker lies in conveying content messages which, in turn, involve organization and production of language in tasks such as giving directions, describing objects or events, making explanations, and giving reasons. Barrier games, those which require speakers to describe or explain information that the listener does not have, offer a structured context for learning, especially when combined with feedback from the listener or from the teacher as to the relevance, clarity, and effectiveness of the message.

Similarly, making requests requires clarity, relevance, and politeness on the part of the speaker. Teachers can facilitate this skill through a modified barrier game format in which one student gives directions to another (e.g., "What do I need to do now?" or "Where does this one go?"). In addition, teachers use games such as Twenty Questions in which the speaker must produce socially acceptable questions in order to receive clues. Finally, they also model and use cues and prompts to promote requesting behaviors.

Response to the Listener. A final area of speaker's responsibility involves being sensitive to the listener's perspective and being responsive to cues and other forms of feedback from the listener. Again, the prerequisite skill of being able to perceive and make accurate judgments about social situations is necessary in order to take in and evaluate feedback. Social interaction techniques such as role playing, which require

speaker and listener to react appropriately to each other, are excellent ways to meet this goal.

Turn-taking. In maintaining the flow of a conversational exchange, the listener and speaker share some responsibilities. These include taking turns in conversation, maintaining a topic, and repairing breakdowns in the conversation. Just as young children often interrupt or speak out impulsively, many students with special needs, especially students with learning disabilities, have not learned the social language skill of waiting for a break in the conversation before speaking (Craig & Evans, 1989). To promote this skill, teachers model and reinforce appropriate turn exchanges and monitor interactions in student pairs and small groups, providing feedback as needed. Owens (1999) suggests the following progression of learning activities to teach turn-taking:

- begin at a nonverbal or physical level (e.g., passing an item back and forth signals a time for each participant to talk; using structured games and motion songs that require turn taking);
- move to a question-answer format to help students take verbal turns;
- decrease questioning and increase nonlinguistic cues (e.g., eye contact, nodding) to signal the student to take a turn;
- teach students attention-getting techniques (e.g., speaking louder) to gain a turn;
- begin conversational turn-taking by pairing with a person the student already initiates talk with frequently;
- move to structuring conversations with other students.

For students who interrupt others, teachers may focus instruction on identifying when speakers have finished their turns, making sure to discuss when interruptions are appropriate (e.g., in emergencies).

Topic Maintenance. Topic maintenance is another tacit but critical conversational skill with which many students with language disabilities have difficulty (McCord & Haynes, 1988). Again, this behavior may be facilitated in a variety of naturally occurring contexts in which teachers monitor and provide feedback during partner and small group interactions. For example, the teacher can keep the student on topic with cues such as, "Tell me more" and "Anything else?" and probes such as, "Then what happened?" (Owens, 1995).

Hess and Fairchild (1988) used a more structured approach called MAP (model, analyze, practice) to teach topic initiation and maintenance to adolescents with learning disabilities. These students participated in six weekly, 1-hour sessions that began with a review of the specific skill that would be the focus of that meeting. Following the review, the students watched videotaped models of the skill. First they viewed models of undesirable interactions, after which they saw a taped version that demonstrated students employing more effective strategies. They compared the two examples, replaying the poor interactions to generate additional ideas about how the conversation could be improved. Building on these ideas, students then role-played a variety of contingent responses. Next, they reviewed the videotapes of their practice exchanges, pinpointed problems with the help of group members, and retaped their revised interactions, critiquing their improvement.

Repairing Communication Breakdowns. Another responsibility of the speaker and listener is to repair breakdowns in the conversation. Repairs require perceiving whether a message is adequate and requesting clarification or elaboration as needed. Some students' responses for requesting clarification are "I don't understand"; "Which one?"; "Say those one at a time." (Owens, 1995). Because of the social nature of these skills and their dependence on context, a useful method of promoting these skills is structuring role playing in a variety of situations, and accompanied with appropriate feedback. In addition, students can practice identification and reaction by clarification requests in ongoing classroom situations.

Content

Vocabulary. Students with disabilities often have trouble learning vocabulary. An initial question to ask when planning instruction is, "What is the core vocabulary necessary for the student to have?" Students' language use (e.g., the vocabulary words used in the curricula) is a natural choices for study. After selecting the vocabulary items, teachers must consider the method of instruction. A general approach reported by Owens (1995) is to (a) link new words to prior knowledge and experience, (b) teach in meaningful contexts, and (c) provide many exposures to the word and to real-life experiences.

Many students with disabilities also experience difficulty understanding multiple meanings and figurative language. Thomas and Carmack (1997) describe the following activities that teachers may use to promote semantic learning.

Multiple Meanings. *Dictionary Match-Up.* On 3″ × 5″ cards paste pictures that represent words with more than one meaning (e.g., *bat*) and on another set of cards print short definitions appropriate to the students' level. Ask students to match the definition to the picture. Another activity that may promote understanding of multiple meaning involves having students complete a form that has four columns headed: (1) Word, (2) Noun, (3) Verb, (4) Adjective. Students look each word up in a dictionary and write the meaning under the appropriate heading. The word *trim*, for example, as a noun means a decoration; as a verb, to cut and to adorn, as an adjective, neat, orderly. Other examples of words that have more than one meaning include: *state, diner, short, turn, pink, coin, phone, break, suit, light, pose, bear, print, glasses, plum*, and *tax*.

Figurative Language. Difficulties with this abstract use of language (e.g., similes, metaphors, idioms) often occur when students have limited vocabulary and experience. Teachers can plan three activities that may help students understand nonliteral meanings: Sense-able Lessons, Word Search, and Explain That.

Sense-able Lessons. Plan sensory experiences to stimulate students' use of metaphors and similes. Bring objects for seeing, tasting, feeling, hearing, and/or smelling. Then ask students to describe the sensation they experience and relate it to something they know. Make a list of student's reactions.

Word Search. To assist students in understanding metaphors and similes in a writing activity teachers may focus on choosing descriptive words, beginning with the concrete and moving to the more abstract. A hummingbird, for example, may be described first as "green," then "like a bug with a beak," and finally, a "tiny helicopter."

Explain That. To help students discover the connection between the literal and figurative meanings teachers show drawings that depict the literal meaning (e.g., sitting on pins and needles). Next, they ask students to talk about the idea/feeling of each picture, and then discuss possible meanings (e.g., This would be an uncomfortable position that a person would be eager to change).

When teaching vocabulary it is important to remember, as Owens (1999) points out, "no one likes to give verbatim definitions" (p. 300). According to him, the teacher should not expect dictionary definitions from students below age 12. The key is to help students use words to discuss relevant topics in context.

Form

Syntax. Many students with special needs also have difficulties with grammar or syntax. Modeling and cueing are particularly useful in teaching syntax. In addition, feedback provided in incidental teaching, activity-based intervention, and a variety of whole language arrangements helps students to generalize productions to natural contexts.

Wh- Questions. Formulating critical questions such as *Who, Where, What,* and *Why* is problematic for many students with disabilities. Educators create and capitalize on a variety of classroom contexts in which students are required to describe, give directions, and make explanations and teachers form questions to provide models of this language behavior.

Knapczyk (1991) designed a structured program to teach students with learning disabilities to ask questions and to generalize question asking and answering skills. The intervention began with a series of sessions conducted in the resource room during which the teacher worked individually with the students. The general education curriculum, which had been videotaped, provided the content for intervention that progressed as follows.

In the first session, as students watched the videotape of a World Geography class presentation, the resource teacher asked them to identify points in the lesson when they did not understand the information being presented, were uncertain about what was being asked, or were unfamiliar with the information that was being discussed. At each of these points, the teacher stopped the tape and answered the questions. In developing their requests for information, students were directed to ask questions that (a) were timed at natural breaks or followed cues the teacher gave to elicit questions and (b) were formulated to elicit the needed information and to be relevant to the content. The teacher reinforced questions that met these criteria and replayed the tape to show examples of appropriate question asking when student questions were poorly timed or incorrectly formulated.

In the second session, teacher and students viewed the same tape again. Students stopped the tape when they had questions and practiced asking questions, which the resource teacher answered. In sessions three through five, the teacher arranged additional practice using different classrooms tapes and offered demonstration and feedback as needed. During the last 2 days of the intervention, the resource teacher met with the students immediately before they went into their mainstreamed class and reviewed the major components of asking questions.

Special Needs of Adolescents

Although many of the techniques described in this chapter are appropriate for students of all ages, adolescents have specific social language needs. Given their age and the fact that many high school students are about to either enter the work force or to go on to higher education, they need to be adept at survival communication skills. These skills include knowing how to conduct banking and other financial transactions, participate in job or school interviews, and interact in social situations, such as dating.

Larson and McKinley (1995) have developed an approach to teaching skills such as these. This approach consists of three components: mediation, bridging, and summation. Mediation and bridging occur in the context of discussion. Specifically the discussion begins with a statement of the topic (e.g., conversation breakdowns) then moves to mediation, which provides an explanation and framework. The next phase of discussion is bridging, in which students adapt the information to different situations; the final phase is a summation of what was discussed.

In mediation, teachers may suggest strategies such as (p. 188):

1. visualizing the information being spoken or listened to (i.e., seeing it in your mind);
2. using a plan to organization information (i.e., what is most important to say first, next, last);
3. concentrating attention on the speaker when in the role of the listener (e.g., blocking out distractions);
4. knowing how and when to ask a question for clarification;
5. using appropriate concepts (e.g., spatial, quantity, quality) to make messages concise, and
6. taking the listener's perspective when producing a model.

In bridging, teachers may ask the following questions (pp. 187–88):

1. In what other situations has it been important to communicate a message clearly?
2. Tell me a time when you were talking and a breakdown in communication occurred? What were the consequences?
3. Give an example of when you asked a question for clarification? How did it prevent a communication breakdown?
4. You have just been prevented from using gestures and eye contact when saying your message. When else are you prevented from using nonverbal communication?

Special Needs of Students from Culturally/Linguistically Diverse (CLD) Backgrounds

Increasing numbers of students from CLD backgrounds are enrolling in schools. It is projected that "by the year 2020 the population of school-aged children will be 48 percent ethnic minority" (Winzer & Mazurek, 1998, p. 21). As Shames and his colleagues (1998) report, although most are typical language learners who can develop competence in the new language without major difficulty, students with language and learning disabilities have more problems in learning the new system of communication. Figure 7–3 illustrates culture-specific customs and conventions that influence communication at many levels. According to these authors, the conventions listed here, coupled with a variety of language and learning difficulties, make language learning difficult and require more than simple exposure to and experiences with the new language and culture.

To meet the needs of this increasingly diverse student population, teachers need additional knowledge and skills. Garcia and Malkin (1997) outline four areas in which educators require information: (a) the language characteristics of learners with disabilities who are bilingual or have limited English proficiency (LEP), that will help teachers create a language use plan, (b) the cultural factors that affect educational planning and services, (c) the characteristics of instructional strategies and materials that are appropriate, and (d) the characteristics of the learning environment that facilitate success for all students. Because assessment of students from CLD backgrounds has been discussed previously in this chapter, this section will focus on the remaining areas, especially on instructional strategies and materials and the learning environment.

To understand more than superficial aspects of cultures (e.g., foods, music, holidays), Thorp (1997) recommends finding and using a "cultural guide" who can act as a translator/mediator in communication with students and families. In addition, it is important that teachers understand the family's perspective. Asking parents

FIGURE 7-3
Influences of cultural diversity.

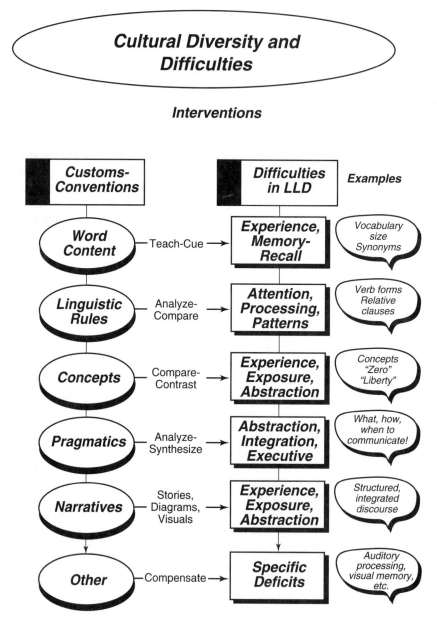

Reprinted with permission from Wiig, E. H., & Wilson, C. C. 1997. *Visual tools for developing language and communication: Content, use, interaction.* Arlington, TX: Schema Press.

questions such as, "What are your expectations for your child in school?"; "What do you value?"; "How do you communicate with your child?"; "What traditions do you hold?"; "What are the standards for acceptable behavior you have for your children and other adults?" can promote understanding (Garcia & Malkin, 1997).

This dialogue also may facilitate educators and the family working together to develop an IEP and help teachers select interventions that will assist the student in attaining the IEP goals and objectives. Table 7-9 outlines key cultural and linguistic factors to consider for IEP development (Winzer & Mazurek, 1998, p. 225).

Many educators (e.g., Merritt & Culatta, 1998) agree that providing supportive, interactive environments in which students and teachers talk about authentic activities is necessary to learning. Bunce (1997) suggests several techniques to increase communicative opportunities for bilingual students that include:

1. Creating a buddy system which provides a peer who can offer explanations and answer questions. (Initially, communication between buddies may be nonverbal, relying on pointing, gesturing, or demonstrating.)
2. Using role-playing to provide contextual support for learning (e.g., act out stories or historical events).
3. Using some group work and cooperative learning that allows peer demonstration and additional practice.
4. Describing what the student is observing to help him or her learn both language content and form.
5. Accepting simplified syntactic forms. Focus on what is being communicated using expansions, discussed in this chapter, to provide a model.
6. Beginning by presenting the whole and then introducing the parts (e.g., give a summary of a story first). Teaching literacy skills through whole-language activities such as language experience stories, choral reading, and predictable books that have recurring lines that facilitate students joining in reading.
7. Making content area books available in the student's first language. This is particularly helpful for older students who have some literacy skills in their first language. An English as Second Language (ESL) teacher may assist in collecting these books.

As Gersten, Baker, and Moses (1998) point out, vocabulary instruction is crucial for English-language development. They suggest using several instructional strategies including teaching vocabulary in the context of mastering new concepts through literature discussion, student conversations, group activities, writing assignments, and visual formats, such as graphic organizers.

In addition, understanding the culture may be necessary to select appropriate materials (Kayser, 1995). Some key considerations in choosing materials involve making sure that they: (a) include the perspectives and contributions of men and women with and without disabilities from CLD backgrounds, (b) identify strengths of so-called "underachieving" diverse populations, (c) represent diverse individuals engaged in a wide range of professional and social activities, and (d) represent culturally diverse content, examples, and experiences that are comparable to those selected from the mainstream culture (Garcia & Malkin, 1997).

Modifications

From the discussion in this chapter it is clear that students with disabilities have a wide range of spoken language difficulties. In addition, they are required to understand and produce complex language in a variety of school settings (e.g., playground, academic classrooms, physical education classes, fine arts programs). The realization that learning varies in different contexts has prompted educators (e.g., Fuchs, Fernstrom, Scott, Fuchs, & Vandermeer, 1994; Wood, 1992) to encourage teachers to evaluate their classroom's physical, social-emotional, and instructional environment. For example, teachers may consider the level of difficulty of their discourse and the demands of language tasks in their class in relation to the abilities of their students, especially students with disabilities. In those areas in which the demands do not match student skills and

TABLE 7–9
Cultural and linguistic considerations related to IEP development

Considerations for IEP Development	Classroom Implications
IEP is relevant to the child's pattern of learning and disability.	Accommodate learning patterns related to specific disabilities as well as communicative and learning styles.
IEP goals and objectives accommodate the student's current level of performance.	At the student's instructional level based on student's cognitive level, not on language proficiency level.
Goals and objectives are responsive to cultural and linguistic variables.	Builds in student's culture, not on it. Takes into account the current cultural home setting, the goals and expectations of the family, and is sensitive to culturally based responses to the disability.
Linguistic variables	Includes a language plan that addresses language development and ESL needs.
English as a Second language (ESL) strategies are used.	Modifications to address the student's disability. Use of current ESL approaches with a focus on meaningful communication.
Interventions provide adequate exposure to curriculum.	Both English and other goals must be integrated. IEP should allow for instruction that assists in the mastery of basic concepts and skills on which future learning will be based. Focus on development of higher level cognitive skills as well as basic skills.
IEP provides for curricular/instructional accommodation, learning styles, and locus of control.	Responsiveness to learning, cognitive, and communication of styles. Stress preferred style of participation (e.g., teacher directed vs. small-group instruction). Reduce feelings of learned helplessness.
Strategies are likely to be effective for culturally diverse and language minority students.	Changes in classroom structure to stress techniques such as cooperative learning and peer tutoring.
IEP provides for multicultural perspectives at students' developmental levels.	Allows for development of cross-cultural competency, learning about diversity, appreciation of other cultures. Brings students' culture into the classroom.
Strategies for literacy are included.	Holistic approaches to literacy development that stress genuine dialogue with students. Language teaching integrated across the curriculum with thematic literature units, language experience approach, journals, and so on.

knowledge, teachers can support and promote learning by making modifications.

Modifications of Language Environment.

Small Groups. Adger (1993) points out that student silence in classrooms is a double-edged sword. The teacher who calls on one student at a time may unwittingly reinforce those students who are proficient in spoken language and on whom the teacher can depend to contribute to the lesson and thereby reduce the opportunities of less able students to participate in class discussions. Providing opportunities such as small group projects, class meetings, cooperative learning discussions, daily news broadcasts, peer and teacher-student conferences, and laboratory and problem-solving partnerships expands the chances for all students to speak and practice using appropriate language. These opportunities can be expanded further by rotating responsibility for reporting to the whole class and by asking different students to be in charge of these activities. Teachers also can extend and refine students responses (e.g., "What does that mean to you?" "Could you tell me more?").

Teacher Discourse.

Teachers must monitor the complexity of their own discourse to increase the understanding of students with language and learning disabilities. For example, teachers may need to be aware of their own language, eliminating idiomatic expressions and complicated verb tenses and minimizing the time spent in teacher talk and maximizing opportunities for students to speak (Winzer & Mazurek, 1998). They also may need to simplify their vocabulary and sentence structure and slow their speaking rate so that students with disabilities understand class expectations, directions, and instruction.

Figure 7-4 summarizes ways in which teachers can modify their presentation to assist students with learning and language disabilities. Moreover, when giving directions, Wood (1992) recommends the following modifications:

1. Get the attention of the group before presenting directions.
2. Make directions clear and simple.

FIGURE 7–4

Consultation suggestions for modifying classroom presentation

Provide contextual cues
State the topic to be discussed.
Supply a prepared outline.
Use visual support, such as writing important information on the blackboard or using charts, pictures or diagrams. For example:

plus
and   } ADD
sum

minus
take away } SUBTRACT
difference

Present questions that review major points to focus student attention on these points.

Provide redundancy
As instructions are given verbally, write them on the board at the same time
Paraphrase information on the lesson, giving each main point several times with different wording each time

Relate new information to what is already known
Help students establish an anticipatory set by asking what they know about the topic
Ask students to talk about personal experiences with the topic.
Personalize information: talk about curriculum topics by using names of students in the class ("Suppose Jose wants to start a rock collection. . . .")

Slow down presentation rate
Talk in a slower-than-normal manner.
Pause for 2 seconds at the end of long sentences.

Adapted from *Language disorders from infancy through adolescence* (p. 469), 1995, by R. Paul, St Louis: Mosby. Originally modified from "Comprehending and Processing of Information in Clinic and Classroom," by E. Lasky, 1991, *Communication Skills in Classroom Success* (pp. 113–134), in C. S. Simon, Ed., San Diego: College-Hill Press. Copyright 1991 by College-Hill Press.

3. Give directions one step at a time.
4. Include procedure(s) students should follow when they do not understand directions and instruction.
5. Present directions in oral and written form.

A recent study that examines the influence of the clarity of adult communication on the learning of adolescents with learning disabilities illustrates the importance of clear directions. Educators found that when adults initially oriented students to a task with clarity, students were able to use focused and coherent logic, such as prior knowledge and efficient cognitive strategies (Shields, Green, Cooper, and Ditton, 1995). An example of directions with high clarity follows.

> We are going to stop with science now and begin our math. First, I would like all of you to put your science books away; next I want you to get your math book out and open it to page 43, and then face the front. Questions? (p. 383)

These directions contrasted both in form and outcomes with the following directions with low clarity:

> Put away your books. Get out your books. Kathy, what is the answer to number 15?. . .Yes, Mike we are in the math book on page 43, why aren't you with us? You're not listening (p. 383).

In addition, teachers may ask students to role-play class expectations, such as rules and routines, to increase understanding of the exact meaning. They also may brainstorm with students how a specific rule would look and sound (Johnson et al., 1994).

Questioning. In addition, Nelson (1993) emphasizes the importance of teachers' asking scaffolding questions. She points out that often when teachers ask higher-order, open-ended questions, they place students with disabilities at a disadvantage in two ways. First, they may not provide cues that let students know appropriate topic(s) for response. For example, a teacher who asks students to discuss "current events," but wants to focus on the upcoming elections requires students to read between the lines and deduce the topic that is targeted for discussion. Phrasing questions so that they convey the topic provides support (e.g., "Today in current events, let's talk about the upcoming elections."). Second, having posed an open-ended question, teachers may hesitate to directly criticize students' responses. They may imply that the answer is not exactly what they had in mind and leave it up to the students to determine whether their answer was correct and

complete. Asking process questions (e.g., "What are the people doing in this picture?") or asking the group to brainstorm possible answers provides opportunities for all students in the class to understand correct and incorrect responses.

Lecturing. Many students with disabilities have difficulty processing spoken language for a variety of reasons, which puts them at a disadvantage in classrooms where lecture is a frequently used format. Masters, Mori, and Mori (1999) report several strategies to improve and augment listening developed by Alley and Deshler:

- Provide organizing cues, such as identifying the main points by writing key elements on the board, overhead transparencies, or in outlines given to each student.
- Teach students to identify nonverbal and verbal cues and use them throughout the lecture, such as facial expressions, hand movements and verbal cues (e.g., "There are three main points", "next", "in summary").
- Identify main and supporting ideas (e.g., use graphic organizers as concept maps).
- Teach and encourage students to ask questions and to provide feedback to the speaker. (See *wh-* questions and indicating level of understanding and giving feedback).

Modifications of Instructional Environment. *Integrating Curricula.* To provide students with an effective learning environment, according to Norris and Hoffman (1993), teachers may consider that less quantity often results in more learning with greater quality, especially for students with less flexible language systems. These educators reason that selecting integrated curricula and providing instruction based on thematic units reduces the need to address the multiplicity of topics subsumed under each content area in traditional curricula. Furthermore, they indicate students with disabilities may not be able to benefit from traditional curricula because their poor oral and written language skills have restricted their learning the general, scientific, or cultural knowledge that is required to interpret and understand grade-level texts. Finally, teachers can select a variety of ma-

TABLE 7–10
Oral-based activities in composition instruction

Skill Domain	Accompanying Composing Processes	Adjuncts to Composing	Cognitive Calisthenics
Invention—discovering subject matter, elaborating, forging topical coherence	Prewriting discussion, interviewing as an information gathering tool	Tape-recording notes, dictating "zero drafts"	Topic sculpting impromptus, forum questioning
Audience awareness—anticipating and adapting to the responses of readers with diverse backgrounds and to their informational and language processing needs	Helping circles, oral "publication," teacher conferencing	"Talk-write" dyads, audience interviews	Role-switching, discussing moral dilemmas
Cooperative discourse—building on what has been said before, both interacting with a particular audience and within a broader cultural context; being relevant, making a contribution, acknowledging sources	Group work in dividing a topic, group reports	Collaborative drafting, group revising	Instruction in listening, peer questioning as a tool for learning how to internalize dialogue
Monitoring—metacognitive awareness, reflecting on and distancing oneself from one's own discourse, adopting a critical stance	Reading aloud to facilitate editing, group critiques	Thinking-aloud composing, discourse-based interviews for self-assessment	Structured forensic discussion, transcribing speech

*Note.*Reprinted with permission from "Divergence and Convergence Between Oral and Written Communication," by D. L. Rubin, 1994, *Best Practices I: The Classroom as an Assessment Arena,* by K. G. Butler, Ed., Gaithersburg, MD: Aspen Publishers. Copyright 1994 by Aspen Publishers, Inc.

terials at various levels to explore themes without stigmatizing students who require less complex materials. See Merritt and Culatta (1998) for a discussion and extended example of planning and implementing a collaborative thematic unit: The Pilgrim's Experience (pp. 409–452).

Integrating Oral and Written Forms. As students move from the predominantly oral discourse of primary classrooms into curricula that

are presented almost exclusively in written form by Grade 4, Wallach (1994) recommends integrating oral-to-written and written-to-oral activities. For example, she helped students appreciate the communication style differences between the two forms in a sports unit. She guided students from informal conversation into the more structured but visual television reporting, then into radio broadcasting, and finally into sports writing. Throughout the progression, she helped students compare spoken and written texts and to understand the ways in which they could say the same thing to different audiences in different contexts. In Table 7-10 Rubin (1994) provides several activities in four skill domains that help students make the transition from oral to written forms.

Retelling. Providing arrangements in which students retell the same information, procedures, or stories to different individuals further supports students' language and learning (Norris & Hoffman, 1993). In this arrangement, speakers have opportunities to adjust their linguistic orientation (e.g., vocabulary, sentence structure, tone) to different audiences. In addition, repetition of the same information helps students refine the organization, content, and form of their message and at the same time to learn the information through repetition. During this process the teacher collaborates with the students to present the information and thereby provide supports.

Finally, educators need to consider modifications for students who come to the classroom from diverse linguistic, cultural, and social backgrounds. Fletcher, Bos, and Johnson (1999) studied the modifications that two bilingual education teachers made for their students with language and learning disabilities. Their findings suggested that adaptations in these classes were similar to those made by teachers in inclusive classrooms. Having observed the bilingual students with disabilities in these classes, Fletcher and his colleagues recommended that educators modify the learning environment by providing peer assistance in cooperative learning and flexible grouping arrangements, planning for individual differences in terms of expectations, assignments, and grading modifications, and contextualizing and infusing the student's native language and culture into teaching and learning activities.

In addition, Winzer and Mazurek (1998) offer these recommendations (p. 376):

- Contextualize language with manipulatives, photographs, drawings.

- Use advanced organizers to outline the structure of the instruction that will follow.
- Preface all remarks with a title, or the main idea of the lesson.
- Use newspapers, magazines, radio, videos, TV as sources of natural and functional language.
- Change the volume and tone of voice to emphasize important points in the lesson.
- When students do not understand, rephrase rather than repeat.
- Encourage students to use their dominant language to learn concepts.

SUMMARY

James Chesbro, past president of the National Communication Association, states that, "lack of communication skills is one of the most critical national problems" (*Education Update,* 1999). School professionals increasingly are acknowledging the importance of communication.

Realizing that language performance is linked to success in and out of school, teachers, SLPs, and families are becoming involved in the assessment and interventions that occur in homes, schools, and communities. Assessment in schools serves several purposes including identification and placement for special education, intervention planning, and progress monitoring. Given the implications of each of these functions, educators want to be as accurate as possible in their evaluation and therefore often use both formal and informal assessment procedures to evaluate the meaning students express, the form of their message, and the intent and the context of their communication. Information about published, norm-referenced tests and informal procedures has been discussed along with their advantages and disadvantages.

Similarly, language instruction and facilitation is moving out of isolated therapy rooms and into inclusive classrooms where specialists and classroom teachers collaborate to meet their students' needs. Considering the heterogeneity of today's classrooms and of students' spoken language needs, teachers require a repertoire of instructional practices and modifications.

TEACHER TIPS

DON'T LEAVE THEM SPEECHLESS

It is sometimes very difficult to elicit spoken language from young children and from students whose language is delayed. This can create a cycle of poor language skills, followed by few attempts to practice using language, resulting in continuing language deficits. Sometimes teachers must arrange situations so that students "have to" use language. To elicit speech try these ideas:

- Put items out of reach so the child must ask for them.
- When the child asks for something, give her the wrong item.
- Give a child a difficult task (opening a tight jar lid) so he has to ask for assistance.
- Perform an easy task incorrectly, so that the child corrects you.
- Talk the child through activities. ("What are we doing now? We're going for a walk. First, we'll put on our coats. What is this? That's right, it's your coat.")
- Use talking toys that repeat common phrases or sounds.
- Play music that encourages children to sing and make sounds.
- Pair students up for activities, letting a nontalker work with student who can model good language skills.

Source: Fad K., & Riddle, M. (1995). *Inclusion notes for busy teachers.* Longmont, Co: Sopris West

TEACHER TIPS

THEY HAVE A VERY CLOSE RELATIONSHIP: PRAGMATIC LANGUAGE AND SOCIAL SKILLS

Older students who lack positive social skills and strong interpersonal relationships may be at risk for a number of associated problems, including underachievement, juvenile delinquency, and dropping out. Prevention of these serious problems may require proactive intervention in the form of social skills training. Because pragmatic language skills are an essential feature of good social skills, many speech-language professionals suggest that direct instruction should be one component of an effective intervention program for secondary students.

Larson and McKinley (1995), in their discussion of speaking skills, list a few of the rules of conversation that encompass both pragmatic speech and social behavior:

- Initiate and close conversations appropriately.
- Select appropriate topics of conversation.
- Make contributions to the conversation truthful.
- Make contributions to the conversation relevant.

(continued)

(continued)

These authors also list some nonverbal communication behaviors that older students may find essential for good social skills:

- matching oral and nonverbal messages
- detecting and displaying emotion through facial expression
- maintaining socially acceptable distance
- maintaining appropriate eye contact

The authors suggest that teachers recognize the importance of these and other pragmatic skills. Social skills that are both age appropriate and situation appropriate are essential for students' success in school and in the community,

Source: Larson, V. L., McKinley, N. (1995). *Language disorders in thinking students: Preadolescents and adolescents.* Eau Claire, WI: Thinking Publications.

TEACHER TIPS

Technology

With the technology available today, powerful and creative applications are being used in the area of communication disorders. Because of this widespread use of technology, the members of the American Speech-Language Association (ASHA) are encouraged to use computers in their clinical work. As more and more clinicians use this technology on a daily basis, the skill level of the ASHA members must be evaluated in order to ensure the delivery of quality therapy to children needing speech and language services. In response to this need, a group of computer experts developed computer competencies for ASHA clinicians (Cockran, 2000). These competencies include:

1. using computers as productivity tools;
2. awareness of technology-related ethical issues;
3. awareness and use of technology-related resources;
4. using computers as diagnostic tools;
5. using computer-based materials as a context for conversation;
6. using computers as instructors;
7. using computers to record and analyze data;
8. using computers as biofeedback devices;
9. using computers to generate clinical materials.

As these competencies are implemented and enforced, Cochran recommends that the education of clinicians, in relation to these technology requirements, should include "hands-on opportunities and should reinforce good clinical practices." This qualification should be underscored as the quality of the therapy, delivered through technology, is a necessary component for student success.

Source: In. J. D. Lindsey (Ed.), Technology and exceptional individuals. Austin, Tx.: Pro-Ed.

Reading: Introduction and Word Recognition

The ability to read is essential for living in today's world; personal independence requires at least functional literacy. Failure to read restricts academic progress because proficiency in Math, English, or Social Studies depends on an ability to read. Most jobs in our society also require at least minimal reading skills. Reading is also a key to personal/social adjustment and to successful involvement in community activities.

Reading, reading failure, and ways to teach reading remain dominant issues today for teachers working with students with special needs. This concern—and appropriate preoccupation by teachers—is clearly underscored by Lyon (1995) in his observations about students with learning disabilities. The concern can be generalized to other students with special needs as well. He states:

> At least 80 to 85 percent of children and adults diagnosed with LD have their most severe difficulties in learning to read. This is unfortunate since the major task in the early school grades is to learn to read, and most activities in the early and later grades, as well as in adulthood, involve and rely upon the ability to read. For example, consider being a child in elementary school, who, at the tender age of seven, cannot read—who cannot do what most others are able to do effortlessly—and knows it. Consider the humiliation and embarrassment that this youngster feels when called upon to read aloud in class and can only respond in a labored and inaccurate fashion. Think ahead to the fourth grade and beyond, where the ability to learn about history, the English language, mathematics, current events, and the rich tapestries of literature and science are inaccessible because all of this learning requires the ability to read rapidly, fluently, and accurately. . . . The eager third graders experiencing reading difficulties become, in turn, the frustrated ninth graders who drop out of school, the barely literate twenty-five-year-olds who read at the fourth grade level, the members of the thirtysomething generation who are unemployed, and the defeated adults struggling to raise families and needing to go on public assistance.

Selecting the correct reading instructional approach has been, perhaps with the possible exception of discipline, the most discussed issue in education, and few agree that any single method is the most effective with all children with disabilities. The responsibility for teaching reading can thus seem awesome, particularly because more than 100 approaches have been identified for teaching beginning reading. A common observation is that teachers' consistent, direct, personal involvement in reading instruction is among the most important influences on achievement.

Although the importance of the correct methods and materials in reading instruction goes without saying, a continuing concern is time spent in learning to read. In 1980 Zigmond, Vallecorsa, and Leinhardt (1980) stressed that the amount of time actually spent reading is the major factor in reading progress. Their report on the classroom routines of 105 elementary students who were learning disabled indicated that only 27 minutes out of the 287 minutes in an average school day were spent reading. An analysis of the students' reading progress established a direct correlation between time spent reading and reading achievement. They concluded therefore that teachers must reorganize the daily classroom schedule to increase the time students are actively engaged in reading if students with learning disabilities are to improve their reading skills.

Has this situation improved over time? Vaughn, Moody, and Schumm (1998) report on the contemporary reading instructional practices of resource teachers. They conclude that their instruction consisted primarily of whole group teaching to large numbers of children (up to 19) and that the emphasis of instruction most often was undifferentiated even though students' ability ranged across 3 to 5 grade levels in a number of instances. Further, the teachers indicated that they used approaches consistent with their school's focus, which in most cases meant an emphasis on whole language. There was minimal evidence of instruction in word recognition strategies and when this occurred, it was frequently incidental rather than explicit and systematic. Ironically, this instructional focus was in opposition to the beliefs of a number of teachers that such explicit instruction was necessary if students were to learn to read.

The pattern that Vaughn et al. (1998) found with resource teachers was a virtual replication of the characteristics of reading instruction in general education classes which they and others had studied earlier. Unfortunately, research has consistently documented that such reading instructional programs are not correlated with acceptable rates of achievement in students with special needs.

Against this backdrop of reading problems, teachers are faced with several key instructional goals. In their classic book on teaching reading, Kirk and Monroe (1940) outline three such goals that help provide a framework for instruction of readers who are disabled. A minimal goal for all students is the ability to *read for protection.* Implicit in this goal is the concept of reading for survival. A second goal, *reading for information and instruction,* is realistic for most students who are mildly and moderately disabled. Implied in this goal is functional reading that allows the individual to deal with job applications, newspaper advertisements, job instruction manuals, telephone books, and countless other sources of information and assistance. The third goal is reading for pleasure. This should be a realistic goal for many adolescents with disabilities and should be a long-range objective of teachers working with all children.

READING IN THE CURRICULUM

The importance of reading within the curriculum of virtually all students is universally accepted. Reading must be a significant part of the school day, and teachers should seek ways to integrate reading instruction into other areas of the curriculum. Given the frequency of significant reading difficulties among students with disabilities, additional practice to maintain and refine skills is warranted. In addition, such opportunities provide a place for students to generalize their reading ability. Thus, adolescents can improve their comprehension skills while acquiring basic vocational competencies from trade books; younger students can benefit from vocabulary development while learning basic science concepts.

Although all agree that reading is critical and that it should be taught and reinforced throughout the day and in multiple venues, agreement on

how best to teach reading was debated throughout the twentieth century and continues into the twenty-first century. While the foci have changed over the last century, in recent years the key players in the debate have been decoding-based emphases (e.g., phonetic analysis approaches that teach sound-symbol correspondences) and holistic approaches (e.g., stressing the necessary emphasis on meaning). The following discussion briefly highlights these concerns as an introduction to these issues and as a basis for illustrating for the reader the arrangement of these two chapters in the text.

Decoding-based programs typically emphasize a skills-based, "bottom-up" approach to reading. Frequently focused on teaching sound-symbol correspondences in language (e.g., c - a- t → cat), they are often characterized by the direct teaching of a sequence of skills that begins with an emphasis on the phonological basis of the English language and thus provides a foundation for the subsequent transfer of skills to actual reading (e.g., comprehension). This general approach has received recent support from the research on phonological awareness difficulties in students with special needs. As Fletcher, Foorman, Francis, and Schatschneider (1998) have summarized it:

> Success in beginning reading reflects the development of fast, efficient decoding skills. Although the primary goal of reading is to comprehend what is read, comprehension is compromised if decoding is not accurate, fluent, and automatic. Underlying both success and failure in word recognition skills is the development of phonological awareness skills. . . . the ability to deal with sound units in speech smaller than the syllable. Children learn to crack what is essentially an alphabetic code by relating language to print. When children learn how print represents the internal structure of words, they become accurate at word recognition; when they learn to recognize words quickly and automatically, they become fluent. This is not hard to learn for many children who seem to develop an awareness of these relationships regardless of how they are taught. For some children, however, learning these skills is not straightforward. The actual number is difficult to determine, but our research indicates that at least 20 to 40 percent of children in kindergarten through second grade may

have these deficiencies. . . .The best evidence that we have indicates that such skills must be explicitly taught in these high-risk children. In the absence of explicit instruction in word recognition and phonological awareness skills, our research suggests that many children will not develop proficiency in word recognition ability, and consequently, are destined to a life of reading failure (p. 3-4).

The holistic approach, generally referred to as a whole language emphasis, focuses on the meaningfulness of language, stresses the importance of the child's language as a bridge to literacy, and includes speaking, listening, and, expressive writing as integral parts of literacy development (Chiang & Ford, 1990; Gersten & Dimino, 1990). This approach builds on the diversity of literary experiences that children are exposed to prior to entering schools. For example, as a result of having been read to by parents, young children often develop an awareness of the structure of texts and understand the implicit relationship between speech and print. Certainly, in instances where this is lacking, a whole language approach primarily emphasizes assisting students in understanding this relationship.

McNutt (1984) describes reading through whole language as consisting of ever-widening spirals in which learning is often unconscious or unintentional. Because of its ongoing and continual nature, learning cannot be broken down into discrete skills. When the whole language approach is used to teach reading, the students' success as language users is emphasized and reading is presented as just one additional use of language as a communication tool (Hollingsworth & Reutzel, 1988). In a classroom in which the whole language approach to teaching reading is used, students are provided more time to read "real" books and write their own stories. Basic to the program is an environment rich in reading choices, with easy access to many resources, as well as an opportunity for students to respond to what they have read in a variety of active and creative ways.

Advocates of the whole language approach point out that countries with the highest literacy rates (e.g., New Zealand) use the whole language approach. (Cutting & Mulligan, 1990). However,

more limited research is available that speaks specifically to the use of whole language with students with disabilities.

Decoding and Whole Language: Perspective

The arguments for the primacy of the direct instruction of decoding skills versus the use of a whole language orientation escalated in the 1990s to the point where teachers may have felt trapped within circles of divisiveness. However, as Mather (1992) asserts, no single reading methodology exists that can meet all the needs of all students. Some students learn to read quite easily, requiring little or no direct instruction. Thus, a meaning-based whole language program is likely to provide appropriate experiences for these students. On the other hand, students with reading disabilities often require intensive, direct reading instruction that is not available in classrooms that have adopted purely whole language philosophy. Mather concludes that whole language reading programs that incorporate various instructional techniques tailored to individuals' needs (i.e., decoding) are a viable option for students with reading disabilities.

Thus, although often presented as opposing viewpoints for teaching reading to students with reading difficulties, the holistic and the skills-based decoding approaches can be successfully combined. When the two are combined, students can benefit from instruction that uses the best elements of both approaches. For example, phonetic patterns needed for decoding can be taught within the principles of whole language (Engelhard, 1991). As Fletcher et al. (1998, p. 6) succinctly state,

> Phonological awareness leads to success in decoding; automatized decoding is a necessary component of good comprehension. All of this can and should be accomplished within a literature-rich environment. Comprehension processes are critical, and there is good evidence that shows that explicit instruction in comprehension skills facilitates the development of reading comprehension skills.

Upon analysis of data from their survey of outstanding literacy teachers, Pressley and Rankin

(1994) note that teachers' classroom practices generally parallel an eclectic approach as described above. Even those who referred to themselves as whole language teachers reported using direct instructional approaches in addition to meaning-based methodologies in their classrooms. Direct teaching of decoding skills, auditory and visual discrimination skills, and letter-sound relationships were listed as techniques used with general education students and with students with reading difficulties in particular. Pressley and Rankin (1994) support Mather's (1992) observation that students with reading disabilities often need reading instruction that goes beyond the scope of whole language programs. Similarly, Gersten and Dimino (1993) propose that, while both direct instruction and whole language approaches have merit, research is needed to identify which approach is best suited to particular teaching contexts.

Both whole language and decoding emphases are useful approaches for children with reading difficulties. The whole language movement reminds us that the goal of reading instruction is comprehension and that good literature is the best way to attract students to books. On the other hand, decoding approaches provide a foundation for recognizing words that is essential for ultimately deriving meaning from reading opportunities. With careful planning, a teacher can develop a successful reading program that includes direct instruction of phonetic and structural analysis skills that complements a meaning emphasis in teaching reading. Rather than having to be seen as opposites, there are numerous creative classroom approaches that have been developed to blend principles of decoding instruction with a meaning orientation (Morgan, 1995).

Given this brief outline of the recent debates in the field of reading, the philosophy of the authors of the text is that teachers of students with special needs—whether in special class, resource or inclusive settings—must be prepared to focus on teaching word recognition and analysis skills as well as on the promotion of meaning through well-designed reading comprehension programs. Thus, while teachers will obviously be influenced by their own philosophies of reading and, frequently in instances of collaboration and inclusive settings, by the approaches favored by other teachers, the purpose of this text is to provide a broad basis for the teaching of reading. Therefore this chapter examines assessment in reading in general and instruction of skills related to word recognition in particular. Chapter 9 then focuses on reading comprehension. The approaches discussed here provide a sound foundation for the development and implementation of a comprehensive reading program.

ASSESSMENT

Reading presents the reader with many challenges and consists of many essential components. The teacher must understand the many facets of the reading task and know how to determine which skills each student does or does not possess. It is also important for the teacher to determine each student's specific reading level before implementing any skills program. Thus, the primary purpose of reading assessment is instructional planning.

Two types of assessment instruments—informal and formal—can assist the teacher in determining an individual's level of reading competency. Instruments of both types can be designed to determine an approximate reading level equivalent for reading as a basis for determining where to begin instruction and how to begin to analyze specific strengths and weaknesses. In general, most reading-assessment devices derive reading levels using similar criteria and comparisons to norm groups or graded materials. Also, most tests assess skill deficits similarly; the major differences are in precision and specificity.

Teacher-Oriented Assessment

Informal Reading Inventories. An informal reading inventory (IRI) is a common informal instrument to assess reading skills. Several IRIs are commercially available; most contain four parts: a word-recognition inventory, oral reading passages, silent reading passages, and comprehension questions to accompany the passages.

Word-recognition inventories are lists compiled from the vocabularies used in instructional materials. The student receives the master copy, and responses are checked on the teacher's score sheet. Administration of the test continues with increasingly more difficult word lists until the student misses 25% of the words. The number of words per grade list usually ranges from 20 to 30.

Three classifications of reading ability can be determined from these inventories. The independent reading level often refers to vocabulary that a student can read without teacher assistance and content that can be comprehended at a high level while still identifying approximately 95% of the words correctly. Library books and seat work instructions should be at the student's independent level. The instructional reading level refers to vocabulary and content that the student can read with some outside assistance. Students should be 85% to 95% accurate at this level. The frustration reading level is that at which the student cannot read with any degree of independence, accurately identifying fewer than 80% of the words. The material at this level is too difficult. These ranges are included for illustration purposes; views vary on precisely what percentage of accuracy is associated with any given level. Teachers should use them as general guidelines in their assessment efforts.

Listening level can also be determined, indicating to the teacher the level at which a student can comprehend material that is read aloud by someone else. Thus, this section of the IRI gives the teacher a basis for deciding the level at which instruction and comprehension testing should begin.

An IRI can also provide for an analysis of errors, which can give added information on specific word analysis difficulties; for this reason mispronounced words should be recorded phonetically. The errors can be classified in common areas, such as incorrect sounds, full reversals, partial reversals, or incorrect beginning, medial, or final consonants. A typical scoring sheet is enclosed in Figure 8-1.

An oral reading inventory samples a student's oral reading and comprehension capabilities at various levels. The format, administrative procedures, and scoring practices may vary. However, it may be advantageous to record the student's reading so that the teacher can listen critically and analyze errors as a basis for instruction.

IRIs can also assess silent reading. Achievement and skill difficulties can be determined by students' responses to comprehension questions.

Classroom Reading Inventory. The commercially prepared Classroom Reading Inventory (CRI) (Silvaroli, 1990) is a diagnostic tool designed for teachers who have had no prior experience with informal reading inventories. It assesses silent and oral reading, listening, and sight-word knowledge. Comprehension is measured by a total of five factual, inferential, and vocabulary questions that follow the oral or silent reading of graded paragraphs. Forms A and B are used to assess elementary school students' word recognition and comprehension skills. Forms C and D differ in that they include high-interest stories for students of high school age or low-functioning adults.

Observation and Checklists. Checklists developed from a summary of reading competencies are also an effective informal diagnostic procedure. The teacher selects a particular area to assess and, during a classroom lesson, observes and records a student's skills on the checklist. To observe comprehension skills during a small group-reading lesson, the teacher might ask questions like the ones on the chart in Figure 8-2.

Language-Based Reading Disabilities Checklist. The awareness of a language basis for many reading problems has given rise to an increased number of assessment approaches and intervention strategies that focus on these concerns. Consistent with this emphasis, Catts (1997) has developed a checklist for speech language pathologists, teachers, and parents that screens for speech-language problems that may be indicative of reading problems. It was intended for use with kindergarten and first grade children but Catts notes that some of the items may be applicable to older children with language-based reading prob-

FIGURE 8–1
Oral reading scoring system

1. Mispronunciations: Write the child's pronunciation above the word.

   (E.g., They bought the bread at the store.) *[brought written above "bought"]*

2. Assistance: Write the letter A above each word pronounced for the child after allowing five seconds to elapse.

   (E.g., Hawkeye performed the delicate operation.) *[A written above "delicate"]*

3. Omissions: Circle each word or portion of word that the student omits.

   (E.g., After the race, the runner was winded.) *["ed." circled]*

4. Letter or Word Inversions: Use the traditional typographical mark to indicate this type of error.

   (E.g., The ball seemed to fly forever—it was a homerun!) *[transposition mark on "homerun"]*

5. Self-correction: Write the letter C above the word if the student corrects an error on his/her own.

   (E.g., They were late but they arrived just in time to ride the train.) *[C and "arose" written above "arrived"]*

6. Insertions: Use a caret to indicate additions inserted by the reader.

   (E.g., She was afraid to go into the haunted house.) *["old" inserted with caret before "haunted"]*

7. Hesitations and Repetitions: Though not errors, these can be noted by a check mark and a wavy line, respectively.

   (E.g., The dog scratched and itched until they put on his flea collar.) *[check mark above "scratched", wavy line under "put on his"]*

Source: Polloway, E. A., & Smith, T. E. C. (1999). *Language instruction for students with disabilities* (2nd ed., rev.). Denver, CO: Love Publishing.

lems. Although no single description confirms a problem, teachers should be aware that a pattern of difficulties is predictive of subsequent problems in learning to read (Figure 8–3).

Curriculum-Based Measurement. Curriculum-based measurement (CBM) is a procedure that measures a student's academic progress by sampling mastery of his actual curriculum. For example, to assess reading progress, 1- to 3-minute oral reading samples can be taken under the assumption that as the decoding process becomes more automatic, more attention can be allocated to comprehension. CBM is a valid, efficient, easily understood, and repeatable assessment procedure (Potter & Wamre, 1990).

FIGURE 8–2
Checklist of comprehension skills

Student names	Main Idea	Sequence	Details	Cause and Effect	Fact v. Opinion
Martha	X	X	X	X	X
Raul		X	X	X	
Lucinda	X	X	X		
Harry		X	X		

FIGURE 8–3

Early identification of language-based reading disabilities: A checklist

This checklist is designed to identify children who are at risk for language-based reading disabilities. It is intended for use with children at the end of kindergarten or beginning of first grade. Each of the descriptors listed below should be carefully considered and those that characterize the child's behavior/history should be checked. A child receiving a large number of checks should be referred for a more in-depth evaluation.

Speech Sound Awareness
- ☐ doesn't understand and enjoy rhymes
- ☐ doesn't easily recognize that words may begin with the same sound
- ☐ has difficulty counting the syllables in spoken words
- ☐ has problem clapping hands or tapping feet in rhythm with songs and/or rhymes
- ☐ demonstrates problems learning sound-letter correspondences

Word Retrieval
- ☐ has difficulty retrieving a specific word (e.g., calls a sheep a "goat" or says "you know, a woolly animal")
- ☐ shows poor memory for classmates' names
- ☐ speech is hesitant, filled with pauses or vocalizations (e.g., "um," "you know")
- ☐ frequently uses words lacking specificity (e.g., "stuff," "thing," "what you call it")
- ☐ has a problem remembering/retrieving verbal sequences (e.g., days of the week, alphabet)

Verbal Memory
- ☐ has difficulty remembering instructions or directions
- ☐ shows problems learning names of people or places
- ☐ has difficulty remembering the words to songs or poems
- ☐ has problems learning a second language

Speech Production/Perception
- ☐ has problems saying common words with difficult sound patterns (e.g., animal, cinnamon, specific)
- ☐ mishears and subsequently mispronounces words or names
- ☐ confuses a similar sounding word with another word (e.g., saying "The Entire State Building is in New York")
- ☐ combines sound patterns of similar words (e.g., saying "escavator" for escalator)
- ☐ shows frequent slips of the tongue (e.g., saying "brue blush" for blue brush)
- ☐ has difficulty with tongue twisters (e.g., she sells seashells)

Comprehension
- ☐ only responds to part of a multiple-element request or instruction
- ☐ requests multiple repetitions of instructions/directions with little improvement in comprehension
- ☐ relies too much on context to understand what is said
- ☐ has difficulty understanding questions
- ☐ fails to understand age-appropriate stories
- ☐ has difficulty making inferences, predicting outcomes, drawing conclusions
- ☐ lacks understanding of spatial terms such as left-right, front-back

Expressive Language
- ☐ talks in short sentences
- ☐ makes errors in grammar (e.g., "he goed to the store" or "me want that")
- ☐ lacks variety in vocabulary (e.g., uses "good" to mean happy, kind, polite)
- ☐ has difficulty giving directions or explanations (e.g., may show multiple revisions or dead ends)
- ☐ relates stories of events in a disorganized or incomplete manner
- ☐ may have much to say, but provides little specific detail
- ☐ has difficulty with the rules on conversation, such as turn taking, staying on topic, indicating when he/she does not understand

Other Important Factors
- ☐ has a prior history of problems in language comprehension and/or production
- ☐ has a family history of spoken or written language problems
- ☐ has limited exposure to literacy in the home
- ☐ lacks interest in books and shared reading activities
- ☐ does not engage readily in pretend play

Comments

Source: Catts, H. W. (1997). The early identification of language-based reading disabilities. *Lanuague, Speech, and Hearing Services in the Schools, 28,* p.88–89.

Criterion-Referenced Tests. Criterion-referenced tests measure specific mastery of individual skills. They do not assess a student's performance in relation to a standardized sample but focus on the ability to perform the specific skill stated in the accompanying behavioral objective. An example of such a test is the *Brigance Diagnostic Inventory of Basic Skills* (Brigance, 1983). The Brigance Inventory is available for students at three levels: preschool, kindergarten through sixth grade, and fourth through twelfth grades. It assesses basic readiness and academic skills in key subjects, including reading, language arts, and mathematics. Specific areas measured in the reading section are word recognition, comprehension, word analysis, and vocabulary. Information obtained from this test indicates a student's specific skills and deficits. The Inventory of Essential Skills is a section for Grades 4 through 12 that assesses minimal competencies and skills commonly identified as necessary for successful life experiences.

Lindamood Auditory Conceptualization Test. (LAC; Lindamood & Lindamood, 1998). The LAC is a criterion-referenced assessment instrument that is individually administered. It is focused on the discrimination of one speech sound or phoneme from another and the segmentation of the spoken word into its component phonemic units. It is intended to identify students who will be at risk for reading and spelling because of poor phoneme-grapheme correspondence ability. Its primary intent is to measure the ability to distinguish and manipulate sounds as a basis for success in reading and spelling.

Formal Instruments

Formal tests are recommended for teachers who need specific guidelines or tools for screening and other administrative purposes, such as program eligibility. The instruments discussed provide teachers with grade-level information as well as assessment data on specific skills. However, teachers must realize that a grade-level score of 4.2 on a format test is misleading; it does not necessarily mean that the student should be placed in a fourth grade reading program. No formal test can guarantee a student's exact reading level, because publishers use different methods to determine reading levels. Nevertheless, the score does supply a starting point. Students should start with material a half-year below the tested reading level. If problems become apparent, the teacher can modify materials until the proper level of difficulty is determined.

Formal instruments can be used to analyze skills in the same way as informal inventories are used. If word lists or paragraphs are read orally by a student, the teacher phonetically records the errors at the time of the reading or later from a tape recording. Once categorized, the errors provide a picture of the student's needs.

The purposes of formal instruments are a continuum ranging from surveying global reading performances to pinpointing specific strengths and weaknesses. They also have been used to determine class placement. Diagnostic tests are used primarily to identify specific problems and to highlight skills needing remediation.

The Wide Range Achievement Test-Revised (WRAT-R) (Jastak & Wilkinson, 1984). The WRAT is an individual achievement test that covers arithmetic, spelling, and reading. The student's test performance determines a grade level, standard score, and percentile rank. The test has two levels: Level 1 is designed for ages 5 to 12 years and Level 2 for 12 years to adulthood. The reading subtest measures word recognition and can be administered in approximately 10 to 15 minutes. It is composed of a group of words that the student reads orally. Words pronounced incorrectly are marked phonetically to aid in determining the need for remedial instruction. Because the WRAT-R assesses only word recognition, no judgments can be made about total reading ability.

The Peabody Individualized Achievement Test—Revised (PIAT-R) (Markwardt, 1989). The PIAT-R tests mathematics, reading recognition, reading comprehension, spelling, and general knowledge. The reading-recognition subtest measures word-attack skills. As with the WRAT-R, errors can be analyzed to determine skills that need to be taught. The comprehension subtest presents paragraphs to be read silently, after which the student is shown four pictures and is instructed to pick the one that best fits the paragraph. The PIAT-R yields grade and age equivalents, percentiles, and a standard score.

The Slosson Oral Reading Test (SORT) (Slosson, 1983). The SORT is an individualized test of a student's reading level using lists of sight words. Word lists progress in difficulty from primer to high school levels, and the test can be repeated to measure the student's achievement annually. It consists of one page of word lists and is easy to administer and score. Results must be used with caution, because the total assessment is derived from isolated sight words.

The Gray Oral Reading Test-Revised (Wiederholt & Bryant, 1986). This test measures oral reading fluency and diagnoses oral reading problems. The test is available in two forms; each contains 13 reading passages ranging in difficulty from pre-primer to college level. Each passage is accompanied by questions that orally measure literal comprehension. Error analysis gives performance levels for meaning similarity, function similarity, and graphic/phonemic similarity.

The Woodcock Reading Mastery Test-Revised (Woodcock, 1986). This test is appropriate for students from Grades 1 through 12. It is an individual test that measures reading achievement and provides specific diagnostic information. The test is available in two forms with subtests for letter and word identification, word attack, word comprehension, and passage comprehension. The test takes approximately 30 minutes to administer.

Test of Phonological Awareness (TOPA) (Torgesen & Bryant, 1994a). This test is intended to measure young children's awareness of individual sounds in specific words. The assumption is that children who are not sensitive to the phonological structure of words will have more difficulty learning to read. The TOPA is intended for kindergarteners who can benefit from phonological awareness activities as a basis for reading instruction. An early-elementary version of the test is intended to assess difficulties in reading that may be present in first- and second-graders.

Use of Assessment Data

Efficient assessment should begin with survey tests that identify major areas of difficulty. Diagnostic tests then pinpoint specific strengths and weaknesses, which are described as precise tasks through informal tests and task analysis. Goals and objectives for individualized educational programs are derived from this test information. Teachers then prepare instructional lessons to teach the specific skills indicated by the diagnosis, using teaching approaches that capitalize on students' strengths. The teachers evaluate the lessons when they are completed and try alternative methods if necessary.

Assessment should always be considered a continuous process, and the initial appraisal process should take no more than 2 weeks. Students do not learn to read through assessment and appraisal but through good, sound teaching practices. Teachers should remember that the best evaluation is ineffective if the findings are not used in planning the instructional program, if the evaluation process becomes so complicated and tedious that it leaves no room for instruction, or if the evaluation process itself becomes a substitute for actual teaching and learning.

Information from assessment is used to individualize reading instruction. Tailoring reading lessons to meet each student's needs may overwhelm the teacher unfamiliar with management systems. However, efficient yet simple record-keeping procedures like those in Figures 8–4 and 8–5 can be helpful. Figure 8–4 represents a form to use to analyze a student's strengths and weaknesses in various reading areas. To use this form teachers should establish criteria for the evaluation of which skills require practice or have been mastered. Figure 8–5 is a sample class profile of word analysis skills in a format that is appropriate for other reading skill areas as well. Figure 8–6 presents some specific questions that teachers can then use to translate assessment information into individualized teaching plans.

FIGURE 8–4

Reading assessment
summary

Student's name:_____ Age: _____
Class placement: _____ Teacher: _____

Key: N = Not acquired   P = Needs practice   M = Mastered

Reading levels: Independent _____   Tests used: IRI _____
                Instructional _____   Survey _____
                Frustration _____   Diagnostic _____
                                                    Other _____

Sight word vocabulary: SORT _____   Dolch list_____   Other _____

Phonics:
  Consonants

b	c	d	f	g	h	j	k	l	m	n	p	q	r	s	t	v	w	x	y	z

Vowels

	a	e	i	o	u	y
Long sound						
Short sound						

Digraphs

ch	sh	th	wh

Variant vowels

ar	er	ir	or	ur	au	al	on	ow	oi	oy

Blends

bl	cl	fl	gl	pl	sl	br	cr	dr	fr	gr	pr	tr	wn	ap	st

Comprehension: Factual questions _____   Main idea _____
               Inferential questions _____   Sequence of events _____
               Application questions _____   Cause and effect _____

Reading interests: _____
Comments: _____
_____

Once information about each student is organized and easily accessible, a teacher can individualize group instruction. Within a reading group, for example, a few students might be assigned a literal-level purpose in reading a selection whereas other students might be required to make inferences. The group can discuss the story together with teacher guidance.

WORD RECOGNITION INSTRUCTION

The remainder of this chapter is devoted to instructional strategies related to enhanced word recognition skills. This focus reflects the fact that the majority of students with special needs often will have difficulty acquiring a sight vocabulary, typically will experience problems in decoding because of difficulties related to phonological awareness and to using sound-symbol correspondences to phonetically analyze words, and will profit from direct instruction in structural analysis and contextual analysis.

Sight-Word Vocabulary

For learners who are disabled, a key component is learning sight words. Through a whole-word approach students learn to recognize important,

FIGURE 8–5
Class profile of word analysis
skills

Skills		Lyndsay P.	Karen C.	Mike E.	Sharon G.	Jason T.	Marcus W.	Tony S.
		Students						
Reading levels	Independent							
	Instructional							
Consonants	Initial consonants							
	Final consonants							
	Consonant blends							
Vowels	Long sound							
	Short sound							
	Variant							
	Prefixes							
	Suffixes							
Comments								

Key: N = Not acquired
      P = Needs practice
      M = Mastered

high-frequency words without analysis. Further, the teacher can use acquired sight words to introduce and teach decoding skills. Students must achieve automaticity with the sight words they have learned—they must recognize them immediately and automatically—to be able to move continuously through a written passage. Fluent readers use their sight vocabulary consistently, applying phonetic analysis only to new words.

To be remembered, sight words must already be in the learner's speaking and comprehension vocabulary. Sight words can be selected from a variety of sources. Language experience stories (see Chapter 9) include words that are important to the student and are therefore an excellent source

of initial words. Survival words, (e.g., *exit* and *poison*) and survival phrases (e.g., *keep out*) are also important (Tables 8–1 and 8–2). If a basal reading series is used, words from the particular program become a focus of sight-word instruction.

With all students, but especially with those experiencing reading difficulty, a variety of strategies should be used to teach sight words. Attention has been focused on the imagery level of the word to be learned (Hargis, 1982). Imagery level refers to the ease with which a word evokes a concrete picture. High-imagery words include *ear, house,* and *bird;* low-imagery words are *democracy, idea, believe,* and *have.* High imagery immediately increases the speed at which students with

FIGURE 8–6

Assessment considerations to assist in instructional planning

1. What are the student's specific strengths?
   a. What specific phonic knowledge is mastered: letter names? letter sounds? blending?
   b. What specific knowledge of structural analysis is mastered: plural endings? prefixes? suffixes? compound words?
   c. What sight-word categories are mastered: Dolch list? content area words?
   d. What specific comprehension skills are mastered: vocabulary? getting the main idea? summarizing? making inferences? recognizing cause and effect?
   e. Does student comprehend best when reading orally or silently?
   f. What is the student's reading level?
2. What skills are priority concerns (based on the school's curriculum guide, skills checklist, or a basal reader's scope and sequence chart)?
3. What is the next needed skill in each area that can be taught to the student at this time?
4. What is the student's attitude toward reading and reading instruction?
5. What possible organizational arrangement for this classroom setting best meets the needs of the student? (Can the student fit into a small group of students in need of instruction on word endings? Does the whole class need instruction in making inferences? Can the student's sight-word knowledge be developed by using a computer program?)
6. What reading program is most appropriate for the student?
7. What independent practice and reinforcement activities can the student engage in successfully (e.g., follow-up worksheets, computer program, group projects, learning center activities, silent reading and reporting, creative activities like illustrating, dramatizing, constructing, manipulating materials)?
8. What serves as a reinforcer for the student (e.g., progress checklists, gold stars for daily progress, frequent verbal praise, grades, progress notes sent home to parents)?

or without disabilities can learn. In some instances, high imagery can be provided for a word by the context in which it is presented. For example, the word *see* in "I *see* a big lion" becomes more concrete and memorable. A rich experiential background enhances a student's wealth of high-imagery words, including traffic signs, restaurant names, store names, and names of tools, cars, and flowers.

Students with disabilities require many repetitions to learn a sight word. Hargis (1982) adapted the estimates of Gates (1931) to arrive at the number of repetitions necessary for students according to their IQ levels. Those estimations appear in Table 8–3.

A reading selection should present a minimum number of new words to a student. Because basal series and high-interest, low-readability books introduce new words at a higher frequency and with fewer repetitions, teachers must provide activities that increase the number of repetitions. Sight-word diagnosis must document known as well as unknown words. The teacher should use words that students can read, no matter how few, to teach new words. This process is difficult when a student has learned only five words, but using these as the contextual setting for high-imagery words and providing numerous repetitions will enable students to steadily increase their vocabulary. A variety of strategies are appropriate to teach sight words.

Fernald Method (Fernald, 1943). The Fernald method is a classic multisensory remedial approach combining language experience

TABLE 8–1
Fifty most essential survival words

Word	n[a]	mean[b]	Word	n[a]	mean[b]
1. Poison	52	4.90	26. Ambulance	54	4.02
2. Danger	53	4.87	27. Girls	54	4.00
3. Police	52	4.79	28. Open	53	3.98
4. Emergency	54	4.70	29. Out	53	3.98
5. Stop	53	4.66	30. Combustible	54	3.94
6. Not	53	4.53	31. Closed	54	3.90
7. Walk	53	4.49	32. Condemned	54	3.90
8. Caution	54	4.46	33. Up	53	3.89
9. Exit	53	4.40	34. Blasting	54	3.87
10. Men	54	4.39	35. Gentlemen	52	3.86
11. Women	53	4.32	36. Pull	53	3.73
12. Warning	53	4.32	37. Down	53	3.72
13. Entrance	53	4.30	38. Detour	53	3.71
14. Help	54	4.26	39. Gasoline	54	3.70
15. Off	52	4.23	40. Inflammable	53	3.70
16. On	53	4.21	41. In	54	3.68
17. Explosives	52	4.21	42. Push	53	3.68
18. Flammable	53	4.21	43. Nurse	52	3.58
19. Doctor	54	4.15	44. Information	54	3.57
20. Go	53	4.13	45. Lifeguard	52	3.52
21. Telephone	53	4.11	46. Listen	54	3.52
22. Boys	54	4.11	47. Private	53	3.51
23. Contaminated	54	4.09	48. Quiet	53	3.51
24. Ladies	53	4.06	49. Look	53	3.49
25. Dynamite	52	4.04	50. Wanted	54	3.46

Note: [a]The number of participants varies because of omissions or errors by raters.
[b]Maximum rating of an item was 5; minimum was 1. From "Survival Words for Disabled Readers," by E. A. Polloway and C. H. Polloway, 1981, March, *Academic Therapy, 16,* p. 446. Copyright 1981 by Academic Therapy Publications. Reprinted with permission.

with visual, kinesthetic, and tactile (VAKT) instructional techniques. The program consists of four basic steps: eliciting a word from the student, writing it large enough for the student to trace, saying the word as the student traces the word, and having the student write the word from memory. These four steps are intended to provide ways to develop a sight vocabulary by offering the students multiple ways of experiencing the word. Words learned by this procedure can then be alphabetically filed in a word bank. When several words have been learned, the student uses them to dictate a story to the teacher. As the student progresses, the procedure can be modified in various ways. For example, tracing can be done with letters made of sandpaper, smooth paper laid on sandpaper, or sand sprinkled on glue. Teachers should focus on the potential benefits of teaching new words through multiple means. Rather than rigid adherence to the se-

TABLE 8–2

Fifty most essential survival phrases

Phrase	n	mean	Phrase	n	mean
1. Don't walk	53	4.70	26. Wrong way	53	3.96
2. Fire escape	54	4.68	27. No fires	54	3.96
3. Fire extinguisher	54	4.59	28. No swimming	53	3.92
4. Do not enter	53	4.51	29. Watch your step	52	3.92
5. First aid	54	4.46	30. Watch for children	54	3.91
6. Deep water	50	4.38	31. No diving	54	3.91
7. External use only	53	4.38	32. Stop for pedestrians	54	3.89
8. High voltage	54	4.35	33. Post office	52	3.85
9. No trespassing	52	4.35	34. Slippery when wet	53	3.85
10. Railroad crossing	52	4.35	35. Help wanted	54	3.85
11. Rest rooms	52	4.35	36. Slow down	53	3.81
12. Do not touch	52	4.33	37. Smoking prohibited	54	3.80
13. Do not use near open flame	53	4.24	38. No admittance	54	3.78
14. Do not inhale fumes	53	4.24	39. Proceed at your own risk	53	3.77
15. One way	53	4.24	40. Step down	52	3.77
16. Do not cross	53	4.17	41. No parking	52	3.75
17. Do not use near heat	53	4.11	42. Keep closed	54	3.74
18. Keep out	53	4.09	43. No turns	53	3.73
19. Keep off	54	4.07	44. Beware of dog	54	3.72
20. Exit only	53	4.07	45. School zone	53	3.72
21. No right turn	52	4.04	46. Dangerous curve	53	3.71
22. Keep away	52	4.00	47. Hospital zone	54	3.70
23. Thin ice	53	3.98	48. Out of order	53	3.66
24. Bus stop	54	3.98	49. No smoking	53	3.66
25. No passing	52	3.98	50. Go slow	52	3.65

Note: From "Survival Words for Disabled Readers," by E. A. Polloway and C. H. Polloway, 1981, March, *Academic Therapy,* *16,* p. 447. Copyright 1981 by Academic Therapy Publications. Reprinted with permission.

quences outlined by Fernald, teachers are encouraged to investigate multisensory strategies that are effective for individual children and enhance their recognition of sight words.

Word Imprinting. Like the Fernald method, word imprinting is a multisensory approach. Students learn sight words in six steps, using tactile and kinesthetic reinforcement (Carbo, 1978).

1. The teacher says the word; the student repeats it.
2. The meaning of the word is discussed and taught.
3. The word's configuration is drawn.
4. The actual word is traced.
5. The student says the word while tracing it.
6. With eyes closed, the student tries to visualize the word and write it in the air.

Word Banks. Words to be learned through this strategy are written on index cards and placed in each student's "bank," a box established for that purpose. The words that are selected typically derive from reading materials

TABLE 8–3
Average number of word repetitions needed
(Across hypothetical functioning levels)

Mean Number of Word Repetitions Required by Varying IQ Levels	
Repetitions	**IQ Range**
20	120–129
30	110–119
35	90–109
40	80–89
45	70–79
55	60–69

Note. From "Word Recognition Development," by C. H. Hargis, 1982. *Focus on Exceptional Children. 14* (9), p. 3. Copyright 1982 by Love Publishing Company. Reprinted with permission.

that have been presented to the student or ones that will be presented in the future. Common examples also come from the student's own oral language vocabulary.

Initially the words are presented by the teacher and reviewed to ensure that the student can say the word initially and that its meaning is clear. Then students prepare cards for their bank by writing the word, drawing the picture, and dictating a sentence for the teacher to write.

These cards are continuously used to practice the words, but they also need to be used in context because repeated practice of words in isolation is the least efficient method of learning sight words. Strategies for repeated use of the words in context are described in the activities section of this chapter. Collecting words in a bank gives students a sense of ownership that may motivate them. It also makes the words easily available for informal practice and reference.

Errorless Discrimination. The errorless discrimination strategy is especially appropriate for students with more severe disabilities who have failed to learn by conventional methods. The teacher presents the word in isolation, reads it aloud, and says, "Point to the word _____." In the

four to six trials that follow, the target word appears among three or four other words. At first the words differ significantly from the target word but converge in appearance as the exercise continues. After the students begin pointing to the word with 100% accuracy, the teacher directs them to "read this word" (Walsh & Lamberts, 1979). This procedure is repeated daily; words can be taped for continued practice at home or independent practice at school. The availability of the words on tape gives students a sense of control over their own learning while providing an opportunity for repetition and drill.

Edmark Program. The Edmark Reading Program, Level 1 (Edmark Associates, 1984) was developed to teach a 150-word sight vocabulary to students in Grades K-1 or individuals with mental retardation. It is appropriate for children who have some verbal skills (i.e., can repeat, can point, and have sufficient receptive language to understand and respond to a teacher). The program comes in kit form with more than 200 lessons consisting of word recognition, storybooks, picture/phrase matching, and a direction book. The goal of Level 1 is to promote acquisition of a sight vocabulary, and it can serve as a good beginning approach to reading, especially for those with more severe disabilities. Level 2 is for students (Grades 1-3) who have completed Level 1 and teaches 200 new words from the Dolch high frequency word list and early elementary basal readers. This level includes storybook lessons with graphics and story lines portraying real-life situations to increase students' involvement. Successful completion of the program should provide students with a solid reading foundation that can be supplemented with phonics instruction.

Functional Reading. A sight-word approach is recommended for initiating functional reading, a level of literacy necessary for information and protection. An understanding of this concept is particularly important for teachers of high–school-age students who must decide how to teach reading. Instruction at this level raises a number of difficult questions: Which reading program should the current teacher select? Is it best in the limited time remaining to teach functional reading so that students will know some words for their own protection and safety? Or is there still time to teach students decoding strategies, aiming toward an acceptable level of literacy?

Teachers of adolescent students continually encounter this dilemma. Choosing the most appropriate approach for each student must depend on a number of critical factors. These include:

- the student's attitude, energy, and motivation for learning to read
- the teacher's assessment of the previously used instructional approaches
- the assessment information that points to the causes of the student's inability to read
- the teacher's knowledge of strategies essential to reading progress for the student
- the identification of the type of program that will provide a successful experience for the student

After weighing these factors, the teacher can decide to concentrate efforts on functional reading, exert a final effort toward teaching remedial skills, or focus primarily on one option but include the other in a less intensive form. Students need to understand clearly what the goal is and how it will be measured at specific intervals. When goals are organized into small steps, adolescent students are motivated by their progress, which suggests that the problem they have faced unsuccessfully throughout their school careers may have a solution.

Reading for protection requires minimal but practical competence. Generally, this is the level of reading achievement that enables minimal survival in today's word-dependent world. Survival words should be taught as sight words, using the strategies described earlier. Comprehension of these words must also be specifically taught. The teacher may need to provide an actual experience that demonstrates the word's meaning, produce a concrete object, or identify a special characteristic of the concept.

Fortunately, with relatively few exceptions, students with disabilities learn to read beyond the level of survival words. The next stage of functional reading addresses what the world of work requires and thus focuses on sufficient skill to fill out applications and related forms, pass a driver's test, follow simple factory check-in directions, order from a restaurant menu, and handle similar life tasks.

Teachers can use a combination of strategies to teach this level of functional reading. Using the whole-word approach, the specific vocabulary of applications and forms can be taught, and then decoding clues can be introduced. The most important step is teaching students to generalize this knowledge by providing practice with a variety of formats and situations that they are likely to encounter. Many workbooks contain samples of forms and applications.

Decoding via Sound-Symbol Correspondences

A crucial foundation to reading is the ability of young students to learn and use the productive relationships between sounds and symbols of their language system. As more careful analyses continue to be conducted, it has become clearer that teachers must attend to this area if problems are to be prevented in children who are at risk for reading failure and if remediation is to be achieved for these young readers who fail to make satisfactory progress.

Recent research by Shaywitz and Shaywitz (1997) further indicates that the difficulties of many children with reading disabilities are related to the limited neurological linkages between the written word and its phonological elements. The implication is that these linkages must be taught to give these children an opportunity to improve their skills (Center for Future of Teaching and Learning, 1996).

The importance of phonetic analysis is best understood by first considering the importance of phonological awareness, that is, the awareness of the phonological structure of words. Research has shown a significant relationship between reading acquisition and phonological awareness (see Fletcher et al., 1998; Jerger, 1996; Mather,

1992; Pressley & Rankin, 1994; Simmons, Gunn, Smith, & Kameenui, 1994) and supports the fact that individuals become better readers if they understand the relationship between phonemic correspondences and the actual reading process. Thus, the basis for the decoding process can be seen as coming from phonological awareness, including phoneme awareness, and the subsequent use of phonetic analysis as a reading/decoding strategy. The rationale for attention to this area is based on the growing evidence that the phonological system is the primary problem area for students with reading disabilities and that it requires explicit instruction for those who do not learn to read independently. At the same time, it is likely to not be a concern for accomplished readers who implicitly learn the sound system and exhibit automaticity at recognizing and linking phonemes.

Phonological awareness includes concern for discriminating between words and between sounds, identifying certain sounds within words, manipulating the sounds in words, identifying phonemes, (e.g., *ax = a/k/s, bake = b/a/k, thing = th/i/ng*), and isolating sounds in words, such as in the initial, medial, and final position.

Instruction based on these considerations promotes the students' ability to be aware of phonemes in words and serves as a foundation for the use and application of sound-symbol correspondences in reading as a component of phonetic analysis. Consistent with this transitional focus, Simmons et al. (1994) thus propose that appropriate prereading instruction include an emphasis on direct teaching of auditory segmenting (breaking words into component parts) and auditory blending (recombining words from smaller parts), as well as letter-sound correspondences. Simmons et al. also recommend that teachers follow these steps in phonological awareness instruction: (a) focus on the auditory components of words initially; (b) introduce the concept of segmenting by starting with sentences and moving to words, then syllables, and finally, phonemes; (c) control task complexity by beginning with words containing fewer phonemes; (d) model and reinforce segmenting and blending skills; and (e) integrate segmenting and blending skills into meaningful contexts of reading, writing, and spelling activities.

Varied exercises can promote the development of phonological awareness in young children: Some examples include:

- Expose children to nursery rhymes to highlight how sounds are stripped from words and replaced with other sounds to make new words.
- Teach phoneme segmentation: What sounds do you hear in the word *hot?*
- Play oddity games: Which last sound is different in *doll, hop,* and *top?* Which middle sound is different in *pin, gun,* and *bun?*
- Play sound to word matching: Is there a /k/ in *bike?*
- Work on sound isolation: What is the first sound in *rose?*
- Teach blending skills: What word do the sounds /m/ /a/ /t/ make?
- Teach children to tap out the number of syllables in a word such as *backyard* or the number of sounds in single syllable words such as *mat, pin, big,* etc.
- Play syllable/phoneme deletion games: Say *backyard.* Now say *backyard* without the *back.* Say *cat.* Now say *cat* without the /t/ sound. (CEC Today, 1995, p. 9).

Phonetic Analysis. Teaching phonetic analysis, traditionally called phonics, builds on phonemic awareness as students begin to learn how to apply their knowledge of the phonological system to the written word. Because of its nature, phonetic analysis is technically "reading for reading," not for meaning. Therefore, a key concern is that a meaning focus must be included subsequently. Phonetic analysis provides a strategy to attack unknown words via verbal mediation; that is, it offers the student a way to decode the unknown by applying a learned rule. Given its crucial role in early reading development, Morgan (1995) notes that one of the unfortunate side effects of inclusion has been the danger that students who need and would profit from instruction in phonetic analysis are placed in general education classes where it is possible that no such instruction may be provided.

In order to use phonics, students must be taught the sounds for consonants and vowels and the ways to blend these sounds. Key words are usually presented to reinforce the memory of each letter sound; for instance, *sun* suggests the *s* sound. Phonics instruction is divided into two basic, complementary methods. The synthetic method teaches letter sounds and blends and then progresses to words, such as *c/a/t->cat*. The analytic method begins with the teacher dictating words to students, who then break the words into their component sounds: *cat->c/a/t*.

Phonetic analysis can be used with students at all educational levels, although it is most appropriate in elementary school. It can be used as an initial step in a developmental program with young students just beginning to learn to read, or it can be used as a remedial technique with students who have developed a strong sight vocabulary but lack the skills needed to analyze unfamiliar words. It can be adapted for learners being taught with a basal series or with a language-experience approach using simple drills and games to reinforce basic rules. In each case the teacher's goal is to produce fluent readers with the necessary skills to decode unknown words. Once decoded, the words should become part of the students' sight word vocabularies so that they can be read without analysis when next encountered.

The sequence for phonetic analysis skills that is described here is adapted from the classic work of Orton (1964). It also includes emphasis on structural analysis skills.

1. *b, s, f, m, t* in initial and final positions
2. short *a*
3. all consonants except the five already learned
4. short *o, i*
5. digraphs (*sh, ch, th, wh*)
6. initial consonant blends (*bl, br, st*)
7. short *u*
8. final consonant blends (*nd, nk*)
9. short *e*
10. long vowels (final *e,* double vowels)
11. syllabication
12. *r*-influenced vowels (*er, ir, ur, ar*)
13. suffixes (*-s, -ing, -ed*)
14. vowel teams (*ai, ea, ow, ea*)
15. diphthongs (*oy, au*)
16. prefixes (*re-, pre-, un-*)

This sequence introduces five consonants, then short *a*. It allows the formation of short words quickly (e.g., *bat, fat, tab*) to provide immediate decoding experience.

The Center for the Future of Teaching and Learning (1996) emphasizes that explicit instructions should be provided on the sound-spelling correspondences that are observed most frequently in the English language. Successful ability to decode based on these sound-spelling relationships are perceived as necessary for learning to read and eliminate the need for the virtually infinite number of potential relationships that could be incorporated within an instructional program (Table 8–4).

Teaching Phonetic Analysis Skills. A variety of strategies for teaching phonetic analysis are available and reflect to some degree the biases and experiences of those using them. Teachers are encouraged to develop their own instructional sequence and then revise it to meet student needs. Two examples are presented below.

Grossen and Carnine (1993, p. 22–24) outline four general steps for successful phonics instruction

1. *Introduce letter-sound correspondence in isolation* Letter-sound correspondences should be taught directly, instead of through implicit approaches in which individual letters are never pronounced in isolation. For example, instead of introducing the letter *s* by its inclusion in *sun* or *soap*, it should be written in isolation and pronounced *sss*. Some instructors would like to see sounds in isolation used carefully and tied as quickly as possible to usage in words.
2. *Teach students to blend sounds to read words* Students should be taught to blend sounds after they have learned two sounds that can be blended, such as *a* and *m*. Breaks in words can be dealt with by instructing students to say the word faster.

TABLE 8–4
The 48 most regular sound-letter relationships

a	as in fat	g	as in goat	v	
m		l		e	
t		h		u-e	as in use
s		u		p	
i	as in sit	c	as in cat	w	"woo" as in well
f		b		j	
a-e	as in cake	n		i-e	as in pipe
d		k		y	"yee" as in yuk
r		o-e	as in pole	z	
ch	as in chip	ou	as in cloud	kn	as in know
ea	beat	oy	toy	oa	boat
ee	need	ph	phone	oi	boil
er	fern	qu	quick	ai	maid
ay	hay	sh	shop	ar	car
igh	high	th	thank	au	haul
ew	shrewd	ir	first	aw	lawn

Source: Center for Future of Teaching and Learning (1996). Thirty years of NICHD research: What we now know about how children learn to read. *Effective School Practices, 15*(3), p.40.

3. *Provide immediate feedback on oral reading errors* Oral reading provides a mechanism by which teachers can identify and immediately correct students' reading errors.
4. *Provide extensive practice* New sounds should be practiced in isolation daily over several days, then incorporated in reading activities.

Kaluger and Kolson (1969) include six instructional steps in their program: introduce, identify, visually cue, synthesize, reinforce, and review.

1. *Introduce*
   a. Write the letter *t*.
   b. Explain that the object is to learn the sound of this consonant.
   c. Write three or four words beginning with *t* that are in the students' sight vocabulary (e.g., take, tent, toe).
   d. Read the words aloud, emphasizing *t*.
   e. Ask students for additional words that begin with *t*.
   f. Write these in another list, underlining the letter *t*.
2. *Identify*
   a. Instruct students to look at all the words and identify how they are alike.
   b. Ask a student to say the sound of the letter *t* as heard in *tent*.
   c. Read the list of words again, pointing to the *t* in each, saying its sound, and reading it.

3. *Visually cue*
   a. Give each student a 3-inch square tagboard card.
   b. Instruct students to draw a picture of a tent and write the letter *t* on the card.
4. *Synthesize:* Introduce activities requiring students to use and manipulate the phonic generalization just learned.
5. *Reinforce*
   a. Assign and supervise practice activities.
   b. Dictate words and syllables that use the newly learned letters and have students write them.
6. *Review*
   a. Remind students that this letter has the sound of the *t* in *tent.*
   b. Ask students for additional words that begin with *t.*

Phonological Awareness and Decoding Programs

Lindamood Phoneme Sequence Program. The Lindamood Program for Reading, Spelling, and Speech (Lindamood & Lindamood, 1998) is a revision of the former Auditory Discrimination in Depth program. The new program focuses on the development of phonemic awareness by enabling learners to identify and sequence individual sounds in their order within words to promote competence in the three areas of reading, spelling, and speech. The key element is learning consonant and vowel sounds through feedback from articulating the sounds. It includes a training manual, a research booklet, videotapes, photos of correct formation for phoneme pronunciation, and a variety of instructional materials. A comprehensive review of related research has been reported by Truch (1998) that focuses on the effectiveness of the Lindamood program within the context of an analysis of the role of phonological processing in reading and spelling.

Phonological Awareness Training for Reading This program developed by Torgesen and Bryant (1994b) was designed to increase phonological awareness in young children with particular emphasis on kindergarten children at risk for failure and first- and second-grade children who have already begun to experience difficulty in learning to read. It is an approximately 12–week-long program that teaches sensitivity to phonological structures. The program includes a training manual, picture word cards, rhyming picture cards, and a variety of other instructional materials. It was based on validation studies conducted by the senior author under the auspices of the National Institute of Mental Health.

Direct Instruction Programs Several direct instruction programs can provide approaches to reading instruction in general, with a focus on decoding. The original DISTAR program developed by Engelmann and Bruner initially was based on the instructional procedures developed by Carl Bereiter and Siegfried Engelmann in the late 1960s for use with young, culturally disadvantaged children. These programs are highly structured, sequence each step of learning, and contain criterion objectives for each learning task as a developmental program in beginning reading instruction for any student but are more commonly is used for remedial purposes. The program currently in use in the elementary schools is *Reading Mastery,* which continues this focus for young learners who experience difficulty in decoding.

The Corrective Reading Program (CRP) (Engelmann, Becker, Hanner, & Johnson, 1989) Another direct instruction program of Science Research Associates, this is a remedial program for upper elementary, middle, and high school students who have not mastered decoding and/or comprehension skills. The program is divided into two strands, decoding and comprehension, each with three levels of skill development. The decoding strand follows the traditional DISTAR approach in presenting decoding strategies; the comprehension strand presents a variety of formats involving real-life survival situations that are excellent for the adolescent learner.

CRP increases and ensures time on task by providing group lesson plans using teaching strategies that require students to answer aloud and in unison. Each lesson is fast paced, keeping students thinking and providing less opportunity for students to become distracted. Because CRP uses the direct instruction approach, it provides a "script" for teachers to follow. Special motivation for adolescent students is provided in a group reinforcement component, with each student receiving additional points based on the group's performance.

Some research (e.g., Polloway, Epstein, Polloway, Patton, & Ball, 1986) indicates that students with learning disabilities as well as those who were mildly retarded increased decoding and comprehension skills after participating in the Corrective Reading Program for an academic year. This study also notes that, although CRP was effective with both groups, those students identified as learning disabled showed overall greater gains.

Glass Analysis for Decoding (Glass & Glass, 1978). Glass analysis is a technique to teach letter clusters; it uses packs of cards organized into 119 clusters, ranging from the most common to the most difficult. Students learn a sound cluster and, through a rapid series of steps, add letters that change and extend the cluster. Students are taught both to see and to hear sounds as letter clusters in whole words. This is a unique technique that can also motivate adolescents still in need of phonics practice and is particularly recommended for students with learning disabilities.

Writing to Read. *Writing to Read* is a computer-based teaching system recommended for beginning readers. It begins with the vocabulary that students already know and goes on to introduce 42 sound/symbol relationships that the author believes children need to learn before writing is introduced. The message conveyed to students is that they make the sounds that form letters and words, which can be seen, read, and written. Students begin by working with the computer, then move to audiotapes, and then to electric typewriters. Some writing is also done on chalkboard and in personal journals. The development of this unique approach to the teaching of reading was funded by IBM, which has also created Writing to Read Centers in numerous schools.

Structural Analysis

Structural analysis skills enable students to use larger segments of words for decoding cues. Recognition of root words, compound words, prefixes, suffixes, contractions, and plurals allows students to use clusters of letters to assist in reading a new word. Structural analysis is an essential word-recognition strategy that directly influences reading fluency; continued letter-by-letter phonetic analysis slows the reading process and will inhibit comprehension. The strategies suggested for teaching phonics also apply to teaching structural analysis.

One key area of structural analysis is syllabication. The method described herein was developed to teach advanced structural analysis skills to readers who are disabled while minimizing their need to learn the many complex rules and exceptions of the English language. Two syllabication rules form the basis for a systematic approach to analyzing polysyllabic words. Using this sequence, students learn to recognize and count syllables, to apply the two rules to words with two or more syllables, to use context clues, and to rely on vocabulary to correct any distortions in pronunciations. Without a multitude of rules to memorize, students can learn to read larger words using the generalizations learned previously.

The first rule, dividing syllables between two consonants, can be illustrated by the word *rabbit*. Instruction would emphasize that rabbit should have two syllables (two sounded vowels), should be divided between *b* and *b* (two consonants together), and then read as two small words and blended. The word *between,* an exception to this rule, would first be pronounced *bet-ween* and then read correctly (*be-tween*) after the student notes the distortion.

The second rule, dividing syllables between a vowel and a consonant, can be illustrated by the word *favor.* Division would fall between *a* and *v* (because of the vowel-consonant-vowel combination), and the word would be read and blended. These two rules can extend to words with more syllables (e.g., *discussion* and *tomato*, respectively) and with both combinations present (e.g., *envelope, remainder*). Polloway and Polloway (1978) present the full 11-step program, which can provide a method of improving word-attack skills for students who have reached approximately third- or fourth-grade reading levels. The steps are (as adapted from Polloway & Smith, 1999):

A. *Objective:*
   1. Student will identify how many syllables are heard in known word.
   2. Student will divide a known word orally.
   Procedure:
   1. Teacher orally explains concept and demonstrates on known words.
   2. Student is given words to divide orally.
   Sample Word List: tomato, sunshine, toe, cucumber
B. *Objective:* Student will recognize that a word has as many syllables as vowels heard.
   Procedure:
   1. Teacher writes known words and student tells how many syllables are heard and how many vowels are seen and heard.
   2. Process continues until student learns that the number of vowels heard equals the number of syllables.
   Sample Word List: tomato, sunshine, toe, cucumber
C. *Objective:* Student will determine how many syllables an unknown word will have.
   Procedure:
   1. Review silent e rule, and rule that when two vowels come together, one sound results.
   2. Teacher writes unknown word; student determines which vowels will be silent and predicts number of syllables.
   Sample Word List: domino, barbecue, stagnate, mouse
D. *Objective:* Student will syllabicate words that follow the *vc/cv* pattern.

Procedure:
   1. Teacher writes and student divides two-syllable words that fit the pattern.
   2. Student practices dividing and pronouncing two syllable *vc/cv* words.
   3. Teacher demonstrates process of dividing longer known words:
      a. Determine number of syllables.
      b. To establish first division, start with first vowel and look for *vc/cv* pattern, then divide.
      c. To establish second division, start with second vowel and look for *vc/cv* pattern, then divide.
      d. Continue procedure until all syllables are determined.
      e. Pronounce word.
   4. Student practices dividing and pronouncing unknown words that contain *vc/cv* pattern.
   Sample Word List:
   1. Teaching words: *rabbit, bitter, pepper, mixture*
   2. Practice words: *Volpone, Vermeer, Bellew, Aspic* [Note: names chosen as unknown words]
E. *Objective:* Student will be able to syllabicate words that contain the *v/cv* pattern.
   Procedure: Follow instructions for Step D, substituting the *v/cv* pattern.
   Sample Word List:
   1. Teaching words: *labor, favor, basic, demand*
   2. Practice words: *Cahill, Zuzo, Theimer, Tatum*
F. *Objective:* Student will syllabicate words that contain both *vc/cv* and *v/cv* patterns.
   Procedure:
   1. Teacher writes and student divides known words that contain both patterns.
   2. Student practices dividing and pronouncing unknown words with both patterns.
   Sample Word List:
   1. Teaching words: *envelope, cucumber, remainder, resulting*
   2. Practice words: *Provenzano, Tedesco, Dannewitz, Oberlin*

G. *Objective:* Student will syllabicate words that have a *vcccv* or *vccccv* pattern.
Procedure:
1. Teacher writes and student divides known words containing *vcccv* or *vccccv* patterns until student recognizes that the division is based on consonant blends and digraphs.
2. Student practices dividing and pronouncing unknown words containing both patterns.
Sample Word List:
1. Teaching words: *concrete, pitcher, contract, merchant*
2. Practice words: *Omohundro, Armentrout, Marshall, Ostrander*

H. *Objective:* Student will syllabicate words that end with *-cle.* (i.e., consonant *-le*)
Procedure:
1. Teacher writes and student divides known words ending with *-le* until student generalizes that when preceded by *cl,* finalize *e* is not silent but produces a syllable that contains *-cle* and the preceding consonant.
2. Student practices dividing and pronouncing unknown words containing the *-cle* ending.
Sample Word List:
1. Teaching words: *candle, rattle, dribble, staple*
2. Practice words: *whipple, biddle, noble, radle*

I. *Objective:* Student will recognize the *y* in the medial or final position as a vowel.
Procedure:
1. Teacher tells student that *y* will be a vowel in the medial or final position.
2. Teacher writes and student divides known words containing *y* in both positions.
3. Student practices dividing and pronouncing unknown words that contain *y* in the medial or final position.
Sample Word List:
1. Teaching words: *funny, my, cranky, style*
2. Practice words: *Snydor, Murtry, Tyson, Gentry*

J. *Objective:* Student will divide and pronounce unknown words containing all patterns.
Procedure: Student practices dividing and pronouncing unknown words containing all patterns.

Sample Word List: Hirshoren, Shirly, Ruckle, Espenshade

K. *Objective:* Student will syllabicate and pronounce unknown words met in context.
Procedure:
1. Student silently reads material on instructional level.
2. After reading is completed, teacher checks student's accuracy in decoding unknown words in context.

This program is intended as a way to use the student's existing graphophonemic skills to analyze longer words beyond the student's current reading vocabulary. To the degree that such a task can be done automatically, it can be incorporated within the process of reading a passage without significant interference with comprehension.

Contextual Analysis

Contextual analysis involves the identification of an unknown word based on its use in a sentence or passage. It functions as a system of syntactic and semantic cueing (Figure 8–7). Context clues not only may help readers identify words but also aid readers to derive word meanings, particularly in content area subjects (Roe, Stoodt, & Burns, 1995). Smith (1988) asserts that context is defined not just by the visual information (e.g., words and sentences) surrounding an unknown word, but by the author's purpose, the reader's prior knowledge and current expectations, and the text as a whole. According to Smith, these factors combine to help the reader bring meaning to the text.

At the primary school level, students' listening vocabulary and comprehension may supercede their decoding skills and thus their ability to use context may be relatively effective. They can use structural and meaning cues to follow the sentences to anticipate forthcoming words and make a guess about one that they might not be able to recognize on sight (e.g., "Susie liked to watch the funny shows on the _____ (television)." "John had a little red _____ (wagon)" (Greene, 1998).

FIGURE 8–7
Contextual analysis skills

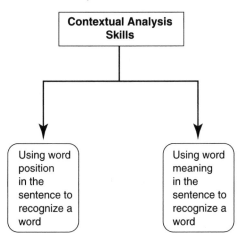

Source: From *Designing Instructional Strategies: The Prevention of Academic Learning Problems* (p. 217) by E. J. Kameenui and D. C. Simmons. 1990. Upper Saddle River, NJ: Merrill/Prentice Hall. Copyright © 1990 by Prentice Hall Publishing Company. Reprinted with permission of Merrill, an imprint of Prentice Hall Publishing Company.

The difficulty in the use of context becomes evident as students move to middle school. As Greene (1998) notes:

a.) New content-area vocabulary words do not preexist in their listening vocabularies. They can guess wagon. But they can't guess circumnavigation or chlorophyll based on context. . . . these words are not in their listening vocabularies.

b.) When all of the words readers never learned to decode in grades one to four are added to all the textbook vocabulary words that don't preexist in readers' listening vocabularies, the percentage of unknown words teeters over the brink; the text now contains so many unknown words that there's no way to get the sense of the sentence.

c.) Text becomes more syntactically embedded, and comprehension disintegrates. Simple English sentences can be stuffed full of prepositional phrases, dependent clauses, and compoundings. Eventually, there's so much language woven into a sentence that readers lose meaning. When syntactically embedded sentences crop up in science and social studies texts, many can't comprehend (p. 76).

Therefore, the challenge for teachers is to find a way to encourage the use of context primarily when it assists in enhancing comprehension of text (e.g., through vocabulary development) and figuring out the occasional word but not to overemphasize it to the point where it becomes a primary strategy used by students. The Center for Future of Teaching and Learning (1996) posits that an overemphasis on prediction from context can have a negative effect on reading and delay successful acquisition. Drawing on the work of Stanovich and Stanovich (1995), the Center indicates that it is incorrect to assume that predicting forthcoming words in sentences is a relatively easy activity and one that results in a high level of accuracy. Rather, it appears that the use of semantic and syntactic cues is a minor aspect of the way that mature readers attack the reading task. Consequently, poor readers are more likely to rely on context to a significant degree when their ability to decode is too weak to assist them in the task.

The Center for Future of Teaching and Learning (1996, p.41) summarizes the challenge for children as follows: "Much research has evaluated the effectiveness of prediction [contextual analysis] as a strategy for word recognition. Though prediction is valuable in comprehension for predicting the next event or predicting an outcome, the research indicates that it is not useful in word recognition".

Using Word Analysis in Reading

The use of contextual analysis is a step in the use of CRUSH, a word-recognition strategy for identifying unknown, polysyllabic words. CRUSH refers to the following:

- Context: Use contextual analysis for periodic (i.e., infrequent) determination of meaning for new vocabulary words.
- Rapid: Rapidly focus on initial consonant, vowel sounds and prefixes and suffixes while reviewing whole words.
- Unimportant: Skip over unimportant words that do not require precise pronunciation (e.g., names).
- Syllabicate: Apply syllabication strategies.

- Help: Seek help (e.g., from teacher, peer, dictionary).

The use of CRUSH represents a teaching strategy that can assist students in thinking about how they will respond when confronted with unknown words. Although research indicates that mature readers are most successful when they respond to the inherent sound-symbol correspondences in their reading, the steps as outlined in CRUSH will give those who experience difficulty ways to generate meaning for new vocabulary words, focus on the most efficient sound-symbol correspondences that provide key graphophonemic cues, ignore the need for pronunciation of words that do not affect meaning, and utilize more complex syllabication strategies when they are necessary to determine the pronunciation of a particular word and/or an understanding of its meaning.

SUMMARY

This chapter focuses on assessment and instruction in reading with special emphasis on decoding. Specific suggestions are made for formal and teacher-oriented assessment that assist in instructional planning. Instructional strategies and programs for promoting word recognition and word analysis are presented. Special emphasis is placed on phonological awareness and phonetic analysis for students with reading disabilities.

ACTIVITIES

The activities listed here are representative of reading strategies that are intended to serve as a basis for reinforcing skill work that is being provided in the area of word recognition. The activities are grouped according to three topics: early reading, word analysis, and sight vocabulary.

Early Reading

1. Make two identical sets of index cards using varied but similar designs. Turn one set of cards face up and spread them on a flat sur-

face. The second group remains face down in a stack. The child draws one card from the pile and places it on its mate. The game can be varied by replacing the designs with pictures, letters, and, for more advanced students, simple two-, three-, or four-letter words.

2. Give students objects (e.g., pencils, finger puppets, crayons, or cards) of three or four colors. When you hold up a colored card, each child should raise the object that is the same color.

3. Letter recognition can become a daily activity by attaching library pockets to the children's desks and placing a tagboard card printed with a letter of the alphabet in each packet. Each time that the class lines up, the teacher calls a letter of the alphabet, and the person with that letter gives it to the teacher and gets into line (Lake, 1987).

4. Have children sort small cardboard tiles with letters or small words on them into small milk cartons or egg-carton sections with a similar letter or word on the outside.

5. Worksheets can be made of primary lined paper with a green margin drawn on the left for *go* and a red margin drawn on the right for *stop*. Each line has a series of geometric figures running across the page. Students put a mark in each figure, starting on the green and stopping on the red, to practice directionality.

6. Show students four objects, discuss them, and then remove one. Have students tell which object was removed.

7. Select one student to come to the front. Have the other students study the child, who then leaves the room. List all things that the other students can remember about the chosen child.

8. Cut strips of construction paper in sizes suitable for making paper chains. Draw paper chains on index cards, using the colors in different sequences on each card. Instruct the students to make their chains in the same sequence shown on the cards. The activity can be varied by using beads or macaroni of different shapes or colors.

9. Use cardboard tiles with letters on them. Arrange two or three tiles in a sequence. Allow

students to match the sequence. Have more advanced students cover the model and re-produce it from memory.

Word Analysis

1. Initial consonant sounds can be practiced by gluing pictures of simple objects on small cards. Have students place the cards on a grid on which each square has a consonant letter corresponding to the beginning sound of an object on the cards. Consonant blends and final consonant sounds can be drilled in the same manner.

2. Make word wheels of word families, changing only the initial consonants. These devices not only give practice in consonant sounds but also are excellent for sound blending. Word wheels are two circles made of oaktag, one smaller than the other and fastened together in the center with a brass fastener so that they can rotate. The different word bases (e.g., -ag, -ad, -at) are written on the exposed edge of the larger circle, and the different initial consonants are written on the edge of the smaller circle. As students rotate the top circle, different words are formed, which students can read aloud to a friend.

3. Make a tape recording of 20 to 25 words. Instruct students to listen to each word and write the sounds they hear at the beginning of each word. The answers can be given at the end of the tape or in an envelope to be opened at the end of the tape. Time can be saved and confusion avoided by providing a sheet for students to write their responses on that has been numbered to correspond with the tape. This activity can also be used with vowel sounds and ending sounds.

4. Make two-part puzzles with an initial sound on one part and a word family on the other. Have students put the puzzles together and pronounce the words. Animal shapes are popular and can be cut between the head and body or body and tail. Use the same idea for contractions, compound words, and root words with endings. Character combinations are popular also: Snoopy and his doghouse, Woodstock and his nest, and Batman and his cape. Three-part puzzles can be made to accommodate adding prefixes and suffixes to root words (e.g., unfolded).

5. Class bookmaking and rhyming phrases can be combined to spark interest and creativity. On the first day read aloud a book that uses repeated phrases or rhymes (e.g., *Brown Bear, Brown Bear, What Do You See?* Martin, 1983) and have students draw a picture of themselves. On the next day have them complete the picture by adding details and activity to it to make it illustrate the repetitive phrase. They should write the phrase and their explanation of the picture below the illustration. Assemble all the pictures for a class version of the story (Hamilton, Miller, & Wood, 1987).

6. Have students make notebooks for sounds. As sounds are presented, students can cut out pictures of objects that begin with each specific sound and glue them into the book. Later, students can write words that they have learned to recognize or spell that begin with each specific sound.

7. List on the board the letters for the vowels, blends, or consonants that have been studied. Have students stand in a large circle with one student in the center. The student in the center tosses a ball to a student in the circle and calls out one of the letters from the board. The student who catches the ball has to say a word that contains the sound that was called. That student then goes to the center and throws the ball.

8. Recognition of prefixes and suffixes can be practiced by listing words on the chalkboard or on a worksheet and having students underline the prefix, suffix, or both. You may also call out words while students write the prefix or suffix they hear in the word, or they may find and write different words containing the same prefix or suffix.

9. Write multisyllabic words on small cards, one word per card. Place the cards in an envelope

and clip it to a manila folder. Inside the folder draw several columns, numbered 2, 3, 4, and so on as room permits. The student counts the number of syllables in the word on the card and writes in the proper column. The cards have the correct number of syllables written on the back, or an answer sheet can be provided for immediate feedback.

10. Draw several worms on a worksheet, and write a root word on each of their heads. Have students cut out circular worm sections containing suffixes and add appropriate sections to each worm. This can be varied using a train or octopus or by drawing the object on the board and letting students take turns adding the suffixes.

11. Give each student a set of index cards, with one number on each card. When you say a word, students should hold up index cards with the number that corresponds to the syllables they hear.

12. Make sound wheels. Place a consonant in the center of each wheel. Have students write or draw words beginning with that sound on the spokes of the wheel.

13. Use a game board and a tape player to help students develop syllabication skills. Make a tape by first recording a new word and then pausing. During the pause students should determine the number of syllables in the word. After the pause, record the correct number of syllables so that students can self-check. Using the on/off switch, students can listen to the tape and move pieces on a game board according to the number of syllables in the words. However, students can move their pieces only if they accurately determine the number of syllables. The first student to the end of the board wins (Aullis, 1978).

Sight Vocabulary

1. List words on the chalkboard. Have two students stand with their backs to the lists. As you call out a word, the students turn; the first to find the word receives a point.

2. Make a gameboard of oaktag with a path of squares. Mark "start" and "finish" squares and various outer squares with directions like "move ahead three squares," "move back three squares," or "short cut" with a path to another square. Laminate the board or cover it with clear Contact paper. Write words that are to become sight vocabulary words in the open squares with a grease pencil. Students then throw dice to determine how far they are to move. They must pronounce the word they land on to remain in the game. The game can be varied by changing the words, and several boards can be made to fit the season of the year.

3. Make a ladder or rocket ship blastoff pad and place a sight word on each level. Have students pronounce words to see how far up they can get.

4. Give students cards with sight words on them. Call out the words, and have students hold the appropriate card up in front of them.

5. Put pictures of words like *ball* or *car* on one side of a card, and write the word on the other side. Make a game board similar to a bingo card, with each sight word written on it for each child. Place cards with the word side up in a pile. Students take turns drawing cards. They must be able to say the word correctly before placing it on their boards. The picture on the back makes the game self-correcting. If the student cannot recognize the word, the card is placed at the bottom of the pile. The first student to get four words in a row in any direction wins the game.

6. Make two sets of cards, one with pictures of sight words and the other with the words written out. Spread the word cards face up on a flat surface. Place the picture cards face up in a pile in the middle. The first student to point to the word matching each picture card takes the picture card, thus exposing the picture of the next word to be identified. The student with the most picture cards at the end of the game wins.

7. Put sight words on index cards, with each word appearing on four different cards. Then

play a variant of "Go Fish" by calling for various words.

8. A form of "Concentration" can be played by making two sets of identical cards with sight words. Begin with five pairs of cards. Place the cards spread out in two areas, face down on a flat surface. The child turns up a card in one set and then tries to find the card that matches in the other set. When a match is made, the student pronounces the word and gets to keep the cards.

9. Use a chart-size pegboard and attach hooks on which index cards can be hung. Write vocabulary words on index cards, punch a hole in each card, and hang the cards from the hooks on the peg board. Give students a rubber jar-ring to toss at a hook on the board. When a ring lands on a hook, that card is removed from the hook, and the student pronounces the word to earn a point. The one with the most points wins. The game can be varied by using bean bags to throw at a card on a board or at cards hung from a miniature clothesline with pins.

10. Encourage students to make comparisons by describing different objects. For example, list the qualities of chalk and of objects that are similar to chalk. Then direct students to write similes, such as "white as snow" or "round as a pencil" (Taylor et al., 1972).

11. Vocabulary words that depict their meaning when heard can be illustrated by students. Secretly assign a vocabulary word to each student, who then illustrates the word and on a separate piece of paper writes a sentence using the word. Then write all of the vocabulary words on the board, and collect the illustrations. Give children paper to record their choices, and hold up the pictures one at a time while students choose the word they think each illustration depicts. Refer to the artist if a question arises (Baroni, 1987).

12. To assist adolescents with vocabulary development, establish a word retirement area on a bulletin board. During the week have students list words that they and their peers overuse. Once a week have the class review the words and choose one or two to focus on. Have students look the word(s) up and agree on the intended meaning(s). Then have them use a thesaurus to find synonyms for the overused word(s). Students should keep a record of their use of the chosen synonym(s) for the next week. At the end of the time period the student using the new vocabulary word(s) the most becomes the manager of the word retirement "home" and is in charge of recording the next week's words (Pearson, 1987).

TEACHER TIPS

Henry (1999) has written an article concerning multisensory teaching for children with dyslexia. In her article she defines multisensory teaching as simultaneously visual, auditory, and kinesthetic-tactile. All of these sensory-based approaches are used to enhance the memory and learning of children with dyslexia. Additionally, Henry states that there is a growing body of evidence supporting the use of multisensory teaching. The National Institute of Child Health and Human Development (NICHD) also supports this approach to teaching of young children with dyslexia. "These multisensory approaches use direct, explicit teaching of letter-sound relationships, syllable patterns, and meaning word parts. Studies in clinical settings showed similar results for a wide range of ages and abilities. The following are recommended multisensory structured language approaches to reading.

- Alphabetic Phonics Based Methods
  Academic Language Therapy Association, 4020 McEwen, Suite 105, Dallas, TX 75244, HELP (972) 907-3924
- The Association Method
  DuBarb School for Language Disorders, The University of Southern Mississippi, Box 10035, Hattiesburg, MS 39406-0035, (601) 266-5223.
- Orton-Gillingham Approach
  Academy of Orton-Gillingham Practioners and Educators, P. O. Box 234, East Main Street, Amenia, NY 12501 (914)373-8919
- The Herman Method
  Herman Method Institute, 4700 Tyrone Ave., Sherman Oaks, CA 91423, (818) 784-9566
- The Slingerland Approach
  The Slingerland Institute, Security Pacific Plaza, 411 108th Avenue, N. E., Bellevue, WA 98004 (425) 453-1190
- The Spalding Method
  Spalding Education Foundation, 2814 W. Bell Road, Suite 1405, Phoenix AZ (602) 866-7801.

- Wilson Reading Program
  Wilson Language Systems, 175 W. Main St., Millbury, MA 01527, (508) 865-3656

Henry, M. K. (1999). How people with dyslexia learn: Multisensory teaching. http://www.interdys.org/parents_.str

TEACHER TIPS

Elementary Level

The state of Texas has put into law (in accordance with the State Board of Education Rule) procedures for instruction of students with dyslexia. After appropriate identification and placements, students with dyslexia can expect to engage in instructional strategies that utilize individualized, intensive and multisensory methods; contain writing and spelling components; and include the following descriptors:

- Graphophonemic knowledge (explicit, synthetic, and analytic phonics);
- Individualized instruction that meets the learning needs of each child;
- Meaning-based instruction that is directed toward purposeful reading and writing;
- Multisensory instruction that incorporates the two or more sensory pathways;
- Phonemic awareness instruction that enables students to detect, segment, blend, and manipulate sounds in spoken language;
- Process-oriented instruction that teaches the strategies of decoding and encoding;
- Language structure instruction that encompasses morphology, semantics, syntax, and pragmatics;
- Explicit direct instruction that is "systematic, sequential, and cumulative and is organized and presented in a way that follows a logical sequential plan and fits the nature of language (alphabetic principle), with no assumption of prior skills or language knowledge. (p.10)

Texas Education Agency, (1998). *Dyslexia and related disorders.* Austin, TX: Texas Education Agency,

TEACHER TIPS

Many secondary students are required to read novels and discuss them within a classroom format. With the onset of technology in the classroom, however, different ways of discussing literature are being formed. Computer-mediated conversations are being used to foster discussions between students. For example, Bean, Valerio, and Senior (1999) conducted a study in which high school students (Juniors) were paired with a university inservice teacher to discuss a novel over electronic mail. The student-teacher pairs discussed the novel by Amy Tan, *The Kitchen God's Wife*. The student-teacher pairs were instructed to talk about the novel by writing at least a one-page e-mail massage to their partner. The results indicated that the pairs tended to write statements that were personal and intertextual in nature—indicating a high level of reader engagement during the discussion. The pairs exceeded their one-page writing goal on a daily basis. A consumer satisfaction measure, indicating how well the students and in-service teachers liked this form of communication/discussion, met with mixed results. Of the high-school students, 42% preferred the e-mail discussions over classroom discussions while 60% of the in-service teachers preferred e-mail over a classroom discussion format. Teachers of students with disabilities might try to engage their students in class discussions by pairing them with other students who are disabled or nondisabled from other schools. Another method might be that the whole class responds together to another class in another state. In this manner more information can be shared and students are not pressured to perform alone when constructing an e-mail message.

Bean, T. W., Valerio, P. C., & Senior, H. M. (1999) Intertextuality and the e-mail discussion of a multicultural novel in secondary American literature. In T. Shanahan & F. V. Rodriguez-Brown (Eds.), *National Reading Conference Yearbook, 48*. Chicago, IL: National Reading Conference, Inc.

Reading: Comprehension

Although word recognition is clearly an important basic skill, it is not the primary goal of a reading instructional program. The goal of reading is comprehension—obtaining meaning from printed material. In their review, Mastropieri and Scruggs (1997) define it as "a process of constructing meaning from written texts, based on a complex coordination of a number of interrelated sources of information" (p. 197). As they note, it can be argued that comprehension is the most important academic skill that is taught in school. It is also one that is particularly problematic for students with special needs. Students' difficulty in understanding abstract concepts and generalizing information often adversely affects their ability to comprehend written material. Therefore, their reading programs must emphasize comprehension skills.

How can reading comprehension be promoted and advanced in learners with special needs? We suggest two opportunities that can be accessed. First, teachers can select and refine a general teaching approach that has as its focus the enhanced ability to derive meaning from the printed word. Second, teachers can rely on strategies that develop specific skills in comprehension and fluency. These two considerations frame the outline for this chapter, which concludes with a discussion of special considerations relative to implementing a successful reading program.

GENERAL APPROACHES

The selection of a general approach or approaches to reading comprehension provides a basis for a program to enhance learning to read. The following examples illustrate some options that teachers have and which, as needed, can be blended in with decoding programs as discussed in the previous chapter.

Regardless of the particular approach to reading, teachers should remember that special considerations are pertinent to the reading instruction of older students. The adolescent who is disabled is likely to have experienced considerable frustration and failure in past efforts to learn

or improve reading skills. Thus, the teacher must overcome not only skill deficits, but also problems in attitude, motivation, and fear related to failure expectancy. A positive, reinforcing manner and realistic expectations should underlie any approach to reading instruction with older students. Materials such as high-interest, controlled-vocabulary readers are particularly suitable for junior- and senior-high readers who are disabled.

Language Experience Approach (LEA)

LEA has been mentioned briefly as an alternative to be used with a basal series, but it need not be used only with other approaches. Even though one of the real strengths of LEA is its versatility as a complement to other techniques, many reading specialists advocate and use LEA as a total initial reading program. Allen and Halvorsen (1961) describe the basis for LEA here:

> What I can think about, I can talk about.
> What I can say, I can write.
> What I can write, I can read. (p 33)

LEA encourages students to verbalize their thoughts and experiences, which are then written down by the teacher or the student and can be read. These stories are reread by the student and by other students as the program progresses. Word lists are made from the words used in the stories to develop word-recognition skills. Phonetic and structural analysis skills are taught when the teacher observes the student's readiness for such instruction. Because LEA lacks the developmental structure of the basal approach, beginning teachers may need to follow the outline of a basal or another sequential program to guide students successfully through an LEA program.

Beginning readers may be introduced to LEA as a class. The teacher should establish a common interest, such as a class animal, field trip, or television program. As students tell about their experiences, the teacher needs to assist them in transcribing the words on paper. Students then receive copies of the stories for their books. Word lists and seat-work activities are made from the stories. Independent reading books are also made available and should be encouraged. The transition from student-written material must be made at some point. Commercial material should be presented early in the program, but it must be well within the student's independent level to ensure success.

The LEA program can be used in remedial fashion with adolescents who have met repeated defeat with printed material. The use of the student's own language and handwriting is a strong motivating tool. With older students, the teacher should write the stories as students dictate. Then students can copy the stories for their books, thus reducing the use of incorrectly spelled words. Because of LEA's versatility and valuable motivational qualities, it is recommended as a supplementary program for students of any age. It is most appropriately used in special programs when it accompanies systematic instruction in word-attack skills.

Whole Language Approach

Whole language is a reading instructional method that represents a logical expansion of the philosophy of the language experience approach. As Englehard (1991) notes:

> Whole language is conceptualized as a philosophy in which children learn naturally and holistically through the integration of reading and writing with good literature, emphasizing meaning and the use of real texts such as familiar stories and content area texts instead of basal readers. Further, all aspects of language (oral and written) are integrated and taught across content areas. (p. 3)

Polloway and Smith (1999), basing their summary on Reid and Kuykendall (1996), provide the following summary of the concepts underlining the whole language approach:

- Language, including speaking, listening, reading, and writing, develop interdependently as well as in a social context.
- Students learn to read using authentic books, not basal readers.
- Students learn to write by engaging in the writing process.

- Students in a whole-language class are allowed to learn at their own pace.
- Teachers serve as mediators during the whole language process, providing support but not interfering with the learning process.
- Students become involved in reading and writing that is connected to their own lives.
- Students should be immersed in an environment that is filled with language materials and activities, including high-interest reading materials, and print that they have helped produce.
- Students must be encouraged and motivated to share their experiences through literature. (p. 317).

Core instructional activities that characterize the whole language approach include (a) teacher-led discussions of stories; (b) sharing book experiences through material such as Big Books; (c) sustained silent reading (i.e., a regular time when students have an opportunity to practice reading using self-selected stories and content silently; Gartland, 1994); (d) silent reading time segments in which students write responses to what they are reading and share these with other students or with the teacher in individual conferences; (e) language experience activities in which children write stories in a group or individually to be used for future reading experiences; (f) time set aside for large group writing instruction, followed by students' writing, revising, editing, and sharing their own writing; and finally (g) reading and writing activities that involve a content area theme such as science or social studies (Chiang & Ford, 1990).

Brand (1989) suggests theoretical reasons why these activities, common in the whole language approach, help to alleviate some of the difficulties children with disabilities bring to the learning situation. Organizing teaching around themes or topics is easier for students with memory or cognitive difficulties than learning isolated skills or changing from one topic to another. Anxieties are often lessened and self-esteem enhanced because whole language provides more opportunities for students to feel personal success when telling or writing an original story or experience. Students are affirmed in what they have to offer.

Because whole language is more self-directed than traditional reading programs, students feel more in control of their own learning. Additionally, whole language can minimize attention deficits because it includes self-direction, freedom of choice, interesting topics, and often a hands-on approach (Brand, 1989). Emphasis shifts from deficits to strengths, and students have the opportunity to learn through their collective experiences in an atmosphere of active involvement (Hollingsworth & Reutzel, 1988).

Clearly, a program based on whole language has much to offer in the area of reading instruction. It provides an emphasis on reading authentic texts rather than the contrived stories that may often appear in basals, it provides a way to blend reading with instruction in the other language arts, and it emphasizes students' active involvement in constructing meaning. At the same time, its success with students with special needs has been somewhat limited. In part this is likely to be due to the fact that whole language advocates have primarily emphasized the use of qualitative (vs. quantitative) research that relies more heavily on case studies than group achievement test data. As Mastropieri and Scruggs (1997) note, such research has typically been more helpful in the description of educational interventions but less helpful in providing documentation of the effectiveness of the interventions. While teachers are encouraged to draw from the tenets of whole language, there also is clear merit in the teaching of specific skills (i.e., decoding, as mentioned in the Chapter 8 and in comprehension skills as discussed through strategies presented later in this chapter).

Source Material Using Literature. A key aspect of whole language programs is the reliance on literature as the source of content for reading opportunities. As Mandlebaum, Lightbourne, and VandenBrock (1994) note, literature (including novels, stories, magazines, and trade books) has the advantages of being authentic, varied, on the market faster, and thus current. It can meet diverse student needs and interests and offers alternative

points of views on topics and issues as well as the opportunity to study topics in depth. Finally, the whole language approach gives students more opportunity to select their own reading material. Mandlebaum et al. present an excellent evaluative list of literature sources that can be considered.

O'Neil (1994) highlights the "revolution" occurring in the use of literature in the elementary classroom. As he notes:

> Perhaps the predominant change in what literature is taught in elementary schools is a new interest in using more "real" literature in the curriculum. Dick and Jane, it seems, are on the way out, and classrooms are filling up with dog-eared versions of children's classics and fiction and nonfiction on every conceivable topic. . . . In general, literature-based programs differ from traditional approaches by surrounding students with rich, authentic, whole pieces of literature from the earliest grades; by teaching reading skills in the context of real literature; and by using literature throughout the curriculum. . . . The books, moreover, are diverse—in topics, culture of the characters and the authors, and difficulty. Students and teachers are talking to each other about their reading. Pupils are using books for information to help them in subjects other than reading or language arts. (p. 2)

Although there have apparently been significant changes in the use of literature in the elementary grades, there has been less change at the secondary level, where the curriculum has remained reasonably similar to traditional patterns (O'Neil, 1994). Particularly for special educators who may be working with English teachers in a cooperative teaching venture, the list in Table 9–1 of the most popular works taught in the school may be of interest.

Predictable Books. Predictable books are children's books or stories that use repetition, as in *Brown Bear, Brown Bear, What Do You See?* (Martin, 1983); a cumulative pattern, as demonstrated in the familiar Gingerbread Man story; or familiar day, month, or time sequences, as found in Maurice Sendak's (1962) *Chicken Soup with Rice.* These three types of predictable stories—through the use of rhythm, rhyme, and redundancy—give

TABLE 9–1
Most popular books in secondary schools

The Most Popular Works

The most popular book-length works assigned in public schools, by grade and the percentage of schools requiring them, are:

Grade	Work	%	
Grade 7	The Call of the Wild	22%	▇▇
	Tom Sawyer	15%	▇
	The Red Pony	15%	▇
	A Christmas Carol	15%	▇
Grade 8	Diary of a Young Girl	34%	▇▇▇
	The Call of the Wild	14%	▇
	The Pigman	12%	▇
Grade 9	Romeo and Juliet	76%	▇▇▇▇▇▇
	Great Expectations	32%	▇▇▇
	To Kill a Mockingbird	16%	▇
	The Pearl	16%	▇
Grade 10	Julius Caesar	64%	▇▇▇▇▇
	The Pearl	31%	▇▇▇
	To Kill a Mockingbird	29%	▇▇
Grade 11	The Scarlet Letter	52%	▇▇▇▇
	Huckleberry Finn	43%	▇▇▇
	The Great Gatsby	39%	▇▇▇
Grade 12	Macbeth	56%	▇▇▇▇
	Hamlet	45%	▇▇▇
	Lord of the Flies	19%	▇
	1984	19%	▇

Note. From "Rewriting the Book on Literature," adapted by J. O'Neil, 1994, *Curriculum Update,* p. 5. Copyright 1994 by Association for Supervision and Curriculum Design. Adapted with permission.

semantic and syntactic language cues that stimulate fluent reading for children with disabilities and can enhance sight word recognition.

To use predictable books as a strategy for promoting reading, the teacher first reads the story aloud to children, using an enlarged version or distributing multiple copies of the material so that children can read along for most of the story. After this, group and individual activities are developed by the teacher to teach and reinforce the sight words and phonics generalizations that are used in the predictable book (McClure, 1985).

High-Interest Low-Difficulty (HILD) Books. These books are designed for students who read at a level 2 years or more below their interest level. For example, a teacher would recommend the HILD book *Specter,* which is about weird events and psychic phenomena, to a 15-year-old interested in such topics, but who reads only at the second-grade level. This book is described by Fearon Education Publishers as having a 1.9 to 2.8 reading level, and an interest level for Grades 7 to 12. For a list of HILD books, see Table 9-2.

TABLE 9–2

High-interest-low-difficulty (HILD) books

Publisher	Title/Topic	Reading Grade Level	Interest and Age Level
STORY HOUSE CORP. Bindery Lane Charlottesville, NY 12036 1-800-847-2105	*Walt Morey Adventure Library (8 titles)* Fast-paced adventure in the rugged world of Walt Morey. It is the land of bears, eagles, cougars, and rugged men and women.	5	10 to adult
	Adventures of Tintin (12 titles) A comic book adventure series set in interesting backgrounds.	5	12 to adult
HIGH NOON BOOKS A Division of Academic Therapy Publications 20 Commercial Blvd. Novato, CA 94949 1-800-422-7249	*Tom & Ricky Mystery Series* (15 titles) Tom & Ricky, two 14-year-old boys, set out to solve strange happenings in their hometown. With the help of their dog, they eventually solve the mysteries.	1	9 to 14
	Meg Parker Mysteries (10 titles) Meg and Kate solve a variety of exciting mysteries, ranging from a bank robbery to a counterfeiting ring.	1 to 2	11 to 15
	High School Highways (10 titles) Exciting novels about Black and Hispanic high school students in inner city settings.	2 to 3	12 to 16
	Prospectives (18 titles) Bike rides through the desert, life on a ranch, space exploration, and white-water rafting are examples of the intriguing encounters of the characters in the series.	3 to 4	12 to 18
	Romance Series Love, romance, growing up, and disappointment are some of the topics for teenagers that characterize this series.	4.5 to 5.0	12 to 18
	Spy Series Stories about the adventures of undercover cops, the FBI, foreign agents, American diplomats, and spies are included in this group.	4.5 to 5.0	12 to 18
	Science Fiction Series Life in the 23rd century, robots, UFOs, and invaders are examples of this suspensefilled series.	4.5 to 5.0	12 to 18

Publisher	Title/Topic	Reading Grade Level	Interest and Age Level
JAMESTOWN PUBLISHERS P.O. Box 9168 Providence, RI 02940 1-800-872-7323	*Jamestown Handbooks* (14 titles) Information about sports is used to motivate reluctant readers. Each book focuses on how to play a particular sport.	5	11 to 18
	Baseball: *Pitching, Catching, Hitting, Base Running, Playing the Infield,* and *Playing the Outfield*	5	11 to 18
	Basketball:*Shooting, Ball Handling, Playing the Defense,* and *Playing Offense*	5	11 to 18
	Women's Gymnastics: *Floor Exercises, Vaulting, Uneven Parallel Bars,* and *Balance Beam*	5	11 to 18
	Attention Span Stories (5 titles) Each of these 5 books contains a single cliff-hanger story told in one-page episodes. Plots include a safari, a trip to outer space, and sports stories. *Time Trip* *Survival Trip* *Sports Trip* *Jungle Trip* *Star Trip*	2 to 3	11 to 14
FEARON/JANUS 500 Harbor Blvd. Belmont, CA 94002 1-800-877-4283	*An American Family* (8 titles) Eight 80-page stories tell the tale of an American family through 200 years, ranging from the settlement of the American colonies through World War I. Examples of titles include the following. 1692 *Colony of Fear* 1827 *The Journey Home* 1920 *A Test of Loyalty*	4.5	12 to 18
	Hopes and Dreams (10 titles) Ten novels, each 80 pages, dramatize experiences of immigrant groups. They tell of all the challenges that a family meets when starting life in a new land. Titles include the following.	4.5 to 5.0	12 to 18

(continued)

TABLE 9–2 *(Continued)*

Publisher	Title/Topic	Reading Grade Level	Interest and Age Level
	O Little Town (German)		
	Hungry No More (Irish)		
	For Gold and Blood (Chinese)		
	A Different Home (Cuban)		
	Boat People (Vietnamese)		
	Nobody Knows (American)		
	The Magic Paper (Mexican)		
	Old Ways, New Ways (Russian)		
	Push to the West (Norwegian)		
	Little Italy (Italian)		
	Fastbacks (74 titles)	4.5 to 5.0	12 to 18
	Sports Series (10 titles)		
	Topics range from horse racing and football heroes to rodeo riders and female jockeys.		
	Crime and Detection Series (10 titles)	4.5 to 5.0	12 to 18
	In *Beginners Luck* an amateur detective becomes the victim of a kidnapper. Others are stories of robbery, murder, detectives, and deception.		
BANTAM DOUBLEDAY Dell Publishing Group School & College Dept. 666 Fifth Avenue New York, NY 10103 212-765-6500	*Be an Interplanetary spy* (12 titles) Full-length fiction stories in which the reader is sent to different galaxies on exciting missions.	3	9 to 13
	Time Machine (8 titles) In these historically accurate novels, the reader travels to another time and place to search for a famous person or event.	4	10 to 15
LITERACY VOLUNTEERS OF NEW YORK CITY Publishing Department 121 Ave. of Americas New York, NY 10013 219-925-3001	*Writers' Voices* (10 titles) A series containing works by contemporary writers. It includes true stories, short stories, and poetry on a variety of topics. Examples of titles include the following. *Elvis and Me* *The Godfather* *The Right Stuff* *Jaws* *Kramer vs. Kramer*	1 to 6	15 to adult

Publisher	Title/Topic	Reading Grade Level	Interest and Age Level
SCHOLASTIC, INC. 2931 McCarty Street P. O. Box 7502 Jefferson City, MO 65102-9968 1-800-325-6149	*Sprint Libraries* (60 titles) This collection includes eight themes: family, winners, fantasy, courage, mystery, achievement, friendship, and science fiction. Six different titles constitute each of them. Teaching guides and activity sheets accompany each theme to provide professional support. Examples of titles include the following.	1 to 3.9	9 to 12
	Elephants Never Forget	1.5 to 1.9	
	Karate Ace	2.0 to 2.9	
	Victory for Jamie	3.0 to 3.9	

Basal Reading Approach

Basal reading programs are used in the vast majority of elementary schools; consequently, such materials are readily available. They usually contain a series of books or stories written at different difficulty levels, with most beginning at preprimer and primer levels and progressing through upper elementary levels. Most readers also have workbooks that allow students to practice specific skills. Although some educators, (e.g., whole language advocates) decry their use, these workbooks are used widely, which makes it essential that educators working with students with special needs (especially in inclusive settings) become familiar with them.

Most basal programs are accompanied by comprehensive, highly structured teacher manuals that completely outline each lesson. They provide skill objectives, new vocabulary, suggested motivational activities, verbatim questions to check comprehension on each page of text, and lesson activities. The lessons follow a hierarchy of specific reading skills. Although some teachers think basal manuals limit creativity, others find their structure and guidance valuable. Beginning teachers typically find the manuals informative and beneficial.

A basal program exposes students to a basic vocabulary that provides for repetition. Although structured in format, basals can be modified to meet individual needs while following a sequential developmental pattern of skill building. They have often been used to assess a student's reading level and subsequent placement in an appropriate reading group. As long as the basal meets students' needs and falls within their interests and abilities, such placement may be temporarily adequate. The basal will not meet all needs, however, so the teacher must be prepared to revise and supplement the program.

Several methods can supplement basals when students begin to have difficulty with the vocabulary or cognitive processes demanded at increasingly higher levels. Teachers should avoid recycling students through the same stories, which can lower students' motivation to read. One alternative is to place students in another basal series at approximately the same level, thus giving them different reading experiences at approximately the same level and allowing for overlearning, which is important to students who are disabled.

A second option is to follow the series outline of skills as the manual presents them, supplementing them with other commercial reading materials. Many low-vocabulary supplemental materials cover interesting topics. A third option is to require students to write their own stories, as in the language experience approach previously discussed. Such an experience can provide practice on reading skills that need reinforcement, and the students' stories can provide reading material. A final option is to discontinue basals in favor of an alternative approach. Teachers should realize that many children cannot learn effectively through basals and should not force such students to fit into a program that is inappropriate for them.

Because basals provide a sequential, detailed, developmental program, they are valuable tools and should be considered one potential avenue for teaching reading to children with special needs. Only in very rare instances, however, can they be expected to furnish the entire program for children with reading difficulties. The Basal series such as Open Court and Caught Reading represent programs that have been designed especially for students with disabilities.

One additional consideration is how the basals are used. For example, according to Marston, Deno, Kim, Diment, and Rogers (1995), the use of direct instruction (DI) instructional principles as a modified approach with basal reading materials proved to be effective with students with mild disabilities in a comparison of six options.

Comprehensive Programs

With the increase in concerns for both phonological processing instruction and comprehension instruction for students with special needs, a number of new programs are being developed to attempt to ensure instructional emphasis on both critical aspects of the reading process. For example, Idol (1997) has developed a program entitled *Reading Success* that endeavors to combine emphases on sound-letter combinations, development of sight vocabulary, reading comprehension, and writing about what has been read. It emphasizes a direct instruction approach to each critical area within reading.

COMPREHENSION STRATEGIES

These general approaches provide a foundation for reading comprehension, but the teacher will also need to rely on strategies that can promote the acquisition of specific skills. Specific skills in comprehension do not fit into a clear scope and sequence to the degree that is often seen with word recognition, but there are clearly areas of emphasis that teachers need to assess (refer to Figure 8–2) and address as part of a comprehensive instructional program.

Literal comprehension refers to information as printed in text. Attention to literal recall includes comprehension for details, sequence of events, and major characters in the story. Most reading programs have traditionally addressed literal comprehension as their primary concern.

Inferential comprehension requires the reader to move beyond the literal information to infer the meaning of text. Although it is often mistakenly referred to as a lower-level skill, deriving the main idea from text is a good example of inferential comprehension. In this case, students are required to consider what they have read and infer the primary focus of the author.

A third level of comprehension is critical, in which the reader is asked to analyze and evaluate the information that has been read typically to develop new perspectives relative to the content. While all comprehension draws on prior knowledge, critical comprehension in particular asks the reader to use new information, for example, to compare and contrast it with other information learned at a prior time.

To complement this model of three levels of comprehension, Idol (1997), summarizing the work of researchers in the field, defines three types of comprehension as follows:

- text explicit: This type of comprehension is text dependent in that the answer is explicitly stated in the text (passage or picture).
- text implicit: This type of comprehension is implied within the text (or pictures). The

derivation of this type of information is based upon two or more nonexplicitly connected details of the passage or picture.

- script implicit: This type of comprehension requires integration of prior knowledge about the subject being read with one or more details from the passage or picture (p. 112).

The strategies that are discussed in the next section of this chapter provide several ways to enhance comprehension. Most can be adapted for variant purposes. The teacher's task is to ensure that appropriate attention is given to different levels of comprehension based on the developmental levels and learning needs of individual students. Through creative teaching, instructors can work with groups of students and incorporate a focus coincidentally on literal, inferential, and critical comprehension questions within the same lesson. Such an approach enhances inclusion efforts for students with special needs when they are participating in larger group instruction with other students whose cognitive abilities may be significantly greater.

Traditionally, many teachers have taught comprehension solely by asking students questions after they have read a specific passage. Thus, instructional lessons might typically be inclusive of questions such as the following after students have completed a reading sample:

- What is the main idea?
- What are the sequential events that took place in the story?
- Who are the main characters?
- What do you conclude about the story?

General questions such as these provide a basis for evaluating whether students have understood the passage they have completed. However, such an approach continually tests students' comprehension without necessarily directing or instructing them in comprehension strategies. The following strategies focus on comprehension in a more multifaceted fashion.

Although a number of reading comprehension strategies exist and many have proven to increase students' comprehension, further research must focus on determining which interventions are most effective given various reading contexts (Talbott, Lloyd, & Tankersley, 1994). Where evaluative information on the relative efficacy of a strategy is known, such information is provided. The following discussion focuses first on some specific strategies and then concludes with some more broad-based ones that can be used for variant purposes.

Teacher-Directed Questioning Strategies

Questioning by teachers is the instructional strategy used most often in teaching reading comprehension. As a general approach, this has frequently been found to be effective, particularly when students are taught to ask themselves questions before, during, and after the reading process.

Questioning permeates the reading process. Factual, inferential, and analytical questions are all essential for comprehension development. However, frequently the majority of questions that teachers ask are factual, and the answers are directly stated in the text, requiring no higher-level thinking by students. Teachers can stimulate students to begin inferential and critical thinking through higher-level questioning. Students who can decode the material adequately can, with guidance and practice, become critical readers. If properly guided and questioned, slow learners as well as gifted students can learn to make inferences from the material they have read. Questions that stimulate thought and motivate students to higher levels of comprehension can be asked on material at any readability level. Evaluative and interpretive questions also apply to every level of readability.

Smith (1979) emphasizes that as people read, listen to speakers, and study, they constantly ask questions. Comprehension occurs when people perceive answers to their own questions or find their predictions validated or refuted. Knowledge and experience directly influence predictions and thus comprehension.

Reading comprehension requires connecting what is read with prior knowledge of the topic. The printed material provides new information;

to understand it, readers use various information sources within their own memories. Thus, each reader's background of concepts directly influences the comprehension of passages read. Most comprehension instruction therefore should be initiated prior to a reading of the material. The teacher must stimulate students' thinking about the topic before oral or silent reading begins.

A variety of teaching strategies make use of questioning as an aid to comprehension. Strategies include setting the purpose for reading to arouse students' prior knowledge, and the use of the directed reading/thinking activity.

Setting the Purpose. Setting the purpose in advance of reading is one way to stimulate students' prior knowledge. A teacher can introduce a reading selection by saying, "As you read, think about what you would do if you were caught in a flood as Van is in this story." Immediately, students' prior knowledge (or lack of it) concerning floods comes to mind and thus helps prepare them for the passage to be read. Wilson (1983) also stresses the importance of teaching students to assume responsibility for their own comprehension. She advocates instructing children to self-monitor by asking themselves periodically, "Is this making sense to me?" Students who realize that they are not comprehending can try a variety of strategies: rereading the material, trying to rephrase it, reading ahead, or, if necessary, asking for help.

Directed Reading/Thinking Activity. One of the most useful questioning techniques to teach comprehension of content or expository material is the directed reading/thinking activity (DRTA). In this activity students are taught to make predictions about what they are going to read before they begin reading the text. While reading, the students test and refine the predictions they made in advance. These predictions generate divergent questions and stimulate expanded thinking. DRTA teaches students to verify and defend their predictions and gives them guidelines for reading to learn. The following procedures comprise the DRTA technique.

1. Students examine the story title, pictures, and subheadings.
2. Individually or in a group, students list information they anticipate finding in the selection.
3. Students read the selection.
4. Students then look at each prediction on their list and decide whether it was correct or incorrect.
5. When uncertainty or disagreement occurs, students defend their positions by locating validating information in the text.

DRTA stimulates students to generate their own questions. Their predictions become questions when they search the text for supportive information.

Student-Directed Questioning Strategies

While teacher questioning is the staple of much that has been done in the area of reading comprehension instruction, students must learn to ask themselves questions in order to become more effective and independent readers. In order to do this, several strategies can be used. These include the direct teaching of self-monitoring strategies as well as instructional programs that involve students working reciprocally with teachers. These are discussed next.

Self-Questioning. Cognitive psychology has fostered the use of self-monitoring of the reading process such as through the development of self-generated questions. The assumption is that children must actively participate in the learning process and take responsibility for their own learning. Empirical work has indicated that one major influence on students' inability to read is that they do not take an active role in their own learning (Brown & Palinscar, 1982; Torgesen, 1982). The lack of metacognitive skills (e.g., self-monitoring, predicting, and controlling one's own attempts to study and learn) limits students' success in learning to read (Wong, 1982). Self-questioning is one way to stimulate development of the poor reader's metacognitive skills and improve comprehension that has proved to be effective for enhancing achievement (Swanson & de la Paz, 1998).

To facilitate a strategy of using self-generated questions, students can first be trained in question phrasing or writing. This orientation includes identification of good and poor questions, discrimination between questions and statements, and awareness of question words. Students are then instructed to read the story, describe what it is about, and generate two questions. Finally, students answer their own questions or exchange questions with peers. Teachers can further enhance students' metacognitive skills by directly teaching and modeling comprehension processing. Students can be instructed to perform the following self-questioning tasks (Schewel & Waddell, 1986).

1. Identify the main idea of a paragraph and underline it.
2. Develop questions related to the main idea and write them where they can be referred to easily.
3. Check those questions with the teacher's models to be certain that they are correctly stated.
4. Read the passage, answer the questions, and learn the answers.
5. Continually look back over the questions and answers to note the accumulation of information.

In emphasizing the use of self-monitoring approaches, Mastropieri and Scruggs (1997, p. 205) report that several common features are characteristic of research on strategies that promote enhanced reading comprehension. These include:

- clear, explicit instruction in a strategy associated with enhancing reading comprehension
- detailed self-monitoring procedures containing cards that require students to mark off steps as they proceed
- informing students about the purpose of the strategy instruction, and
- attributing success to controllable factors (e.g., reminding students that the use of a strategy would be beneficial to them and would influence success)

In Table 9–3, a series of steps that facilitate student use of a variety of comprehension strategies is presented.

Reciprocal Teaching. One strategy that involves questioning and additional activities related to active comprehension is reciprocal teaching. This approach was developed by Brown and Palinscar and is based on the relatively simple assumption that comprehension is enhanced when students read a text and then take turns leading small-group discussions to help their peers also understand what was read (Reid, Baker, Lasell, & Easton, 1993; Schulz, 1994).

Reciprocal teaching includes four specific and related strategies. These include questioning about the content read, summarizing the most important information, clarifying concepts that are unclear, and predicting what is occurring. An example from the work of Ann Brown illustrates the process:

> A group of second-grade students in Jill Walker's classroom at John Swett School are beginning a new book on a topic they have been researching. Tyrone, the designated teacher for this session, begins by reading aloud the book's title, *Read About Animals That Live in Shells.* Next, Tyrone asks if anyone has questions. The teacher's aide prompts the quiet group by asking, "What are shells?" Katie responds that shells provide coverings for soft-bodied animals and names snails as an example. Tyrone then asks the group to predict what information might be found in the book. After the students list possible topics, Tyrone begins reading. Katie and Kendra assist him with difficult words. Next, Tyrone asks if any words need to be clarified. Katie asks, "What are exoskeletons?" Several incorrect guesses are ventured. The teachers' aide suggests that the group think about the topic in order to answer the question. Katie summarizes their reading and announces, "Oh! I think it means skeletons on the outside!" (Schulz, 1994, pp. 21, 24).

In research by Marston et al (1995), reciprocal teaching was confirmed as one approach to comprehension that resulted in achievement improvements. The key to the effectiveness of reciprocal teaching is that it enables students to learn specific strategies that foster their comprehension

TABLE 9–3
Developing self-regulated comprehension strategies

1. _Describe the target comprehension strategy._ Explicitly describe the strategy steps, and discuss _why_ the strategy should be used, _what_ it accomplishes, and _when_ and _where_ the strategy may be used.

2. _Activate background knowledge._ Review information students may have learned previously that is necessary for learning the target strategy.

3. _Review current performance level._ Provide feedback to students regarding their current level of functioning and reiterate potential benefits of the strategy. Goals for and commitment by the students should be reached collaboratively.

4. _Modeling of the strategy and self-instructions._ Demonstrate how to use the strategy in a meaningful context, and use relevant self-regulatory behaviors by thinking out loud. Self-statements include ideas such as "What should I do first?" "I am using this strategy so that I can understand what I am reading better . . ."; or "I need to take my time," which show students the purpose of the procedures and how to manage their performance.

5. _Collaborative practice._ Provide _several_ opportunities for student practice using the strategy and self-statements as a whole class, in small groups, or in pairs. Monitor students' progress in following the strategy steps. Facilitate students' success in using the strategies by prompting them to complete steps if they are omitted or by providing assistance in completing strategy steps accurately. It may be necessary to reexplain or model some of the more difficult aspects of the strategies, based on student need.

6. _Independent practice and mastery._ After determining that the students know and understand the steps of the strategy, each student practices using the target strategy and self-statements without help. Continue to give guidance, reinforcement, and feedback. Gradually fade assistance until each student is capable of using the strategy without any help.

7. _Generalization._ Discuss with students throughout the week whenever situations arise where it is appropriate for students to apply the strategies. In addition, during collaborative and independent practice sessions, provide students with different types of materials (e.g., lookbacks are useful with narratives, expository text such as science book chapters, and learning rules to play a game) so that students learn to use the strategies flexibly.

Source: Swanson, P.N., & de la Paz, S. (1998). Teaching effective comprehension strategies to students with learning and reading disabilities. _Intervention in School and Clinic, 33,_ 211.

rather than simply asking them questions about what they have read. By using this approach, a variety of questions can be modeled, practiced, and used in an active fashion. The planned outcome then would be that students would be more able to generate appropriate questions themselves while reading.

Graphic-Aid Strategies

These strategies use visual formats or structures to assist students in organizing information for better comprehension. Several graphic aids apply to teaching students who are disabled. The use

of graphic aids provides a way to enhance the teacher-directed and student-directed questioning strategies that are being used to build comprehension skills. Graphic aids provide systems where students can organize their thoughts, make notes on what they are going to read or have read, and ultimately promotes recall and provides a basis for further study.

Graphic strategies frequently serve as advanced organizers that provide an introduction or an overview of the passage to be read. One example of this is an outline containing major headings with space for students to fill in the supporting details (Graham & Johnson, 1989). Students with learning disabilities using and discussing the outline before attempting content area textbook reading scored higher on comprehension measures than those in the control group. The comprehension of students with learning disabilities also improved after they were given prompts to be used with basal reader stories prior to reading. Prompts included asking, "Does the title give a clue to the story?"; looking for, saying, and discussing new or difficult words; and skimming for the story setting.

Several graphic-aid strategies are discussed next and have a number of overlapping qualities. Collectively they represent effective strategies to enable students to develop "maps" of stories and are associated with enhanced comprehension (Swanson and de la Paz, 1998).

Story Frames. Story frames constructed by the teacher also help students organize and summarize information. This strategy guides comprehension by helping students to sort out the important concepts and ideas of the material. Fowler (1982; Fowler & Davis, 1986) describes the five steps necessary for constructing a story frame.

1. Identify the problem of the story on which you want students to focus.
2. Write a paragraph about that problem.
3. Delete words, phrases, and sentences that are not necessary to guide one through the paragraph.

4. Under selected spaces, place a clue to ensure that students can follow the frame.
5. Modify the frame for subsequent selections.

Story frames can focus attention on character comparison or analysis, plot, or setting. Figure 9-1 is an example of a story frame focused on plot. When first introducing story frames, the teacher should read a story to the students, and together they should discuss and fill in the blanks on the frame. Following this direct instruction, students should be able to complete story frames successfully and with minimal assistance. They can then begin working through frames independently.

Semantic Mapping. A strategy to aid in reading comprehension, semantic mapping is based on the concept of schema theory, which postulates that new information is learned and understood when it is integrated with prior knowledge. The theory is based on the concept that information is stored in the brain in categories known as schemata. When a student is introduced to new information through reading or other experiences, the new knowledge is learned as it is stored in the brain with similar schemata.

In relation to schema theory, the reading teacher's role is twofold: to continually work on building students' knowledge background through experiences, discussion, and literature and to teach

FIGURE 9–1
Story frame focused on plot

In this story the problem starts when _____.

After that _____ . Next, _____

_____ . Then, _____

_____ . The problem is finally

solved when _____ . The story ends _____

_____ .

From "Developing Comprehension Skills in Primary Students Through the Use of Story Frames," by G. L. Fowler, 1982, *The Reading Teacher, 36*(2), p. 176. Copyright 1982 by the International Reading Association. Reprinted with permission of the International Reading Association and G. L. Fowler.

students to stimulate their own schemata about a topic before beginning to read a passage. The teacher might instruct students in the use of self-questioning (e.g.,"What do I already know about the Civil War?") or prediction strategies. Children with disabilities often have limited experiential backgrounds and need additional guidance in gaining knowledge from the experiences they encounter.

Brainstorming is an essential element in the mapping process. The student's active participation in this activity stimulates prior knowledge and encourages students to associate new information with what is already part of their schemata (Schewel, 1989).

Semantic mapping is a method of promoting reading comprehension that stimulates a student's prior knowledge of the topic. Semantic maps are diagrams developed by students and teacher before students read an assigned selection. The maps can be reused after reading to further stimulate comprehension. The semantic mapping procedure is as follows.

1. The teacher presents a stimulus word or a core question related to the story to be read.
2. Students generate words related to the stimulus word or predict answers to the question, all of which the teacher lists on the board.
3. With the teacher's help, students then put related words or answers in groups, drawing connecting lines between the topics to form a semantic map.
4. After reading the selection, students and the teacher discuss the categories and rearrange or add to the map.

Semantic mapping can appear in various forms. Figure 9–2 presents one possible semantic map as an illustration of some of the information in this chapter.

When using semantic mapping, students are actively engaged in a strategy that stimulates retrieval and organization of prior knowledge. It is also useful as a post-reading exercise to enhance comprehension and as a study skill technique (Heimlich & Pittelman, 1986).

FIGURE 9–2

Example of semantic mapping

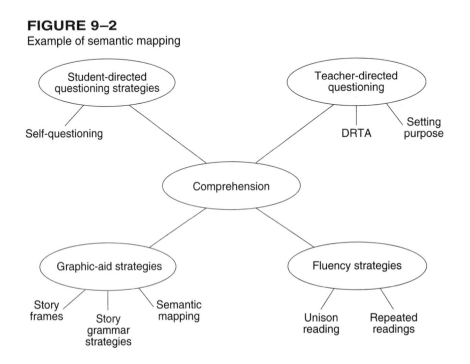

Story Grammar Strategies. The use of story grammar strategies has become a popular way to enhance the reading and writing skills of students and in particular students with special needs; the concept builds on many of the aforementioned strategies. Story grammar strategies are included here although they can complement a variety of graphic and nongraphic approaches to promoting comprehension. Hagood (1997) outlines a series of strategies that provide ways to enhance learning for students.

- Teach students to use self-questioning techniques to increase their comprehension of a narrative text (i.e., Who is the story about? Where does it take place? What is the problem in the story? How is the problem solved? How does the main character feel about the solution?) (Figure 9–3).
- Teach students to use story maps to organize a story's components (i.e., use visual organizers to enable students to enhance their understanding) (Figure 9–4).

- Develop group narrative dramatizations through the use of visual, auditory, and kinesthetic learning channels (e.g., use multisensory activities to enhance students' involvement with understanding and communicating stories).
- Teach students to analyze and critically compare the story elements of two similar stories (e.g., use graphic organizers to discuss similarities and differences between specific stories).
- Teach students to manipulate and analyze the components of story grammar (e.g., rewrite stories by changing, for example, the setting of a story and modifying other elements that necessarily change when the setting does).

Fluency Strategies

Although the development of fluency is not an approach to comprehension per se, the process of reading through passages continuously and smoothly can enhance comprehension. For this reason, these methods are discussed here. The

FIGURE 9–3
Sample story map questions

1. Where did this story take place?

2. When did the story take place?

3. Who were the main characters in the story?

4. Were there any other important characters in the story? Who?

5. What was the problem in the story?

6. How did the character(s) try to solve the problem?

7. Was it hard to solve the problem? Explain.

8. Was the problem solved? Explain.

9. What did you learn from reading this story? Explain.

10. Can you think of a different ending?

Source: Idol, L. (1997). *Reading success: A specialized literacy program for learners with challenging reading needs.* Austin, TX: Pro-Ed, p. 61.

FIGURE 9-4
Sample story map

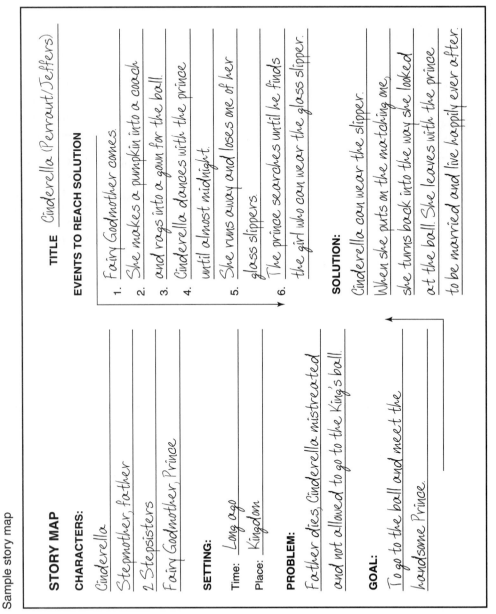

STORY MAP

TITLE Cinderella (Perrault/Jeffers)

CHARACTERS:

Cinderella

Stepmother, father

2 Stepsisters

Fairy Godmother, Prince

SETTING:

Time: Long ago

Place: Kingdom

PROBLEM:

Father dies, Cinderella mistreated

and not allowed to go to the King's ball.

GOAL:

To go to the ball and meet the

handsome Prince.

EVENTS TO REACH SOLUTION

1. Fairy Godmother comes.

2. She makes a pumpkin into a coach
and rags into a gown for the ball.

3. Cinderella dances with the prince
until almost midnight.

4.

5. She runs away and loses one of her
glass slippers

6. The prince searches until he finds
the girl who can wear the glass slipper.

SOLUTION:

Cinderella can wear the slipper.

When she puts on the matching one,

she turns back into the way she looked

at the ball. She leaves with the prince

to be married and live happily ever after.

From "Constructing Meaning: An Integrated Approach to Teaching Reading," by K. D. Barclay, 1990, *Intervention in School and Clinic, 26,* p. 88. Copyright 1990 by PRO-ED, Inc. Reprinted with permission.

techniques described here were designed to help students become more fluent readers in terms of both word recognition and ultimately comprehension and are applicable to a variety of students.

Repeated Readings. With repeated readings or multiple oral readings, students receive a selection approximately 200 words in length with instructions to practice reading it orally while listening to a tape of the same material. When students decide they are ready, their time and errors are recorded. After further oral practice, another time/error check is made. This procedure continues until the student reads 85 words per minute, at which time the process begins again with new material. Samuels (1979) reports that after practice with this technique, students required fewer readings with each new selection and comprehension continuously improved. He concludes that comprehension improved because the attention required for decoding was minimized and automaticity was enhanced. Graham and Johnson (1989) note that three readings of the same passage noticeably improve reading comprehension and fluency of students with learning disabilities.

In their review of research, Mastropieri and Scruggs (1997) conclude that reading the same passage three or four times did have a positive effect on fluency and also on passage comprehension. However, they caution that additional readings would yield diminishing returns and that repeated readings of a given text may have a positive effect on other texts only to the extent that there are significant overlaps in words.

Unison Reading. Several approaches represent forms of unison reading. With the *neurological impress method* (NIM), the student and the teacher read aloud in unison or echo fashion. The instructor sits behind the student and reads slightly faster and louder, pointing to the words as they are read (Ekwall & Shanker, 1988). As reading improves, students may begin the finger movements themselves. This method is recommended for use 10 to 15 minutes daily up to a maximum of 8 to 12 hours. Because progress

usually occurs quickly, this strategy should be terminated if no improvement is noted in a reasonable period of time. NIM does not use questioning or discussion to encourage comprehension. Because research on the technique has been mixed, teachers should evaluate its effectiveness when using it.

Bos (1982) found that a combination of repeated readings and the neurological impress method resulted in improved word recognition and comprehension skills for intermediate and junior–high-aged students reading at the primary level. She used the following procedure.

1. The teacher begins by reading the first 15 to 30 words in the story to the student.
2. The teacher and the student reread the passage together, with the teacher pointing to the words, until the student is ready to read the passage aloud without assistance.
3. As the student reads orally, the teacher notes the words the student does not recognize.
4. Student and teacher discuss the message of the selection. The teacher teaches and reviews unknown words from the story, using a variety of activities.

By increasing fluency, this combination of two techniques allowed the student to focus attention on comprehension (Bos, 1982).

While the NIM approach has the teacher reading just before the student, teachers may also want to use *imitative reading,* which is a similar procedure for improving the fluency of students with severe reading difficulties. In this case, unison reading is technically not used. The teacher reads very simple, short segments aloud as the student follows silently. The student then tries to read the same phrase or sentence aloud. The procedure is repeated until the student reads the material with fluency. Gradually the teacher increases the length of the sections being read to the student (Henk, Helfeldt, & Platt, 1986).

In *paired reading,* two students who work well together and who have similar instructional reading levels read aloud in unison (Henk et al., 1986). Material familiar to both students is used in the initial stages of paired reading. After the two develop a sense of trust and cooperation, less familiar text can be introduced. As they work together, one student can assist when the other hesitates or makes an error. Tape recordings of these oral reading sessions can help both students evaluate their reading fluency.

GENERAL INSTRUCTIONAL CONSIDERATIONS

Grouping for Instruction

A key question that is always integral to planning for instruction is the issue of grouping. In Chapter 2, there was an extensive discussion of grouping strategies that promote acquisition and maintenance/proficiency learning. In no place is the question of grouping more critical then in the area of reading.

Traditionally, successfully matching individual readers to appropriate reading materials has required that students be divided into small groups for reading instruction. The advent of inclusion has challenged the assumption that students will be taught to read in small, homogenous groups. For example, Moody, Vaughn, and Schumm (1997) have recently provided a detailed analysis of the grouping practices of general education and special education teachers, respectively. For the former, the most commonly used strategy was whole class grouping with students of mixed ability combined within the group. The most common finding was that general educators use smaller groups for practice and reinforcement activities but not for teacher-led instruction and, when the groups are used for that purpose, the students are of mixed ability.

On the other hand, special educators reported that they were much more likely to use groups of similar ability. Further, they reported that they had greater autonomy making decisions about how students were grouped. Consequently, the traditional pattern of homogeneously set up groupings appeared more common with this group of teachers. Moody et al. caution that the implications for reading are quite different when the grouping strategy used is largely whole-class. The obvious associations of such an approach with a whole language program is apparent. However, to the extent that students need work on specific skills, particularly in the area of phonological processing as discussed in the previous chapter, it would appear that large group instruction with mixed-ability groups would not be consistent with effective instructional practices.

Although there is much benefit in the use of skills-based grouping for students with special needs, too often such groups have remained static; reading-achievement level has been the primary determinant of group placement. Instead, teachers should consider options that introduce change and flexibility into grouping procedures. Interest and skill groups, as well as pupil pairs, should be incorporated into the program at regular intervals.

Interest groups can be formed around a common theme (e.g., spaceships, baseball) regardless of reading-achievement level. The teacher can assign trade book material at levels appropriate for each student, with questions and activities suitable for the group. In skill groups, students periodically meet with the teacher to work on a specific skill deficit. Here again, students of varying levels of reading achievement work together on a common problem. A stronger student assisting a weaker one constitutes a pupil pair. With planning assistance from the teacher, this peer tutoring approach can be as motivating and instructional for the tutor as it is for the tutee.

Scaffolding

Scaffolding has become an increasingly popular term to describe interactions between teachers and students that facilitate the learning process. Stone (1998) describes the scaffolding "metaphor" as follows:

> In providing temporary assistance to children as they strive to accomplish a task just out of their competency, adults are said to be providing a scaffold, much like that used by builders in erecting a building. [Scaffolding] connotes a custom-made support for the "construction" of new skills, a support that can be easily disassembled when no longer needed. It also connotes a structure that allows for the accomplishment of some goal that would otherwise be either unattainable or quite cumbersome to complete (p. 344).

In scaffolding instruction, teachers think aloud or talk through the steps they follows to reach a specific conclusion. As students begin to understand the process, they gradually take over this talking-through procedure and the teacher acts only as a coach, providing prompts when needed. As a teaching strategy, it can be seen across all curricular domains; it is mentioned here to provide teachers with this additional perspective on reading instruction.

An example of a scaffolding procedure is seen in this exercise, which focuses student attention on story grammar. The teacher begins by modeling the scaffolding steps, thinking aloud by saying to the students after they have read to a designated point in the story, "I see a problem." The teacher states the problem and writes it on a notesheet that students can see. The teacher then describes the attempts in the story to solve the problem or conflict and gives an analysis of the events that led to the solution of the problem. After the teacher models these steps, the students begin to talk themselves through a story following the same steps (Gersten & Dimino, 1990). This is another example of a strategy that leads students into being active participants in the reading process. When used, students' responses to both lower- and higher-level questions improve.

Oral Reading

Oral reading is an important component of a total reading program. It is particularly necessary in the early stages of reading instruction because it gives the teacher insight into the beginning reader's knowledge of sight words and decoding skills. With most children, oral reading has three major purposes: diagnosis, conveying directions or instruction, and personal pleasure. For learners with special needs, oral reading has four additional purposes: articulation and vocabulary practice, memory reinforcement, rereading for better comprehension, and group participation.

Oral reading can assist development of correct word pronunciation by providing the disabled reader who seldom verbalizes with a structured opportunity to speak. When reading aloud, the student takes in information both auditorily and visually, adding an additional pathway to learning that is often necessary for memory. Rereading a passage orally after it has been read silently assists comprehension, particularly when the teacher designates a purpose for each reading.

Continuing oral reading for students with special needs longer than for average children is often beneficial. However, the students also clearly need practice and guidance in the transition from oral to silent reading (directed and encouraged by the teacher), because silent reading is the critical skill to develop. The previous discussion on self-questioning illustrated ways in which students can be taught to monitor their own reading in order to ensure that the silent reading process is effective in promoting comprehension.

SUMMARY

This chapter focuses on enhancing reading comprehension in students. It begins with a discussion of three general approaches: language experience, whole language, and the use of basal readers. It then provides information on a variety of specific strategies related to teacher-directed questioning, student-directed questioning, graphic-aid strategies, and fluency strategies. The chapter concludes with attention to several special considerations including instructional grouping of reading, scaffolding strategies in instruction, and the role of oral reading.

ACTIVITIES

The activities below relate to specific aspects of enhanced reading comprehension.

1. Make worksheets with several lists of words on them. Put several directions at the bottom of the sheet for students to follow (e.g., "Circle two animal names with red," "Draw a blue line under two things to wear.")
2. Make worksheets containing sentences and groups of words. Have students put "yes" behind those that are sentences and "no" behind those that are not sentences. This activity can be varied by adding questions to the

items and having students put a question mark behind items that are questions.

3. Have students read to remember instead of reading to find out and answer questions. Tell them to read to remember something they can share with their peers. When they finish, have them volunteer information to the class and write their statements on the board. At first begin with three pieces of information from each student. Write these statements on the board and have the students place them in the sequence in which they occurred in the story. As students improve, more statements can be required and/or the remembered information can be written (Harden, 1987).

4. Make a reading kit for adolescents by gathering interesting reading materials that correspond to students' reading ability levels. Record identifying information on cards that you number and laminate and prepare discussion questions separately. Place the laminated cards in a file box. Have students obtain a card, read for recreation, and then set up a private student-teacher conference for them to discuss the material with you (Machart, 1987).

5. To encourage the use of the library and promote independent reading, have students help rate books. With the librarian's assistance, ask students to help the teachers and the rest of the students at the school by reading the books in the library that fall within their reading ability. As a group, have them establish a system for evaluating and recommending books to others. (Jamison & Shevitz, 1985).

6. Make worksheets with simple drawings of several different objects. Have students cut out the objects and glue them on a sheet of extra paper according to written directions that contain prepositional phrases (e.g., "Put the cat under the tree," "Put the apple on the tree.")

7. Write short paragraphs for which students choose titles.

8. An activity that includes reading for information, survival, and amusement uses menus from the community's restaurants, fast food chains, or food counters. Give students specific assignments to compare prices, develop lists of meals, or identify the top 10 places to go on a special date. Students might also construct a composite menu to be printed in the graphics department and used for personal review. This menu can provide a basis for a variety of exercises to develop vocabulary, attack skills, and word recognition.

9. Read mystery stories to encourage students to make inferences and draw conclusions. Students like who-done-it stories and usually enjoy figuring out the final outcome of an unclear chain of events. Brainstorming as part of the activity might assist them in drawing conclusions (Cole & Cole, 1980).

10. Have students report on books they have read by acting out a phone conversation about the book, using visual aids to illustrate an episode in the book, making comic strips depicting scenes in the book, drawing a mural, selecting friends to act out scenes, or developing advertisements for the book (Bailey, 1975).

11. Newspaper articles from different sections of the paper can help students get the main idea of a story. Separate headlines from stories and place them in random order. Have students match titles to stories (Taylor et al., 1972).

12. Show the words to a popular song on the overhead projector. Without naming the song, choose someone to read the lyrics orally. As soon as others recognize the words, they can elect to sing it together. Words can be memorized as they are sung and visually tracked (Bailey, 1975).

13. Have students complete follow-up activities.
    - Write a letter to a main character in the book suggesting other ways the character might have solved the problem or acted in the situation.
    - Write sentences from the story that show that someone was excited, sad, happy, or ashamed.
    - Draw a picture of something in the story that indicates the setting is past, present, or future.
    - Find three pictures in magazines that remind you of the main characters in the

story. Under each picture write your reasons for selection.

- Draw a picture of one of the memorable scenes from the story, showing as many details as possible.
- Make a poster advertising your book.

14. Students can motivate others to read by sharing a book they have enjoyed. Some creative ways for them to share are listed here.

- Publish a book review column for the school paper with short reviews and reactions to books read.
- After reading a biography or book of fiction, describe the main characters and their common problems. Tell how these problems were or were not solved.
- Prepare a collection of something the class has read about (e.g., rocks, coins, stamps), with appropriate information for an exhibit.
- Make a poster (either flat or three-dimensional) showing a scene or stimulating interest in a book.
- Make and decorate a book jacket; write an advertisement to accompany the book.
- Write a letter to a friend or a librarian recommending a book you especially liked.
- Dress as one of the characters in a book and tell about yourself.

15. Students of all ages and abilities comprehend and retain information better if they are active readers.

- Always give students a purpose for reading and gradually train them to set their own purposes.
- Teach them to make predictions about content before beginning to read.
- After reading, have students defend or reject their predictions.
- Encourage students to ask themselves after each paragraph, "What is the main idea?"

16. Journal writing can be used to enhance comprehension. In character journals, students can comment on a story they have read in the voice of one of the characters. In this way, they may think more about what they are reading. Further, when students do not agree with a character's actions or attitudes, they may

come away with an improved sense of their own identity (Gartland, 1994, p. 20).

17. In groups, have students write and produce a videotaped commercial advertising a novel they have read. Each student will serve on their group's "ad committee," which will determine the type of commercial to be produced (e.g., public service announcement, testimonials) and how the information will be presented. The goal of each group should be to create an informative, entertaining commercial about their book, which will convince "viewers" to read that book. Commercials may also be shared with other classes and teachers.

18. Read a short story out to the class and stop before reaching the conclusion. Provide students with a variety of possible conclusions, some more closely related to the story than others. In groups, have students select the most appropriate conclusion and discuss why it was selected. As a class, discuss group conclusions and compare against the original ending of the story (Heilman, Blair, & Rupley, 1986).

19. After reading a selected story or novel, ask the students to paraphrase the story and develop a script for a class play or puppet show. The students make props, costumes, and puppets if desired. For a shorter version, students role-play parts of the story without verbalizing the information. The remainder of the class guesses the part of the story that is being dramatized. This activity reinforces the events of the story and improves comprehension.

20. In cooperative learning groups, students are responsible for finding a story element assigned to them (e.g., the problem) while reading a short story or chapter silently. Next, the students discuss what they read and the particular story element given to each group member. Then the group writes the answers in the story map.

21. Gartland (1994) encourages students to consider *K-W-L* as a technique to focus attention, with *K* representing what is known, *W* what the student wants to know, and *L* what has been learned.

TEACHER TIPS   Elementary Level

In a recent study researchers (Lipson, Mosenthal, & Mekkelsen, 1999) interested in the assessment of young children's reading comprehension skills found that several variables can influence reading comprehension outcome measures. Lipson and her colleagues conducted an investigation to measure how children retell stories that they have read in school. The researchers used the Development Reading Assessment (Beaver, 1997) to assess 7,500 second graders' reading comprehension.

The results of this study indicated that teachers should consider reading comprehension abilities of children on several dimensions. For example, the children in this study showed an understanding of stories through retelling. Interestingly, the children's recall proficiency was greater when the story's major events were illustrated. The results also suggested that the performance of children may be enhanced when teachers made minor changes in their teaching and gave greater attention to the children's skill of retelling stories.

Another dimension that may influence reading comprehension abilities (at least on this assessment measure) concerned text characteristics of the text. Text difficulty variables seem to influence children's recall of story elements when they were embedded in well-written text and had a clear character perspective. This finding indicated that teachers should carefully consider this aspect of a story when selecting text for assessment purposes.

These researchers discuss the use of retelling stories as a form of reading comprehension. They make the case that most assessment is limited to the answering of questions about the story. Libson and her colleagues argue that teachers may wish to understand children's construction of meaning in the story. Perhaps a child's meaning/understanding is central in assessment rather than questions that might be leading in nature. Of special note is that the quality of a child's retelling ability is more important than the quantity of the retelling.

Lipson, M. Y., Mosenthal, J. H., & Mekkelsen, J. (1999). The nature of comprehension among grade 2 children: Variability in retelling as a function of development, text, and task. In T. Shanahan & F. V. Rodriguez-Brown (Eds.). *National Reading Conference Yearbook 48,* Chicago, IL: National Reading Conference, Inc.

Beaver, J. (1997). *Developmental reading assessment.* Glenview, IL: Celebration.

TEACHER TIPS

Reading is an essential element for academic success. Many students with disabilities have difficulty in this area. Additionally, students entering secondary schools with limited English proficiency struggle with academic subjects due to reading difficulties. English as a Second Language (ESL) is burdensome to these students as they have as they have difficulty understanding teachers and reading subject matter in a language they do not fully comprehend.

Nuwash (1999) provides several rationales for investigating this aspect of reading. One rationale is that researchers have found that although less skilled readers preferred listening to reading as a learning mode, poor readers generally have poor listening skills. Nuwash further notes that studies have indicated a strong relationship between reading and listening in native English. Unfortunately, there is little research identifying the relationship between reading/listening and second-language acquisition. Hence, Nuwash presents a study to examine whether: (a) ESL students with strong educational backgrounds understand what they read in English better than what they listen to in English; and (b) ESL students with poor educational backgrounds, but with exposure to English, understand what they hear in English better than what they read in English.

Nuwash studied 204 secondary students that ranged from 13–21 years of age (98 were male). The student came from 18 different countries, with 10 languages being represented. Of these students, 156 were Spanish speakers of different countries. As a group, the exposure to English ranged from 6–12 months. Additionally, all the students filled out a questionnaire indicating their language learning and educational background.

Due to the difficulty in finding suitable assessment measures, Nuwash developed her own battery of tests. Her battery consisted of three tests in either listening or reading formats and were identical in every way except the mode of acquiring the knowledge. The tests were field-tested with mono-lingual students.

In spite of her small sample size, Nuwash found that regardless of educational backgrounds, ESL students had an easier time reading English than listening to English in the academic setting. Indeed, fluency in academic listening may be more difficult to acquire than teachers realize. Although these findings are preliminary, teachers of content areas may wish to couple reading and listening activities so ESL students can gain content and acquire English listening skills at the same time.

Nuwash, C. (1999). Reading and listening in English as a second language. In T. Shanahan and F. V. Rodriguez-Brown (Eds.), *National Reading Conference Yearbook, 48.* Chicago, IL: National Reading Conference.

TEACHER TIPS

In a small descriptive study of developing reading comprehension skills with students who are deaf, Lissi and Schallert (1999) present the use of computer-networked conversations between students and their reading teacher. These researchers discuss that students who are deaf have difficulty acquiring English speaking and writing skills and often score low on reading achievement tests. Also, the lack of English writing skills is of some concern as writing is an accessible way of communication (after sign language) for these students.

In part, this discussion is not surprising if we think that students who are severely and profoundly deaf face language acquisition difficulties and could be considered as second language learners, with sign language being their first language and English being their second. In fact, these researchers state that the reading problems of students who are deaf are not the result of poor decoding or comprehension difficulties, but rather as a consequence of poor English language knowledge. Thus, this study looked at the use of computer conversations between students and reading teachers in order to enhance English language skills and improve reading comprehension levels.

The researchers used a local-area computer network, developed by Batson and Peyton in the 1980s for Gallaudet University and which has been broadened to include deaf and hearing students (elementary and secondary) to engage students in conversations by writing about what they read in their reading class. This type of intervention is often called computer-mediated communication. Several descriptive measures were taken and analyzed through qualitative methodology.

The results indicated that computer-mediated communication did influence the students' meaningful conversations in written English. Although the students were still reading below grade level, they were addressing questions posed by the teacher, asking their own questions to the teacher and other students, and sharing information. Other outcomes included reacting to other student messages and generally having fun with the their new found form of communication.

Lissi, M. R. & Schallert, D. L (1999). A descriptive study of deaf students and their reading teacher participating in computer-networked conversation. In T. Shanahan & F. V. Rodriguez-Brown (Eds.). *National Reading Conference Yearbook 48*. Chicago, IL: National Reading Conference.

Written Language

The development of written language skills represents the summit of the language hierarchy. Built on and closely related to listening, speaking, and reading, writing is a critical component and an important goal within programs of language development. Written language subsumes the areas of handwriting, spelling, and written expression and thus demands that the communicator have a variety of mechanical, memory, conceptual, and organizational skills. It is not surprising that writing can present a variety of significant challenges to students with special needs, who may have existing linguistic deficits in oral language and/or reading, low societal expectations for success, and limited encouragement and reinforcement for appropriate usage. The importance of writing to such students, however, should be apparent because it opens another avenue for communication. At initial or minimal levels, students must develop the capability to write their names and other personally identifying information. At more advanced levels they need to take notes, respond to test questions, particularly within inclusive classrooms, and write letters of inquiry and complete job applications, as they transition into adult life. As Graham (1992) aptly states, "writing has increasingly become a critical occupational skill. Successful performance in a variety of occupations requires the ability to write in a clear . . . manner" (p. 137).

In recent years written language has received increased attention, particularly within general education, and the trend toward inclusion has obvious implications for students with disabilities. Advances in research and programming have come at an opportune time. A 1986 media report from the federal government indicated that 80% of all high school students in the general population write inadequately, more than 50% do not like the process of writing, and approximately 80% cannot write well enough to ensure that they will convey their meaning. A 1992 report confirms that many students have difficulty producing effective pieces of writing, whether their purpose is informative, narrative, or persuasive (Olson, 1994). These problems are found to an even greater extent in students with special needs. Vallecorsa

and deBettencourt (1992) note that students with learning disabilities have problems with basic mechanical and technical skills (e.g., difficulties in spelling, handwriting, capitalization, punctuation, sentence structure) as well as with composing (e.g., they write short and less cohesive compositions with less appropriate text structures). However, it is important to keep in mind that the writing difficulties of children and adolescents who have disabilities are also experienced by large numbers of other students.

WRITTEN LANGUAGE IN THE CURRICULUM

The role of handwriting, spelling, and written expression within the total curriculum is determined by the functioning levels of the individuals for whom the curriculum is designed. For the young child, handwriting and spelling instruction need to stress letters and then words having the most relevance for that individual (e.g., name, address, common lexicon). As students progress, these skill areas become tool subjects that support the ability to communicate through writing.

To promote an overview of written language and to illustrate the role of handwriting and spelling as supportive skills to written expression, a model is presented in Figure 10–1.

There are a number of specific facets of writing that serve as general programming considerations. Writers must *draw on previous linguistic experiences.* Thus, prior problems in listening, speaking, or reading may be reflected and perhaps magnified in the area of writing. In order to write in a coherent, understandable manner, *one must be able to think, read, and comprehend in a logical way.*

Writing involves a complex blend of *ideation as content* and *technical skills as craft.* Particularly when teaching the more mechanical aspects of writing (e.g., handwriting, spelling, grammar), teachers should remember that the goal is to use craft to enhance the expression of content. Thus, work on technical skills is more effective if learners see it not as boring but as engaging or interesting (e.g., games, student choice, peer

FIGURE 10–1

Model for writing

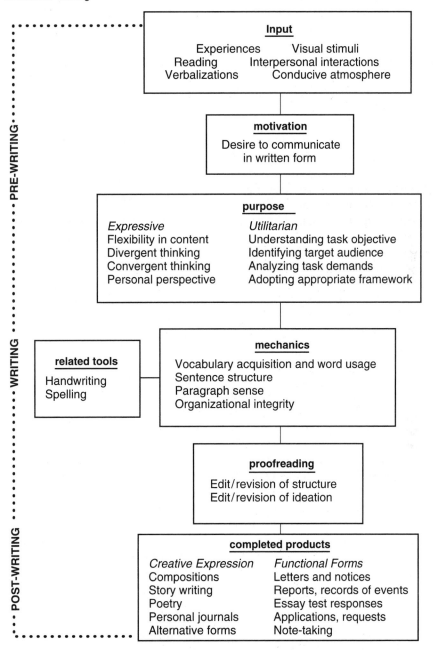

Source: Adapted from Polloway, E. A., Patton, J. R., & Cohen, S. B. (1983). Written language for mildly handicapped children. In E. L. Meyen, G. A. Vergason, & R. J. Whelan (Eds.), *Promising practices for exceptional children: Curriculum implications.* Denver: Love, (p. 289).

collaboration), if the skills taught offer a high rate of return because of their relative importance and usage, and if the skills are directly used in subsequent writing assignments (Graham, 1999).

Writing must be viewed as both process and product. Products typically serve as our primary goal. However, educators need to ensure that students learn how to reach that goal. For example, some students may have the mistaken impression that the textbooks used in various subject areas were written by an obscure scholar who simply transcribed thoughts directly to the finished product. These children need to understand the process behind the product, which provides an opportunity to emphasize the concept of the "rough draft." Writing provides a communication link for personal expression. In this sense, writing is not simply a goal but also a vehicle. Writing can provide opportunities for the expression of feelings and attitudes.

A comprehensive program provides for the development of both creative and functional uses of written language. The creative emphasis stresses individual expression and can promote personal and social adjustment. The functional emphasis serves a more utilitarian purpose, stressing skills that are directly applicable to independent living. Teachers, particularly at the secondary level, should carefully evaluate both current writing ability and expected future needs to determine which skills will benefit each student most.

Finally, teachers of writing should consider their own roots as writers. Graves (1994) encourages teachers to consider their own experiences with writing instruction in order to take a fresh look at writing themselves.

HANDWRITING

Handwriting has been a staple of the school curriculum for years. However, recently some educators have questioned whether technological advances have rendered it an unimportant skill. Nevertheless as Smith, Polloway, and Beirne-Smith (1995) note,

> Although the advances made in technology have clearly impacted on the everyday use of handwriting for some people, competencies in this skill definitely remain important. Without the ability to communicate with handwriting, individuals will be unable to make notes, take down information quickly, or communicate with others. (p. 2)

Some have argued that, rather than technology bringing about the end of the importance of handwriting, it may rather lead to its resurgence. As Murphy (1998, cited in *Academe Today,* 1998), states, as handwriting becomes less of "a daily utilitarian workhorse, it may well become even more a cherished means of interpersonal transmission— for the sorts of messages that one sets aside to preserve" (p. 2).

Greenland and Polloway (1995) highlight, in particular, issues related to first impressions associated with handwriting: Does an employer disregard sloppy and/or illegible applications? Does a teacher initially regard a student with poor handwriting as academically inferior? Are credit applications reviewed from a less favorable perspective? Graves (1994) stresses that while meaning in writing is paramount, it should not result in the handwriting being ignored.

Many children are delayed or disabled for reasons that also may impact their handwriting skills. For example, they may have deficits in attention or visual memory, or they may have physiological problems that inhibit the development of fine motor skills. In addition, they may be more susceptible to the effects of poor teaching or carelessness (Wallace, Cohen & Polloway, 1987). Because writing combines fine motor skills, sequencing, language, memory, attention, thinking skills, and visual-spatial abilities, it may be quite difficult, especially for those students with learning disabilities. Negative feelings about one's own handwriting may further aggravate the problem (Levine, 1990).

All students, but especially those with disabilities, are disadvantaged when handwriting is not taught correctly and frequently. Because handwriting is a critical skill, it is of concern that it is so often neglected (Dyer, 1992), especially among older students (Hammill & Bartel, 1990). One reason may be that most teachers assume that children learn to form letters merely by looking at them and writing them repeatedly (Dyer, 1992). Another reason may be that teachers have the knowledge and understand the need, yet choose not to emphasize it because of the time and attention required.

In instructing learners with special needs, teachers should remember the ultimate goal is legibility. Efforts to achieve perfect reproduction are most often doomed to fail; even when successful, they are frequently short-lived triumphs because most students develop a personal style. Therefore, instructional programs should avoid stressing the perfect reproduction of recognized standards and instead encourage a legible yet unique style (Wallace et al., 1987).

Assessment of Handwriting Skills

If a student has not formally started to write or is experiencing difficulty in acquiring a certain writing skill, the teacher must be able to assess the pupil's potential to develop this skill. Probably the best method of assessment is visual inspection; the teacher watches the student forming letters and determines which particular actions in the formation process are causing problems. Teachers can also refer to a commercial writing workbook that contains examples of general and specific handwriting errors and lists steps to correct them.

Many screening devices, such as the Wide Range Achievement Test (Jastak & Wilkinson, 1984) and the Slingerland (Slingerland, 1962), have sections that require students to demonstrate mechanical handwriting skills. These tests, however, provide little diagnostic information per se. Other alternatives are the Test of Written Language-3 (Hammill & Larsen, 1996), which evaluates handwriting according to graded scales and is discussed later in this chapter, and the Test of Legible Handwriting (Larsen & Hammill, 1989) which can be used with the TOWL-3. However, neither instrument is intended to provide information on strengths and weaknesses to develop an intervention program (Hammill & Bartel, 1990).

Given the limited diagnostic options available, the most common assessment tools are teacher observations and related informal techniques. Thus, once screening has been accomplished, a close visual examination should give the teacher information upon which to build a program to help a pupil develop or improve specific handwriting skills.

Handwriting Prerequisites

The development of prewriting skills demands adequate visual acuity and its coordination with motoric movements. Therefore, when students who are disabled enter formal schooling they must engage in the same type of visual and motoric activities that average children have probably mastered by that time. Two objectives—developing visual/motor integration and establishing handedness—are central concerns at this stage. To achieve these goals, numerous activities have typically been suggested: manipulation of objects, tracing of objects with the index finger in sand, manipulation of scissors for cutting paper, crayon and finger painting, and connecting dots and completing figures. Visual-motor activities adjusted for differences in chronological age also may be helpful for older students. For example, fine motor skills can be developed in shop classes and in vocational training.

Several important concerns arise about such activities. First, some activities (e.g., cutting with scissors) are clearly important for their own worth, regardless of their relationship to writing. However, there is no empirical support for the theory that these exercises directly assist in refining existing writing skills. Instead, some argue, the focus on nonwriting fine motor activities simply takes time away from direct instruction in writing. Another caution concerns the use of visual-motor activities with children with limited writing skills; overemphasizing fine motor skills may not be the most beneficial approach. The handwriting process itself provides fine motor practice and thus can accomplish both linguistically relevant goals (i.e., objectives that promote language development) and motoric goals (Decker & Polloway, 1989; Wallace et al., 1987). As Hammill (1986) notes, so-called prerequisites often can be naturally developed by directing students to write letters and words rather than giving extensive readiness instruction.

Manuscript Writing

Since manuscript writing is the initial instructional focus for most students, the teacher's first planning tasks are to determine an instructional sequence of letters and to select instructional methodology. There is no correct letter to start with in teaching manuscript writing; however, certain letters lend themselves to that function. For example, the letters of a child's first name have high utility value and motivate learning.

To ensure an appropriate instructional sequence, the teacher can group different letters by their shapes (Figures 10-2 and 10-3) or can follow the letter sequence in one of many commercial manuscript workbooks available. Another alternative is to follow the order in which letters are introduced for reading. Attention should be given to the relative similarity of strokes required for the letters.

For students who experience difficulty at the beginning stages of writing, modifications of the writing implement should be considered; the greatest problem often encountered is the correct grip on the utensil. A variety of aids have been used to facilitate appropriate grip, including the larger primary-sized pencils, tape wrapped around the pencil, use of a multisided large pencil, and the adaptation of a standard pencil with a Hoyle gripper (a three-sided plastic device that requires the child to place two fingers and the thumb in the proper position).

FIGURE 10–2

A sequential grouping of lowercase manuscript letters according to common features

o a d g q / b p / c e /
t l i k / r n m h / v w
x y / f j / u / z / s

FIGURE 10–3

A sequential grouping of uppercase manuscript letters according to common features

L H T E F I / J U /
P R B D K / A M N
V W X Y Z / S /
O Q C G

Although research on handwriting instruction has not demonstrated the necessity of modifying writing utensils (Graham & Miller, 1980), the database has not been generated from problem learners. Thus, it seems prudent to assess the grip of individual students who are experiencing difficulties in order to determine whether an adaptation is warranted. Norton's (1985) suggestion that students be allowed to select the size of utensil most comfortable for them seems particularly apt.

The most effective approach to teaching specific letters and words is one in which teacher presentation is consistent. Most programs assume that these forms are best taught in isolation but that opportunities must be provided for their use in actual writing exercises. Graham and Miller (1980) provided an excellent review of effective instructional techniques and sequence to facilitate letter formation. The procedure that follows is based on the specific steps they outline for instruction.

The first step is for the teacher to demonstrate the formation of individual letters while students observe the specific strokes involved. Students' attention should be directed to the distinctive features of these letters and their comparison with letters previously learned. As the children begin to transcribe letters, the teacher should use *prompting* (e.g., manual guidance during writing, directional arrows) and tracing to facilitate the task. When there is no longer a need for intrusive prompting, instruction becomes a function of copying—typically, from near-point (i.e., from a paper on the student's desk) and then from far-point (i.e., from the chalkboard). While copying and when writing from memory, students should be encouraged to engage in self-instruction by verbalizing to themselves the writing procedures being followed. After a letter can be written from memory, repetition of the form is needed to ensure learning and enhance proficiency. Finally, corrective feedback from the teacher, extrinsic reinforcement, and/or self-correction can be used so that the letter will be retained and increased legibility will be achieved.

As students master the formation of additional letters, they should be encouraged to write more about events occurring in the environment. Many teachers make good use of natural events by writing about them in the daily "class news." Teachers should watch for opportunities to record dictated thoughts on paper so that students can associate speaking, reading, and writing. One of the best uses of language experience charts is to help students perceive that what they say can be written down and read later. To prepare adolescents for the world of work and for the forms and applications that so frequently specify "Please print," teachers should continue to provide practical opportunities for using manuscript writing at the secondary level.

Once the student has made appropriate progress acquiring competence in the formation of manuscript letters, the transition to cursive should begin. This usually occurs in the third grade in most school divisions. Criteria for the transition include manuscript proficiency, ability to write all letters from memory, and self-initiated imitation of cursive forms.

Cursive Writing

The set of skills acquired while learning manuscript writing is helpful to students when they begin to learn how to write in cursive form. The movement to cursive should stress the key features of that style: paper positioning, the pencil remaining on the paper throughout the writing of individual words, all letters starting at the base-line, a left-to-right rhythm, an appropriate slant to the right, connection of letters, and spacing between words. Students should be encouraged to begin with manuscript letters that directly evolve into cursive forms.

Generally, instruction in cursive writing should follow the same format used with manuscript form: (a) start with letters that students are presently working with while following a predetermined sequence (Figures 10–4 and 10–5) based on common features or follow the sequence found in a commercial cursive writing workbook; (b) consistently use uppercase and lowercase to describe a letter; and (c) work with previously written words at the beginning of students' cursive writing experiences to promote transfer and overlearning. In addition, teachers must always tell students whether they should be writing

FIGURE 10–4
A sequential grouping of lowercase cursive letters according to common features

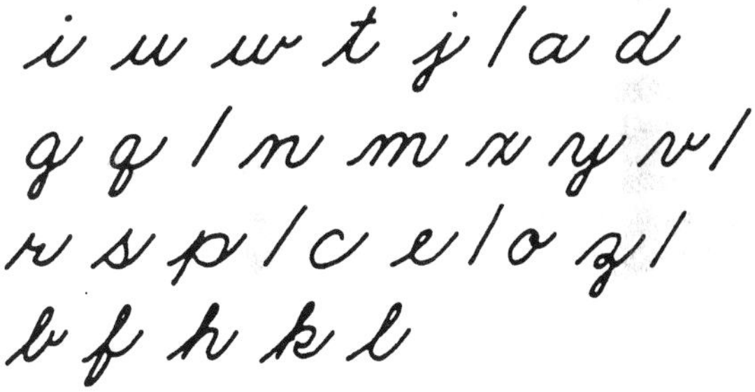

FIGURE 10–5
A sequential grouping of uppercase cursive letters according to common features

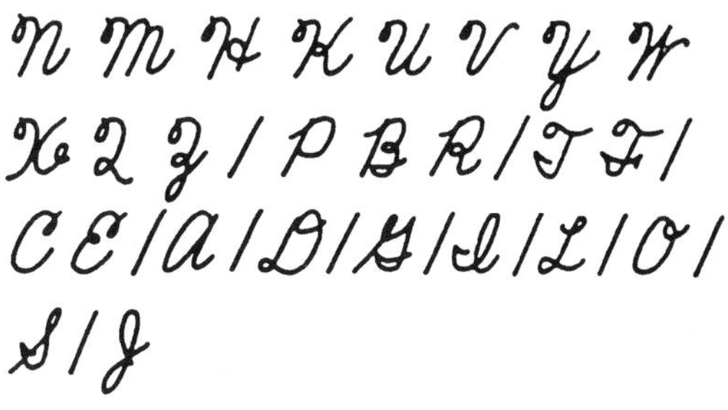

they can read. The close ties among spelling, reading, and writing should lead to integrated instruction in these areas.

Word Selection. The first words that students write are very meaningful to them, not just because they are new, but because they are usually the names of people, places, and things with which the students are familiar. Teachers should make other new words as meaningful as possible, perhaps by using new words to make up stories about students' immediate environment, thus facilitating a transition from the old to the new, or by placing new words in colorful sequence on a bulletin board, thereby causing students to be interested in finding out what the words are and how to spell them.

Word selection can be made from a variety of sources. Based on a student's ability and interest level, a teacher can select from frequency-of-use-in-writing lists (e.g., see Table 10–1), linguistic word families (e.g., fan/tan/pan), words used regularly within a student's oral expressive vocabulary, lists from specific remedial programs, commonly misspelled words, and words taken from the student's list of mastered reading words.

Students also should have as many functional words in their spelling vocabularies as possible. Functional words help young students communicate more effectively and help older individuals gain and maintain employment, adjust to environmental and social demands, and thus achieve social independence. Teachers are in the best position to draw up a list of community-relevant, functional words for students to learn. Functional word lists can be integrated into the reading program and can help students develop skills not only for spelling but for life in general.

General Teaching Strategies. A variety of instructional strategies can assist students who are having difficulty with spelling. Teachers should plan a program allowing for regular, systematic instruction while drawing from a variety of word-study techniques that are effective for particular students. The most successful word-study techniques use multisensory approaches, promote revisualization of words, assist students in formulat-

ing specific rules for accurate spelling, or promote self-correction. Some selected techniques outlined by Graham and Miller (1979), and Polloway and Smith (1999) are presented in Table 10-2.

The classic example of a word study technique is the Fernald (1943) multisensory approach. It is one of the best-known educational techniques for use with learners with disabilities, although it is actually applicable to all learners. The following specific procedures for teaching spelling are based on Fernald's directions for children learning new words. The techniques provide an example of the multisensory nature of the approach.

1. Look at the word very carefully and say it over to yourself.
2. See if the word can be written just the way you say it.
3. Shut your eyes and see if you can get a picture of the word in your mind. If you cannot . . . , you can remember the parts that are written the way you say them. Pronounce the word to yourself or feel your hand make the movements of writing the word.
4. When you are sure of every part of the word, shut your book or cover the word and write it, saying each syllable to yourself as you write it.
5. If you cannot write the word correctly after you have looked at it and said it, ask the teacher to write it for you. Trace the word with your fingers. Say each part of the word as you trace it. Trace the word carefully as many times as you need to until you can write it correctly. Say each part of the word to yourself as you write it.
6. If the word is difficult, turn the paper over and write it again.
7. Later in the day, try writing it from memory.
8. Make your own dictionary.

An emphasis on spelling rules can also be beneficial within a spelling program. Because within the English language there is a productive relationship between sounds and symbols, such an emphasis can be important as a mediating influence. The classic instructional sequence provided by Brueckner and Bond (1967, p. 374) can be helpful in teaching generalizations.

TABLE 10–2
Selected techniques for word study

Fitzgerald Method (Fitzgerald, 1951)

1. Look at the word carefully.
2. Say the word.
3. With eyes closed, visualize the word.
4. Cover the word and then write it.
5. Check the spelling.
6. If the word is misspelled, repeat Steps 1 through 5.

Horn Method (Horn, 1954)

1. Pronounce each word carefully.
2. Look carefully at each part of the word as you pronounce it.
3. Say the letters in sequence.
4. Attempt to recall how the word looks; then spell it.
5. Check this attempt to recall.
6. Write the word.
7. Check this spelling attempt.
8. Repeat the above steps if necessary.

Simultaneous Oral Spelling (Gillingham & Stillman, 1960)

1. Select a regular word and pronounce it.
2. Repeat the word after the teacher.
3. Say the sounds in the words.
4. Name the letters used to represent the sounds.
5. Write the word, naming the letters while writing them.

Fernald Method (Fernald, 1943) (Modified)

1. Make a model of the word with a crayon, grease pencil, or magic marker, saying the word as you write it.
2. Check the accuracy of the model.
3. Trace over the model with your index finger saying the word at the same time.
4. Repeat Step 3 five times.
5. Copy the word three times correctly.
6. Copy the word three times from memory correctly.

Cover-and-Write Method

1. Look at the word; say it.
2. Write the word two times.
3. Cover and write it one time.
4. Check work.
5. Write the word two times.
6. Cover and write it one time.
7. Check work.
8. Write the word three times.
9. Cover and write it one time.
10. Check work.

---

6. Review the rule systematically on succeeding days. Emphasize its use, but do not require pupils to memorize a formalized statement.

Another effective word study approach is the corrected-test method. Under a teacher's direction students correct specific spelling errors immediately after being tested. This strategy enables students to observe which words are particularly difficult, identify the part of the word creating the difficulty, and correct the errors under supervision (Graham & Miller, 1979).

Goddard and Heron (1998) provide examples of two self-correction strategies. Of particular note is letter-by-letter proofreading in which students are taught proofreading marks to check and correct their spelling. Figure 10–7 shows a five-column practice sheet that students use to practice new words. To proceed, Column 1 is completed by the teacher with the lesson's

FIGURE 10–7
Letter-by-letter proofreading

COLUMN 1	COLUMN 2	COLUMN 3	COLUMN 4	COLUMN 5
horse	hou̶se (r)	horse	horse	√
better	bettt̶er	better	better	√
passage	passg̶ae	passage	passg̶e (a)	passage
brain	brian	brain	brain	√
forget	forgo̶t (e)	forget	forgt̶ (e)	forget
measure	mee̶sure (a)	measure	mesure (a)	measure
target	target	√	target	√
activate	activate	√	activate	√
forty	foty (r)	forty	forti (y)	forty
pinnacle	pineccal (na e)	pinnacle	pinacal (n e)	pinnacle

From Goddard, Y. L., & Heron, T. E. (1998). Please, teacher, help me learn to spell better. *Teaching Exceptional Children, 30,* 41.

stimulus words; this column is folded back. Students then write the word from dictation in Column 2 and compare it to Column 1, making corrections where needed (as noted in the example). In Column 3, they write the corrected form or make a check if they were correct. Then Columns 4 and 5 are used for additional practice. This approach provides an apt transition to the use of strategy training in spelling.

Strategy Training. Accurate spelling of difficult words can also be facilitated through the use of strategy training. One approach is through mnemonic devices such as have been found useful in teaching students memory tasks in reading and recalling information to be learned in content areas. As Greene (1994) notes, mnemonic techniques are effective when they associate several items together, are unique, add concreteness to abstractions, have multisensory appeal, and provide rhythm or repetition. The task of learning a series of mnemonic devices, however, can place as much strain on the student's memory as the memory task itself. Therefore, the use of mnemonic techniques in spelling should be limited to examples that students can retain and use regularly (e.g., "a principal is your pal") (Polloway & Smith, 1999).

To facilitate retention, having students generate their own mnemonics is a plus; the following were developed by middle-school students (Burns, 1988).

- fowl—foul:An owl is a fowl.
- dessert—desert:Which would you like to have two of?
- hangar—hanger:An airplane is stored in a hangar.
- Caribbean:I drove a car in the Caribbean while I was eating some ribs and beans.
- niece:Ellen is my nice niece.
- Courtesy—curtsy:You have to show a lot of courtesy when you're in court.

Another key strategic approach to spelling success is the development of a word-study method that can be used by the student on an independent basis after interaction and support by the teacher. One useful approach is the method referred to as *copy-cover-compare.* Students study the word, copy it, cover it, develop an image of it, write the word, and then compare it with the original. The precise steps can be modified for a particular student and/or situation. The strategy is a simple one to use in spelling and provides for a straightforward approach to word study. Figure 10-8 provides a sample word list worksheet format for this approach.

This approach is consistent with the recommendation made by Greene (1994) for the use of a procedure called Look, Cover, Write, Check (LCWC). This strategy is as follows:

Students begin their lesson by looking at a word they are learning to spell and saying the letters out loud (verbal rehearsal). This is followed by the student closing his/her eyes and attempting to visualize in his/her mind the letters in the word (visual imagery). The student then looks at the spelling word again to verify the accuracy of the visual image and covers the word with his/her hand and writes it from memory. Following this step, the student checks for spelling accuracy once again and either repeats the procedure for the next word

FIGURE 10–8

Copy-cover-compare

Name _____

Spelling Worksheet

1. Word to practice	2. Spelling	3. Copy Word	4. Cover/Compare	5. Spelling
about				
after				
again				
all				
also				
always				
am				
an				
and				
another				
any				
are				
around				
as				
asked				
at				
away				
back				
be				
bear				
because				

From McLaughlin, T. F., & Skinner, C. H. (1996). Improving academic performance through self-management: Cover, copy and compare. *Intervention in School and Clinic, 32,* 114.

in the spelling list or starts over with the steps of LCWC on the present word until mastery is achieved. (p. 35)

Program Design. In addition to these general approaches to spelling instruction, a number of specific considerations can assist in designing an effective spelling program either for the inclusive or special education setting. The following suggestions are derived from Gordon, Vaughn, and Schumm (1993), Graham (1999), Graham and Voth (1990), McNaughton, Hughes, and Clark (1994), and Polloway & Smith (1999):

1. Instruction should focus initially on high-frequency words and misspelled words from the student's own writing efforts.
2. Words should be organized into small units (6 to 12 words) that emphasize a common structural element.
3. Students should be directed to name letters and words during practice to enhance attention and retention.
4. Teaching phonological awareness (see Chapter 8) is particularly useful for young learners.
5. Because overuse of direct phonemic spelling may cause problems, students also should be taught how to recognize and retain the patterns of words by focusing on morphemic analysis (e.g., suffixes, root words).
6. Students should be provided with immediate error-correction procedures.
7. Students should be taught strategies for word study to help them with their spelling and should use a systematic study procedure to study words missed on a pretest.
8. Students should practice missed words on succeeding days using games and other interesting activities to improve fluency and accuracy.
9. Long-term maintenance of correct spelling of words should be ensured through periodic review activities.
10. The teacher should work to establish links between instruction in spelling and the students' writing. Written products should be examined to determine if learned spellings are being generalized.
11. Reinforcement strategies related to spelling should be considered to ensure that motivation is sufficient for learning.
12. Motivation can be increased by giving students options for the motoric act of spelling practice, including the use of keyboarding and by using peer tutoring and group assignments.

Technology affords a useful approach for spelling practice. However, computers are not necessarily substitutes for "pencil and paper tasks". Table 10–3 provides a research summary of these options. Graham (1999) cautions that a key issue is whether the motoric demands are a confounding variable. Needless to say, teachers can observe students using the different approaches to evaluate their relative effectiveness.

Regardless of the word list selected or the approach utilized, spelling instruction can be effective only if students have opportunities to use the target words in written assignments and to proofread their work for possible errors. Although learning words in isolation is recommended to facilitate acquisition, maintenance and generalization are achieved only when students are encouraged to make regular use of the words they have learned. However, because students risk an interruption in the conceptual task of writing when they ponder the correct form of a difficult word, they can be encouraged to write an approximation of the word initially and then review it and correct it as necessary during the postwriting phase.

Invented Spellings

A new educational practice of the 1990s has been the use of invented (or creative) spellings, often a component of whole language instructional programs. The assumption of invented spellings is that students should be able to express themselves initially in writing without having to be concerned with spelling accuracy. Without question, when students invent their own spellings, teachers are naturally provided with helpful assessment data. Further, it is assumed that the use of invented spellings will have a positive effect

TABLE 10–3

Comparison of research on pencil versus computer in spelling

	Cunningham & Stanovich, 1990	Vaughn, Schumm, & Gordon, 1992	Berninger et al., 1998
Age of Children	24 first graders, mean = 6 years-10 months in 3rd and 4th months of 1st grade (Study 1); 24 first graders, mean = 7 years-3 months in 6th and 7th months of 1st grade (Study 2)	24 nonlearning disabled first graders, mean=7 years-7 months at end of school year; 24 learning disabled students who had completed first or second grade, mean = 8 years-6 months	48 children who had completed second grade, mean = 8 years-6 months
Socioeconomic Background of Children	predominantly middle class	lower middle class	diverse (lower to upper middle class)
Learning Characteristics of Children	normally developing (no IQ reported)	normally achieving and learning disabled (Mean IQ on WISC-R=89, *SD*=9.24)	all at risk for spelling disabilities; half also at risk for learning disabilities (*Mean* Verbal IQ on WISC-III=101; *SD* =14.88)
Duration of Intervention	4 teaching days (1/2-hour sessions), 1 testing day	4 teaching days (1/2-hour sessions) 1 pretesting day 1 posttesting day	6 teaching days (1 hour each) 1 pretesting 1 midtesting 1 posttesting
Spelling Words	30 words (6 homonyms) (no pretesting)	30 words—only words no child recognized at pretest (9; the same as used by Cunningham & Stanovich) (3 homonyms).	48 words organized by level of sound-spelling, predictability and reliance on word-specific information (1 homonym).
Method of Intervention	Simultaneous oral spelling method: Teacher names word. Child repeats name. Child reproduces word with pencil, keyboard (child finds keys), or tile and either names letters or hums as spelling word. Child	Same as Cunningham and Stanovich but eliminated the condition of naming letters vs. humming which yielded no main effect. Corrective feedback.	Derived from multiple-connections model: emphasized sound-spelling connections at whole word and subword level and representation of words in the "mind's ear and eye." Corrective feedback. Pencil or *(continued)*

TABLE 10–3 (*Continued*)

	Cunningham & Stanovich, 1990	Vaughn, Schumm, & Gordon, 1992	Berninger et al., 1998
Findings	repeats name of word. Corrective feedback. Learned to spell words better with pencil writing than with computer keyboard or tiles. No effect for letter-naming.	No differences among pencil, tile, computer condition in learning to spell words; no differences between non-learning disabled and learning disabled in learning to spell words.	keyboard response (tutor finds keys). No differences between pencil and computer, except computer was better for difficult words over time. Children with handwriting difficulties spelled worse than those without handwriting difficulties at pretest and throughout intervention.

Adapted from Berninger, V. et al. (1998). Teaching spelling to children with learning disabilities:The mind's ear and eye beats the computer or pencil. *Learning Disability Quarterly, 21,* 108.

on writing fluency and creativity by not interfering with the writing process.

The efficacy of invented spellings used with students with special needs is largely unexplored territory (Graham, in press) and there remains disagreement as to whether acceptace or encouragement to create new spelling ultimately will have a positive effect on the writing of students. Teachers therefore should consider invented spelling only as an experimental method and should evaluate its effectiveness and continue its use only if it is having positive results. With students with special needs, the use (or nonuse) of this approach often will be determined by one or more of the following: how spelling is taught within the inclusive setting in which students spend a portion or all of their instructional day; how transfer will be achieved from a pull-out program to the general education classroom; and what approach best promotes success in the inclusive setting (Polloway & Smith, 1999).

WRITTEN EXPRESSION

The technical skills of handwriting and spelling warrant attention for particular benefits of their own but their primary purpose is to serve as tools in written communication and expression, which builds on all of the skills acquired in other language domains. The process of writing can best be conceptualized as a multicomponent model, a series of sequential stages that not only define the process but also guide the necessary instruction. Writing models typically divide the process into the three stages: prewriting, inclusive of planning and organizing; writing, or drafting of ideas into sentences and paragraphs; and postwriting, or revision and editing (see Fig. 10-1).

Prewriting consists of what the would-be writer considers prior to the act itself. Input includes the various forms of stimulation that assist in forming a basic intent to write, such as environmental experience, reading, listening, and media exposure. Motivation includes the effects of various stimulating activities, as well as the external factors that reinforce writing. In addition, purpose must be established to assist in organization.

The *writing stage* encompasses handwriting and spelling as previously discussed, as well as the other craft aspects and content of written language. Considerations include vocabulary, meaning and description, sentence form, paragraph sense and the overall sequence of ideas, consistency, clarity, and relevance. The *postwriting* stage focuses on the importance of proofreading and includes editing of the craft aspects of writing and revising the content, with both emphases having the goal of improving the written product.

Viewing these three stages of writing as distinct and significant enables instruction to focus on the specific tasks facing the would-be writer. However, it is important to realize that, in practice, these phases are not perfectly discrete (Isaacson, 1987; Scarmadalia & Bereiter, 1986). For example, planning continues to take place during the postwriting stage, and revising takes place during the drafting stage. Nevertheless, an initial focus on the stages of writing does provide a process-type approach, which can assist students in thinking about what they are to do (Thomas, Englert, & Gregg, 1987).

Assessment

Even though writing produces a permanent product to aid teachers in assessment, a number of problems have typically complicated such evaluation. Some of these are the relative paucity of formal tools and the emphasis of existing tests on contrived formats (e.g., multiple-choice items) that assess only the mechanical aspects of writing; this latter problem is particularly common in achievement-oriented tests with written language subtests.

One diagnostic tool that can provide a more comprehensive analysis of written language abilities is The Test of Written Language-3 (TOWL-3) (Hammill & Larsen, 1996), which was developed to assess the adequacy of abilities in handwriting, spelling, and the various other components of written expression. The test includes scales

for vocabulary, thematic maturity, word usage, and style. Both spontaneous and contrived formats provide a basis for assessment, with primary emphasis on evaluating an actual writing sample. The TOWL is the best-designed, most diagnostically useful formal tool available for analyzing the writing of students with disabilities.

Because formal tools cannot fully evaluate the total scope of written expression, informal assessment approaches should receive primary attention. Emerging assessment strategies in writing are comprehensive in scope and rely on data from a variety of sources. According to the ASCD (1997), qualities that should be assessed in writing are as follows:

- *Ideas and Content*—is the message clear? Does the paper hold the reader's attention?
- *Organization*—Does the paper have an inviting introduction? Are supporting details placed in a logical order? Can the reader move easily through the text?
- *Voice*—Does the writer speak directly to the reader? Is the writer sensitive to the needs of an audience?
- *Word Choice*—Are the words chosen specific and accurate? Do lively verbs energize the writing?
- *Fluency*—Does the writing have a cadence and easy flow? Do sentences vary in length as well as structure?
- *Conventions*—Does the writer demonstrate a good grasp of standard writing conventions, such as grammar, punctuation, and paragraphing? Is punctuation accurate? Is spelling generally correct? (p. 5).

While a full discussion of these concerns is beyond the scope of this chapter, teachers working in special or inclusive settings do need to rely on a repertoire of writing assessments.

The techniques described in Table 10-4 facilitate informal analysis of a number of aspects of writing. The key to using any of the procedures listed in this table is to analyze students' writing samples. Frequent opportunities to communicate must be part of the weekly experiences of all students possessing basic skills in the area. Teach-

TABLE 10–4
Informal written language assessment procedures

Technique	Description	Methodology	Example	Comment
Type token ratio	Measure of the variety of words used (types) in relation to overall number of words used (tokens)	$\dfrac{\text{Different words used}}{\text{Total words used}}$	type = 28 token = 50 ratio = $\dfrac{28}{50}$ = .56	Greater diversity of usage implies a more mature writing style.
Index of diversification	Measure of diversity of word usage	$\dfrac{\text{Total number of words used}}{\text{Number of occurrences of the most frequently used word}}$	total words = 72 number of times word *the* appeared = 12 index = 6	An increase in the index value implies a broader vocabulary base.
Average sentence length	Measure of sentence usage (number of words per sentence)	$\dfrac{\text{Total number of words used}}{\text{Total number of sentences}}$	total words = 54 total sentences = 9 words per sentence = 6	Longer length of sentences implies more mature writing ability.
Error analysis	Measure of word and sentence usage	Compare errors found in a writing sample with list of common errors		Teacher can determine error patterns and can prioritize concerns.

T-unit length (Hunt, 1965)	Measure of writing maturity	1. Determine the number of discrete thought units (T-units)
		2. Determine average length of T-unit: $\dfrac{\text{Total words}}{\text{Total number of T-units}}$
		3. Analyze quantitative variables:
		  a. no. of sentences used
		  b. no. of T-units
		  c. no. of words per T-unit
		4. Analyze qualitative nature of sentences
			"The summer was almost over and the children were ready to go back to school."
			Quantitative
			(1; 2; 5 + 10)
			Qualitative:
			1. compound sentence
			2. adverbs:
			  of degree—"almost"
			  of place—"back"
			3. adjective—"ready"
			4. infinitive—"to go"
			5. prepositional phrase adverbial of place—"to school"
				This technique gives the teacher information in relation to productivity and maturity of writing skills.

Note. From "Written Language for Mildly Handicapped Students," by E. A. Polloway, J. R. Patton, and S. B. Cohen, 1983, *Promising Practices for Exceptional Children: Curriculum Implications* (pp. 300–301), by E. L. Meyen, G. A. Vergason, and R. J. Whelan, Eds., Denver: Love Publishing. Copyright 1983 by Love Publishing Company. Reprinted with permission.

ers should plan a sequence of skills that will be evaluated on an ongoing basis and should resist the temptation to provide corrective feedback for all types of errors simultaneously. Error analysis should thus focus on an individual skill deficit as a basis for remediation. An overriding concern, however, is that assessment should not focus just on skills but on the overall communicative effectiveness of the written product (Ballet, 1991).

Portfolios are particularly appropriate for writing assessment. Portfolios enable teachers to involve the students in the evaluation of their own writing samples, particularly by selecting samples to be kept and then working with them to compare changes in writing over time. Three types of portfolios that are likely to be used in inclusive classes are:

- *Sampling of Works*—This type of portfolio is often used in primary grades to compare early writing samples with later writing samples. . . . These portfolios are often sent on to the student's next teacher.
- *Selected Works*—In these portfolios, students collect samples of their writing in response to a teacher prompt.
- *Longitudinal*—These portfolios are oriented toward district goals for student achievement and [essentially yield pre- and post-test measures] to provide an accurate assessment (p. 51). (adapted from ASCD, 1997).

Instruction

Given the challenges that students with special needs face in writing, the most important consideration in instruction is sufficient opportunity for students to develop their writing ability. Thus, they need a substantial amount of time to write. Further, as Graham (1992) notes, this opportunity to write should involve meaningful tasks (i.e., written for an authentic audience, important and/or interesting to the author, designed to serve a true purpose in communicating). Graham (1992, p. 137) notes the following suggestions for providing frequent and meaningful writing opportunities:

1. Encourage students to decide for themselves what they will write about.

2. Ask students to establish goals for what they hope to achieve.
3. Arrange the writing environment so that the teacher is not the sole audience for students' writing.
4. Provide opportunities for students to work on the same writing project across days or even weeks if necessary.
5. Incorporate writing as part of a larger, interesting activity.
6. Select writing activities that are designed to serve very specific and real purposes.

As noted, the writing process involves three semidistinct stages. Although the lines between these stages can blur, and although writers shift back and forth among them, they are presented here separately for ease in presentation.

Prewriting. Instruction taking place during the planning stage should reflect the reality of the way students present themselves for instruction. In particular, assumptions should not be made that pupils with disabilities have had the necessary experiential prerequisites to develop ideation, that they have a desire to communicate via written means, or that they understand their purpose in writing and the nature of their intended audience. Each of these factors should be addressed by instruction.

The first concern at this stage is *stimulation.* Teachers should strive to provide opportunities to expose students to varied experiences through listening and reading; provide them with a chance to discuss and clarify ideas on a given topic, thus encouraging active thinking about the task at hand; promote brainstorming with peers; develop story pictures, outlines, and webs with students to organize ideas; and establish a conducive, supportive classroom atmosphere. Concerned teachers working with learners with special needs must stimulate students before giving them a chance to write. While stimulation alone does not promote the acquisition of writing skills (Phelps-Gunn & Phelps-Terasaki, 1982), it does provide for conceptualization and offers an organizational picture; it starts writers thinking clearly.

When provided with an opportunity for creative writing, students can be stimulated by topics of personal interest. Teachers should generate a collection of possible themes to use as general assignments. Table 10-5 presents some examples that can be used in general and special education classes.

The second concern at this stage is *motivation,* which is particularly important for adolescents with disabilities. A substantial amount of research focused on the writing of students without disabilities argues that motivation must come from within; teachers can stimulate students, but they cannot actually motivate them. According to this logic, if students have something meaningful and/or interesting to think about, their writing will reflect it. This premise in remedial and special education, however, presents some difficulty because writing just does not happen much of the time. Teachers of students with special needs should consider ways to promote motivation, such as using external reward systems to complement the internal motivation of reluctant writers.

Alley and Deshler (1979) in their classic text on adolescents with special needs provided several apt observations on motivation. Identifying attitude toward writing as a key concern, they suggest the following strategies: encourage students to focus initially on ideation rather than mechanical skills so that they feel comfortable with writing before trying to achieve perfection (thus sensing failure); expose students to a variety of experiences to build their knowledge base for writing; use tape recorders as a way to record thoughts, followed by subsequent efforts to transcribe and revise these thoughts; and have students write daily or weekly journals without corrective feedback.

The third aspect of planning is that of *setting the purpose.* The writer must have a clear understanding of who the audience is and thus what the purpose is. Expressive and functional writing have different intents and thus require different formats.

Writing. The writing or drafting stage is the broadest of the three components. Consequently, it is of little surprise that problems and deficits in this phase are common in students who are disabled. The educator's key concern is to determine how skills are most effectively learned and most effectively taught. With this focus, it is useful to consider the distinctions discussed by Isaacson (1987, 1989) between the two roles inherent in the writing process: the author and the secretary. Whereas the author role is concerned with the formulation and organization of

TABLE 10–5
Sample writing themes

Topics for Writing Assignments

I knew something was wrong when I heard that sound . . .

When I was a baby . . .

The day I became a . . . (name an animal)

The day at the circus

A TV character I would like to be

My favorite movie

My summer vacation

My favorite sports hero

The secret clubhouse

The Western character I would most like to be

If I could be anybody in the world for one day, I would most like to be . . .

I wish I could spend my summer vacation in . . .

My best friend is . . . because . . .

Why colors remind me of moods

Spending the day with my favorite rock group

Summer camp

If I could change one thing in my past, I would change . . .

My hobbies

What I look for in a friend

My first job

The day I got my license to drive

The first thing I want to do when I turn 18 is . . . because . . .

If I were a millionaire, I would . . .

ideas and the selection of words and phrases to express those ideas, the secretarial role emphasizes the physical and mechanical concerns of writing, such as legibility, spelling, punctuation, and grammatical rules. Obviously, both roles are critical to a writer's success, and both have influenced instructional practice.

Sink (1975) distinguishes between a focus on teach-write and one on write-teach. The former corresponds reasonably well with the secretarial role of writing; it emphasizes formal grammar instruction, structure, skills exercises, perhaps the diagramming of sentences, and often a reliance on worksheets and workbook pages. Even though this approach is common in classrooms, it does not have proven effectiveness. For example, Sherwin's extensive 1964 review of 50 years of literature on this topic found little evidence of the effectiveness of this approach with learners without disabilities. There is even less reason to believe that the teach-write approach is effective with learners with special needs. A major concern is that the instructional activities required can be completed without opportunity for actual writing. Additionally, the approach can have a negative effect on motivation (Gould, 1991) and remind students that they "can't" write (Lynch & Jones, 1989). At the same time such activities can damage motivation to write by usurping a major block of time, something that writing programs may have in only limited supply. Thus, although skills are important, they may not be truly learned—that is, applied—in this fashion.

The alternative is the write-teach focus, with initial stress on the primacy of the author role, on ideation over form, with structure emphasized later. The write-teach approach capitalizes on the desire to write without stifling that effort. Structure can then be taught within the context of actual writing opportunities. The approach is more holistic in nature, since learning to write comes through the process of writing (Gould, 1991).

Graves (1985) succinctly states the case for a write-teach approach:

> Most teaching of writing is pointed toward the eradication of error, the mastery of minute, meaningless components that make little sense to the child.

Small wonder. Most language arts texts, workbooks, computer software, and reams of behavioral objectives are directed toward the "easy" control of components that will show more specific growth. Although some growth may be evident on components, rarely does it result in the child's use of writing as a tool for learning and enjoyment. Make no mistake, component skills are important; if children do not learn to spell or use a pencil to get words on paper, they won't use writing for learning any more than the other children drilled on component skills. The writing-processing approach simply stresses meaning first, and then skills in the context of meaning. (p. 43)

If this option is adopted, there are a number of clear implications for instruction. Most significant is that for writing to improve, students need to write regularly. Graves (1985) recommends that students write at least 4 days per week and indicates that irregular instruction merely reminds students of their inability to write. Daily journal writing is an approach that has been used effectively for this purpose. The increased trend toward inclusion may enhance the amount of time available for writing because special education settings too frequently have stressed remedial reading and math activities to the virtual exclusion of the development of writing.

Once the opportunity to write is confirmed, the development of structural or mechanical skills needs to be considered. The dilemma here is to find an appropriate approach to enhance the acquisition of skills without interfering with the writing process. Graham (1992) offers three well-reasoned tenets to assist with instructional decision making. These include: (a) maintain a balanced perspective between the extremes of decontextualized teaching of mechanics (including handwriting and spelling) and complete deemphasis on skills information to the extent to which acquisition becomes incidental; (b) focus on teaching skills that are likely to benefit the student rather than unlikely to produce generalizable benefits (e.g., learning to spell high-frequency words versus learning to diagram sentences); and (c) tie instruction on skills to the context of real writing opportunities. Students should be shown that these skills reflect conventions followed to enhance communication. As Graves (1994) notes in reference to teaching children to write, "If I take the view that conventions are there to help me, and that each one offers a better opportunity to understand what I am trying to say, then I want them in my repertoire of tools for writing" (p. 192).

One approach consistent with these concerns is selective feedback, which focuses on a limited number of skills at a given point in time. Selective feedback is a preferred alternative to both extremes of inordinate corrections or relatively meaningless comments about "good work." One way to accomplish selective feedback is through teacher conferencing (Barenbaum, 1983). With this technique the teacher proofreads written assignments and provides feedback directly to students, most often in an oral conference. Such an approach provides an opportunity to introduce and reinforce specific skills and conventions.

Experience rather than empirical data serves as the support for the write-teach approach with students with disabilities. One should not assume that the more students write, the better their writing will become. Rather, constant application of the skills developed in written language should be actively encouraged. When students develop specific written language skills, teachers must give students many chances to use these skills. The key is instruction that results in embedding skills work in the students' own writing (ASCD, 1997).

Vocabulary Development. A major instructional concern is vocabulary building. Because students' oral vocabulary is larger than their written vocabulary, teachers should look for ways to facilitate transition from oral vocabulary to writing. This can be accomplished by introducing them to objects and experiences outside their daily lives and assisting them in writing about these events.

The language experience approach (LEA) offers a natural lead in by combining attention to listening, speaking, reading, and writing. With LEA, students dictate stories that teachers transcribe for subsequent reading. Students then revise the stories, establishing the link between oral and written expression.

Within the context of specific writing tasks, several strategies may promote vocabulary development. Students can generate specific words that might be needed in a writing assignment, and the teacher can write them on the chalkboard for illustration and later reference. A list of words can also be kept on a bulletin board for students to copy and place in a notebook for later use. This is especially helpful with high-frequency words (e.g., Dolch words) that may also be spelling demons. Having the accurate spellings of words that are likely to be used minimizes interruptions in the conceptualization process (Wallace et al., 1987). Instructional activities should also focus on the development of descriptive language. Students might brainstorm alternative words to use in a specific instance and then systematically substitute them in their own written compositions. This exercise can target synonyms as well as adjectives and adverbs to increase the descriptiveness of writing. However, for older students who may still have very limited writing abilities, the most appropriate goal is the acquisition and correct use of a limited number of functional words.

Vocabulary building can also be facilitated by various reward systems. A variety of contingency arrangements has been reported; collectively, they indicate that reinforcement for specific targets, such as use of unusual words, not only produces gains in that area but often produces generalization to related skills (Polloway et al., 1983).

Sentence Development. Another significant aspect of writing instruction is sentence development. The sentence is the nucleus of structural work with students and the basis for teaching about appropriate syntax. Often, the poor writer's efforts are characterized by either safe, repetitive, short sentences or rambling prose without any structure. It is important to balance an emphasis on "real writing" with focused instruction on patterned sentence guides and structures (Isaacson, 1987). With such guides, students can enhance their efforts to communicate effectively. The simplest form of patterned guide presents a picture for which students must write a sentence, following a set pattern (e.g., "The [dog] is [running]").

Several other instructional alternatives are also available. The Fitzgerald Key (Fitzgerald, 1966) was developed for children with hearing impairments based on the assumption that written language would help them improve in oral language. Essentially, this tool analyzes sentences into a series of *Wh*-questions (who, what, when, and where) instead of labeling nouns, verbs, adjectives, adverbs, and prepositions. This alternative is promising for students with disabilities, because it avoids the density of instruction in parts of speech. It keeps instruction meaningful and relevant by focusing on things that students can deal with directly. A modified Fitzgerald Key was used in the Phelps Sentence Guide (Phelps-Terasaki & Phelps, 1980), which involves a structured sequence for generating, elaborat-

ing, and ordering sentences based on various stimuli and a series of questions posed to students. Subsequently, this program was revised as the Teaching Competence in Written Language Program (Phelps-Terasaki & Phelps-Gunn, 1988), which contains 44 lessons ranging from writing subjects in sentences to paragraph development. A sample lesson is shown in Figure 10–9.

A *sentence extension* model can be used in two ways. One approach is to take a sentence and analyze it according to specific word categories, thus outlining the specific parts of a sentence. The second option is to have students generate a series of words or phrases to fit in each of these columns; at that point a sentence or series of sentences can be synthesized. Both exercises emphasize a direct relationship between words and sentences and facilitate sentence sense. Either approach enables students to appreciate how lexical items can vary sentence usage, sentence sense, and sentence generation.

FIGURE 10–9
Teaching competence in written language program

LESSON 10: Review and Practice 1

The Sentence Guide for Lesson 10 has ten sentences. These are not good sentences. Each sentence has one of the following mistakes:

1. The Who/What? column is blank.
2. The Doing What? column is blank.
3. The time is wrong.
4. The sentence does not paint a clear mind picture.

Look at the picture below. Use this picture to help you correct the mistakes in the sentences.

Sentence Guide

Connectors	Who/What?	Doing What?	Details
And First Second Next Then Last	Which? What kind of? How much? How many?		Why? (because, since, so that) What? When? Where? How?
		Is putting out	the fire with a firehose.
	The black-and-white dog		
	The fire	started	tomorrow.
	It	is hanging	on the fire truck.
		is climbing	up the ladder.
	A boy and a girl		
	The fire truck	came	next week.
	He	is carrying	an ax.
		is parked	by the house.
	The orange cat		

From Phelps-Terasaki, D., & Phelps-Gunn, T. (1988). *Teaching Competence in Written Language: A Systematic Program for Developing Writing Skills,* p. 9 (Student Tablet) and p. 12 (Student Lesson Book). Austin, TX: PRO-ED. Copyright 1988 by PRO-ED, Inc. Reprinted with permission.

A further step in sentence development is *sentence combining,* which expands simple sentences into more complex ones. Research has indicated that sentence combining is an effective way to increase syntactic maturity and improve the overall quality of writing (Isaacson, 1987; Scarmadalia & Bereiter, 1986). Among the most commonly used programs of sentence combining is one developed by Strong (1973, 1983), which asks students to combine clusters of sentences; they are informed that this can be accomplished in a variety of ways and that no specific response is indicated. A sample cluster from Strong's (1973) original program is shown here.

1. Most of us remember Groper.
2. We remember him from our high school days.
3. He was angular.
4. He was muscled.
5. He had huge hands.
6. The quarterback would send him down.
7. The quarterback would send him out into the flat.
8. And then the football would come.
9. It looped in an arc.
10. The arc spiraled.
11. Groper would go up.
12. He would scramble with the defense.
13. The defense clawed at his jersey.
14. He was always in the right place.
15. He was always there at the right time (p. 38).

Even though Strong's program does not begin with true writing, it does encourage students to expand and develop their own creation. Individual tasks finish with an invitation to finish the story. While the program provides a model for instruction in this area, the lessons are not extensive enough to provide the necessary amount of practice for students with special needs. Therefore, teachers need to supplement the program by developing their own sentence clusters to promote additional practice and enhance mastery.

Paragraph Development. Just as sentences are the transition from words to organized thoughts, paragraphs represent the transition from sentences to a unified composition.

Instruction in paragraphing thus provides training in organization. Students need to learn that paragraphs are a matter of making assertions and elaborating on those assertions; they have an introductory sentence that asks "why," which is followed by two or three sentences that give the "because" (Buchan, 1979). To begin, teachers can identify a topical sentence and students can provide elaboration. Then students can generate the first sentence and the teacher can monitor their efforts. Later, teachers can have students support their topic sentences with three follow-up sentences and one clincher sentence.

To give some meaning to paragraph writing, teachers can assign functional tasks for initial instruction, because their purpose is often more apparent. One example is a one-paragraph letter ordering a particular item from a catalog.

A helpful technique to assist in building paragraphs as well as a useful skill for writing in general is paraphrasing. One example of a paraphrasing strategy is identified as RAP (Schumaker, Deshler, & Denton, 1984, cited in Ellis & Sabornie, 1986). The acronym comes from *Read* a paragraph, *Ask* yourself what the main ideas and details in the paragraph were, and *Put* the main idea and details into your own words.

Composition Writing. Composition writing is the goal of most teachers working with students having difficulties with written language. Included within this area are initial considerations of story writing and then extensions of skills into further opportunities for expository writing. Several general considerations that can enhance students' composition writing in both areas are worthy of initial note.

Teachers should provide students with models that exhibit the desired behavior. Numerous methods can accomplish this: (a) the teacher can model the desired behavior by writing short stories, paragraphs, or essays that students copy; or (b) students who are approaching or have reached the desired outcome can exhibit their work for other pupils to view, thereby demonstrating correct behavior from a student perspective.

Special sensitivity should be accorded to students with cultural backgrounds different from the instructor's. Specifically, language production should be promoted initially, regardless of form, with subsequent efforts then geared to assist students in "saying that (i.e., writing it) in another way" if it is necessary for standard English to be used in a given assignment or communicative act.

To facilitate story writing, Graves and Hauge (1993) recommend the use of a story grammar cuing system. Students are to learn to focus on a series of specific story elements: the *setting* of the story to be written, the main and supporting *characters,* the *problem* in the story and the *plan to solve* it, and the *ending* or resolution. The cuing system is a checklist on which students check off each of these five elements as they plan and write it. The checklist should then be practiced and maintenance and generalization should be emphasized.

To support students' ability to understand the specific story elements discussed, it is helpful to have them discuss each of them and derive specific concepts. One particularly problematic area may be understanding problems and plans within the story. Montague and Leavell (1994) present specific ideas about these considerations, which were generated by the students themselves in response to a topic to be written about. These can be summarized on a poster for student reference (Table 10-6).

Another important component of story writing is the development of characters. Leavell and Ioannides (1993) encourage teachers to provide explicit instruction in character development by focusing students' attention on the attributes of physical appearance, speech and actions, and thought and emotions. Table 10-7 provides a list of thought and emotion words that they provided to assist students to further their ability to develop characters.

For students who have significant difficulties with writing production, the process of developing composing skills is a challenging task. Teachers will need to consider which students can profit from relatively brief targeted instruction to enhance stories that they are already writing and which students' deficiencies will necessitate more intensive instruction in order to operationalize compositional elements within their writing (Montague & Leavell, 1994).

In addition to story writing, students also need to be taught expository writing skills. For many students with disabilities, this is a daunting challenge. Assisting these students to understand

TABLE 10–6
Problems and plans in composing

Problems set the action of the story in motion.
Plans tell how the character(s) will solve the problem(s).

Problems can be internal (inside the character)
  or external (outside the character).

Some Examples are Problems With

Money	Work	Heartbreak	Insanity
Family	Friends	Sickness	War
Business	Love	Death	Being trapped/
Personal issues	School	Abuse	stranded
Crime	Weather	Nature	Addiction

Note. From Montague, M., & Leavell, A. G. (1994). "Improving the Narrative Writing of Students with Learning Disabilities." *Remedial and Special Education, 15,* 23. Copyright 1994 by PRO-ED, Inc. Reprinted with permission.

TABLE 10–7
Thoughts and emotions chart

Thought Words			
wanted	realized	thought	wished
noticed	reasoned	hoped	felt
knew	needed	wondered	believed
understood	remembered	pondered	

Emotion Words			
happiness	hate	sadness	anxiety
satisfaction	nervousness	boredom	worry
amazement	tension	jealousy	fear
excitement	surprise	panic	loneliness
depression	envy	love	compassion
joy	agony	frustration	sympathy

Note. From Leavell, A. & Ioannides, A. (1993). "Using Character Development to Improve Story Writing." *Teaching Exceptional Children, 27,* 1993, 43. Copyright 1993 by The Council for Exceptional Children. Reprinted with permission.

the various structures inherent in such writing requires a significant commitment.

One helpful way to teach expository text structures is to teach students to use advanced organizers as vehicles for enhancing their planning and writing. Figure 10-10 presents a framework that highlights specific questions that are associated with the task of explanation. Englert and Mariage (1991) also present models for assisting with writing narratives and comparisons and contrasts as well as further information on the use of such text structures to promote effective writing.

Postwriting. The general goal of writing instruction is to enable students to communicate effectively with others while achieving personal satisfaction in the process. To achieve this goal, the revision stage must become a routine and integral part of the writing process. Students must be sold on the concept of the "working draft" as the initial effort to get on paper the information to be shared. The revision stage must acquire a positive association, removed from any connection with punitive action. Students should be

assisted in deriving personal satisfaction from writing that comes from looking at it as a process rather than as a polished product.

Postwriting requires the active involvement of the writer in the careful review and revision of what has been previously written. Initially, students must have the opportunity to establish the concept and activate the skills. Training can begin with anonymous papers and direct instruction to, for example, identify correct and incorrect sentences, find three spelling errors, and/or correct all punctuation errors on a given page. After reaching an acceptable criterion, students can shift to their own work.

Focusing on the full spectrum of revision and editing is an overwhelming task for any student who has difficulties with writing. Therefore, only one or two skills should be stressed at any time. A helpful approach for the organization of the initiation of revising and editing activities is the error-monitoring strategy indicated by the acronym COPS (Schumaker et al., 1981):

■ Capitalization: Have I capitalized the first word and proper nouns?

FIGURE 10–10
Explanation organization form

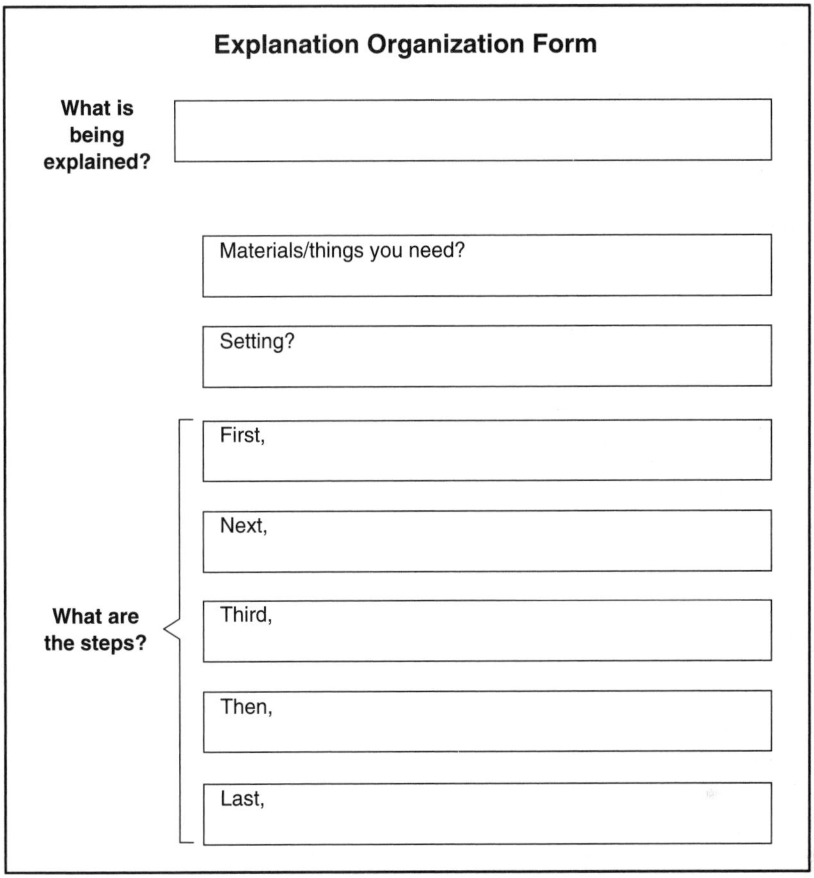

Explanation Organization Form

What is being explained?

Materials/things you need?

Setting?

What are the steps?

First,

Next,

Third,

Then,

Last,

From Englert, C. S. & Mariage, T. V. (1991). "Shared Understandings: Structuring the Writing Experience Through Dialogue." *Journal of Learning Disabilities, 24,* 334. Copyright 1991 by PRO-ED, Inc. Reprinted with permission.

- Overall appearance: Have I made any handwriting, margin, messy, or spacing errors?
- Punctuation: Have I used end punctuation, commas, and semicolons correctly?
- Spelling: Do the words look like they are spelled right? Can I sound them out, or should I use the dictionary?

The COPS process is intended to be introduced one step at a time. Students should first learn a particular skill and then learn to edit for that skill. After they have been trained to proofread for each of the components separately, they can be directed to use all four at the same time. The procedure can be used effectively with students in both general and special education and has proven effectiveness for students who are at or above the middle-school level (Shannon & Polloway, 1993).

However, there is far more to the postwriting stage than checking for capitalization, overall appearance, punctuation, and spelling. If students acquire these skills, instruction should then focus on the higher levels of editing, with special attention to content and organization.

Postwriting should focus on the revision of the content in writing as well as the craft. MacArthur, Schwartz, and Graham (1991) recommend an approach to the revision of composition based on the interaction of two peers. Such an approach encourages the sense of a "community of learners" that represents an important component of effective instruction. The peer revising strategy is based on the suggestions that two students give each other on ways to revise their respective writing efforts. Steps include:

- Listen to each other's papers and read along.
- Tell what your partner's paper is about and what you liked best.
- Reread your partner's paper and make notes. Is everything clear? Can any details be added?
- Discuss your suggestions with your partner.

- Revise your own paper and correct errors.
- Exchange papers and check for errors in:

    Sentences
    Capitalization
    Punctuation
    Spelling (p. 141).

A similar approach is recommended by Levy (1996) who describes a peer-critiquing strategy originally developed by Polinko (1985) called the "helpful audience."

"Helpful audience" provides a purpose and an audience for the writing. The teacher first explains the structure of a helpful audience group and, when necessary, models how it works. Groups form as writers are available to discuss their writing . . . Each student uses a teacher-prepared questionnaire

FIGURE 10–11
Helpful audience questions: a peer-critiquing strategy

1.   Ask the writer . . . What is the main idea of your paper?

      [Write what you think the writer has said]

2.   Now include what you think the main idea of the paper is.

3.   Help the writer by indicating what you believe are the strongest parts of the paper.

      Some ideas to consider are:
      (a) Did the writer include all parts of the composition?
      (b) Was the vocabulary used effectively?
      (c) Were sentences varied and interesting?
      (d) Did everything fit correctly with the topic?
      (e) Have you been persuaded by the argument? Why? Why not?
      (f) Was the purpose (thesis) clearly stated?
      (g) Is enough evidence given to support the thesis?

4.   Give at least two concrete suggestions for improving the paper.

From Levy, N. R. (1996). Teaching analytical writing: Help for general education middle school teachers. *Intervention in School and Clinic, 32,* 100.

to guide peer critiquing discussion (Figure 10-11). In groups of three to four, students read their essays to one another in order to listen to and comment about one another's writings. The physical composition of the student peer groups may vary, depending on which students first complete this stage of writing. Occasionally, the teacher rearranges groups so that a balance is maintained among more and less efficient learners (p. 99).

Technological support also can be used on a regular basis to enhance writing and particularly to support the skills associated with postwriting. Word-processing opportunities can have a positive effect on the length and quality of writing efforts and, importantly, on the way that the revision and editing process is viewed

(Morocco & Neuman, 1987; Vallecorsa & deBettencourt, 1992).

Strategy Training

Strategy training provides a vehicle for enabling students to enhance their writing across all stages of the writing process. A variety of options are available for this purpose. The key element is to encourage students to think about, and talk to themselves about, the writing process. Table 10-8 provides a good starting place for students' thinking aloud and then developing their "inner voice." A key aspect of the writing process is *planning*. For students with special needs—and for many other students in inclusive settings as well—planning is an area given insufficient attention.

TABLE 10–8
Strategies for writing subprocesses

Subprocesses	Strategies	Self-Talk
Planning	Identify audience.	Who am I writing for?
	Identify purpose.	Why am I writing?
	Activate background knowledge; brainstorm.	What do I know? what does my reader need to know?
Organizing	Identify categories of related items.	How can I group my ideas?
	Label related ideas.	What can I call each set of ideas?
	Identify new categories and details.	Am I missing any categories or details?
	Order ideas. What comes first?	How can I order my ideas?
Drafting	Translate plan into text.	When I write this up, I can say . . .
	Check text against plan.	Did I include all my categories?
	Add signals to aid comprehensibility and organization.	What signal word will tell my reader what this idea has to do with other ideas?
Editing/revising	Monitor for comprehensibility.	Does everything make sense?
	Check against plan.	Did I include all the ideas in my plan?
	Revise as necessary.	Do I need to insert, delete, or move ideas?
	Monitor from audience's perspective.	
	Is my paper interesting?	Did I answer all my readers' questions?

Note. From Stevens, D. D. & Englert, C. S. (1993). "Making Writing Strategies Work." *Teaching Exceptional Children, 26,* 37. Copyright 1993 by The Council for Exceptional Children. Adapted with permission.

TABLE 10–9
Expository writing planning strategy

Planning strategy: STOP	Instructions for each planning step:
1. *S*uspend judgment	Read the prompt and do TAP (identify *task*, *audience*, & *purpose*). Brainstorm ideas about the purpose. Use webbing, umbrella-type maps, lists, or other ways to jot down ideas.
2. *T*ell your thesis statement	Read your ideas. Write your thesis statement on your planning sheet. Decide whether you will put your thesis statement first or whether you will "start with an attention getter."
3. *O*rganize ideas	Choose ideas that are strong and decide how to organize them for writing. To help you do this, put a star by *major points* and a dot or some other mark by *elaborations* of the main points. Number major points in the order you will use them.
4. *P*lan more as you write	Use the essay sheet, your cue cards, and **DARE:**
	Different kinds of sentences
	Avoid first-person pronouns if you can
	Remember to use good grammar
	Exciting, interesting, $100,000 words

Note. In the second step, "***T*ell your thesis statement**," each writer makes the decision how to introduce the thesis statement, based on his/her reaction to the topic. Cue cards suggest how to introduce the thesis sentence, list transition words for different paragraphs, and repeat DARE. In the last step, "***P*lan more as you write**," students initially use a form, called an essay sheet, to write their five-paragraph essay.

From de la Paz, S. (1997). Strategy instruction in planning: Teaching students with learning and writing disabilities to compose persuasive and expository essays. *Learning Disability Quarterly, 20,* 244.

Table 10-9 depicts a planning strategy. Intended for expository writing, the strategy promotes a series of steps to follow in preparing to write.

Beyond the planning stage, students need to be taught specific strategies for writing that enable them to enhance their basic writing skills as well as to develop advanced compositional skills. A good example was introduced by Harris and Graham (1992) to assist students in writing stories. This approach includes a series of story grammar elements that are summarized in the mnemonic W-W-W, What-2, How-2. The letters of this mnemonic correspond to these elements:

- Who? (is main character)
- When? (does it take place)
- Where? (does it take place)
- What? (does main character want to do)
- What? (happens when she does it)

- How? (does it end)
- How? (does the character feel)

This mnemonic is then embedded within a self-instructional strategy training procedure that includes the following steps:

1. Provide pretraining (prerequisite skills).
2. Review current strategies/motivation.
3. Describe the executive strategy.
   a. Look at the picture.
   b. Let your mind be free.
   c. Write down the story reminder: W-W-W, What-2, How-2.
   d. Write down story ideas for each part.
   e. Write your own story, use good parts, and make sense.
4. Model the strategy.
5. Promote mastery (repeat necessary steps).

6. Provide controlled practice.
7. Encourage independence and generalization.

Another useful strategy is Rooney's 1989 *Wheels for Writing*. This approach includes a focus on the use of circles or wheels to provide a visuo-graphic organizer for planning and writing. With this approach, the student is taught to begin with five wheels: the first for the "start" of the paper, the next three for the three main ideas within the composition, and the fifth a "therefore" or conclusion. These five wheels then become circles around which specific ideas in the forms of details can subsequently be developed (Fig. 10–12).

Graham, Harris, MacArthur, and Schwarz (1991) reviewed the extensive research literature on strategy training that had been used particularly with students with learning disabilities; they conclude that there is strong evidence that such training results in enhanced quality as well as improvements in structure and length of compositions. In some instances, these gains superseded those of students who did not have disabilities but who did not have the benefits of study training.

FIGURE 10–12
Wheels for writing (overview).

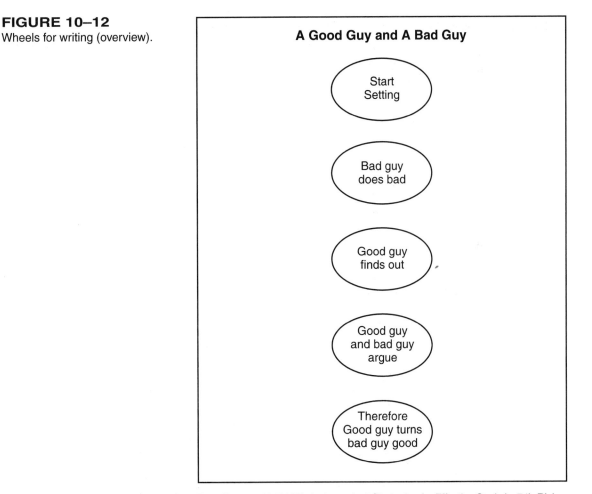

From Rooney, K. (1989). *Independent Strategies for Effective Study* (p. 74). Richmond, VA: Educational Enterprises. Copyright 1989 by Educational Enterprises, Inc. Reprinted with permission.

Notetaking

A special writing challenge for learners with disabilities is notetaking from class lectures. Particularly because the lecture format is used at the middle and high school level (as well as in postsecondary education), students need to develop strategies for making notes for later review and study.

While a variety of strategies are available to enhance notetaking, a full review is beyond the scope of this chapter. In Figure 10–13 one representative strategy is presented. CALL-UP was developed for middle school students in inclusive classes. The full process of teaching and learning to proficiency and generalization took 6 months according to Czarnecki, Rosko, and Fine (1998). The strategy instructional sequence was consistent with the learning strategies instructional model (see Chapter 6). In addition, Czarnecki et al. also present a parallel lecture notes revision strategy ("A" NOTES) intended for secondary school

FIGURE 10–13

A notetaking strategy: CALL UP

Memory Device	Intended Associations (What each step cues the student to do)
Copy from board or transparency	1. Be aware that teachers usually write the main ideas on the board or on a transparency—copy these.
	2. Listen and look for cue words or phrases that will identify main idea and copy them down next to the margin and underline them.
Add details	3. Listen and look for details and add them to your notes. Write them one inch from the margin with a line (-) in front of the detail.
Listen and write the question	4. Listen to the question that the teacher asks and that students ask and write it down if it helps your understanding. Put a "Q" in front of the question to signal that it is a question. Indent this, just like the details, under the main idea.
Listen and write the answer	5. Listen to the answer to the question and write it down. Put an "A" in front of the answer to signal that it is an answer. Indent this just like the details, under the main idea.
	6. Continue adding details and questions and answers to the main idea. If the teacher discusses another main idea, skip six lines before writing the next main idea.
Utilize the text	7. At home; utilize your textbook to help you review and understand the information. Read about the main idea in your textbook.
Put it in your own words	8. Put the information in your own words and write these statements in your notes. Write your statements under the main idea on the six lines that you skipped in #6. Write the page number where you found the information in the book in the margin so you can go back later if needed.

Linking Device to the Strategy

1. Use the CALL UP Notetaking Strategy to help you CALL UP your memory.

2. This strategy also helps you to CALL UP your attention by helping you to be more focused on what is being said in class.

From Czarnecki, E., Rosko, D., & Fine, E. (1998). How to call up notetaking skills. *Teaching Exceptional Children, 30,* 14.

students. Further information on related aspects of notetaking will also be presented in Chapter 13, which focuses on study skills and strategies.

SUMMARY

This chapter addresses assessment and instructional concerns across the three areas of written language. The discussion of handwriting focuses on the relative value of skill development in this area and the importance of initial instruction and maintenance and proficiency. In spelling, particular attention is given to common problems and teacher- and student-directed strategies. For written expression, emphases are placed on the three stages of writing, on mechanical skills and content development considerations, on the value of strategy learning, and on notetaking.

ACTIVITIES

Differentiation is not made below between younger and older students but specific activities that are particularly relevant for older students are so noted. Teachers should select activities based on the interest and level of functioning of their students.

Manuscript Writing

1. Make name tags for all students, and have them copy their names.
2. Write students' names at the top of a sheet of primary writing paper, and have them copy their names.
3. Make dot letters and have pupils form the letters by connecting the dots.
4. After a series or group of letters has been learned, have the children write the letters on primary writing paper.
5. Make letters on the chalkboard, and let pupils add or take away some part of the letter to make another letter.
6. Dictate letters for students to write that they have previously learned, and check for formation, shape, and size.
7. Using flash cards with lowercase letters on them, ask students to write the uppercase form of each letter shown.

8. Have students look at maps and find geographical locations that begin with given letters.
9. Give groups of students large sheets of chart paper, and have them use fine-point markers to make lists of given topics (e.g., animals, foods, popular music groups).
10. As pupils learn more letters of the alphabet, have them combine the letters to form words. The words chosen can be copied from a chart of words already in the students' vocabulary.
11. Have the class dictate several sentences about some event that has previously occurred, and then have students copy the sentences that you have written on the board or chart paper.
12. Play a game of "Something Is Wrong" by putting lowercase letters at the beginning of sentences and incorrect punctuation at the end of sentences. Have pupils find the errors and correct them.

Cursive Writing

1. Make dot cursive letters and have students form the letters by connecting the dots.
2. Play "Concentration" using cards with manuscript or cursive letters copied on them. Ask students to match the cursive and manuscript forms of a letter.
3. Using an overhead projector, let students take turns writing on transparencies or tracing letters projected on the chalkboard.
4. Make lists of words to be written alphabetically in cursive.
5. Dictate for students to copy all letters that they have previously learned, and check for formation.
6. Let students collect samples of cursive writing to share and compare. Signatures from staff members, parents, or other community members can be interesting.
7. A classroom mailbox encourages students to write notes to their friends during specified times of the day or at home. Notes must be legible in order to be read and answered. The students especially want to use their best handwriting when they are writing to someone spe-

cial outside the classroom (e.g., principal, last year's teacher, nurse).

8. As students get older, a handwriting goal is to increase speed without loss of legibility. The students write an assignment for a certain amount of time. When time is up, each letter is evaluated against preset criteria. One point is given for each correctly formed letter. The writing assignment can be content material, classmates' names, ABCs, or sentences that contain all the letters of the alphabet (Alston & Taylor, 1987).

Spelling

1. Have each child spell different words by changing the initial or the final sounds.

2. Have younger children trace words in different media.

3. Have pupils keep words that they can spell in a box so that these words can be reviewed periodically. They can also be used for spelling games, alphabetizing, homework assignments, or creative writing.

4. Students can keep their own dictionaries of words that they are learning to spell. A notebook with a page for each letter of the alphabet can be used for recording weekly words, words written incorrectly on assignments, or words that required teacher assistance. The notebooks can then be used for reference and studying.

5. The Dolch and other word lists can be grouped into different sets of words (e.g., nouns, adjectives). Have pupils pick out words that they do not know how to spell.

6. Pupils can be taught to use the dictionary to help check their spelling. Picture dictionaries are extremely helpful in developing dictionary as well as spelling skills.

7. Show the children that there is some linguistic regularity to English by giving them a word or stem and having them form and spell other words (e.g., -ad: had, dad, mad; -amp: damp, lamp, stamp; -oe: hoe, foe, toe).

8. Give children groups of letters (nonmeaningfully arranged) and have them spell as many words as they can, using only those letters (e.g., lliks: skill, kills, ill, sill).

9. Write words on the board or on a sheet of paper with a letter missing, and have pupils fill in the missing letters.

10. After spelling words have been introduced to the class, prepare charts with the individual words written in a variety of different styles. This activity will help students with inconsistent form and those who lack the ability to retain letter sequence when the written style changes (Wulpe, 1968).

11. Divide the class into two teams and list spelling words on the chalkboard in short columns. While students from each team stand with their backs to the board, pronounce a word. The students then turn and find the word on the board; the first person to find the word gets a point for the team.

12. Older students may enjoy opportunities to make, as well as solve, spelling puzzles. Students can make word searches by placing spelling words in different spaces on graph paper (diagonally, horizontally, vertically) and then filling in the other blocks with random letters. The puzzles can then be exchanged and solved by classmates.

13. Play Bingo. Give each student a playing card. Instruct students to write a word from a current spelling list on each square of their cards. Collect and redistribute the cards. The game proceeds until the first student to cover the appropriate squares says "Bingo!"

14. Students may enjoy academic activities that have a sports flavor, such as Spelling Baseball. The class is divided into two teams. Batters must correctly pronounce and spell a given word. If they do, they move to first base; the next batter does the same, and movement around the bases parallels regular baseball.

15. Pass out loose alphabet letters. Have students select the letters of their entire name and spell it out. Then they scramble the letters and spell as many words as possible, using only the letters of their name. Each word should be listed on a sheet of paper. Introduce anagrams with other words (Coleman, 1978).

16. Provide proofreading activities useful in enhancing spelling skills: providing a short list of words that includes misspelled words to be located, providing a passage with errors ranging from easy ones to spelling demons, listing the total number of words purposely misspelled in a written composition, and alternatives (Graham & Miller, 1979).

17. Greene (1994) encourages the use of visual mnemonics that can be built into the students' spelling lists and/or presented on flash cards, with the mnemonic on one side and the standard spelling on the other. Visualization exercises are then recommended to enable students to retain the image (Figure 10–14).

Written Expression

1. At the beginning of the day, set aside a silent writing time for students to write in their journals. The aim of this activity is to foster enjoyment in writing; therefore, entries should not be evaluated.

2. Develop visual imagery as a prerequisite to writing. Students can imagine making an angel in the snow, flying a kite in March winds, eating ice cream on a hot summer day, or burying a friend in a pile of leaves. Initially, have students relax and think at their desks. Later, have students list adjectives associated with their images. Finally, direct students to write sentences or paragraphs.

3. Wiener (1981) suggests an activity called "boasts" that is particularly appropriate for adolescents. Assign students the task of writing four or five sentences about what makes them exceptional. It can be what they know, what they have done, or how they look.

4. Direct adolescents to write responsible letters to local elected officials. Help students express their opinions on various political or social issues. These letters can be the foundation for a discussion on civic responsibility.

5. Have younger students keep a class diary. As a group, the class can discuss one topic as the teacher records comments on the board. Students then copy the writing in their notebooks, and after fifteen or so topics, the diaries can be sent home (Kline, 1987).

6. Have students develop family folklore scrapbooks. Students can write down and illustrate stories told to them by older relatives. Possible themes include good stories from hard times, practical jokes, and stories of when others were young (Brooke, 1986).

7. Have students write poems. Start by reading poetry aloud. Introduce unrhymed poetry before rhymed poetry. Print a booklet (complete with illustrations) of the students' poems for their parents and others in the school to read.

8. Progressive writing exercises are interesting activities. The object is to pick up where a classmate has left off and write for 2 or 3 minutes. The final writer should write a conclusion. One student can read the finished prod-

FIGURE 10–14
Visual mnemonic aids for spelling

From "Research into Practice: The Magic of Mnemonics" by Greene, G., 1994, *LD Forum, 19* (3), p. 35.

uct. Later, improvements and corrections can be made.

9. Pretending to be an inanimate object, such as a rock on the road, students can write sentences containing gripes from the object's point of view (Wiener, 1981).

10. A class newspaper can help students improve their written expression. Assignments can be made according to ability and interest. Class, school, community, national, or international topics can be reported.

11. Use pictures to teach students topic sentence development. Start by describing the photograph, and then write sentences and paragraphs.

12. Guide students in writing a letter to the editor of a local paper. Their perspective on an issue might be greatly appreciated. Instruct them to keep the letter concise and to the point (Wiener, 1981).

13. A motivating activity is "Contest Week." Many contests merely require students to place their name and address on a postcard and mail it to a company or radio station. Others require them to express ideas or opinions. Students can search through newspapers and magazines and be alert to contests advertised on the radio or television.

14. Make a worksheet with sentences—all in lowercase letters and no punctuation. Have students capitalize and punctuate as necessary.

15. Cut pictures out of the newspaper and remove the captions. Students must write a title and caption based on what they think is happening in the picture. Students read their ideas to the class and then write a short article about what they believe is going on.

16. Have students obtain a copy of, or transcribe the lyrics of, a favorite rock or rap song. Then have them rewrite the words in standard English.

17. Many students have trouble writing sentences that include details. Often their sentences are merely statements of fact, or telling sentences. One way to add detail is by changing telling sentences into showing sentences. Write a telling sentence on the board (e.g., "The dog is mean.") Have students write as many showing sentences as they can that will convey the idea in the telling sentence. Then have the students share their sentences.

18. To help students expand their sentences while at the same time reinforcing the concepts of subject and predicate, have them write a simple sentence on the board, dividing it into subject and predicate (e.g., "The dog barks."). Working in pairs, have students add details to both parts. Then have students share their expanded sentences. Discuss the differences between the simpler sentences and the expanded versions.

19. Have students work in groups and provide each student with a topic with which he and the rest of the class are familiar (e.g., brushing teeth). Each student writes one sentence to begin a paragraph about that topic. Students then pass their papers to the right. That person reads the sentence and writes one more sentence to continue that thought. This process continues until each paragraph has reached a conclusion. Have students share the paragraphs.

TEACHER TIPS

As teachers consider how to teach writing skills to children with disabilities, they must be aware of the metacognition constructs related to writing. These include:

- Awareness of the writing—This construct refers to a student's awareness of clarity, organization, and evocation of interest in readers. These cognitions are higher order processes that imply the student understands that writing involves planning, sentence generation, and revision.
- Awareness of the process of revision—This construct refers to the identification or detection of unsatisfactory parts of a student's writing. This process implies that the student can establish criteria to assess the quality of the writing and make appropriate changes.
- Self regulation in writing—This construct refers to a student's awareness of the writing process and the cognitive process of writing. Students must understand the writing process and be able to evaluate their strengths and weaknesses related to the process. Once the weaknesses are identified, students can work to develop strategies to correct the problems.

Teachers should note that most students with learning disabilities perseverate on their secretarial problems of neatness and spelling. In order to advance in their writing skills, these students need to learn the metacognitive process of writing.

Wong, B. Y. L. (1999). Metacognition in writing. In R. Gillmore, L. P. Bernheimer, D. L. MacMillan, D. L. Speece, & S. Vaughn (Eds.). *Developmental perspectives on children with high-incidence disabilities*. N J: Lawrence Erlbaum Associates.

TEACHER TIPS

LOOKING FOR WRITING OPPORTUNITIES?

Improving and maintaining skills in almost any area requires practice, practice, practice. Writing skills are especially difficult for many students to master, so it is important to provide students with frequent opportunities to practice their skills. Since many students find writing difficult or boring, provide them a wide variety of writing opportunities. Instead of assigning another paper you could ask your students to write:

- job or college applications
- letters requesting freebies
- written math problems
- thank you letters
- want ads
- imaginary obituaries
- advice columns
- recipes
- descriptions of items for magazine advertisements
- critiques of TV shows or movies
- book reviews
- travel brochures
- jokes or riddles
- business letters

TEACHER TIPS

As educators move beyond the use of computers for drill and practice, they will find that students with special needs will benefit greatly from the enhancement of their written language. Today, writing tools such as word processing, spelling checkers, speech synthesis and word prediction programs, writing prompts, and media composing tools are available to enhance the written language of students. Additionally, tools for organizing content information are available. These tools include outlining and concept mapping programs that work to organize student's thoughts prior to and during the writing process. The mapping program can act as a tool to facilitate the acquisition of content-area information, too.

In many schools students from ages six to 18 are required to access material outside the classroom in order to complete writing projects. When these demands are made, students with special needs can access authoring tools. Working together in groups to obtain electronic reference materials can be done through the internet, databases, and CD-ROM materials. For example, students with disabilities can work with nondisabled peers to produce multimedia projects in social studies (Okolo, 2000).

As much as technology has become a part of our lives, the reality of many schools is that teachers are limited to the number of computers they have and the information that can be accessed by these computers. In such cases, Okolo (2000) stresses that educators must prioritize the goals and purposes for which the technology will be used. She indicates that "if instructional technology is to have optimal impact, it must be used by teachers in a systematic manner as part of their ongoing instructional program." In essence, instructional technology must be integrated into the curriculum if academic gains are to be made.

Okolo, C.M. (2000) Technology for individuals with mild disabilities. In J. D. Lindsey (Ed.), *Technology and exceptional individuals.* Austin, TX: ProEd.

Mathematics

Mathematics is an important part of everyday life. Although not always obvious, math pervades much of what we do at home, on the job, and in the community. Many common activities involve mathematical concepts and skills, with money handling being perhaps the most important.

Interestingly, much of the math we use on a daily basis involves problem solving and the estimation of solutions rather than precise calculations. For instance, in determining how long it will take to drive somewhere, we consider when we need to be at our destination, the route we will take, and the potential for traffic, among other factors. Ultimately, we estimate how long it will take us and then plan our departure accordingly.

Many professionals are suggesting that we rethink the math programs we offer to students with disabilities in light of their needs as adults. Curricular decisions and the instructional strategies to accomplish them must be guided by sensitivity to the current and future needs of students (Polloway, Patton, Epstein, & Smith, 1989). The type of math students need in order to be successful in their subsequent environments (e.g., college, employment) should determine the emphasis of their math programs. However, the life-related math skills that are necessary for dealing effectively with the demands of adulthood and community living must be taught to all students.

We must be concerned about the skill levels in mathematics of students with mild disabilities as they exit formal schooling. Cawley, Baker-Kroczynski, and Urban (1992), in summarizing research efforts, report that these students may attain math proficiency at the fifth- to sixth-grade level and that they do not perform well on required minimum competency tests. Couple this information with the dropout and outcome data and there is much cause for alarm.

This chapter should assist teachers in their attempts to develop instructional approaches that are sensitive to the current and future needs of students. We share the perspective of Cawley and colleagues for accomplishing this task: "To pro-vide these students with the best and most appropriate education in mathematics, teachers must break out of the traditional mold from which they themselves were educated in math, and be willing to be innovative and creative" (1989, p. 69). In addition, teachers must incorporate the principles of effective instructional practice into their math programs.

GOALS OF MATHEMATICS INSTRUCTION

Most educators consider development of mathematic competence a high priority. Evidence of this in the area of mild disabilities can be seen in the amount of literature in this area (Cawley et al., 1992). Currently, mathematics education is too often focused on the mastery of computational skills and memorization of basic facts, with little emphasis being placed on their application. From a life skills perspective, the development of thinking and problem-solving abilities is far more important to students than the rote learning typically associated with computation.

National Initiatives

Over the years a number of efforts have been initiated to establish new directions in math education. In 1977 the National Council of Supervisors of Mathematics (NCSM) identified 40 basic skill areas that need to be included in the math curriculum: (a) problem solving; (b) applying mathematics to everyday situations; (c) alertness to the reasonableness of results; (d) estimation and approximation; (e) appropriate computational skills; (f) geometry; (g) measurement; (h) reading, interpreting, and constructing tables, charts, and graphs; (i) using mathematics to predict; and (j) computer literacy (p. 20). Although these areas are postulated for regular mathematics education, they are appropriate for special populations too. In fact, the first two items, which embody many of the other skills, are critically important.

The National Council of Teachers of Mathematics (1980) (NCTM) next presented a list of eight recommendations related to the future direction of mathematics education. Five of the eight recommendations have direct relevance to students with special needs.

1. Problem solving must be the focus of school mathematics
2. The concept of basic skills in mathematics must encompass more than computational facility
3. Mathematics programs must take full advantage of the power of calculators and computers at all grade levels.
4. The success of mathematics programs and student learning must be evaluated by a wider range of measures than conventional testing.
5. More mathematics study must be required of all students, and a flexible curriculum with a greater range of options should be designed to accommodate the diverse needs of the student population. (p. 1)

These recommendations are important because they helped spell out the needed changes in mathematics education and shaped reform efforts.

The NCTM updated its position on mathematics education in 1989 by publishing the Curriculum and Evaluation Standards for School Mathematics. The new standards were developed to judge mathematics curricula and to provide a basis for reform. The major goals promoted in this document encourage students to do the following:

■ learn to value mathematics
■ learn to reason mathematically
■ learn to communicate mathematically
■ become confident of their mathematical abilities
■ become mathematical problem solvers

Although the document does not offer a set scope and sequence, it does provide 40 curriculum standards across three grade ranges and 14 evaluation standards in three areas (Table 11–1). Also included in these standards is a strong push for the use of calculators and computers within math programs.

With regard to these curriculum standards, Cawley et al. (1992) remark that "both the standards and the extent to which they are ultimately implemented in the schools have deep implications for professionals involved with the education of children with disabilities. . . . No comparable statement of goals and outcomes for mathematics exists within the special education community" (p. 40). They further raise the question of whether professionals in special education can arrive at some consensus about the goals of mathematics education for students with special needs.

If the ultimate goal in mathematics instruction of learners with special needs is to help them prepare for using math at a later point in their lives, programs must include content that is based on the type of mathematics that will be needed. For instance, the math programs appropriate for students going on to higher education must be different from programs designed for students who will be entering the work force immediately after leaving school.

A fundamental goal of all programs should be to teach consistent methods for solving number-related problems encountered in everyday situations. If this is so, then teachers must be aware of the major life demands of adulthood that require math proficiency. Furthermore, students must receive systematic, direct instruction so that they will acquire a range of mathematical skills extending beyond computational competence. Concepts of money management, time, estimation, and geometry are likely to play greater roles in a person's life than computational skills (Sedlak & Fitzmaurice, 1981). Implicit within the goals of mathematics education for students with learning problems is the idea that these students must receive opportunities, encouragement, and instruction on using fundamental math skills to solve everyday problems.

While professionals in special education must decide on the goals for mathematics education

TABLE 11–1
Curriculum standards and evaluation standards (NCTM, 1989)

Curriculum Standards	Evaluation Standards
Grades K to 4	
1. Mathematics as problem solving	**Grades K to 12**
2. Mathematics as communication	General Assessment
3. Mathematics as reasoning	1. Alignment
4. Mathematical connections	2. Multiple sources of information
5. Estimation	3. Appropriate assessment methods and use
6. Number sense and numeration	Student Assessment
7. Concepts of whole number operations	4. Mathematical power
8. Whole number computation	5. Problem solving
9. Geometry and spatial sense	6. Communication
10. Measurement	7. Reasoning
11. Statistics and probability	8. Mathematical concepts
12. Fractions and decimals	9. Mathematical procedures
13. Patterns and relationships	10. Mathematical disposition
Grades 5 to 8	Program Evaluation
1. Mathematics and problem solving	11. Indicators for program evaluation
2. Mathematics as communication	12. Curriculum and instructional resources
3. Mathematics as reasoning	13. Instruction
4. Mathematical connections	14. Evaluation team
5. Number and number relationships	
6. Number systems and number theory	
7. Computation and estimation	
8. Patterns and functions	
9. Algebra	
10. Statistics	
11. Probability	
12. Geometry	
13. Measurement	
Grades 9 to 12	
1. Mathematics as problem solving	
2. Mathematics as communication	
3. Mathematics as reasoning	
4. Mathematical connections	
5. Algebra	
6. Functions	
7. Geometry from a synthetic perspective	
8. Geometry from an algebraic perspective	
9. Trigonometry	
10. Statistics	
11. Probability	
12. Discrete mathematics	
13. Conceptual underpinnings of calculus	
14. Mathematical structure	

and how its teaching is to take place for students with special needs, general educators of mathematics have taken detailed steps toward deciding how to teach mathematics to students in general education. The NCTM (1991) professional standards are based on the assumptions that teachers are the primary people involved in changing the methods used for teaching and learning mathematics and that they require long-term support as well as adequate resources in order for this change to take place. The standards are meant to provide guidance "about the kinds of teaching environments, actions, and activities, that are needed to realize the goals for students" to become mathematically powerful (NCTM, 1991, p. 189). This standard, along with the Curriculum and Evaluation Standards for School Mathematics, is meant as a "long-term commitment to provide direction for the reform of school mathematics" (p. 2).

To further emphasize this shift away from teaching mathematics through rote learning and the accumulation of facts, the NCTM (1991) stressed the following:

> Effective teachers are those who can stimulate students to learn mathematics. Educational research offers compelling evidence that students learn mathematics well only when they construct their own mathematical understanding. To understand what they learn, they must enact for themselves verbs that permeate the mathematics curriculum: "examine," "represent," "transform," "solve," "apply," "prove," "communicate." This happens most readily when students work in groups, engage in discussion, make presentations, and in other ways take charge of their own learning. (pp. 58–59)

The 18 standards put forth in this latest document are contained under four headings. These headings include (a) standards for teaching mathematics, (b) standards for the evaluation of the teaching of mathematics, (c) standards for the professional development of teachers in mathematics, and (d) standards for the support and development of mathematics teachers and teaching. Table 11-2 outlines in detail the professional standards for teaching math.

Assessment

Let us assume that Ashley responds to the following algorithm as indicated: $13 - 7 = \partial$. Is the response right or wrong? The teacher's decision may depend on any number of factors, such as knowledge of the student and/or the objectives that have been established for this activity. For instance, if Ashley frequently writes the numeral 6 this way, the teacher may accept her response as correct arithmetically. The important point is that teachers sometimes need to dig a little deeper to understand fully how a student is performing, and they need to remember what information they are evaluating.

Educational assessment is the systematic process whereby information about students is collected and used to make decisions about them. One of the more educationally relevant questions that should be asked and answered is, What are the student's strengths and weaknesses? In other words, a major instructional reason for assessing students is to obtain diagnostic information. Other motivations for assessing students may stem from a need to determine eligibility for services, to choose the most suitable placement option, or to evaluate student progress or program effectiveness. All these reasons for assessing students occur daily in educational settings and are inexorably entwined with providing appropriate education. Nevertheless, the problems inherent in this process demand caution.

Typically, assessment is equated with testing. Although testing is one way to answer some educationally relevant questions, it is not the only way. Information about students can and should be obtained through other techniques as well: direct observation of students' behaviors; interviews, checklists and rating scales; and examination of students' work. Assessment in mathematics should utilize all of these techniques but should not be limited solely to a demonstration of arithmetic skills. Affective dimensions (e.g., how students feel about math) as well as communication and process evaluation (e.g., how students are able to communicate their math

TABLE 11-2

Professional Standards for Teaching Mathematics: standards for teaching mathematics

Standards for Teaching Mathematics

Standard 1: The teacher of mathematics should pose tasks that:

- are based on sound and significant mathematics
- are based on knowledge of students' understandings, interests, and experience
- are based on knowledge of the range of ways that diverse students learn mathematics
- engage students' intellect
- develop students' mathematical understandings and skills
- stimulate students to make connections and develop a coherent framework for mathematical ideas
- call for problem formulation, problem solving, and mathematical reasoning
- promote communication about mathematics
- represent mathematics as an ongoing human activity
- display sensitivity to, and draw on, students' diverse backgrounds and experiences and dispositions
- promote the development of *all* students' dispositions to do mathematics

Standard 2: The teacher of mathematics should orchestrate discourse by:

- posing questions and tasks that challenge students' thinking
- listening carefully to students' ideas
- asking students to clarify and justify their ideas orally and in writing
- deciding what to pursue in depth from among the ideas that students bring up during a discussion
- deciding when and how to attach mathematical notation and language to students' ideas
- deciding when to provide information, when to clarify an issue and when to model, when to lead, and when to let a student struggle with a difficulty
- monitoring students' participation in discussion and deciding when and how to encourage each student to participate

Standard 3: The teacher of mathematics should promote classroom discourse in which students:

- listen to, respond to, and question the teacher and one another
- use a variety of tools to reason, make connections, solve problems, and communicate
- initiate problems and questions
- make conjectures and present solutions
- explore examples and counterexamples to investigate conjectures
- try to convince themselves and one another of the validity of particular representations, solutions, conjectures, and answers
- rely on mathematical evidence and argument to determine validity

Standard 4: The teacher of mathematics, in order to enhance discourse, should encourage and accept the use of:

- computers, calculators, and other technology
- concrete materials used as models
- pictures, diagrams, tables, and graphs

Standards for Teaching Mathematics

- invented and conventional terms and symbols
- metaphors, analogies, and stories
- written hypotheses, explanations, and arguments
- oral presentations and dramatizations

Standard 5: The teacher of mathematics should create a learning environment that fosters the development of each student's mathematical power by:

- providing and structuring the time necessary to explore sound mathematics and grapple with significant ideas and problems
- using the physical space and materials in ways that facilitate students' learning of mathematics
- providing a context that encourages the development of mathematical skill and proficiency
- representing and valuing students' ideas, ways of thinking, and mathematical dispositions

and by consistently expecting and encouraging students to:
- work independently or collaboratively to make sense of mathematics
- take intellectual risks by raising questions and formulating conjectures
- display a sense of mathematical competence by validating and supporting ideas with mathematical argument

Standard 6: The teacher of mathematics should engage in ongoing analysis of teaching and learning by:

- observing, listening to, and gathering other information about students to assess what they are learning
- examining effects of the tasks, discourse, and learning environment on students' mathematical knowledge, skills, and disposition

in order to:
- ensure that every student is learning sound and significant mathematics and is developing a positive disposition toward mathematics
- challenge and extend students' ideas
- adapt or change activities while teaching
- make plans, both short- and long-range
- describe and comment on each student's learning to parents and administrators, as well as to the students themselves

Note. Adapted from National Council Teachers of Mathematics (1991). *Professional Standards for Teaching Mathematics.* Reston, VA. The National Council of Teachers of Mathematics Inc.

knowledge as well as their critical thinking skills) are worth investigating too.

Standardized Measures of General Achievement

General achievement instruments are formal devices that usually assess a range of skill domains (e.g., reading, mathematics, written language) and result in a variety of derived scores (e.g., percentiles, standard scores, grade equivalents). These norm-referenced tests are designed to show how a student's score compares with the scores of other students on whom the test was standardized. From an instructional perspective, such tests do provide some general indication of the skill/subject areas in which students are strong or are having difficulty. However, these instruments are not intended to be diagnostic and therefore offer little information and guidance about student needs or where to start teaching.

There are two major types of achievement tests: individual and group. Individual tests have enjoyed a great deal of popularity in special education. Some of those more commonly used include tests such as the Wide Range Achievement Test-Revised (Jastak & Wilkinson, 1984) and the Diagnostic Achievement Battery-2 (Newcomer, 1990). Most individual achievement tests are developed for school-age populations. If one requires standardized data related to math performance for adult populations, then one is referred to tests that extend coverage to this age range [e.g., Wide Range Achievement Test-Revised (WRAT-R)] or to tests that are developed specifically for adult groups (e.g., Scholastic Abilities Test for Adults).

Group achievement tests, such as the Stanford Achievement Test (SAT) (Gardner, Rudman, Karlsen, & Merwin, 1982) and the Metropolitan Achievement Tests (MAT6) (Prescott, Balow, Hogan, & Farr, 1984), are also used frequently in schools. Like individual achievement tests, group tests assess multiple skills—one domain of which is math. For instance, the SAT has three subtests in this area: concepts of number, mathematics computation, and mathematics applications. These instruments have the advantage of administration to large numbers of students at one time. Both types of achievement tests are limited from an instructional perspective, as they give only one or two different samples of any major skill area. As a result, they may not tap certain skills at all and do not provide enough examples to establish error patterns.

Standardized Diagnostic Measures of Arithmetic Functioning

Instruments that assess specific academic areas in more detail than the general achievement measures help teachers determine particular problems and strengths of students. For the most part, instruments in this category are attractive be-

cause of their potential diagnostic usefulness; they usually contain a number of mathematically related subtests; some of the more frequently used instruments are featured in Table 11–3.

Some of these tests may not be as diagnostic as teachers would like them to be. There are a limited number of behavioral samples for specific subskills within each subtest and, if derived scores are the only items used, diagnostic usefulness decreases. Thus, to obtain the information necessary to plan instructional interventions, teachers must augment these tests with informal, teacher-constructed measures. For example, if a student has difficulty with two items on an addition subtest (66 + 4 and 86 + 29), then it is advisable to explore this skill with additional problems (16 + 8, 19 + 15, 37 + 20, 66 + 44, 145 + 159, 390 + 148, 524 + 386). Such an analysis provides a more detailed assessment of the pupil's ability to do two- and three-digit addition problems that require regrouping and handling a zero.

Other Formal Diagnostic Techniques

There are several formal, nonstandardized instruments available for obtaining diagnostic information. Two of these types of instruments are described briefly here.

Diagnostic Test of Arithmetic Strategies (DTAS). The DTAS (Ginsburg & Mathews, 1984) is an individually administered diagnostic instrument designed to analyze the strategies that students use to perform arithmetic calculations in addition, subtraction, multiplication, and division. It is useful to teachers who work with students who are having difficulty in these computational areas. Each subtest is divided into four parts:

- setting up the problem: setup only, no calculations are performed.
- number facts: students respond to basic problems presented to them visually.
- written calculation: students work problems while verbalizing what they are doing.
- informal skills: students work problems using pencil and paper while verbalizing what they are doing.

TABLE 11–3
Formal, standardized diagnostic tests

Test	Grade Appropriateness	Subtests	Results	Remarks
KeyMath-Revised: A Diagnostic Inventory of Essential Mathematics (KeyMath-R) (Connolly, 1988)	Grades K–8	3 areas/13 subtests/ 43 domains: Basic concepts Numeration Rational numbers Geometry Operations Addition Subtraction Multiplication Division Mental computation Applications Measurement Time and Money Estimation Interpreting data Problem solving	Derived scores for total test and area composites: Standard scores (mean = 100, std. deviation = 15) Grade equivalents Age equivalents Percentile ranks Stanine Normal curve equivalents Derived scores for Individual subtests: Standard scores (mean = 10, std. deviation = 3 Percentile ranks Domain perfor- mance scores	Individually administered Two Forms - A and B Two easels Each subtest composed of 3–4 domains Written re- sponses required on subtests in operations Software avail- able for con- verting scores and developing profiles
Stanford Diagnostic Mathematics Test (SDMT) (Beatty, Gardner, Madden, & Karlsen, 1985)	Grades 2–12	3 subtests: Number system and numeration Computation Applications	Center-referenced scores Norm-referenced scores Percentile Stanines Norm curve equivalents Scaled scores	Group administered Four overlap- ping levels: Red: Grades 2–4 Green: Grades 4–6 Brown: Grades 6–8 Blue: Grades 8–12
Test of Mathematical Abilities (TOMA - 2) (Brown, Cronin, & McEntire, 1994)	Grades 3–12	Five subtests: Vocabulary Computation General Information Story Problems Attitude Toward Math	Derived scores for total test and composites: Standard scores (mean = 100, std. deviation = 15) Percentiles Age equivalents Grade equivalents	All subtests ex- cept general information can be group administered

The stimulus items for the "Written Calculations" part of the DTAS are presented in Figure 11-1. Each problem the student is asked to perform and verbalize is analyzed with the help of the checklist shown in Figure 11-2. If used appropriately, this form can assist teachers in pinpointing where a student is having basic fact or procedural problems.

Brigance Diagnostic Inventories.
These inventories (Brigance, 1980, 1983) are also useful for obtaining diagnostic data. The Diagnostic Inventory of Basic Skills (Grades K to 6) in-cludes subtests on computation, measurement, and geometry. The Diagnostic Inventory of Essential Skills (Grades 7 to 12) includes subsets on computation, fractions, decimals, percents, and measurement.

Curriculum-Based Measures

The most instructionally useful methods of assessing mathematical performance and diagnosing math difficulties are measures based on the curriculum being used. This approach allows an in-depth probe of specific skills based on the types

FIGURE 11–1
Written calculations part of DTAS

From *Diagnostic Test of Arithmetic Strategies* by H. P. Ginsburg and S. C. Mathews, 1984, Austin, TX: PRO-ED. Copyright 1984 by PRO-ED. Reprinted with permission.

FIGURE 11–2
Checklist for written calculations

	Problems 5	6	7	8	9	10	11	12	13	14	15	16
1. Answer												
Correct (circle)	96	48	903	736	558	322	17,520	18,390	4,958	2,660	111,537	133,056
Incorrect (write in)	—	—	—	—	—	—	—	—	—	—	—	—
2. Standard school method	—	—	—	—	—	—	—	—	—	—	—	—
3. Informal method	—	—	—	—	—	—	—	—	—	—	—	—
4. Number fact error	—	—	—	—	—	—	—	—	—	—	—	—
5. Bugs												
A. Units by units, tens by tens	—	—	—	—	—	—	—	—	—	—	—	—
B. Partial product problems		—	—						—	—	—	—
C. Addition errors					—	—	—		—	—	—	—
D. Crutch difficulties					—	—	—		—	—	—	—
E. Zero makes no difference							—	—				
F. No need to write zero							—	—				
G. Left to right	—	—	—	—	—	—	—	—			—	—
H. Other	—	—	—	—	—	—	—	—			—	—
6. Slips												
A. Skips numbers	—	—	—	—	—	—	—	—			—	—
B. Multiplies or adds twice; uses wrong number	—	—	—	—	—	—	—	—			—	—
C. Other	—	—	—	—	—	—	—	—	—	—	—	—

Notes: _____

of problems encountered in everyday instructional situations and instructional goals set for students.

A procedure that can be followed in collecting curriculum-based data is to ask students to complete a sheet containing multiple samples of math skills that are being taught (Fig. 11-3). Students are given 2 minutes to solve as many of these items as they can. This sheet and alternative forms of it are administered on a regular basis. The results of each data collection can be graphed; decisions can be made as to whether students are progressing toward the intended goal.

Advantages of curriculum-based approaches are many. For example, (a) items or problems assess a specific skill; (b) tests include enough problems to ensure knowledge or lack of knowledge regarding a specific skill; (c) if the teacher

FIGURE 11–3
Sample curriculum-based
assessment sheet

12 + 23	33 + 26	43 + 44	26 + 51	55 + 23
56 + 11	42 + 20	52 + 32	66 + 33	71 + 24
55 + 44	68 + 21	16 + 52	79 + 10	30 + 56
37 + 12	17 + 72	76 + 22	62 + 36	45 + 41
83 + 13	35 + 34	78 + 11	24 + 33	63 + 33
48 + 31	29 + 30	57 + 32	21 + 41	23 + 35

has any doubts about the test results, similar problems can be constructed and given to the pupil, and those results can be checked against previous results; and (d) student-specific data can guide instructionally meaningful decisions.

Informal Diagnostic Techniques

One way to obtain diagnostically useful information is to expand on and/or subdivide concepts and skills found in formal instruments. For instance, a student might miss items on the WRAT-R designed to assess the concepts of "more" and "less" because of an inability to identify or recognize the numerals (or their value) or because of a lack of understanding of the concepts of more and less. (The specific WRAT-R assessment items are "Which is more: 9 or 6?" and "Which is more: 42 or 28?"). In this case, to determine numerical identification and recognition, the teacher might present index cards to the student with one numeral on each card and have the student respond by naming each numeral. If the student hesitates or misses a particular numeral, the card should be presented again later to assess consistency. Another approach would be to present a group of numerals on a sheet of paper, pronounce a number, and ask the student to respond by pointing to that numeral. To determine whether numerical values are understood, the teacher might present an index card with a numeral on it and instruct the student to give the teacher the corresponding number of checkers. The task can be varied by instructing the student to select two checkers, five checkers, nine checkers, and so on.

By subdividing and expanding the concepts and skills assessed by informal tests, teachers can begin to pinpoint the difficulties students have in acquiring specific arithmetic understanding, comprehension, and skills. Some effort is required here, as most standardized instruments do not provide guidance or assistance in analyzing individual responses. The following diagnostic techniques may be used to analyze individual student responses.

Error Patterns. Carefully examining the work samples of students often provides clues to patterns in the types of errors they are making. Look at the series of subtraction problems presented here. Upon close examination, a teacher can determine the error pattern a student is demonstrating, then reteach to correct the problem.

It is possible to classify computational errors into different categories. One possible system is outlined here.

- random responding (RR): Student errors are without any recognizable reason.
- basic fact error (BF): Student performs the operation correctly, but makes a simple error (addition, etc.)
- wrong operation (WO): Student performs the wrong operation (e.g., adds instead of subtracting).
- defective algorithm (DA): Student does not perform the operation appropriately; the steps involved are out of sequence or are performed improperly.
- place value problems (PV): To some extent this category is a subset of the previous category. Student knows the facts and the beginning stages of an operation but is deficient in some aspect of place value.

Whether teachers use this or another system, recognizing students' systematic errors is a diagnostic skill that has great bearing on determining the focus of instruction.

Task Analysis. The process of task analysis can be utilized to determine a hierarchical sequence. Diagnostic information may be obtained from checklists corresponding to thorough task analyses of specific computational operations. These lists can be found in commercial materials (e.g., DTAS) or they can be developed by teachers based on their understanding of different arithmetic procedures. Table 11–4 is an example of one such task analysis. Knowledge of the steps involved in solving this particular subtraction problem can be used to help isolate specific problems.

Student Verbalizations. An extremely useful practice for determining the nature of problems students are experiencing in math is to have them verbalize the procedure they are employing in solving a given task. This process is similar to the analysis used in the Diagnostic Test of Arithmetic Strategies, discussed earlier. After such an analysis, teaching strategies can be developed to address the specific problems. This is not a difficult procedure to use, but it does require teachers to structure their class periods such that they have an opportunity to work individually with students. The benefits of scheduling time for this activity far outweigh the hassles of scheduling the time.

Current Trends in Mathematics Assessment

A recent trend in mathematics is to build a math curriculum based on changing students' concep-

TABLE 11–4

Task analysis of a subtraction problem

$$\text{Computational Task:} \quad \begin{array}{r} 400 \\ -175 \\ \hline \end{array}$$

Prerequisite Skills Required

1. Visually discriminate numbers
2. Write numerals
3. Follow written or oral directions
4. Name numerals
5. Match numerals
6. Identify the minus sign
7. Given the minus sign, state the concept of take-away
8. Compare basic subtraction facts
9. State the concept of regrouping for computing problems that require regrouping

Math Procedures Required

1. Identify the problem as subtraction
2. Identify the starting point
3. Recognize state, refuse to compute 0 minus 5
4. Move to the tens column to regroup
5. Recognize, state, refuse to group 0 tens
6. Move to the hundreds column
7. Identify 4 hundreds as a number than can be regrouped
8. Regroup the hundreds
   a. Cross out 4
   b. Write 3 above 4
   c. Place 1 on tens column
9. Regroup tens
   a. Cross out 10
   b. Write 9 above 10 in tens column
   c. Place 1 on ones column
10. Subtract 10 minus 5
11. Write 5
12. Subtract 9 minus 7
13. Write 2
14. Subtract 3 minus 1
15. Write 2
16. Read the answer correctly (225)

tions about math and adopting more constructive and sophisticated approaches toward models of mathematics (Wilson, 1992). Traditional mathematics assessment tools do not necessarily identify how students approach a mathematical problem or are able to communicate their mathematics knowledge. Traditional methods of assessment evaluate student skills in math facts, computation skill, and algorithms. These traditional methods score items as "right" or "wrong" rather than identifying where unexpected holes or gaps in a student's knowledge are occurring. Therefore, we don't necessarily know how students actually process a mathematics problem, what their belief systems are about the problems they are solving, or how their processing of a problem may be different from the instruction being given. Given this research and information, we might wish to reconsider how we attempt to measure student learning in the area of math problem solving and decision making. The following discussion outlines three problem-solving assessment techniques that are being considered by different mathematics educators and researchers.

Interviews. Researchers such as Clark, Stephens, and Waywood (1992) have investigated the advantages of evaluating students' communication and learning of mathematics through interviewing techniques. The hypothesis that students can learn through guided self-questioning and suggested self-management of learning (Briggs, 1988) is being tested by asking questions that reflect the students' ability to communicate their mathematics knowledge as well as give the instructors insight into their problem-solving ability. Generic questions such as (a) "What was the best thing to happen in mathematics?" (b) "What is the biggest worry affecting your work in mathematics?" (c) "How do you feel in mathematics class?" and (d) "How could we improve mathematics classes?" are found to show students' conceptions of mathematics as well as an increased use of technical mathematical terms (Clark, 1987). Other, more specific questions or directives such as (a) "What

would you most like more help with?" (b) "Write down one particular problem that you found difficult." (c) "Write down one new problem that you can now do." and (d) "How could we improve mathematics classes?" are beneficial in that students report attitudes and say whether procedures are useful to them. In response to these questions, teachers seem to take a proactive approach to teaching by engaging in more organization, instruction, individual assistance, and counseling. Clark (1985) also reports that several instances were documented in which teacher reaction to interview questions led to positive changes in student attitude and achievement.

Journal Writing. Journal writing is an opportunity to introduce self-evaluation skills to students in connection with mathematics learning. Through journal writing, teachers may be able to identify whether students are choosing to use mathematical procedures, principles, and facts without being cued or questioned on tests. Journal writing may be able to identify when students are distinguishing strategies within the problem-solving process. Additionally, students may be able to report in their journals a systematic approach of reviewing what they know. Such approaches may include the discussion of planning, decision making, verifying, and evaluating their solutions. Finally, journal writing can show teachers whether students are motivated in the mathematics classes, whether they are developing appropriate work habits, and their "beliefs about the nature and purpose of mathematical activity" (Clark et al., 1992). When students are asked to write in their journals after every mathematics class, a continuous dialogue between students and teacher can result.

Clark et al. (1992) note that despite the benefits of journal writing, students may find it a challenging experience, demanding of their time and concentration. Teachers who use journal writing do, however, report that improvement in students' journal writing is seen over the year and particularly across several years. This leads one to believe that good journal writing is taught to students over time.

Portfolio Assessment. The Vermont Mathematics Portfolio Assessment Program is an example of the use of portfolio assessment to evaluate mathematical problem solving. In this program, the best three work examples of each student—selected by the teacher and student—are placed in the portfolio under the following problem-solving areas: (a) understanding of the task; (b) quality of approaches, procedures, and strategies; and (c) decision making, findings, conclusions, observations, connections, and generalizations the students reach. Each section is rated by a specific criterion based on a four-point scale (e.g., a rating of 1 would indicate that the student totally misunderstood the task; a rating of 4 would indicate that the student generalized, applied, or extended the task) that is evaluated by a designated team of professionals. The project report indicates that the portfolios do provide insight to student progress, the rating scales seem to work in assessing learning, and additional specification of portfolio content is necessary to provide an equitable basis for evaluating student performance.

General Instructional Considerations

A variety of general factors should guide programming in mathematics. Many of these issues are closely related and are as applicable to other subject areas as they are to mathematics. Nevertheless, they are of particular importance when teaching mathematical skills.

Relationship of Arithmetic to Mathematics

Prior to our discussion on instruction, clarification of the terms *arithmetic* and *mathematics* is warranted. Although these terms are used somewhat interchangeably, they are different. Mathematics is best described as a "way of thinking" (Johnson & Rising, 1972) that involves quantities, their relationships, and ways of reasoning. Various branches of mathematics include arithmetic, geometry, algebra, and calculus, among others. Arithmetic is a subcategory of mathematics and refers to "the study of number, counting, notation, and operation with numbers" (Ballew, 1973, p. 460). For obvious

reasons, it is the foundation of most elementary school mathematics programs. However, it should not be the only focus of instruction; other areas of mathematics such as algebra and geometry should also be part of the curriculum.

Curricular Implications

Although a more complete discussion of this topic appears in Chapter 7, a number of important points bear repeating here. At the elementary level the focus of the curriculum is developmental/remedial, with the intent of establishing a fundamental understanding of math and proficiency in various math skills that will be used later in applied ways. Far too often, the emphasis of the elementary program is on the rote learning that relates to proficiency in that skills can be performed quickly and accurately. This outcome comes with a price: students can solve algorithms but do not understand math or how to apply math skills.

Every school system has a scope and sequence for math skill development. Most math programs are developed in compliance with the organization suggested by such systems. Some (Polloway et al., 1989) argue that the scope of math programs for students with special needs should be reexamined in light of what they will need as adults. Others (Cawley et al., 1989) have raised questions about the sequencing (i.e., when math topics are covered) of math programs. Cawley and his colleagues suggest that we do not have to adhere to the traditional sequence of teaching addition and subtraction before multiplication and division.

Many learners with special needs require that their programs reflect a realistic examination of their subsequent environments. If postsecondary education is not likely, then the curriculum should reflect a strong orientation toward the life skills and knowledge needed to survive in the community and on the job; that is, an adult outcomes mathematics curriculum (Cronin & Patton, 1993). Students for whom higher education is likely should be in programs that will prepare them for these settings. School systems must remain sensitive to a range of student needs, individual personal goals, and probable subsequent environments when developing programs.

Effective Instructional Practices

Mathematics instruction requires attention to all of the components of the effective instruction model depicted in Figure 2-2. Selected aspects of effective instruction practice as they apply to math instruction are discussed in this section.

Scheduling. Of the various precursors to teaching, an important consideration is the organization of the math period. One way to schedule the class period includes the following components: review of previously covered material; teacher-directed instruction of new content when acquisition stage learning occurs; a time for independent practice, typically during seat work; and allocated time for assigning homework. Managing these components is complicated by the nature of the students in the class (i.e., the skill level of students) and the number of math groups that exist.

Many teachers have found a daily timed test (about 2 or 3 minutes long) to be effective for collecting curriculum-based data on students' performance as well as for management purposes. Students tend to get on task quickly when they know that they have only limited time to perform the tasks required.

Student Motivation. Many students find math uninteresting and lose any desire to pursue it later in their school careers. The subject can be taught so that it becomes a fun time of the school day. Teachers should attempt to make math instruction engaging by incorporating intriguing activities and topics in their lessons. Math games and brain teasers are some of the ways this can be done; relating mathematics to other academic areas can also be effective.

Demonstration/Guided Practice/ Independent Practice Paradigm. Of particular importance among the teaching behaviors is ensuring that every student receives some teacher-directed instruction as part of the demonstration/guided practice/independent practice routine. Students with mild learning problems are not apt to acquire basic skills from workbooks or worksheets alone; they need to be taught these skills directly. Acquired skills can then be improved through practice. Unfortunately, some commercially available math materials do not provide enough practice, and few offer suggestions for presenting teacher-aided practice.

Clear Communication. Students get very confused when material is presented to them in disorganized and unclear ways. Teachers must take time to be sure that their verbal explanations are precise and meaningful to the students with whom they are working. Instructional attention needs to be given to the language of instruction, the types of examples used to explain a topic, and the manner in which instruction is delivered. In the absence of this attention, students will be confused and fail to understand the concepts being presented, which may result in them losing their motivation to remain engaged in the lesson.

Informational Feedback. Foremost among follow-up activities is the need to give students feedback. For students who do not enjoy or see the relevance of mathematics, external systems may be required to provide motivational feedback. Such systems must be implemented consistently and fairly. All students require informational feedback on their performance, particularly if their responses are incorrect. Informational feedback implies that teachers solicit student explanations (i.e., verbalizations) about how they arrived at their answers. This evaluation will often result in reteaching some concepts if students fail to understand them. All too often student work is evaluated in terms of product rather than process. In other words, the only feedback students may receive is the number of items that are incorrect or correct.

Concept and Skill Development

Within the field of mathematics education in general there is some debate over two different instructional approaches: didactic and discovery. The didactic approach stresses initial instruction in basic skills development, followed by the application of these skills to problem solving. The discovery approach allows students to establish an individual understanding of the process needed to solve a problem prior to formal instruction in the basic skills. Advocates of a discovery approach believe that such an orientation enhances concept and skill development.

Teachers of students with disabilities must confront this dilemma as well. Recognizing that a discovery approach implies minimizing various prompts and teacher direction, Bartel (1990) warns that such an approach may not be warranted for those students who need various degrees of prompting.

Cawley and his colleagues (Cawley, Fitzmaurice-Hayes, & Shaw, 1988; Cawley et al., 1989) have stressed the importance of teaching students to understand mathematical concepts rather than forcing them to memorize rote responses to basic facts or algorithms:

> Many concepts are understood by young children long before they can perform skills. For example, young children deal quite effectively with the division of a whole number by a fraction in real situations, such as cutting an apple into halves or near-halves, even though these children have no idea of the computational algorithm. (Cawley et al., 1989, p. 1)

Any discussion of skill development needs to address the question of generalization. Opportunities for applying basic skills to new situations must be programmed systematically. Teachers should give students many chances to apply their acquired skills in new contexts and settings. One way to do this is to integrate math into other subject areas. This can be done easily in a subject like science but it can also be done in other subjects.

Accommodating Individual Differences and Diversifying Instruction

Even though drill and practice are essential to mastering certain math skills, the learning process need not be as tedious as it sometimes becomes.

Variety in instructional techniques continues to be suggested (Bartel, 1990), yet it is often absent in classrooms.

Many students with learning problems need more practice than other students require. It is essential that teachers ensure fluency and mastery of specific math skills by developing novel practice activities (Bott, 1988). Many good teachers incorporate variety into their instruction as a matter of course, and these teachers serve as good resources for ideas and assistance.

Another source of ideas for programming variety is the interactive unit model originally developed by Cawley et al. (1976). This model focuses on the interaction of teacher, students, and skill area while allowing a great deal of instructional variation. The teacher can provide instruction by:

- manipulating something (e.g., physical action)
- displaying something to the students (e.g., materials or pictures)
- saying something (e.g., verbal instructions or directions)
- writing something (e.g., on worksheet or chalkboard)

The student can respond in four ways:

- by manipulating something (e.g., working with physical materials)
- by identifying something (e.g., pointing to or circling)
- by saying something (e.g., responding verbally)
- by writing something (i.e., using some form of graphic symbols—numerals or words).

The various combinations of teacher action and student response allow 16 ways to vary instruction. The virtue of this model is that it allows the teacher great flexibility when planning instruction for a variety of student needs; moreover, it allows the teacher to program instructional variation into math lessons. Figure 11–4 illustrates how this interactive idea can be used with three groups of students working on distinctly different skills: addition, geometry, and fractions. It also shows how the teacher-student interaction can be scheduled to provide direct

FIGURE 11–4
Interactive unit model

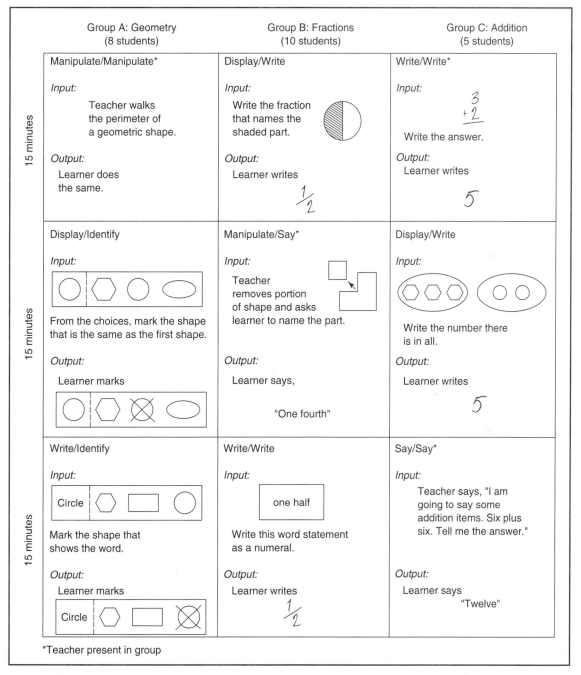

From *Developmental Teaching of Mathematics for the Learning Disabled* [p. 246] by J. F. Cawley (Ed.), 1984, Austin, TX: PRO-ED. Copyright 1984 by PRO-ED, Inc. Reprinted by permission.

teacher contact for all groups. This conceptual model provides a framework for a set of curricular materials called Project MATH, discussed later in this chapter.

Many students will need certain modifications to their curriculum, instructional materials, and/or teaching procedures. Table 11–5 provides a list of suggestions that may be appropriate for accommodating specific needs. Close inspection of the table shows that the ideas contained in the interactive unit model can serve as a resource for making needed modifications.

Relevance

Those who have encountered much frustration with the acquisition of the skills they will need as adults must first find skills relevant to their present as well as their future needs. This is particularly true of older students, who feel the greatest cumulative effect of frustration and lack of interest. Sternberg and Sedlak (1978) relate this need for relevance to the idea of ecological meaning; they encourage applying target skills to students' real-life experiences.

Teaching students math-related life skills is very much needed. These skills can be addressed in any type of placement, whether it is a special class or general education class. The instructional options range from the development of life skills course work to integrating these topics into existing curricula. This idea is discussed in detail in Chapter 16.

A useful way of making math more interesting to more students is to provide many examples of how math can be used in everyday life. One tool for doing this is the Math Applications Kit (Friebel & Gingrich, 1972). The idea behind this material is to provide students with activities that require them to apply the math skills they have learned to fascinating real-life situations. The most important feature of this resource is that it can stimulate the development of other ideas that are relevant to the local area in which students live. Figure 11–5 is an example of one such extension.

Related to the idea of making math instruction personally relevant is the notion of making

students active learners. Torgesen (1982) suggests that students with mild learning problems are only passively engaged in the tasks that are presented to them in school and making instruction more relevant can improve the chances of actively engaging them.

Student interest and motivation are closely tied to relevance and to instructional diversity. Programming variety and life–skills-relevant topics can make math exciting for both the students and the teacher. Teacher enthusiasm is something that students perceive and react to just as easily as they sense lack of interest and boredom.

Suggestions

A number of general warnings are provided here. Teachers must be sensitive to individual student personalities and needs in relation to the following practices:

- language: Be aware of students' language levels. Be careful not to confuse students initially (i.e., acquisition stage) by using different expressions to convey the same meaning (e.g., using terms like *less, take away,* or *minus* interchangeably). Eventually, students will need to understand various terms describing a concept, but it is best to be consistent at first.
- boardwork: Understand that some students experience a great deal of stress when they are at the chalkboard in front of the class, attempting to solve a problem given to them. This activity can be terrifying.
- worksheets: Do not base a math program on worksheets. Furthermore, be cognizant that worksheets can be overused.
- games: Realize that games can be used instructionally, but there are potential problems associated with them. They require gamesmanship skills: they can result in unproductive competition; they may not be as interesting to some students as you may think; and they may not really serve instructional objectives.
- homework: Remember that acquisition learning should not be done as homework. Homework is ideal for proficiency-building and maintenance activities and should be assigned

TABLE 11–5
Modification of instruction in mathematics for students with learning disabilities

Instructional Modification (Stage of Learning)	Description	Examples
Modify the content (acquisition).	Alter the type or amount of information presented to a student, substitute content.	A unit on rate-time-distance algebraic problems is not taught to a seventh-grade student; instead, the student is given extra practice learning how to balance a checkbook. A third-grade student is provided with the correct answers to a set of story problems—the student's task is only to describe how the correct answer was obtained.
Modify the nature of teacher input (acquisition and generalization).	Alter the input from the teacher (e.g., manipulate, display, say, write); repeat or simplify instructions; read the questions to the student (rather than telling the student to read).	Before having a second-grade student begin work on a page of subtraction and addition problems, the teacher requires the student to point to the operation sign of each problem and orally state whether the problem requires addition or subtraction.
Adjust the instructional pace or sequence (acquisition, proficiency, and generalization).	Alter the length or frequency of instructional periods; slow down the rate of presentation; defer the introduction of certain content; provide more frequent reviews.	The teacher plans two 15-minute math periods each day rather than one 30-minute period. Worksheets are kept to a maximum of six problems each.
Use alternative teaching techniques (all stages).	Change some aspect of verbal instruction, demonstration, modeling, rehearsal, drill and practice, prompts and cues, feedback, reinforcement, or error contingencies.	The teacher provides step-by-step direct supervision for each of three long division questions during the acquisition stage of instruction; feedback is given on each step of the process.
Alter the demands of the task (all stages).	Allow use of a calculator; allow the student to make pointing rather than oral responses or oral rather than written responses.	The teacher allows a third-grade student to use counting beads as an adjunct to completing a worksheet. The teacher works orally for a few minutes each day with a first-grade student who has difficulty writing.

(continued)

TABLE 11–5 (*Continued*)

Instructional Modification (Stage of Learning)	Description	Examples
Change the instructional delivery system (all stages)	Change the *primary instructional personnel* (use peer tutors, classroom aides, or itinerant or consultant teachers); change the *instructional format* (use computer-assisted instruction, or programmed instruction); change the *instructional context* (use small-group instruction or one-to-one instruction).	The teacher assigns a peer to play a number game and to use multiplication flashcards with a student for 3 days before any independent written work is required. For a review of making change with money, a small group of third-grade students are permitted to "play store." As a reward for completing an assignment, a student is permitted to use the computer for a game-format drill and practice on division facts.

Note. From Hammill, D. D., & Bartel, N. R. (1990). *Teaching students with learning and behavior problems,* (5th ed.) Copyright © 1990 by Allyn and Bacon. Reprinted with permission.

regularly in reasonable amounts, as discussed in Chapter 2. For a list of homework suggestions, see Patton (1994).

Oberlin (1982) offers an explanation for why many students dislike math. She feels that the following classroom practices contribute to this phenomenon:

- assigning the same work to everyone in the class regardless of individual needs
- going through the book methodically, problem by problem, page by page
- assigning written work every day—ignoring the need to include variety into lessons
- insisting that there is only one correct way to solve each problem—forgetting that there are often alternative strategies for solving math problems
- assigning mathematics as a punishment for misbehavior
- using long drill-type assignments with many examples of a similar problem (e.g., 30 long-column addition problems)
- insisting that every problem worked incorrectly be reworked until it is correct—this is

especially tragic when no informational feedback is given

APPROACHES TO TEACHING MATHEMATICS

With increasing attention being given to mathematics, new programs and materials appear on a regular basis. Some of the most recent instructionally useful materials are microcomputer software programs and other multimedia programs. This section presents major approaches to mathematics instruction that can be used with students who have problems in this area.

Basal Textbook Approach

The most frequently employed approach to teaching math is the use of basal textbooks, which all major publishers produce. It is important to remember that these textbooks are written primarily for students in general education math classes; however, most teacher's editions included in these series offer suggestions for addressing the needs of students with learning-related problems. Nevertheless, teachers of students who are experiencing

FIGURE 11–5
Math applications—Hawaiian style

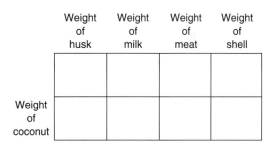

SCIENCE

What makes a coconut weigh so much?

How much of the coconut's weight makes up the husk, shell, meat, and milk?

You'll need...

1 coconut
1 hammer
1 screw driver
2 strong arms
4 large plastic containers
(of the same weight)
1 spoon
1 scale
data sheet
pencil

Note: For safety reasons, ask your teacher to have the coconut ready for husking.

Husk
Shelf
Meat
Milk

PROCEDURE

1. Label your containers 1, 2, 3, and 4.
2. Set the scale at 0 and make sure it is balanced for weighing.
3. Weigh the coconut and record the weight across the paper as shown on the data sheet.
4. Place one empty container on scale and set a 0 balance.
5. Peel the husk and place all the husk pieces into container 1.
6. Place shell into container 2 and crack open the shell using a hammer and/or screw driver.
7. Drain milk into container 2.
8. Scrape meat from the shell and place it into container 3.
9. Place empty shell into container 4.
10. Weigh each container and record the appropriate weight on the data sheet.
11. To find what fraction each part is to the whole coconut, divide the weight of each pan by the weight of the coconut.

For example: Weight of husk = .2 oz.
Weight of coconut = 1.6 oz.

Calculate: $\dfrac{.2}{1.6} = \dfrac{1}{8}$

Interpretation: The weight of the husk is 1/8th the weight of the coconut.

	Weight of husk	Weight of milk	Weight of meat	Weight of shell
Weight of coconut				

EXPLORING

Discuss ways to recycle each part of the coconut.

What are the related occupations?

How many coconuts would be needed to fill a 5-pound bag of shredded coconut flakes?

difficulties in math must be prepared to augment and/or adapt these texts as necessary.

Although there are many commonalties across basal series, there are notable differences as well. Before selecting a specific series, teachers should evaluate the instructional features of each thoroughly. In particular, attention should be directed to the teacher's edition, the student textbook/workbook, and any supporting materials that accompany the series. A sample page from a teacher's edition is presented in Figure 11-6.

The more attractive series include specific suggestions for dealing with diverse needs and offer ways to augment lessons. A key variable to consider is the amount of practice included to achieve mastery of the skill(s) being taught. Many commercially available textbooks now come with sets of supplementary hands-on materials as well, which must be evaluated in terms of students' needs.

Textbook usage with students who have learning problems has distinct advantages as well as some disadvantages that may be characteristic of some books. Some of the advantages are:

1. Skill development is laid out in a comprehensive and sequential fashion.
2. A number of primary and supplemental materials are provided: text, teacher's edition, student workbook, ditto masters, quizzes and placement tests, and record-keeping procedures.
3. Some series are oriented to real-life situations and use student-relevant examples.
4. Some series provide a hands-on, activity-oriented approach.

Some of the disadvantages are:

1. Teacher's editions do not provide specific teaching strategies for acquisition stage learning (e.g., scripted instructions for teachers).
2. Enough practice may not be provided (proficiency stage).
3. Movement from one skill/topic to another may be too rapid.
4. Sometimes there is not enough review of previously acquired skills and knowledge (maintenance stage).
5. Linguistic and conceptual complexity may inhibit student understanding.

6. Types of activities may have limited variety.
7. The activities may lack relevance to students.
8. Problem-solving applications are often too contrived.

Comprehensive Math Programs

Another approach to teaching mathematics is the use of math programs that cover a wide range of math skills. Two such programs are described in this section. Some of these programs are published as kits or an assemblage of materials, usually containing teacher's manuals, student materials, and supplementary items or resources. Other programs may also include a teacher's resource book.

Project MATH. Project MATH (Cawley et al., 1976) is a comprehensive developmental program that attempts to meet three major goals. These goals include (a) providing students with a wide range of math experiences, (b) minimizing the effects of inadequately developed skills and abilities on mathematics performance, and (c) using the qualities of mathematics and experiences that can be generated via mathematics to enhance the learner's affective and cognitive status. Project MATH has four levels: prekindergarten to Grade 1, Grades 1 and 2, Grades 2.5 through 4, and Grades 4 through 6. Each level contains directed activities in six strands of mathematics: geometry, sets, patterns, numbers, measurement, and fractions.

Project MATH incorporates the interactive unit (IU) model as the framework for a multiple-option curriculum; activities represent various combinations of teacher presentation formats and student responses. The activities have been developed with consideration for the requirements of learners with special needs.

The heart of the curriculum is the instructional guides (Fig. 11-7). Each guide is in card form, is coded for easy access, and focuses on one particular concept. Included in each guide is information about instructor input and learner output as well as information on activities to be performed, materials needed, relevant supplemental activities, and a brief informal evaluation

FIGURE 11–6
Sample page from a teacher's edition

STUDENT OBJECTIVE
To interpret information from a mileage chart and relate the information to problem solving.

VOCABULARY
kilometer (km)

TEACHING SUGGESTIONS
Talk about distances between cities. (Materials: large map of the United States) Display the large map of the United States. Discuss the locations of many of the major cities listed on the mileage chart. It may be an interesting exercise to have the students estimate how far it is from our city to another. Their responses may be in miles. At this point, introduce the vocabulary word, *kilometer*, explaining that it is part of the metric system, which they will be learning more about as the year progresses.

READINESS
For students who need help reading charts.

Readiness for 60–61

Mileage Chart

City	Atlanta	Boston	Chicago	Dallas
Atlanta		1108	706	785
Boston	1108		1004	1753
Chicago	706	1004		421
Dallas	785	1753	421	

How many miles is it from:

1. Atlanta to Boston? _1108_
2. Atlanta to Chicago? _708_
3. Boston to Chicago? _1004_
4. Chicago to Dallas? _421_
5. Dallas to Boston? _1753_
6. Dallas to Atlanta? _785_

Copymaster S82 or Duplicating Master S82

"Who can tell me what this chart is used for?" Has anyone in your family used a chart like this to plan a trip? A mileage chart helps us plan trips by showing the distance between cities and towns. For example, to find the distance between Atlanta and Boston, place the index finger of your left hand on the Atlanta and the index finger of your right hand on Boston. Move your left index finger straight across to the right and your right index finger straight down until your fingers touch. Did you touch on *1108*? That is about the number of miles between Atlanta and Boston."

Have the students find Chicago on the left and Chicago at the top. Ask why that box is blank. Assign the page.

PROBLEM SOLVING
Interpreting a Table

Many people work for airlines. Some fly the planes. Other work with passengers. Still others work on the planes.

Modern jets can fly long distances. The chart below shows the air distance in kilometers between certain cities of the world.

Air Distance in Kilometers between Cities

City	Chicago	Hong Kong	London	Montreal	Moscow	New York	Peking	San Francisco
Chicago		12,475	6,333	1,192	7,979	1,142	10,586	2,974
Hong Kong	12,475		9,584	12,378	7,099	12,896	1,947	11,048
London	6,333	9,584		5,206	2,502	5,550	8,118	8,587
Montreal	1,192	12,378	5,208		7,042	530	10,422	4,069
Moscow	7,979	7,099	2,502	7,042		7,493	5,771	9,416
New York	1,142	12,896	5,550	530	7,493		10,950	4,115
Peking	10,566	1,947	8,118	10,422	5,771	10,950		9,469
San Francisco	2,974	11,048	8,587	4,069	9,416	4,115	9,469	

USING THE PAGES
Explain the use of the distance chart on page 60.

To find the distance from New York to Hong Kong, the students should go down the left side of the chart until they find New York. They should move a finger across the row until they have located Hong Kong at the top of the chart. The number that coincides with New York and Hong Kong will tell them the distance in kilometers between these two cities. Do exercises 1–6 as a class.

To find the total distane between three or four cities, the students will have to record each separate distance and then find the sum. Do exercise 12 on the chalkboard. Have a student record the separate distances. Have another student add the numbers together.

CLASSWORK/HOMEWORK

Textbook Assignments	Basic	Average	Enriched
Exercises 1-17	✔	✔	✔
Keeping Skills Sharp	✔	✔	✔
Extra Problem Solving set 2 page 381	✔	✔	
Optional Materials			
Readiness Worksheet	✔	✔	
Basic Worksheet	✔		
Enrichment Worksheet		✔	✔
Excursion Worksheet			✔
Calculator Worksheet	✔	✔	✔
Creative Problem Solving section 3	✔	✔	✔

From *Health Mathematics: Teacher's Edition* [p. 60] by W. E. Rucker, C. Dilley, and D. W. Lowry, 1987, Lexington, MA: D.C. Heath and Company. Copyright 1987 by D.C. Heath and Company. Reprinted by permission.

FIGURE 11-7

An instructional guide from Project MATH

LEVEL 2   **N137**

PROJECT MATH INSTRUCTIONAL GUIDE

STRAND	Numbers	INPUT	OUTPUT
AREA	Subtraction		
CONCEPT	Role of Zero		

BEHAVIORAL OBJECTIVE	**INSTRUCTOR**	LEARNER
	States subtraction number expressions.	Constructs representations of the number expressions.

ACTIVITIES

1. **Review.** Review with the learners the different types of subtraction problems. State a subtraction problem, and have a learner construct the answer. For example, say, "I had five books on my desk. Two belonged to Mrs. Jones, so I gave them back to her. Show me how many books I would still have on my desk." You may also state expressions such as, "Five take away three." and have a learner construct the remainder set.

Also review problems with a number other than the difference missing (e.g., ____ – 2 = 4. 6 – ____ = 4). Say, "I had some books, I gave two away. Now I have four. Show me how many I started with." Ask a learner to make the set of four and then to add to it the set of two books that were given away to find out how many books there were at the outset. Repeat the activity using other examples.

2. **Role of Zero.** Explain, "In subtraction problems, the number zero (Write "0" on the chalkboard.) plays an important part. When we subtract to take away zero from a number, the answer is always that number. The answer is identical to, or the same as, the number from which you subtract the zero. For example, five blocks take away zero blocks is five blocks because nothing was taken away from the five blocks."

State different subtraction expressions in which 0 occurs. At the same time, give some blocks to a learner, and ask him to construct the sets in each expression. He should demonstrate his understanding by not taking any blocks away.

MATERIALS

Classroom objects, blocks or discs.

SUPPLEMENTAL ACTIVITIES N137: a, b.

EVALUATION

Give the learner blocks of discs, and ask him to construct representations of four subtraction expressions such as the following:

           3 – 2   3 – 0   5 – 1   5 – 0

From *Project MATH* by J. F. Cawley, H. A. Goodstein, A. M. Fitzmaurice, A. Lepore, R. Sedlak, and V. Althaus, 1976, Tulsa OK: Educational Development. Copyright 1976 by Educational Development Corporation. Reprinted by permission.

procedure to determine whether a student is ready to proceed to the next instructional task.

The teacher considering Project MATH must also become familiar with the administrative guide, which presents the conceptual basis for the program as well as procedures for appropriate use. Of particular importance is the topical skill sequence, which relates the strand/area/concept being taught to a specific instructional guide. This feature is essential for identifying activities to be presented.

Other materials included in this curricular program are learner activity books, supplemental activity books, class and individual progress forms, and manipulative materials. An assessment tool, the Math Concept Inventory, is included for use either as a screening device to determine the proper placement of students in the Multiple

Option Curriculum or as a curricular-based instrument to determine whether students have mastered a specific block of instruction.

The authors of Project MATH recognize the importance of problem-solving skills for special learners and include a verbal problem-solving component with the program. This portion of the Project MATH curriculum is discussed later in the chapter.

The program also includes an assessment component. The authors suggest that the teacher first determine at which point to begin teaching by giving each student the Math Concept Inventory. After determining placement and grouping, the teacher can select the appropriate instructional guide, following the sequence of instructional activities outlined in the program to mix the six mathematical strands or select the strands they deem instructionally relevant. This program also allows teachers to be creative. With the interactive unit approach, teachers can develop other suitable instructional activities to capitalize on the multiple input/output options. Project MATH can also be used to supplement an existing math program. It is possible to correlate topics addressed in any math program with the activities provided on the instructional guides. An example of this is provided later in this chapter.

Overall, Project MATH is a powerful instructional program. It covers a wide range of mathematical skill areas while allowing for differences in learning abilities and limitations.

Direct Instruction Mathematics. A direct instruction approach to teaching mathematics is teacher directed, structured, and demonstrative of the components of effective instruction presented in Chapter 1.

According to the authors of this program, "Direct instruction provides a comprehensive set of prescriptions for organizing instruction so that students acquire, retain, and generalize new learning in as humane, efficient, and effective a manner as possible" (Silbert, Carnine, & Stein, 1990, p. 1). Direct Instruction Mathematics is predicated on careful consideration of three major elements: (a) instructional design, (b) pre-

sentation techniques and (c) organization of instruction. The attitude that almost all students can learn mathematics is inherent in this program.

This program provides techniques for constructing effective lessons and developing specific instructional procedures. The authors suggest an eight-step sequence.

1. Specify objectives that are observable and measurable.
2. Devise problem-solving strategies that can be useful across situations.
3. Determine necessary preskills and teach those first.
4. Sequence skills in an appropriate order.
5. Select a teaching procedure related to the three types of tasks required of students (motor, labeling, and strategy).
6. Design instructional formats, including the specifics of what the teacher does and says, correction procedures, and anticipated student responses. (See Fig. 11–8 for a sample instructional format.)
7. Select examples based on what students are learning and what they have been taught previously.
8. Provide practice and review, including guided and independent practice.

Additional instructional suggestions address maintaining student attention, teaching to criterion, selecting various instructional materials, augmenting commercial materials, assessing students, and grouping for instruction.

Problem-Solving Approaches

Cooperative Learning. Cooperative learning approaches involve the grouping of students so that a particular goal is accomplished by the group members. In the past, researchers (Johnson & Johnson, 1989a; 1989b; Slavin, 1987; 1989) have applied the cooperative learning method to mathematics instruction and have reported effective instructional results in primary grades.

Implementing a cooperative learning program in mathematics requires that teachers structure the group work to promote a group effort toward meeting the academic goal. Slavin (1989) states

FIGURE 11–8

Sample instructional format for reducing fractions in Direct Instruction Math

Day	Part A Structured Board Problems	Part B Structured Worksheet Problems	Part C Less Structured Worksheet Problems	Part D Supervised Practice Problems	Part E Independent Practice Problems
1-2	4				
3-4	2	6			
5-6		2	6		
7-8			2	6	
9-Until accurate				8	
Until fluent					8-12

PART A: Structured Board Presentation

TEACHER   **STUDENTS**

Write on board: $\dfrac{8}{12} = \left(\right)$—

1. "WE'RE GOING TO REDUCE THIS FRACTION. WE REDUCE BY PULLING OUT THE GREATEST COMMON FACTOR OF THE NUMERATOR AND DENOMINATOR. HOW DO WE REDUCE A FRACTION?"

   "Pull out the greatest common factor of the numerator and denominator."

2. "WE WANT TO REDUCE 8/12. WHAT IS THE GREATEST COMMON FACTOR OF 8 AND 12?" Pause.

   "4"

   TO CORRECT: Tell correct answer. Explain why student's anwer is incorrect.

3. "SO WE PULL OUT THE FRACTION 4/4. WHAT FRACTION DO WE PULL OUT OF 8/12?"

   "4/4"

   Write on board:
   $$\dfrac{8}{12} = \left(\dfrac{4}{4}\right)\text{—}$$

4. "LET'S FIGURE OUT THE TOP NUMBER OF THE REDUCED FRACTION." Point to symbols as you read. "EIGHT EQUALS FOUR TIMES WHAT NUMBER?"

   "2"

   Pause.

   Write on board:
   $$\dfrac{8}{12} = \left(\dfrac{4}{4}\right)\dfrac{2}{}$$

5. "LET'S FIGURE OUT THE BOTTOM NUMBER OF THE REDUCED FRACTION." Point to symbols as you read. "TWELVE EQUALS FOUR TIMES WHAT NUMBER?" Pause, signal.

   "3"

   Write on board:
   $$\dfrac{8}{12} = \left(\dfrac{4}{4}\right)\dfrac{2}{3}$$

6. "THE FRACTION IN PARENTHESES EQUALS 1. WE DON'T CHANGE THE VALUE OF A FRACTION WHEN WE MULTIPLY BY 1. SO WE CAN CROSS OUT 4/4." Cross out. "WHEN WE PULL OUT THE FRACTION OF 1, THE REDUCED FRACTION IS 2/3. WHAT IS THE REDUCED FRACTION?"

   "2/3"

From *Direct Instruction Mathematics* (2nd ed.) [p. 338] by J. Silbert, D. Carnine, and M. Stein, 1990, New York: Merrill/Prentice Hall. Copyright 1990 by Merrill/Prentice Hall Publishing Company. Reprinted by permission.

that cooperative learning is most effective when group goals and individual accountability are incorporated in the cooperative learning lesson.

One cooperative learning model is the Think-Pair-Share model (McTighe & Lyman, 1988). Using this model, students are required to follow three steps: (a) think, (b) pair, and (c) share. During the "think" step, students are required to listen to a question or presentation about a mathematic situation and then allowed to "think" how they might solve the problem.

After the children are able to think about a solution, they are grouped together to undertake the "pair" step of this model. Within their groups of "pairs," students must share their ideas and solutions with their partners; this allows the students to communicate in mathematical language with one another and practice their skills in a safe, manageable, small-group atmosphere.

The final step, the "share" step of the model, requires the teacher to place the students in larger groups. The students are then encouraged to share their "paired" discussions within a larger group framework. In this way different ideas are shared and students realize that there is more than one way to solve a problem.

Cognitively Demanding Instructional Approach. The Cognitively Demanding Instructional Model (Sosniak & Ethington, 1994) is based on studies that looked at the successful student scores in the Second International Mathematics Study (SIMS). These researchers looked at two groups of teachers and students: (a) those teachers whose students scored high on the SIMS tests—successful teachers and students, and (b) those teachers whose students did not score high on the SIMS tests—unsuccessful teachers and students. These two groups were selected because the pretest scores for the two groups of students were similar. Sosniak and Ethington wanted to isolate what teaching variables could be accounting for the more successful student scores at the end a particular academic period. Keeping stringent experimental control over their studies, the authors developed a notion of what a cognitively demanding instructional

model in problem solving might be; they identified the following four components.

The first component of a successful problem-solving program is to emphasize the most difficult mathematics concepts and skills rather than focusing on the basic or easier concepts of problem solving. Sosniak and Ethington believe that teachers should emphasize the students' Opportunity To Learn (OTL) more difficult mathematics ideas and skills. They emphasize different problem-solving activities or word problems in this area. Their studies indicate that the more opportunities students have to learn mathematical problem solving, the more they learn about mathematics.

The second component of a successful problem-solving program relates to the type of materials the teachers use in their teaching. These authors found that the successful teachers rely on teacher-created sets of materials rather than district mandates or school-selected materials. These teachers seem to personalize their teaching of problem-solving skills through carefully prepared lessons and materials that they themselves conceptualize.

The third component of a successful problem-solving program focuses on the teacher behaviors of getting other students involved in the process of learning. Although the authors did not discuss time-on-task issues, they did emphasize that successful teachers call on students who do not volunteer answers as well as on students who do volunteer answers. These teachers promote an atmosphere of participation regardless of whether the students' answers are right or wrong. It is more important to know how students are conceptualizing mathematics and that they are able to communicate their thoughts than to establish whether a student has a right or wrong answer. Thus, an atmosphere of openness and acceptance of students as well as the notion of help with mathematics seems to prevail.

The fourth component of a successful problem-solving program looks at the teachers' beliefs about mathematics itself. Successful teachers think that mathematics is principally an intellectual matter or subject; unsuccessful teachers believe that mathematics is a procedural matter or a efficient methods for calculating (e.g., use of a calculator), (c) predicting what the answer might be, (d) using the language of estimation (e.g., about, nearly, almost, close to, etc.), and (e) estimating what the answer will be. Each of these skills allows students to approximate an answer. The correct answer in these cases may not be as important as the procedure used or as important as arriving at an answer that is an estimate of the exact answer.

Another effective strategy with older students uses a sequence of tasks to be performed each time a word problem format is encountered.

1. Read (or listen) carefully.
2. Write a few words about the kind of answer needed (e.g., kilometers per hour).
3. Look for significant words and eliminate irrelevant information.
4. Highlight the numbers that are important.
5. Draw a diagram or sketch when appropriate. This graphic does not have to be a work of art but should depict what the problem is describing.
6. Decide on the necessary calculations, and identify a math sentence for this situation.
7. Perform the calculations.
8. Evaluate the answer to determine its reasonableness.
9. Write the answer with the appropriate units.

Although this strategy is straightforward, each step requires considerable instruction.

Students with language or vocabulary problems may wish to use the strategy of retelling the problem in their own words. A teacher can check for understanding through this method. If for some reason students cannot paraphrase or use their own words, teachers may wish to read the word problem aloud. Using different variations of the problem, ask the students to choose the correct one (Bley & Thornton, 1995). Remember that students with auditory and sequencing problems may have difficulty with this strategy.

Bley and Thornton (1995) also provide some teacher tips for teaching problem solving to children. These authors recommend that teachers make problem solving more attractive to students by using interesting problems that are within the students' experiences. Also, encourage students to give an estimate of the answer rather than exact answer. Additionally, provide visual props or use concrete objects such as drawings or diagrams as the problem is read orally to the students. Another tip is to foster creative thinking about problem solving by letting students think of different ways to solve a problem—often there is more than one way to solve an open-ended problem. These authors also recommend that students be given opportunities to recognize and identify relevant and irrelevant information within a word problem. The identification of the necessary information is often the key to continuing the procedure of problem solving.

Cawley and his colleagues (Cawley et al., 1988; Cawley, Fitzmaurice, Shaw, Kahn, & Bates, 1979b) suggest the development of word problems that vary according to different linguistic demands. They provide many examples of word problems that have various linguistic features.

Some students whose reading skills limit their ability to comprehend word problems encounter great difficulty dealing with the linguistic demands of math materials. For these students Cawley (1984) recommends using reading materials that the student can handle and infusing mathematical features into these passages. From this adapted material, word problems can be developed using language that the student understands. An example of this idea is provided in Figure 11-9.

Thus, the most effective ways to develop and enhance reasoning skills in arithmetic involve clearly defining the terms used, teaching strategies to identify significant words and to ignore nonessential information, using verbal mediation strategies to work through to the solution of a given problem, and providing procedures for systematically solving math problems.

Research-Based Practices for Teaching Problem-Solving Skills. Miller et al. (1998) showcase five problem-solving studies that yielded excellent student outcomes. The studies looked at the teaching of cognitive or metacognitive

	Applied Skills					
Life Demand	Money	Time	Capacity/ Volume	Length	Weight/ Mass	Temperature
home repair/ maintenance	X	X	X	X	X	X
financial management:						
-checking/ savings account	X					
-ATM	X			X		
-credit cards	X	X				
-insurance	X	X				
-taxes	X	X				
-investment	X	X				
individual/ family scheduling		X		X		
automobile:						
-payments	X	X				
-maintenance	X	X	X	X	X	X
-repair	X					
-depreciation	X					
-fuel costs	X		X			
thermostat		X				X
cooking	X	X	X	X	X	X
yard maintenance	X	X	X	X	X	X
home remodeling	X	X	X	X	X	X
decorating	X	X	X	X	X	X
shopping:						
-comparing prices	X	X	X		X	
laundry	X	X	X			X
Leisure Pursuits						
travel	X	X		X	X	X
membership fees	X	X				
subscription costs	X	X				
reading newspaper	X	X	X	X	X	X
equipment costs:						
-rental or purchase	X	X				
sports activities	X	X		X	X	X
entertainment (e.g., movies, videos, performances, sporting events)	X	X		X		X
cards, board games, electronic games	X	X				
lottery	X	X				
hobbies	X	X	X	X	X	X

(continued)

TABLE 11–7 (Continued)

Life Demand	Applied Skills					
	Money	Time	Capacity/Volume	Length	Weight/Mass	Temperature
Personal Responsibility and Relationships						
dating	X	X				
scheduling		X				
anniversaries/ birthdays/etc.	X	X				
correspondence	X	X	X		X	
gifts	X	X				
Health						
physical development:						
-weight					X	
-height				X		
-caloric intake				X		
-nutrition	X	X			X	
physical fitness program	X	X		X	X	
doctor's visits	X	X		X	X	X
medications	X	X				
medically related procedures (e.g., blood pressure)		X	X			X
Community Involvement						
scheduling		X		X		
voting		X		X		
direction				X		
public transportation	X	X		X		
menu use	X	X				
tipping	X					
financial transactions:						
-making/receiving change	X					
-fines/penalties	X	X				
phone usage	X	X				
using specific community services	X	X		X		
emergency services	X	X		X		X
civic responsibilities:						
-voting		X		X		
-jury duty		X				

Note. Patton, J. R., Cronin, M. E., Bassett, D., & Koppel, A. (in press). Preparing students with learning disabilities for the real-life math demands of adulthood: A life skills orientation to mathematics instruction. Journal of Learning Disabilities.

TABLE 11–8
Examples of math through children's literature books

Book Title	Math Concept	Author	Publisher/date
The Shape Race in Outer Space	Shapes	Calvin Irons	Mimosa Publishing 1998
Baker Bill	Telling time, money, and fractions	Calvin Irons	Mimosa Publishing 1998
A Week Away	Days of the week, time	Calvin Irons	Mimosa Publishing 1998
The Icky Sticky Trap	Subtraction	Calvin Irons	Mimosa Publishing 1998
Clarence the Clock	Telling time	Calvin Irons	Mimosa Publishing 1998
The Crocodile Coat	Measuring	Calvin Irons	Mimosa Publishing 1998
Fishy Scales	Weighing	Calvin Irons	Mimosa Publishing 1998
The 500 Hats of Bartholomew Cubbins	Counting	Dr. Suess	Vanguard Press 1965
26 Letters and 99 Cents	Counting	Tana Hoban	Mulberry Paperback books, 1995
The Dinosaur Who Lived In My Backyard	Size and weight	B. G. Hennessy	Puffin Books 1988
Count Your Way Through China	Counting, culture, geography, foreign language	Jim Haskin	Carolrhoda Books Inc. 1987
One Hundred Hungry Ants	Multiplication concepts	Elinor Pinczes	Houghton Mifflin 1993
What is Cooking, Jenny Archer?	Time, estimating, money, word problems	Ellen Conford	Little, Brown & Co. 1989
If You Made a Million	Money concepts	David M. Schwartz	Mulberry Paperback Books, 1989
How Much is a Million?	Number concepts	David M. Schwartz	Mulberry Paperback Books, 1985
Tooster's Off to See the World	Addition and subtraction	Eric Carle	Simon & Schuster Books, 1972

Alternative Delivery Systems

In the area of math instruction, alternative delivery systems in the classroom consist of instruction that is facilitated through some mechanism (e.g., computer, literature books) or by other individuals such as classroom peers. In this discussion, alternative delivery systems include computer-assisted instruction (CAI), instruction facilitated by peer tutors, and math instruction through literature.

Computers. As computers become more and more a part of our instruction in the classroom,

the effectiveness of CAI in the area of math must be investigated. Miller et al. (1998) reviewed 10 studies that investigated the use of CAI when teaching computation and problem-solving skills. The authors of these studies evaluated (a) CAI versus teacher-assisted instruction (TAI), (b) computer-based feedback, (c) computer practice formats, (d) computer-assisted problem solving, and (e) videodisk instruction in fractions. Results from these studies were inconclusive with regard to whether computer games or computer practice were more effective. What seemed to be evident was that computer feedback produced better performance scores. Based on this limited review of the literature, one might suggest that the area of CAI need to be researched further to determine how best to use this technology in the area of math instruction.

Peer Tutors. The use of tutors to enhance instruction has been well documented. Miller et al. (1998) emphasize this enhancement when they review recent studies that look at the use of tutors for the purpose of math instruction. As with all other studies in this area, the use of tutors proved to be beneficial in enhancing the learning of math through the use of counting-on procedures, rote memorization, oral and written drills, and practice using flashcards. Additionally, the use of corrective feedback by the tutors seemed to be an important component in the tutoring of students with learning disabilities.

Math Through Children's Literature. In the early 1990s the idea of integrating math and literature was met with enthusiasm by proponents of the integrated curricula and the whole language approach (Bradden, Hall, & Taylor, 1993). Since that time teachers have been using children's books that facilitate the learning of math concepts as well as math skills. For example, by integrating math and literature, word problems can use familiar stories to allow students to address the mathematical functions rather than struggle with unfamiliar vocabulary. Table 11–8 outlines a few books that can facilitate math concepts and math skills if appropriate discussion and activities accompany the reading of the book.

Although teachers can use children's books as independent or alternative systems of teaching math, some math curricula companies are now incorporating short stories that incorporate the math concept being presented in the unit lesson; two such companies are Mimosa Publications and Silver Burdett & Ginn.

ACTIVITIES

Precomputation

1. To develop the ability to count from 1 to 10, have pupils play rhyming games such as "Buckle My Shoe."
2. Make different cutouts of three basic shapes (circles, triangles, rectangles); have pupils identify each shape. After pupils can identify each different shape, have them compare the sizes of the different shapes to determine which is larger, smaller, and so on.
3. Pupils can learn the concepts of "more" and "less" by comparing groups of objects. Start with one object in one group and two or more objects in another group. Have the pupil identify which group has more and which has less. This activity could also be used to teach sameness.
4. Draw a line of objects, such as applies; have a pupil put an X on the number of objects designated by the numeral at the beginning of the line.
5. Have pupils match strings to kites, sails to boats, or stems to flowers to help develop an understanding of one-to-one correspondence.

6. Make up ditto sheets with similar but different-sized figures (e.g., animals, toys, buildings) in each of several boxes. Have pupils cross out the largest and/or smallest figure in each box.

7. Using a felt board or pocket chart, have pupils match a set of objects with a numeral. For example, they might match two apples with the numeral 2.

8. Using a felt board or pocket chart, have pupils match a number word with a set of objects. Next, have pupils match a numeral and a number word with a set of objects.

9. Group objects in sets from 1 to 10; place several numerals next to each set and instruct pupils to circle the correct numeral.

10. Instruction in writing numerals from 1 through 9 should be started when a pupil is learning to write in manuscript. Have pupils trace the numerals to be learned, make the numerals by connecting dots, and finally write the numerals independently.

11. Have students complete dot-to-dot puzzles of simple designs (e.g., circle, square, triangle) and then of more complicated pictures (e.g., boats, animals, cars).

12. Spring-type clothespins can be used as counting devices. Attach cards with a numeral on each (1 to 10) to coat hangers; instruct youngsters to clip that many clothespins to the hanger (Crescimbeni, 1965).

13. Cut numerals from old calendars and paste each on cardboard. Ask pupils to arrange the numbers in proper sequence without using the calendar page (Crescimbeni, 1965).

14. Request students to count silently the number of times you bounce a ball or buzz a buzzer. Challenge a pupil to state the correct number; if correct, ask that student to take your role.

15. Make seasonal puzzles with numbers as cues (e.g., jack-o-lanterns with different numbers of teeth, turkeys with different numbers of tail feathers, Christmas trees with different numbers of decorations). The student must count the items, find the puzzle piece with the corresponding numeral, and fit the pieces together.

16. Make dittos with several different shapes on a page. At the top of the page, color code a sample of each shape. Instruct pupils to color each matching figure with the designated color (Lettau, 1975).

17. To aid in numeral recognition, make a ditto sheet with overlaid geometric patterns creating a design with numerous individual sections. In each section place a numeral, and color code each numeral at the top of the page. Instruct students to color all sections of the design to match the color code (Lettau, 1975).

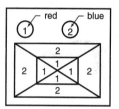

18. To give students practice matching numbers and numerals, make dittos with designs like those in Activity 17, but this time place a different number of objects in each section of the design. Again, put numerals at the top of the page and color code each (Lettau, 1975).

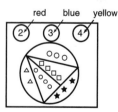

Computation

1. Have students make combinations of less than 10 by first counting real or pictured objects and then writing the correct number:

2. To ensure understanding of addition (or any other operation), introduce the concept of

the missing element. This can be done in a way that is similar to the following example:

$$1 + 4 = \underline{\hspace{1cm}} \quad 1 + \underline{\hspace{1cm}} = 5 \quad \underline{\hspace{1cm}} - 4 = 5$$

3. An abacus is a good, concrete way to introduce students to the idea of place value. Show pupils when they get to 10 beads in the same row on the combinations and then write the number indicated on the abacus.

4. Have students play counting games in which the counting changes direction every time a bell rings.

5. Strengthen concepts of "before" and "after" by having pupils find the missing number in a series.

before $\boxed{}\boxed{2}\boxed{3}\boxed{}$ $\boxed{6}\boxed{7}\boxed{}$ after
$\boxed{}\boxed{4}\boxed{5}\boxed{}$ $\boxed{5}\boxed{6}\boxed{}$

6. Help students learn to carry by covering all but the number column they are working with in a given problem.

7. Start work with fractional numbers by having students actually manipulate the fractional part to see that all parts are equal.

8. As students manipulate equal fractional parts, give them a chance to label them; for instance, if there are four parts, then each part should be labeled one fourth or ¼.

9. As students learn to count and write numerals, encourage them to make their own number line using tape or some other material.

10. Beginning instruction in subtraction should focus on actually taking away concrete objects, then crossing out pictures of objects, and finally working with pure abstraction.

11. Help students perceive the relationship of addition and subtraction by having them first add two sets of numbers and then subtract the two numbers from the derived sum.

12. Since multiplication involves grouping of sets, show students an arrangement like the following, requesting that they make several similar sets.

$$\underset{2}{\circ\circ} \mid \underset{2}{\circ\circ} \mid \underset{2}{\circ\circ} = 6 \qquad 3 \times 2 = 6$$

13. Make a ditto sheet with objects in sets like those in Activity 12. Have pupils write how many objects are in each set. Then instruct pupils to write the same statements, using only numbers.

14. To show the relationship between addition and multiplication, have students first add the same number several times and then multiply that number by the number of times it was added.

$$\underline{3 + 3 + 3 + 3 + 3 = 15} \qquad \underline{3 \times 5 = 15}$$
$$6 + 6 + 6 = 18 \qquad\qquad 6 \times 3 = 18$$

15. Concepts of "more" and "less" can be further developed by using multiplication facts. Require pupils to underline which is more or less.

more	*less*
2 threes or 5	3 fives or 18
3 twos or 7	4 twos or 10

16. A pupil with a short attention span can sometimes do as much work as another pupil if arithmetic work is broken into smaller segments. To achieve this goal, cut a worksheet into small parts (e.g., rows of problems) or make up arithmetic problems on three-by-five cards that the pupil picks up each time a problem is completed.

17. After students learn basic division facts, have them show how a given number is divided into several equal parts.

$$6 = \underline{\hspace{1cm}} \text{ twos} \qquad 6 = \underline{\hspace{1cm}} \text{ threes}$$
$$12 = \underline{\hspace{1cm}} \text{ sixes} \qquad 12 = \underline{\hspace{1cm}} \text{ threes}$$
$$12 = \underline{\hspace{1cm}} \text{ twos} \qquad 12 = \underline{\hspace{1cm}} \text{ fours}$$

18. A highly motivating type of worksheet is a shade-in math puzzle. Instruct the student to shade in the puzzle parts with numbers divisible by 2, shade in all multiples of 3, or shade in all problems with correct answers. The shaded puzzle parts form a picture. Prentice-Hall has two excellent books of math puzzles, one for primary students and one for older students: *Contemporary Math Shade-Ins/Primary* and *Contemporary Math Shade-Ins.*

For Older Students

1. Make a math center using index cards with basic computational skills of addition, subtrac-

tion, multiplication, or division on each card. Arrange the cards according to sequential skills (i.e., basic addition facts, carrying, and so on). Students can check their own recording sheets to show individual growth. Commercially prepared activity cards, such as Contemporary Math Facts Activity Cards (Prentice Hall Learning Systems), cover all math areas.

2. Many recently developed electronic games can be used to teach or reinforce math skills. Students also can check their work with them.

3. Simple calculators can be used to check work. In addition, these devices can be used for motivation: a student who finishes work on time or ahead of time can check it with the calculator.

4. More metric-related activities are needed to help students with disabilities understand the different systems of measurement. To show the difference in liquid measurement, empty a liquid from a container with a known measure to a container showing the metric equivalent.

5. Play the game "Greatest Sum Wins." Use poker chips and flashcards showing addition problems. Mix up the flashcards and place them face down. Each student picks up a card and the player with the greatest sum wins a chip. The player who has the most chips at the end of the game wins. Play the game with division, multiplication, and subtraction facts (Rucker & Dilley, 1981).

6. Discuss the concept of symmetry through examples, such as a person's face or body. Ask the class to find as many examples of symmetry as they can in magazines and newspapers (Schminke & Dumas, 1981).

7. Using pictures of various items that can be bought in restaurants, direct students to make up menus and choose what they will eat. Have them write the name of the food and its price, and then add the prices to determine the total bill.

8. Give students practice reducing fractions to the lowest terms by making fraction cookies. Reduce all the fractions in the recipe and follow the directions as given.

Ingredients:

$\frac{4}{2}$ cup of sugar
$\frac{2}{4}$ cup of milk
$\frac{3}{3}$ stick of margarine
$\frac{4}{8}$ cup cocoa

Bring ingredients to a boil in a saucepan. Cool slightly. Add $\frac{2}{2}$ cup peanut butter and $2\frac{2}{4}$ cup oatmeal. Drop on waxed paper. Makes $1\frac{4}{4}$ dozen cookies.

9. Mercer (1979) suggests using money cards, like the ones in Illustration 1, to find correct change. Students mark out the amount of a purchase; the remaining amount is the correct change.

10. Let two students roll dice to practice addition facts. The object of the game is to be the first player to score 100 points from the totals on the dice rolled. The players take turns rolling the dice; each may continue to roll as long as neither die shows a 1 but may stop voluntarily at any point. When either die does show a 1, the player gives up the turn and loses all points earned during that turn. If a 1 is rolled on both dice, the player gives up the turn, loses all points, and starts again at zero (Mercer, 1979).

Illustration 1

Purchase	$10.00 Money Card									Change
6.00	$	$	$	$	$	$	$	$	$	3.00
.70	10	10	10	10	10	10	10	10	10	.20
.07	1	1	1	1	1	1	1	1	1	.03
6.77										3.23

Illustration 2

Ten Thousand	Thousand	Hundreds	Tens	Ones

11. Have three students play "Divido." One player, the dealer, has a set of cards with division facts. The other two players have a set of answer cards. The dealer places a dealer's card (one with a division fact on it) on the table. The student putting the correct answer card down first wins the dealer's card and takes it. The player with the most cards at the end is the winner (Dumas, 1971).

12. Have each student draw a place-value chart like the one in Illustration 2. Draw a card from a deck of 10 with a digit (0 to 9) written on each. Direct students to record that digit in any column they wish. Continue drawing until five cards have been drawn. The student with the largest number wins. Require the winner to read the winning number correctly. Modify as appropriate.

13. Cut a piece of tagboard into a circle as large as the center of a car tire. Tape the tagboard into the center of a tire. Write these directions on the circle: (a) measure the radius of the circle, (b) tell the diameter of the circle, (c) find the circumference of the circle. Use different types of tires and other circular items to vary this activity.

TEACHER TIPS

Elementary Level

INTEGRATE MATH AND LANGUAGE ACTIVITIES: MY FATHER'S DRAGON

The book *Simple Ways to Make Teaching Math More Fun,* by Algozzine and Ysseldyke (1994), offers many suggestions for making math more enjoyable for young students. One idea described (pp. 71–72) is to integrate math and language by using the book *My Father's Dragon* by Ruth Stiles Gannett.

In the book, a little boy packs his knapsack to leave home. During his trip he uses some of the things he packed. The story offers some excellent opportunities to develop addition and subtraction activities. Students can calculate how many things are in the boy's knapsack at the beginning of the trip, then recalculate the total as the trip progresses. Some of the other activities that could be developed for students include:

- Read the story aloud to your students, allowing them to take notes and add up items as you read.
- Have students create packing lists and complete them as though they were making the trip.
- Then, have students change their totals as the trip progresses.
- Have students pretend they are taking a trip somewhere else. Help them create their own trip logs that answer questions about the items they take (what to take, how much, how many, and how many would be left).

Making math fun for young students is important because it may have a positive impact on their attitudes toward math for years to come. There are many stories that could be used as the basis for both reasoning and calculation activities.

Algozzine & Ysseldyke (1994)

TEACHER TIPS

Real Life Math: Living on a Paycheck is a math-based consumer education simulation program. Students move out of their parents' homes to Willow, U.S.A., the city where they get their first jobs and their first apartments. Students hunt for and choose apartments. They sign leases, pay security deposits, start paying rent, and move in. They buy starter furniture and basic household needs. Students who think they will have trouble affording an apartment on their own choose roommates and begin making joint decisions.

After filling out applications and being interviewed, students get a job. They receive paychecks based on actual school attendance. For 70 simulated days, they budget their money to:

- rent and furnish their apartments
- buy cars and gas fill-ups
- pay bills
- buy groceries
- pay for leisure activities
- buy clothes
- pay for medical care
- take care of personal needs

The 70 simulated days can translate to either a one or two semester course. Choosing possible shortcuts, limiting elaboration, keeping all students working together, and doing activities in groups as needed to stay on track will allow the program to be completed in one semester. Although students choose their jobs from the want ads, part of their job duties include the billing, banking, and other paperwork involved with the simulation. Students also create and maintain the Willow Shopping Center where they do their shopping.

TEACHER TIPS

Teachers now have access to numerous web sites to enhance the teaching of math in their classrooms. Of particular interest are the following web sites.

- AskERIC Lesson Plans: Enigmas. This web site was developed by the Educational Resources Information Center (ERIC) of the National Library of Education. The web site can be found at the following link: http://ericir.syr.edu/virtual/lessons/Interdisciplinary/INT0017.html
  The goal is to teach about mysterious elements of literature, math, science, and technology.
- Education in Science, Technology, Engineering, and Math (ESTEEM). You can reach this web site at the following link: http://www.sandia.gov/ESTEEM/home.html
  This website presents the Education of Science, Technology, Energy, Engineering, and Math (ESTEEM) program of the U.S. Department of Education. It includes information for teachers and students from middle school to college.
- Knowledge Adventure. This web site is a collection of web sites for children. It offers access to games and activities in the area of art, early language, entertainment, Math, reading, Science, study skills, typing for all ages.
  A teacher can link up to this web site by typing in: http://www.knowledgeadventure.com/home/
- KidsClick. This web site features KidsClick which is a collection of links to online resources for children. The site was initiated under a Federal Library Service and Technology Act (LSTA) grant. Contains links to many categories including math.

  A teacher can link up to this web site by typing in: http://sunsite.berkeley.edu/kidsclick%21/

CHAPTER 12

Science and Social Studies

Students are typically curious about their surroundings and about the people and things inhabiting them. As a result, they have a natural interest in seeking information about their environment and the events occurring within it. Teachers should take advantage of this curiosity by exposing students to science and social studies topics that capitalize on their interests and backgrounds. These two subject areas are rich with topics and issues that provide wonderful opportunities for active student involvement.

Traditionally, science and social studies have often had a low priority in the educational curriculum for students with mild/moderate disabilities (Patton, Polloway, & Cronin, 1987; 1994). However, as students with mild learning problems remain for longer periods of the instructional day in general education, these academic areas become critically important. The importance of these two subjects is reflected in the competencies required by many states for graduation from high school. In considering why these subjects have been deemphasized in the past, Price, Ness, and Stitt (1982) suggest that the overwhelming thrust in many programs for students with mild disabilities is on the development/remediation of basic skills. In addition, personnel-preparation programs have neglected these areas; few special education training programs require or even offer course work in these subjects. Patton et al. (1987, 1994) found that a significant number of special education teachers reported that they had received no training of any type (i.e., preservice or in-service) in these areas. Not surprisingly, most special education personnel feel unprepared and uncomfortable teaching these subjects. However, many of them are assigned to teach in these areas, especially at the secondary level, and often find themselves teaching credit-generating science and social studies courses to students in diploma-track programs.

General educators also feel unprepared to work with special learners in these areas. Atwood and Oldham (1985) highlight the three major presenting problems of students who have learning-related problems when placed in activity-oriented general education settings: (a) deficiencies in language (i.e., reading, listening, writing, speaking); (b) difficulty with new concepts and vocabulary; and (c) inappropriate behaviors. These concerns are legitimate and suggest that general education teachers be exposed to techniques for accommodating students with such needs in their classes.

How to accommodate the needs of students with mild disabilities, especially in terms of science and social studies, is still not adequately covered in the preservice programs of many teachers. Method courses in science and social studies that preservice general education teachers take allot very little time to accommodative practices. Courses taught through special education departments that are specifically designed for general educators and that cover accommodative techniques typically do not go into enough detail for teaching these subjects to students with special needs. Only a few books written to help general educators address the needs of special learners actually provide specific information in these curricular areas (cf., Schulz, Carpenter, & Turnbull, 1991; Wood, 1993).

Instructional suggestions for working with students with diverse learning needs have not usually been effectively conveyed to general education personnel on an in-service basis either. For this reason, special education personnel who work cooperatively with general educators need to be able to assist them in this task. To do so, however, means that special education personnel need to know about the subject areas of science and social studies.

Two other important factors are administrative in nature. The first involves the placement of students with learning problems in general education science and social studies classes. Far too often these students are unable to read the textbooks or participate appropriately in class discussions and activities. The results are minimum learning and increased undesirable behaviors. The other problem occurs when students receive scheduled special services (e.g., counseling, remedial reading) during periods when these subjects are being taught, resulting in their missing potentially valuable instructional time.

Science and social studies should be recognized as basic subjects that have major life skill implications (Patton, 1995). As a result, these subjects must be taught to all students, utilizing different emphases depending upon the current and future needs of the students. There are many reasons for doing so, including the following important benefits of quality science and social studies programs.

1. Firsthand experiences particularly help students become familiar with their surroundings (Jacobson & Bergman, 1991).
2. Basic skills can be applied in meaningful contexts (Cronin & Patton, 1993; Price et al., 1982).
3. A rich experiential background can be developed to establish "knowledge frameworks into which students can integrate new ideas, relationships, and details" (Jenkins, Stein, & Osborn, 1981, p. 37).
4. Students have the opportunity to develop higher thinking skills and problem-solving strategies (Carnine, 1992; Woodward & Noell, 1992).
5. Certain topics covered in science and social studies are essential for dealing successfully with the demands of adulthood and are useful for lifelong interests (Cronin & Patton, 1993).

ASSESSMENT IN SCIENCE AND SOCIAL STUDIES

A number of techniques are available for collecting information on students' knowledge and skills in science and social studies. The major ways of measuring performance include standardized testing, curriculum-based measurement, behavioral techniques, rubrics, and portfolio assessment. All of these are discussed below.

Standardized norm-referenced group achievement tests are given to students throughout the United States. Most of these tests have subtests on science and social studies; some of the more commonly administered tests are listed in Table 12–1. The validity of such tests as an index of a student's knowledge and skill development in science is questionable, as the tests concentrate on facts and may not match well with a student's particular curriculum of study. As a result, scores should be interpreted cautiously.

Curriculum-based measures are generally teacher-made, nonstandardized tests that reflect the actual curriculum to which students are being exposed and other teacher-produced assessments. Examples of curriculum-based measures in science can be found in Idol et al. (1986).

Interviews are useful not only to determine what a student has learned but also to determine interest. If there is sufficient time to do this, teachers are encouraged to gather information through conversations with students as an adjunct to other techniques.

If an activity-oriented science program is used, some type of observational measure is extremely useful for assessing performance. For this to work well it is advisable to have predeveloped checklists with predetermined objectives that will be observed. Some commercial programs publish materials designed specifically for evaluating student performance through teacher observation.

Similar to behavioral checklists is the rubric assessment (Finson & Ormsbee, 1998). A rubric assessment refers to the use of specific guidelines to help navigate the grading of the student's work. A teacher may use *analytic rubrics* that outline specific criteria to determine the level of a student's performance. This type of rubric is objective in nature. A more subjective assessment is the *holistic rubric,* which implies that a teacher assesses and rates the overall quality of the student's work (e.g., as superior, acceptable, inadequate, or unacceptable). Either rubric can be used for the assessment of a science and social studies project/performance.

Portfolio assessment implies the accumulation of student products to reflect their performance. This increasingly popular method is attractive for use with students with special needs because it deemphasizes the need for optimal demonstration of competence in a standardized format. Instead, it allows students to show their best work that has been generated over time.

TABLE 12–1
Selected standardized group achievement tests

| Test | Publisher | Age/Grade Appropriateness for Science/ Social Studies | Subtests | | Type of Derived Scores |
			Science	Social Studies	
Iowa Test of Basic Skills (ITBS)	Riverside Publishing (1993)	K to 9	X	X	Percentile rank Grade equivalents Stanines Standard scores Normal curve equivalents
Metropolitan Achievement Test (MAT) (6th ed.)	The Psychological Corporation, Harcourt Brace Jovanovich (1985)	K to 12	X	X	Percentile rank Grade equivalents Stanines Scaled scores Normal curve equivalents
Stanford Achievement Test	The Psychological Corporation, Harcourt Brace Jovanovich (1995)	K to 12	X	X	Percentile rank Grade equivalents Stanines Standard scores Normal curve equivalents

TEACHING SCIENCE TO SPECIAL LEARNERS

Science is very much a part of everyone's daily life. It includes topics that can have a major impact on our personal, family, workplace, and community needs so it is not difficult to make science meaningful to students as well as relevant to their current needs. It is essential to interest students of both genders with special needs in science early and maintain this interest over their school careers.

Of all the subject areas taught, science may be one of the most fascinating as well as one of the most feared by many teachers. The following example, although it involves a student with unusually advanced language skills, illustrates both points.

Not long ago, I was invited to go on a "reef walk" with a class of gifted third and fourth graders. It is very educational to do such a thing with this type of youngster. While we were wading in some shallow water, we came upon a familiar marine organism called a "feather duster." Being cognizant of being with a group of young students but forgetting that they were students with vocabularies which were well advanced of their nongifted age peers, I was about ready to say something like "Look how that thing hangs on the rock." Before I could get my highly descriptive statement out, Eddie, one of the students who always amazes us with his comments, offered the following: "Notice how securely anchored the organism is to the stationary coral." All I could say was "Yes, I do." (Patton, Blackbourn, & Fad, 1996, p. 216)

How exciting to be out on a reef actually seeing, touching, and experiencing nature; but how threatening to realize that a student may know more about something than you do or that someone may ask you a question for which you do not have an immediate answer. Many teachers who do not have extensive science training express reservations about teaching anything connected with science. Nevertheless, by using effective instructional techniques as outlined in Chapter 1 and discussed in Chapter 4, by refusing to feel intimidated by the subject itself, and by recognizing the intriguing aspects of this subject area, teachers can provide dynamic and socially valid science programs.

It is important for teachers to acquire a comfort level with the subject of science. This includes a recognition that no one will ever know every science fact or even be able to recall instantaneously information that was formerly in one's memory. It might be helpful to think of the teacher's role as that of a travel guide who leads students on a wonderful journey.

Nature of Science Education for Students with Special Needs

Teaching science can be exciting and rewarding. Few subject areas are as inherently interesting to teach, actively involve students as much, and can be made as relevant to students of varying backgrounds. Interestingly, a teacher's attitude may be the most critical variable. It has been found that enthusiasm on the teacher's part can lead to excitement in students as well as to higher academic achievement and lower rates of off-task behavior (Brigham, Scruggs, & Mastropieri, 1992). However, not every student will share this enthusiasm. Even though many students are stimulated by an engaging science program, others are not in such fashion and may require other motivational strategies.

Science instruction must be designed for all students, not just those who will be future scientists (Jackson, Jackson, & Monroe, 1983). Traditionally, much of what has been taught to students is appropriate for approximately 3% of high school graduates (Kyle, 1984). Patton et al. (1994) found in their study of special education teachers that substantial numbers of students were not receiving any science instruction and that those who did, did not have much time allocated to this subject area each week.

Before examining the general approaches to and specific strategies for teaching science, some basic guidelines and suggestions are warranted. Although offered in the early 1970s, Boekel and Steele's (1972) general guidelines about science are still appropriate today. They suggest that science is discovery, solving problems, broadening curiosity, nurturing interests, and finding answers to questions. They warn that science is not hit-or-miss lessons, pure memorization, or just substantive knowledge. Rossman (1985) suggests that science is a way of whetting the appetites of students and that we should make every student a scientist. Gurganus, Janas, and Schmitt (1995), in summarizing the trends in recent reform movements in science education, note the following four common elements: less is more—spend more time on fewer topics; more curricular integration; learning that results from constructing knowledge based on exploration and later concept development; and use of assessment techniques that are tied more closely to instruction.

Students who are having difficulty learning will present specific challenges when we attempt to teach them science. Rakes and Choate (1990) have identified a number of skills that students need in order to understand the many facets of science instruction. These skills have been organized according to three major dimensions: information acquisition skills (observation, listening, reading, study skills, directed experimentation); information-processing skills (organization, analysis, measurement, classification); and integration skills (synthesis, hypothesis, independent experimentation, generalization, evaluation). Many of these skills relate closely with inquiry skills discussed later in the chapter that are part of the scientific process. Nevertheless, it is important to be cognizant of the skill demands of science, particularly in the area of information acquisition, in terms of the special needs of students.

Certain competencies are desirable in science teachers. The following list is not exhaustive; however, it can serve as a preliminary checklist.

- knowledge of basic content in the area of science
- understanding of certain laboratory skills
- ability to follow a preestablished curriculum or to develop one
- knowledge of various approaches to and materials for teaching science to students with special learning needs
- ability to adapt materials and techniques to accommodate the individual needs of special learners
- knowledge of skills needed to plan and carry out science investigations
- familiarity with print and community resources
- ability to apply relevant science education research to the educational programs of special populations
- ability to relate science topics and concepts to real, everyday situations and adult outcomes
- ability to work cooperatively with general education teachers in delivery of science to students with special needs.

Content of Science Instruction

Different sources yield different goals for science education. In summarizing the findings of a major research effort that examined science education, Yager (1989) offers the following four goal clusters for science education.

- science for meeting personal needs
- science for resolving societal problems
- science for career awareness
- science for preparation for further study (p. 151)

While all these goal clusters may be appropriate for students with special needs, some of these goals are likely to be more important than others for certain students.

On an instructional level, three major objectives are woven throughout science education: the acquisition of relevant content and knowledge, the development of various inquiry-related skills, and the nurturing of a scientific attitude. Many of us have experienced science instruction that focused largely on content acquisition with little opportunity for hands-on activities. In recent years more emphasis has been given to the importance of skill acquisition, and attention is being directed toward the attitudinal/affective domain associated with science topics. All these objectives are important, and none should be emphasized to the detriment of the others.

Although there is no generally accepted curricular sequence in science education and some (e.g., Rossman, 1985) would suggest that science is every place we cast our attention, science programs typically include subject matter from three areas: life science (the study of living things including biology, zoology, botany, ecology); physical science (the study of nonliving things including chemistry and physics); and earth science (the study of such topics as astronomy, meteorology, and geology).

The National Science Education Standards (draft version), developed by the National Research Council (1996), recommends the following eight categories of science content standards for grade levels K-12.

- unifying concepts and processes in science
- science as inquiry
- physical science
- life science
- earth and space science
- science and technology
- science in personal and social perspective
- history and nature of science (p. 6)

Gurganus et al. (1995) suggest that a set of common themes or concepts exists that can serve as a guide for what should be covered in science education. Cawley (1994) indicates that "the use of themes is both a provocative and potentially powerful curriculum organizer" (p. 70). A vast number of topics could be incorporated into a science curriculum, but, given the trend to cover fewer topics while spending more time on each, one must select topics to the exclusion of others. It is possible to address major concepts by selecting appropriate related units of study. Figure 12–1 lists important science concepts along with suggested activities for studying them.

Elementary Level. The importance of quality science programs at the elementary level is generally recognized because this level of science instruction provides the foundation in skills, knowledge, and attitudes for further science study that supports a sound science education program. Most elementary programs still rely greatly on textbooks as the primary source of scope and sequence. As Idol, Nevin, and Paolucci-Whitcomb (1986) note, science curricula are often spiraling

FIGURE 12–1
Concepts of science

Concepts	Examples
Systems	Life in an aquarium, home heating systems
Models	Map of community, model of human heart
Scale	Inflation of a balloon, amount of moisture held by air
Change	Seasons of the year, growth of a seedling
Stability	Properties of sugar dissolved in water, phases of the moon
Diversity	Elements of an ecosystem, fingerprints
Structure/Function	Types of teeth, operation of a solar collector
Matter	Mixing liquids, dissolving solids into liquids
Energy	Effect of sunlight, heat produced through friction

From "Science instruction: What special education teachers need to know and what roles they need to play," by S. Gurganus, M. Jonas, and L. Schmitt, 1995, *Teaching Exceptional Children, 27*(4), *7–9.*

curricula. For example, a topic like plants will be introduced at an early grades level and covered a number of times in subsequent grade in more conceptually complex ways. Figure 12–2 outlines an elementary science curriculum.

Secondary Level. The nature of science programs for students with special needs will depend upon the curricular orientation these students are following. If students are in a general education curriculum, they will take courses such as life science/biology, physical science or earth and space science. If students are in a curriculum that parallels the general education curriculum, materials and procedures may not differ significantly from those used in the general education setting. If students are in an alternative curriculum, they may be exposed to functional science content related to life skills and/or vocational applications. Alternative coursework that is geared toward teaching life skills required in typical adult settings might include the following three courses: Science for Living (related to life science); Everyday Science (related to physical science); and Science in the World (including earth/environmental science topics). The "Science for Living" course was developed in Dubuque, Iowa, and was intended to address the real needs of students in the context of a viable life science course. The major life demands covered in the course are presented in Chapter 16.

Teaching Science to Diverse Students with Disabilities. In addition to the challenges of teaching science to children with disabilities, a special challenge involves teaching science to such children who are from culturally and linguistically different backgrounds. Although few studies have been devoted to the teaching of science to diverse learners, Raborn and colleagues (Raborn, 1988; Raborn & Daniel, 1999; Voltz, 1998) indicate that these children learn best when science lessons include inquiry-based and hands-on activities that provide high context and meaningful opportunities. These types of lessons promote reciprocal interactions necessary for second-language acquisition with Spanish-English bilingual students with disabilities.

FIGURE 12–2

Delta Science Modules II for elementary students

	Life	**Earth**	**Physical**
K-1	From Seed to Plant Observing an Aquarium	Finding the Moon Sunshine and Shadows	Investigating Water Properties
Grades 2–3	Using Your Senses Butterflies and Moths Classroom Plants Plant and Animal Populations	Amazing Air Weather Watching Soil Science	Force and Motion Length Sink or Float? States of Matter
Grades 3–5	Animal Behavior Dinosaur Classification Food Chains and Webs Insect Life Plant and Animal Life Cycle Small Things and Microscopes	Earth Movements Solar System Water Cycle Weather Instruments	Electrical Circuits Looking at Liquids Magnets Measuring Powders and Odors Sound
Grades 5–6	Fungi—Small Wonders Pollution Pond Life You and Your Body	Erosion Oceans Rocks and Minerals Solar Energy Weather Forecasting	Flight and Rock Color and Light Electromagnetic Lenses and Mirrors Simple Machines
Grades 6–8	DNA—From Genes to Protein Plants in Our World	Astronomy Earth, Moon and Sun Earth Processes	Chemical Interaction Electrical Conduction Newton's Toy

Interdisciplinary
Famous Scientists
If Shipwrecks Could Talk

Approaches to Teaching Science

Traditional elementary science programs have consisted primarily of a basic textbook and very few hands-on activities. As statistics show, many students have not found science engaging and have not chosen careers related to it. Fortunately, science educators are changing the way that science is taught; unfortunately, these changes are not yet evident in a significant number of settings.

There are a number of general approaches to teaching science. Saul and Newman (1986) conceptualize the various orientations to teaching science in a fascinating way. Their categorization, as well as the advantages and disadvantages of each approach, is presented in Table 12-2. Teachers are encouraged to think about the points Saul and Newman make about the different orientations.

The remainder of this section will discuss approaches to providing science instruction from the perspective of how content is presented. The major approaches covered include commercial programs (textbooks, hands-on programs, and special programs designed for students with special needs) and customized programs that usually are developed locally. A substantial amount of research on the first two approaches has been conducted by Mastropieri, Scruggs and their colleagues (Mastropieri & Scruggs, 1994; Scruggs, Mastropieri, Bakken, & Brigham, 1993).

Textbook Approach. This traditional approach continues to be used frequently today, especially at the upper elementary and secondary levels (Mastropieri & Scruggs, 1994). Yager (1989), in referring to regular education science pro-

TABLE 12–2
Advantages and disadvantages of various science orientations

Orientation	Advantages	Disadvantages
Gee–whiz Science	Is engaging Provides an entry point to more in-depth science	Gives only isolated bits of information Should not be the only format for teaching science
Learn-the-facts Science	Gives students information with which to work Allows students to formulate questions and initiate investigations Minimizes the need to look up information	Can lead to the presentation of meaningless and useless pieces of information
Theoretical Science	Provides students with frameworks for organizing and categorizing what they encounter Is not only for the brighter students	Can be a turn-off for students if this is the only way science is taught May exceed the conceptual levels of some students
Hands-on-Science	Is activity/experiment-oriented Provides students with experience working with the materials of science Calls for exploration Promotes the idea that science can be done by everyone Is fun	Is more difficult to provide—many materials may be needed May not dispel naive misconceptions Requires different type of teaching behavior
Eclectic Science	Combines elements of all previous orientations	Can lead to gaps in students' programs

grams, remarks that "textbooks are in use over 90% of the time by 90% of the science teachers" (p. 148). Reality for most students is that they are introduced to science by means of the textbook and continue to be exposed to this type of material as the primary "vehicle of instruction throughout their science education (Memory & Uhlhorn, 1991).

In their study of science education in special education settings, Patton et al. (1994) found that nearly 60% of the teachers who taught science used a regular education textbook in some fashion. This figure is only 60% primarily because many students in special education simply cannot use a regular education textbook.

Teachers can use commercially published textbooks in various ways. For most a textbook is the primary vehicle of the science program, with students regularly reading and consulting it. A class discussion/lecture format usually accompanies this type of approach, which emphasizes a verbal mode of presenting information (Scruggs & Mastropieri, 1993).

Textbooks can also be used in a supplementary way, as part of a program that utilizes additional sources of science information and activities. In certain science programs textbooks are used only as occasional reference materials, as in the Science for All Children program (Cawley, Miller, Sentman, & Bennett, 1993). Nearly all textbook series now include activities for students to perform and an assortment of laboratory materials to assist them in doing so.

Textbook use has both advantages and disadvantages. Textbooks can serve as excellent teacher resources, can be of great assistance to the beginning teacher, can help organize a science program, and are durable. On the other hand, they require complex literacy and study skills competence, are often abstract, typically have readability levels above the reading levels of students, may be the only source of science information, become outdated, and may not be in concert with the curricular needs or goals for students.

Student inability to read grade-level materials looms as the most significant barrier to using science texts with special populations. However, as Armbruster and Anderson (1988) note, problems with textbooks can also arise because of three other factors: structure (arrangement of ideas), coherence (smoothness in the way ideas stick together), and audience appropriateness (suitability to reader's level of knowledge and skills). Certainly, teachers do not have the time to regularly rewrite textual material to meet the needs of their students, nor should they do so. However, if the textbook approach is used, certain textbook series are worth considering because of their deemphasis on reading and their hands-on orientation. Two such texts are the Addison-Wesley and the Houghton Mifflin science programs.

Another problem related to reading ability is the need for certain reading skills for effective comprehension of information. Carnine, Silbert, & Kameenui (1990) highlight some characteristics of content-area materials that can be problematic for students with restricted reading abilities.

- vocabulary: It is usually more difficult than that used in narrative material.
- content: Often the information presented is not familiar to students and can cause conceptual problems.
- style and organization: There may be extensive use of headings/subheadings. Writing is very succinct and matter-of-fact.

- special features: Graphics and illustrations play an important part in presentation of information.

Suggestions for addressing these potential problems are provided later in this chapter.

Hands-On/Activity-Based Approach. Hands-on approaches to science stress the use of process/inquiry skills more than the accumulation of substantive information. They underscore doing and discovery. These programs include those associated with the first wave of science curriculum reform in the 1960s and 1970s, as well as newer programs developed in recent years.

Boekel and Steele (1972) believe that many aspects of these approaches can be used with students with disabilities, and others (Davies & Ball, 1978; Esler, Midgett, & Bird, 1977) have documented the use of process-oriented materials with special students. Most importantly, Scruggs et al. (1993) found that students with learning disabilities who were exposed to activity-oriented science experiences performed better on follow-up unit testing than those students who used a textbook approach. Atwood and Oldham (1985) found that this type of curricular orientation worked well for students with special needs who were mainstreamed into regular education settings.

For the most part these approaches require teachers to be facilitators of learning rather than distributors of information or fonts of knowledge. Not every teacher is comfortable with these curricula because of this facilitating role, but Kyle, Bonnstetter, McClosky, and Fults (1985) found that students tend to prefer this type of science program to more traditional approaches.

To help teachers who are reticent to try activity-based or hands-on experiences with their students, Salend (1998) suggests several guidelines for success. The first guideline involves the use of a structured learning cycle when introducing activity-oriented lessons. This instructional cycle involves a sequence of learning phases: (a) engagement; (b) exploration; (c) development; and (d) extension (Guillaume, Yopp, & Yopp, 1996). The *engagement phase* is designed so that real-life activities or problems are used to motivate the students to want to learn the content area and to assess prior knowledge of the topic. The *exploration phase* involves the development of hypotheses. Students generate ideas and ask questions concerning the real-life problem. Once these ideas and questions are formulated, the students explore/manipulate the contents/equipment of the problem to predict how the problem might be addressed. The third phase of teaching is the *development phase*. In this phase students gather information and make conclusions. The resources the students use to gather information are usually multimedia sources as well as qualified professionals. The final phase involves the *extension phase* of the students learning by applying their acquired knowledge to new or similar situations.

Another guideline that Salend (1998) provides emphasizes the use of real-life situations. For example, the instructional cycle can be applied to summer jobs. A teacher might *engage* the students with the content of establishing the job of cutting lawns for the summer. To do so, he brings in several broken lawn mowers; the students can *explore* the mowers, *develop skills* to fix them, and finally *extend* their knowledge to fixing other machines or appliances.

A final guideline concerns the organization of instruction around "big ideas" (Salend, 1998). These refer to "important concepts or principles that help students organize, connect, and apply material so that they see a meaningful relationship between the material and their own lives" (p. 70). Interdisciplinary themes are good ways to develop big ideas. For example, science, music, art, literature, and social science can be integrated under a common theme that will (a) motivate students; (b) provide opportunities to teach high-level content; and (c) relate content to real life (Savage & Armstrong, 1996).

Regardless of the guidelines and programs that can be used with learners with mild disabilities, attention to classroom and behavior management is essential because the instructional situations encourage more movement and less overt structure. Furthermore, hands-on activities may involve the use of equipment and materials that can be dangerous if used improperly. Some students require more instructional structure and direction than is suggested in these programs. For instance, it may be necessary to prepare data collection sheets ahead of time to help students. Students may also require some teacher-directed intervention to understand certain vocabulary concepts and facts. It is important that teachers become familiar with these programs and the roles they will be required to play before trying to use the materials (Price et al., 1982; Shymanksy, 1989).

A variety of commercial programs that accentuate a hands-on approach to teaching science are available. These programs are worth considering for use with students who have learning-related disabilities because they emphasize relevance to students, fewer topics covered, active engagement in the activities, integration of science with other subject areas, and better balance of content and process. Table 12–3 lists some of these programs and provides descriptive information about them.

Programs Designed for Special Students. Although not plentiful, materials developed specifically for special populations are available. Four programs are discussed here (Table 12–4). The first program, Science Activities for the Visually Impaired (SAVI)/Science Enrichment for Learners with Physical Handicaps (SELPH) is a major adaptation of selected topics from the Science Curriculum Improvement Study (SCIS) program. SAVI was the original program and was later modified for other special populations and labeled SELPH. The three other curricula—Me Now, Me and My Environment, and Me in the Future—were developed by the Biological Sciences Curriculum Study (BSCS). These programs were originally designed for students with mental retardation and include multicomponent kits for conducting science activities. Their attraction is that they avoid the problems associated with programs that require reading and focus on topics that are relevant to students. The teacher manuals provide precise directions for carrying out the activities.

Customized Approaches. Many special education teachers who teach science in self-

TABLE 12–3
The new science programs

Science Program	Source	Features
Delta Science Modules	Delta Education	■ allows schools to develop their own scope and sequence by selecting modules that relate to local situation
		■ modules designed for 3–5 week duration
		■ emphasizes the application of scientific concepts and higher order thinking
		■ integrates science-technology issues whenever possible
		■ hands-on
Full Option	*Encyclopedia Britannica*	■ 27 modules designed for grades K-6
		■ hands-on
Science and Technology for Children	National Science Resource Center Smithsonian Institute	■ thematic-based program
		■ activities-oriented
		■ intensive teacher in-service component

contained settings have developed their own curricula. With this approach the content of the program needs careful consideration. If students are to be moved into regular class settings, content should be similar to that of the general education curriculum. For other students a more functional science program based on life skills needed in adulthood might be more appropriate.

Regardless of the specific content, however, a customized program must be sequenced appropriately with regard to concept development and teaching strategies (Price et al., 1982). Teachers interested in designing their own curricula should first consult other resources. One such resource is the scope and sequence chart of a commercial program. Another resource of note is an instructor's manual from any of the Hubbard materials

(e.g., Me and My Environment); each includes a good discussion on developing science curricula.

Another type of customized approach being implemented in some settings is integrated programming. The major objective of this type of programming is to integrate science and other subject and skill areas. Although this programming model has been used effectively with gifted students (e.g., Nakashima & Patton, 1989), it can also be used with students with mild disabilities (Patton & Nakashima, 1987). An example of how a science topic can be integrated with other subject and skill areas will be highlighted later in this chapter.

Instructional Practices

Like any other subject area, science requires sound instructional practices that maximize the

TABLE 12–4
Description of specialized programs

Program	Publisher	Grade Range	Features	Topics/ Content	Components
Science Activities for the Visually Impaired (SAVI)/ Science Enrichment for Learners with Physical Handicaps (SELPH)	Center for Multisensory Learning (Lawrence Hall of Science, University of California, Berkeley)	1 to 10	Life and physical science program designed for students with visual (SAVI) or physical and learning problems (SELPH) SAVI and SELPH contain the same content Activity-oriented Multisensory Can be used in a range of settings	Measurement Structures of life Scientific reasoning Communications Magnetism and electricity Mixtures and solutions Environments Kitchen inter-actions Environmental energy	Activity folios for each module Training manual Materials kit (special equip-ment designed for visually im-paired students is available)
Me Now	Hubbard	Upper elemen-tary	Life science program designed for stu-dents who are mildly retarded Two-year sequence Primary focus on systems of the human body Activity-oriented Inquiry-oriented Functional language used Reading minimized Activities present in small, discrete units	Digestion and circulation Respiration and body waste Movement, support, and sensory pro-cesses Growth and development	Teacher's guides Multimedia supple-mentary materials Supplies kit Student work-sheets Evaluation material
Me and My Environment	Hubbard	Junior high school	Environmental science program designed for stu-dents who are mildly retarded Three-year sequence Activity-oriented	Exploring my environment Me as an envi-ronment Energy rela-tionships in my environment	Teacher's guides Multimedia supple-mentary materials (e.g., slides, games) Supplies kit Student worksheets

(*continued*)

TABLE 12-4 *(Continued)*

Program	Publisher	Grade Range	Features	Topics/Content	Components
			Inquiry-oriented Reading minimized Career education focus	Transfer and cycling of materials in my environment	
Me in the Future	Hubbard	High school	Culmination of other Hubbard programs Activity-oriented Adult interest level Low readability level	Vocations Leisure Daily living skills	Teacher's guides Multimedia supplementary materials Supplies kit

probability that learning will occur. The components of effective instruction discussed in Chapters 1 and 4 also apply to science instruction.

Selected instructional practices are highlighted here.

Classroom Management and Organization. Teachers must be able to control their classrooms. This objective can be achieved by establishing rules and procedures for specific tasks and appropriate functioning, as mentioned earlier. This requirement is especially important for science activities of a hands-on nature that use potentially dangerous materials. It is helpful to establish systematic procedures for distributing and collecting materials before, during, and after an activity or class period. One method is to designate part of the room as the science area and to conduct most science instruction in this area. Within this area or wherever science instruction occurs, tables should be used as much as possible.

Safety is a primary concern. Teachers should anticipate and prepare for potential problems. All planned science activities should be performed ahead of time, and equipment should be checked to ensure that it is in proper working condition. Students' eyes should be protected, fire extinguishers should be readily available, and safety in-

structions should be demonstrated and practiced regularly. Dangerous or potentially dangerous materials should be secured and off-limits signs posted to protect students from injury and the teacher from liability. It is also advisable to consult the safety guidelines of the school district.

Inquiry Skills. One of the goals of science instruction is skill development. Many different abilities can be addressed, including organizational, basic academic, and social/behavioral skills. Other specific inquiry-oriented skills are not only extremely useful in science but also beneficial in other areas of school and life as well. These skills are described here (as adapted from Cain & Evans, 1984, pp. 8–9).

- observation: using the senses to find out about subjects and events
- measurement: making quantitative observations
- classification: grouping things according to similarities or differences
- communication: using the written and spoken word, drawings, diagrams, or tables to transmit information and ideas to others
- data collection, organization, and graphing: making quantitative data sensible, primarily through graphic techniques

- inference: explaining an observation or set of observations
- prediction: making forecasts of future events or conditions, based on observations or inferences
- data interpretation: finding patterns among sets of data that lead to the construction of inferences, predictions, or hypotheses
- formulation of hypotheses: making educated guesses based on evidence that can be tested
- experimentation: investigating, manipulating, and testing to determine a result

These inquiry skills should be included regularly in science activities. Most activities require some of these skills; however, the goal is to get students to use as many of them as often as possible. An example of each inquiry skill can be demonstrated from one of the subtopics from a marine biology unit of study. Students worked regularly with hermit crabs and in so doing they used all of the inquiry skills, as listed in Table 12-5.

Elements of a Science Lesson. Effective instruction incorporates variety and systematic presentation of material. Some science lessons might be devoted to discussing a topic of current interest, using educational media, reading science materials, listening to a guest speaker, going on a field trip, or carrying out activities in the classroom. However, all science lessons should be planned to accommodate individual differences and follow an organizational schema that provides a certain structure that is helpful to teachers and to students. The actual format of the instructional period depends to a great degree on the nature of the lesson. For most lessons, the class session can be organized into five major components: introduction, attention getting and motivation, data gathering, data processing, and closure (Cain & Evans, 1990).

The first component of a lesson should be an introduction to the day and an update on what was done previously. The primary purpose of this piece of the lesson is administrative and management related. The teacher's goal should be to get the students settled, prepared, and focused. If done properly, it will serve as a nice transition to the beginning phase of the actual science lesson.

Attention-getting and motivating techniques attempt to engage students in the lesson. They

TABLE 12–5
Examples of inquiry skills

Inquiry Skill	Hermit Crab Activity
Observation	Identification of body parts
Measurement	Timing of crab races
Classification	Species identification
Communication	Description of habitat poetry
Data collection, organization, and graphing	Shells preferred by crabs
Inference	How crab attaches to inside of shell
Prediction	Location/movement of crabs as a function of time of day and tides
Data interpretation	Conclusions derived from information collected (e.g., species data)
Hypothesis generation	Generation of ideas about how often crabs change shells based on growth patterns
Experimentation	How crabs will react to changes in their habitats

FIGURE 12–4
Graphic organizer for "Supporting the Body" chapter

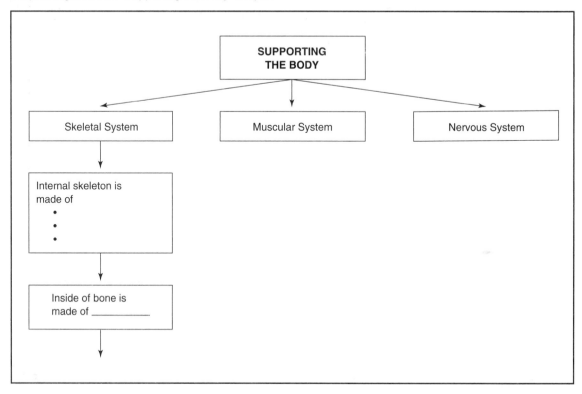

Mnemonic Strategies. Mnemonic strategies are useful for helping students deal with vocabulary, scientific terminology, and other label tasks that are associated with science instruction. Mastropieri and Scruggs (1995) describe mnemonic strategies as the "pairing of unfamiliar, new terminology with acoustically similar, familiar words (keywords) and associating the keyword with the definition" (pp. 11–12). Figure 12-5 provides examples of this technique for remembering the meaning of deciduous and evergreen trees.

Conceptual Models. Since students with special needs who are placed in regular education courses at the secondary level are beset by a deluge of science information, techniques need to be implemented to assist them to master the content presented. Woodward and Noell (1992) suggest that less material should be covered and that con-

ceptual models should be taught to students. They remark, "When scientific models relate common, underlying principles to a variety of events or phenomena, they communicate sameness" (p. 42). If students are to truly understand the content that is being presented in secondary-level science courses, students with special needs must recognize this sameness across different topics.

Adapting Laboratory Materials. It may be necessary to provide adaptations to many elements of an activity-oriented general education program. Science materials at the secondary level, even if they include hands-on activities through laboratory experiences, often require some reading and the understanding of more complex vocabulary and advanced concepts. Sasaki and Serna (1995) demonstrate how a middle school science program developed for general education, the Foundational Approach to Science Teaching I

FIGURE 12–5

Mnemonic illustration of
deciduous and evergreen trees

From "Reconstructive Elaboration: Strategies for Adapting Content Area Information,"
by M. A. Mastropieri and T. E. Scruggs, 1989, *Academic Therapy, 24*(4), p. 394. Copyright 1989 by PRO-ED, Inc. Reprinted with permission.

(FAST 1) (Pottenger & Young, 1992) could be adapted for use with students with mild disabilities. Through the use of techniques such as notebooks, direct vocabulary development, and thorough introduction to laboratory procedures, students were able to perform successfully in these general education materials.

SCIENCE ACTIVITIES

1. Have students build the lightest possible device capable of keeping a raw egg unharmed when dropped from a height of 10 to 20 feet.
2. Experiment with decomposition by burying various items in a container filled with soil. Mark the items with a stick and label. Add moisture periodically. After a few weeks examine the buried items, record what is found, and discuss the results (Cain & Evans, 1984).
3. Study anatomy by examining parts of a chicken. This is an easy animal to get, and it lends itself well to study because students are familiar with it.

4. Have pupils collect plant seeds or small plants; ask them to describe what they see when the seeds are planted or the plants are small. Have them make periodic written observations to demonstrate that plants do change. Have them place the plants under different conditions—no water, no sun, too much water—and observe the results.
5. So that pupils can better understand weather changes, have them keep weather charts that record temperature on different days, rain or snow accumulation, and other data students may want to collect. Questions to ask are, "Does it rain when the sun shines?" "What happens to water when you freeze it?" "What does snow look like close up?"
6. Science in the home provides a wealth of opportunities for a science unit: What makes an iron work? What causes cakes to rise? What causes bread to mildew?
7. Depending on students' ages and the area from which they originate, take students to farms where food is grown and/or animals

are raised. Older pupils or pupils who live in farming regions can actually grow food products or raise farm animals.

8. Build small models of simple machines, such as a pulley, wheel and axle, wedge, screw, and inclined plane. Use a spring scale to measure the amount of energy saved by using the machines to move and raise books or other heavy objects.

9. A study of different types of plants and flowers can be aided by keeping a log of the plants found for the project. The log can be most effective if the plants are sketched or pressed. (To press, put the plant in a catalog with heavy objects on top and leave it for approximately 4 to 6 days.)

10. To aid students with the vocabulary that they encounter in science, have them make small books for each unit. They should take white paper and divide it into fourths. In each quarter they should write a vocabulary word, define it in their own words, illustrate it, and explain their illustration. Then have them design a title page for the unit, cut out the pages, and staple the book together (Heukerott, 1987).

11. To aid students in memorizing information, first state the information for them in a sentence. Then have the students repeat the sentence to you and act out the meaning of the sentence motorically. To test their memory, cue the students with the main verb, and have them state the entire sentence (Freides & Messina, 1986).

12. Vocabulary usage and comprehension can be strengthened by having students participate in round-robin stories. After science vocabulary has been introduced, have the students sit in a circle. Choose a student to begin a story, following the rule that one of the words just introduced must be included. At some point tell the student to stop and ask the next student to continue the story. Continue this pattern around the circle until all the words have been used. Be sure that the task of continuing the story rests with you once in a while (Kotting, 1987).

13. Science at work requires adolescents to identify basic elements of science that they encounter in their work settings. This activity can involve notebooks, essays, oral reports, or whatever the teacher decides is appropriate to students' abilities, work roles, industry or business, and understanding of science principles. For example, one student may demonstrate the sterilization of eating utensils at the school cafeteria, and another may report on the necessity of lubrication for machines.

14. Many students have trouble comprehending the concept of environment. Direct students to make notes on their surroundings on an index card. Have them print their first and last names in the center of the card. In the upper right corner they should write the average temperature of their environment; in the upper left corner, the name of an animal that lives in their environment. Have them write something they really like about their environment. In the lower left corner they can give the name of something they think would improve their environment; in the lower right corner, the name of a plant that lives in their environment (Richardson, Harris, & Sparks, 1979).

15. Examine different types of soil to see which holds water best. To make a sieve, punch holes in the bottom of a cup. Place a jar underneath the cup. Ask students to bring in soil from a garden and around the school. Try to sample clay, sand, and humus. Fill the sieve with one type of soil, and use a watch to record how fast water runs through. Discuss why soil is important for plants to grow in the garden. Encourage students to create their own gardens (Sund, Tillery, & Trowbridge, 1970).

16. Make insect mounts. Direct students to collect insects around their home and near the school. Obtain carbon tetrachloride from the science department. To kill the insects, place a false bottom in a jar, place a cotton ball soaked in carbon tetrachloride under it, and place the insect on top of the false bottom. This will keep the insect from getting entangled in the

cotton. Pin the insects to cardboard. Make labels for identification. Discuss insect behavior and the variety of insects.

17. Obtain a set of teeth from a dentist and place them in a glass of soft drink. Have students make observations over several days. Place a tooth in plain water as a control. Discuss the effect of sugar on tooth decay. Invite a dental hygienist to speak to the class about dental care.

18. Aquariums and terrariums in the classroom give students an opportunity to observe the behavior of communities of organisms. Many books show how to construct these items.

19. To find out what color absorbs the sun's heat the most, take students outside and place an ice cube on various colors of construction paper. Which cube melts first? Would a white shirt be cooler than a brown shirt? Would a house with a white roof be cooler than a house with a dark roof? (Oak Ridge Associated Universities, 1978).

20. Arrange a field trip to a local zoo so that students can observe the behaviors of a variety of animals. Encourage students to take cameras and use their pictures as part of a bulletin board display. The purpose for the trip should be clearly stated, and a handout to guide observations at the zoo is helpful. Encourage students to ask questions of the zoo keepers.

21. Explore ways that machines transfer force and make work easier. The egg beater and bicycle are great examples. Have students note how gears change the direction of force. What turns the big wheel? The small wheel? Have the students count the number of turns the rear wheel makes for one turn of the pedal on a bicycle. Look at general merchandise catalogs for pictures of different kinds of machines. Demonstrate care and maintenance of bearings, gears, and so on (Blough & Schwartz, 1974).

22. Explore the composition, construction, and operation of a book of matches or a cigarette lighter. Talk about the three elements essential to fire: oxygen, heat, and fuel (the fire triangle).

Discuss ways to extinguish fire by removing one of the three elements.

23. Discuss the effects of air temperature on the activity level of humans and insects. Collect a black cricket. Have students count the number of times it chirps in 14 seconds. Add 40 to that number to find the approximate air temperature. Compare the estimate with the actual thermometer reading. Discuss the reason for this relationship (Howe, Joseph, & Victor, 1971).

24. Find out whether birdseed is alive or dead. Ask students to suggest a way to find out. Make observations and measurements. Draw conclusions about dormancy and its purpose. This is an excellent activity for introducing the scientific method, because it triggers curiosity (Baker, 1981).

TEACHING SOCIAL STUDIES TO SPECIAL LEARNERS

More and more attention is being paid to the adult adjustment needs of special learners. As a result, preparing them to be active, competent citizens and contributing members of their communities has become a major goal of education. Perhaps as much as any other subject area, social studies attempts to do this. At its very core is citizenship education. Moreover, social studies promotes informational skills and value development that contribute substantially to an understanding of human diversity, societal complexity, and general world knowledge.

We know very little about how best to teach social studies to students with special needs (Passe & Beattie, 1994). Of all the subject areas to which students with special needs are exposed, social studies has been studied and written about the least. In recent years much more attention has been paid to science than to its companion subject area, social studies; special issues of different journals (*Remedial and Special Education* and *Teaching Exceptional Children*) have been dedicated to science instruction and students with mild disabilities.

Nature of Social Studies Education for Students with Special Needs

The specific goals of social studies are not generally agreed upon but can be extracted from various sources—professional organizations and councils, state program objectives, competency requirements, and professional literature. Goals have also been predicated on the pervading philosophy of the times.

Prior to the late 1970s, the "new social studies" movement was prevalent, espousing inquiry-oriented techniques and including disciplines beyond history, geography, and civics (Birchell & Taylor, 1986). This orientation was replaced in the late 1970s and early 1980s by a "back-to-basics" movement that emphasized five primary areas: reading skill development; American history and heritage; geography (including map and globe skills); American government; and tradition, values, attitudes, and beliefs (Birchell & Taylor, 1986). A new orientation has arisen in response to the criticism of social studies programs that emerged during the 1980s. McGowan and Guzzetti (1991) summarize the spirit of these reforms.

> Reformers advance a "kinder, gentler" social studies, founded on a content framework largely drawn from history and geography, but enhanced with teaching strategies encouraging student engagement, subject matter integration, global awareness, social participation, and the formation/application of significant ideas. (p. 16)

In 1992, the Board of Directors of The National Council for the Social Studies (NCSS) adopted the following definition of social studies:

> Social studies is the integrated study of the social sciences and humanities to promote civic competence. Within the school program, social studies provides coordinated, systematic study drawing upon such disciplines as anthropology, archaeology, economics, geography, history, law, philosophy, political science, psychology, religion, and sociology, as well as appropriate content from the humanities, mathematics, and natural sciences. The primary purpose of social studies is to help young people develop the ability to make informed and reasoned decisions for the public good as citizens of a culturally diverse, democratic society in an interdependent world.

The NCSS (1994) has also issued curriculum standards for social studies, which include ten thematic strands that should pervade every level of schooling. The strands are interrelated and draw from all the disciplines associated with this area. The ten thematic strands include:

- culture
- time, continuity, and change
- people, place, and environment
- individual development and identity
- individuals, groups, and institutions
- power, authority, and governance
- production, distribution, and consumption
- science, technology, and society
- global connections
- civic ideals and practices

As regards whether these themes apply to special students, if we want these students to be well-adjusted, contributing members of society, then these goals are well worth our attention. However, program planning must be guided by a realistic appraisal of student values and abilities, as well as current and future needs.

A significant number of learners with mild disabilities are not receiving social studies instruction. In a study of special education classes for students with mild and moderate learning problems, Patton, Polloway, and Cronin (1987) found that no social studies instruction was occurring in almost one third of classes where it should be taught. What could not be determined was the appropriateness of the social studies programs that were offered.

Social studies is a subject area that contains many complex topics, issues, and concepts. For instance, the concept of "community" is abstract, requiring certain cognitive and conceptual skills. The subject also favors students with rich experiential backgrounds, who find many topics more meaningful. In addition, most social studies classes demand proficiency in a variety of areas, particularly reading, writing, oral expression, study, and library skills. Smith and Smith (1990) suggest that students need a significant set of social studies skills, as indicated here.

- acquiring information: reading, study skills, information search, technical skills (e.g., computer)
- organizing and using information: classifying, interpreting, analyzing, summarizing, synthesizing, evaluating, decision making
- participating socially: personal skills, group interaction, social and political skills (i.e., related to group dynamics) (p. 5)

Another concern related to social studies instruction is the training background of special education teachers, many of whom feel unprepared to teach social studies. Patton et al. (1987) found that 43% of the special education teachers they surveyed had no training in how to teach this subject. Many secondary-level special education teachers, in particular, are unfamiliar with curriculum, instructional practices, and appropriate materials in this area. With the increasing numbers of students with special needs being taught in inclusive settings, teachers will need to be able to accommodate their needs in the context of the demands of the general social studies classes.

Nonetheless, teachers need not be intimidated by this subject area and must realize that difficulties can be overcome. Much like science, social studies can be extremely interesting and relevant to students.

Content of Social Studies Instruction

The content (i.e., scope and sequence) of any social studies program for special education students is likely to depend on where the student receives such instruction. If students are placed in general education classes, the nature of the curriculum will be dictated by that program. A program that parallels the regular curriculum is indicated for some students who remain in special education settings but for whom the topics covered in the general education program are appropriate; others, especially students at the secondary level who will not go on to postsec-

ondary education, can benefit from a program that emphasizes life skills and content that will be useful to them in adjusting to adulthood.

For the most part the K through 12 curricular sequence in social studies has been fairly standard in classrooms across the nation. The common themes by grade level are reflected in Table 12-8, which reveals two major patterns: a focus in Grades K to 6 on expanding environments (movement from family/neighborhood to world perspective), followed by recurrent attention (Grades 7 to 9 and 10 to 12) on contracting environments. Other subjects like economics may be taken as well.

This sequence represents social studies curricula in general, even though not all commercially available textbook series adhere to this. The newly issued themes designed to guide social studies curriculum are to be woven into the sequence depicted in Table 12-7. The scope of the social studies curriculum at the high school level may vary considerably from one state to another; however, courses such as U.S. history and world history are typically required for gradua-

TABLE 12–8

Typical social studies themes by grade level

Grade Level	Theme
K	Self, school, community, home
1	Families
2	Neighborhoods
3	Communities
4	State history, geographic regions
5	United States history
6	World cultures, western hemisphere
7	World geography or history
8	American history
9	Civics or world cultures
10	World history
11	American history
12	American government

tion. In addition, particular states commonly require that students take units pertaining to their own state histories and cultures (e.g., fourth- and eleventh-graders in Hawaii take a course entitled *Hawaiiana*).

Approaches to Teaching Social Studies

How social studies should be taught and what should be addressed have always been debatable topics. Yet certain emphases or orientations have been observed at various times, as reported earlier in the chapter.

Of the various ways to cover social studies content, the most frequently used technique in regular education is the textbook, lecture, and discussion format. This was the case in the 1970s (Turner, 1976) and remained so during the 1980s and in to the 1990s (Hayes, 1988; Steinbrink & Jones, 1991; Woodward, Elliott, & Nagel, 1986). Furthermore, Patton et al. (1987) found that approximately 37% of the special education teachers who teach social studies use a textbook as the basis of their program. It is also likely that many of the teachers (an additional 40%) who indicated that they used a combination of approaches used textbooks as the primary vehicle for covering content.

The major approaches discussed in this section fall into three categories: traditional content approach, inquiry approach, and balanced approach. These approaches are based on Brophy's (1990) categorical distinctions, which resulted from his study of social studies instruction. All of them are discussed here and summarized in Table 12–9.

Traditional Content Approach. This approach is characterized by an emphasis on textbooks, lectures, and discussion. Teachers familiar with textbook series in social studies know that the most significant problem is readability or, more specifically, students' inability to comprehend the material. Woodward and Noell (1992) note the complexity of the problem.

Important topics in social studies texts, for example, are discussed insufficiently, references are ambiguous, too many concepts are presented in too short a space, and a considerable amount of background knowledge is simply assumed (p. 40).

Shepherd and Ragan (1982) corroborate the problems associated with textbooks, suggesting that elementary social studies textbooks may have the highest readability levels of any textual material at a particular grade level. This fact remains problematic for at least two reasons. First, many students with special needs are not effective readers and have a difficult time comprehending grade-level materials. Second, as implied by Woodward and Noell (1992), readability is compounded by a number of other dimensions, thus complicating the comprehension process. These factors need to be considered in the selection of any material-textbook, supplement, or worksheet.

In their evaluation of 10 eighth-grade history textbooks, Kinder, Bursuck, and Epstein (1992) found that the readability of all the textbooks was 1 or more years above the grade level. They also found important differences in certain organizational dimensions of the textbooks that have an effect on a student's ability to use them successfully.

Most major publishers have developed a social studies series, and some of the series seem to accommodate individual differences better than others. Teachers should examine these series closely, looking for certain features in the student materials (e.g., controlled reading levels, organization, language demands, conceptual level) and in the teacher materials (e.g., guidelines for modifying instruction, additional activity-oriented ideas for covering the topic, supplemental materials).

Two commercial series have been adapted extensively for use with visually impaired students through Project MAVIS (Materials Adaptations for Visually Impaired Students in the Social Studies), a federally funded project awarded to the Social Science Education Consortium. The two programs adapted were the Houghton Mifflin Windows on Our World and the Silver Burdett Social Science series. One very interesting conclusion derived from the project was that large-scale literal adaptation, although useful to teachers and students, is not feasible because of its expense and the tendency of materials to become dated too quickly (Singleton, 1982).

Inquiry Approach. This approach, also referred to as a process approach, puts a premium on skills used in solving problems or addressing issues, much like the process-oriented approach discussed in the science section. Kelly (1979) indicates that this approach is "conducive to development of initiative, judgment, and good study habits" (p. 130). Although attractive in many ways, this approach requires that students possess certain abilities and prerequisite skills such as the social studies skills previously mentioned. Teachers also need specific skills, and for this reason many find the approach unattractive (Jarolimek, 1981).

A totally inquiry-oriented approach for teaching social studies to learners with special needs must be used with caution. As in science, the use of process approaches with special students is not prohibited, but a certain amount of structured instruction that helps students make connections across topics and concepts (Kinder & Bursuck, 1993) is probably necessary. Thus, it is important first to assess whether students can effectively use inquiry skills and then to present a schema of substantive information via a systematic teaching paradigm.

Curtis and Shaver (1980) report that a social studies program that is inquiry oriented and focuses primarily on the study of contemporary problems relevant to students can be employed effectively with special students. They contend that such a program is interesting to students because it deals with local community issues and helps develop decision-making skills. These authors also stress that special students "can engage in more sophisticated studies than those described in many social studies curriculum guides" (p. 307). Special learners are too infrequently afforded opportunities to experience innovative, dynamic programs. Such programs should be considered, but their effectiveness should be evaluated.

Others in the field of social studies (Evans, 1989; Massialas, 1989) promote the use of issue-centered approaches for teaching social studies. To date, programs that are totally devoted to this approach have found only limited acceptance.

Balanced Approaches. Many teachers have developed social studies programs that combine features of the traditional content approach with inquiry- or issue-oriented techniques. For example, a program might use a textbook but also regularly include inquiry-oriented activities. Some programs have incorporated the use of a newspaper as a supplement to the text (Gregory, 1979); other programs have used a newspaper as the primary vehicle for instruction.

Many of these programs are developed at a local level. They can be engaging, relevant, and appropriate for special learners. However, teachers should consult available resources for assistance in developing such curricula. It may be important that the customized curriculum not deviate too much from the regular curriculum in terms of general content even though methodology and selected topics may be very different.

Instructional Practices

We have little documented information on how to teach social studies effectively to special learners (Passe & Beattie, 1994). However, we do know that many of the instructional principles discussed in Chapter 4 and in this chapter's section on science instruction are equally relevant to this subject area. Other techniques are described here.

General Instructional Suggestions. Teaching social studies can involve many different instructional practices. Within the classroom setting, teachers can employ discussions, demonstrations, and learning centers. Other intriguing techniques involve simulation activities, role playing, or dramatic improvisation (Wagener, 1977). The efficient use of media is another way of making content interesting and instructionally relevant. A substantial number of videotapes and CD-ROM media are available for instructional use. Another approach is to immerse students in a culture. For example, if the topic under consideration is a particular foreign country and its culture, then students might be introduced to its food, dress, music, and any other identifiable characteristics.

Outside the classroom, field experiences to museums, historical sites, and community locations can be engaging. The local neighborhood can serve as a plentiful and primary source of in-

TABLE 12–9

A summary of instructional approaches in social studies

Approach	Positive Features	Negative Features	Components
Traditional content	Has been simplified in recent series (Birchell & Taylor, 1986) Includes good aesthetic features (e.g., illustrations) Includes good resource/reference materials Introduces content-related terms (Armstrong, 1984) Lessens teacher's workload (i.e., preparation time)	Presents readability problems Introduces language complexity Develops too many concepts too quickly Lacks sufficient organizational aids (e.g., headings and subheadings (Adams, Carnine, & Gersten, 1982) Makes understanding difficult because of superficial and disconnected coverage of topics (Woodward, Elliott, & Nagel, 1986) Does not adequately accommodate special learners in teacher's guides Is typically used only in combination with discussion	Teacher's guide Student text Student workbook Supplemental materials (e.g., filmstrips)

formation. Weitzman (1975) has capitalized on this idea in his excellent book *My Backyard History Book.* For instance, the history and culture associated with any local cemetery are bountiful but often overlooked. Another outside resource is people from the community who can easily augment and embellish most social studies programs.

It is also well worth the effort to obtain materials such as maps, globes, charts, diagrams, and graphs. In addition, teachers should keep uptodate on the multimedia software being developed today.

Integration with Other Curricular Areas. Social studies, like science, relates easily to other subject and skill areas. One successful example involves a unit on ecology. The unit starts off with the old Marvin Gaye song "Mercy, Mercy, Me . . . the Ecology." It then explores topics such as government regulation and historical examples of the effect of pollution on the environment. Another example has been demonstrated by Oyama (1986), who took a commonly used basal reading series by Ginn and developed social studies topics for each story.

Music is a great way to demonstrate how other subject areas can be worked into social studies. Much popular music can be easily integrated for this purpose. For instance, songs like Madonna's "Papa, Don't Preach," the Pretenders' "My City Was Gone," and Billy Joel's "We Didn't Start the Fire" all address issues worthy of discussion within a social studies class.

Approach	Positive Features	Negative Features	Components
Inquiry	Emphasizes organizational problem-solving skills Is student-centered Capitalizes on student curiosity and interests	Requires organizational and problem-solving skills Demands self-directed behavior (i.e., independent learning) Requires the use of outside materials that may not be readable and/or available (e.g., in Braille or on tape) Requires special skills of the teacher	Tradebooks Reference materials Library work Field work Media Resource persons Student reports (oral or written) Microcomputers
Balanced	Focuses on students and teacher Is relevant to students' interests and experiences Uses local context Can be student generated Should be activity-oriented Can include a combination of instructional practices Can integrate curricular areas	Typically requires considerable teacher effort May be conceptually confusing Can result in too narrow a focus	Texts Trade books Media Role-playing Simulations Group work Microcomputers

Another method for integrating social studies with other areas is the use of a literature-based approach to instruction (McGowan & Guzzetti, 1991). In this system the primary mechanism for covering social studies topics is through tradebooks. An example of such a resource is the book, *Literature-Based Social Studies: Children's Books and Activities to Enrich the K-5 Curriculum* (Laughlin & Kardaleff, 1991). Many publishers now incorporate literature within elementary-level basal programs.

Computer Applications and Electronic References. Microcomputers are well suited for use in social studies. Years ago software was limited graphically; better products are now being developed regularly, primarily through the growth of CD-ROM media. One of the most exciting uses of microcomputers in this subject area is with CD-ROM and interactive videos, even if this interactive technology is not being used as extensively as would be hoped (Ehman & Glenn, 1991). Other applications are listed here.

- simulations: (e.g., SimCity, Oregon Trail)
- word processing/desktop publishing: school newspapers, reports
- databases: data on community demographics, information on legislators, CD-ROM encyclopedias
- spreadsheets: economic trends, census data
- graphics: demographic information

■ communications: electronic field trips, online data bases, e-mail

In addition to microcomputer applications, electronic references can be of great benefit to teachers of social science. For example, Partin (1998) offers teachers a valuable resource in his *Online Social Studies Resources: 1000 of the most valuable social studies web sites, electronic mailing lists and newsgroups.* In this book, Partin introduces the teacher to the Internet as an educational resource. He offers resources in the areas of (a) general social studies; (b) American history; (c) world history; (d) consumer economics; (e) sociology; (f) psychology; (g) geography; (h) American government; and (i) current events.

Accommodations for Inclusive Settings

A number of techniques can be implemented that will enhance the probability that students with special needs will learn social studies content. Table 12–10 provides many recommendations for accommodating student needs as a function of the typical types of demands/activities encountered in the social studies classroom. Selected suggestions contained in Table 12–9 are discussed in further detail.

Textual Material. Because of the problems many students have with comprehending the content of textbooks, all the suggestions for adapting textual material discussed in the section on science apply here as well. Three social studies examples are provided for reference. An example of a graphic organizer is presented in Figure 12–6. It demonstrates how material can be organized for students in manageable ways. Figure 12–7 is a social studies example of a mnemonic illustration to help students to remember the meaning of "corduroy road."

Potter (1978) suggests using textbook inventories that ask students questions about the structure and organization of the textbook itself. She also recommends reading guides to help students to comprehend the literal information of a reading passage. Another suggestion calls for activities that ask students to restate the material they have read using a cloze procedure (see Chapter 8), Schneider and Brown (1980) suggest using various types of study guides as well as an assortment of concept and vocabulary development activities. Downey (1980) presents the interesting idea of using pictures with historical relevance, often found in history texts, for instructional purposes. Such pictures "can add to the students' intellectual experience . . . [and] can be used to give students practice in critical thinking and in interpreting visual evidence" (p. 93). Felton and Allen (1990) recommend the use of visual materials of a historical nature with students who are poor readers, as they may be able to engage in the discussion on a particular topic if reading is not a factor.

Easy-reading textbooks are a recommended alternative to the traditional regular education textbook. These alternative materials are especially important for students at the secondary level, and most such books serve this population by matching topics that are covered at secondary levels. Memory and McGowan (1985) promote the use of these materials in regular education classes; however, such texts are equally appropriate for use in special classes.

Cooperative Learning. Cooperative learning arrangements are particularly well suited for social studies. Most of the various cooperative learning methods (e.g., jigsaw, teams-games-tournaments) can be used to develop effective instruction. Manning and Lucking (1991) in their discussion of cooperative learning state that cooperative learning can result in increased achievement and self-esteem as well as social benefits.

Linkages. As for history, Kinder and Bursuck (1993) recommend teaching students a schema for analyzing historical events. This schema provides students with a method by which they can see similarities across events. The technique involves having students analyze historical events by applying a "problem-solution-effect" framework. This strategy seems consistently to capture the elements of vari-

50 states, sayings like the following can help: Charles Ton lives west of his friend, the Rich Man (Charleston, West Virginia, and Richmond, Virginia).

17. Study cards can help special needs' learners prepare for exams. On one side of an index card print the important event, name, or place covered in the chapter. On the back make a mark of any sort to use as a key. On another card print information that explains, defines, or identifies the word printed on the first card. Place the same symbol on the back of this second card. Students can then study at school or at home by reading the study cards and matching them. The cards are self-checking, provide instant reinforcement, and let students work on information in small, manageable pieces.

18. Combine practice of written expression and reference skills by having your class make a travel brochure for a state or region of study. Have students use library sources to gather interesting information about a specific area, tourist attraction, or culture found within this region. Then have them prepare a paragraph that highlights the facts and sparks interest in visiting that spot. They can also find pictures that add meaning to their writing. Both pictures and paragraphs can be cut, pasted, and copied to make a brochure for all to read.

19. A number of law-related activities may be appropriate for many special learners. Bogojavlensky et al. (1977) suggest activities related to a variety of topics, such as FBI wanted posters, children's rights, and shoplifting.

20. To develop more ethnic awareness, have students conduct a community survey focusing on different ethnic groups in the area (King, 1980).

21. Have students conduct opinion polls on several topics. This exercise requires students to use various data gathering and interpretative skills.

22. Have students use graphing skills as often as possible. Activities requiring graphing can be found in almost any area; for example, students can graph the number of brothers and sisters they have.

23. As you begin to study a particular time period or event, read aloud to the students from a book that tells about that period. The book should be one that interests them and pulls them into the time (de Lin, DuBois, & McIntosh, 1986). Book bibliographies can be found in social studies periodicals (e.g., Social Education, April/May 1987, pp. 290–300).

24. To combine written expression and thoughts on social issues, have students write. Place a topic on the board and allow them to write on it for 5 minutes. Let the students know that their work will be evaluated on quantity, not quality. This approach encourages them to write freely and helps special needs students to express their thoughts fluently (Tamura & Harstad, 1987).

SUMMARY

It is important to revisit the metaphor of going on a journey introduced earlier in the chapter. The expansive nature of science and social studies makes it impossible to cover all possible topics, just as it is impossible for any of us to visit all national or foreign destinations. However, as good tour guides we can make sure that our travelers, our students, can get the most out of the destinations that we do visit. We cannot guarantee that every student will like where we go, but we have the opportunity and the duty to put together an exciting, meaningful itinerary for them.

TEACHER TIPS

REINVENTING THE CLASSROOM

Combining entrepreneurial skills with academic and social survival skills is a great way to teach students about real life while also motivating them to do well in school. In classrooms like Ronni Cohen's in Wilmington, Delaware, students invent, produce, and market their own products. Ms. Cohen's gifted and talented students at J.H. Burnett Elementary School must master skills in creative thinking, research, math, reading, writing, time management, and budgeting.

With each entrepreneurial project, students are required to keep an inventor's portfolio, in which they write a design abstract and log their thoughts, progress, difficulties, research, and amount of time spent thinking about and working on their projects. A brainstorming session is used to come up with a name for the product, which often uses word play and unusual lettering. Students must design their invention on paper; list the land, labor, and capital requirements needed to produce it; and calculate the cost involved. Students then conduct a market survey, graph a supply schedule, and determine the market clearing price. They create an advertising campaign and when they are done, the students, their peers, and the teacher evaluate each product based on a demonstration.

A recent project, called "Pastamania," required students to invent something that would help people eat spaghetti more neatly. The demonstrations included "Leyla's Loony Linguini Looper," the "Super Slicer Spaghetti Sweeper," and "Spingetti." Final products were required to be demonstrated by a student bystander, who had to figure out how to use the instrument by following the inventor's written instructions.

Ms. Cohen has received many awards for her entrepreneurial education program, including "Entrepreneurship Educator of the Year" and a stipend for summer study at the Kauffman Foundation Center for Entrepreneurial Leadership. She believes that the study of economics can make school exciting for all students.

Garrison (1994).

TEACHER TIPS

McCleery and Tindal (1998) published a study that looked at three different teaching approaches when teaching science to middle school children who are at risk and with learning disabilities in inclusive settings. The experimental conditions included a pull-away group and a Period A group with a comparison group (Period B). The pull-away group received both direct instruction and administration of the outcome measure from a trained teacher. These children were taught concepts, explicit rule-based instruction, and hands-on activities. Period A received hands-on constructivistic instruction from a science teacher but had the final lab and outcome measure administered by the trained teacher who emphasized the concepts within the explicit rule basis. The third group, the comparison group, received only the constructivistic hands-on instruction (no concepts or explicit rules were presented). The results of this experiment showed that the pull-away and Period A group performed at higher levels than the comparison group. The study was quite revealing in terms of the importance of science instruction for all children. The authors recommended the following:

> Although hands-on instruction may be important in framing conundrums and engaging students in the process of scientific inquiry, it cannot replace instruction. Even the use of single lesson lab (provided to period A students) was helpful in improving performance, indicating that instruction in the scientific method should include at least some degree of structured teaching. This structure should be framed on concepts taught with explicit rules. To achieve this kind of literacy, science instruction must move beyond minimally introducing facts or simply exposing students to hands-on activities in a constructivist manner. Rather, direct, systematic instruction must focus on the conceptual knowledge and introduce guided rule-based activities. The planning and implementation of a curriculum must remain clearly connected, as the pull-away intervention demonstrated. Students need to make connections when learning (Patton, 1995; Willis, 1995) .
> . . . . Furthermore, all students need thoughtful instruction, including those with learning disabilities and a risk for failure. With instruction that is conceptually focused and explicit, it may be possible to compensate for the language and background knowledge deficits these students often possess." (pp. 16-17)

McCleery J. A., & Tindal, G. A. (1999). Teaching the scientific method to at-risk students and students with learning disabilities through concept anchoring and explicit instruction. *Remedial and Special Education, 20*, 1, pp. 7–18.

CHAPTER 13

Study Skills

Study skills are essential for all students at all grade levels. Although the appropriate use of study skills is particularly essential at the elementary, middle, and secondary levels, acquisition of study skills should begin early in the educational career. Hoover and Patton (1995) emphasize the need for integrated study skills programs throughout one's schooling and as life-long skills.

Current literature suggests the need for increased study skill development in students with learning problems (Hoover, in press). McKenzie (1991b) stresses that teachers need to provide opportunities for students to use study skills. Strichart and Mangrum (1993) write that some students with learning problems often do not possess adequate study skills for success in schools. Unfortunately, adolescent students with learning disabilities generally have not been taught study skills during elementary education, and as secondary students they often lack sufficient skills to meet their various educational demands (Campbell & Olsen, 1994). Deficiencies are often found in the listening, note-taking, test-taking, time-management, and organizational abilities of secondary students with disabilities. Hoover (in press) and Brown (1995) discuss students' lack of self-management abilities. Deficient test-taking skills in students with mild disabilities are noted by Hoover and Rabideau (1995) and Mercer and Mercer (1996). Thus, evidence continues to suggest the need for an increased emphasis on effective study skills for students with special learning needs at both the elementary and secondary levels of education.

Study skills include those competencies associated with acquiring, recording, organizing, synthesizing, remembering, and using information and ideas. Such skills assist students in confronting the educational tasks associated with the learning process. Students with learning problems often lack strategies for organizing and remembering information (Day & Elkins, 1994). Thus, study skills facilitate mastery of learning components, several of which are listed and defined here.

- acquisition: the crucial first step involved in learning, the first experiences encountered by learners
- recording: any activity in the classroom that requires the learner to record responses, answers, or ideas, including both written and verbal forms of communication
- location: seeking and finding information
- organization: arranging and managing learning activities effectively
- synthesis: integrating elements or parts to form a whole, creating something that was not clearly evident prior to synthesis
- memorization: remembering learned material, storing and recalling or retrieving information

For a more detailed discussion the reader is referred to Hoover and Patton (1995) and Hoover (1995).

TYPES OF STUDY SKILLS

Various study skills exist, including reading at different rates, listening, note-taking/outlining, report writing, making oral presentations, using graphic aids, test taking, using the library, using reference materials, managing time, and managing behavior. Table 13–1 briefly identifies the importance of each of these skills.

Reading at Different Rates

The ability to use different reading rates is an important study skill (Harris & Sipay, 1990) that is most evident as students progress through the grades. Teachers at the elementary and secondary levels must often teach their students how to develop reading rate skills. Although various terms are used to describe the different rates, reading rates include skimming, scanning, rapid reading, normal reading, and careful, or study-type, reading.

Skimming refers to a fast-paced reading rate used to grasp the general idea of material. As students quickly skim materials, they may deliberately gloss over different sections. *Scanning* is also a fast-paced reading rate, used to identify specific items or pieces of information. Students might scan material to search for a name or a telephone

TABLE 13–1
Study skills for effective and efficient learning

Study Skill	Significance for Learning
Reading at different rates	Reading rates should vary with type and length of reading assignments.
Listening	Listening skills are necessary to complete most educational tasks of requirements.
Note-taking/outlining	Effective note-taking/outlining skills allow students to document key points of topics for future study.
Report writing	Report writing is a widely used method of documenting information and expressing ideas.
Making oral presentations	Oral presentations provide students an alternative method to express themselves and report information.
Using graphic aids	Graphic aids may visually depict complex or cumbersome material in a meaningful format.
Test taking	Effective test-taking abilitites help to ensure more accurate assessment of student abilities.
Using the library	Library usage skills facilitate easy access to much information.
Using reference materials	Independent learning may be greatly improved through effective use of reference materials and dictionaries.
Managing time	Time management assists in reducing the number of unfinished assignments and facilitates more effective use of time.
Managing behavior	Self-management assists students to assume responsibility for their own behaviors.

Note. From *Teaching Students with Learning Problems to Use Study Skills: A Teacher's Guide* (p. 6), by J. J. Hoover and J. R. Patton, 1995, Austin, TX: PRO-ED. Copyright 1995 by PRO-ED. Inc. Reprinted with permission.

number. *Rapid reading* is used to review familiar material or grasp main ideas. In rapid reading, some details may be identified, especially if the reader needs the information only temporarily.

Normal rate is used when students must identify details or relationships, solve a problem, or find answers to specific questions. *Careful* or *study-type reading* is a slow rate used to master details, retain or evaluate information, follow directions, or perform other similar tasks (Harris & Sipay, 1990).

The nature of the material being read helps to determine the need for varied reading rates; different activities also require different reading rates. In many reading situations two or more rates must be employed. For example, a student may scan several pages to locate a name and then use normal or study-type reading to learn the details surrounding that name. Varied reading rates, when used appropriately, can be highly effective and important study skills for students with learning problems.

Listening

Listening also is involved in many different activities. Gearheart, Weishahn, and Gearheart (1995) estimate that listening-related activities comprise approximately 66% of a student's school day. Similarly, much instruction in elementary and secondary school relies heavily on the listening abilities of students. Listening includes both hearing and comprehending a spoken message. As was noted earlier in this text, listening involves the ability to receive information, apply meaning, and provide evidence of understanding what was heard. Effective listening is required in formal presentations, conversations, exposure to auditory environmental stimuli, and attending to various audio and audiovisual materials (Gearheart, Weishahn, & Gearheart, 1995). Carlisle and Felbinger (1991), and Lerner (1996) suggest that listening skills can be improved through teaching and practice. Teachers must ensure that classroom conditions facilitate effective listening.

Note-Taking/Outlining

Note-taking/outlining requires students to document major ideas and relevant topics for later use to classify and organize information. Note-taking becomes less difficult once outlining skills have been acquired. Furthermore, study skills associated with reading, listening, thinking, and using vocabulary may improve significantly as students develop effective note-taking abilities. These involve summarizing ideas and organizing information into a useful format for future use. Instruction in this study skill area is particularly appropriate for students with learning problems as they often experience difficulties with organizing and recording information. With sufficient practice and systematic instruction, these students are capable of acquiring note-taking/outlining skills, even though they tend to exhibit some difficulty in the process.

Report Writing

Report writing involves the various skills necessary to organize and present ideas on paper in a meaningful and appropriate way. Included are topic selection, note-taking, organization of ideas, outlining, spelling and punctuation, and sentence structure. Since students with learning problems often have writing problems (Scott, 1991; Welch & Jensen, 1990), teachers must provide direction in each area associated with written reports to ensure satisfactory growth and progress.

Making Oral Presentations

Many skills necessary for report writing are also important in oral presentations of various types—interviews, debates, group discussions, and individual or group presentations. Caution should be used to ensure that oral presentations occur in a nonthreatening environment to minimize student anxiety. Oral presentation tasks should be clearly defined and students need preparation time, guidance, and structure in planning their oral presentations. On occasion, oral reports can be an effective supplement to or substitute for written assignments on occasion.

Using Graphic Aids

Graphic aids—materials such as charts, graphs, maps, models, pictures, or photographs—can be an effective tool to facilitate learning. Graphic aids may (a) assist students in more easily comprehending complex material; (b) facilitate the presentation of large abstractions in small, more manageable pieces; and (c) assist students in ascertaining similarities within and differences among cultural, geographic, and economic situations. Thus, numerous important concepts or events can be addressed through visual materials. Students with disabilities can benefit from graphic aids if they are taught what to look for and attend to while reading and interpreting visual material.

Test Taking

Students in any grade are frequently subjected to various forms of assessment and evaluation. Even though tests are one of the primary means of assessing students in school, many students do not possess sufficient test-taking skills (Good & Brophy, 1995). Test-taking skills are those abilities necessary to prepare and study for tests, take tests, and review test results (Hoover, 1995). They are important to ensure that tests accurately measure students' knowledge rather than their poor test-taking abilities. Test-taking skills include reading and following directions, thinking through questions prior to recording responses, and proofreading and checking answers. Students who lack these abilities can learn them through instruction and practice (Good & Brophy, 1995).

Using the Library

Library activities are periodically required of students at every grade level. Library use requires skills in locating library materials, including using computerized systems; locating films, filmstrips, resource guides, and curriculum materials; and understanding the general layout and organization of the library. Knowledge of the role of the media specialist is also important. Although library use becomes especially important at the secondary level of education, it should be taught gradually and systematically through a student's schooling.

Using Reference Materials

Other study skills become important when students locate materials within the classroom or school library. Students must be knowledgeable about the uses and functions of dictionaries and various other reference materials and must be familiar with various aspects of their design. They must be able to use a table of contents and an index; to alphabetize and use chapter headings; and to understand how content is arranged in dictionaries, encyclopedias, and other reference books. Use of encyclopedias and reference materials on computerized CD-ROM discs is also a necessary reference material study skill. Students with disabilities are capable of acquiring these skills if they receive guided instruction and practice (Lerner, 1996).

Managing Time

Time management involves using time effectively to complete daily assignments and carry out responsibilities. It includes allocating time and organizing the environment to study, complete projects, and balance various aspects of individual schedules effectively. Deshler, Ellis, and Lenz (1996) emphasize that some students with special needs lack awareness of time. Lewis and Doorlag (1998) believe that some students have difficulty with the organization and management of time, which may lead to incorrect or unfinished assignments. As students enter secondary school and work loads increase, effective time management becomes increasingly important. Teachers of learners with disabilities must structure learning situations to encourage students to manage their time responsibly throughout elementary and secondary schooling.

Managing Behavior

Another important tool necessary for learning is the ability to manage one's own behavior, especially during independent work time. Inappropriate behavior can seriously interfere with task completion. Students learn to assume responsibility for their own behavior only when educational programs emphasize self-management and behavior control (Brown, 1995). Self-management assists students to mediate their own behaviors (Swicegood, 1994). Hughes, Korinek, and Gorman (1991) find that self-management training assists with academic improvement for students with special needs. In addition, self-monitoring is effective in increasing time on task and reducing time required to complete tasks. Self-monitoring also reduces the demands on teachers for data collection (Lewis & Doorlag, 1998). In addition, the very act of self-recording or monitoring a behavior often results in desirable changes in that behavior (McCarl, Svobodny, & Beare, 1991). Several programs concerned with self-control and self-management currently exist (Workman & Katz, 1995); the reader is referred also to Chapter 3 for more comprehensive coverage of this topic.

ASSESSMENT OF STUDY SKILLS

Numerous instruments exist for assessing study skills; they include norm-referenced, criterion-referenced, and standardized devices as well as informal and teacher-made checklists. Table 13–2 identifies a variety of such devices. The appropriate use of the various types of instruments is discussed here; selected devices are presented to familiarize the reader with existing instruments, not to provide valuative judgments. The reader should consult each instrument's manual or cited references for additional information and evaluative reviews. Table 13–3 summarizes additional information about selected norm- and criterion-referenced instruments. It is based on information provided by Harris and Sipay (1990); McLoughlin and Lewis (1994); and Salvia and Ysseldyke (1998).

Norm-Referenced Instruments

Although norm-referenced general achievement tests are used in most schools, these measures tend to produce a low estimate of students' performance (McLoughlin & Lewis, 1994). In addition, this type of test may pose particular problems to students who are disabled because such instruments are often timed and require students to record their own answers.

Norm-referenced tests attempt to separate student results into a distribution of scores (Salvia & Ysseldyke, 1998). Such tests assume that students have sufficient independent work habits to monitor their own time and behavior and to sustain attention to the various tasks presented by the tests (McLoughlin & Lewis, 1994). Furthermore, these tests frequently include only a small number of items to assess study skills and thus may not adequately assess student abilities. Nonetheless, group tests are often appropriate as screening devices to identify students who require additional assistance (Salvia & Ysseldyke, 1998). When study-skill assessment does include use of group-administered, norm-referenced general achievements tests, results must be interpreted carefully.

Criterion-Referenced Instruments

Salvia and Ysseldyke (1998) write that criterion-referenced tests measure one's development of skills in terms of absolute levels of mastery. They suggest that criterion-referenced tests be used to assist classroom teachers in program planning. The criterion-referenced tests listed in Table 13–3 may assist in identifying specific study skills that students have or have not mastered.

Standardized Devices

Standardized devices designed to specifically assess study skills also exist. The Study Habits Checklist is designed for students in Grades 9 to 14 and assesses a variety of study-skill areas, providing scores for 37 study skills and habits (Harris & Sipay, 1990). The Study Skills Counseling Evaluation is another instrument normed with secondary and postsecondary students. This instrument contains 50 items within several study-skill areas, including study-time distribution, test-taking, study conditions, and note-taking (McLoughlin & Lewis, 1994).

Informal Devices

Several informal inventories and teacher-made checklists for assessing study skills also exist. The reader is referred to Hoover and Patton (1995) and Strichart, Iannuzzi, and Mangrum (1998) for examples of informal study skills inventories and assesments. Various study habits inventories assess skills including time management, note-taking and outlining, use of graphic aids, reading rates, library use, reference material/dictionary use, and report writing. Despite the availability of these instruments, many teachers find themselves needing to develop their own informal checklists to assess study skills efficiently, as areas requiring further assistance are identified (McLoughlin & Lewis, 1994). Informal analysis of students' study skills may be the easiest aspect of diagnosis for helping students improve their learning abilities. Hoover and Patton (1995) identify several steps that should be followed in an informal assessment of study skills.

TABLE 13–2
Study skills assessment
instruments

Norm-Referenced General Achievement Tests

California Achievement Tests (CTB/McGraw-Hill)
Comprehensive Tests of Basic Skills (CTB/McGraw-Hill)
Iowa Silent Reading Tests (Harcourt Brace Jovanovich)
Iowa Tests of Basic Skills (Riverside)
Sequential Tests of Educational Progress (STEP) (Addison-Wesley)
SRA Achievement Series—Reading (Science Research Associates)
Test of Achievement and Proficiency (Riverside)

Criterion-Referenced Instruments

Analysis of Skills: Reading (Scholastic Testing Service)
BRIGANCE Diagnostic Inventories (Curriculum Associates)
Diagnosis: An Instructional Aid: Reading (Science Research Associates)
Fountain Valley Reading Skills Tests (Zweig Associates)
Individual Pupil Monitoring System—Reading (Riverside)
System for Objective-Based Assessment—Reading (Science Research
    Associates)
System FORE (Foreworks Publications)
Wisconsin Tests for Reading Skill Development (NCS/Educational Systems)

Standardized Study Skill Instruments

Study Habits Checklist (Science Research Associates)
Study Skills Counseling Evaluation (Western Psychological Services)

Informal and Teacher-Made Checklists

Checklist of Reading Abilities (Maier, 1980)
Reading Difficulty Checklist (Ekwall, 1985)
Study Habits Inventory (Devine, 1987)
Study Skills Checklist (Estes & Vaughan, 1985)

1. Identify study skills necessary to complete various tasks or courses.
2. Construct a teacher checklist based on the items identified in Step 1.
3. Construct a student self-analysis checklist similar to the teacher checklist.
4. Develop and implement evaluative activities requiring the student to employ desired study skills.
5. Observe the student during these activities, record results, and have the student complete the self-analysis form.
6. Compare teacher and student checklist results and design a study-skills program to address areas requiring further assistance.

If commercial study-skill devices are inappropriate for a particular situation or student, teachers may want to develop an inventory like the one provided in Figure 13–1.

TEACHING THE DEVELOPMENT OF STUDY SKILLS

Study skills are best learned and used within the actual context of completing meaningful academic tasks (Hoover & Rabideau, 1995). This chapter presents numerous study skill strategies and teaching suggestions; however, these must be used within the overall classroom structure as well as within specific teaching practices. As with any area of edu-

TABLE 13–3

Norm (NR) and criterion-referenced (CR) assessment devices

Test	Type	Subtest	Grade Level
Analysis of Skills: Reading	CR	Study Skills	1 to 8
Brigance Diagnostic Inventories	CR	Reference Skills/Graphs and Maps	K to 12
California Achievement Tests	NR	Reference Skills	3.6 to 12.9
Comprehensive Test of Basic Skills (CTBS)	NR	Reference Skills	1 to 6
Diagnosis: An Instructional Aid: Reading	CR	Study Skills	1 to 6
Fountain Valley Reading Skills Test	CR	Study Skills	1 to 6, Secondary
Individual Pupil Monitoring System	CR	Discrimination/ Study Skills	1 to 6
Iowa Silent Reading Tests	NR	Directed Reading	6 to 14
Iowa Tests of Basic Skills	NR	Reference Materials	1.7 to 9
Sequential Tests of Educational Progress (STEP)	NR	Study Skills	3 to 12
System for Objective-Based Assessment— Reading	CR	Study Skills	K to 9
System FORE	CR	Study Skills	K to 12
Tests of Achievement and Proficiency	NR	Sources of Information	7 to 12
Wisconsin Tests for Reading Skills Development	CR	Study/Reference Skills	K to 6

FIGURE 13–1
Study-skills inventory

Name:_____

Date (pre):_____ Date (post):_____

Rating scale: 1 = not mastered; 2 = partial/mastered/needs improvement; 3 = mastered

Study Skills	Pre	Post	Study Skills	Pre	Post
Reading Rates Scanning			Uses organized note card format		
Skimming			**Report Writing** Organizes thoughts		
Normal rate			Uses proper punctuation		
Rapid reading			Uses proper spelling		
Careful reading			Uses proper grammar		
Listening Attends to listening tasks			**Oral Presentations** Participates freely		
Applies meaning to verbal messages			Organizes presentation		
Filters out auditory distractions			Uses gestures		
Note-taking/Outlining Appropriately uses headings			Speaks clearly		
Takes brief and clear notes			**Use of Graphic Aids** Attends to relevant elements		
Records important information			Understands purposes		
Uses for report writing			Incorporates in presentations		
Uses during lectures			Develops own visuals		
Test Taking Organizes answers			Uses guide words		
Proofreads			Understands uses of each		
Reads and understands directions			Uses for written assignments		
Identifies clue words			Identifies different reference materials		
Properly records responses			**Time Management** Organizes daily activities		
Answers difficult questions last			Completes tasks on time		
Narrows possible correct answers			Organizes weekly/monthly schedules		
Corrects previous test-taking errors			Understands time management		
Library Usage Use of card catalog			Reorganizes time when necessary		
Ability to locate materials			Prioritizes activities		
Organization of library			**Self-Management of Behavior** Monitors own behavior		
Role of media specialist			Changes own behavior		
Reference/Dictionary Usage Identifies components			Thinks before acting		
Makes well-organized outlines			Is responsible for own behavior		

From *Teaching Students with Learning Problems to Use Study Skills: A Teacher's Guide* (pp. 14–16), by J. J. Hoover and J.R. Patton, 1995, Austin, TX: PRO-ED.

cation, the teaching and learning of study skills must be individualized to meet unique learning needs. While the development and application of each study skill is specific to that study skill, a general process may be followed for learning and using study skills in the classroom to assist students in their development. One such process is presented next, followed by a discussion of two effective classroom practices for facilitating additional study skills use for students with learning problems.

Steps to Teaching Study Skills

The classroom development and use of study skills should follow a circular process that begins with assessment and is refined through ongoing evaluation. The four-step process developed by the author includes assessment, selection, implementation, and evaluation. Each of these is discussed next.

Assessment. The initial step in the process of teaching study skills to learners is to assess particular need areas within the classroom to determine the study skills the student must acquire. During this assessment stage, specific study skill areas requiring some development or refinement are determined (e.g., time management, report writing, listening during lectures, etc.). This process is specific to individual learners as unique classroom needs often arise. The process for assessing needed study skills was discussed in a previous section in this chapter and the reader is referred to those procedures. The steps for informally assessing study skills is most appropriate in this process although general information may be obtained through standardized measures. Once the specific study skill areas requiring development have been determined though assessment the second step begins.

Selection. In this second step two major decisions must be made: (1) which study skill area(s) will be initially addressed; and, (2) which methods or strategies will be selected to help the student learn the identified study skill(s). The selection of the study skill(s) to initially address should be determined based on classroom needs,

immediate academic needs, as well as student motivation. Once the study skill to address has been selected, one or more methods or strategies for developing the skill must be determined. Numerous strategies for assisting students with the different study skills are presented in this chapter. Some of these are individual teaching strategies (e.g., follow a consistent form of notetaking, ensure proper reading rates are used, reward effective use of time, review test-taking errors); others are fully developed student strategies that contain procedures where a specific process is outlined and followed (e.g., SQ3R, Guided Lecture Procedure [GLP], COPS, TOWER, ReQuest). In the selection step, the teacher and student must identify the study skill area to address (i.e., reading rate, time management, etc.) and then select teaching and student strategies that will assist the learner to develop and use the targeted study skill more successfully. Once this process has been completed, the third step begins.

Implementation. During the implementation step, the study skill teaching strategies and student strategies are reviewed and applied within actual classroom situations whenever the targeted study skill is needed. Teaching suggestions can easily be incorporated into various lessons and activities to help the student focus on the appropriate use of the study skill. The use of selected student strategies (e.g., ReQuest) requires some preparation and training on the part of the teacher. These student strategies (Table 13–4) each contain specific steps to follow to be properly used in the classroom and learning situation. Initial development of these student strategies should include time for practicing and learning the steps. Most of these contain a few easy steps through which students may easily progress. Once the learner is familiar with and has practiced the steps within the selected strategy, its use should be applied on a regular basis when needing the targeted study skill; (for example, if COPS is selected it should be used regularly when completing written reports). The use of selected teaching suggestions and student study strategies should be continued for a specified amount of

TABLE 13–4

Study skill strategies

Strategy	Task Areas	Process	Description

CAN-DO	Acquiring Content	Create list of items to learn
		Ask self if list is complete
		Note details and main ideas
		Describe components and
		  their relationships
		Overlearn main items
		  followed by learning details
			This strategy may assist with
			  memorization of lists of items
			  through rehearsal techniques.

COPS	Written Reports	Capitalization correct
		Overall appearance
		Punctuation correct
		Spelling correct
			This strategy provides a
			  structure for proofreading
			  written work prior to
			  submitting it to the teacher.

DEFENDS	Written Expression	Decide on a specific position
		Examine own reasons for
		  this position
		Expose position in first
		  sentence of written task
		Note each reason and
		  associated points
		Drive home position in
		  last sentence
		Search for and correct
		  any errors
			This strategy assists learners to
			  defend a particular position
			  in a written assignment.

EASY	Studying Content	Elicit questions (who, what,
		  where, when, why)
		Ask self which information
		  is least difficult
		Study easy content initially,
		  followed by difficult content
			EASY may assist learners to
			  organize and prioritize
			  information by responding
			  to questions designed to
			  identify important content
			  to be learned.

FIST	Reading
	  Comprehension
		First sentence is read
		Indicate a question based on
		  material in first sentence
		Search for answer to question
		Tie question and answer
		  together through
		  paraphrasing
			This questioning strategy
			  assists students to actively
			  pursue responses to
			  questions related directly to
			  material being read.

Strategy	Task Areas	Process	Description
GLP	Note-taking	Guided Lecture Procedures	GLP provides students with a structure for taking notes during lectures. Group activity is involved to facilitate effective note-taking.
PANORAMA	Reading	Preparatory Stage - identify purpose Intermediate Stage - survey and read Concluding Stage - memorize material	This strategy includes a three-stage process to assist with reading comprehension.
PARS	Reading	Preview Ask questions Read Summarize	PARS is recommended for use with younger students and with those who have limited experiences with study strategies.
PENS	Sentence Writing	Pick a formula Explore different words to fit into the formula Note the words selected Subject and verb selections follow	PENS is appropriate for developing basic sentence structure and assists students to write different types of sentences by following formulas for sentence construction.
PIRATES	Test Taking	Prepare to succeed Inspect instructions carefully Read entire question, remember memory strategies and reduce choices Answer question or leave until later Turn back to the abandoned items Estimate unknown answers by avoiding absolutes and eliminating similar choices Survey to ensure that all items have a response	PIRATES may assist learners to more carefully and successfully complete tests.

(Continued)

TABLE 13–4 *(Continued)*

Strategy	Task Areas	Process	Description
PQ4R	Reading	Preview Question Read Reflection Recite Review	PQ4R may assist students to become more discriminating readers.
RAP	Reading Comprehension	Read paragraph Ask self to identify the main idea and two supporting details Put main idea and details into own words	This strategy assists students to learn information through paraphrasing.
RARE	Reading	Review selection questions Answer all questions known Read the selection Express answers to remaining questions	RARE emphasizes reading for a specific purpose while focusing on acquiring answers to selection questions initially not known.
RDPE	Underlining	Read entire passage Decide which ideas are important Plan the underlining to include only main points Evaluate results of the underlining by reading only the underlined words	This strategy assists learners to organize and remember main points and ideas in a reading selection through appropriate underlining of key words.
REAP	Reading Writing Thinking	Read Encode Annotate Ponder	REAP is a method which assists students to combine several skills to facilitate discussion about reading material.
ReQuest	Reading Questioning	Reciprocal Questioning	Teacher and student ask each other questions about a selection. Student modeling of teacher questions and teacher feedback are emphasized as the learner explores the meaning of the reading material.

Strategy	Task Areas	Process	Description
RIDER	Reading Comprehension	Read sentence Image (form mental picture) Describe how new image differs from previous sentence Evaluate image to ensure that it contains all necessary elements Repeat process with subsequent sentences	This visual imagery strategy cues the learner to form a mental image of what was previously learned from a sentence just read.
SCORER	Test Taking	Schedule time effectively Clue words identified Omit difficult items until end Read carefully Estimate answers requiring calculations Review work and responses	This test-taking strategy provides a structure for completing various tests by assisting students to carefully and systematically complete test items.
SQRQCQ	Math Word Problems	Survey word problem Question asked is identified Read more carefully Question process required to solve problem Compute the answer Question self to ensure that the answer solves the problem	This strategy provides a systematic structure for identifying the question being asked in a math word problem, computing the response, and ensuring that the question in the problem was answered.
SQ3R	Reading	Survey Question Read Recite Review	SQ3R provides a systematic approach to improve reading comprehension.
SSCD	Vocabulary Development	Sound clues used Structure clues used Content clues used Dictionary used	SSCD encourages student to remember to use sound, structure, and context clues to address unfamiliar vocabulary. This is followed by dictionary usage if necessary.

(Continued)

TABLE 13–4 (*Continued*)

Strategy	Task Areas	Process	Description
TOWER	Written Reports	Think Order ideas Write Edit Rewrite	TOWER provides a structure for completing initial and final drafts of written reports. It may be used effectively with COPS.
TQLR	Listening	Tuning in Questioning Listening Reviewing	This strategy assists with listening comprehension. Students generate questions and listen for specific statements related to these questions.

Note. From *Teaching Students with Learning Problems to Use Study Skills: A Teacher's Guide* (p. 107–109), by J. J. Hoover and J. R. Patton, 1995, Austin, TX: PRO-ED. Copyright 1995 by PRO-ED, Inc. Reprinted with permission.

time (e.g., 2 school weeks; next five written reports) and the impact on the targeted study skill should be documented. For example, if COPS is used for the next five written reports document how the reports have improved in punctuation and capitalization. Once the targeted study skill has been determined and implementation of relevant teaching and student study strategies has begun, the final step occurs.

Evaluation. As discussed in the preceding step, the teacher should determine a specific amount of time each strategy will be used. The evaluation of the effectiveness of the strategy use on the targeted study skill must also be determined. That is, How will you know the strategy is working? Use of simple checklists or anecdotal logs will facilitate regular and easy documentation of the effectiveness of the strategy on the student's use of the targeted study skill (e.g., better written reports, more effective use of time, more organized lecture notes, etc.). As the study skill strategies are used by the learner, the effects on the use of the study skill will become apparent and should be documented. Use of the strategies should continue for the specified amount of time. Using the ongoing documentation as a

guide, the use of the strategy to assist with the targeted study skill should be evaluated. If sufficient progress has been made, its use should continue. If not, other strategies should be tried following the procedures outlined in the second and third steps of the procedure.

This four-step process provides a general framework for teachers to teach study skills to students as well as to assist students to apply the strategies in appropriate classroom situations.

In addition to the four-step process for teaching study skills, other popular and widely used classroom practices facilitate study skills development. Two of these are *semantic webbing* and *cooperative learning*. Both these teaching practices facilitate the development, maintenance, and generalization of study skills while also assisting students with learning problems with various academic tasks. When used in conjunction with the preceding steps, varied experiences and opportunities are provided for students to develop and use the study skills discussed in this chapter.

Semantic Webbing and Study Skills

The use of semantic webs is frequently discussed as an effective teaching practice to assist with reading comprehension and related areas of learning (Harris & Sipay, 1990). Through semantic webbing students relate new knowledge to existing knowledge. Semantic webbing is also useful in assisting students to learn and apply study skills within actual classroom situations (Hoover & Rabideau, 1995). Semantic webbing or mapping is discussed in Chapter 9; the reader should refer to this chapter or to Hoover and Patton (1995) for an overview of this teaching practice.

Semantic webbing allows students to build systematically on their previous study skill knowledge and experiences, no matter how inexperienced the student may be in using study skills

(Hoover & Rabideau, 1995). Table 13–5 lists several of the most important study skills discussed in this chapter, along with several suggested semantic web topics for which subordinate ideas may be generated by the students.

As Table 13–5 shows, many different semantic web topics and subtopics exist to help learners use their study skills. These may easily be adapted and expanded. Figure 13– 2 provides an example of a completed semantic web for helping students learn how to take multiple-choice tests. In this example the teacher identifies the main topic (test taking: multiple choice) and the subtopics (studying for the test, taking the test, reviewing completed test). The items surrounding

TABLE 13–5
Semantic web topics for major study skills

Study Skills	Semantic Web Topics
Test Taking	Essay tests, mulitple choice tests, short answer tests, *studying for tests, taking the test, reviewing the completed test*
Library Usage	Cataloging system, library organization, media specialist role
Reference Materials/ Dictionary Usage	Dictionary, encyclopedia, atlas, *material's purpose, finding information, guide words, table of contents, glossary*
Presenting Information	Written reports, oral presentations, visual presentations, *topic selection, organizing thoughts, proper grammar, punctuation using visuals, speaking mechanics*
Note-taking/Outlining	Formal papers, draft papers, research project, *organizing notes, sufficient details, headings, and subheadings, organizational format, collecting ideas*
Time Management	Task identification, prioritizing tasks, recording task completion, daily, weekly, monthly
Listening	Formal lectures, small group discussions, audio-visual presentations, *attending to message, clarifying speaker's ideas, applying meaning to message, remembering message*
Reading Rate	Fast-paced, slow-paced rates, *getting main idea, locating details, determining sequence of ideas, retaining information*
Self-Management of Behavior	Monitoring own behavior, assuming responsibility, changing own behavior

Note. Main semantic web topics appear in roman type; suggested subtopics appear in italics. From "Teaching Study Skills Through Semantic Webs," by J. J. Hoover and D.K. Rabideau, 1995, *Intervention School and Clinic, 30,* p. 293. Copyright 1995 by PRO-ED, Inc. Reprinted with permission.

FIGURE 13–2

Semantic web of the test-taking multiple choice study skill

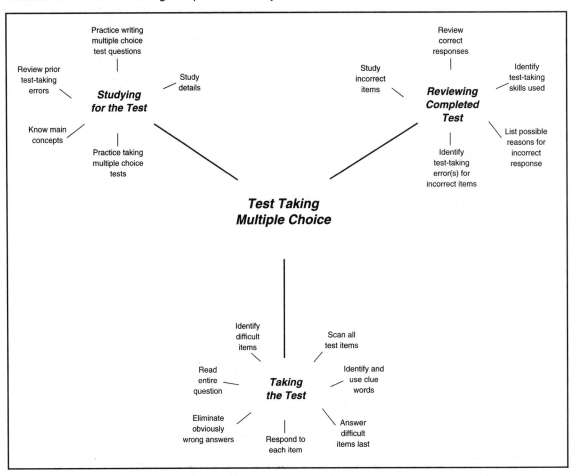

From "Teaching Study Skills Through Semantic Webs." by J. J. Hoover and D. K. Rabideau, 1995. *Intervention in School and Clinic, 30,* p. 29. Copyright 1995 by PRO-ED, Inc. Reprinted with permission.

subtopics are examples of student-generated ideas for using the study skill and applying the subtopics to their test taking. Once the web has been completed by an individual or a small group of students, all learners should receive copies of the semantic web and select one or two ideas from the web to begin to apply in their learning. After students complete a multiple-choice test, they should analyze why and in what ways the web ideas helped them and what they can do in the future to best study for, complete, and review multiple-choice tests.

This test-taking example is only one of many that teachers can model and adapt as they use semantic webbing to help students use study skills in the classroom. Students who have learning problems may require specific training or coaching to successfully complete semantic webs for study skills development. A critical follow-up in the use of semantic webs is to develop and use study skills in actual classroom situations. As students share their successes with their study skill webs, they will assist others to become more proficient in test taking. Use of the various study strategies and teaching suggestions discussed in this chapter will help students apply the study skills they have identified through semantic webbing.

Teaching Study Skills Through Cooperative Learning

A classroom structure built on cooperative learning and its principles may also teach essential study skills. The use of cooperative learning on a regular basis in the classroom is a decision left to each individual teacher. However, should cooperative learning be used, study skills education should be an integral part of each student's academic and social growth. The following discussion provides a general overview of cooperative learning, along with consideration of ways to teach study skills through this method.

Essential Elements of Cooperative Learning

Although researchers in this area have identified various ways of implementing cooperative learning, several common elements are frequently discussed. These include (Roy, 1990)

- positive interdependence
- individual accountability
- positive interactions
- interpersonal training
- group processing

Within the context of cooperative learning, students perceive that their goals are achieved through shared work with other students. The five elements identified facilitate this shared work, whether in the area of study skills development or in any content area. Each is briefly summarized (Johnson & Johnson, 1990; Roy, 1990).

Positive Interdependence. This occurs when each student in the cooperative group or pair feels a sense of mutual goals and rewards. Each student understands that all members must complete the assigned tasks for the group's work to be complete. Students learn the material or task themselves and assist others in acquiring the information.

Individual Accountability. Individual accountability means ensuring that each member demonstrates mastery of the assigned task, skill, or content. Each student's mastery levels are assessed along with the cooperative learning team's mastery levels. Cooperative learning does not exclude or excuse individuals from participating or from acquiring the material; rather, it uses the strengths of each group member to facilitate the learning of the task or skill by each individual student.

Positive Interactions. Students are encouraged to assist others in learning material. This includes exchanging ideas, providing feedback, encouraging student efforts, discussing concepts and skills, and supporting one another's involvement. This positive and constructive interaction not only helps those who are being given assistance but also provides a valuable learning experience for those helping other students. Although the quantity and quality of these types of student interactions will vary, regular practice in facilitating student assistance and interactions strengthens the cooperative sharing of information.

Interpersonal Training. Interpersonal training addresses the issue of preparing students for successful interactions in cooperative learning teams. Teachers must assist students with communication, conflict management, decision making, leadership, and other group-oriented interaction skills. Students with special learning needs may require assistance and encouragement in this area. In conjunction with the teacher intervention, the use of pairs or groups of three students, some of whom possess these skills, allows students the opportunity to share their skills with others. The success of cooperative pairs or groups depends greatly on proper student preparation by the teacher in how the teams should function. In many situations, directly teaching specific study skills (e.g., self-management of behavior, note-taking/outlining, time management) will facilitate this student preparation.

Group Processing. Group processing provides students and teachers the opportunity to determine how well the pair or group functioned in specific tasks. Team members discuss their contributions to the group, ways to improve overall member interactions and contributions, and recommendations for future cooperative team efforts. Having a student or teacher observe the group's activities may facilitate processing of the group's interactions.

Study Skills and Cooperative Learning

Earlier in this chapter, study skills were defined as competencies or support skills students must employ to effectively and efficiently record, organize, synthesize, and evaluate tasks and skills in the overall process of learning. As students engage in learning, regular and consistent use of study skills is necessary. Efficient use of study skills becomes even more important as tasks and concepts become more complex. Whether students are working independently or in a cooperative learning group, they must develop and use a variety of study skills to meet the demands associated within assigned tasks.

A direct relationship exists between effective use of study skills and the efficient implementation of cooperative learning. Table 13–6 provides an overview of how study skill development is a natural and integral part of a cooperative learning structure. It shows how the five essential elements associated with cooperative learning are directly impacted by students' use of study skills. How well students use study skills affects the overall performance of members within the group or pair; the identification, development, and maintenance of various study skills; the sharing of strategies for effective use of study skills; the importance of different study skills to the overall process of cooperative learning; and the reflection of study skills use by group or pair members. For example, inefficient use of time, poor self-management of behavior, inappropriate library and reference material use, poor test-taking skills, or ineffective use of reading rates will interfere with the successful learning of most tasks or content through cooperative learning. On the other hand, these skills can be strengthened by effective cooperative group interactions and learning.

The reader is advised to consider the importance of incorporating an ongoing study skill program into cooperative learning as well as into the various content areas and classroom structures. The use of semantic webbing as a teaching practice also enhances the development of study skills as students learn and apply the following strategies.

IMPLEMENTING A STUDY SKILLS PROGRAM

A four-step process and two effective teaching practices—semantic webbing and cooperative learning—have been discussed within which study skills can be taught. However, no matter what classroom structure a teacher elects to implement, a study-skills program should introduce simple variations of study skills in lower elementary grades and gradually increase in complexity as students progress through the grades (Hoover & Patton, 1995). The age, ability, and individual needs of special learners must determine the extent of that complexity; however, early efforts may prove beneficial throughout the entire educational program, particularly since problems with study-skill use become more visible as students progress through school (McKenzie, 1991b). Hoover and Patton (1995) outline several guidelines for teachers to follow in developing and/or improving their study skills programs. Although the guidelines can be applied to all students, they are of particular significance for teachers of students who have special learning needs.

1. Introduce simple variations of the different study skills in the early grades.
2. Gradually increase to the more complex elements associated with each study skill as students progress through the grades.
3. Identify specific goals and objectives for a study skills program prior to program implementation.
4. Let students' individual strengths and weaknesses guide decision making concerning what study skills to emphasize at any particular time.

TABLE 13–6
Study skill development and cooperative learning

Cooperative Elements	Study Skills Development
Positive Interdependence	Effective study skills usage by each member affects in a positive way the actions and learning of all members within a cooperative learning group or pair.
Individual Accountancy	As individuals within a group recognize their own study skill strengths and weaknesses, they are able to identify ways to best contribute to the group and ways the group may best assist them with their study skill development. Pre-post assessment of study skill abilities will ensure that individual accountability is maintained.
Positive Interactions	Once individual strengths and weaknesses in the use of study skills have been identified, students are better prepared to help others with study skills they may already possess as well as learn from others. Exchanging study skill ideas and strategies that have been effective and that are relevant to completion of the cooperative learning task at hand will serve to strengthen the study skill abilities of group members. It will also provide a basis for constructive interactions and decision making required for effective cooperative learning to occur.
Interpersonal Training	A major goal of any comprehensive study skills program is to promote greater independence in learning. As teachers engage students in interpersonal training activities, study skills should be an integral part of this training. As students become proficient with skills such as time management, self-management of behavior, note-taking, and library usage, they will be better prepared to engage in interpersonal interactions relative to a cooperative learning academic task. Interpersonal training will not be complete unless these and similar study skills are mastered.
Group Processing	As students engage in discussions and reflect on how well their group or pair functioned relative to specific tasks, the specific study skills used to facilitate completion of the task or learn the content should be addressed.

Note: From *Teaching Students with Learning Problems to Use Study Skills: A Teacher's Guide* (p.25), by J. J. Hoover and J. R. Patton, 1995, Austin. TX: PRO-ED. Copyright 1995 by PRO-ED, Inc. Reprinted with permission

5. Know what motivates students to use different study skills and emphasize these motivations in program implementation.

6. Explain and demonstrate the proper use of each study skill.

7. Expect students to use different study skills appropriately through guided practice and planned learning experiences.

8. Provide continued opportunity for practicing study skill use to assist students in acquiring and maintaining mastery of the skills.

9. Facilitate the use of study skills in natural classroom settings and on a regular basis as the need arises in different subject areas and learning activities.

10. Assist students in generalizing acquired study skills through an emphasis upon more complex use of the skills once initial mastery of the basic study skills has been achieved.

Students at any grade level, especially students with disabilities, require direct teacher guidance in study skill areas. In addition to the general guidelines just presented, teachers may find more specific instructional strategies useful in implementing a study skills program. For additional teaching suggestions the reader is referred to Hoover and Patton (1995).

Reading Rates

1. Ensure that proper reading rates are used for different reading activities.
2. Establish clear purposes for each reading assignment.
3. Ensure that each student is familiar with each type of reading rate.
4. Provide opportunities for the appropriate use of each reading rate.

Listening Skills

1. Reduce distractions and deal quickly with classroom disruptions.
2. Encourage each student to speak loudly enough so that all can hear.
3. Repeat and emphasize important items in the verbal message.
4. Summarize the verbal message at strategic points in the lecture.
5. Use visual materials to support oral presentations.

Note-Taking/Outlining

1. Encourage students to follow a consistent note-taking/outlining format.
2. Teach students to identify and focus on key topics and ideas.
3. Discuss with students the uses and advantages of making outlines and taking notes.
4. Model different note-taking/outlining formats for students.

5. Begin with simple note-taking/outlining activities, and gradually introduce more complex types of activities.

Report Writing

1. Clarify the purpose for each writing assignment and assist students in organizing their ideas.
2. Begin writing activities with simple, less complex written assignments and gradually introduce more difficult types of written reports.
3. Insist that students use a dictionary and other reference materials when necessary and that they proofread their written work.
4. Work with students as they complete different stages of writing assignments.
5. Provide periodic review and encouragement to students as they complete writing reports.

Oral Presentations

1. Allow sufficient time for students to prepare for oral presentations.
2. Conduct oral presentations in a nonthreatening environment to minimize peer criticism.
3. Provide different situations for oral presentations (e.g., with students seated or standing by their desks, standing in front of a small group, addressing the whole class).
4. Ensure that students know and understand the purposes for oral presentations.

Use of Graphic Aids

1. Allow students to use graphic aids with, or as alternatives to, oral and written reports.
2. Ensure that students know why specific material is presented in graphic form.
3. Incorporate visual material into oral presentations.
4. Assist students in focusing on important aspects of graphic aids.
5. Provide sufficient time for students to read and interpret graphic aids presented during lectures.

Test Taking

1. Discuss with students the purposes of tests and show them how to complete different types of tests.
2. Explain the different methods of study necessary to prepare for various types of tests (e.g., objective, essay).
3. Review test-taking errors with students.
4. Ensure that students know the time allotted for completion of each test.
5. Explore test-taking procedures with students to ensure that they are familiar with different types of test questions.

Library Use

1. Review the uses and importance of a library, and familiarize students with the organizational layout of a library.
2. Structure assignments so that students must use a library to complete them.
3. Be sure that students know the purpose of using the library in any library activity.
4. Teach students to consult media specialists and other library personnel as necessary.

Reference Materials Usage

1. Ensure that dictionaries are readily available to all students.
2. Structure various assignments to require students to use reference materials.
3. Be sure that each student possesses sufficient skills to successfully use general reference and dictionary materials when these are required.
4. Create situations that help students understand the uses of reference materials.
5. Familiarize students with the different components of general reference materials and dictionaries prior to requiring their use in assignments.

Time Management

1. Reward effective use of time.
2. Structure classroom activities so that students are required to budget their own time periodically.

3. Praise on-task behaviors, especially during independent work times.
4. Ensure that students know the amount of time allotted for completion of each activity.
5. Provide sufficient time and opportunity for students to manage their own time and to complete assigned tasks.

Self-Management of Behavior

1. Be sure that students know specific behavioral expectations.
2. Establish student self-management programs and monitor associated progress.
3. Assist students in setting realistic and attainable goals in a self-management program.
4. Be consistent in enforcing behavioral expectations of students.
5. Allow sufficient time for a self-management program to be implemented before the effects of the program are tested.

Study Strategies

Students' application of study skills can be improved through the use of various study-skill strategies. Study strategies help students to complete tasks in different content or skill areas (Hoover, 1995). Several of the more frequently discussed strategies were presented earlier in Table 13–4. Each strategy in the table is presented relative to specific study skills areas. None is appropriate for all students with special learning needs; individual needs and abilities must be considered. Some of these strategies are part of a learning-strategies model that presents a problem-solving approach not restricted to applications specific to the context in which the strategy is taught.

Study Skills and Technology

Using computers and other technology to improve the personal productivity of students with disabilities has become popular. Okolo (1993) notes that using word processors, databases, and electronic networking can help students with mild disabilities improve their efficiency and proficiency as learners. Technology provides unique opportunities for students in the development and use of study skills. For example, learning how to use a database to keep lists of assignments may enable the student to transfer this skill to organizing information collected for a research paper later. Use of computerized databases to locate references in local and regional libraries may also facilitate effective study in students. Additionally, CD-ROM encyclopedias, computer spell-check programs, grammar and sentence structure computer programs, and use of the Internet to locate materials and specific sources of information are all examples of how technology can facilitate study skill development in the areas of reference materials, time management, note-taking, library use, and report writing. When developing an overall classroom study skills program, students' access to computers, the Internet, CD-ROM materials, and other technology should be identified and used to help learners use study skills as efficiently and effectively as possible.

LEARNING STRATEGIES

This chapter concludes with a general overview of six learning strategies that are appropriate for use with students who exhibit learning or behavior problems. Learning strategies have often been viewed as a subset of study skills. These six were selected because of their relevance in meeting the needs of students with special needs. They are not all-inclusive; rather, they represent additional types of study strategies effective in meeting academic and educational needs. Learning strategies emphasize learning how to learn and complement use of existing study skills known to the student. For additional information about the learning strategies discussed in this section, the reader is referred to Hoover (1991) and Hoover and Collier (1992), as well as to Deshler, Ellis, and Lenz (1996) and Good and Brophy (1995).

Active Processing

Active processing involves the use of self-talk or self-questioning in order to activate knowledge. This strategy also assists students to elaborate on

a particular content area in order to complete a task. Skills such as summarizing, scanning, questioning, and predicting may be used. When using this strategy, teachers must make certain that students know that self-talk is appropriate and acceptable to help them define, evaluate, monitor, and complete a task.

Analogy

Analogy allows an individual to recall previously acquired learning and knowledge and relate these to a new topic or experience. This strategy may use schema, metaphor, or cloze procedures as students learn new material. The effective use of analogy in the classroom requires that teachers help students to recall prior learning and then compare, contrast, substitute or elaborate upon that knowledge in order to learn and retain new information.

Coping

Coping is a problem-solving learning strategy that enables students to confront issues and tasks systematically and objectively. A variety of problems may be addressed as the learner confronts issues, develops solutions, identifies necessary assistance, attempts solutions, persists with a task, and eventually generates successful resolution to the problem or learning task. Teachers should be sensitive to students' values and problem-solving preferences when assisting them to develop this learning strategy.

Evaluation

Evaluation helps students to become aware of what is needed to successfully complete a task and monitor whether that task has been completed. Self-monitoring, reflection, prediction, generalization, and feedback skills are all used with this strategy. Independent work skills of students may improve through this strategy. Teachers should demonstrate to students how to check answers, monitor progress towards task completion, reflect upon procedures and results of the completed task, and transfer skills to new tasks or situations. Successful mastery of these and similar skills will facilitate effective use of the evaluation strategy.

Organization

The strategy of organization emphasizes student abilities to group or cluster items, tasks, ideas, and skills. A variety of organizational patterns may exist for specific items or skills, and specific instructional situations may dictate the use of different organizations (e.g., broad versus narrow groupings). Students may initially experience problems knowing what types of categories or clusters are acceptable or appropriate for different learning situations. Teachers should employ direct teaching to help learners explore possible ways to categorize and then evaluate effectiveness.

Rehearsal

Rehearsal helps students to think about a task prior to beginning the task, while working at it, and upon its completion. Elements such as reviewing, reciting, and recalling different aspects related to an assignment are important in rehearsal. This strategy allows students to think through what they are doing as they proceed in task completion. This, in turn, minimizes problems and facilitates more effective use of time. Pausing, questioning, visualizing, and summarizing are important features of this strategy, and teachers should help students practice these as tasks are completed.

The six learning strategies discussed above will help students in their overall study skill development. In actual practice these strategies are frequently used with each other or with other study skills. Table 13-7 illustrates how these may be used in combination. As shown in the table, a visual cue is associated with sample instructions for the use of each strategy. An example of a "key" word or words is also provided to further enhance their effective use in the classroom. Figures 13-3 through 13-8 provide teacher guides for identifying student learning strategy needs in the classroom. These should be completed relative to the actual classroom tasks that students complete. The items in each guide reflect important skills needed to successfully use the strategy and offer a quick way to begin student assessment in this area. Additional guides for teachers and for students using these learning structures in the classroom can be found in Hoover (1991).

SUMMARY

This chapter emphasizes that study skills are essential for students across all grade levels. For students with disabilities, learning and using these skills is particularly problematic. Several study skills have been identified as critical to academic and postsecondary success, including differential reading rates, listening, notetaking, report writing, presentations, test taking, and time management. A variety of approaches can be used to informally assess skills within this domain.

Study skills instructional programs can be designed to include a variety of elements. These include the use of semantic mapping, cooperative learning strategies, specific curricular components emphasizing individual study skills, and the use of learning strategies. A variety of specific learning strategies were presented that have applicability for teaching students with special needs.

TABLE 13–7
Combined use of study strategies

Strategy	Key Words	Visual Cue	Instructions
Active Processing Coping Rehearsal	Stop and think	STOP	Students are asked to remember when "look before you leap" has been valuable to them. Also discussed are the benefits of reflection.
Active Processing Evaluation Rehearsal	The five Ws	W — HO, HAT, HY, HERE, HEN	Students are led to use these elements in their self-questioning exercises. Also discussed are ways to elaborate upon them.
Analogy Rehearsal	Practice	PRACTICE	The benefits of "practice makes perfect" and rehearsals are discussed. Analogies to previous experiences are elicited.
Active Processing Evaluation	Check your work	✓	The benefits of self-monitoring and evaluating are discussed. Ways that students can assess accurately are discussed.
Coping Evaluation Organization	Break it into smaller parts		Students are shown how to group information into smaller pieces and discuss the benefits of taking smaller bites. Also discussed is how to put things back together.
Active Processing Rehearsal	Make notes	SCRIBBL SCR	Students are led to use self-generating visual cues or notes as aids in questioning, rehearsing, and organizing information.
Analogy Organization	Organize		The benefits of organizing information are discussed using analogies from students' own experiences. The students think of their minds as houses and how keeping things in particular room/places facilitates access.
Active Processing Coping Rehearsal	Take time/takes time		Students are reminded that learning and development take time. Cultural differences in time use and biorhythms are discussed, as well as the effective use of time.
Analogy Organization	Look for patterns	✗ ⊙ ✗ ⊙ _ _	The benefits of identifying and using patterns are discussed. Students are shown how to make analogies in using patterns. Patterns learned in students' own languages and cultures are used to illustrate transfer and flexibility.
Analogy Coping	Think about other things you know about the topic		Students are led to generate questions that will elicit prior knowledge about the topic.

Note: From *Cognitive Learning Strategies for Minority Handicapped Students* (pp. 50–51), by C. Collier and J. J. Hoover, 1987, Boulder, CO: Hamilton. Copyright 1987 by Hamilton Publications. Adapted with permission.

FIGURE 13–3

Guide for identifying use of active processing

Name: _____ Date: _____

Classroom: _____ Completed by: _____

Instructions: Place a check next to each item if it is exhibited by the student on a regular and consistent basis. Summarize the student use of active processing to complete the guide.

The student uses self-talk or self-questioning to...

_____ identify the task to be completed

_____ clarify how to go about completing a task

_____ check completed written work for accuracy of responses

_____ examine the appropriateness of the method or strategy used to complete a task

_____ reinforce his or her efforts related to the task

_____ clarify potential mistakes made while completing the task

_____ identify possible methods to prevent making similar mistakes

_____ evaluate his or her progress toward task completion if an alternative method is used

_____ verify that the task was completed

_____ congratulate self for successful completion

Summary Comments:

From *Classroom Applications of Cognitive Learning Styles* (p. 91), by J. J. Hoover, 1991, Boulder, CO: Hamilton Publications. Copyright 1991 by Hamilton Publications. Reprinted with permission.

FIGURE 13–4

Guide for identifying use of analogy

Name: _____ Date: _____

Classroom: _____ Completed by: _____

Instructions: Place a check next to each item if it is exhibited by the student on a regular and consistent basis. Summarize the student use of analogy to complete the guide.

The student...

_____ identified items or situations previously experienced that are similar to a current task or topic of study

_____ compares similar characteristics of like items

_____ is able to identify differences between dissimilar items

_____ identifies similar uses for similar types of items

_____ applies knowledge from prior experiences to better understand a current situation or topic of study

_____ is able to substitute items or situations showing how they may be used or studied interchangeably

_____ is able to provide examples, based on own experiences, that are relevant to the study of current topics

_____ recognizes the fact that one effective way to study an unknown topic is to draw similarities to previous topics already learned

_____ elaborates on prior knowledge relative to new information

_____ recalls previously learned patterns of study and uses them to acquire new information

Summary Comments:

From *Classroom Applications of Cognitive Learning Styles* (p. 94), by J. J. Hoover, 1991, Boulder, CO: Hamilton Publications. Copyright 1991 by Hamilton Publications. Reprinted with permission.

FIGURE 13–5

Guide for identifying use of coping

Name: _____   Date: _____

Classroom: _____   Completed by: _____

Instructions: Place a check next to each item if it is exhibited by the student on a regular and consistent basis. Summarize the student use of coping skills to complete the guide.

In order to cope with a problem or situation, the student is able to...

_____ divide a problem into component parts

_____ prioritize elements within a problem in order of importance

_____ identify any assistance that may be required to help resolve the problem, situation, or conflict

_____ identify people who may provide necessary assistance to help resolve the situation

_____ provide self with a verbal or visual cue when ready to begin to resolve the problem

_____ persevere when confronted with resistance or setbacks while attempting to resolve the situation

_____ attempt a variety of possible solutions until the problem is resolved

_____ modify plans as necessary

_____ recognize when the problem or situation is resolved

_____ congratulate self when the problem or situation has been successfully resolved

Summary Comments:

From *Classroom Applications of Cognitive Learning Styles* (p. 97), by J. J. Hoover, 1991, Boulder, CO: Hamilton Publications. Copyright 1991 by Hamilton Publications. Reprinted with permission.

FIGURE 13–6

Guide for identifying use of organization

Name: _____   Date: _____

Classroom: _____   Completed by: _____

Instructions: Place a check next to each item if it is exhibited by the student on a regular and consistent basis. Summarize the student use of organization skills to complete the guide.

The student is able to...

_____ determine similarities and differences between situations

_____ identify various ways to sort and organize items, tasks, or situations

_____ cluster similar characteristics in a meaningful way in order to complete various tasks

_____ provide an accurate name or title for grouped items or tasks

_____ adjust the organization of the grouping of required tasks if the initial clustering does not facilitate successful completion of the tasks

_____ review the process used to group items or assignments and adjust in future groupings, if necessary

_____ group items of a topic or skill in a way that facilitates learning and remembering the items

_____ remember group names or titles as well as items within those titles

_____ continually search for additional meaningful ways to group topics or items to best learn new skills and retain information

Summary Comments:

From *Classroom Applications of Cognitive Learning Styles* (p. 103), by J. J. Hoover, 1991, Boulder, CO: Hamilton Publications. Copyright 1991 by Hamilton Publications. Reprinted with permission.

FIGURE 13–7

Guide for identifying use of rehearsal

Name: _____   Date: _____

Classroom: _____   Completed by: _____

Instructions: Place a check next to each item if it is exhibited by the student on a regular and consistent basis. Summarize the student use of rehearsal skills to complete the guide.

The student is able to...

_____ recall what has just been heard

_____ recall what has just been seen or read

_____ describe a mental image associated with a topic recently studied

_____ ask a variety of who, what, where, why, and when questions in order to remember information

_____ verbalize a process to follow in order to create a mental picture of a skill or topic

_____ review the critical elements of a topic or skill recently learned

_____ verbalize the steps to be followed to complete a task prior to beginning the task

_____ periodically stop during the completion of a task to review the process being followed to make certain it is similar to that which was previously outlined

_____ generate and organize key questions to ask oneself in order to determine steps to follow to effectively complete a task

_____ use responses from the generated questions to plan, implement, and review the process used to remember essential information and complete tasks

Summary Comments:

From *Classroom Applications of Cognitive Learning Styles* (p. 106), by J. J. Hoover, 1991, Boulder, CO: Hamilton Publications. Copyright 1991 by Hamilton Publications. Reprinted with permission.

FIGURE 13–8

Guide to using evaluation strategies

Student's Name: _____   Date: _____

Instructions: Identify the task to be completed and for each step, write a statement in your own words or draw a picture to help you select methods to complete the task.

Task _____

1. The outcome of this task is:

2. The materials or resources that I need to complete the task are:

3. Steps to follow to complete the task are:

4. Methods that have worked in the past to complete similar tasks are:

5. The method that I will use to complete this task is:

6. The steps to follow to use this method are:

7. If this method does not work, I will try:

8. The method(s) I used to complete the task worked because:

From *Using Study Skills and Learning Strategies in the Classroom: A Teacher's Handbook* (p. 98), by J. J. Hoover, 1990, Boulder, CO: Hamilton. Copyright 1990 by Hamilton Publications. Reprinted with permission.

TEACHER TIPS

Instruction of study skills can and should begin at the elementary level. Integrating study skills development into the curriculum at the elementary level enhances the probability that students with special needs will be able to handle the demands of inclusive settings. One of the study skills discussed in this chapter is self-management. This skill is considered under this topic because of the importance that self-regulatory behaviors can play in a student's academic success.

Various techniques that assist a student in managing their own behaviors can be very helpful. An example of such a technique is a weekly checklist (see below) to which a student can refer to make sure that certain behaviors are performed. These behaviors would be generated based on the needs of the student. The student would place a check in the box when the behavior has been performed. The form could be tailored to use for each class or for an entire school day.

CHECKLIST ITEMS

Name _____   Date _____

	M	T	W	T	F
Have all necessary supplies	☐	☐	☐	☐	☐
Assignments completed	☐	☐	☐	☐	☐
Assignments turned in on time	☐	☐	☐	☐	☐
Papers organized in notebook	☐	☐	☐	☐	☐
Arrive on time	☐	☐	☐	☐	☐
If absent, obtain missed assignments	☐	☐	☐	☐	☐
Total Complete	__	__	__	__	__

X = student rating (mark for each completed task)
+ = teacher verification (mark for each completed task)

Source: Lovitt, T. C. (2000). *Preventing school failure* (2nd ed.). Austin: Pro-Ed. Reprinted by permission.

TEACHER TIPS

When one seriously thinks about it, study skills are actually life-long skills. We use most of them frequently in our everyday lives. For this reason, a strong case can be made for ensuring that these skills are taught to students with special needs. The following list provides examples of how study skills are part of our lives.

- Reading Rate
  - Reviewing an assigned reading for a test
  - Looking for an explanation of a concept discussed in class
- Listening
  - Understanding instructions about a field trip
  - Attending to morning announcements
- Note-taking/Outlining
  - Capturing information given by a teacher on how to dissect a frog
  - Framing the structure of a paper
- Report Writing
  - Developing a book report
  - Completing a science project on a specific marine organism
- Oral Presentations
  - Delivering a personal opinion on a current issue for a social studies class
  - Describing the results of a lab experiment
- Graphic Aids
  - Setting up the equipment of a chemistry experiment based on a diagram
  - Locating the most densely populated regions of the world on a map
- Test Taking
  - Developing tactics for retrieving information for a closed-book test
  - Comparing notes with textbook content
- Library Usage
  - Using picture files
  - Searching a computerized catalog
- Reference Materials
  - Accessing CD-ROM encyclopedias
  - Using a thesaurus to write a paper
- Time Management
  - Allocating a set time for homework
  - Organizing a file system for writing a paper
- Self-Management
  - Assuring that homework is signed by parents
  - Rewarding oneself for controlling temper

Source: Hoover, J. J., & Patton, J. R. (1995). *Teaching students with learning problems to use study skills: A teacher's guide.* Austin, TX: Pro-Ed.

TEACHER TIPS

Teachers can now log on to different websites to enhance the study skills of the students. Of particular interest is the site put out by Educational Resources Information Center (ERIC) of the National Library of Education. The lesson plans outline the grade level of each lesson, objectives, materials needed, and procedures to implement the lessons. Examples and links that can be found on this web site are as follows:

- AskERIC Lesson Plans: Request Reciprocal Teaching. This site can be found at the following link: http:/ericir.syr.edu/Virtual/Lessons/Lang_arts/Reading/RDG0006.html. The goal of the lessons in "Request Reciprocal Teaching" is to improve students' questioning skills.

- AskERIC Lesson Plans: Reinforcing Alphabet Names/Sounds. This site can be found at the following link: http:/ericir.syr.edu/Virtual/Lessons/Lang_arts/Reading/RDG0005.html. The goal of the lessons in "Reinforcing Alphabet Names/Sounds" is to reinforce skills for beginning readers.

- AskERIC Lesson Plans: Our Day at School. This site can be found at the following link: http:/ericir.syr.edu/Virtual/Lessons/Lang_arts/Reading/RDG0033.html. The goal of the lessons in "Our Day at School" is to enhance students reading and writing skills.

- AskERIC Lesson Plans: Interviewing. This site can be found at the following link: http:/ericir.syr.edu/Virtual/Lessons/Lang_arts/Journalism/JNL0002.html. The goal of the lessons in "Interviewing" is to teach students about developing questioning skills and using the computer to present interviews in a class newsletter.

Social Competence and Self-Determination Skills

This chapter provides information for teachers wanting to establish a social and self-determination skills program for students exhibiting failure in the classroom and community. Several topics are addressed. First, the history of social and self-determination skills instruction and definitions of social competency, social skills, social problem-solving skills, and self-determination skills are presented. Second, assessment procedures are reviewed. Third, the contents of social and self-determination skills programs for children and adolescents and the teaching procedures used to effectively teach these skills are described. Fourth, strategies that promote the generalization of social and self-determination skills across situations, persons, and environments are summarized. Fifth, sequenced procedures for establishing a social and self-determination skills program conclude the chapter.

HISTORY AND DEFINITIONS

Although a complete history of social and self-determination skills teaching has yet to be written, the work of Wolpe (1958) is often singled out as the most influential antecedent to the development of these fields. Initially Wolpe emphasized the use of behavioral principles and techniques to ameliorate adult psychiatric patients' problems with interpersonal interaction. He and his colleagues introduced the idea of teaching assertive and self-advocacy behaviors to people who were experiencing such problems due to stressful life events. Wolpe's assertion teaching was said to reduce the emotional distress that was inhibiting the patient's ability to interact successfully with other people.

B. F. Skinner's research was also beginning to have an impact on the clinical treatment of people with behavioral problems. Behavioral principles of shaping and chaining were soon applied to the teaching of many new behaviors (Bandura, 1977). Simultaneously, Argyle (1967; Argyle & Kendon, 1967) was developing a body of knowledge that attempted to explain appropriate social interactions between two or more individuals. Argyle noted that several skills were necessary. These skills included the ability to accurately (a) determine social goals (e.g., the need to make friends); (b) perceive, interpret, and act upon cues in the environment (e.g., determine which peers would be most receptive to becoming a friend, determine whether a peer would be an appropriate friend, and introduce oneself to the peer); and (c) understand and respond to the feedback given (e.g., interpret whether the peer positively responds to the initiation of friendship). Once these models were established, several researchers (Argyle, 1967; Bellack & Hersen, 1979; Liberman, King, DeRisi, & McCann, 1975) developed social skills teaching programs for various populations. The positive results achieved sparked the enthusiasm of many professionals in the fields of child and adolescent psychology and special education.

As researchers worked to promote the success of children and adolescents, they realized that certain personal or self-determination skills were not being learned. In addition, many children with disabilities were not well accepted by peers without disabilities or by teachers (Bryan, 1983). Reports on adolescents with various disabling conditions indicated a rise in the number of students dropping out of school, having difficulties establishing relationships, deciding upon inappropriate life goals, and a decrease in those exhibiting independent behaviors and maintaining long-term jobs (Furnham, 1986; Henderson & Hollin, 1986; Schumaker, Hazel, Sherman, & Sheldon-Wildgen, 1982; Serna & Lau-Smith, 1995). Many self-determination skills were lacking, and students were not being taught to develop goals for themselves, collaborate with others to attain goals (e.g., seek out mentors), and solve problems that present barriers to goal attainment (Serna & Lau-Smith, 1995). It seems therefore that teachers were being given the responsibility of ameliorating behavioral problems as well as developing appropriate social interactions and personal competence skills (i.e., self-determination skills) among children and adolescents with special needs.

In response to this need, professionals in the field of special education and psychology have not only developed several programs and procedures to teach social skills (Goldstein, Sprafkin, Gershaw, & Klein, 1998; Hazel, Schumaker, Sherman, & Sheldon-Wildgen, 1981a), but have begun to develop self-determination skills programs (Abery, Rudrud, Arndt, Schauben, & Eggebeen, 1995; Hoffman & Field, 1995; Martin & Huber-Marshall, 1995; Serna & Lau-Smith, 1995; Wehmeyer, 1995) for children and adolescents with disabilities. The following discussion introduces the concepts of social and personal (i.e., self-determination) competence by defining three dimensions: social skills, social problem-solving skills, and self-determination skills.

Social and Personal Competence

Professionals define the constructs of social and personal competence as a person's overall ability to achieve his or her goals and desires in the personal and social aspects of life (Ford, 1985; Foster & Richey, 1979). Ford elaborates by identifying three different components that interact to comprise the concept of social and personal competence: self-perception (i.e., an individual's ability to recognize and set goals for oneself), behavioral repertoire (i.e., a person's ability to effectively perform social skills, problem-solving skills, role-taking abilities, assertive skills, and language/communication skills), and effectiveness (i.e., a person's ability to determine whether set goals and desires are achieved).

Ford (1985) continues by outlining three additional factors that interact with the components of social and personal competence: (a) motivation; (b) development; and (c) environment. Motivation is a factor that interacts with social and personal competence in that an individual may have the desired skills (i.e., setting goals, behaving appropriately, and evaluating achievement) in his or her behavioral repertoire but may not be motivated to use these skills. Development, on the other hand, interacts with social and personal competence in that a person's age or developmental growth may influence the type of goals set and achieved by an individual. For example, the social and personal goals of a preschool child would be different from the goals of an adolescent graduating or leaving school and going out into the

community. Finally, environment pertains to the culture, society, or family expectations that influence the social and personal behavior of an individual (e.g., some Native American populations do not believe in long-term goal setting). A socially and personally competent person is able to move from one environment to another, recognizing the social rules of each setting and acting accordingly. The individual who consistently demonstrates the ability to shift from one environment to another and exhibit appropriate social behavior in each setting is considered a socially competent person. The person who demonstrates the ability to set and achieve goals, make appropriate decisions, and persist through difficult times by using problem-solving skills is considered a personally competent individual.

Social Skills. Since the 1970s, the definition of social skills has been modified to reflect the knowledge that researchers have acquired concerning social behavior. For example, Libet and Lewinsohn (1973) define social skills as "the complex ability both to emit behaviors which are positively or negatively reinforced and not to emit behaviors that are punished or extinguished by others" (p. 304). This definition directly reflects the influence of applied behavior analysis and social learning theory (Bandura, 1977; Eisler, Miller, & Hersen, 1973) whereby a person modifies his or her behavior according to the responses of others. Schumaker and Hazel's 1984 behavioral definition of social skills included overt behaviors as skill components necessary in the interactions between two or more people and also cognitive functions (i.e., covert behavior). Overt behaviors include observable nonverbal behaviors (e.g., eye contact and facial expression) and verbal behavior (what words are used and how the person communicates a message). Covert behaviors consist of a person's ability to empathize with another person and discriminate social cues. The appropriate and fluent use of these behaviors is rewarded by the attainment of the person's goal.

Eventually, the definition of social skills was broadened to eliminate the possibility that an individual would use specific social skills to manipulate, intimidate, or violate a person's rights. Phillips (1978), for example, defined a socially skilled person according to "the extent to which he or she can communicate with others in a manner that fulfills one's rights, requirements, satisfactions, or obligations to a reasonable degree without damaging the other person's similar rights, requirements, satisfactions, or obligations, and shares these rights, etc., with others in free and open exchange" (p. 13). This definition is quite encompassing in that it includes the reciprocal interactions of both individuals involved in the social exchange. Phillips (1985) explains that this definition disallows one person to be taken advantage of by another person. For instance, Phillips states that a teacher cannot use intimidation or threats to induce a student to complete an academic task. Phillips also states that a parent or supervisor must use reciprocal interactions to avoid inhibiting a child's or employee's expression of emotions. Thus, social skills should be proactive, prosocial, and reciprocal in nature; in this way the participants of the interaction share in a mutually rewarding experience.

Social Problem Solving. Bijou and Baer (1978) define problem solving as a sequence or an algorithm of behaviors. When we are able to identify this sequence or algorithm of behaviors, we are able to teach it to others. Because problem solving is a covert or cognitive behavior, much of its analysis must be done through language. Social problem solving is the sequence of behaviors that is developed to ameliorate a particular social interaction problem. We are able to identify the social problem-solving process through the analysis of a person's language about a particular social event.

Several researchers propose an algorithm for teaching social problem solving (D'Zurilla & Goldfried, 1971; D'Zurilla & Nezu, 1980; Nezu & D'Zurilla, 1981; Spivack & Shure, 1974). These authors outline five components to be used in a social problem-solving algorithm: (a) problem orientation, (b) problem definition and formulation, (c) generation of solutions, (d) decision making,

and (e) implementation of plan and evaluation and verification of the outcome. This algorithm may include other covert behaviors that influence the effectiveness of the problem solving. These additional covert behaviors include empathy, moral judgment, the ability to process nonverbal cues, and the ability to make inferences.

Self-Determination Skills. The area of self-determination skills for students with disabilities is relatively new. When federally funded projects were initiated between 1990 and 1993, self-determination was researched, skills were identified, and curricula were developed for adolescents with disabilities and for those who are at risk for failure in their communities and schools. The definition of self-determination is currently evolving as the research in this area continues to develop. All the definitions in the current literature, however, are similar in considering that goal-setting skills, decision-making skills, problem-solving skills, social skills, and self-evaluation skills are among the behaviors needed to identify a self-determined person (Field & Hoffman, 1993; 1994; Schloss, Alper, & Jayne, 1994; Ward, 1988). For the purposes of this chapter, the following definition is offered:

> Self determination refers to an individual's awareness of personal strengths and weaknesses, the ability to set goals and make choices, to be assertive at appropriate times, and to interact with others in a socially competent manner. A self-determined person is able to make independent decisions based on his or her ability to use resources, which includes collaborating and networking with others. The outcome for a self-determined person is the ability to realize his or her own potential, to become a productive member of a community, and to obtain his or her goals without infringing on the rights, responsibilities, and goals of others. (Serna & Lau-Smith, 1995, p. 144)

Individuals who are self-determined also exhibit the skill of persistence through problem solving. In meeting goals, everyone is faced with barriers or problems. In order to succeed in accomplishing these goals, the ability to overcome barriers is needed. Usually, this is done through continuous use of the skill of problem solving. With all this in mind, individuals pursue their goals through ethical and appropriate strategies.

ASSESSMENT

The previous discussion concerning the definitions of social competence, social skills, social problem solving, and self-determination skills is important inasmuch as it directly relates to the assessment of child and adolescent behaviors. The construct of social competence, for instance, introduces global behaviors as well as several dimensions of social behaviors. The assessment instruments for social competence therefore are usually global in nature, addressing many behaviors that contribute to a student's total behavior in school and community environments. The instruments designed for the assessment of social skills and social problem solving, however, are more specific in nature. They identify specific nonverbal and verbal behaviors that are required to complete a successful social interaction with another person. The assessment measures for self-determined behaviors are still developing and are in the initial stages of validation on a large population of students.

In the following discussion each assessment category is discussed by presenting brief descriptions of the assessment instruments, how the instruments are implemented, and the advantages and disadvantages of each assessment category. Particular attention is given to the assessment of specific social, problem-solving, and self-determination skills. These assessments are most accessible to teachers and most relevant in establishing social skills and self-determination programs for students in any type of classroom environment.

Assessment of Social Competence

To date, the literature reveals that there are many assessment instruments related to social competence. These instruments usually collect global information and are particularly useful when screening a student for a certain program. Assessment measures under this category are sociometric ratings, ratings by teachers and other adults, and self-report measures.

Sociometric Ratings. Sociometric ratings are assessment instruments that typically have an adult or peer evaluate the student according to some designated dimension (e.g., best friend, most popular, etc.). These assessments are commonly used for identifying the socially competent child or adolescent and attempt to target the student's social status in comparison to the peer group (Foster & Richey, 1979). The most common procedures used with children and adolescents are (a) nominations by peers with regard to who is liked or disliked and (b) peer ratings of each student in the classroom (usually on a Likert-type scale) according to how much the student is liked. For example, a teacher may gather information from peer ratings by giving students a list of their peers (or by displaying snapshots of peers) and asking them to identify their best friend or with whom they would most like to play or work. Scores taken from the Peer Nominations and Peer Rating Scales are compiled to determine the student(s) who are most liked or most disliked.

One advantage of using sociometric measures is that they generally exhibit reliability and validity in predicting the student who is at risk for behavior problems (Asher & Hymel, 1981; Foster & Richey, 1979; Roff, 1972). A disadvantage or limitation of the sociometric procedures is that they often do not provide teachers with information concerning specific behaviors that must be taught or ameliorated. At most, the teachers know that a student receiving votes in the "dislike" category is in need of an intervention.

Ratings by Teachers. Several standardized adaptive behavior scales have been developed as screening instruments for identifying children and adolescents at risk for behavior problems (Dodge & Murphy, 1984). Some of the most common and well validated scales are the Vineland Adaptive Behavior Scales (Sparrow, Balla, & Cicchetti, 1984), AAMR Adaptive Behavior Scales (Nihira, Foster, Shellhaas, & Leland, 1974), Quay-Peterson Behavior Problem Checklist (Quay & Peterson, 1967), the Devereux Adolescent Behavior Rating Scale (Spivack, Sports, & Haines, 1966), and The Social Skills Rating System (Gresham & Elliott, 1990); see Table 14–1.

Implementation of the scales may be demonstrated by the Social Skills Rating System developed by Gresham and Elliott (1990). This adaptive scale not only identifies students at risk for behavior problems but also provides teachers with information on specific social skill deficits. Gresham and Elliott developed an assessment tool for elementary and secondary students. Parents, teachers, and students are asked to rate a student's behavior on the following dimensions: (a) cooperation (e.g., helping others, sharing); (b) assertion (e.g., asking for information); (c) responsibility (e.g., ability to communicate about property and work); (d) empathy (e.g., behaviors showing concern or respect); and (e) self-control (e.g., behaviors that emerge during conflict situations). Ratings are based on the memory of parents, teachers, and students with regard to the frequency (i.e., *never, sometimes, very often*) that a specific behavior occurs. Additionally, a second assessment requires teachers, parents, and students to rate the importance of each behavior. Gresham and Elliott report high validity and reliability scores for the parent and teacher scales but note that the reliability and validity scores for the student scales are less impressive.

Perhaps the most valuable aspect of the Social Skills Rating System is that the authors provide several examples that illustrate how to use the results of the assessment to target specific social skills and develop an intervention program for a student. Teachers should remember, however, that the assessment relies on the memory of the rater and does not indicate the exact frequency with which the behaviors occur (i.e., we don't know what "sometimes" means). Finally, unless several raters fill out the assessment on each child, the teacher cannot be sure if the problem behaviors are due to social deficits or motivation problems within the classroom environment.

Assessment of Specific Social, Problem Solving, and Self-Determination Skills

Dissatisfaction with social competence assessment tools of global behaviors (for example, because the instruments rely on memory or subjective interpretation of past behavior) has led researchers to develop direct observation assessment procedures that require a student to respond to specific instructions or stimuli and then allow observers to rate the performance of the student in that particular situation. These assess-

TABLE 14–1
Adaptive behavior scales commonly used

Assessment Skills	Authors	Publisher
AAMR Adaptive Behavior Scale	Lambert, N., Nihira, K., & Leland, H., 1993	American Association on Mental Retardation/ProEd
Devereux Adolescent Behavior Rating Scale	Spivack, Spotts, & Haines, 1966	Devereux Foundation
Quay-Peterson Behavior Problem Checklist	Quay & Peterson, 1967	Children's Research Center
The Social Skills Rating System	Gresham & Elliott, 1990	American Guidance Service
Vineland Adaptive Behavior Scales	Sparrow, Balla, & Cicchetti, 1984	American Guidance Service

ments are usually related to specific social skills and can help the teacher or tester identify specific nonverbal and verbal behavioral component deficits of a particular skill. For example, a teacher can assess a student's nonverbal skills of eye contact, facing a person, posture, and facial expression while a student is trying to ask for help. Similarly, a teacher can assess the verbal components (i.e., verbal statements as well as voice tone, interrupting, etc.) a student exhibits while trying to ask for help. This direct observation assessment procedure provides information concerning the student's performance of specific skill components (e.g., eye contact) of a particular social skill and in a specific situation. Additionally, the observation can determine whether the social skill is absent due to skill deficits or motivation to use the social skill. Teachers wanting to pursue this form of assessment may want to initiate the following procedures when developing an assessment instrument for their particular classroom of students (Table 14–2).

Step 1: Task Analyze the Social Skill. Once the teacher identifies a problem area (e.g., student is unable to attend to and follow the teacher's instructions), the teacher can develop a social skill that meets the needs of the student (e.g., following instructions skill). The teacher should consider the nonverbal and verbal components of the social skill. In most social skills

TABLE 14–2
Procedures used to establish direct observation assessments of specific social skills

---

Steps

1. Task analyze the social skill.
2. Develop definitions for each behavioral component of the skill.
3. Implement a rating scale to assess the defined behavioral components.
4. Secure a reliability observer.
5. Generate real-life situations that require the student to use the targeted social skills.
6. Plan for individual test sessions.

---

four nonverbal behaviors can be identified: facing the person, eye contact, facial expression (e.g., serious or smiling), and posture (e.g., straight or relaxed). The paraverbal behaviors of voice tone (e.g., pleasant or serious) and volume are also considered during the observation of the social skill. The teacher can then task analyze the verbal components of the "following instructions" skill. For example, after listening to the instruction, students may need to clarify the instructions and then say that they will follow the instructions. The task analysis will require a step-by-step sequence of behaviors that must be executed while following instructions. Table 14–3 exhibits a task analysis of the "following instructions" skill (Hazel et al., 1981a). Notice how the

TABLE 14–3
Task analysis of the "following instructions" skill

Skill Sheet

Following Instructions

1. Face the person.
2. Maintain eye contact.
3. Keep a neutral facial expression.
4. Use a normal tone of voice.
5. Keep a straight posture.
6. Listen closely to the instruction so that you will know what to do and remember to give feedback with head nods and by saying "mm-hmm" and "yeah."
7. Acknowledge the instruction, "*OK.*"
8. Ask for more information if you don't understand the instruction. "*But I don't understand . . .*"
9. Say that you will follow the instruction. "I'll do it . . ."
10. Follow the instruction.
11. Throughout, give polite, pleasant responses.
12. Do not argue with the person about the instruction: follow it and talk to the person later about problems.

Note. From *ASSET: A Social Skills Program for Adolescents* (p. 113), by J. S. Hazel, J. B. Schumaker, J. A. Sherman, and J. B. Sheldon-Wildgen, 1981, Champaign, IL: Research Press. Copyright 1981 by the authors. Reprinted with permission.

verbal components of the skill are labeled and followed by a verbal example. This analysis is important when working with students who exhibit verbal expression problems.

Step 2: Develop Definitions for Each Behavioral Component of the Skill. This step requires that the teacher develop a definition of each behavioral component of the skill. For instance, the nonverbal behavioral component of "face the person" may be defined as "the student's shoulders are positioned parallel to the person giving the instruction, with face and eyes directed toward the person." An approximation of this nonverbal behavioral component may be defined as the "student's shoulders are positioned at a 45-degree angle away from the person giving the instructions, but the face and eyes are still directed toward the person." A definition that describes an inappropriate use of this behavioral component may state that the "student turns the whole body away from the person giving the instructions."

Step 3: Implement a Rating Scale to Assess the Defined Behavioral Components. Although there are a variety of rating scales to be adopted, one of the most efficient scales is the one advocated by Hazel et al. (1981b). These authors use a 2, 1, 0 rating scale for each behavioral component of a skill. For example, a score of 2 is recorded when the student is performing the behavioral component exactly as defined. A score of 1 is recorded when the student approximates the defined behavior (see Step 2). A score of 0 is recorded if the student exhibits the behavioral component inappropriately or does not perform the behavior at all. When the rating scale is applied to the definition of each behavioral component of a skill, the teacher can determine what behavioral components need intervention. Additionally, the teacher can secure a mean score for the student's performance of the skill in a particular situation.

Step 4: Secure a Reliability Observer. In this step, the teacher is required to seek out another individual who can observe the student's performance and reliably score the behaviors according to the definition criteria developed in Step 3 of these procedures. The teacher should instruct the observer by explaining the definitions of the

behavioral components in each skill and demonstrating the desired behaviors. The teacher and observer should practice the scoring procedures by independently observing a student performing a skill (e.g., following instructions) and then comparing their scores. When the teacher's and observer's scores agree on 80% or more of the behavioral components, the teacher can feel confident that the scoring of the behavioral components (according to the stated definitions) is accurate.

Step 5: Generate Real-life Situations that Require the Student to Use the Targeted Social Skills. After the definitions, scoring, and reliability observer are secure, the teacher generates several situations that require the student to use the targeted skills. These situations are used during role-play test sessions (i.e., the teacher and student act out the situation so the student's performance can be evaluated). The situations should be based on real-life incidents that occur in many different settings (home, school, community); for example, when a parent asks a child to take out the trash. The situation may read as follows: "You are in the kitchen when your mother asks you to take out the trash. I'll be your mother and let's act out the situation. '_____' would you take the garbage out to the trash bin?'" This particular situation is used during a role-play test session that assesses the student's performance for the following instructions skill.

Step 6: Plan for Individual Test Sessions. The final step in developing a skill-specific assessment procedure is to plan individual test sessions for each student. There are three methods of collecting the assessment information. First, the teacher can wait for naturally occurring interactions to take place in the classroom and then score the behavior. Although this is the most preferable method to use, it can be problematic if there are few opportunities for the behavior to occur or if the behavior does not occur at all. A second method, the use of confederates, can also be employed if the teacher desires to obtain information in the natural setting. With this method, the teacher must secure the cooperation of other peers or teachers to set up situations so that the student can respond to the peer's (or teacher's) initiations. This method is advantageous if the peers are cooperative, do not prompt the student to use certain behaviors, and do not tell the student that they were asked to participate in this endeavor.

A third method of assessing a student's social skill behavior is during a simulated role-play situation. Using this method, the teacher should begin a test session by securing a private room for the student, teacher, and reliability observer. Once the teacher has eliminated as many distractions and interruptions as possible, the student is told that he or she will be role-playing (acting out) several situations with the teacher. Because preteaching assessments do not require the student to act in accordance with the targeted social skill, the student is instructed to be himself or herself and respond as normally as possible. The teacher then reads the situation (developed in Step 5) to the student, making sure that the student understands the scenario before beginning. Once the student understands the situation, the role-play interaction begins. During the interaction the teacher must not prompt the student and must observe the student's behavior carefully in addition to acting out the role designated in the situation. After this brief role-play interaction (it should not last more than 2 or 3 minutes), the teacher and reliability observer should score each nonverbal and verbal behavior of the social skill according to the designated definitions rating scale (Steps 2 and 3). This procedure continues until all the targeted social skills are assessed.

Regardless of the test method used, the teacher can assess the student's behavior on specific social skills. Multiple assessments (at least three), using different situations and different methods, should be gathered to obtain an overall performance score. With this information, a student's mean scores (or cluster of scores) can be graphed or recorded so that pretest and after-teaching scores can be compared.

Assessment of Self-Determination Skills

Assessment tools for self-determination skills are beginning to be developed. These emerging as-

sessment tools reflect the work of researchers who developed self-determination skills curricula (e.g., Hoffman & Field, 1995; Martin & Huber-Marshall, 1995; Serna & Lau-Smith, 1995). The following description outlines criterion-referenced and curriculum-based assessment tools, as well as behavioral observation checklists, designed for each of five self-determination curricula described later in this chapter.

Assessment Tools for the Steps to Self-Determination Curriculum. Hoffman and Field (1995) describe two assessment tools developed to accompany their curriculum. The first assessment tool, the Self-Determination Observation Checklist (SDOC) is comprised of a teacher-administered behavioral observation checklist that identifies 38 behaviors that are correlated with self-determination skills found in the classroom. The second assessment tool is called the Self-Determination Knowledge Scale (SDKS). This tool is a 30-item structured response test designed to assess the students' cognitive knowledge of different self-determination skills.

Assessment Tools for the Learning with PURPOSE Curriculum. Three assessment tools were developed to complement the Learning with PURPOSE Curriculum (Serna & Lau-Smith, 1995). The first assessment involves a behavioral checklist for each self-determination skill covered in the seven-domain curriculum. Each component of each skill is rated on a three-point rating system to determine if the student was able to demonstrate the skill component as described, approximated the skill component, or did not exhibit the skill component. The second assessment form is a teacher and parent general report in which the individual is required to rate the student's skill competency on a seven-point Likert scale for each of the seven skill areas. Complementing the teacher and parent report is a student self-report measure in which students rate themselves according to perceived skill proficiency in each of the skill areas. The third assessment tool is a 75-item report filled out by the teacher, parent, and student. Each individual is required to rate the student's skill according to proficiency in the skill, the frequency of the skill being used, and the importance of the skill.

Assessment Tool for the ChoiceMaker Curriculum. A criterion-referenced tool was developed by Martin and Huber-Marshall (1995) to be used in conjunction with their curriculum that emphasizes self-determination skills to be used during Individual Education Planning meetings (IEP meetings). The teacher is required to rate the student's self-determination skills and whether opportunities to use the skills occur in the school settings.

Assessment Tools for the Life-Centered Career Education Curriculum. Brolin (1993) developed a career education curriculum that includes a criterion-referenced test that allows the teacher to determine the student's knowledge, performance, and perceptions of each self-determination skill outlined in the curriculum. A second measure, a 40-question self-report measure, was developed to gain information from the student's point of view.

Assessment Tools for the Classroom-Based Competency-Building Curriculum. Abery and his colleagues (Abery et al., 1995) describe two assessment tools that were developed for their curriculum. The first assessment is a criterion-referenced measure, the Self-Determination Skills Evaluation Scale (SDSES), that allows the teacher to determine the student's self-determination knowledge, performance, and perceptions. It consists of a 75-item observation whereby the students are rated on the self-determination skills they exhibit over a 3-month period. The second measure is entitled the Opportunity and Exercise of Self-Determination Scale (OESDS) and consists of a 200-item self-report rating scale for the student, teacher, and parent. This scale asks the individual to assess the extent to which students have the opportunity to exercise personal control in different situations or at least attempt to exercise control when opportunities allow them to do so.

SOCIAL SKILLS AND SELF-DETERMINATION SKILLS: CURRICULA AND INSTRUCTION

Social Skills Curricula

To date, several commercially produced social skills curricula are available to teachers of students with special needs. Many of these social skills programs have been developed by experts in the field of child and adolescent behavior disorders (e.g., Goldstein et al., 1980; Hazel et al., 1981a) and have been field tested to ensure their adaptability to the classroom environment. Among the most notable of these available social skills programs for children in the elementary grades are Skillstreaming the Elementary Child (McGinnis, Goldstein, Sprafkin, & Gershaw, 1998) and the ACCEPTS Program (Walker, McConnell, Holmes, Todis, Walker, & Golden, 1983). Two very popular social skills programs for adolescents with special needs are Skillstreaming the Adolescent (Goldstein et al., 1998) and the ASSET Program (Hazel et al., 1981a). A relatively new adolescent social skills curriculum is the Social Skills for Daily Living (Schumaker, Hazel, & Pederson, 1989). The authors of these programs have developed very adaptable curricula that are recommended for the use of teachers in their classrooms. Whether or not teachers decide to use any one of these programs depends on their preference, the adaptability of the program to the students' needs, and the teachers' familiarity with social skills instruction.

The following discussion will briefly describe each of the social skills curricula mentioned with regard to the assessment procedures recommended, skill content, instructional material, and instructions to the teacher. (Table 14–4 summarizes this discussion.)

Skillstreaming the Elementary Student. Skillstreaming the Elementary School Child: A Guide for Teaching Prosocial Skills (McGinnis et al., 1998) is one of the most popular social skills programs for students in the elementary grades. Packaged in a paperback book for teachers, this program is designed to provide the

TABLE 14–4
Social skills curricula

Social Curricula	Assessment Procedures	Skill Content	Instructional Materials	Instructions to Teacher
1. Skillstreaming the Elementary School Child (McGinnis et al., 1998)	Student skill checklist Teacher skill checklist Group chart	Classroom survival Friendship making Dealing with feelings Alternative to aggression Dealing with stress	Samples of home-work reports Contingency contracts Self-monitoring Home journals	Beginning a group Constructing a structured learning group Suggestions Managing behavior problems
2. ACCEPTS Program (Walker et al., 1983)	Teacher questionnaire Screening checklist Observation forms Placement test Recess rating form Behavior rating form	Classroom skills Basic instructions Getting along Making friends Coping skills	Videotapes	Direct instruction Teaching scripts for each skill Behavior management procedures
3. Skillstreaming the Adolescent (Goldstein et al., 1998)	Skill checklist Group chart Master record	Beginning skills Advanced skills Dealing with feelings Alternative to aggression Dealing with stress Planning skills	Videotapes	Structured learning procedures Selection and grouping Managing behavior problems
4. The ASSET Program: A Social Skills Program for Adolescents (Hazel et al., 1981a)	Criterion checklist Pre- and posttraining checklist Parent questionnaire Parent satisfaction Participant satisfaction	Giving positive feedback Giving negative feedback Accepting negative feedback Negotiation Following instruction Problem solving Resisting peer pressure Conversation	Skill sheets Videotapes Home notes Sample parent letter Sample telephone conversation with parent	Starting a group Basic teaching steps Group leader steps Conducting group meetings Group rules and behavior problems Maintaining skills Quick reference guide
5. Social Skills for Daily Living Program (Schumaker, Hazel, & Pederson, 1989)	Awareness quiz Practice checklist Group practice checklist Mastery role play Surprise mission checklist Bonus mission checklist Instructor surprise missions Teacher rating scales Student rating scales	Prerequisite skills Conversation and friendship skills Skills for getting along with others Problem solving	Skill book Comic book Workbook Practice cards Surprise missions Bonus missions Class plan Student activity record Progress charts Missions plan Missions point sheet	Instructor's manual for each skill area

teacher with different assessment options from direct observation to sociometric ratings. Particular emphasis is placed on teacher frequency ratings of the students' skill performances. The authors recommend this assessment when deciding on the social skills to be targeted for teaching. The social skills presented in this program are divided into five groups: (a) surviving-in-the-classroom skills, (b) friendship-making skills, (c) dealing with feelings, (d) using alternatives to aggression, and (e) dealing with stress. The skills are task analyzed so that each skill has up to six general steps outlined for the student. However, the teaching of each step in the social skill must be extended by teachers through modeling, discussion, and prompting. Finally, a social learning approach/ direct instructional procedure is outlined for teachers to use when teaching the social skill. A set of transcripts, used as examples of instruction, is provided for teachers.

ACCEPTS Program. The Walker Social Skills Curriculum: The ACCEPTS Program (Walker et al., 1983) was developed to promote teacher-student and peer-to-peer interaction skills. The program includes a placement test, direct instructional procedures for teachers, guidelines for teaching, scripts for teaching the social skills, and activities that enhance the skill learning. A behavior management procedure and a videotape are also available with the program. Five social skill areas are emphasized in this program: (a) classroom skills (e.g., listening, following rules); (b) basic interaction skills (e.g., eye contact, starting, taking turns); (c) getting-along skills (e.g., sharing, assisting others); (d) making friends skills (e.g., smiling, complimenting); and (e) coping skills (e.g., when to say "no").

Skillstreaming the Adolescent. Skillstreaming the Adolescent: A Structured Learning Approach to Teaching Prosocial Skills (Goldstein et al., 1998) is packaged in an easy-to-handle paperback book for teachers. The authors begin by introducing the history of social skills in the field of education and continue with a description of the social learning approach to social skills instruction. Following these preliminary chapters,

they present the teacher with a rating scale for evaluating the social behavior of their students. Like the teacher rating scales described under the assessment section of this chapter, the authors list the target skill (e.g., saying "thank you"), give an example of the skill (e.g., "Does the student let others know that he or she is grateful for favors, etc.?"), and then provide a frequency rating scale of 1 to 5 (i.e., a rating of 1 would indicate *Never* and a rating of 5 would indicate *Always*). The assessment of these 50 skills allows the teacher to target the most deficient skills in the student's repertoire.

Once the deficient skills have been targeted, the authors present the 50 skills categorized under six groups: (a) beginning social skills (e.g., listening, starting a conversation, question asking); (b) advanced social skills (e.g., asking for help, joining in, following instructions); (c) skills for dealing with feelings (e.g., knowing your feelings, dealing with fear); (d) skill alternatives to aggression (e.g., asking permission, sharing something, negotiation); (e) skills for dealing with stress (e.g., making a complaint, dealing with embarrassment, responding to persuasion); and (f) planning skills (e.g., deciding on something to do; setting a goal; making a decision). Each skill is then task analyzed into three- to four-step directions for the student. The authors then instruct the teacher by providing transcripts of social skill instruction groups. These transcripts provide examples of the direct instructional procedures and how to prompt a student to use each step of the targeted skill. A videotape instructing teachers how to conduct a social skills group is available under separate cover.

ASSET Program. The ASSET Program: A Social Skills Program for Adolescents (Hazel et al., 1981a), consists of a leader's guide manual and skill sheets that are used during the skill teaching sessions. The authors introduce their program with an overview of the program. The second chapter describes the essential components in developing and starting a social skills teaching group. Chapters 3, 4, and 5 of the leader's manual focus on the teaching skills (i.e., direct instructional procedures) needed to conduct a social skills group.

Research associated with this social skills program reveals that the investigators socially validated the eight skills presented in the curriculum. Teachers, court officers, and professionals working with adolescents identified eight skills they thought were the most beneficial for adolescents to learn in order to be successful in the academic, home, and community environments (Hazel et al., 1981b). These skills include giving positive feedback, giving negative feedback, accepting negative feedback, resisting peer pressure, problem solving, negotiating, following instructions, and conversing. The program is designed so that a teacher will teach all eight skills to students.

The best feature of this program is the skill sheets that are provided for the teacher and students. Each skill sheet involves a step-by-step task analysis of each skill, divided into nonverbal, verbal, and some covert skill components (e.g., listening). Each verbal step of the skill is accompanied by a verbal example of what an adolescent might say in a certain situation. This feature is advantageous for students who require verbal prompts and possess limited English/verbal skills. The skill sheets are also adaptable to all grade levels by modifying the number of skill steps and the difficulty of the language used. The final section of the teacher's guide includes sociometric measures for teachers, parents, and students. Instructional videotapes are also available under separate cover but are not necessary to conduct an effective social skills program.

Social Skills for Daily Living Program.

The Social Skills for Daily Living Program (Schumaker et al., 1989) presents 30 social skills for adolescents with special needs. The authors include several instructional materials to enhance their direct instructional approach to teaching each social skill. These additional materials include workbooks, skill books, comic books, and practice cards (for role playing). Assessment materials consist of a practice checklist, group practice checklist, and mastery checklist for each skill.

This social skills program presents each skill in the same fashion as the ASSET Program (Hazel et al., 1981a). Each skill is task analyzed in a step-

by-step format with the nonverbal and verbal components outlined in sequential order. The program exceeds the ASSET Program, however, in that the comic books and workbooks enhance each step of the direct instructional procedure (e.g., definitions, rationales, and examples) used to teach the skills. This feature is particularly advantageous for students who are able to read at or above a fifth-grade level. However, teachers are cautioned when using this program that the many features of the program must be carefully coordinated and planned if the skill teaching is to be successful. The instructional materials do not take the place of effective teacher modeling, role playing, and feedback to the students.

Social and Self-Determination Curricula for Young Children

So far most of the social and self determination curricula have been developed for adolescents with disabilities. Ultimately, however, skill building in this area should begin as early as possible (Kamps & Tankersly, 1996; Tankersly, Kamps, Mancina, & Weidinger, 1996; Forness et al., in press). If children are taught following-instruction, self-evaluation, self-advocacy, self-regulation, problem-solving, and decision-making skills at an early age, numerous social and mental health issues that plague young children can be prevented (Forness et al., 1996; Serna, Forness, & Nielsen, 1998).

One attempt to develop a curriculum for young children is now in progress (Serna, Nielsen, & Forness, 1997). After socially validating five social and self-determination skills for young children (i.e., following instructions, sharing, self-regulations, problem solving, and decision making) a curriculum based on story telling was initiated. This story telling process involves the orchestration of carefully developed animal stories with direct instructional procedures embedded throughout the introduction, plot, and resolution of the story (see Fig. 14-1 for an example of a storyline that introduces the skills "saying hello" and "giving a compliment"). The teacher begins by (a) introducing the animals in the story (e.g., "What is a

FIGURE 14–1
Teaching social and self-determination skills through stories: An example of a story that teaches how to say hello and give compliments.

The Ballad of Sammy the Scorpion
By Dwayne Norris

Larry the Lizard came loping along.
Shuffling his shoes and singing a song.

When looking around at the dry desert land
His eyes did spy a scorpion named Sam.

"Hola, partner," the lizard exclaimed.
"They call me Larry. What is your name?"

The scorpion lashed his stinger at Larry; how rude!
Larry jumped back and said, "What's wrong with you, dude?"

"I didn't mean to offend you," said Sammy so slow.
"I was only trying to tell you 'Hello.'"

"That's an odd way to greet someone, Sir Scorpion.
It's easy to see why you don't have many friends.
But, if you will listen, I'll try to explain
How to tell someone you like them without causing pain."

"Would you, oh could you?" the scorpion asked.
"Certainly, there's very few steps to the task...
When you meet a new person who you really dig,
Square your shoulders with them, don't dance a jig."
That lets them know that you care what they say.
Now keep eye contact with them and don't turn away.
Smile when you're talking and you'll be surprised
How a glow of warm friendship will fill your friend's eyes.

Now, when you're facing the person, eyes meet and teeth flashed,
Remember to keep a posture that says you're relaxed.
And don't be afraid to point out things that you like
About your friend's tail or stinger or bike."

"Wow, that's so cool. I never thought about that.
I will have to try some of this positive feedback."

Just then Pete the Prairie Dog appeared from the ground
Burrowing, out of his prairie dog mound.

He said: 'What's up? What are you guys doing?"
And Sammy remembered that he shouldn't sting.

A new friend, rather, he turned clockwise,
Squared his shoulders with Pete and looked at his eyes.
He smiled at the rodent with a body most calm.
He said: "Hello! I like your buckteeth and how you tunnel along.
The Lizard was happy, singing "Way to go, Sam."
And Sammy and Pete became very good friends.

(Printed with the author's permission)

porcupine?"), (b) reading the story, (c) talking about each section of the story that emphasizes a directional step, (d) modeling the skill steps introduced in the story, and (e) requiring each child to practice the steps.

Once the children learn the self-determination/social skill in the story-time portion of the day, a learning center is available for the children to practice their newly acquired skill. The practice is monitored by the teacher and feedback is given to each child. Generalization of the skill is prompted and reinforced at other learning centers and during outside play time.

Although the curriculum is still being developed, preliminary data and observations indicate that very young children can learn these social/self-determination skills (Serna, Nielsen, & Forness, in preparation). Longitudinal studies, however, are required to establish the maintenance and long-term effects of this type of teaching for young children.

Self-Determination Curricula for Adolescents

The Office of Special Education and Rehabilitative Service initiated a series of grants to fund demonstration projects in the area of self-determination. Approximately 26 demonstration models were funded between the years 1990 and 1993. These researchers were asked to investigate and develop self-determination programs that taught youth to become more independent and future oriented. Of these projects, five socially validated programs are outlined below.

Steps to Self-Determination Curriculum. The Steps to Self-Determination program, developed by Field and Hoffman (1992), consists of six steps to independence and self-determination. These steps include: (a) knowing yourself, (b) valuing yourself, (c) planning, (d) acting, (e) experiencing outcomes, and (f) learning. Each of these steps is divided into 16 class sessions where the students are taught specific skills of self-evaluation, goal setting and planning, risk taking, decision making, independent performance, and adjustment. The program is designed to be implemented in a one-semester period and involves parents and community members as support people during the program. Figure 14–2 represents the curriculum model that Field and Hoffman advocate.

Learning with PURPOSE. Learning with PURPOSE: Self-Determination Skills for Students Who are At Risk for School and Community Failure (Serna & Lau-Smith, 1994; 1995) is a curriculum developed for the use of teachers who work in inclusive settings with students who (a) have

FIGURE 14–2

Model for self-determination

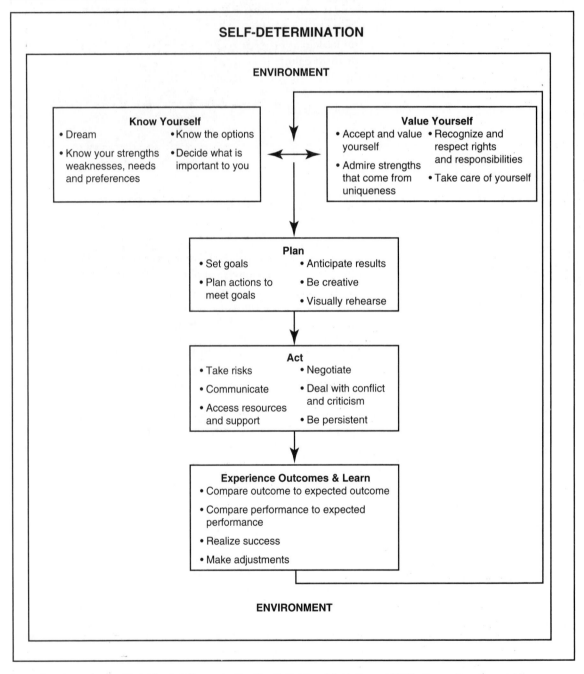

SELF-DETERMINATION

ENVIRONMENT

Know Yourself
- Dream
- Know your strengths weaknesses, needs and preferences
- Know the options
- Decide what is important to you

Value Yourself
- Accept and value yourself
- Admire strengths that come from uniqueness
- Recognize and respect rights and responsibilities
- Take care of yourself

Plan
- Set goals
- Plan actions to meet goals
- Anticipate results
- Be creative
- Visually rehearse

Act
- Take risks
- Communicate
- Access resources and support
- Negotiate
- Deal with conflict and criticism
- Be persistent

Experience Outcomes & Learn
- Compare outcome to expected outcome
- Compare performance to expected performance
- Realize success
- Make adjustments

ENVIRONMENT

From "Development of a Model for Self-Determination," by S. Field and A. Hoffman (1994), *Career Development for Exceptional Individuals 17,* 165. Copyright © 1994 by CDEI. Reprinted with permission.

mild to moderate disabilities, (b) are at risk for failure in their school and community, and (c) are in the general education classroom. The teaching model of the curriculum was piloted with students who were high, regular, and at-risk achievers as well as students receiving special education services. Based on this research, Figure 14–3 lists those skills that many high achievers exhibit as compared to students who are at risk for failure in the classroom and community and shows how the curriculum skills address these deficits areas.

The curriculum contains seven domain areas with a total of 34 skills and three guideline areas. The domain areas consist of (a) prerequisite social skills, (b) self-evaluation skills, (c) self-direction skills, (d) networking skills, (e) collaboration skills, (f) persistence and risk-taking skills, and (g) stress management. The program is designed to be used during a 5-year period (Grades 8 through 12). For example, eighth-grade students could begin learning the skills of communication and assertiveness (social skills) as well as self-direction skills. By the time they are in the twelfth grade, they should be learning the skills of collaboration and formal networking to prepare them for their transition into the community and work place.

ChoiceMakers. ChoiceMakers (Martin & Huber-Marshall, 1995) is a curriculum that specifically focuses on the leadership of students during their IEP meeting. This curriculum contains three basic sections: (a) choosing goals, (b) expressing goals, and (c) taking action. Within these three sections, seven concepts are taught in the form of skills areas. These areas include (a) selfawareness, (b) self-advocacy, (c) self-efficacy, (d) decision making, (e) independent performance, (f) self-evaluation, and (g) adjustment. All skills taught in the curriculum address transition areas and student attainment during their high school years. The goal is to plan and prepare students for a successful transition into the world of work and the community outside school. Table 14–5 outlines the curriculum concepts and their associated skills.

Life-Centered Career Education Curriculum. This well-established curriculum was originally developed by Brolin (1993) for youth with developmental disabilities. As part of the federally funded self-determination projects, Wehmeyer (1995) adapted and field tested the curriculum to promote self-determination skills for adolescents with disabilities. The curriculum includes 350 lesson plans for students who are 12 to 18 years of age. Self-determination lessons are intended to be used sequentially beginning with Lesson 10 (goal setting), yet all lessons enhance the learning of independence among adolescents.

Classroom Competency Building Program. Abery and his colleagues (Abery et al., 1995) developed a 10-module curriculum that includes the following skill areas: (a) self-awareness, (b) self-esteem, (c) perceptions of personal control, (d) personal values, (e) goal setting, (f) assertive communication, (g) choice making, (h) self-regulation, (i) problem solving, and (j) personal advocacy. The curriculum is designed for students with mild to moderate developmental disabilities and is for the most part experiential in nature to encourage active learning among the students. A parent program also was incorporated along with this curriculum; Table 14–6 illustrates the the curriculum skill modules.

Direct Instruction of Social and Self-Determination Skills

The teaching process typically employed in social skills instruction is structured learning or direct instruction. This behavioral approach to teaching consists of modeling, role playing, corrective feedback, and planning for generalization (Goldstein et al., 1980). Another variation of the structured learning model is a teaching interaction procedure perfected by Phillips, Phillips, Fixsen, and Wolf (1974). This procedure requires the teacher to engage in specific steps that can be used with an individual and in a group situation. The steps include the following: (a) beginning with a positive statement about the student, (b) defining the social skill to be learned, (c) giving a rationale regarding the importance of the skill, (d) giving an example of when the skill could be used, (e) introducing and explaining

FIGURE 14–3

Comparison of successful and at-risk student behaviors and ways the Learning with PURPOSE curriculum meets these students' needs.

A Comparison of Successful and At-Risk Student Behaviors		Identification of Self-Determination Skills Needed to Be Successful — Identified Self-Determination Skills							
In many cases, successful students:	In many cases, at-risk students exhibit:	Social Skills	Self-Evaluation	Self-Direction	Informal and Formal Networking	Collaboration	Problem Solving & Decision Making	Stress Management	Family Program
• Suceed in areas of academics, art, drama, and sports.	• Difficulties in school (e.g., work habits, coping, peer relations).	•		•			•	•	
• Exhibit survival skills in different situations.	• Functional skills only in their subculture (e.g., gangs).	•					•		
• Exhibit healthy communication and social skills.	• Communication and social skill problems.	•							•
• Gain positive attention from others.	• Self-defeating behaviors to gain negative attention.	•							
• Make statements of positive self-regard, indicating self-esteem.	• Behaviors that indicate self-esteem problems vary according to situation.	•	•						
• Use reflective/self-evaluation skills.	• No or few self-evaluation skills.		•						
• Exhibit ability to delay gratification.	• Impulsive behavior—need immediate gratification.	•		•				•	
• Maintain future orientation/goals.	• No self-direction or goal-setting skills.			•				•	
• Acquire supportive and encouraging teachers, peers, and adults.	• No acquisition of teacher support or few collaboration and networking skills.	•			•	•		•	
• Seek help when needed.	• Asking for help skills, but not always.	•			•	•			
• Exhibit locus of control through decision-making skills.	• Little or few decision-making skills.						•		
• Overcome problem/barriers.	• Few problem-solving skills.	•					•		
• Learn to survive stress and use humor.	• Inappropriate stress-management skills (e.g., drugs).						•	•	
• Use negative situations to learn from and for future positive outcomes.	• Listless, nonproductive behavior due to their negative view of personal situation (e.g., depressed, hopeless).		•		•	•	•		
• Experience positive parent discipline and interactions.	• Behaviors that indicate fluctuating family environments.	•		•					•

TABLE 14–7
Teaching interaction

Nonverbal Behavior
1. Face the student.
2. Maintain eye contact.
3. Maintain a neutral or pleasant facial expression.

Paraverbal Behavior
4. Maintain a neutral tone of voice.
5. Speak at a moderate volume.

Verbal Teaching Behavior
6. Begin with a compliment related to the student's efforts and achievements.
7. Introduce the social skill and define what the social skill means.
8. Give a rationale for learning the skill and for using the skill with others.
9. Share an experience when you used the social skill or could have used the social skill.
10. Specify each behavior (e.g., nonverbal and verbal behavior) to be considered when exhibiting the skill.
11. Demonstrate or model the use of the skill.
12. Have the student rehearse the social skill. (Observe the student's behavior.)
13. Provide positive corrective feedback.
    State what the student did correctly.
    Provide suggestions for improvement.
    Demonstrate the corrective suggestions.
14. Practice the social skill with the student. (Make sure you do not prompt.)
15. Continue to provide corrective feedback to practice until the student masters (100%) the social skill in a novel situation.
16. Plan, with the student, when and where to use the social skill.

Remember: Make sure the student participates throughout the lesson. To do so, ask questions and let the student share ideas and thoughts. Always praise the student for participating and rehearsing the social skill.

ful implementation of the teaching interaction is to involve the student in the teaching procedure. For example, before defining the targeted social skill, teachers should ask students if they know what the skill means. Likewise, asking students to provide rationales for why the skill is important to learn allows them to think of how the skill can be integrated into everyday social interactions. By personalizing the social skill, the teacher may find that students are more willing to use the skill.

Generalization of Social, Problem-Solving, and Self-Determination Skills

As social, problem-solving, and self-determination skills instruction has assumed increasing importance in the promotion of competent behaviors, the effectiveness of direct instructional procedures is well noted in the literature. Yet the success of acquiring these skills in the instructional setting is only half the journey toward fluency of skills and eventual social and personal competence. Since the mid-1970s researchers and educators have identified the problem of skill generalization as the other key factor in promoting social and personal competence (Lovejoy & Routh, 1988; McConnell, 1987; Schumaker & Hazel, 1984; Stokes & Baer, 1977).

Haring and Liberty (1990) define generalization in broad terms such as "responding appropriately to new situations." Specifically, the generalization of social or self-determination skills is defined as the use of acquired skills (a) with people other than the social or self-determination skills instructor, (b) across environments other than the instructional settings, and (c) in to situations other than those experienced during instruction of the social or self-determination skill.

In the past, the generalization of any skill was thought to be a phenomenon that just happened (Stokes & Baer, 1977). Teachers were accustomed to the idea that once a skill was taught, a student could naturally perform the skill when needed. However, generalization was quickly recognized as the performance of acquired skills through the use of procedures specific to the skill.

Acknowledging the problems with generalization of social and self-determination skills, researchers are currently investigating the use of different generalization strategies. A majority of these strategies are the outcome of the work by Stokes and Baer (1977). In their classic article, the authors outline a technology of generalization that can be used to facilitate the use of any acquired skill with different people, in different settings, and in varied situations. The following discussion outlines strategies that are based on the work of Stokes and Baer and provides examples of the identified strategies.

Generalization Strategies and Examples

Stokes and Baer (1977) identify nine strategies that can be used to facilitate generalization of skills. These strategies will be presented under four categories: (a) antecedent strategies, (b) setting strategies, (c) consequent strategies, and (d) other strategies (Haring & Liberty, 1990). When available, examples of the strategies will be taken from investigations concerning the generalization of social skills for students who exhibit mild to moderate disabilities.

Antecedent Strategies. Haring and Liberty (1990) suggest that two generalization strategies (outlined in Stokes & Baer, 1977) can be categorized as antecedent strategies, or strategies introduced during the teaching of the social skill. By using antecedent strategies during instruction of the social skill, teachers are incorporating environmental factors that may prompt or maintain the use of the social skill outside the teaching setting. The use of antecedent strategies may accomplish the goal of acquisition and generalization through one intervention. The first antecedent strategy, program common stimuli, uses a predominant factor or a salient stimulus that is common to both the instructional setting and a generalization setting. A teacher therefore should consider what stimuli are present in both settings and then employ the salient stimulus (or stimuli) during the instruction of the social skill. A very obvious salient stimulus is exemplified by classroom peers. Using peers (especially peers from general education classes)

to participate in the teaching, learning, or monitoring of social skills can facilitate the use of social skills wherever the designated peers may appear (McConnell, 1987). The second antecedent strategy used to facilitate generalization is sufficient exemplars. This strategy incorporates the teaching of several examples using the same direct teaching procedures, so generalization of social skills to new settings and new situations and responses can occur. An example of teaching sufficient exemplars can be seen in the study by Hazel et al. (1981b). These authors taught sufficient exemplars during the rehearsal portion of their teaching interaction. A new situation was used each time a student rehearsed the social skill. This continued until the student rehearsed the skill to 100% criteria in a novel role-playing situation. The outcome was generalization to hypothetical situations presented during posttesting of the social skills.

Setting Strategies. The second category of generalization strategies involves a strategy intervention that is implemented whenever the social skills behavior is desired. This strategy, called *sequential modification,* is a tactic of planning a social skills program in every condition (i.e., across people, setting, or situation) in which generalization is desired. Kelley and Serna (in preparation) conducted a study in which the social skills instruction was provided in one classroom and the generalization of the acquired skills was assessed in different desired settings (mainstream classroom, cafeteria, and playground). When generalization of the skills did not occur in the different settings, the authors taught the social skills sequentially in each setting until generalization occurred over all the desired settings.

Consequence Strategies. Haring and Liberty (1990) propose that a third category of generalization strategies is one that deals with the reinforcement of social skill behaviors in the natural setting (outside the instructional setting). The reinforcement or punishment (i.e., consequences) of the social skills directly relates to the continued use of the social skill and therefore directly relates to the generalization of the behavior. The authors target three generalization strategies (Stokes & Baer, 1977) under this category: (a) introduce to natural maintaining contingencies, (b) use indiscriminable contingencies, and (c) train to generalize.

The first generalization strategy under the category of consequences involves introducing the student to natural maintaining contingencies. This strategy deals with the use of people (or outcomes) who may reinforce the student for appropriate use of the social skill in the natural environment. Teaching the social skill to fluency can facilitate this strategy as well as ensure that the student experiences reinforcement for social skill performances. Although empirically based studies demonstrating the effectiveness of this strategy were not found in the social skills literature, teachers employ this strategy throughout the school year when they inform teachers and parents that a student has learned a particular skill and should be praised for the use of the skill in their classrooms or at home.

The use of reinforcement is highly desirable when one wishes to maintain a skill in any environment. Researchers in the area of behavior analysis demonstrate that the use of intermittent reinforcement can maintain a behavior for long periods of time (Ferster, Culbertson, & Boren, 1975). The use of indiscriminable contingencies therefore becomes another generalization strategy under the category of consequent strategies. This strategy is recognized when a student is unable to determine when reinforcement is going to occur for a desired behavior. Not knowing when reinforcement will occur, students are more likely to engage in the behavior in the hope that a positive outcome will emerge. Kazdin and Polster (1973) conducted a study in which the acquired social interactions of two students were reinforced with tokens. One student received continuous reinforcement, the other intermittent reinforcement; only the student receiving intermittent reinforcement continued appropriate interactions with peers.

The last strategy under the category of consequent strategies is the train-to-generalize strategy. This strategy can be described as a systematic use of instruction to facilitate generalization. A teacher can tell the student about generalization, model the generalized use of the social skill, and ask the student to use the skill. Blackbourn (1989) reports that after a shop teacher instructed a student to use the desired behavior, the social skill was observed in the shop class.

Other Strategies. Haring and Liberty (1990) created a fourth category for the Stokes and Baer (1977) generalization strategies. Having no particular focus, this category may be called a catch-all category of other strategies. The strategies under this category are: (a) train loosely, (b) mediate generalization, and (c) train and hope. Training loosely is described as teaching social skills during every appropriate opportunity during the school day. This means that a teacher may elect to teach social skills using the context of the presenting classroom or school environment. By doing so, the teacher can enhance the possibility that students will begin to use their social skills in a variety of settings, with other people, and in different situations. This strategy has not been investigated through experimental procedures but can be demonstrated when teachers and parents use every opportunity to teach social skills to a student (e.g., parents often teach their children to say "please" and "thank you" at every available opportunity).

Using the generalization strategy, a teacher will instruct students in the use of covert or overt behaviors that will help them to remember how and when to use a social skill. Most exemplified in the literature on social skill generalization for adolescents is the self-monitoring or self-control procedure. Self-monitoring procedures are taught to students so they can remember to use the learned social skills in settings outside the teaching environment (e.g., Kiburtz, Miller, & Morrow, 1984).

Finally, authors in the field of generalization (Stokes & Baer, 1977; Haring & Liberty, 1990) identify the "train and hope" practice that is employed by many researchers and teachers alike. Actually, *train and hope* signifies the nonexistence of any generalization strategy. Providing social skills instruction and then "hoping" the skills will occur across different settings, people, or situations exemplifies this aspect of generalization.

ESTABLISHING A SOCIAL OR SELF-DETERMINATION SKILLS PROGRAM

Once a teacher decides that a social or self-determination skills program should be made part of the school curricula, preparation for implementing the program must begin. To do so the teacher should follow the presented sequence of events: (a) identify students through observation and assessment, (b) develop students' social skills profiles, (c) consider the grouping of the students, (d) prepare for program implementation, (e) implement social skills teaching procedures, (f) evaluate student performances after each skill is taught, and (g) program for generalization of the learned social skills to the natural environment.

Identify Students

The first step in establishing a social or self-determination skills program is to identify the students who exhibit interpersonal and personal problems in or outside the classroom environment. This may be done by observing student behaviors during classroom activities, using standardized adaptive behavior scales, and surveying significant other people (i.e., other teachers, parents, and peers) concerning the students' social behaviors. Once the teacher has gathered this first and secondhand information, an analysis of the data may reveal that specific social skills are lacking. At this point, the teacher will broaden the scope of information by isolating a set of specific social or self-determination skills and assessing the student's performance of each skill during simulated situations. From this information, the teacher can identify whether (a) skill components (e.g., recognizing that a skill should be used, nonverbal behaviors, verbal behaviors) of each skill are present in the student's repertoire; and (b) stu-

dents are choosing not to use social skills that are in their repertoire (motivation problem). From this analysis, a final set of social or self-determination skills can be targeted for the overall needs of the students.

Develop Student Profiles

After the teacher compiles a set of targeted skills for each student, a skills profile may be developed. The profile will illustrate the student's competency level on each skill and indicate which skills need to be taught. When a profile is constructed for each student, the teacher may wish to identify a group of social skills that seem to be common across all the students.

Group Your Students

If a teacher plans to implement a social or self-determination skills program with a select number of students (rather than the entire class), it is wise to identify several aspects of the group's composition (Goldstein et al., 1980; Hazel et al., 1981a). An important consideration may be grouping students who are friends and would enjoy learning the social skills together. Although this may work well for the students, a teacher also must consider if such a group would exhibit unmanageable behaviors; if so, a different grouping may be considered. Most often authors of social skills curricula (e.g., Goldstein et al., 1998; Hazel et al., 1981a) suggest that teachers compose a group that is heterogeneous (males and females) in nature. Also, a group of students with varying intelligence is possible because students needing help can be paired with a peer who already knows the skill. The two students can work together in a tutor-tutee relationship.

Finally, a teacher may wish to consider the size of the skills instruction group. Although an entire class (15 or more) can engage in the skills program, teachers might find the behavioral rehearsal of the skills (role playing) difficult to manage. This monitoring is especially crucial when establishing mastery performance criteria. On the other hand, more student participants can add to the diversity of the shared problems so that everyone can learn that other students have similar or worse problems. Sharing these experiences, coupled with learning how to deal with situations through the use of social and self-determination skills, may facilitate the generalization of the social skills among peers.

Socially Validate Your Program

One of the most important preparation steps is to make sure that the skills you are going to teach are necessary and appropriate for the children. The purchase of a social skills or self-determination skills program does not guarantee that desirable skills will be taught. One way to ensure that the appropriate skills are being taught to students is to socially validate the program (Wolf, 1969) by developing a list of all the skills that may be taught. Ask parents, teachers, and counselors (and students, if possible) to review the skill list and rank the skills in the order of importance based on the needs of the children. The skills with the highest rankings are the skills that others feel are important to teach.

Prepare for Program Implementation

Once the assessment and student groupings are established, preparation for the social skills teaching must take place. This preparation includes deciding when and where the teaching will occur (e.g., three times a week), making sure the teaching procedures are well understood (refer to the skill teaching section of this chapter), and explaining the program to the students (e.g., describing the social skills that will be learned, explaining the benefits of learning the social skills, enlisting their cooperation and creating enthusiasm for learning the social skills).

Implement the Program

The direct instructional procedures outlined in this chapter and in social and self-determnation skills curricula have been experimentally evaluated to be some of the most effective methods for teaching skills to children and adolescents. In addition to these procedures, however, Hazel et al. (1981a) stress that teachers must exhibit other teaching behaviors. These behaviors include (a) controlling off-task behavior, (b) using students' names, (c) programming for student participation throughout the teaching process, (d) teaching at a lively pace to avoid boredom, (e) using praise continuously, (f) exhibiting enthusiasm during the teaching of social skills, (g) using humor whenever possible, (h) being sincere and interested in the successful acquisition and mastery of the social skills, (i) displaying a pleasant manner, and (j) being empathetic with the students.

Another aspect of the teaching of social skills that is not usually emphasized is teaching to mastery. Teachers should make sure the students have learned the components of each social skill (e.g., use a learning strategy or memorize the skill for long-term retention) without hesitation and can then exhibit 100% mastery in the skill in a novel role-playing situation during the social skills teaching sessions.

Evaluate Student Performances

Once the students have reached a 100% mastery level in the social skill teaching setting, the teacher should evaluate the students' performances in the test setting or in the natural environment. Assessments that take place in the test setting allow the teacher to evaluate the student's individual performance in novel simulated situations in a setting outside the teaching environment. Assessing the students' social skill performances in the natural environment may involve using confederate peers or teachers or arranging the environment so that the teacher can observe whether a student recognizes the need for the social skill and then engages in that particular social or self-determination skill. In either case, teachers are assessing some aspect of skill generalization and should use the information to program for further teaching of the social skill or to progress to the teaching of a new skill.

Program for Generalization

Once the teacher determines that the students have acquired the targeted social skills, an analysis must be made of whether the social skills are generalizing to the natural environment. If students are not using their newly acquired skills, teachers should plan for and employ the generalization strategies suggested by Stokes and Baer (1977). Additionally, classroom activities may be planned so that students have opportunities to use their learned social and self-determination skills and teachers have opportunities to reinforce the students' use of their social and self-determination skills. The ideas in the Activities section may facilitate the generalization of specific social and self-determination skills to the natural environment.

SUMMARY

In a society where emotional ills, verbal and physical aggression, and failure among youth are becoming the most predominant problems within schools, the importance of social competence and self-determination skills must not be underestimated. Teachers who exhibit the skills to teach these behaviors are equally important. It is necessary therefore to make deliberate efforts to train future teachers in the area of social skills and self-determination skills. Through concerted efforts, teachers and parents may foster independent behaviors and appropriate interactions that contribute to successful individuals.

The purpose of this chapter is to provide information to teachers who want to establish a social and self-determination skills program for students exhibiting failure in the classroom and community. A history of the area of social skills is presented, with a rationale for teaching social competency skills (social skills and social problem-solving skills) to students. With knowledge of this history and rationales, the reader is introduced to assessment procedures and program content in the area of social skills and self-determination skills. This discussion includes examples of different social skills programs as well as new and innovative self-determination skills programs. The chapter then addresses the instruction of these skills and how to promote generalization of social and self-determination skills. Of utmost importance is the presentation

of activities that teachers can use when facilitating the use of social or self-determination skills in their classroom.

These activities should not be confused with instruction in these skills. For students to gain the benefits of these skills, the following components must be initiated: (a) structured learning, (b) guided practice, (c) individual practice, and (d) planned generalization of the skills.

ACTIVITIES

1. Institute a regular "Friday Shakes" activity in which students line up at the door before Friday dismissal and the teacher shakes the hand of each student and gives him or her some personalized compliment or praise.

2. As students learn appropriate behaviors and social skills in the classroom, they should start identifying these behaviors in other students. Place a box with a slot in a prominent location and label it the "Praise Box" (or whatever creative title desired). As you and the students (stress student participation) observe someone doing acts of kindness, consideration, encouragement, and learning social skills in and out of the classroom, have them write it down (or write a note yourself telling of the appropriate activity, noting the time, the place, and the name of the person doing the behavior.) At the end of the day or week, open the box and give all praise notes to the named students. Be sure that each student gets at least one "praise" note per time (Hayden, 1980).

3. In class, during specified time, have each student find and say one thing he or she likes about two classmates.

4. Develop specific routines to welcome new students to the classroom. During class meetings, ask the students, "What things would you want to know if you were new in this school?" Make a list of informational facts about the school so that the students can answer any questions a new student might have.

5. Develop a specific skill for welcoming visitors to the classroom. Each week, assign a student

to greet visitors, ask them to sit down, and perform any other task that may make the visitor more comfortable in the classroom.

6. Assign "buddies" to new students in your classroom. The buddy is responsible for introducing the new student to peers and other teachers as well as for asking the new student to participate in different social situations (e.g., eat lunch together, play games, sit together at school assemblies).

7. Develop a "secret buddy." Each week, each student selects the name of another student in the classroom. During the week, the secret buddy is responsible for doing "nice" things for the student whose name was selected. These can involve leaving a "hello" note for the buddy, bringing a surprise, or helping the buddy with a class assignment. At the end of the week, students guess their secret buddies.

8. Read a story involving a particular social interaction problem or issue. Through a class discussion, let the students identify the problem, list possible solutions and the outcomes of each solution, and decide which solution would be most beneficial to all involved.

9. Instead of just playing team sports, the students work together to decide the best offensive and defensive strategies to use during a game. The position of each team member can be discussed and agreed upon by the team as a whole instead of being assigned by the coach.

10. During the morning class meeting, have students talk about personal or interpersonal problems concerning the school and the community. Conduct a problem-solving session where peers provide possible solutions to the problems. Then, as a class, decide on the best solution for all involved and how the solution will be implemented. Role-play the implementation of the solution, since it often requires the use of many social skills. Always follow up to see if the implemented solution worked.

11. Have a student bring an item or something of value to school. Have the student tell about it and why he or she likes it. If the item was given to the student, have the student talk about that person and the relationship between the item, student, and person.

12. Have students identify feelings that can be associated with items that are valued (e.g., "My grandma gave me this stuffed bear for my birthday. I like my grandma because . . . She knew I wanted a stuffed bear. I think of my grandma when I play with my bear.")

13. Each time a group of students seem to be disagreeing, have them resolve the conflict by each "giving and taking" a little through the skill of negotiation. Make sure you foster a "win-win" situation.

14. Teach students the skill of negotiation. Each week, select a student to be the peer mediator, who will facilitate a conflict resolution when it occurs between two or more persons. Make sure the peer mediator is well liked and respected among the peers.

15. Have students develop goals that relate to their learned social skills. For example, one goal may be this: "I will use my skill of saying "thank-you" three times this week." Have students monitor their achievement with goal accomplishment sheets and graphs.

16. Have each student think of a social skill upon which he or she would like to improve and write this goal on a card (e.g., "I will use my Accepting Criticism skill with Mr. K_____"). The students check off each time they used or did not use the skill on the card (which is filed in a box in the classroom) every day for 2 weeks. At the end of 1 week and at the end of 2 weeks, have the students discuss their progress and any changes they recognize.

17. A self-determination activity that will promote long-term goal setting is to have the students create a picture of what they wish their lives to look like 10 years from today.

18. A self-determination activity that will promote long-term goal setting is to ask the students to list what they would like to learn during the academic year. Let them choose a subject area and state what they want to accomplish in a 1-month, 3-month, 6-month, and 9-month period.

19. Promote self-evaluation skills by having the students create self-portraits. Self-portraits may be drawn from memory or through the use of mirrors (Canfield & Wells, 1994).

20. Place butcher paper across the classroom. Have your students draw pictures of "professional" people. Then have them draw a picture of what a professional person can do to help them. After they have drawn their pictures, have a discussion about the advice or information we can acquire from professionals.

21. Arrange for professionals from the community to come visit your class. People such as real estate people, dentists, telephone operators, and so forth can provide information that students can seek out. Take pictures of the professionals and start a scrapbook of who the students can talk to when they need to seek advice, opinions, or information.

22. For younger children who need to learn how to express their feelings to alleviate stress, read the book: *Alexander and the Terrible, Horrible, No Good, Very Bad Day.* After the story is read, ask the children how they think Alexander was feeling. Explain that it is all right to feel sad and mad and that sometimes it helps to tell someone or express how you are feeling. Have the students write or draw pictures of a terrible, horrible day that happened to them (Freeman, 1992).

23. Keep a problem box in your classroom. Students may write down problems and put them in the box. Once a week, take time to discuss the problems in a group. Have students generate solutions to the problems and discuss the possible outcomes to each problem. Emphasize that problem solving is a way to persist toward a certain goal or to overcome a barrier.

24. Teachers do not often ask students what they want out of class or how the teacher and classmates could do things differently to make learning easier or more fun. Ask the students to write down what they want to be different in the class. Follow up by providing students with choices in the classroom.

25. Teach your students how to manage their time by filling out time cards of what they do after school. Then make a time card for the classroom. After an entire day, have the students divide the day up into a "pie graph." This will show the students how much time is devoted to different activities and what can be changed.

TEACHER TIPS

Past knowledge of friendships of students with learning disabilities (LD) indicated that these children had few friends and were not among the popular peer-nominated classmates. In addition, early reseachers thought that there was a correlation between the unpopular status and the self esteem of children with LD. New developmental studies, however, shed a different light on the friendships of children with and without LD. For example, recent investigations indicate that friendships are not exclusive to classmates and their peers are not primary agents influencing self esteem. What researchers are finding is that friendships and self-esteem have several dimensions.

Vaughn and Elbaum (1999) report that elementary aged children with learning disabilities look very much like their nondisabled peers with regard to friendships. Although the young children with LD had slightly fewer friends, the differences were not great. Young children with LD also indicated that some of their friends were not necessarily classmates; a response that mirrored their nondisabled peers. As for the quality of the friendships, young children usually attributed activities to the quality of their friendships.

As children grow into their middle and high school years, the students with LD continue to have a comparable (but slightly lower) number of friends than their nondisabled peers. The two groups of students are still identifying other peers outside of school among their group of friends. At this point, however, the students with LD are indicating less quality in their friendships as their peers are indicating more intimate factors as a measure of friendship quality. It seems that students with LD are equating peer support in academic matters as a quality factor in friendships whereas their nondisabled peers are becoming independent of academic matters when evaluating friendship quality.

Finally, Vaughn and Elbaum indicate that self-esteem is not dependent on friends per se. Depending on the dimension of self esteem, they found that students with and without LD gain their self esteem primarily from their parents, then their close relatives (e.g., grandparents and siblings) and friends, and last of all from their teachers. They go on to report that self-esteem with regard to academic matters is different than other aspects of life requiring a measure of self-esteem. Unfortunately, academic self-esteem remains low among children with LD regardless of age.

Vaughn, S., & Elbaum, B. (1999). The self-concept and friendships of students with learning disabilities and developmental perspectives. In R. Gillmore, L.P. Bernheimer, D. L. MacMillan, D. L. Speece, & S. Vaughn (Eds.). *Developmental perspectives on children with high-incidence disabilities.* Hillsdale, NJ: Lawrence Erlbaum Associates.

TEACHER TIPS   Secondary Level

Steven Covey is the author of several books that have guided people toward their own self-determined behavior as well as success in their personal and professional life. Some of his books are:

- The 7 Habits of Highly Effective People
- First Things First
- Principle-Centered Leadership
- The Power Principle
- The 10 Natural Laws of Successful Time and Life Management
- The 7 Habits of Highly Effective Families

Most recently, however, Covey has written a book entitled *The 7 Habits of Highly Effective Teens.* This book is written specifically for teenagers and has been adopted by secondary schools across the nation as a way to motivate and empower teenagers. The purposes for developing the habits are outlined as (a) getting control of your life, (b) improving your relationships with your friends, (c) making smarter decisions, (d) getting along with your parents, (e) overcoming addiction, (f) defining your values and what matters most to you, (g) getting more done in less time, (h) increasing your self-confidence, (i) being happy, and (j) finding balance between school, work, friends, and everything else.

The habits that Covey covers in his book are as follows:

Habit 1: **Be Proactive**
Take responsibility for your life
Habit 2: **Begin with the End in Mind**
Define your mission and goals in life.
Habit 3: **Put First Things First**
Prioritize, and do the most important things first.
Habit 4: **Think Win-Win**
Have an everyone-can-win attitude.
Habit 5: **Seek First to Understand, Then to Be Understood**
Listen to people sincerely.
Habit 6: **Synergize**
Work together to achieve more.
Habit 7: **Sharpen the Saw**
Renew yourself regularly. (p.9)

In addition to the habits, Covey works on getting students to take "baby steps" when trying to implement each habit or lesson.

Covey, S. (1998). *The 7 habits of highly effective teens.* New York: Fireside/Simon & Schuster, Inc.

TEACHER TIPS

Technology

Teachers and students must constantly be aware of their self-determined behaviors in all aspects of their lives. This self-monitoring also applies to the use of technology in educators' lives. Donna Baubach and Mary Bird (1999) are very much aware of this aspect of teachers' lives and, using Steven Covey's book as their inspiration, they have adapted his principles for technology-using educators. The following outline is a summary of what Bauback and Bird developed:

1. **Be Proactive.** Effective technology-using teachers don't wait for the perfect software or the perfect situation to use technology. They work with what they have and overcome barriers to obtain their goals. They are realists and know that effective use of technology doesn't mean that everything will be perfect or smooth operating.
2. **Begin with the end in mind.** "Effective technology-using teachers plan, plan, plan and then, knowing things happen with technology, create a Plan B . . . . Effective technology-using teachers choose hardware, software and technology with desired student outcomes in mind. It becomes an integral part of the instruction, not an add-on." (p.13)
3. **Put first things first.** The first thing in school and in education is the student. Not technology. It can only help us do more for our students.
4. **Think win/win.** "Effective technology-using teachers don't spend their time trying to convert the un-willing . . . Effective technology-using teachers do share their expertise with those who show in-terest and . . . a willingness to reciprocate." (p.14)
5. **Seek first to understand, then to be understood.** "If we can learn to listen and start with the (technol-ogy) needs of others instead of our own agendas, we can begin to see the bigger picture." (p. 14)
6. **Synergize.** This habit means that an effective technology-using teacher gets people to work cooper-atively and collaboratively to help the school survive and thrive. Be aware of your goals and estab-lish them as a priority.
7. **Sharpen the saw.** Effective technology-using educators preserve and enhance their greatest assets: themselves. Take care of yourself by eating right, exercising, and learning to manage stress.

Baumback, D. & Bird, M. (1999). The seven habits of highly effective technology-using educators. *Special Education Technology Practice, 1* (2). 12–14.

CHAPTER 15

Creative Arts: Visual Arts, Music, Dance, and Drama

Glenn H. Buck

The creative arts (i.e., visual arts, music, dance, and drama) have always held a position of importance in the human community. Their expression has been, and remains, universal (Pascale, 1993). We see evidence of this universality across cultures and historical periods (Cohen & Hoot, 1997) and in everyday life, such as when we observe a child drawing on the sidewalk, or when a group of adolescents sing and dance while listening to the radio.

The creative arts enjoy universal appeal for a number of reasons. On the group level they provide a means by which a society defines, redefines, and perpetuates cultural values and norms of self- and group expression. On the individual level, they extend the human experience by introducing novelty into our world and establishing ritual in our lives. The creative arts strengthen personal connection with the world because they require us to think, create, feel, move, appreciate, express, and share—activities that form the basis of the human experience.

Despite their universality, access to the creative arts have historically been somewhat restricted for persons with disabilities. Even as late as the 1980s many people with disabilities were often excluded from school and community arts programs. The affirmation of the notion that access and participation in the creative arts is an inalienable right for *all* people is a recent development (Harlan, 1993). Today, more people with disabilities than ever are involved in a variety of community-based arts programs, such as performing in or attending concerts and plays (Blandy, 1993). Moreover, growing numbers of individuals with disabilities pursue careers, and in some cases gain national recognition, as writers, musicians, dancers, actors, and artists. This positive trend has been the result of both legislation (e.g., Americans with Disabilities Act) and increased efforts on local levels to normalize environments for persons with disabilities (Harlan, 1993). Although this trend is encouraging, it is still important to remember that individuals with disabilities are less likely than their nondisabled peers to belong to school or community arts groups. Unfortunately, the leisure time of many

individuals with disabilities is spent on passive activities such as viewing television rather than participation in community-based creative arts activities (Salend, 1994; Wilkening, 1993).

This chapter introduces basic guidelines for incorporating a variety of creative arts activities into the educational programs of students with disabilities. Both general and specific teaching techniques are presented. It should be noted, however, that even though this book focuses on teaching methods for students with high incidence (i.e., mild) disabilities, instructional strategies effective for *all* severity levels have been included in this chapter. This broad approach is based on several factors. First, special educators in today's special education classes may work with students from a wide range of severity levels, no matter how they were trained or how the classroom is defined (such as resource/mild disabilities). Therefore teachers who have a variety of instructional techniques are better prepared to meet the challenges of teaching in diverse classrooms. Second, many teaching ideas for the severe population can be adapted for students with mild disabilities. And third, because many special educators are collaborating with general education and arts-specific teachers (e.g., choral directors), it is important that they know the wide array of teaching strategies in the creative arts. A basic knowledge of the arts helps special educators to be more effective collaborators; this chapter can serve as a reference for them.

RATIONALE FOR CREATIVE ARTS INSTRUCTION

Whereas all students can benefit from involvement of the creative arts, students with disabilities benefit most of all. Some of these benefits include improved cognition, literacy and basic language skills, verbal and nonverbal communication skills, self-expression, self-discipline, self-awareness, self-esteem, mutual respect, trust, and decision making skills (Cohen & Hoot, 1997; de la Cruz, Lian, & Morreau 1998). The creative arts also stimulate intellectual curiosity, develop motor skills, reduce levels of physical and emotional stress, and foster appreciation for cultural heritage and human diversity. When combined with academic subject areas, the creative arts can provide novel and enjoyable means of learning new information.

For persons with severe disabilities especially, involvement in the creative arts can lead to the development of certain leisure-related skills, such as those related to self-expression, communication, and social behavior, which are learned as a consequence of such participation. Acquisition of such skills (a) allows persons greater freedom in making choices about how to utilize free time, (b) allows persons to access more complex leisure and recreation activities, and (c) reduces the dependency on others for lifelong leisure participation (Buck & Gregoire, 1996; Hawkins, 1994).

Schools can play an important role in helping students with disabilities to gain benefits from the creative arts. Formal groups (e.g., band) and planned classroom arts activities offer opportunities for students to develop artistic skills as well as experience the enjoyment that comes with involvement in the arts. Students benefit from the arts especially when they engage in arts activities with their nondisabled peers. Unfortunately, however, creative arts opportunities in many schools are presented in ways that reduce their effectiveness for students with disabilities (Henley, 1990). Some of these problems include:

- Often, rehearsals are scheduled before or after school hours, times after which the special education bus has left.
- Arts-related teachers often lack information about the needs of special students, because these teachers tend to work in isolation and have few opportunities to collaborate. As a result, creative arts teachers tend to rely on traditional instructional practices (e.g., large-group instruction with minimal efforts toward individualization) that are not always effective with students with disabilities (Pfeuffer-Guay, 1993a).
- Special and general educators often incorporate the arts into their curricula in a random

and haphazard manner (Carter, 1993). Often, creative arts activities are provided infrequently or they are planned as time fillers rather than as valuable learning experiences. When creative arts activities are provided in an unconnected manner, teachers reinforce the idea that art is less important than other subjects. Such an idea is misplaced because the benefits of creative arts activities, especially when they occur across a variety of settings, are numerous. If the benefits of education in the creative arts are to be realized, teachers must provide arts activities in a broader and more holistic manner.

- The current decline in arts opportunities for all students across school districts reduces the opportunities for involvement in the arts for all students. This situation has resulted from overall reductions in financial support for creative arts programs. Ironically, expensive special education programs often deplete the resources needed to maintain arts programs that would benefit the students with disabilities.

Taken together or separately, these factors may in part explain negative attitudes some art and music teachers hold toward the inclusion of students with disabilities in their classes (Pfeuffer-Guay, 1993a; Sideridis & Chandler, 1996). Given the fact that the creative arts are often the first areas within which special students are mainstreamed (because they require less reading and fewer other academic-related skills) this potential negativity on the part of arts teachers presents a disconcerting paradox.

Fortunately, some of the problems inherent in the education of students with disabilities in the creative arts can be resolved by effective collaboration. Special educators can assist creative arts educators by providing knowledge of the learning and behavioral characteristics of students with disabilities (Oi, 1988; Pfeuffer-Guay, 1993a). In turn, creative arts educators can provide special and general educators with knowledge about creative activities, procedures, and materials that can be used in classroom activities. Through such collaboration, art teachers become more positive toward and knowledgeable about working with students with disabilities, and special educators become more skilled at integrating creative arts activities into their classes.

GENERAL INSTRUCTIONAL GUIDELINES

Teachers should consider several guidelines when planning and implementing creative arts activities. While effective for all students, these guidelines are especially relevant to students with disabilities. Creative arts should be

- *integrated:* Creative arts activities should be integrated throughout the curriculum, not just added on as isolated activities used to fill up time. Pfeuffer-Guay (1993b) observed a special education teacher who turned a measuring and cake baking unit into a celebration of Van Gogh's birthday; another teacher led students to create box sculptures that represented first-aid kits during a unit on safety. These two examples point to the idea that the creative arts do not have to occur in an isolated time period but can be used in a variety of contexts.

When arts activities are incorporated in an integrated fashion, students learn the skills and attitudes necessary for lifelong participation in the creative arts. For students with disabilities, who typically have difficulty generalizing skills, integration of the arts throughout the curriculum promotes transfer of learned behaviors and attitudes across multiple settings.

- *student-centered:* Creative arts activities should be based on students' interests, preferences, and abilities. Teachers who include students in the planning of creative arts activities increase student motivation. Students also develop independence when given choices and when they are allowed to express preferences. According to Harlan (1993), "creativity flourishes where individuals have choices . . . a variety of art materials and open-ended activities

allow participants to take initiative and to express their preferences" (p. 1).

- *age-appropriate:* Any creative arts activity should be planned with consideration of the students' chronological and developmental age. Secondary teachers who require their students to sing nursery school songs continue the image of the older student with disabilities as being childlike. Likewise, elementary-level students are rarely successful when they are required to create intricate art products that require them to follow complex directions.

For young children, creative arts activities should focus on self-expression, exploration, and experimentation. Students should be able to play with colors, shapes, three-dimensional objects, textured materials, sound, sound-producing toys, and unstructured movement. In drama, children should have opportunities to engage in make-believe, role-playing, simple story telling, puppetry, and pantomime.

As students get older, activities should gradually change to the development of skills and attitudes that will result in lifelong participation in the arts. Learning the history of great artists, musicians, and theatrical personalities, as well as learning how to recognize styles and characteristics of an art form, leads to appreciation. By focusing on the technical skills related to the production of artistic products and the social behaviors and attitudes necessary for participation in an organized community arts group, students increase their potential for access, participation, and enjoyment in arts opportunities throughout life.

- *process-oriented:* No matter what the chronological age, teachers should never lose sight of the fact that the act of creating is often more exciting and fun than completing a product. For example, for young children, watching colors mix together is often much more exciting than finishing a picture. This simple observation-type learning is a necessary developmental step that should be allowed because it serves as a basis for more complex creativity later. Unfortunately, too many teachers have an unrelenting desire to see young children *make* something—any product that approximates what the teacher rather than the child had in mind. This push to make young children artistic clones of adults frequently results in children feeling inadequate. Often, children end up avoiding arts activities because of frustration and a belief that they cannot draw, paint, sing, dance, or act as well as they should. How many adults avoid singing in public because they were told at a young age they couldn't carry a tune?

This criticism of teacher directed, product-oriented activities is not to be interpreted as a call for their elimination. Children who spend all their efforts in 'free-form' creativity activities may never learn basic skills needed for more complex creative endeavors. As a result, they may never have the opportunity to achieve satisfaction from a product well done. Any future artist, musician, dancer, or actor must learn fundamental skills. However, teachers should balance activities with both high and low structure. Basic skills can be taught in fun, creative ways.

- *multisensory:* Students with disabilities often retain new information for longer periods of time when lessons include opportunities to learn information by using a variety of senses. Lessons that incorporate music, art, movement, and drama (separately or in combination) allow students to acquire and practice new skills and concepts in multiple ways. Students who are learning about Native Americans, for example, will remember information about the culture if they have opportunities to experience the culture through song, art, dance, and drama.

- *multidimensionally taught:* Students tend to learn when they have opportunities to learn from each other and when they become actively engaged in the learning process. One of the criticisms of traditional arts programs has been the overemphasis on teacher-directed instruction (Platt & Janeczko, 1991). While students with disabilities benefit from arts activities that are task-analyzed and taught via a direct instruction model, creativity is reduced

when these approaches are the sole form of instruction. This shortcoming has been documented in current literature, and arts educators now are recommending the use of a variety of teaching methods for students with disabilities. Advocates are calling for more extensive use of the cooperative learning and peer tutoring models (e.g., Platt & Janeczko, 1991; Spencer, 1992). Other recommendations for enriching arts activities include teaching students to access arts opportunities on the Internet and using field trips, guest speakers, video recordings, and other nontraditional approaches.

- *set in a creative environment:* Teachers should make their classrooms places where creativity is allowed to flourish. One of the best ways for teachers to accomplish such a goal is for them to model creative behaviors themselves and to show sincere interest in the creative arts. Specifically, teachers can incorporate the arts throughout their curriculum, display art in their classrooms, and report about concerts, art exhibits, dance and theatrical performances attended. During arts activities, teachers can provide nonfrustrating and age-appropriate materials, reinforce students' efforts as well as their products, and remain nonjudgmental, helping students take pride in their creativity.

INSTRUCTION IN THE VISUAL ARTS

Painting, drawing, sculpting, collage, and photography represent the most common types of visual art forms found in most schools. Students experience these art forms in formal art classes and when their classroom teachers incorporate art activities into lessons. Modification and activity ideas related to these five visual arts are addressed in this chapter. However, teachers should investigate the use of other arts and crafts activities that often are enjoyed, particularly by secondary students. Some of these include jewelry making, gem crafts, metalworking, woodworking, plastic crafts, silkscreening, leather crafts, papier-mâché, weaving, shell crafts, and ceramics. Books on these topics are available in most libraries and bookstores.

Table 15-1 includes an observation checklist of skills related to the visual arts. Teachers may find this checklist useful when they incorporate this art form into their programs, or by special educators as they collaborate with general educators. Depending upon the goals targeted for an individual student, this list can be modified and some of the skills rewritten as objectives and included in the student's IEP, or in the general educator's lesson plans.

Adaptations

Across all settings, students with disabilities frequently need material and instructional adaptations in order for them to participate fully in the creative process. In deciding which adaptations are appropriate, teachers should focus on individual abilities and preferences. A sample list of prerequisite skills that are often required when participating in visual arts activities is presented in Table 15-2. While deficits in any of these skill areas certainly do not preclude participation, such deficits often necessitate certain adaptations (listed in the following section).

General Adaptations. Although students with cognitive and behavioral difficulties constitute a highly heterogeneous population, several adaptations can be made to improve their ability to participate in art activities. (The following adaptations have been adapted from Pascale, 1993; Pfeuffer-Guay, 1993a.)

1. Reduce the number of materials (in order to reduce the number of decisions students have to make).
2. Break down complex procedures into small sequential steps (task analysis).
3. Provide hand-over-hand assistance (when needed).
4. Make directions simple and direct.
5. Provide activities that involve cutting and gluing for students who work too quickly.

TABLE 15–1
Visual arts skill checklist

Observation
_____ 1. Student communicates feelings evoked while observing a work of art.
_____ 2. Student identifies details and characteristics in a work of art (e.g., colors, shapes, objects, themes).
_____ 3. Student defines the concept "art gallery."
_____ 4. Student behaves appropriately while visiting an art gallery.

Participation
_____ 5. Student prepares the work area before initiating an art activity.
_____ 6. Student begins working without prompting.
_____ 7. Student manipulates materials.
_____ 8. Student completes an art activity.
_____ 9. Student displays his or her art work.
_____ 10. Student cleans up the work area.

Appreciation
_____ 11. Student critiques his or her art work, or the work of others.
_____ 12. Student participates in discussions about art.
_____ 13. Student reports about a public arts event that she or he attended.

TABLE 15–2

Prerequisite skills for participation in visual arts activities

---

_____ 1. Student is able to hold and manipulate an art tool (e.g., brush).

_____ 2. Student is able to distinguish colors and shapes.

_____ 3. Student is able to distinguish same and different concepts.

_____ 4. Student is able to hold and manipulate pieces of materials of various sizes.

_____ 5. The student is able to communicate preferences.

Adaptations for Students with Physical Limitations. Students who have difficulty with reaching, grasping, or keeping hands steady can benefit from art activities that require them to manipulate materials. With adaptations, students with physical limitations strengthen fine and gross motor skills and improve overall range of motion (i.e., the extent to which a person can move various parts of the body). Specific adaptations for students with physical limitations (as adapted in part from Ensign, 1992, 1994; Platt & Janeczko, 1991; Pfeuffer-Guay, 1993b) include:

1. Use large-handled brushes, attach Hoyle pencil grippers (see Chapter 10) to brushes, or attach brushes to hands using Velcro straps. Allow students to hold brush by teeth or toes.
2. Use large, chunky crayons or oaktag.
3. Melt crayons and let them cool. The resulting mass is easier for students with manual dexterity problems to grasp.
4. Give hand-over-hand assistance if needed.
5. Attach a turntable to top of work table so that students with restricted reach are better able to access materials.
6. Secure paper to the desk for drawing and painting. Paper can be secured with tape (or magnets if working on a metal surface).
7. Attach a small easel to the top of the work table.
8. Raise or lower the height of the table depending on wheelchair size.
9. It may be easier for some students to work on the floor, with an angled wedge provided to support the arm. (Consult with physical or occupational therapist.)
10. Use less frustrating materials (e.g., use yarn instead of string, sponge instead of brushes, cardboard or thick paper instead of construction paper).
11. Provide adaptive scissors.
12. Place finger paints on a cookie sheet or in a baking pan.

Adaptations for Students with Visual Impairments. Participation in art activities that are primarily dependent on sight can be a challenge for persons with limited vision. When developing art activities, teachers should gather as much information about a student's visual impairment as possible, because the type and severity of the impairment will determine the type and number of adaptations that need to be made. Information often can be obtained from the student's family or by consulting with the student's ophthalmologist. Generally, the following guidelines can be considered when teaching a student with a visual impairment:

1. Alter the amount of light in the work area. Depending upon the type of vision problem, a student may need to work in an area where the amount of light has been increased or reduced. (Consult with family or student's ophthalmologist.) For students who see better in less light, placement away from sources of light (e.g., windows, overhead lights) or the utilization of a study carrel can be effective in reducing the amount of light in a work area.
2. In order to reduce glare, have students work on light grey or light brown colored paper.
3. Provide high-contrast materials. Magic markers that produce dark primary colors may have better visibility against contrasting paper than lighter-colored primary or secondary-color markers. Materials that are shiny or fluorescent also may assist visual discrimination.

4. In order to prevent spills, put paints in travel coffee cups (i.e., cups that are wide on the bottom and narrow on the top). Also, paints can be placed in a baking pan to keep them contained.

5. Rubber gloves or boots can be cut up and glued to the bottom of containers to prevent sliding.

6. Provide magic markers, pencils, and brushes with large tips so that lines and marks will appear large on the paper.

7. Glue a small piece of cardboard in the middle of the paper to serve as a reference point. An alternative to the reference point is to punch holes in the corners of the paper (Platt & Janeczko, 1991).

8. Place materials in an ordered fashion in the work area (e.g., always place the crayons in the upper left corner of the table).

Art Activities

Painting. Free-form painting is one of the most common art activities used in the classroom. Painting helps students practice combinations of gross and fine motor movements and extend range of motion, as well as allowing them to experiment with color. Teachers should provide ample opportunities for students to paint with a variety of colors, textures, and painting tools (e.g., brushes, fingers, wooden blocks, string). Some recommendations for the use of painting in the classroom include:

1. Students can paint while listening to different styles of music. Encourage the students to discuss feelings evoked by the music.

2. Have students paint by a variety of means—painting with fingers, feet, paintbrushes, sponges, or blocks. Students often enjoy placing paint on paper and blowing on the paint through a straw to create interesting designs.

3. Write students' names or other letters of the alphabet in very large letters (36 inches tall) on large paper (can be obtained from newspaper printers). Have students fill in the letters with tempera paints.

4. Show the students a well-known art work. Discuss the theme of the picture. Follow up with the students creating their own pictures on a similar theme (Livermore, 1996).

5. Have students lie in a supine position on a large piece of paper. Trace each child's body. Have students paint inside the tracing.

6. Let students work together to create a large mural. Murals are large pictures that are made on walls or on large pieces of paper attached to a wall. Murals can have a particular theme (e.g., children around the world) although this is not necessary.

7. Have students lie down on a very large sheet of paper (obtained from newspaper printers). Draw around them individually and let them color in eyes, nose, mouth, and other facial details. Have children color in clothes they are wearing and cut the figures out.

8. Have pupils paint large macaroni. (Use water color or tempera paint.) When the macaroni is dry, have children string it into a necklace. (Use kite string or shoelaces.)

9. Have students paint half of the outside bottom of an egg carton, adding eyes and pipe cleaner antennae to make a caterpillar. Draw a butterfly outline on paper and have the children decorate it and cut it out. Then glue it onto a pinch clothespin. Coordinate this idea with the concept of caterpillars changing into butterflies.

10. Have students help design and produce backdrops for school plays and musical productions.

11. For students prone to eating paint, use homemade, nontoxic finger paints. Mix over low heat: 3 tablespoons sugar and $\frac{1}{2}$ cup cornstarch; add 2 cups cold water; stir until thick; divide mixture into medium-sized cupcake tins; add a drop or two of food coloring and allow to cool. Mixture can be stored in refrigerator between uses (Ensign, 1992).

Free Form/Object/Figure Drawing. The ability to draw is highly variable, depending on a variety of abilities (e.g., manual dexterity, attention; Spencer, 1992). However, teachers should encourage drawing for all students, because it helps them observe details in the world (e.g., shape, size, proportion, perspective) and it allows them to represent the world in two-dimensional form. For free-form drawing especially, the process of creating a picture expands a student's imagination and provides an excellent forum to promote social interaction with peers (as students discuss each other's pictures). Some recommendations for the use of drawing in the classroom include:

1. Encourage students to draw pictures of real or imagined objects. Students can be given actual objects to use as models. It is especially important to let students with visual difficulties manipulate the objects before drawing. Also, there is some evidence that students tend to draw with more detail when they work on large paper (Spencer, 1992).
2. Have students draw pictures using a variety of writing and drawing tools, such as rules, compasses, stencils, protractors, etc.
3. Encourage students to draw self-portraits or portraits of each other, their families, or the teacher. Students can share these with each other.
4. Teach students simple elements of perspective (e.g., objects that are far away are drawn smaller than closer objects).
5. Provide activities in which students copy simple pictures. While copying certainly would not be considered to be a highly creative activity, it does have value in helping students develop the mechanical skills necessary for more complex creative work. According to Spencer (1992), copying helps students acquire graphic schemata necessary for later representational drawing. When copying activities are used, teachers should keep them simple by limiting the number of details in the prompts.
6. Draw part of a picture for the student, based on a particular theme or topic. Let the student finish the drawing. A series of creative workbooks based on this idea is available through the Owl Book Company. The workbooks are known as the Anti-Coloring Books and are available in most school supply stores.

Sculpting. Sculpting (i.e., creating three-dimensional objects) can be an effective means for developing students' fine and gross motor skills and for developing a sense of size, shape, and proportion. A variety of materials can be used in the sculpting process, some of which include clay, playdough, mud, sand, plaster, cardboard, and styrofoam. Some recommendations for the use of sculpting in the classroom include:

1. Give students ample opportunities to explore with different sculpting materials. Often, students enjoy repetitive movement patterns, such as rolling, pushing, pounding, and chopping. These basic movements should be encouraged, because they form the basis for later, more complex, work.
2. For representational sculptures, move from simple to more complex projects. For instance, it is better for students to start with sculpting representations of mountains and valleys in a sand box rather than sculpting representations of people. However, students' individual preferences should be allowed to influence the process and product.
3. Have students create sculptures from objects and materials found in the immediate environment. For example, a leather glove can be positioned upside down, filled with water (provided it doesn't leak), and suspended in a freezer by string and clothes pins. Once the water has frozen, students can quickly cut the glove from the ice. Through this type of activity, students learn the idea of casting. Follow-up information about art forms that use this type of process (e.g., ceramics) can be incorporated into the lesson.
4. Have students mold numbers or letters (such as the letters in their names) from clay or playdough. Let them dry and then have students paint them with water colors or tempera paint.
5. Let students mold clay to form animals, foods, people, and objects, and have them tell you what they are making. Rolling pins and cookie cutters can be used.
6. Teach mathematical concepts such as fractions, addition, and subtraction by requiring children to count clay balls and tear clay into more than one part.

7. For students prone to eating clay, teachers can use homemade, nontoxic playdough. Add 1 package unsweetened Kool-Aid mix to 2 cups of water in a pan; add 2 cups flour, 2 tsp cream of tartar, ½ cup of salt, and 2 tbsp oil to the pan. Cook over medium heat for 5–10 minutes, stirring constantly. Playdough is done when color deepens and it comes together in a ball. Let cool and cover tightly to store.

Collage. Collage (French, meaning "to paste") is an effective medium for self-expression. Just about any material can be used in the making of a collage (Pascale, 1993; Table 15-3). Collage making requires students to select, cut, and manipulate various-sized materials and to make decisions about their placements on the paper. Collages can be personalized by including pictures of students or by including pictures cut from magazines that represent students' interests. However, not all collages need to look like something; often, students enjoy creating a collage without any theme. Instead, they may focus on color, shape, or size of materials (Pascale, 1993). Some recommendations for the use of collage in the classroom include:

1. Limit the amount of material that is available for students to use in making the collage, depending on the abilities and learning style of students.
2. Cut up the collage and make a mobile.
3. Students can make a collage by cutting pictures from magazines that reflect their interests, hobbies, or future career and life desires.
4. Take a walk or have a scavenger hunt to collect flowers, leaves, nuts, and seeds. Have students glue these to a sheet of paper to make a picture or put them in between sheets of waxed paper, iron the sheets together (low setting), and make a place mat. Coordinate this with a discussion about changing seasons (fall or spring). Talk about things found in the woods or coordinate with a unit on ecology.
5. Have pupils collect leaves in the fall and bring them to class. Using white or brown paper, place different-sized leaves under different pieces of paper. Then have students rub

TABLE 15-3
Sample materials used in collage

Tinsel	Cut-up balloons
Wallpaper samples	Yarn
Gift wrap	Cotton balls
Doilies	Sandpaper
Foil	Corrugated paper
Newspaper	String
Cellophane	Tape
Sheet plastic	Glue
Ribbon	Glue cups
Assorted contact paper	Stick
Magazines	Scissors
Brass fasteners	Paper plates
Napkins	Material scraps
Scrap paper	Sawdust

Note. From *Multi-arts Resource Guide,* by L. Pascale, 1993, Boston: Very Special Arts Massachusetts. (ERIC Reproduction Service No. ED 370 330)

crayons over the top of the paper. After outlines of the leaves are formed on the paper, have students cut the leaves out. These cutouts can be put on a bulletin board or made into student scrapbooks.
6. Obtain scrap wallpaper from paint stores. Let students develop appreciation for shape by making wallpaper collages.
7. Art and reading can be combined in book review collages. Students should select a book they have completed and then cut out words and pictures from magazines and newspapers to illustrate the idea of the book (Crisculo, 1985).

Photography. Photography can be an effective instructional medium for all students. Given a camera's ability to capture reality, students are able to record events and things of interest to them that have real-life relevance. According to Bildman (1982), students become more in touch with their environments and learn a sense of sequence in events along with a perception of time and space. Students not only learn to use a camera, they also learn to make decisions about what to photograph. Students may wish to photograph objects of beauty or situations that represent social injustices. It should be remembered that photography does not have to be restricted to the use of a 35-mm camera. Students also can use a video camera to record events. Whichever type of camera used, some specific recommendations for using photography in the classroom include:

1. Have students take photos of each other engaged in activities they enjoy (e.g., sports, music) and make a mobile or collage of the photos.
2. Have students take photos of an outside object at different times throughout the school year. Place the photos side by side and have the students discuss or write about how the scenery changes according to the seasons.
3. Have students take slide pictures of school events and activities. Later, students can give slide shows in other classrooms (good for developing some public speaking skills).
4. Have students develop their own personal portfolios of photos they have taken. Have an open house where students get to show off their portfolios to visitors.

INSTRUCTION IN MUSIC

Attention to the relationship between music and human behavior has a long history. Through the centuries, poets, writers, and philosophers have written about the power of music to evoke images, emotions, abilities, and belief systems (Marshall & Tomcala, 1981). Today, music is very much a part of everyday life. Think about how many times music enters our lives each day and how it affects us.

Music plays a major role in the everyday and special day lives of most people. It has frequent applications ranging from simple sounds for improving the environment to complex, integrated, artistic works forming the core of life's important ceremonies. . . . Music is used whenever humanity wishes to transcend, when humans want to mark the most important ceremonies of transition in life, when events are to be made memorable, when it is important to unify groups, and to

achieve physical sedation or stimulation. (Duerksen, 1981, p. 1)

Music plays an important role in the curriculum of most schools. Although students with disabilities have access to musical opportunities, it should be remembered that for all students, the extent to which they participate in music activities and the types of music activities that are provided are relative to school type. Elementary students often receive instruction in a general music class where they are introduced to the basic elements and history of music, group singing, and musical instruments. In middle school, students often continue in general music class; however, the content becomes more sophisticated. Students are expected to have a basic understanding of musical notation, harmony and theory, and music history. Many schools introduce basic keyboarding skills at this time. In middle school, students also are provided opportunities to participate in an organized music ensemble such as a choir, band, or orchestra. On the secondary level, however, it is unusual for students to receive general music classes. At this level, music involvement is typically focused on the organized ensembles (with admittance often contingent upon a tryout and continued participation dependent on the maintenance of a certain level of competence) (Buck & Gregoire, 1996).

Students with disabilities should participate in general music classes with nondisabled peers. Depending upon level of interest, they should also be given the opportunity to participate in music ensembles. Such participation may require that adaptations be made. For example, a student with manual dexterity problems may be able to play a bass drum more easily than a snare drum (which requires a high degree of hand and finger movements). Likewise, the arrangement of choir sections on risers may need to be changed before a concert (e.g., the tenors placed on the bottom row risers), so that a student with cerebral palsy will not have to stand in a location separate from his or her section because of accessibility problems.

In whatever context music participation occurs, teachers should take into account the variability among student abilities, interests, and preferences.

To assist teachers in the identification of these musical abilities, a checklist is presented in Table 15-4. Teachers can use this checklist, or a modified version, to identify students' level of performance and thereby derive sample objectives and ideas for instruction. Also, depending on the involvement of the music teacher or the goals for a given student, some of the objectives can be written into the IEP. The checklist is divided into six areas. The items under each area are sequenced from easiest to most complex. The teacher circles the item that best represents the present level of performance for a student. The IEP objective is the item directly below the circled item, because the lower item is the next skill in sequence. Classroom teachers may need the assistance of the school music teacher in the assessment of these skills.

Adaptations

Although no student should be denied participation in music activities, instructional adaptations are often necessary in order for students with disabilities to have successful musical experiences. The following is a list of adaptations that may prove useful.

TABLE 15–4
Musical abilities checklist

Participation

_____ 1. Student becomes agitated and prefers to leave room/area during music activities.

_____ 2. Student prefers to stay in room/area during music activities.

_____ 3. Student sits on the sidelines and watches the group during music activities.

_____ 4. Student sits on the sidelines but participates by singing, clapping, etc.

_____ 5. Student sits with the group, but does not participate.

_____ 6. Student sits with group and participates with adult prompting.

_____ 7. Student sits with group and actively participates without adult prompting.

_____ 8. Student will lead group in music activities when invited (e.g., leading the group in singing).

Melodic Abilities

_____ 9. Student appears agitated while others are singing.

_____ 10. Student makes no sound while others are singing.

_____ 11. Student tries to sing while others are singing, but sounds are unintelligible.

_____ 12. Student sings while others are singing, but pitches do not relate to group pitches.

_____ 13. Student sings while others are singing, pitches approximate group pitches.

_____ 14. Student sings on pitch.

_____ 15. Student sings a familiar melody without assistance.

_____ 16. Student creates and sings a new melody.

_____ 17. Student expresses desire to sing in formal singing ensemble (i.e., choir).

_____ 18. Student expresses a desire to sing in front of class (solo or in a small group).

Rhythm

_____ 19. Student attempts to clap, move, or play a rhythm instrument while listening to music.

_____ 20. Student consistently claps, moves, or plays a rhythm instrument while listening to music, without prompting.

(continued)

TABLE 15—4 (*Continued*)

Rhythm

_____ 21. Student matches beat of teacher (by clapping, moving, or playing a rhythm instrument).

_____ 22. Student matches the beat while listening to a song (by clapping, moving, or playing a rhythm instrument).

_____ 23. Student maintains a steady beat for a brief period of time (0–20 seconds).

_____ 24. Student maintains a steady beat for prolonged period of time (more than 20 seconds).

Basic Music Theory

_____ 25. Student identifies dynamics of music (i.e., loud, soft) while listening to music, singing, or playing an instrument.

_____ 26. Student identifies tempo of music (i.e., fast, slow) while listening to music, singing, or playing an instrument.

_____ 27. Student identifies differences in pitch (i.e., same, different, high, low) while listening to music.

_____ 28. Student recognizes familiar melodic phrases or rhythmic pattern that reoccur in a song.

_____ 29. Student reads basic musical notation.

Music Appreciation

_____ 30. Student sings or asks for a favorite song.

_____ 31. Student identifies one or more traditional musical instruments.

_____ 32. Student identifies different musical genres (e.g., classical, jazz).

_____ 33. Student identifies well-known composers within musical genre.

_____ 34. Student demonstrates knowledge of how music is produced (in terms of acoustics).

_____ 35. Student demonstrates knowledge of how music is recorded.

_____ 36. Student attends community music events.

General Adaptations. Cognitive and behavioral disabilities certainly do not reduce a person's interest and motivation to participate in musical activities. Adaptations include:

1. Use more demonstration and practice when learning new musical concepts.
2. Teach new songs at a slower tempo (i.e., speed).
3. Use songs with repetitive melodies or phrases.
4. Use songs in combination with movement.
5. Keep songs simple (i.e., simple words and melodies).

Adaptations for Students with Physical Limitations. Playing a musical instrument is an effective means of increasing a student's manual dexterity, large-muscle strength, coordination, and range of motion. With practice, students

with physical limitations benefit from playing musical instruments (i.e., rhythm instruments used in circle time activities, and traditional band instruments). Specific adaptations include:

1. Alter the position of a musical instrument. For example, a guitar can be positioned flat on a student's lap or on a table if the student finds holding the instrument in the traditional manner too difficult. Instruments also can be secured to a lap or table using straps to secure positioning.
2. Use electronic keyboards rather than traditional pianos in the classroom because their height can be adjusted (often necessary for students who use wheelchairs) and the fact that the keys of an electronic keyboard are much easier to press down than traditional keys on a piano makes them easier to use.

3. For students with respiratory limitations, playing a recorder (i.e., a simple wind instrument that is available from most music stores) is much easier than playing a flute; very little breath is required to produce sound on a recorder.
4. Songs can be shortened for students with endurance problems.
5. Use peer tutors to help hold instruments.

Adaptations for Students with Sensory Impairments. There are several ways in which to adapt music activities for students with hearing and visual impairments. Adaptations for hearing-impaired students can include:

1. Incorporate sign language into singing.
2. Place the student away from ambient noise (e.g., air conditioners).
3. Place the student in front of room and in a location where he or she can see the teacher's face.
4. Use visual aids and visual models when teaching a concept (e.g., use different-colored lighting to denote certain types of mood present in a musical selection).
5. Use sound equipment that has good clarity.
6. Match student's hearing range with an instrument that produces sound in the same range. For example, if a student hears sounds in the lower ranges, playing a tuba or bass drum would be more appropriate than playing a flute or piccolo.
7. Focus on teaching drum techniques (due to the visual and rhythmic nature of the instrument).
8. Emphasize rhythmic and percussive qualities of music rather than the melodic.

For students with visual impairments:

9. Use concrete objects to teach concepts (e.g., use real musical instruments rather than pictures).
10. Use large-print song books and other music manuscripts.
11. Teach music notation using Braille.

Music Activities

Singing. Almost everyone loves to sing. Singing can be used for the expression of emotions, a reward, free time, socialization, or as a means of celebrating an important event. Teachers should incorporate singing in a variety of contexts. Some suggestions include:

1. Personalize songs by inserting a child's name into the song.
2. Make up new words to old melodies. Words about holidays and other special events can replace words in traditional melodies (Hildebrandt, 1998).
3. Sing songs at a slower tempo (i.e., speed). One of the problems with many of the commercial music recordings for children is that they have songs that are recorded at too fast a speed. For students with speech and language difficulties, fast tempos often lead to frustration (i.e., students get frustrated because they cannot sing all of the words). Teachers need to consciously slow their tempos while singing. Slowing down, however, is not easy. It feels unnatural and it is too easy to speed up without realization. Some teachers put a yellow sign on the wall that says *slow down* as a memory prompt.
4. Use singing as part of a reward contingency included in a student's behavior management plan. For instance, take the song, 'The Ballad of Davy Crockett.' Switch the name Davy Crockett with the student's name. Sing the song to the child when he or she has met the criteria for a good behavior day.
5. For shy students, start a singing group at the beginning of the year. After students have learned several songs well, ask for three or four volunteers to come to the front of the room and lead the rest of the group in singing. Over time, gradually reduce the number of student leaders to two (a duo) and then to one (soloists). Shy students may be more comfortable singing with one or two other students rather than doing a solo. Eventually, however, the student may elect to go solo.

6. Shy students can also be motivated to get in front of groups of people with the 'air band' strategy. Air band is a method of entertainment in which a small group of people pretend to perform in a rock-and-roll band. They dress and behave like real rocks stars while they lip-synch (pretend they are singing) to recordings.

7. For students with learning disabilities and an elementary reading level, reinforcing reading skills (e.g., sight word vocabulary and speed) using the popular music video disk machine (known as *karaoke*) can be effective (Brick & Wagner, 1993). Students sing words to a song displayed on a video monitor while a musical accompaniment is played in the background.

8. Many popular children's songs can be related to a theme connected with social studies. For example, as children are learning about our country, they could also learn the song 'This Land Is Your Land'; or when studying transportation, they could learn such songs as 'City of New Orleans.'

9. All adolescents like to feel that they are an integral part of the school society. One way of increasing the sociability of students with disabilities is to teach them school-related songs, such as the alma mater or school fight song. These same songs can provide many pleasurable moments for students on bus trips, hiking experiences, and camping expeditions.

Playing Musical Instruments. Involving students in the production of music is a very motivating and beneficial activity. Simple musical instruments can be purchased or made and used in a variety of ways. Figure 15–1 shows examples of easy-to-make instruments. Specific activity ideas include:

1. Collect a number of empty plastic gallon milk containers. Use them as conga drums. Have a local drummer come to class or to the playground and demonstrate basic conga rhythms. Students can imitate the rhythms or create their own. Another activity would be to have a student read a story about the jungle and have one or two other students play quiet drum sounds in the background. Record the story.

2. Have students tap on a drum the number of syllables that are heard in a particular word.

3. Have students listen for rhythms that occur in the natural world, such as the ticking of a clock or the rhythm of someone skipping on a sidewalk. Discuss the importance of rhythm in our lives.

4. Play rhythm games in which students must imitate rhythms or move when a certain rhythm is heard.

5. A variety of software programs have been developed recently to provide specific instruction in rhythm. Consult with your school's music teacher or a local music store.

Active Listening. Students should learn how to listen attentively to music. Specifically, they should learn to focus on certain elements of style, such as volume, rhythm, melody, and texture, and they should learn how to express their reactions to music. Time should be set aside for students to listen to a variety of musical styles and to discuss personal reactions to the music. Specific activities could include:

1. Take students on a walk through a variety of environments (e.g., forests, urban areas). Have them record all the sounds they hear. Make comparisons between the sounds in terms of the way the sounds make them feel. Record the sounds.

2. Play a game in which short sound segments are played on a tape recorder, and have the students guess what each sound is. For instance, play the sound of water dripping and ask the students to identify the sound. Follow this activity up with playing commercially made environmental recordings (such as recordings of the rain forest, whales, etc.).

3. Have students watch different types of movies and note the type of music that is played during the movie. Discuss how the music affects the mood of a scene. Teachers can also black out the monitor while the movie is playing, so students can hear the dialogue and the music

FIGURE 15–1
Easy-to-make musical instruments

Rhythm blocks
Use a cross-cut saw and make scraps of wood into two blocks of the same size; sand them smooth. Nail spools or narrow blocks of wood on the backs as handles.

Maracas
Apply papier maché around a light bulb or small balloon. After it dries, break the light bulb or pop the balloon and fill the cavity with rice and dried beans. The open end can be filled with plaster of paris.

Brass tube triangle
Use a 12-inch length of brass tubing (1/4-inch thick) for the triangle and a 6-inch brass rod for the striker. Drill holes so that it can be threaded with string and hung up.

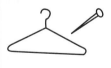

Coat hanger triangle
Use an unpainted coat hanger, hold it by the hook, and tap it with a heavy nail.

Cap tinkles
Make wooden handles 2 inches wide and 6 inches long; sand them smooth. Pry the linings out of bottle caps, hammer the caps flat, punch a hole in the center of each and put a nail through those holes into the handle, being sure not to hammer the nail so deeply that it prevents the caps from jingling.

Flowerpot bells
Attach a string to the bottoms of earthenware flowerpots. Suspend the pots upside down from a wooden rod so that they hang freely and are in descending order of size (and tone). Place the rod over the backs of two chairs. Strike the pots with a wooden stick or toy hammer.

Kettle drums
A metal tray can serve as a drum. Make a beater with a broom handle covered with a wool sock that is tied on with a rubber band or string.

Drums
Make drumsticks from unsharpened pencils with eraser tops, or glue large wooden beads on small paintbrush handles. Strike the bottoms of empty oatmeal or shortening containers.

but cannot see the picture. Discuss whether the music has the same effect on mood when you cannot see what's going on.

4. Have students listen to the recording of the classical masterpiece *The Moldau*, by Smetana. This programmatic musical work represents through sound the progress of a river that flows through Eastern Europe. The river starts out as a trickle and grows steadier. The music parallels this progression by its increasing complexity. Other well-known programmatic classical works include *Symphonie Fantastique* by Berlioz, *Romeo and Juliet* by Tchaikovsky, and *Danse Macabre* by Saint-Saens.

5. After students listen to a musical selection, have them draw a picture or write a story relating to how the music makes them feel.

6. Take the students to a public concert. Some local music groups will present concerts in schools.

7. Invite local musicians to come in and present information about their musical activities, their musical instruments, and their lives as musicians.

8. Expose students to various types of ethnic music, especially when studying different cultures in social studies. Miller and Brand (1983) suggest studying ethnic music to promote understanding and appreciation of other cultures. They recommend the Bowmar record and filmstrip series (Bellwin-Mills Publishing Company), which introduces music from Latin American as well as Arabic, Oriental, African, and Jewish cultures.

Background Music. Background music is everywhere—in shopping centers, on elevators, and in classrooms. Although not everyone likes it, a survey conducted in Florida (Buck, 1993) found that a sizable proportion (37%) of general and special education teachers who responded to the survey played background music in their classrooms. Reported purposes of playing music included: creating an enjoyable environment, calming their students (and themselves), increasing student creativity, teaching relaxation techniques, providing novelty, promoting higher-level thinking, and/or improving students' academic performance. Background music was played during independent seat work, free time, art, and creative writing activities. Several teachers also reported using background music as a cue for students at transition times (they paired specific songs with clean-up time). Interestingly, the most frequently used styles of music were classical and easy listening, although some teachers were using various esoteric music styles such as Native American flute music and Scottish bagpipe music

Musart. *Musart* is a term that refers to the combining of music and visual arts into a single multisensory experience (Nowak, 1981). Lessons are developed on particular concepts or themes, and art activities are implemented while music is being produced or listened to. The following is an example of a musart activity: Given the theme "sweet and sour," students are given a variety of art activities, such as painting yellow lemons with real lemon halves on green paper cut into the shape of trees. While the students paint, the teacher leads them in a modified version of the 1960s' popular song, *Lemon Tree*. Modified lyrics:

> Lemon tree very pretty,
> And the lemon smells so sweet,
> But the juice of the lemon,
> Tastes so sour when we eat.
> Take lemon in your hand,
> Put a lemon on the tree,
> Yellow lemons grow so pretty,
> Won't you count them now for me?
> (words modified by Nowak, 1981).

Other similar activities that relate to the theme follow this musart activity (such as cooking with lemons or reading a story about a "sweet" grandmother). The focus of this approach is on the bombardment of the senses while concepts are simultaneously reinforced in a continuous fashion.

INSTRUCTION IN DANCE AND CREATIVE MOVEMENT

Moving to music is one of the most basic characteristics exhibited by humans. Whether we are tapping our feet, clapping our hands, or moving our entire bodies, the power of music to elicit physical response is remarkable. The benefits of dance and creative movement for all people are numerous and include such outcomes as improved physical coordination, emotional well-being, social interactions, and identification with one's cultural background or the cultural backgrounds of others (Bond & Deans, 1997).

Unfortunately, in most schools, dance and creative movement activities are restricted to physical education classes or weekend social events (i.e., school dances). In classrooms, dance and movement activities typically are limited to lower grades and narrowly defined movements (e.g., marching). For most older students, dance opportunities often are accessed only through expensive private lessons. This limited attention to dance and creative movement in schools is unfortunate given the number of benefits that can be derived from their inclusion in the curriculum. For students with disabilities, especially, benefits from this art form can lead to leisure-related skills and interests that last a lifetime.

Dance and creative movement activities can be incorporated easily into the curriculum. For instance, students can choreograph a simple dance that reflects the events in a story or the mood of a poem. Students also can learn about other cultures through exposure to a variety of dances taught by people living in the community who represent diverse cultural backgrounds. Movement activities also can facilitate the acquisition of academic content when, for example, students move in letter or number patterns.

Whatever context dance and creative movement activities occur in, movements should be shaped and controlled in a structured environment (Valeri & McKelvey, 1985). Young children in groups especially can get hurt when movements are without purpose. Teachers who are untrained in dance and movement may want to consult a local dance instructor. Dance instructors can be an excellent source of information on basic dance steps and how to adapt the steps to a diverse population of students.

Movement activities should also take into account students' gross motor, vision, and hearing abilities; ability to concentrate, and understanding of basic vocabulary (e.g., *up, down, under over, jump, stop, start, together, fast, slow*). Teachers often will need to consult with a student's physical or occupational therapist, speech therapist, physician, family, and other teachers in order to gather information about abilities and limitations, as well as interests and preferences. This information is important because a student's ability to move, see, hear, attend, and understand concepts will significantly influence the level of participation. The more impairment present in any of these areas, the greater the level of instruc-

tional adaptations that need to be made. Table 15–5 includes an observation checklist of skills related to dance and movement that can be used by teachers incorporating this art form into their programs. Depending upon the goals targeted for an individual student, some of these skills can be rewritten as objectives and included in the student's IEP.

Adaptations

Most instructional adaptations in dance are focused on modifying the environment and complexity of the movements. The following is a listing of adaptation ideas in these two areas:

Environmental Adaptations. Environmental adaptations in this arts area are primarily concerned with space. Teachers will need to

TABLE 15–5
Observation checklist for dance and creative movement

_____ 1. Student shows interest in dance and creative movement activities (watches others while movement activities are occurring).

_____ 2. Student engages in dance and creative movement activities without prompting.

_____ 3. Student follows directions for initiating a movement activity (e.g., lines up, gathers materials such as streamers).

_____ 4. Student follows directions during movement activities (e.g., responds to words like start, stop, jump, crawl, freeze).

_____ 5. Student demonstrates required movements during activities (e.g., marching, skipping, turning, stepping, bending, leaning, twisting).

_____ 6. Student behaves appropriately during activities (e.g., does not touch others when not supposed to, does not leave activity area).

_____ 7. Student finishes activity when directed.

_____ 8. Student is able to create new movements during spontaneous dance activities.

consider modifying the movement area when assisting students who are not able to deal with confined areas, who may be unable to control aggressive behaviors, who use wheelchairs, or who may have vision difficulties. The following ideas are suggested:

1. Provide an area that is large and free of obstacles.
2. Make the movement area boundaries clearly pointed out to students.
3. Be especially careful when students in wheelchairs are on a stage. Accidents can happen when wheelchairs get too close to the edge.
4. Place large cardboard cylinders (accessible from a cloth store) upright on the floor and give directions to the students that they are only to move around their own cylinders. The cylinders are reference points from which students are able to define their own space. This is especially good for students who have tendencies to wander or to invade the space of their peers. For students with visual difficulties, the cylinders may have to be painted a highly visible color to improve visibility.

Procedural Adaptations. Because of the physical and cognitive limitations of many students with disabilities, modifications will need to be made in terms of simplifying directions, procedures, and physical requirements demanded in the activities. Specifically:

1. Teachers should focus on basic dance steps rather than complicated choreographed movements that require a lot of imitation. Basic steps should be modeled for students, with plenty of opportunities for practice. Steps can include stepping, jumping, turning, bending, leaping, crawling, skipping, hopping, and sliding.
2. Use warm-up activities, such as stretching, 'Simon Says,' or 'Follow the Leader' (Broughton, 1986).
3. Teachers should teach simple commands, directionality words, and form concepts. Command words can include *start, begin, move, go, slower, faster, stop, freeze follow the leader, no touching,* and *help a friend.* Directionality

words can include *above, below, forward, backward, under, over, beside,* and *inside.* Form concepts can include *together, apart, separate, divide, split, connect,* and *circle.* Valeri and McKelvey (1985) recommend that teachers use an auditory stimulus to cue students when to change movements, such as a whistle or tambourine to signify *freeze* or *stop.*

4. Alternative movements can be required for students with severe physical limitations, such as requiring a student to wave the fingers instead of the entire arm. In such cases, students can be asked which movements they prefer to use in activities.
5. When dancing, use popular music that has a strong, steady, and distinctive beat. The tempo (i.e., speed) of the music should be appropriate to the abilities of the students.

Dance Activities

Dance. Dance can be used either during structured group activities or during free time. Students can create dances individually or in cooperative groups, or they can learn dances taught by students in other classes or by adults from the community. Dance can be used to commemorate an important current or historical event, to learn about another culture, or simply as an enjoyable means of self-expression or social interaction. Activities can include:

1. Students should be provided opportunities to attend school and community dance performances and to learn about the profession of dance. Students can learn how dance has changed throughout history and how each culture has developed a unique form of dance.
2. For younger children, play a modified version of "Simon Says." During circle time students are directed to do a series of behaviors, such as: put your hands over your head, under your chin, above your eyes, beside your ears. These movements can be done while listening to music, with the movements timed with the music's tempo.
3. Have students create a dance that represents different seasons. For example, during spring,

students can create a dance that represents the growth of flowers and trees, the melting of snow, or the migration of birds.

4. Students can march in a classroom or playground parade. While marching, students can wave streamers, flags, or hats. Many students also enjoy playing rhythm instruments as they march.

5. Have students move the way the music makes them feel. Students may crawl on the floor during slow, quiet music, and skip during fast music.

6. Young children like to move like animals while listening to music. Playing the recording of the 'Baby Elephant Walk,' for example, is appropriate when moving like an elephant.

7. Have students wear costumes when dancing. Parents often enjoy making dance outfits that can be left in the classroom for continued use.

8. Develop wheelchair dances. Students who are in wheelchairs hold onto one side of a hula-hoop and an adult or peer holds onto the other side. While music is playing, the adult or peer guides the student in a wheelchair around the dance area (Morris, 1991). Certain movements can be incorporated for expressiveness.

9. Incorporate manual signing into dances.

10. Students can make pencil drawings following a dance activity. The drawing can reflect their feelings.

11. Integrate poetry and movement (see Boswell & Mentzer, 1995, for activity ideas).

12. Learn simple dances of other cultures. Invite a community member from a different culture to the class to demonstrate and teach ethnic dances.

INSTRUCTION IN CREATIVE DRAMATICS

The abilities that allow us to imagine, pretend, improvise, act, entertain, and create and communicate stories are uniquely human characteristics. These abilities begin to develop early in life.

Very young children often are observed in play activities where they pretend to be a teacher, a parent, or an animal. Such spontaneous play activities are a child's attempt to mimic and interpret reality, a process that stands as the basis of what we consider creative drama. Through creative play, children practice expressing the emotions and activities that are necessary for functioning within the world. This process is the same for all children, regardless of disability.

As we become older, imaginative and pretend activities become more elaborate and formalized. In schools, children are engaged in reading and interpreting literature, acting in classroom or school plays, and sometimes being members of a drama club. As adults, unless we become involved in a community theater group, participation in drama is usually limited to passive observation (i.e., attending theater events).

Whether we are young or old, actively or passively engaged in dramatic activities, creative drama allows us to think imaginatively, to define and redefine our realities, to experience the diversity of emotions, and to interact with the human community. Through drama we learn about our own and other cultures. For students with learning disabilities, drama can serve to remediate difficulties in oral language and social skills (de la Cruz, Lian, & Morreau, 1998).

There are several forms of drama that can be incorporated in educational settings. The ones addressed in this chapter include spontaneous improvisation, puppetry, pantomime, story telling, role playing, and more advanced acting. Table 15–6 includes a observation checklist of skills related to creative drama that can be used by teachers incorporating this art form into their programs. Depending upon the goals targeted for an individual student, this list can be modified and some of the skills can be rewritten as objectives and included in the student's IEP.

Adaptations

When developing creative drama activities, teachers should be conscious of the abilities and limitations manifested by the participating students

TABLE 15–6
Observation checklist for creative drama

_____ 1. Student shows interest in play activities (watches others during dramatic play activities).

_____ 2. Student engages in dramatic play activities, alone or with others (picks up and engages with toys for prolonged periods of time).

_____ 3. Student engages in group creative drama activities (i.e., role playing, puppets) without prompting.

_____ 4. Student follows directions for initiating a drama activity (e.g., lines up, gets in correct position).

_____ 5. Student follows directions during drama activities (e.g., responds to words like start, stop, look toward).

_____ 6. Student behaves appropriately during drama activities. (e.g., delivers spoken lines, shows expression, does not touch others when not supposed to, does not leave activity area).

_____ 7. Student finishes activities when directed.

_____ 8. Student is able to create ideas for new dramatic activities.

with disabilities. The following is a listing of adaptation ideas that may be pertinent:

1. Teachers should take a greater role as leaders and participants in the planned activities. This is especially true in early childhood, when children with disabilities tend to not engage in imaginative play for prolonged periods of time. For example, in the play kitchen area, while other children are playing tea party, children with disabilities tend to walk to the area, pick up a toy cup, bang the cup on the table, and leave the area within a very short period of time. Although these children may learn more sophisticated play behaviors incidentally by watching their nondisabled peers, teachers can speed up the learning process by creating and leading play situations that encourage higher levels of thinking and attending. Some of the ways facilitation can occur include

   - cuing the child in the play area through a series of tasks (such as telling the child to pick up and pour tea [imaginary] from the tea kettle)
   - providing prompts that facilitate imagination (such as handing children cut-up pieces of construction paper that serve as tickets when children pretend that they are taking a train trip)
   - modeling imaginative thinking by using pantomime _during_ play time (such as pretending to cut an imaginary person's hair)

2. When role playing, teachers should begin with simple activities that are nonthreatening, comfortable, and familiar to the students. For instance, having older students with disabilities act out all the complex behaviors required in a job interview may be less effective than having them practice a few job-interviewing behaviors (such as shaking hands and making eye contact).

3. Teachers should engage students in individual, one-to-one activities (e.g., puppets, one-to-one story telling) before moving on to small-group and large-group activities.

4. Teachers can use group responding methods instead of one person responses during creative drama activities with shy students. For instance, instead of calling on each individual student to tell the group what's in their imaginary boxes, ask all of them to respond at the same time. Listen for the shy student's response, call attention to the student's response, and positively reinforce it.

5. Many students with learning disabilities enjoy making up and telling a story or reciting one from memory, rather than always reading a story. Teachers can serve as models when they create stories or tell well-known folk tales during group sessions. Students can provide the parameters for the teacher's story, such as when and where the story takes place.

6. Teachers can provide props for dramatic activities. Many students enjoy dressing up when playing certain characters.

Creative Dramatic Activities

Spontaneous Improvisation. Teachers can provide opportunities for students to act out certain themes or scenarios. For instance, students learning about transportation safety can act out a scenario about the importance of buckling seatbelts. Depending upon the students' abilities, the scene can be done without preparation (spontaneous improvisation) or planned ahead of time. Teachers and students can set certain parameters for the scene (such as determining the number and type of characters). Similarly, teachers can give students the beginning of a scenario and then ask the students to finish the scene. For example, the teacher can say, "Mrs. Bear is having an awful night. She is not able to fall asleep." Following this, the teacher asks students why they think Mrs. Bear is not able to sleep. Students decide on one specific reason and then act out the scene. Other ideas for encouraging spontaneous improvisation include:

1. Placing a large, gutted-out television in the play area can be a great motivator for young children to engage in solitary or group improvisation.
2. Putting out a box of various adult clothing will invariably lead children to put on the clothing and act out certain parts.
3. Giving students a real microphone and telling them to develop a show in which some of them are comedians and others are singers or dancers can be very motivating.
4. Have students practice verbal exchanges in pairs or small groups to replicate real or imagined human encounters. Students or teacher can set parameters for exchanges.

Puppetry. A number of concepts and facts can be taught with puppets. For example, some teachers use puppets to sensitize students to different social issues (e.g., unfair treatment of different types of people), while other teachers use puppets to convey academic information, de-

velop vocabulary, and increase the frequency and quality of verbal communication.

Whatever their purpose, puppets do not have to be the expensive commercial type. Puppets can be made by drawing faces on a hand, a paper bag, or a sock (Pascale, 1993). Ensign (1992) recommends making puppets by recycling stuffed animals, opening their seams, removing the stuffing, and sewing a child's tube socks inside them. Some activities that can be done with puppets include:

1. Use puppets that represent people of diverse cultural backgrounds, but do not perpetuate inaccurate stereotypes.
2. Teach students academic concepts by having puppets complete academic problems correctly and incorrectly. For example, students can tell the puppets how to do two-digit math problems correctly.
3. Have students resolve conflicts with puppets. Students talk to each other through their puppets.
4. Set out several puppets during free play time.

Pantomime. Pantomime (also referred to as *mime*) is one of the most underused educational methods in schools. It rarely appears in the educational literature and it is infrequently observed in classrooms. This lack of attention is unfortunate because pantomime can be used to increase imagination, social behavior, and conceptual development. Teachers who pantomime life-related activities (such as reading an imaginary newspaper) serve as models to students who often are delayed in their level of imaginative thinking and interpersonal behaviors.

Pantomime can be used effectively in structured group activities. During group time activities, teachers can ask students to guess what is being pantomimed. Concepts such as hygiene, social manners, and career activities can be conveyed through pantomimes. Students often sit spellbound as the teacher pantomimes some of the following:

■ waking up in the morning (getting dressed, washing hands and face, brushing teeth, combing hair, eating breakfast, leaving for school)

- reading a book
- cutting someone's hair
- playing a piano
- running (in the Special Olympics)
- building a house

Teachers also can have students pantomime certain activities. Especially good for students with dysarthria, pantomiming eating ice cream (with exaggerated tongue movements), eating spaghetti (with exaggerated sucking movements of the lips), and blowing on hot coffee can be therapeutic. Providing opportunities for students to pantomime various life roles or vocations (e.g., waiter, astronaut, parent, police officer, or mail carrier) is also beneficial.

Storytelling. Stories have been told and retold throughout human history. Often, students love hearing stories as much as they like stories being read to them. The act of telling stories and the act of listening to stories are very basic to human nature. Unfortunately, the advent of modern technology has made storytelling a much more passive and visual process than it was in the past. Many have criticized technology's influence on children, pointing to the reduced creativity that occurs when stories and information are presented without opportunities for human interaction, where all visual images are supplied to the perceiver (Maguire, 1985).

Infusing story telling into classrooms can have several benefits. Turner and Oaks (1997) point out that storytelling improves academic skills by enhancing children's observation abilities, creativity, and problem-solving and decision-making skills. Storytelling also introduces children to the symbols and traditions that characterize their cultural backgrounds.

Teachers can encourage storytelling both by serving as a model and by providing opportunities for students to engage in the activity themselves. Stories can be either created spontaneously or memorized in advance, and they can be used with students of all ages.

Spontaneous stories are easy to develop when teachers relate subject matter to students' interests. Knowing that Jason has an interest in UFOs can lead to a story about three aliens who descended in a space craft and taught villagers how to improve their environment by recycling and saving endangered species. Likewise, knowing that Sara has an interest in dolphins can lead to a story about a young girl who befriends a dolphin. Students can follow up these types of stories with gathering information about the topics, writing the stories down on paper, and creating related stories. Often, students enjoy hearing their own names interjected into the story.

Memorized stories are often good to use when teachers do not feel confident creating their own spontaneous stories. Reading a favorite book repeatedly often results in the teacher's memorizing the story. Often students enjoy just sitting and listening to the story, rather than looking at the pictures in the book.

For teachers who use storytelling in their classrooms, the following ideas are suggested:

1. Some students need to be taught the difference between fact and fantasy. According to Kelner (1993), children need to be told that what they will be doing or hearing is pretend. At the end of the story or activity, some children need to be told that they are back in reality. For students with disabilities, this recommendation may be especially relevant.
2. Exaggerate events, characters, and behaviors in stories. A big, old, near-sighted owl who lost his spectacles in the stream is certainly more interesting than just a wise, old owl. Likewise, a little girl who makes many friends because she is kind and generous (something she learned from her grandmother, who lives in a one-room apartment) is more interesting than a little girl who makes a lot of friends because she is nice.
3. Do not perpetuate traditional and inaccurate stereotypes in stories. Not all doctors are men nor are all teachers women.
4. Storytelling and gossiping are clearly not the same thing and students should be taught the difference. We do not make up stories about familiar friends and family. Also, we do not tell stories about people we know that are true

and that might hurt their feelings if they knew we told them.

5. Use exaggerated inflections, different dialects, and words or phrases in different languages when telling stories. Encourage students to do the same when they tell stories.

6. Have students work in small groups to shape and highlight the sounds of interesting poems with vocal inflection, coloring, and orchestration. Have them generalize these behaviors to their own spontaneous storytelling.

SOURCES OF TEACHING IDEAS

Teachers often express the concern that they feel untrained in the creative arts. As a result, they tend to have a limited repertoire of activities and those activities that they do use tend to get used repeatedly. Fortunately, there are many sources of information from which to collect a variety of creative arts teaching ideas. One of the most comprehensive sources of teaching ideas is The Very Special Arts Program. This is a national organization that provides (a) ongoing support for the training of teachers in the creative arts, and (b) opportunities for students with disabilities to participate in a variety of creative arts activities (frequently in the form of an annual festival). Teachers should contact their state departments of education to see if any districts in their state participate in the Very Special Arts program. Sometimes, state groups publish a teachers' guide that includes numerous teaching ideas across all the creative arts areas. A guide by the Very Special Arts in Massachusetts can be accessed on microfiche (see Pascale, 1993). Teachers can also gain a number of ideas

from attending a local, state, or national Very Special Arts Festival. If a Very Special Arts organization does not exist in a local district, teachers may want to write to the national office and request information about how to form a group.

Teachers can gain movement and dance activity ideas from local dance instructors. Basic movements can be demonstrated and taught to students. Teachers can ask dance instructors for catalogs from which they can purchase cassette tapes of music that is appropriate for dance activities.

The Internet also is a source of information for teaching ideas. If teachers have access to the Internet, they should contact their school district's computer specialist and inquire about home pages that would be of interest to teachers. Internet directories also can be useful for finding information; they can be purchased in most local bookstores.

SUMMARY

This chapter presents information that will assist educators to include the creative arts (i.e., visual arts, music, dance, and drama) into educational settings. Following a discussion that outlines the rationale for including the arts in special education, general instructional guidelines (relevant across all creative arts areas) are outlined. Next, specific areas of the creative arts are presented, with each of these sections including (a) a short description of the arts area, (b) specific strategies for adapting instruction in the arts area for persons with disabilities; and (c) curriculum activities. The chapter ends with suggestions for locating additional sources of teaching ideas related to the creative arts.

USING POETRY AND MOVEMENT WITH CHILDREN WHO HAVE LEARNING OR BEHAVIORAL DISABILITIES

Want to increase students' appreciation of poetry and also allow them to release excess tension? You can do both at the same time with a movement poetry program. Boswell and Mentzer (1995) describe a teaching style, lesson plan format, and a program that combines creative movement and presentation of poetry. The movement poetry program lessons include three phases: warm-up, movement to poems, and closure. Using an interesting poem with a sequence of action words can motivate students to listen to and read poetry; foster peer interactions; and provide a healthy, productive way to release pent-up energy. Just imagine how much fun your students could have with a poem like this one suggested by Boswell and Mentzer.

'Jump or Jiggle' by Evelyn Beyer

Frogs jump	Seagulls glide
Caterpillars hump	Mice creep
Worms wiggle	Deer leap
Bugs jiggle	Puppies bounce
Rabbits hop	Kittens pounce
Horses clop	Lions stalk
Snakes slide	But—
	I walk!

Boswell & Mentzer (1995)

INTEGRATING SCULPTURE INTO CONTENT AREA UNITS

Innovative teachers are always creating new ways to link core subject areas with the arts. Khilnani and Culhane (1995) describe a unit that used sculpture in a unit on habitats. The teacher and an artist worked with a class of 13-year-olds with learning disabilities. Their final products included individually sculpted habitats and a class mural depicting forests, mountains, and deserts. Instructional strategies included

- brainstorming discussions to generate ideas and words (used later in writing assignments)
- instruction from an artist in the technical aspects of the project
- step-by-step procedures for construction of their habitats from the ground up.

Concepts in language arts (descriptive words), science (characteristics of plants and animals), math (fractions), social studies (land forms), social skills (following directions), and art (mixing colors) were all part of the habitat unit.

When using art activities as part of thematic units, be creative. Your evaluation process can include individual portfolios, a group celebration, individual presentations, or a group video that records everyone's contributions. Students will enjoy the hands-on nature of the assignments and may learn more from the activities than they would from more traditional pencil-and-paper tasks.

Khilnani & Culhane (1995)

For those educators and students who wish to continue their education in the area of the arts and technology, here is a new web site that will allow you to go to school and receive a degree through the use of your computer. The Interarts and Technology (ITECH) program is a program with a unique curriculum in the training and aesthetic guidance for student artists who love technology. "ITECH was conceived as a non-specialized multidisciplinary study in the arts which integrates the visual, sound, and movement arts." The program is designed to provide an interdisciplinary experience using computer animation, digital video, and sound technologies. A graduate of this program may pursue careers in audio/video production, graduate studies in the electronic arts, multimedia performance, and computer entertainment industry. Computer-Integrated Courses are offered in three core areas: Visual Arts, Sound Arts, and Movement Arts. Check the ITECH web page for more information.

CHAPTER 16

Transitions, Transition Planning, and Life Skills Education

This final chapter of the book focuses on the articulation that should exist throughout the schooling process. Although it provides closure to the many topics covered in the previous chapters, it is more than just final thoughts. This chapter addresses three major topics. First, it explores the important school-related transitions that students with special needs are likely to encounter and provides tactics for preparing for them. Second, the chapter covers the important topic of transition planning, as mandated by IDEA, for students who are exiting school. Last, the chapter provides a framework for covering real-life topics that are extremely important for students with special needs.

We all experience many transitions in our lives. Some of the transitions that students might encounter in their lives are depicted in Figure 16-1. Although the focus of this chapter is on those transitions that occur during school years, it is worthwhile to think about transitions as a lifelong reality.

Certain important elements are associated with increasing the chances of any transition being successful (Bruder & Chandler, 1996; Patton & Dunn, 1998). The three key elements, identified by Patton and Dunn, include:

- Comprehensive planning;
- Implementation of a plan of action; and
- Coordination.

Comprehensive planning involves two major activities: needs assessment and individual planning. Assessment should include two separate but related activities: (1) the evaluation of the demands and requirements of the setting to which the person is going and (2) the evaluation of the

FIGURE 16–1
Vertical and selected horizontal transitions

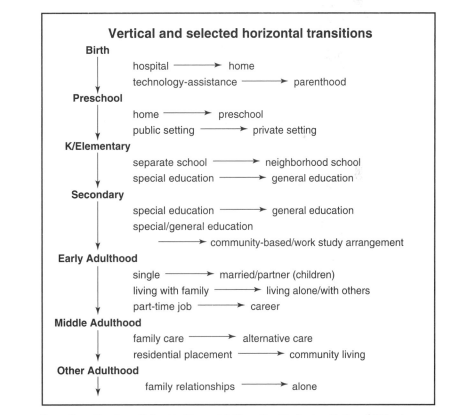

From *Transition from School to Young Adulthood for Students with Special Needs: Basic Concepts and Recommended Practices,* by J. R. Patton and C. Dunn, 1996. Unpublished manuscript. Copyright 1996 by J. R. Patton. Adapted with permission.

individual's competence (i.e., knowledge and skill levels) to deal with these impending demands. Individual planning is the formal or informal process of formulating an action plan to address areas of concern. The action phase refers to the follow-through on the planning that was previously done. Wonderful needs assessment and resulting comprehensive planning are meaningless if the plans are not carried out in an efficient and effective way. Coordination refers to the cooperative efforts between the sending environment (school) and any number of receiving settings (e.g, employment). Ideally, representatives from specific receiving settings would participate actively in the individual planning phase; however, this is often not possible. As a result, coordination implies good communication.

If transition planning is not conducted at all or is conducted ineffectively, several problems are likely to arise. They may include the following.

- Interruption of needed services
- Termination of needed services through oversight or lack of information
- Inadequate preparation of the student in the sending environment
- Inadequate preparation of the receiving environment

TRANSITIONS ACROSS AND ALONG THE SCHOOL YEARS

Throughout life we all experience many different transitions. Some (e.g., beginning kindergarten, moving from elementary to secondary school) are predictable or normative and most people experience them. These types of transitions have also been referred to as *developmental* or *age-based* (Wolery, 1989) and *chronological* (Lazzari, 1991). In this chapter they are referred to as *vertical transitions.*

Other transitions (e.g., major illnesses or accidents) are nonnormative—more individual-specific and not as predictable. Some people experience them, others will not. Wolery (1989) describes these as *nondevelopmental* in nature and Lazzari (1991) as *ongoing.* These types of

transition are referred to as *horizontal transitions* in this chapter.

The school years include many of these normative and nonnormative transitions. As mentioned, most vertical transitions are common to all students, while many of the horizontal transitions are person-specific and are relevant to certain school-age students. It should be noted that the horizontal transitions highlighted in Figure 16–1 represent only some of many different changes that can occur. This chapter will focus in some detail on important vertical and horizontal transitions that occur during the school years and to which teachers should attend.

Vertical Transitions

Important vertical transitions occur throughout a student's school career. The transition from early-intervention programs to preschool settings is extraordinarily important and is addressed elsewhere (e.g., Hansen & Lynch, 1995). The transition that has received the most attention in recent years is from school to adult living; preparation for it is required by IDEA. This transition is so important that the next major section of this chapter is devoted to it. The following discussion centers on two other developmental transitions: the onset of schooling and the move from elementary to secondary education.

Entry into School. Preschool-age students with special needs come to kindergarten from a variety of settings. Some of these children were identified during their first 2 years of life. For these young children, an Individualized Family Service Plan (IFSP) should have been developed, and as a part of the IFSP, transition planning should have occurred. This mandated transition planning is intended to enhance the movement from early intervention services to a variety of settings available when the child is 3 years old.

In addition to the youngsters described above who enter the special education system at an early age, other students with special needs will be identified during their preschool years (3 to 5 years of age). Comprehensive planning, thoughtful action, and coordination with various personnel is essential to maximize children's opportunities to succeed as they move from preschool to school settings. These elements of successful transitions are especially critical in achieving our main goal of having these young students included in regular kindergarten classes.

The vast majority of students who eventually receive special education and related services enter school unidentified because their needs are not formally recognized until later in their school lives. Some students who are at risk for school failure do receive services such as Head Start that are designed to provide the types of experiences that will enhance their ability to cope with the demands of school; transition planning for these children is equally important (Fleck, 1995).

All students benefit from being prepared to enter school, whether the sending environment is home, a regular preschool program, an early childhood special education program, or some other program such as Head Start. The importance of this is reflected in the attention it has been given in the early childhood literature (e.g., Carden-Smith & Fowler, 1983; Chandler, 1992; Conn-Powers, Ross-Allen, & Holburn, 1990; Haines, 1992; McCormick & Kawate, 1982; Wolery, 1989).

The transition skills of young children who are moving into kindergarten or other elementary school settings should be assessed to ascertain their competence in a range of skills that will be demanded of them in these receiving settings. Chandler (1993) generated a list of transitions that a child may need to cope successfully with the requirements of a kindergarten program; these skills are presented in Table 16-1.

The development of an actual transition planning document, a tactic that is recommended as a way of achieving effective individualized planning, can be accomplished in a number of ways. Although federal mandate does not require systematic planning upon entry to formal schooling, we believe that a written plan is very useful. Fiechtl, Rule, and Innocenti (1989) promote the use of a Parent Transition Plan (Fig. 16–2). As can be seen in their example, important transition-related activities are noted and the responsibility for accomplishing them is delegated. A timeline

is also a crucial feature of the document. Regardless of the actual format used, the rationale for advocating such a document is that the transition activities are written down for all parties to use for reference. A written document does not guarantee follow-through, but it can increase the chances that the planned activities will be accomplished. Putting an assignment in writing emphasizes the importance of the responsibility.

Movement from Elementary to Secondary Education. One of the most neglected developmental transitions during the school years is from elementary school to the secondary level, including middle school and high school. Unique challenges exist as a child moves from elementary to middle school (Robinson, Braxdale, & Colson, 1985) and from middle to high school (Wells, 1996). The time when a student leaves the element setting and moves on to middle school is one of major biological change in the students; how the schooling experience is structured and how education is delivered also changes. For students with special needs, the experience is like being a English-speaking traveler in a non–English-speaking country. Given the significant differences that exist between elementary and secondary schooling, it is extremely important that systematic transition planning occur, especially for those who will be in inclusive settings.

Like all other transitions, the successful movement from the sending school to the receiving school is dependent on (a) the identification of the skills required in the receiving environment, and (b) the assessment of student competence vis-à-vis these demands. As McKenzie and Houck (1993) point out, this must be accomplished before students arrive at the secondary level by maximizing communication and implementing pretransition programs (i.e., the essence of coordination).

Certain features of the secondary school setting make it particularly alien to the new arrival. Some of the most obvious features include: larger student population; more teachers to deal with; curricular emphasis on content areas; need for more self-regulated behavior; different in-school

TABLE 16–1
Transition skills related to successful transition from preschool to kindergarten

Social Behaviors and Classroom Conduct
- Understands role as part of group
- Respects others and their property
- Interacts and defends self without aggression
- Plays cooperatively; shares toys and materials
- Expresses emotions and affections appropriately
- Takes turn; participates appropriately in games
- Is willing to try something new
- Follows class rules and routines
- Lines up and waits appropriately
- Imitates peer actions
- Sits appropriately
- Plays independently

Communication Behaviors
- Follows two- to three-part directions
- Initiates and maintains peer interactions
- Modifies behavior when given verbal feedback
- Asks peers or teachers for information or assistance
- Recalls and follows directions for tasks previously described
- Follows group instructions
- Relates ideas and experiences
- Answers questions
- Communicates own needs and wants

Task-Related Behaviors
- Finds materials needed for tasks
- Does not disrupt peers during activities
- Complies quickly with teacher instructions
- Generalizes skills across tasks and situations
- Follows task directions in small or large group
- Replaces materials and cleans up work space
- Monitors own behavior; knows when a task is done
- Begins and completes work at appropriate time without extra teacher attention
- Makes choices
- Stays in own space
- Follows routine in transition
- Uses a variety of materials
- Seeks attention appropriately
- Attends to teacher in a large group

Self-Help Behaviors
- Recognizes when a problem exists
- Locates and cares for personal belongings
- Avoids dangers and responds to warning words
- Takes outer clothing off and puts it on in a reasonable amount of time
- Tries strategies to solve problems
- Feeds self independently
- Cares for own toileting needs

Note. From "Steps in Preparing for Transition: Preschool to Kindergarten," by L. K. Chandler, 1993, *Teaching Exceptional Children, 25,* p. 48. Copyright 1993 by Council for Exceptional Children. Reprinted with permission.

procedures (e.g, use of lockers); and different type of class scheduling.

In addition, other demands are placed on students that relate to their academic success and social acceptance. Robinson, Braxdale, and Colson (1985, pp. 3–4) highlight three areas that are crucial to school success.

- Academic demands: behaviors/competence associated with successful performance in the classroom leading to completion of a course

with a passing grade or better; heavy emphasis on reading, listening, and writing.

- Self-management/study skills demands: behaviors associated with preparation for learning, maximizing the acquisition of material presented in class, and appropriate demonstration that material presented has been learned—typically through testing.
- Social/adaptive demands: behaviors that lead to acceptance by peers, balanced by compliance with school-based and classroom-based

FIGURE 16–2
Parent transition plan

PARENT TRANSITION PLAN

Child: _____ Missy _____

The following plan states the steps that the parents (and/or guardian) of the above named child and the staff of the Preschool Transition Project (PTP) will take, at the beginning of the 2000/01 school year, to ensure an orderly transition to the school district for the child.

Recommended Placement: _____ Regular Kindergarten _____

Neighborhood School: _____ Seven Oaks Elementary _____

In completing this plan, please write out the step to be taken, who will be responsible for the step, and by what date the step will be accomplished.

Step	Person Responsible	Target Date	Date Accomplished
1. Missy is recommended for enrollment in regular kindergarten at Seven Oaks Elementary. Parents will contact the principal to discuss Missy's physical status and capabilities.	Parents	May 30, 2000	
2. Send records to school principal, district special education office and provide the parents with copies of preschool reports for their file.	B. Fiechti, teacher	June 2, 2000	
3. Provide kindergarten teacher with preschool teacher's report, stressing Missy's skills and possible adaptations for the environment.	B. Fiechti, teacher	June 9, 2000	
4. Monitor Missy's progress throughout the year; inform kindergarten teacher whenever physical status changes.	Parents	2000-01 school year	
5. Contact psychologist if advice needed or problems occur.		2000-01 school year	

This plan has been read and agreed to by the following parties. A signature on this plan imparts permission for the person responsible to contact other significant persons (e.g., teachers, principals) necessary to complete the step. These contacts are only to include information relevant to completing the objective of the step.

Persons	Title	Date
_____	_____	_____
_____	_____	_____
_____	_____	_____

From "It's Time to Get Ready for School," by B. Fiechtl et al., 1989, *Teaching Exceptional Children, 21* (2), p. 64. Copyright 1989 by Council for Exceptional Children. Reprinted with permission.

rules and procedures; this latter point is particularly problematic as explicit and implicit classroom-specific rules and procedures vary from one teacher to another and are often difficult for students with special needs to recognize.

The message embedded in this discussion is that the demands of the secondary level must be recognized and the necessary competencies must be addressed in the last 2 years of elementary school. Robinson et al. (1985) recommend that a transition curriculum (Fig. 16-3) be implemented during this time. As can be gleaned from examining the topics listed in the figure, this type of curriculum includes skill development in areas that most teachers do not typically cover at the elementary level.

Essentially, the key ingredients for preparing students with special needs for the secondary level are orienting them to structural and organizational changes, developing useful academic support skills to handle the rigors of the secondary curriculum and instructional format, and readying them socially and emotionally. With the proper assessment of needs, planning, and instruction, many of the usual problems of adjusting to secondary school can be addressed.

Transition from School to Postsecondary Settings. Along with the transition from services provided to infants and toddlers under Part C of IDEA, this is the only other transition for which planning activities are mandated. Because of the importance of this particular transition for students at the secondary level, it is covered in depth in a subsequent section of this chapter.

Horizontal Transitions

Horizontal transitions refer to those movements that affect certain students, as a function of their individual situations, when they move from one situation to another. Two types of ongoing transitions (Lazzari, 1991) are addressed in this section: movement from segregated educational placements to inclusive ones and movement from an ouside facility in a public school setting.

Inclusion in General Education Classrooms. Arguably, the topic that has received the most attention in recent years in the field of special education is inclusion. There has been some emotionally charged debates on the topic, with much of the controversy focusing on the issue of "full" inclusion. Based on the reality that many students are being included in general education classrooms and on the assumption that many more students will be included in this set-

FIGURE 16-3
Skills taught in the transition curriculum

Academic Skills

1. Reading for the purpose of content comprehension (Deemphasis on decoding)
   1.1 Paraphrasing/Summarizing
       1.1.1 Written paraphrasing/taking notes from text
   1.2 Text analysis

Self-Management/Study Skills

2. Listening
   2.1 Following oral directions
   2.2 Notetaking from lectures
3. Self-Management
   3.1 Planning Work Time
       3.1.1 Planning time use at school
       3.1.2 Planning study time at home
       3.1.3 Organization of materials
   3.2 Record-Keeping Techniques
       3.2.1 Assignment record keeping
       3.2.2 Assignment completion
       3.2.3 Self-evaluation of assignments before submission
4. Test Taking
   4.1 Test preparation
   4.2 Test taking

Social/Adaptive Behavior

5. Interactive Learning
   5.1 Appropriate questioning
   5.2 Interpreting feedback
   5.3 Group discussion skills

General Orientation to Junior High School Setting

Note. From "Preparing Dysfunctional Learners to Enter Junior High School. A Transition Curriculum," by S. M. Robinson et al., 1985, *Focus on Exceptional Children, 18*(4), p. 5, Copyright 1985 by Love Publishing. Reprinted with permission.

ting, this section of the chapter addresses the transitional needs of students who are making the move from special classes. Some students who are identified as needing special education and/or related services have never left the general education classroom or are pulled for such a short time that this transition is not a major problem. However, these students also need to demonstrate the survival skills required for success in the general education classroom.

Our discussion is divided into two subsections—one with an elementary focus and the other with a secondary focus. Once again the overriding principle is that comprehensive planning (systematic assessment of needs and individualized planning), reasonable action, and coordination enhance a student's chances for success in the general education classroom.

Many students with special needs who are in the elementary grades are likely candidates for placement in general education classes for most, if not all, of their school day. Some professionals are aware of the need to plan for this transition and several informal transition measures have been developed.

Wood and Miederhoff (1989) generated a three-part checklist that assesses the student's current levels of competence in relation to the demands of the classroom setting. The three major domains addressed by the instrument are classroom (physical variables, instructional variables, counseling); interpersonal/social relations (student interaction, peer attitudes, dress/appearance); and related environments (cafeteria, physical education, music/art).

George and Lewis (1991) were interested in students' readiness to move to more inclusive settings and they developed the *Classroom Inventory Checklist* to examine various dimensions of the receiving classroom. The intent of the assessment is to create conditions in the special education setting that are similar to those in the general education classroom to provide students with a sense of what is to come and to teach certain skills that will be needed.

Another instrument that is useful for preparing students for the transition to general educa-

tion settings is the *Classroom Survival Skills Inventory* (Smith, 1986), shown in Figure 16–4. The four domains that comprise this inventory (self-related skills, task-related skills, interpersonal skills, and environmental awareness) are extremely important demands of most general education classrooms. This device can serve as a prototype for looking at critical survival skills but should be modified to increase its ecological validity for a particular classroom.

One caution must be mentioned in regard to the types of transition measures just described. While these can serve an important function in identifying transition needs, they also have the potential for excluding students from moving into more inclusive settings. For instance, this can happen when a student demonstrates too many deficiencies in the eyes of the receiving teacher. It is important to keep in mind that students with special needs are not likely to show mastery-level competence in all the demands of the general education classroom. The value of these instruments is in their ability to target areas that should be addressed prior to the transition.

The differences noted earlier between the elementary and secondary levels justify some additional considerations. As stressed previously, the assessment of the receiving environment (i.e., general education classroom), in terms of the many different demands that a student is likely to encounter, should be part of the transition process. The notion of classroom survival skills, as depicted in Figure 16–4, is appropriate for the secondary level as well. Furthermore, the demands associated with secondary-level schooling noted by Robinson et al. (1985) and highlighted in Figure 16–3, although presented as a vertical transition, are operative here as well. They can easily be considered from a horizontal perspective if the student is moving into inclusive settings at the secondary level.

To date, one of the best instruments for comprehensively examining the explicit aspects of the secondary-level classroom is the *Classroom Variables Analysis Form* developed by Salend and Viglianti (1982). Although the orginal instrument needs to be adapted somewhat to match today's

FIGURE 16–4

Classroom survival skills inventory

I. Self-Related Skills	1	2	3	4	5	Comments
Demonstrates ethical behavior						
Accepts consequences for own behavior						
Accepts constructive criticism						
Demonstrates a positive self-attitude						
Is responsible for own actions, belongings, and items						
Has self-care/hygiene abilities						
Expresses feelings; communicates verbally						
Controls impulsivity						
Adapts appropriately to change in routine or environment						
Is self-motivated to learn and to control behavior						
Attends class; is on time and prompt						
Brings materials to class						
Occupies free time in constructive manner						

II. Task-Related Skills	1	2	3	4	5	Comments
Follows directions						
Completes tasks within time allotted						
Completes tasks with accuracy						
Focuses on and maintains attention to work						
Listens to speaker; does not interrupt						
Begins task independently after instructions are given						
Remains on-task independently						
Takes part in group activities and discussions (participates/listens appropriately)						
Is able to perform before others, (i.e., presents task results)						
Makes effort before giving up						
Demonstrates task persistence						
Follows class routine						
Makes smooth, appropriate transition from one task to the next						
Seeks help/attention appropriately						

III. Interpersonal Skills	1	2	3	4	5	Comments
Cooperates during play (organized or informal)						
Shows respect for others' feelings and property						
Has positive attitude toward others						
Interacts appropriately and works well with others						
Accepts authority and complies with rules						
Copes with temper, anger, and stress without aggression or conflict						
Requests help appropriately						
Greets others						
Helps others/recognizes needs						
Is able to initiate or terminate conversation						
Initiates play						
Plays and cooperates appropriately for reasonable amount of time						
Does not interrupt others						
Does not disrupt others						
Demonstrates good manners (shares, takes turns, says please/thank you, tells truth)						
Seeks teacher or peer permission appropriately						
Is not easily distracted						
Interacts well with teacher						
Is able to read body cues						

IV. Environmental Awareness	1	2	3	4	5	Comments
Deals with emergency calmly (fire drills, tsunami warnings)						
Moves appropriately about the classroom						
Shows care for environment and classroom materials						
Demonstrates appropriate behavior in other environments (i.e., music, art, PE, lunchroom, playground)						
Locates and replaces materials						
Shows responsibility for classroom responsibilities and chores						
Enters and leaves premises appropriately						

Note. From *Classroom Survival Skills: Requisites to Mainstreaming,* by C. L Smith, 1986. Unpublished master's thesis, University of Hawaii at Manoa. Honolulu, HI.

classrooms (i.e., include more technology features), it still can serve as a useful reference. The instrument covers seven critical areas that should be examined to determine areas in which a student may need skill development and/or in-class support. The major domains, under which there are multiple questions, include the following:

- Instructional materials and support personnel
- Presentation of subject matter
- Learner response variables
- Student evaluation
- Classroom management
- Social interactions
- Physical design

In reality, we will never be able to prepare students completely for moving into inclusive settings. However, the more we know about the receiving setting along with an accurate sense of the student's competence to deal with the demands of this environment, the more likely it will be that we can increase the student's chances for academic and social success. Without such assessment, planning, and preparation, students with special needs are truly strangers in a strange land.

Movement from Nonschool Facilities to School. Examples of this type of transition are sending environments such as private schools, correctional facilities, rehabilitation facilities, and residential treatment facilities. In all these cases, communication and knowledge of both the sending and receiving environments are desperately needed because far too often there is limited or no communication between settings.

One area that has received some attention is the re-entry to school of students who have suffered traumatic brain injury (TBI) and who have been hospitalized and/or receiving rehabilitation over an extended period of time. Tyler and Mira (1999) emphasize that transition planning must include preparing school staff, parents, classmates, along with the student with TBI. They also point out that the school environment must be evaluated and often modified according to the specific needs of the student who is re-entering

school. Accommodations should be guided by the following dimensions.

1. What is the best setting in which to provide the student's instruction?
2. How structured does the environment need to be?
3. How much organization needs to be added to the program?
4. What instructional devices (i.e., assistive technology) must be available to the student on return to school?

Tyler and Mira have developed various checklists that are very useful for planning for the transition of students with TBI back into the school setting.

The notion of vertical and horizontal transitions is intricately tied to the concept of connections. Instructionally, what we teach students should always be influenced by consideration of the next environment(s) in which students are likely to be. Every succeeding environment is preceded by a transition.

TRANSITION FROM SCHOOL TO POSTSCHOOL SETTINGS

A major goal of education is to prepare individuals to be responsible, contributing members of their communities, functioning competently in a number of adult roles. Yet the complexities and many demands of adulthood require a vast array of competencies that often extend beyond the explicit content of the typical school curriculum. Many requisite life skills are learned outside school—either at home or through some type of community-based experience. However, many learners with special needs must be introduced to the realities of "life after high school" in a systematic, programmed way.

Traditionally, if any school-based preparation for the realities of adulthood occurred, it probably focused on vocational needs, certainly an important consideration. Most adolescents with learning problems are fully capable of moving into the work force or some type of postsecondary education and should be appropriately prepared. Many students with mild disabilities who are in strictly academic tracks (i.e., diploma track) can benefit from some vocational experiences as well, as many of these students will not enter postsecondary education.

Vocational concerns, however, are not the only ones that need to be addressed. Students also must also acquire the skills to be competent family members, knowledgeable consumers, wise users of leisure time, and resourceful community members. As a result, transition planning must address the life skills needed to deal successfully with the demands of adulthood.

Conceptualizing the Transition from School to Young Adulthood Process

The driving force of life skills education, vocational training, and transition planning is to enhance the chances that a person will be successful in dealing with the daily demands of adulthood. It is a re-sponsibility shared by the school, the home, the individual, and, to a certain extent, adult agencies/settings who will serve these individuals, as illustrated in Figure 16-5.

A simple explanation of the model suggests that a person's quality of life is a function of being personally fulfilled. Fulfillment comes from being able to deal successfully with the demands of adulthood. (This is a variation of the concept of quality of life proposed by Halpern, 1993). Those who deal effectively with the day-to-day demands of life typically possess usable knowledge and display needed skills. In addition, these individuals utilize appropriate supports and services.

The probability of achieving this status is increased by comprehensive preparation and planning. As mentioned earlier, families often contribute considerably to this preparation. The degree to which the individual student is able to participate in his or her own life skills preparation depends to some extent on the nature of the

FIGURE 16–5
Adulthood implications of the transition process

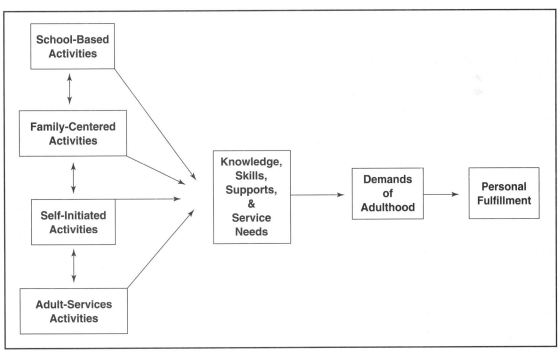

Source: Patton & Dunn (1998)

disability and to a great extent on how well she or he has been prepared to participate in this endeavor. Adult agencies also contribute to the process by participating in planning activities or, at very least, communicating information to schools, families, and students. As expected, the best outcomes of systematic transition services are achieved when school-based personnel, the family, adult agencies, and especially the student work together to determine needs, plan how to meet these needs, and carry out these plans.

The Transition Mandate

The initial focus on transition, spearheaded by the Office of Special Education and Rehabilitative Services (OSERS) (Will, 1984), was largely a response to the alarming data on the high dropout rates of students and the high rates of unemployment and underemployment of adults with disabilities. Major efforts to provide an appropriate education for students with disabilities were not paying off. The model of transition espoused by OSERS centered primarily on the school-to-work linkage and was followed a year later by a more comprehensive model developed by Halpern (1985). Unquestionably, these models have provided the backdrop for much subsequent work in this area.

A universally recognized and clear definition of this transition from school to community does not exist (Martin, 1986), yet certain elements are obvious. Clearly, the concept of transition links the two themes of adolescence and adulthood. Key components of the process are highlighted here.

- school-related activities/issues at the secondary level (e.g., curriculum, transition planning)
- transitional management issues (e.g., linkage between school and adult/postsecondary services)
- community issues (e.g., availability of adult/postsecondary options)

Articulating a set of goals for transition planning is as difficult as trying to define the concept. Nevertheless, three general objectives can be identified (Hawaii Transition Project, 1987).

- Arrange for opportunities and services that will support quality adult living.
- Prevent the interruption of needed services.
- Maximize the independence, community participation, and productivity of adolescents with disabilities who are entering young adulthood.

The transition initiative has been present to a certain extent since the passage of the Education for All Handicapped Children Act in 1975. However, it was not until the 1990 reauthorization of IDEA that there was a mandate to conduct transition activities. Stodden (1998) chronicled the key features of the transition initiative, as captured in the various reauthorizations of IDEA (see Fig. 16–6).

The idea that transition is an "outcome-oriented process," originally espoused in the mid 1980s, was maintained in the 1990 reauthorization to IDEA. In this legislation, transition services were defined as:

> A coordinated set of activities for a student, designed within an outcome-oriented process, which promotes movement from school to post-school activities, including post-secondary education, vocational training, integrated employment (including supported employment), continuing and adult education, adult services, independent living or community participation, (602(a)19)

Guiding Principles of Transition Planning

Effective transitional planning should follow principles that adhere to the goals of transition while respecting variances in the organizational structures, procedures of different localities, and family values. A complete discussion of key principles can be found elsewhere (Patton & Dunn, 1998). Some of the key principles include the following ideas.

- Transition efforts should start early.
- Planning must be comprehensive.
- Student participation is essential.
- Family involvement is crucial.
- The transition planning process must be sensitive to diversity.
- Transition planning is beneficial to all students.

FIGURE 16–6
Progress of the transition initiative within IDEA

1975 IDEA (P. L. 94-142)	1983 IDEA (P. L. 98-199) REAUTHORIZATION	1990 IDEA (P. L. 101-476) REAUTHORIZATION	1997 IDEA (P. L. 105-17) REAUTHORIZATION
■ Ensured FAPE for children with disabilities ■ Outlined due-process procedures ■ Established an Individualized Education Planning (IEP) process for each child with a disability	■ Federal funds were provided to demonstrate transition models ■ OSERS transition model was developed ■ Transition outcomes were specified in legislative language	■ Transition services are defined in legislation ■ Legislation included a statement of needed transition services in the IEP for each student, aged 16 or younger ■ Promoted educational planning focused on postschool goals	■ Focused on self-determination for students and families in transition planning ■ Focused on short- and long-range goals rather than objectives within the IEP ■ Focused on student planning and participation in the general education curriculum ■ Focused on integrating transition planning within the process of educational planning starting at age 14 years ■ Based educational planning and programming on postschool results

Source: Stodden, R.A. (1998). School-to-work Transition: Overview of disability legislation. In F. R. Rusch & J. G. Chadsey (Eds.), *Beyond high school: Transition from school to work.* Belmont, CA: Wadsworth.

Of these principles, none is more important than getting students to be as actively involved in their own transition planning as they can possibly be. Legally, transition goals should be based on students' preferences and interests.

Transition Planning Process

A general model of the transition planning process is presented in Figure 16–7. The first task is the assessment of transition needs, which ideally involves obtaining information from school-based sources, the student, and the family. Although getting to this point may require further assessment, after needs are identified a comprehensive transition plan should be developed. With the needs of the student in mind, this plan should include knowledge and skill acquisition goals as well as linkage goals. Knowledge and skills goals relate to those academic, social, and life skill areas for which

IEP goals should be written and instruction provided. Linkage goals are important for connecting the student with supports and services that will be needed when school is over. This section of the text identifies the skills and domains on which transition assessment should be based and for which transition planning should be done. It also highlights ways to assess transition needs and provides suggestions for developing useful transition plans.

Key Areas of Transition Planning. Various organizational schemes are available for conceptualizing the different areas of adulthood, as evidenced by the different transition domains used by different states. In many instances, emphasis has been given to the employment/education domain. However, equal attention needs to be given to other adult domains as well. The major domains that are being addressed in select

FIGURE 16–7
Transition planning process

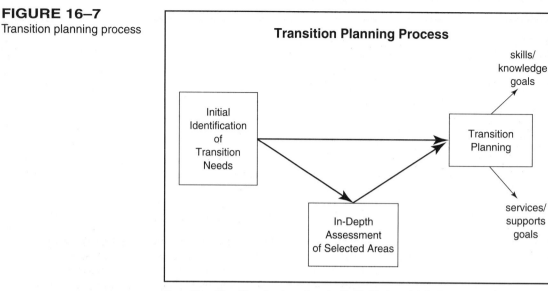

From *Transition Planning Inventory,* by G. M. Clark and J. R. Patton, (1997). Austin, TX: PRO-ED. Copyright 1997 by PRO-ED, Inc. Reprinted with permission.

states, as analyzed by Clark and Patton (1997), include the following transition planning areas.

- Community participation
- Daily living
- Employment
- Financial/income management
- Health
- Independent living
- Leisure/recreation
- Postsecondary education
- Relationships/social skills
- Transportation/mobility
- Vocational training

Assessing Transitional Needs. A number of techniques exist for assessing the transition needs of students. In our opinion, information may be needed in many of the areas highlighted in the previous section. Some instruments have been developed specifically for the purpose of assessing transition needs. A brief description of selected instruments is presented in Table 16–2.

One instrument, the *Transition Planning Inventory* (TPI), is designed specifically for conducting a transition needs assessment. The TPI includes three different forms: a student form, a

school form, and a home form. A portion of the school form is illustrated in Figure 16–8. Each form contains the same 46 questions that are organized according to the following transition planning areas: employment, further education/training, daily living, leisure activities, community participation, health, self-determination, communication, and interpersonal relationships. The information that is gathered can lead directly to the generation of transition-related goals. Often, however, results from administering the TPI suggest that further assessment is needed. A resource, the *Informal Assessments for Transition Planning,* is provided for this purpose.

Planning Based on Needs Assessment. According to the most recent reauthorization of IDEA, a statement of transition needs is required by age 14 for all students who qualify for special education. A statement of needed transition services is required by age 16. Simply stated, the statement of transition needs provides guidance for planning a student's high school program. The statement of transition services serves as a mechanism for planning for a seamless transition from school to community.

TABLE 16–2
Current examples of transition-referenced assessment instruments

Instrument/ Procedure Game	Target Group	Features
Social and Prevocational Information Battery—Revised (Halpern et al., 1986)	Adolescents and adults with mild mental retardation or low-functioning students with learning disabilities.	1. Subscales include Banking, Budgeting and Purchasing Skills, Job Skills and Job-Related Behavior, Home Management, Health Care, Hygiene and Grooming, and Ability to Read Functional Words 2. Orally administered except for items on functional signs 3. Designed especially for secondary school students 4. True-false item format 5. 277 items in the battery 6. 20–30 minutes' administration time
Tests for Everyday Living (Halpern et al., 1979)	All junior high students and average to low functioning senior high school students in remedial programs, including those labeled as having learning disabilities or learning handicaps	1. Subtests include Purchasing Habits, Banking, Budgeting, Health Care, Home Management, Job Search Skills, and Job-Related Behavior 2. Orally administered except where reading skills are critical to an item 3. 245 items across seven subtests 4. Diagnostic at the subtest level 5. 20–30 minutes' estimated administration time per subtest
Transition Behavior Scale (McCarney, 1989)	Any disability group; mild to severe levels of severity.	1. Subscales include Work-Related Behaviors, Interpersonal Relations, Social/Community Expectations 2. Ratings are completed by at least three persons 3. Items are rated on a 3-point scale 4. Estimated completion time is 15 minutes 5. Scores in percentile ranks are based on national standardization sample
LCCE Knowledge Battery (Brolin, 1992)	Mild cognitive disabilities; moderate to severe learning disabilities; mild to moderate behavioral disorders; Grades 7–12.	1. Curriculum-based assessment related to LCCE Curriculum 2. 200 multiple-choice items covering 20 of 22 LCCE competency areas 3. Standardized on a national sample
Transition Planning Inventory (Clark & Patton, 1997)	All disability populations, ages 14–25; mild through severe levels of disability.	1. Areas covered in the inventory include Employment, Further Education/Training, Daily Living, Living Arrangements, Leisure Activities, Community Participation, Health, Self-Determination, Communication, and Personal Relationships 2. 0–5 rating scaled completed independently by student, parent/guardian, and a school representative 3. Administration may be self-administration, guided administration, or oral administration

(continued)

TABLE 16–2 (*Continued*)

Instrument/ Procedure Game	Target Group	Features
		4. 56 inventory items plus open-ended items on the student form (optional on parent form) related to preferences and interests
		5. A profile sheet permits visual comparisons of the respondents' responses to each item
		6. Planning notes form encourages transformation of relevant assessment data into IEP goals, objectives, and interagency linkages
Enderle-Severson Transition Rating (Enderle & Severson, 1991)	Any disability group; mild to severe levels of disability; ages 14–21	1. The scale is an informal, criterion-referenced instrument
		2. Subscales include Jobs and Job Training, Recreation and Leisure, Home Living, and Postsecondary Training and Learning Opportunities.
		3. Scale is completed by the student's teacher and a parent or primary caregiver; framework for transition planning
LCCE Performance Battery (Brolin, 1992)	Mild cognitive disabilities; moderate to severe learning disabilities; mild to moderate behavioral disorders; Grades 7–12	1. The battery is a nonstandardized, criterion-referenced instrument providing skill rather than knowledge assessment of critical life skills
		2. Items are based on skills related to LCCE Curriculum
		3. Estimated time for administration is 3–4 hours
Life Skills Inventory (Brigance, 1995a)	All disability populations, high school ages and adults; mild cognitive disabilities with reading grade levels 2–8	1. Subscales including Speaking and Listening, Functional Writing, Words on Common Signs and Warning Labels, Telephone Skills, Money and Finance, Food, Clothing, Health, Travel, and Transportation
		2. Administered individually or in groups; administration may be oral or written
		3. Criterion-referenced assessment, providing specific knowledge and skill assessments for life skill items paired with instructional objectives
		4. Learner Record Book provided to show color-coded record of performance and instructional objectives generated from the results
		5. Optional Program Record Book is available to track progress of a group or class; optional Rating Scales are available to evaluate behavior, attitudes, and other traits related to life skills and employability
		6. Comparison assessment to Employability Skills Inventory (Brigance, 1995b)

Note. From "Transition Planning Assessment for Secondary-Level Students with Learning Disabilities," by G. M. Clark, 1996. *Journal of Learning Disabilities, 29,* pp. 86–87. Copyright 1996 by PRO-ED. Reprinted with permission.

FIGURE 16–8

TPI

Transition Planning Inventory
School Form

Student's Name _____

Date _____

Birth Date _____ Age _____ Sex M ☐ F ☐

School _____ Grade _____

Name of Person Completing Form _____

Section II. Likely Postschool Setting(s)

Directions: Fill in based on what you expect will happen after high school.

EMPLOYMENT/FURTHER EDUCATION OR TRAINING

☐ work
   ☐ competitive   ☐ full-time
   ☐ supported   ☐ part-time
   ☐ other _____
☐ community-based employment training
☐ vocational/technical school
☐ GED
☐ college/university
☐ other _____

LIVING ARRANGEMENT

☐ live by himself/herself
☐ live with parents or other relatives
☐ live with others who are not related to him/her (without adult supervision)
☐ live with others who are not related to him/her (with adult supervision)
☐ other _____

Section III. Planning Area Inventory

Directions: Rate the student based on his/her current level of competence for each statement listed, using a scale of 0 (for *strongly disagree*) to 5 (for *strongly agree*) to indicate your level of agreement with each statement. Circle the number that reflects your rating.

If a statement is not an appropriate outcome for planning for the student, circle "NA" (for "not appropriate"). If a statement is appropriate but you do not know the student's level of competence on which to base your decision, circle "DK" (for "don't know").

Planning Areas	Not Appropriate	Strongly Disagree 0	1	2	3	4	Strongly Agree 5	Don't Know
EMPLOYMENT								
1. Knows the requirements and demands of his/her preferred occupations.	NA	0	1	2	3	4	5	DK
2. Makes informed choices among occupational alternatives, based on his/her own interests, preferences, and abilities.	NA	0	1	2	3	4	5	DK
3. Knows how to get a job.	NA	0	1	2	3	4	5	DK
4. Demonstrates general job skills and work attitudes preferred by employers for keeping a job and advancing—may include supported employment.	NA	0	1	2	3	4	5	DK
5. Has the specific knowledge and skills needed to perform a particular skilled, semi-skilled, or entry-level job—may include supported employment.	NA	0	1	2	3	4	5	DK

Referring back to Figure 16-7, two types of goals should be generated as a result of a comprehensive transition needs assessment: instructional goals (knowledge and skills development) and linkage goals (connection with needed supports and services). The actual planning phase is relatively easy if the assessment phase provided useful information across a range of crucial adult areas.

Transition Plans. The document that will contain transition goals will vary from state to state. Some states require an individual transition plan (ITP), which is a separate document from the IEP. Other states include transition components within the existing IEP. Regardless of whether or not an ITP is used, the critical issue is that both instructional and linkage goals are developed for transition areas where needs have been identified.

The intent of the ITP may differ substantively from the purpose of the IEP in that the ITP is very often a plan for services rather than a plan for skill or knowledge acquisition. Moreover, it should reflect the individual's as well as the family's values, plans, and needs. Like IEPs, ITPs have no set format; unlike IEPs, ITPs do not have required elements. Typically, ITPs are organized around the key areas of transition or adulthood adopted by a state or local school district. As a result, variations exist in how transitional planning is incorporated into the IEP. One example of an ITP format is presented in Figure 16-9.

Another tool with great utility for students, parents, school personnel, and adult service providers is the transition portfolio. A portfolio should contain a significant amount of important information about students and their specific transitional plans. It is a compendium of materials that will be of great help to students as they exit school and can be beneficial to them later during their young adult years as well. A comprehensive portfolio should be organized according to some set of major transition planning areas. Most of the information can be completed while students are still in school; however, some relevant information must be added at later dates.

Community Linkages. Someone within a secondary school setting must assume the role of coordinator of the transitional process. In some settings transition specialists or transition coordinators have been hired to facilitate the transitional planning for students with special needs. In other locations teachers have taken on these duties in addition to their instructional duties. To effectively serve as a transition coordinator, one must not only be knowledgeable about the school component of this process but must also be aware of the adult/postsecondary arena. Information (i.e., eligibility, services provided) on typical state/federal agencies that are often needed by young adults with disabilities must be acquired. A good source of such information is provided by Cozzens, Dowdy, and Smith (1999).

The business community represents an important linkage for two reasons. It is a source of training sites, and it contains a large number of potential employers. Job placements must be found, developed, and maintained.

Another important linkage should be established and maintained with the state vocational rehabilitation agency, whose primary function is to provide services to persons at or near an employable age who are having or are apt to have employment problems. School systems and vocational rehabilitation agencies have now entered into cooperative agreements whereby the rehabilitation agencies provide services for students of school age with disabilities. Currently, state vocational rehabilitation agencies continue to provide services as needed after students graduate. Among some of the services provided are testing and evaluation to determine job potential and skills, training, placement in temporary or permanent jobs, follow-up and adjustment counseling, and evaluation.

Other community organizations that should be considered in the development of comprehensive transitional networks include the following organizations and agencies.

- Institutions of higher education (community colleges, 4-year colleges, universities).
- Trade and technical schools.
- Private/nonprofit organizations that provide services/assistance.
- Rehabilitation centers.

FIGURE 16–9
Individual Transition Plan 15

I. Career and Economic Self-Sufficiency

1. Employment Goal	Darlene will be employed as a truck driver.
Level of present performance	Darlene has participated in 1 year of career exploration. Darlene has decided that she wants to be a truck driver.
Steps needed to accomplish goal	(1) Darlene and teacher will identify truck driving schools that have credibility and job placement; (2) parents will use community contact to help as well; and (3) student will serve as an intern at a moving company.
Date of completion	1/01
Person(s) responsible for implementation	special educator, Darlene, and parents
2. Vocational Education/Training Goal	Darlene will participate in activities that allow practice on completing job applications, interviewing, using critical thinking skills, and obtaining a license to drive a truck.
Level of present performance	Darlene has decided to train as a heavy truck driver.
Steps needed to accomplish goal	(1) Darlene will practice completing job applications; (2) Darlene and vocational education will role play job interviewing skills; and (3) vocational and special educators will provide Darlene with necessary internship training experience.
Date of completion	6/01
Person(s) responsible for implementation	vocational educator, special educator, and Darlene
3. Postsecondary Education Goal	Darlene will enroll in one heavy truck driving academy.
Level of present performance	Darlene has expressed a strong interest in driving heavy trucks.

(continued)

FIGURE 16–9 (*Continued*)

Steps needed to accomplish goal	(1) Darlene will apply to truck driving academy; and (2) Darlene will meet with advisor from school to discuss job placement after training.
Date of completion	9/01
Person(s) responsible for implementation	Darlene

4. Financial/Income Needs Goal	Darlene will write and follow a monthly budget.
Level of present performance	Darlene has a part-time job.
Steps needed to accomplish goal	(1) Darlene will purchase a spiral notebook. Darlene will list monthly expenses and demonstrate how to add and subtract expenses and income.
Date of completion	12/00
Person(s) responsible for implementation	Darlene and classroom teacher

II. Community Integration and Participation

5. Independent Living Goal	Darlene will use the phone book to identify community resources.
Level of present performance	Darlene does not know how to use a phone book. She knows its purpose but has not demonstrated proficiency.
Steps needed to accomplish goal	Darlene will read through the index of the phone book. Darlene will practice looking up the names and telephone numbers of various agencies.
Date of completion	11/00
Person(s) responsible for implementation	special educator and Darlene

6. Transportation/Mobility Goal	Darlene will be able to read road maps.
Level of present performance	Darlene has a driver's license and borrows the family car often.
Steps needed to accomplish goal	(1) Darlene will use sense of direction to locate north, south, east, and west; and (2) she will highlight route on map and will follow route and check landmarks.
Date of completion	6/00
Person(s) responsible for implementation	special educator and Darlene
7. Social Relationships Goal	Darlene will take women's self-defense class at the YMCA.
Level of present performance	Darlene currently travels alone on many occasions.
Steps needed to accomplish goal	(1) Darlene will use phone book to locate phone number of the YMCA; (2) Darlene will call to get information; (3) she will enroll in self-defense class; and (4) she will evaluate skills as class progresses.
Date of completion	6/00
Person(s) responsible for implementation	Darlene, YMCA instructor
8. Recreation/Leisure Goal	Darlene will join the community volleyball team.
Level of present performance	Darlene has expressed an interest in participating in the activities at the Community Recreation Center.
Steps needed to accomplish goal	Darlene will sign up for team and will practice with team. Darlene will play as a member of the team.

(continued)

FIGURE 16–9 *(Continued)*

Date of completion	7/00
Person(s) responsible for implementation	Darlene and recreation instructor

III. Personal Competence

9. Health/Safety Goal	see Social Relationships Goal
Level of present performance	
Steps needed to accomplish goal	
Date of completion	
Person(s) responsible for implementation	

10. Self-Advocacy/Future Planning	N/A
Level of present performance	
Steps needed to accomplish goal	
Date of completion	
Person(s) responsible for implementation	

Student Career Preference

Work in the transportation industry

- Mental health centers.
- Military services.
- Recreational programs.
- Government agencies that provide services to persons with disabilities.

Time Line for Transition Planning

A crucial dimension in effective transition planning is a systematic time line of critical events. Historically, one of the major problems in appropriately preparing students for adulthood has been the lateness of the attention. In the past, too many students and their families suddenly realized during the last year of high school that they have to make some important choices about life.

The reauthorization of IDEA in 1997 now requires that the transition planning process begin at the middle school level, given that a statement of transition needs should be in place by age 14. It is essential that students, their parents/guardians, school personnel, and adult service providers recognize that early and sequential planning increases the likelihood of successful transition. Students need to be prepared to become active participants in their transition planning. Moreover, parents/ guardians should be encouraged to become actively involved in these activities, as they will often have to function as the service coordinators for their adult children when school is completed.

LIFE SKILLS EDUCATION

Functioning in community settings requires many varied skills. Unfortunately, most students are directly taught very few of the requisite skills needed to deal with the demands of adulthood. The assumption that students automatically adjust to community living after exiting formal schooling is erroneous, as the evidence from the many follow-up studies has shown (Wagner et al., 1993). In general, the adult outcomes data base paints a generalized picture of unemployment and/or underemployment, low pay, frequent job changes, nonengagement with the commu-

nity, limitations in independent functioning, and restricted social life.

Demands of Adulthood

A variety of taxonomies exist depicting the demands of adulthood. One general source on which to base the organization of functionally oriented curricula is the transition assessment area. Instruments like the TPI provide a format of important adult domains. However, other sources from the curricular literature also are available.

Two curricular sources of information include Brolin's (1997) Life-Centered Career Education (LCCE) model and Cronin and Patton's (1993) Major Life Demands model. The LCCE model includes 22 competencies that are divided into 97 subcompetencies. The Major Life Demands model is organized according to six adult domains, 23 subdomains, and 147 major life demands. Table 16–3 provides an overview of these two models.

The list of major life demands developed by Cronin and Patton (1993), the competencies and subcompetencies used by Brolin (1997), and the life skill topics that can be found in other sources tend to correlate with one another. One resource is not necessarily any better than another; they all represent valid efforts to help practitioners develop meaningful programs for students.

Once the major life demand areas are recognized, the specific life skills can be identified. This is the most important level of activity because it addresses local needs and personal relevance. Specific life skills refer to those competencies needed to deal with a major life demand for an individual living in a given location. It is common for many different specific life skills to relate to any given major life demand.

Curricular Considerations

There continues to be a great need to provide comprehensive life skills curricula to students with special needs. As detailed in Chapter 6, such curricula must be responsive to students' present and future needs. The need to make the

TABLE 16–3
Models of Adult Functioning

Model	Adult Domain/ Curriculum Area	Subdomains/ Competency Areas
Domains of Adulthood (Cronin & Patton, 1993)	Employment/education	General job skills General education/training considerations Employment setting Career refinement and re-evaluation
	Home and family	Home management Financial management Family life Childrearing
	Leisure pursuits	Indoor activities Outdoor activities Community/neighborhood activities Travel Entertainment
	Community involvement	Citizenship Community awareness Services/resources
	Physical/emotional health	Physical health Emotional health
	Personal responsibility and relationships	Personal confidence/understanding Goal setting Self-improvement Relationships Personal expression
Life Centered Career Education (Brolin, 1997)	Daily living skills	Managing personal finances Selecting and managing a household Caring for personal needs Raising children and meeting marriage responsibilities Buying, preparing, and consuming food Buying and caring for clothing Exhibiting responsible citizenship Utilizing recreational facilities and engaging in leisure Getting around the community
	Personal-social skills	Achieving self-awareness Acquiring self-confidence Achieving socially responsible behavior Maintaining good interpersonal skills

Model	Adult Domain/ Curriculum Area	Subdomains/ Competency Areas
		Achieving independence
		Making adequate decisions
		Communicating with others
	Occupational guidance and preparation	Knowing and exploring occupational possibilities
		Selecting and planning occupational choices
		Exhibiting appropriate work habits and behavior
		Seeking, securing, and maintaining employment
		Exhibiting sufficient physical-manual skills
		Obtaining specific occupational skills

Source: Patton, Cronin, & Wood (1999)

curriculum more relevant to students has been underscored by secondary-level teachers (Halpern & Benz, 1987).

Once a comprehensive list of life skills has been identified at a local level, the next important task is to organize these topics so that they can be presented to students in their programs. Life skills preparation involves different things for different students. For example, students for whom higher education is a possibility should have access to academically oriented programs in general education that is balanced with the exposure to other important adult outcome areas. Other students, for whom high school may be the termination of formal schooling, are likely to be in a different course of studies. The challenge for school administrators, curriculum development specialists, and teachers is how to cover important life skills topics within existing curricular structures. Figure 16-10 depicts a continuum of options for teaching life skills.

Coursework. The first option for teaching life skills is the development of a sequence of life skills courses. The intent of this option is to offer course work that is life skills-oriented, that relates to the typical subject areas (i.e., science, math, so-

cial studies, English), and that could be either noncredit or credit. Cronin and Patton (1993) suggest the following course offerings: personal finance, practical math, health and hygiene, everyday science, practical communication, community awareness and involvement, occupational development, and interpersonal relations.

The next two options in the continuum involve the creation of a single life skills course. One variation of this single course idea is a course that is life skills-oriented but focuses on one topical area such as math or science. For instance, a course titled "Math in the Real World" might cover many math skill areas related to everyday life.

Another example of how a single life skills course might look is provided by Helmke, Havekost, Patton, & Polloway (1994). A course entitled "Science for Living" was developed using the "major life demands" (Cronin & Patton, 1993) as a way of identifying important topics that should be covered in this life science course. The major life demands chosen as the framework for the course are listed in Figure 16-11.

Another variation of the single course approach would be a course that covers a range of life skills topics cutting across more than one top

FIGURE 16–10

Options for organizing life skills content for formal instruction

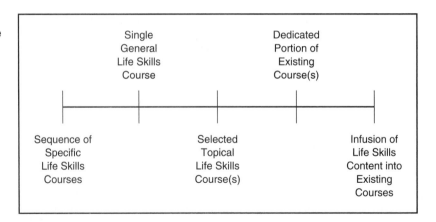

ical area. This might be used in settings where the development of a sequence of courses is not possible or where there is a need for an elective course. An example might be a course titled "Functional Living Skills" or "Life 101."

Integrating Real-life Topics into Existing Content. Another option involves the integration of life skills topics into the predetermined content of existing course work. This scenario

occurs most commonly when students are placed in general education courses or remain in special education courses in which general education content is taught. Two variations of the integration technique exist: augmentation and infusion.

One method of covering real-life topics is to augment existing courses by extending the coverage of set topics into more meaningful, life-related areas. This can be accomplished by dedicating a portion of a course to such topics (e.g, one session

FIGURE 16–11

Major life demands for "Science for Living" course

- Planning nutrition and diet
- Administering simple first aid
- Exercising
- Using medicine
- Knowing basic anatomy
- Knowing and identifying illness (adult, childhood, communicable)
- Seeking regular physical and dental checkups
- Using proper dental hygiene and dental care
- Decision making about substance use and abuse
- Knowing appropriate dress for the weather
- Knowing how the body fights disease
- Preventing illness and mishaps
- Recognizing signs of health problems
- Dealing with emergencies

- Seeking a healthy lifestyle
- Recognizing the physical changes of aging
- Recognizing family genetic features
- Recognizing health risks
- Understanding sexuality
- Dealing with depression
- Managing stress
- Managing life changes
- Dealing with anxiety
- Dealing with the separation or death of a family member
- Dealing with relationships
- Seeking personal counseling
- Recognizing signs of emotional problems
- Exploring career options

Note. From "Life Skills Programming: Development of a High School Science Course," by L. M. Helmke et al., 1994, *Teaching Exceptional Children, 26(*2), p. 53. Copyright 1994 by Council for Exceptional Children. Reprinted with permission.

every week or two). In a consumer math course, for instance, a teacher might include additional lessons that address the economics of dating or the life skills associated with maintaining an apartment.

In the fusion approach, the objective is to infuse into existing content real-life topics that relate directly to information being covered. This approach can be either spontaneous (i.e., capitalizing on teachable moments) or planned (i.e., careful examination of course content to identify "infusion points"). A more detailed discussion of infusion procedures along with 17 examples of how to do infusion are provided by Patton, Cronin, and Wood (1999). One of the examples from this resource is shown in Figures 16–12 and 16–13. In this third-grade example, one can see in the infusion guide (Fig. 16–13) how certain "infusion points" found on the textbook page (Fig. 16–12) were used to generate some real-life discussion topics.

Special education teachers, who are working in consultative and/or cooperative roles with general education teachers, can use their knowledge of major life demands and specific life skills to enhance their efforts to make instruction more relevant for all students. Most general education teachers will greatly appreciate the benefits of such contributions.

Instructional Considerations

The importance of applying various academic skills to and demonstrating social competence in real-life situations cannot be overemphasized. The intent of teaching life skills is to prepare individuals to use foundational skills in ways that will make their lives more productive and meaningful, leading to some sense of personal fulfillment. It is very easy to apply skills associated with reading, speaking, listening, writing, computing, and problem solving to the context of adult situations. Figure 16–14 provides numerous selected examples of how this can happen.

The major features that should characterize innovative life skills programming and instruction for most students with learning-related problems include the following: adult-referenced; compre-

hensive; relevant to students; empirically and socially valid (i.e., appropriate to one's specific situation); flexible; community-based when possible; and sensitive to cultural and family values.

Career Development Emphasis

The concept of career development is akin to the idea of life skills instruction. It was used often in the early 1970s but never caught on in the field of education as it should have. Because of its historical significance and its close relationship to the focus of this chapter, this concept is discussed briefly below.

Definitional Perspective. Career development suggests that individuals should be presented with information that is related to a variety of situations (i.e., careers) associated with community living. The term *career* can be misleading because it is often viewed solely from an occupational perspective. However, the broader notion of career includes various adult roles (e.g., in the home and community).

> Career education is not simply preparation for a job. It is also preparation for other productive work roles that comprise one's total career functioning. This includes the work of a homemaker and family member, the participation as a citizen and volunteer, and the engagement in productive leisure and recreational pursuits that are of benefit to oneself and others. (Brolin, 1986, p. vii)

Goals. It is important to consider career development as a lifelong process that begins at the preschool level and continues past retirement. This view has been espoused by the Division on Career Development and Transition (DCDT) of the Council for Exceptional Children. DCDT advocates the following principles for providing career development and transition education (Clark, Carlson, Fisher, Cook, & D'Alonzo, 1991).

- Education for career development and transition is for individuals with disabilities at all ages.
- Career development is a process that begins at birth and continues throughout life.
- Early career development is essential for making satisfactory choices later.

FIGURE 16–12   Infusion guide: Text example

People also exchanged mandarin oranges happily. The oranges are symbols of happiness and prosperity. Yang loved the New Year's celebration. It was her favorite holiday because it was a very happy time, and there was lots of merrymaking and good food.

After breakfast, Yang and her family started on their visits. Everywhere, happy people greeted them. Everyone said "Kong Hee Fatt Choy." That means "We wish you prosperity."

From *Reading Milestones: An Alternative Reading Program,* Level 6, Orange Reader 9 (2nd ed., p. 36), by S. P. Quigley, C. M. King, P. L. McAnally, and S. Rose, 1991, Austin, TX: PRO-ED. Copyright 1991 by PRO-ED, Inc. Reprinted with permission.

FIGURE 16–13   Infusion guide

Content Referent	Possible Life Skills Topics	Adult Domain
Celebration	■ List family celebrations other than the typical holidays.	Home and Family
Celebration	■ Identify some neighborhood celebrations that occur throughout the year.	Leisure Pursuits
Symbols	■ Identify symbols you see every day in your community (e.g., traffic signs, parking for drivers who are disabled, hospital signs, railroad signs, deer crossing).	Community Involvement
New Year's	■ Name some New Year's resolutions that people make to improve their health.	Physical/Emotional Health

■ Significant gaps or periods of neglect in any area of basic human development affect career development and the transition from one stage of life to another.

■ Career development is responsive to intervention and programming when the programming involves direct instruction for individual needs.

Guided by these principles, schools and adult services should strive to provide mechanisms for facilitating lifelong career development.

Stages of Career Development. The first career development activities are likely to begin during the elementary years. The typical stages include: career awareness, career orientation, career exploration, and career preparation. Clark (1979) suggests some objectives that should be included in an elementary-level career education program.

■ Provide instruction and guidance for developing positive habits, attitudes, and values toward work and daily living.

■ Provide instruction and guidance for establishing and maintaining positive human relationships at home, at school, and at work.

■ Provide instruction and guidance for developing awareness of occupational alternatives.

■ Provide instruction for an orientation to the realities of the world of work, as a producer and as a consumer.

■ Provide instruction for acquiring actual job and daily living skills. (p. 13)

The crucial ingredient for implementing Clark's suggestions is preparing teachers to undertake such a venture; unfortunately, there is little evidence that preservice teachers are required to take course work in this area (Jenkins, Leigh, & Patton, 1996).

Efforts must be made to provide teachers with appropriate information, resources, and techniques for teaching about careers. Accentuating the importance of career education, demonstrating its educational and personal relevance, and providing ways for incorporating it into the existing curriculum will assist in its successful implementation.

Because of the close relationship of career education to transition planning, we suggest that additional goals be added to Clark's list to highlight other roles that become important as individuals enter young adulthood.

1. Explore the variety of leisure activities, including hobbies and recreational activities.
2. Discuss what is expected of and required from a contributing member of the community.

FIGURE 16–14

Relationship of scholastic/social skills to adult domains

Content Areas

Scholastic Social Skills	Employment Education	Home and Family	Leisure Pursuits	Community Involvement	Emotional/ Physical Health	Personal Responsibility/ Relations
Reading	Reading classified ads for jobs	Interpreting bills	Locating and understanding movie information in a newspaper	Following directions on tax forms	Comprehend-ing directions on medica-tion	Reading letters from friends
Writing	Writing letter of application for job	Writing checks	Writing for information on a city to visit	Filling in voter registration form	Filling in medical history or forms	Sending thank-you notes
Listening	Understanding oral directions of a procedure change	Comprehending directions	Listening for forecast to plan out-door activity	Understanding campaign ads	Attending lec-tures on stress	Taking turns in a conversation
Speaking	Asking boss for a raise	Discussing mor-ning routines with family	Inquiring about tic-kets for a concert	Stating opinion at the school board meeting	Describing symptoms to a doctor	Giving feedback to a friend
Math causes	Understanding difference between net and gross pay	Computing cost of doing laundry in a laundromat vs. at home	Calculating the cost of a dinner out vs. eat-ing at home	Obtaining information for a building permit	Using a ther-mometer	Planning costs of a date
Problem Solving	Settling a dispute with a co-worker	Deciding how much to budget for rent	Role playing appropri-ate behaviors for var-ious places	Knowing what to do if victim of fraud	Selecting a doctor	Deciding how to ask someone for a date
Survival Skills	Using a prepared career planning packet	Listing emergency phone numbers	Using shopping center directory	Marking calendar for important dates (e.g.,recycling,gar-bage collection)	Using a system to remember to take vitamins	Developing a sys-tem to remember birthdays
Personal/ Social	Applying appropriate interviews skills	Helping child with homework	Knowing rules of neighborhood pool	Locating self-improvement classes	Getting a yearly physical exam	Discussing how to negotiate a price at a flea market.

Note. From *Life Skills for Students with Special Needs: A Practical Guide for Developing Real-Life Programs* (p. 33), by M. E. Cronin and J. R. Patton, 1993, Austin, TX: PRO-ED. Copyright 1993 by PRO-ED, Inc. Reprinted with permission.

3. Examine the responsibilities of maintaining a house or an apartment, assuming both an owner's and a renter's perspective.

As the need for specific occupational preparation becomes more urgent, other program goals arise.

- Enhance the occupational awareness and aspirations of students through career counseling.
- Conduct an assessment of each student's vocational interests and skills.
- Integrate the assessment findings into the individual education program and lesson planning of each student.
- Develop a comprehensive individual transition plan that is closely related to the Individualized Education Plan (IEP) and predicated on the probable subsequent needs of the student.
- Provide students with community-based training opportunities.
- Ensure the development of entry-level job skills.
- Provide job placement for and support to students as needed.

Developing a Positive Work Attitude. United States culture is result oriented. Many of the results that are usually accorded positive treatment in our society are work related (i.e., those who hold a job are held in higher esteem than those who do not hold a job). The individual with a results- or work-oriented attitude is in a better position to obtain a job than the individual who is negative or naïve about work so it is clear that education should assist students in developing strong positive work personalities with habits and attitudes that will ultimately lead them to become what they are interested in and capable of becoming.

During the preschool stage, youngsters observe the daily living and working habits of those around them. Their observations, as well as interactions with older persons in their environment, begin to yield the perceptions of life that will ultimately cause these individuals to develop a particular type of work personality. It is readily apparent that the family has a tremendous influence on the child. Families who are consistent in meeting family members' needs or who are work-oriented tend to produce persons who behave in the same fashion. Families who are not consistent in meeting family members' needs or who are not work oriented tend to produce young adults who exhibit these latter types of behaviors. Certainly, there are exceptions to this generalization, but it depicts the tremendous importance of the family to the preschool child.

During the elementary school stage, students form a clearer, more precise perception of the world and their immediate surroundings. Parks (1976) reports that stereotyping of career roles can occur even at this age. She further states that evidence supports the finding that children at this level are developing their own values, interests, and concerns about work. As students engage in academic and nonacademic endeavors, teachers need to be aware of the importance of their developing behaviors that will lead to positive work habits and positive work personalities, for example, starting a task on time, cooperating with others, being neat, or cleaning up and putting things away. As children get older and can accept more responsibilities, they should be given more important jobs in school. Students should also be given tasks that require them to express their ideas and understanding about different vocations. For example, students might be asked to write a composition or tell a story about a certain job, such as being a plumber, or students might role-play the actions of different persons, such as a park ranger, magician, or bricklayer.

An additional activity that is appropriate for elementary or middle-school students is maintaining job-awareness notebooks containing articles and advertisements relative to one or more of the 15 career cluster areas presented in Figure 16–15. Students should acquire information to answer some of the following questions: What occupations are included in the cluster? Who works in these occupations? What is the lifestyle of the workers? Whom do they work with? Where are their jobs? How do the workers accomplish their jobs? Activities such as these expose students to the different roles of different workers and also

FIGURE 16–15

Occupational clusters identified by the U.S Office of Education

Career Groups

Agriculture agribusiness	Hospitality and recreation
Business and office	Manufacturing
Communication and media	Marine science
Construction	Marketing and distribution
Consumer education and home economics	Natural resources and environment
	Personal services
Fine arts and humanities	Public service
Health	Transportation

aid students in clarifying alternatives for future study and consideration.

The secondary school period is a crucial stage in the life of the potential worker. Most adolescents with learning problems require a comprehensive curriculum that is responsive to their current needs and consistent with their transitional needs across the life span. Initially, transition planning must be initiated and a realistic appraisal must be made of each student's postsecondary environment. For students with mild learning problems, further educational possibilities can be considered.

FIGURE 16–16

School-based vocational training

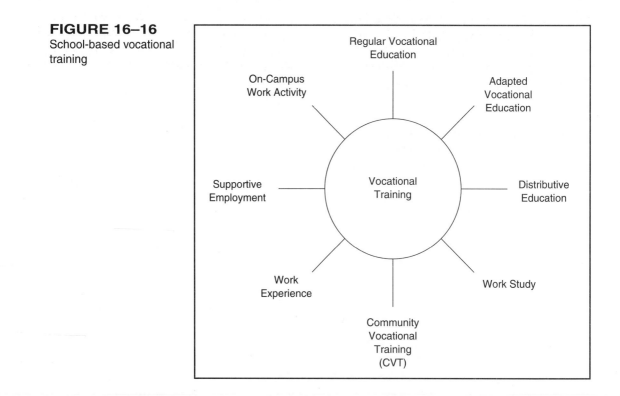

In the postsecondary stage, individuals usually obtain a job or continue their education/training and begin to assume their roles in the community and/or within their families. However, changes often occur in jobs (e.g., layoffs, promotions) and in families (e.g., offspring, divorce), requiring a reeducation process for many people. As a result, some of the early phases just described may have to be repeated at a later point in life.

Vocational Training Options. A number of school-based options for vocational training may be available in a school system. The various alternatives are graphically depicted in Figure 16–16. It is extremely important for many students with special needs to receive some form of vocational experience and skill development prior to exiting from formal schooling. This is critical because many of these students will not access such training at a later time. Unfortunately, many students with special needs leave school without any vocational skills. This often results from the fact that they may be in academically oriented programs that do not allow time for vocational training. It may also result because not all of the vocational options highlighted in Figure 16–15 are available to students with special needs.

SUMMARY

This chapter addresses the numerous aspects of preparing students with special needs for the many vertical and horizontal transitions that they will encounter in their school careers. Special attention is given to the challenges that await them in everyday living.

A significant amount of attention is given to the transition planning process. An overview of the transition planning process, along with more specific information about certain aspects of it (i.e., assessing transition needs, generating transition goals, and establishing links to postschool services and supports) is discussed.

A key part of the chapter is devoted to life skills education. Individuals need to acquire competence in a number of areas to deal successfully with the everyday challenges. Two major approaches (coursework and integration) for addressing life skills in the curriculum are highlighted and accompanied by specific examples. Instructional guidelines for teaching life skills are also provided.

Career development is discussed and related to the notion of life skills and transition planning. The development of a positive work attitude is presented in depth because this is crucial for students with special needs.

TEACHER TIPS   Elementary Level

As has been mentioned throughout this book, the precursors of many adult-referenced competencies can be taught at the elementary level. The following examples show how various transition planning domains [i.e., those used in the Transition Planning Inventory (Clark & Patton, 1997)] can be addressed at the elementary level. The examples provided are most appropriate for upper elementary levels.

EMPLOYMENT

Assign students to keep a journal for a week, writing about their interests, hobbies, strengths, and preferred lifestyles. Have them incorporate these into the "perfect job" for themselves.

FURTHER EDUCATION/TRAINING

Explain to the students what vocational/technical school is and what kinds of occupations are served in these schools. Also, introduce resources to access a vocational/technical school.

DAILY LIVING

Set up a mock store in the classroom with fake checkbooks, cash, and different things to buy. The students can practice making change and balancing checkbooks.

LEISURE ACTIVITIES

Ask the students to discuss their favorite "hangouts," and explain why they like them.

COMMUNITY PARTICIPATION

Have the class as a whole take part in a community volunteer program. For example the class could "adopt" a stretch of road near the school that they could keep clean by picking up trash. Time can be provided weekly, or every few weeks, for students to work on it.

HEALTH

Have each student tell the class what he or she does when feeling bad in order to cheer up. The students can make a book with these ideas for reference.

SELF-DETERMINATION

Assign the students to write about things in their lives about which they would like to make decisions, or about decisions that they have already made. This can be done in journals or as a separate writing assignment.

COMMUNICATION

Have the students keep a daily journal.

INTERPERSONAL RELATIONSHIPS

Have students write descriptions of both positive and negative qualities that their best friends possess.

TEACHER TIPS

More students with special needs than ever before are pursuing postsecondary education. Transition planning should include activities that not only examine the competencies of the student demanded by postsecondary settings, but also assist the student and his or her family in selecting an appropriate institution. Webb (2000) describes a systematic, yet practical, method to help students, their families, and school-based personnel in the decision-making, planning, and preparation processes that will result in college enrollment. Her suggestions are based on the Opportunities in Postsecondary Education through Networking (OPEN) model. The key steps in this model are described below.

- *Deciding* to attend: Making the decision to attend college—which should occur early and involve consideration of possible career paths.
- *Planning* for postsecondary education: Providing information to students and their families that will ensure a planned foundation from which they can complete the college selection and enrollment process with a focus on academic, career, and personal-social planning.
- *Preparing* for postsecondary education: Focus on preparing students for the postsecondary setting in terms of knowledge and skill development.
- *Exploring* postsecondary choices: Examination of the postsecondary educational options available and accessible to students.
- *Selecting* a college or university: Actual selection of a college or university based on a student's interests, abilities, and needs—with a focus on the services that are available at a specific institution.
- *Applying* to a college or university: Features instructions and suggestions for completing the application process—including the application for financial aid.

Source: Webb, K. W. (2000). *Transition to postsecondary education: Strategies for students with disabilities.* Austin, TX: Pro-Ed.

TEACHER TIPS

The selection of appropriate assistive technologies for young adults with special needs requires careful consideration of four interrelated factors (Raskind, 1998): the individual; the specific tasks that need to be performed; the specific technology to be used; and the nature of the context in which the technology is to be used. Key issues associated with each of these factors are listed below.

- *Individual:* Consideration of strengths and weaknesses in relation to various skill areas to enable the identification of areas of difficulty and areas on which to capitalize.
- *Technology:* Consideration of certain factors: technology's effectiveness in accomplishing its primary compensatory purpose; reliability/dependability of the technology over time; compatibility with other technologies; ease of learning and use; technical support; and cost.
- *Task:* Observation of the person's use of a technology to compensate for a specific difficulty; some factors to consider are: effectiveness of the technology; ease and extent of use; individual's interest and comfort level; degree to which the technology taps a person's strengths; and general psychological and behavioral response.
- *Context:* Consideration of the use of a specific technology across differing settings in which a person functions with attention to practical and social appropriateness.

Source: Raskind, M. H. (1998). Literacy for adults with learning disabilities through assistive technology. In S. A. Vogel & S. Reder (Eds.), *Learning: Learning disabilities, literacy, and adult education* (pp. 253–268). Baltimore: Paul H. Brookes Publishing.

References

Abery, B., Rudrud, L., Arndt, L., Schauben, L., & Eggebeen, A. (1995). Evaluating a multicomponent program for enhancing the self-determination of youth with disabilities. *Intervention in School and Clinic, 30*(3), 170–179.

Abrams, B. J., & Segal, A. (1998). How to prevent aggressive behavior. *Teaching Exceptional Children, 30* (4), 10–15.

Abruscato, J., & Hassard, J. (1978). *The earthpeople activity book: People, places, pleasures and other delights.* Santa Monica, CA: Goodyear.

Academe Today, (May 21, 1998). How technology changes the way we read and write. *Academic Today Daily Report.*

Adams, A., Carnine, D., & Gersten, R. (1982). Instructional strategies for studying content area texts in the intermediate grades. *Reading Research Quarterly, 18*, 27–55.

Adger, C. T. (1993). No talking is no good: Student voices in academic discourse. *LD Forum, 18*(2), 26–28.

Affleck, J. W., Edgar, E., Levine, P., & Kortering, L. (1990). Post-school status of students classified as mildly mentally retarded, learning disabled or non-handicapped: Does it get better with time? *Education and Training in Mental Retardation, 25*, 315–324.

Alberto, P. A., & Troutman, A. C. (1995). Applied behavior analysis for teachers (4th ed.). Upper Saddle River, NJ: Merrill/Prentice Hall.

Alexander, J. E. (1988). *Teaching reading.* Glenview, IL: Scott, Foresman/Little, Brown.

Algozzine, B., & Korinek, L. (1985). Where is special education for students with high-prevalence handicaps going? *Exceptional Children, 51*, 388–394.

Algozzine, B., & Ysseldyke, J. (1994). *Simple ways to make teaching math more fun* (Elementary school edition). Longmont, CO: Sopris West.

Algozzine, B., & Ysseldyke, J. (1995). *Tactics for improving parenting skills.* Longmont, CO: Sopris West.

Allen, R. V., & Halvorsen, G. C. (1961). *The language experience approach to reading instruction.* Boston: Ginn.

Alley, G., & Deshler, D. (1979). *Teaching the learning disabled adolescent: Strategies and methods.* Denver, CO: Love.

Alliance for Drama Education. (1983). *An overview to getting dramatic.* Kaneohe, HI: Alliance for Drama Education.

Alston, J., & Taylor, J. (1987). *Handwriting: Theory, research, and practice.* New York: Nichols.

American Association on Mental Retardation (1994). AAMR Board approves policy on facilitated communication. *AAMR News & Notes, 7*(5), 2.

American Speech-Language-Hearing Association. (1982). Definitions: Communicative disorders and variations. *ASHA, 24*, 949–950.

American Speech-Language-Hearing Association. (1983). Position paper: Social dialects. *ASHA, 25*, 23–24.

American Speech-Language-Hearing Association. (1991a). Augmentative and alternative communication. *ASHA, 33 (Suppl. 5)*, 8.

American Speech-Language-Hearing Association. (1991b). A model for collaborative service delivery for students with language-learning disorders in the public schools. *ASHA, 33 (Suppl. 5)*, 44–50.

Anesko, K. M., Schoiock, G., Ramirez, R., & Levine, F. M. (1987). A problem checklist: Assessing children's homework difficulties. *Behavioral Assessment 9*, 179–185.

Archer, A., & Gleason, M. (1989). *Skills for school success.* North Billerica, MA: Curriculum Associates.

Archer, A., & Gleason, M. (1995). Skills for school success. In P. T. Cegelka & W. H. Berdine (Eds.), *Effective instruction for students with learning difficulties* (pp. 227–263). Boston: Allyn & Bacon.

Argyle, M. (1967). *The psychology of interpersonal behavior.* London: Penguin.

Argyle, M., & Kendon, A. (1967). The experimental analysis of social performance. In L. Berkowitz

(Ed.), *Advances in social psychology.* New York: Academic Press.

Armbruster, B. B., & Anderson, T. H. (1988). On selecting considerate content area textbooks. *Remedial and Special Education, 9,* 47-52.

Armstrong, D. G. (1984). Helping youngsters grapple with textbook terminology. *The Social Studies, 75,* 216-219.

Armstrong, D. G. (1990). *Developing and documenting the curriculum.* Boston: Allyn & Bacon.

Asher, S. R., & Hymel, S. (1981). Children's social competence in peer relations: Sociometric and behavioral assessment. In J. D. Wine & M. D. Smye (Eds.), *Social competence.* New York: Guilford Press.

Association for Supervision and Curriculum Development (Spring, 1997). Teaching young writers. *Curriculum Update* (no volume/number cited).

Association for Supervision and Curriculum Development (1999). Speaking and Listening: The first basic skills. *Education Update, 41,* 6-7.

Atwood, R. K., & Oldham, B. R. (1985). Teachers, perceptions of mainstreaming in an inquiry-oriented elementary science program. *Science Education, 69,* 619-624.

Aullis, M. (1978). *Developmental and remedial reading in the middle grades.* Boston: Allyn & Bacon.

Axelrod, S., Hall, R. V., & Tams, A. (1979). Comparison of two common classroom seating arrangements. *Academic Therapy, 15,* 29-36.

Bailey, E. J. (1975). *Academic activities for adolescents with learning disabilities.* Evergreen, CO: Learning Pathways.

Baker, M. (1981). *Focus on life science.* Upper Saddle River, NJ: Merrill/Prentice Hall.

Ball, D. W. (1978). *ESS/Special education teacher's guide.* St. Louis: Webster/McGraw-Hill.

Ballet, L. L. (1991). Written language test reviews. In A. M. Bain, L. L. Ballet, & L. C. Moats (Eds.). *Written language disorders: Theory into practice* (pp. 165-188). Austin, TX: Pro-Ed.

Ballew, H. (1973). *Teaching children mathematics.* Upper Saddle River, NJ: Merrill/Prentice Hall.

Bandura, A. (1977). Self-efficiency: Toward a unifying theory of behavior change. *Psychological Review, 84,* 191-215.

Bandura, A. (1986). *Social foundations of thought and action: A social cognitive theory.* Upper Saddle River, NJ: Prentice Hall.

Bandura, A. (1989). Self-regulation of motivation and action through internal standards and goal system. In L. A. Pervin (Ed.), *Goal concepts in personality and social psychology* (pp. 19-38). Hillsdale, NJ: Erlbaum.

Bandura, A. (1991). Social cognitive theory of self-regulation. *Organizational Behavior and Human Performance, 50,* 248-287.

Bankson, N. (1990). *Bankson language test* (2nd ed.). Austin, TX: Pro-Ed.

Barclay, K. D. (1990). Constructing meaning: An integrated approach to teaching reading. *Intervention, 26,* 84-91.

Barenbaum, E. M. (1983). Writing in the special class. *Topics in Learning and Learning Disabilities, 3*(3), 12-20.

Baroni, D. (1987). Have primary children draw to expand vocabulary. *The Reading Teacher, 40,* 819-820.

Barrish, H. H., Saunders, M., & Wolf, M. M. (1969). Good behavior game: Effects of individual contingencies for group consequences on disruptive behavior in a classroom. *Journal of Applied Behavior Analysis, 2,* 119-124.

Bartel, N. R. (1990). Problems in mathematics achievement. In D. D. Hammill & N. R. Bartel (Eds.), *Teaching children with learning and behavior problems* (5th ed., pp. 289-343). Boston: Allyn & Bacon.

Barton, L. E., Brulle, A. R., & Repp, A. C. (1983). Aversive techniques and the doctrine of least restrictive alternative. *Exceptional Education Quarterly, 3*(4), 1-8.

Bassett, D. S. (no date). *Content area reading teaching packet.* Unpublished guide. Anchorage, AK: University of Alaska.

Bateman, B. D. (1971). *The essentials of teaching.* Sioux Falls, SD: Dimensions.

Bateman, B. D. (1982). Legal and ethical dilemmas of special educators. *Exceptional Education Quarterly, 2*(4), 57-67.

Bates, E. (1976). *Language in context.* New York: Academic Press.

Bates, E., Thal, D., & MacWhinney, B. (1991). A functionalist approach to language and its implications for assessment and intervention. In T. M. Gallagher (Ed.), *Pragmatics of language: Clinical practice issues.* San Diego, CA: Singular Publishing.

Bauwens, J., & Hourcade, J. (1995). *Cooperative teaching.* Austin, TX: Pro-Ed.

Bauwens, J., & Korinek, L. (1993). IEPs for cooperative teaching: Developing legal and useful documents. *Intervention in School and Clinic, 28,* 303-306.

Beatty, L. S., Gardner, E. G., Madden, R., & Karlsen, B. (1985). *Stanford diagnostic mathematics test* (3rd ed.). San Antonio, TX: Psychological.

Beck, J., Broers, J., Hogue, E., Shipstead, J., & Knowlton, E. (1994). Strategies for functional community-based instruction and inclusion for children with mental retardation. *Teaching Exceptional Children, 26* (2), 44–48.

Becker, W. C., & Carnine, D. W. (1980). Direct instruction. In B. B. Lahey & A. E. Kazdin (Eds.), *Advances in clinical child psychology* (vol. 3, pp. 429–473). New York: Plenum.

Becker, W. C., & Carnine, D. W. (1981). Direct instruction: A behavior theory model for comprehensive educational intervention with the disadvantaged. In S. W. Bijou & R. Ruiz (Eds.), *Behavior modification: Contributions to education* (pp. 145–210). Hillsdale, NJ: Lawrence Erlbaum.

Becker, W. C., Engelmann, S., & Thomas, D. R. (1971). *Teaching: A course in applied psychology.* Chicago: Science Research Associates.

Beirne-Smith, M., & Thompson, B. (1992). Spelling instruction. In E. A. Polloway & T. E. C. Smith (Eds.), *Language instruction for students with disabilities* (pp. 347–376). Denver, CO: Love.

Bellack, A. S., & Hersen, M. (1979). *Research and practice in social skills.* New York: Plenum.

Bereiter, C., & Engelmann, S. (1966). *Teaching disadvantaged children in the preschool.* Upper Saddle River, NJ: Prentice Hall.

Bergeron, B. (1990). What does the term whole language mean? Constructing a definition from the literature. *Journal of Reading Behavior, 22,* 301–330.

Bergland, B., & Hiffbauer, D. (1996). New opportunities for students with traumatic brain injuries. *Teaching Exceptional Children, 28,* 54–56.

Berliner, D. C. (1988). The half-full glass: A review of research on teaching. In E. L. Meyen, G. A. Vergason, & R. J. Whelan (Eds.), *Effective instructional strategies for exceptional children* (pp. 7–31). Denver, CO: Love.

Berninger, V., et al. (1998). Teaching spelling to children with learning disabilities: The mind's ear and eye beats the computer or pencil. *Learning Disability Quarterly, 21,* 106–122.

Bernstein, D. K., & Tiegerman, E. (1993). *Language and communication disorders in children* (3rd ed.). Upper Saddle River, NJ: Merrill/Prentice Hall.

Bernstein, D. K., & Tiegerman-Farber, E. (1997). *Language and communication disorders in children* (4th ed.). Boston: Allyn & Bacon.

Bickel, W. E., & Bickel, D. D. (1986). Effective schools, classrooms, and instruction: Implications for special education. *Exceptional Children, 52,* 489–500.

Bigge, J. L., & Stump, C. S. (1999). *Curriculum, assessment, and instruction for students with disabilities.* Belmont, CA: Wadsworth Publishing Company.

Bijou, S. W., & Baer, D. M. (1978). *Behavior analysis of child development.* Upper Saddle River, NJ. Prentice Hall.

Bing, S. B. (1988). Remediate or circumvent. *Academic Therapy, 23,* 509–514.

Birchell, G. R., & Taylor, B. L. (1986). Is the elementary social studies curriculum headed back-to-basics‡? *The Social Studies, 77,* 80–82.

Bishop, K., & Jubala, K. (1994). By June, given shared experiences, integrated classes, and equal opportunities, Jaime will have a friend. *Teaching Exceptional Children, 27,* 36–40.

Blackburn, J. M. (1989). Acquisition and generalization of social skills in elementary-aged children with learning disabilities. *Journal of Learning Disabilities, 22,* 28–34.

Blagden, C. M. (1991, April). *Whole language: The natural way to improve language skills.* Paper presented at the Council for Exceptional Children Conference, Atlanta, GA.

Blalock, G. (1991). Paraprofessionals: Critical team members in our special education programs. *Intervention in School and Clinic, 26*(4), 200–214.

Blalock, G., Bassett, D., & Donisthorpe, L. (1989). *Team strategies for serving special needs students in vocational programs.* Unpublished manuscript, University of New Mexico.

Blalock, G., Mahoney, B., & Dalia, J. (1992). *Albuquerque Public Schools job coach training manual.* Albuquerque, NM: A.P.S. Transition Services Project.

Blalock, G., Rivera, D., Anderson, K., & Kottler, B. (1992). A school district/university partnership in paraprofessional training. *LD Forum, 17*(13), 29–36.

Blalock, V. E. (1984). *Factors influencing the effectiveness of paraprofessionals with disabled populations.* Unpublished doctoral dissertation, University of Texas at Austin.

Blanchard, K., & Johnson, S. (1982). *The one-minute manager: The quickest way to increase your own prosperity.* New York: Morrow.

Blandford, B. J., & Lloyd, J. W. (1987). Effects of a self-instructional procedure on handwriting. *Journal of Learning Disabilities, 20,* 342–346.

Blandy, D. (1993). Community-based lifelong learning in art for adults with mental retardation: A rationale, conceptual foundation, and supportive environment. *Studies in Art Education, 34,* 167–175.

Blatt, B. (1987). *The conquest of mental retardation.* Austin, TX: Pro-Ed.

Bley, N. S., & Thornton, C. A. (1989). *Teaching mathematics to the learning disabled.* Austin, TX: Pro-Ed.

Bley, N. S., & Thornton, C.A. (1995). *Teaching mathematics to students with learning disabilities* (3rd ed.). Austin, TX: Pro-Ed.

Bloom, L., & Lahey, M. (1978). *Language development and language disorders.* Upper Saddle River, NJ: Merrill/Prentice Hall.

Blosser, P. E. (1986). What research says: Improving science education. *School Science and Mathematics, 86,* 597–612.

Blough, G., & Schwartz, J. (1974). *Teaching elementary science.* New York: Holt, Rinehart & Winston.

Boehm, A. E. (1986). *Test of basic concepts: Revised.* New York: Psychological.

Boekel, N., & Steele, J. M. (1972). Science education for the exceptional child. *Focus on Exceptional Children, 4*(4), 1–15.

Bogojavlensky, A. R., Grossman, D. R., Topham, C. S., & Meyer, S. M., III. (1977). *The great learning book.* Menlo Park, CA: Addison-Wesley.

Bolster, L. C., et al. (1978). *Mathematics around us: Skills and applications.* Glenview, IL: Scott, Foresman.

Bond, K., & Deans, J. (1997). Eagles, reptiles, & beyond: A co-creative journey in dance. *Childhood Education, 73,* 366–371.

Bos, C. S. (1982). Getting past decoding: Assisted and repeated readings as remedial methods for learning-disabled students. *Topics in Learning and Learning Disabilities, 1*(4), 51–57.

Bos, C. S., & Vaughn, S. (1998). *Strategies for teaching students with learning and behavior problems* (4th ed.). Boston: Allyn & Bacon.

Boswell, F. F., & Mentzer, M. (1995). Integrating poetry and movement for children with learning and/or behavioral disabilities. *Intervention in School and Clinic, 31,* 108–113.

Bott, D.A. (1988). Mathematics. In J. Wood (Ed.). *Mainstreaming: A practical guide for teachers.* Upper Saddle River, NJ: Merrill/Prentice Hall.

Bracken, B. A. (1984). *Bracken basic concept scale.* Upper Saddle River, NJ: Merrill/Prentice Hall.

Bradden, K. L., Hall, N.J., & Taylor, D. (1993). *Math through children's literature: Making the NCTM standards come alive.* Englewood, CO: Teacher Ideas Press.

Brand, S. (1989). Learning through meaning. *Academic Therapy, 24,* 305–314.

Bray, J., & Wiig, E. H. (1987). *The "Let's Talk" Inventory for Children.* Upper Saddle River, NJ: Merrill/Prentice Hall.

Brick, J., & Wagner, M. (1993). Using karoake in the classroom. *Music Educators Journal, 77*(7), 44–46.

Bricker, D., & Cripe, J. J.W. (1993). *An activity-based approach to early intervention.* Baltimore, MD: Paul H. Brookes.

Bricker, D. D. (1986). *Early intervention for at-risk and handicapped infants, toddlers, and preschool children.* Palo Alto, CA: VORT.

Brigance, A. H. (1980). *Brigance Diagnostic Inventory of Essential Skills.* Billerica, MA: Curriculum Associates.

Brigance, A. H. (1983). *Brigance Diagnostic Inventory of Basic Skills.* Billerica, MA: Curriculum Associates.

Briggs, J. (1988). The role of metacognition in enhancing learning. *Australian Journal of Education, 32,* 127–138.

Brigham, F. J., Scruggs, T. E., & Mastropieri, M.A. (1992). Teacher enthusiasm in learning disabilities classrooms: Effects on learning and behavior. *Learning Disabilities Research & Practice, 7,* 68–73.

Brinton, B., Fujiki, M., & Sonnenberg, E. (1988). Responses to requests for clarification by linguistically normal and language-impaired children in conversation. *Journal of Speech and Hearing Research, 53,* 383–391.

Brizzi, E. (1982). *Developing a partnership: A resource guide for working with paraprofessionals.* Downey, CA: Los Angeles County Superintendent of Schools.

Brolin, D. (1993). *Life-centered career education: A competency-based approach* (4th ed.). Reston, VA: Council for Exceptional Children.

Brolin, D. E. (1982). Life-centered career education for exceptional children. *Focus on Exceptional Children, 14*(7), 1–15.

Brolin, D. E. (1986). *Life-centered career education: A competency-based approach* (rev. ed.). Reston, VA: Council for Exceptional Children.

Brolin, D. E. (1989). *Life-centered career education: A competency-based approach* (rev. ed.). Reston, VA: Council for Exceptional Children.

Brolin, D. E. (1997). *Life centered career education: A competency-based approach* (5th ed.). Reston, VA: The Council for Exceptional Children.

Brolin, D. E., & Kokaska, C. (1984). *Career education for handicapped children and youth.* Upper Saddle River, NJ: Merrill/Prentice Hall.

Brooke, P. (1986). Exploring family folklore. *Instructor, 96,* 114–120.

Brophy, J. (1990). Teaching social studies for understanding and higher-order application. *The Elementary School Journal, 90,* 351–417.

Brophy, J., & Good, T. L. (1986). Teacher behavior and student achievement. In M. C. Wittrock (Ed.), *Handbook of research on teaching* (3rd ed.). Upper Saddle River, NJ: Merrill/Prentice Hall.

Brophy, J. E. (1979). Teacher behavior and its effects. *Journal of Teacher Education, 71,* 733–750.

Broughton, B. (1986). *Creative experiences: An arts curriculum for young children including those with special needs.* Chapel Hill, NC: Training Outreach Project. (ERIC Document Reproduction Service No. ED 331 634)

Brown, A. L., & Palinscar, A. (1982). Inducing strategic learning from texts by means of informed, self-control training. *Topics in Learning and Learning Disabilities, 2*(1), 1–17.

Brown, L. (1995). Evaluating and managing classroom behavior. In D. D. Hammill and N. R. Bartel (Eds.), *Teaching students with learning and behavior problems* (6th ed., pp. 291–345). Austin, TX: Pro-Ed.

Brown, V. L., & McEntire, E. (1984). *Test of mathematical abilities.* Austin, TX: Pro-Ed.

Bruder, M. B., & Chandler, L. (1996). Transition. In S. L. Odom & M. E. McLean (Eds.) *Early intervention/early childhood special education: Recommended practices* (pp. 287–307). Austin, TX: Pro-Ed.

Brueckner, L. J., & Bond, G. L. (1967). Diagnosis and treatment of learning difficulties. In E. C. Frierson & W. B. Barbe (Eds.), *Educating children with learning disabilities.* New York: Appleton-Century-Crofts.

Bruner, J., Goodnow, J. J., & Austin, G. A. (1977). *A study of thinking.* New York: Science Editions.

Bryan, T. (1983, October). *The hidden curriculum: Social and communication skills.* Paper presented at Lynchburg College, Lynchburg, Virginia.

Bryan, T., Donahue, M., & Pearl, R. (1981). Learning-disabled children's peer interactions during a small-group problem-solving task. *Learning Disability Quarterly, 4,* 13–22.

Bryan, T., Donahue, M., Pearl, R., & Strum, C. (1981). Learning-disabled children's conversational skills—The TV talk show. *Learning Disability Quarterly, 4,* 250–259.

Bryan, T., & Pflaum, S. (1978). Social interactions of learning-disabled children: A linguistic, social, and cognitive analysis. *Learning Disability Quarterly, 1,* 70–79.

Bryan, T., Wheeler, R., Felcan, J., & Henek, T. (1976). "Come on, Dummy": An observational study of children's communications. *Journal of Learning Disabilities, 9,* 53–61.

Bryan, T. H., & Bryan, J. H. (1978). Social interactions of learning-disabled children. *Learning Disability Quarterly, 1,* 33–38.

Bryant, D. P., Patton, J. R., & Vaugh, S. (2000). *Step-by-step guide for including students with disabilities in state and district-wide assessments.* Austin: Pro-Ed.

Buchan, V. (1979, September–October). By using the why and because method. *Today's Education,* 32–34.

Buck, G., & Gregoire, M. (1996). Teaching recreation and leisure skills to students with disabilities through music. *Teaching Exceptional Children 29,* 44–47.

Buck, G. H. (1993). Teachers' use of background music in general and special education classrooms. *Dissertation Abstracts International, 55,* 07A.

Buck, G. H., & Gregoire, M. A. (1996). Teaching music-related leisure skills to secondary students with disabilities. *Teaching Exceptional Children.*

Buck, G. H., Polloway, E. A., & Mortorff-Robb, S. (1995). Alternative certification programs: Implications for special education. *Teacher Education and Special Education, 18,* 39–48.

Buckman, D. C., King, B. B., & Ryan, S. (1995). Block scheduling: A means to improve school climate. *NASSP Bulletin, 79*(571), 9–18.

Bulgren, J. A., Schumaker, J. B., Deshler, D. D. (1988). Effectiveness of a concept teaching routine in enhancing the performance of LD students in secondary-level mainstream classes. *Learning Disability Quarterly, 11* (1), 3–17.

Bulgren, J. A., Schumaker, J. B., & Deshler, D. D. (1993). *The concept mastery routine.* Lawrence, KS: Edge Enterprises.

Bulgren, J. A., Schumaker, J. B., Deshler, D. D. (1994). *The concept anchoring routine.* Lawrence, KS: Edge Enterprises.

Bunce, B. H. (1997). Children with culturally diverse backgrounds. In L. McCormick, D. F. Loeb, & R. L. Schiefelbusch (Eds.), *Supporting children with communication disorders in Inclusive settings: School-based language intervention* (pp. 467–506). Boston: Allyn & Bacon.

Burns, J. (1988). *Spelling mnemonics.* Unpublished manuscript, Lynchburg College, Lynchburg, Va.

Bursuck, W. Munk, D. D. & Olsen, (1999). The fairness of report card grading adaptations: What do students with and without learning disabilities think? *Remedial and Special Education, 20.*

Bursuck, W., Polloway, E., Plante, L. M., Epstein, M. H., Jayanthi, M., & McConeghy, J. (1996). Report card grading and adaptations: A national survey of classroom practices. *Exceptional Children, 62,* 301-308.

Butera, G., Klein, H., McMullen, L., & Wilson, B. (1998). A state-wide study of FAPE in school discipline policies. *The Journal of Special Education, 32,* 108-114.

Butzow, C. M., & Butzow, J. W. (1989). *Science through children's literature: An integrated approach.* Englewood, CO: Libraries Unlimited.

CEC Today (1995). Research shows phonological awareness key to reading success. *CEC Today, 2* (4), 1,9,15.

Cain, S. E., & Evans, J. M. (1984). *Sciencing: An involvement approach to elementary science methods* (2nd ed.). Upper Saddle River, NJ: Merrill/Prentice Hall.

Cain, S. E., & Evans, J. M. (1990). *Sciencing: An involvement approach to elementary science methods* (3rd ed.). Upper Saddle River, NJ: Prentice Hall.

Callahan, K., Rademacher, J. A., & Hildreth, B. L. (1998). The effect of parent participation in strategies to improve the homework performance of students who are at risk. *Remedial and Special Education, 19*(3), 131-141.

Calvert, M. B., & Murray, S. L. (1985). Environmental communication profile: An assessment procedure. In C. S. Simon (Ed.), *Communication skills and classroom success: Assessment of language learning-disabled students* (pp. 135-165). Austin, TX: Pro-Ed.

Campbell, P., & Olsen, G. R. (1994). Improving instruction in secondary schools. *Teaching Exceptional Children, 26*(3), 51-54.

Canfield, J., & Wells, H. C. (1994). *100 ways to enhance self-concept in the classroom* (2nd ed.). Boston: Allyn & Bacon.

Canody, R. L., & Rettig, M. D. (1995). *Block scheduling: A catalyst for change in high schools,* Princeton, NJ: Eye on Education.

Carbo, M. L. (1978). A word-imprinting technique for children with severe memory disorders. *Teaching Exceptional Children, 11,* 3-5.

Carden-Smith, L., & Fowler, S. A. (1983). An assessment of student and teacher behavior in treatment and mainstreamed classes for preschool and kindergarten. *Analysis and Intervention in Developmental Disabilities, 3,* 35-57.

Carlisle, J. F., & Felbinger, L. (1991). Profiles of listening and reading comprehension. *Journal of Educational Research, 84,* 345-354.

Carnine, D. (1983). Direct instruction: In search of instructional solutions for educational problems. In *Interdisciplinary voices in learning disabilities and remedial education* (pp. 1-60). Austin, TX: Pro-Ed.

Carnine, D. (1992). Introduction. In D. Carnine & E. J. Kameenui (Eds.), *Higher-order thinking: Designing curriculum for mainstreamed students* (pp. 1-22). Austin, TX: Pro-Ed.

Carnine, D., Silbert, J., & Kameenui, E. (1990). *Direct instruction reading.* (2nd ed.). Upper Saddle River, NJ: Prentice Hall.

Carrow-Woolfolk, E. (1974). *Carrow Elicited Language Inventory.* Allen, TX: DLM Teaching Resources.

Carrow-Woolfolk, E. (1985). *Test for auditory comprehension of language-revised.* Allen, TX: DLM Teaching Resources.

Carter, S. (1993). The forgotten entity in art education. *Art Education, 46*(5), 52-57.

Cartledge, G., & Milburn, J. F. (1986). *Teaching skills to children: Innovative approaches* (2nd edition). New York: Pergamon Press.

Cartledge, G., & Milburn, J. F. (1995). *Teaching skills to children: Innovative approaches* (3rd edition). New York: Pergamon Press.

Caskey, H. J. (1970). Guidelines for teaching comprehension. *The Reading Teacher, 23,* 649-654.

Cates, D. L., McGill, H., Brian, L., Wilder, A., & Androes, T. (1990, April 23-27). *Severely and profoundly handicapped students in the regular classroom: It is happening now.* Paper presented at the 68th Annual Convention of the Council for Exceptional Children, Toronto, Canada.

Catts, H. W. (1997). The early identification of language-based reading disabilities. *Language, Speech, and Hearing Services in Schools, 28,* 86-89.

Cawley, J. F. (Ed.). (1984). *Developmental teaching of mathematics for the learning disabled.* Austin, TX: Pro-Ed.

Cawley, J. F. (1994). Science for students with disabilities. *Remedial and Special Education, 15,* 67-71.

Cawley, J. F., Baker-Kroczynski, S., & Urban, A. (1992). Seeking excellence in mathematics education for students with mild disabilities. *Teaching Exceptional Children, 24,* 40-43.

Cawley, J. F., Fitzmaurice, A. M., Shaw, R. A., Kahn, H., & Bates, H. (1979a). Mathematics and learning disabled youth: The upper grade levels. *Learning Disability Quarterly, 1,* 37-52.

Cawley, J. F., Fitzmaurice, A. M., Shaw, R. A., Kahn, H., & Bates, H. (1979b). Math word problems: Suggestions for LD students. *Learning Disability Quarterly, 2,* 25-41.

Cawley, J. F., Fitzmaurice-Hayes, A. M., & Shaw, R. A. (1988). *Mathematics for the mildly handicapped: A guide to curriculum and instruction.* Boston: Allyn & Bacon.

Cawley, J. F., Goodstein, H. A., Fitzmaurice, A. M., Lepore A., Sedlak R., & Althaus, V. (1976). *Project MATH.* Tulsa, OK: Educational Development.

Cawley, J. F., Miller, D., & Carr, S. (1989). Arithmetic. In G. A. Robinson, J. R. Patton, E. A. Polloway, & L. R. Sargent (Eds.), *Best practices in mental retardation* (pp. 67-86). Reston, VA: Division on Mental Retardation, Council for Exceptional Children.

Cawley, J. F., Miller, J., Sentman, J. R., & Bennett, S. (1993). *Science for all (SAC).* Buffalo: State University of New York at Buffalo.

Cazden, C. B. (1988). *Classroom discourse: The language of teaching and learning.* Portsmouth, NH: Heinemann.

Center for Rehabilitation Studies, University of North Texas. (1990). *Employment specialist training workshop manual.* Denton, TX: Author.

Center for Teaching and Learning (1986). Thirty years of NICHD research: What we now know about how children learn to read. *Effective School Practices, 15*(3), 33-46.

Chalfant, J. C., & Pysh, M. V. (1989). Teacher assistance teams: Five descriptive studies on 96 teams. *Remedial and Special Education, 10*(6), 49-58.

Chandler, L. K. (1992). Promoting young children's social competence as a strategy for transition to mainstreamed kindergarten program. In S. L. Odom, S. R. McConnell, & M. A. McEvoy (Eds.), *Social competence of young children with disabilities* (pp. 245-276). Baltimore, MD: Paul Brookes.

Chandler, L. K. (1993). Steps in preparing for transition: Preschool to kindergarten. *Teaching Exceptional Children, 25,* 52-55.

Chaney, A. L., & Burk, T. L. (1998). *Teaching oral communication in grades K-8.* Boston: Allyn & Bacon.

Check, J. F., & Ziebell, D. G. (1980). Homework: A dirty word. *The Clearing House, 54,* 439-441.

Chiang, B., & Ford, M. (1990). Whole language alternatives for students with learning disabilities. *Learning Disabilities Forum, 16,* 31-33.

Christenson, S. L., Ysseldyke, J. E., & Thurlow, M. L. (1989). Critical instructional factors for students with mild handicaps: An integrative review. *Remedial and Special Education, 10*(5), 21-31.

Clark, D. J. (1985). *The IMPACT project: Project report.* Clayton, Victoria, Australia: Monash Centre for Mathematics Education.

Clark, D. J. (1987). The interactive monitoring of children's learning of mathematics. *For the Learning of Mathematics, 7*(1), 2-6.

Clark, D., Stephens, M., & Waywood, A. (1992). Communication and the learning of mathematics. In T. A. Romberg (Ed.), *Mathematics assessment and evaluation: Imperatives for mathematics education* (pp. 184-212). Albany, NY: State University of New York Press.

Clark, G. M. (1979). *Career education for the handicapped child in the elementary classroom.* Denver, CO: Love.

Clark, G. M., & Patton, J. R. (1997). *Transition Planning Inventory.* Austin, TX: Pro-Ed.

Clark, G. M. (1996). Transition planning assessment for secondary-level students with learning disabilities. *Journal of Learning Disabilities, 29,* 79-92.

Clark, G. M., Carlson, B. C., Fisher, S., Cook, I. D., & D'Alonzo, B. J. (1991). *Career development for students with disabilities in elementary schools: A position statement of the Division on Career Development.* Reston, VA: Division on Career Development, Council for Exceptional Children.

Clark, G. M., Field, S., Patton, J. R., Brolin, D., & Sitlington, P. (1994). Life skills instruction: A necessary component for all students with disabilities. *CDEI, 17,* 125-134.

Clark, G. M., & Kolstoe, O. P. (1990). *Career development and transition of education for adolescents with disabilities.* Boston: Allyn & Bacon.

Clark, G. M., & Patton, J. R. (1997). *Transition Planning Inventory.* Austin, TX: Pro-Ed.

Cochran, P. S., & Bull, G. L. (1993). Computers and individuals with speech and language disorders. In J. D. Lindsey (Ed.), *Computers and Exceptional Individuals* (2nd ed., pp. 143-158). Austin, TX: Pro-Ed.

Cochran-Smith, M. (1995). Color blindness and basket making are not the answers: Confronting the dilemmas of race, culture, and language diversity in teacher education. *American Educational Research Journal, 32*(3), 493-522.

Cohen, H., & Staley, F. (1982). Integrating with science: One way to bring science back into the elementary day. *School Science and Mathematics, 82,* 565-572.

Cohen, M. D., & Hoot, J. L. (1997). Educating through the arts: An introduction. *Childhood Education, 73,* 338-340.

Cohen, R. (1983). Self-generated questions as an aid to reading comprehension. *The Reading Teacher, 36,* 770-775.

Cohen, S., & deBettencourt, L. (1983). Teaching children to be independent learners: A step-by-step strategy. *Focus on Exceptional Children, 16*(3), 1-12.

Cohen, S. B., Perkins, V. L., & Newmark, S. (1985). Written feedback strategies used by special education teachers. *Teacher Education and Special Education, 8,* 183-187.

Cohen, S. B., & Plaskon, S. P. (1980). *Language arts for the mildly handicapped.* Upper Saddle River, NJ: Merrill/Prentice Hall.

Cohen, S. B., Safran, J., & Polloway, E. A. (1980). Minimum competency testing and its implications for retarded students. *Education and Training for the Mentally Retarded, 15,* 250-255.

Cole, M., & Cole, J. (1980). *Effective intervention with the language impaired.* Rockville, MD: Aspen Systems.

Coleman, J. (1978). Using name anagrams. *Teaching Exceptional Children, 11,* 41-42.

Combs, W. E. (1975). Sentence combining practice aids reading comprehension. *Journal of Reading, 21,* 18-24.

Conn-Powers, M. C., Ross-Allen, J., & Holburn, S. (1990). Transition of young children into the elementary education mainstream. *Topics in Early Childhood Special Education, 9*(4), 92-105.

Connolly, A. J. (1988). *Keymath revised: A diagnostic inventory of essential mathematics.* Circle Pines, MN: American Guidance Service.

Cook, L., & Friend, M. (1995). Co-teaching: Guidelines for creating effective practices. *Focus on Exceptional Children, 28*(3), 1-16.

Cooke, N. L., Heron, T. E., & Heward, W. L. (1983). *Peer tutoring: Implementing classwide programs in the primary grades.* Columbus, OH: Special Press.

Cooper, H., & Nye, B. (1995). Homework for students with learning disabilities: The implications of research for policy and practice. In W. D. Bursuck (Ed.), *Homework: Issues and practices for students with learning disabilities* (pp. 7-25). Austin, TX: Pro-Ed.

Corno, L. (1989). Self-regulated learning: A volitional analysis. In B. J. Zimmerman & D. H. Schunk (Eds.), *Self-regulated learning and academic achieve-ment: Theory, research, and practice.* New York: Springer Verlag (pp. 111-141).

Cotton, P. (1991). A flowing start to handwriting. *Times Educational Supplement, 3906,* 9.

Council of Chief State School Officers. (1986). *Disabled students beyond school: A review of the issues.* A position paper and recommendations for action. Washington, DC: Author.

Cozzens, G., Dowdy, C., & Smith, T. E. C. (1999). *Adult agencies: Linkages for adolescents in transition.* Austin: Pro-Ed.

Crago, M. & Cole, E. (1991). Using ethnography to bring children's communicative and cultural worlds into focus. In T. M. Gallagher, (Ed.), *Pragmatics of language: Clinical practice issues* (pp. 99-132). San Diego, CA: Singular Publishing.

Craig, H., & Evans, J. (1989). Turn exchange characteristics of SLIO children's simultaneous and non-simultaneous speech. *Journal of Speech and Hearing Disorders, 54,* 334-347.

Crescimbeni, J. (1965). *Arithmetic enrichment activities for elementary school children.* West Nyack, NY: Parker.

Crisculo, N. P. (1985). Creative approaches to teaching reading through art. *Art Education, 38*(6), 13-16.

Critchlow, D. (1996). *Dos amigos verbal language scale.* Novato, CA: Academic Therapy Publications.

Cronin, M. E. (1988). Adult performance outcomes/life skills. In G. Robinson, J. R. Patton, E. A. Polloway, & L. R. Sargent (Eds.), *Best practices in mental disabilities* (vol. 2). Des Moines: Iowa Department of Education, Bureau of Special Education.

Cronin, M. E., & Gerber, P. J. (1982). Preparing the learning-disabled adolescent for adulthood. *Topics in Learning and Learning Disabilities, 2*(3), 55-68.

Cronin, M. E., & Patton, J. R. (1993). *Life skills for students with special needs: A practical guide for developing real-life programs.* Austin, TX: Pro-Ed.

Cronin, M. E., Patton, J. R., & Polloway, E. A. (1991). *Preparing for adult outcomes: A model for developing a life skills curriculum.* Unpublished manuscript, University of New Orleans, Louisiana.

Cullinan, D., & Epstein, M. H. (1985). Teacher-related adjustment problems of mildly handicapped and nonhandicapped students. *Remedial and Special Education, 6,* 5-11.

Curtis, C. K., & Shaver, J. P. (1980). Slow learners and the study of contemporary problems. *Social Education, 44,* 302-309.

Cutting, B., & Mulligan, J. L. (1990). Learning to read in New Zealand. *Teaching K-8, 21,* 62-65.

Czarnecki, E., Rosko, D., & Pine, E. (1998). How to call up notetaking skills. *Teaching Exceptional Children, 30,* 14-19.

Dale, F. J. (1993). Computers and gifted/talented individuals. In J. D. Lindsey (Ed.), *Computers and Exceptional Individuals* (2nd ed., pp. 201-223). Austin, TX: Pro-Ed.

Damico, J. S. (1991). Descriptive assessment of communicative ability in limited English proficient students. In E. V. Hamayan & J. S. Kamico (Eds.), *Limiting bias in the assessment of bilingual students.* Austin, TX: Pro-Ed.

Damico, J. S. & Oller, J. W. (1985). *Spotting language problems: Pragmatic criteria for language screening.* San Diego, CA: Los Amigos Research Associates.

Damico, J. S., Smith, M., & Augustine, L. E. (1995). Multicultural populations and language disorders (pp. 272-299). In M. D. Smith & J. S. Damico (Eds.), *Childhood Language Disorders.* New York: Thieme Medical Publishers.

Daniels, J. L., & Wiederholt, J. L. (1986). Preparing problem learners for independent living. In D. D. Hammill & N. R. Bartel (Eds.), *Teaching students with learning and behavior problems* (4th ed., pp. 294-345). Austin, TX: Pro-Ed.

Davies, J. M., & Ball, D. W. (1978). Utilization of the elementary science study with mentally retarded students. *Journal of Research in Science Teaching, 15,* 281-286.

Day, V. P., & Elkins, L. K. (1994). Promoting strategic learning. *Intervention in School and Clinic, 30,* 262-270.

Decker, T. W., & Polloway, E. A. (1989). Written language. In G. R. Robinson, J. R. Patton, E. A. Polloway, & L. Sargent (Eds.), *Best practices in mild mental retardation* (pp. 109-131). Reston, VA: Council for Exceptional Children, Division on Mental Retardation.

De la Cruz, R. E., Lian, M. J., & Morreau, L. E. (1998). The effects of creative drama on social and oral language skills of children with learning disabilities. *Youth Theater Journal, 12,* 89-95.

de Lin, G., duBois, B., & McIntosh, M. E. (1986). Reading aloud to students in secondary history classes. *The Social Studies, 77,* 256-259.

de La Paz, S. (1997). Strategy instruction in planning: Teaching students with learning and writing disabilities to compose persuasive and expository essays. *Learning Disability Quarterly, 20,* 227-248.

Demchak, M. A., & Koury, M. (1990). Differential reinforcement of leisure activities: An observation form for supervisors. *Teaching Exceptional Children, 22*(2), 14-17.

Deshler, D. D., Ellis, E. S., & Lenz, B. K. (1996). *Teaching adolescents with learning disabilities: Strategies and methods.* Love Publishing.

Deshler, D. D., & Schumaker, J. B. (1986). Learning strategies: An instructional alternative for low-achieving adolescents. *Exceptional Children, 52,* 583-590.

Deshler, D. D., & Schumaker, J. B. (1988). An instructional model for teaching students how to learn. In J. L. Graden, J. E. Zins, & M. J. Curtis (Eds.) *Alternative educational delivery systems: Enhancing instructional options for all students.* Washington, DC: National Association of School Psychologists.

Deshler, D. D., Schumaker, J. B., Lenz, B. K., & Ellis, E. (1984). Academic and cognitive interventions for LD adolescents: Part II. *Journal of Learning Disabilities, 17,* 170-179.

DiGangi, S. A., Maag, J. W., & Rutherford, R. B., Jr. (1991). Self-graphing of on-task behavior: Enhancing the reactive effects of self-monitoring on on-task behavior and academic performance. *Learning Disability Quarterly, 14,* 221-230.

Dodge, K. A., & Murphy, R. (1984). The assessment of social competence in adolescents. In P. Karoly & J. J. Steffen (Eds.), *Adolescent behavior disorders: Foundations and contemporary concerns.* Lexington, MA: Lexington Books.

Donahue, M. (1994). Differences in classroom discourse of students with learning disabilities. In D. Ripich & N. Creaghead (Eds.), *School discourse problems.* (2nd ed.). San Diego, CA: Singular Publishing.

Donahue, M., Pearl, R., & Bryan, T. (1982). Learning-disabled children's syntactic proficiency on a communicative task. *Journal of Speech and Hearing Disorders, 47,* 22-28.

Donahue, M., & Zigmond, N. (1990). Academic grades of ninth-grade urban learning disabled students and low-achieving peers. *Exceptionality, 1,* 17-27.

Donahue, M. L. (1984). Learning disabled children's conversational competence: An attempt to activate the inactive listener. *Applied Psycholinguistics, 5,* 21-35.

Donaldson, R., & Christiansen, J. (1990). Consultation and collaboration: A decision-making model. *Teaching Exceptional Children, 23,* 22-25.

Dougherty, E. H., & Dougherty, A. (1977). The daily report card: A simplified and flexible package for classroom behavior management. *Psychology in the Schools, 14,* 191-195.

Dowdy, C., Patton, J. R., Smith, T. E. C., & Polloway, E. A. (1998). *Attention deficit disorders.* Austin, TX: Pro-Ed.

Dowdy, C. A., Patton, J. R., Smith, T. E. C., & Polloway, E. A. (1998). *Attention-deficit/hyperactivity disorder in the classroom.* Austin, TX: Pro-Ed.

Downey, M. T. (1980). Pictures as teaching aids: Using the pictures in history textbooks. *Social Education, 44,* 93–99.

Doyle, W. (1986). Classroom organization and management. In M. C. Wittrock (Ed.). *Handbook of research on teaching* (3rd ed., pp. 392–431). New York: Macmillan.

Dreikurs, R., Grunwald, B. B., & Pepper, F. C. (1982). *Maintaining sanity in the classroom: Classroom management techniques* (2nd ed.). Philadelphia: Harper & Row.

Duchan, J. G. (1982). The elephant is soft and mushy: Problems in assessing children's language. In N. Lass, L. McReynolds, J. Northern, & D. Yoder (Eds.), *Speech, language and hearing: Pathologies of speech and language.* Philadelphia: Saunders.

Dudley-Marling, C. (1985). The pragmatic skills of learning-disabled children: A review. *Journal of Learning Disabilities, 18,* 193–262.

Duerksen, G. L. (1981). Music for exceptional students. *Focus on Exceptional Children, 14*(4), 1–11.

Dumas, E. (1971). *Math activities for child involvement.* Boston: Allyn & Bacon.

Duncan, J. R., Schofer, R. C., & Veberle, J. (1982). *Comprehensive system of personnel development: Inservice considerations.* Columbia: University of Missouri, Department of Special Education.

Dunlap, L. K., Dunlap, G., Koegel, L. K., & Koegel, R. L. (1991). Using self-monitoring to increase independence. *Teaching Exceptional Children, 23*(3), 17–22.

Dunn, C. (1996). A status report on transition planning for individuals with learning disabilities. *Journal of Learning Disabilities, 29,* 17–30.

Dunn, L. M., & Dunn, L. M. (1981). *Peabody Picture Vocabulary Test—Revised.* Circle Pines, MN: American Guidance Service.

Durkin, D. (1978–1979). What classroom observations reveal about reading comprehension instruction. *Reading Research Quarterly, 14,* 481–533.

Dyer, S. K. (1992). A multisensory approach to handwriting instruction. *Education Digest, 57,* 70.

D'Zurilla, T. J., & Goldfried, M. R. (1971). Problem solving and behavior modification. *Journal of Abnormal Psychology, 78,* 107–126.

D'Zurilla, T. J., & Nezu, A. (1980). A study of the generalization of alternatives: Process in social problem solving skills. *Cognitive Therapy & Research, 4,* 67–72.

Edgar, E. (1987). Secondary programs in special education: Are many of them justifiable? *Exceptional Children, 53,* 555–561.

Edgar, E. (1988). Employment as an outcome for mildly handicapped students: Current status and future directions. *Focus on Exceptional Children, 21*(1), 1–8.

Edgar, E., & Polloway, E. A. (1994). Education for adolescents with disabilities: Curriculum and placement issues. *Journal of Special Education, 27,* 438–452.

Edgington, R. (1968). "But he spelled them right this morning." In J. I. Arena (Ed.), *Building spelling skills in dyslexic children* (pp. 23–24). Belmont, CA: Academic Therapy.

Edmark Associates. (1974, 1982, 1984, 1986). *Edmark reading program.* Bellevue, WA: Author.

Education Update (June, 1999). Speaking and listening: The first basic skills. Alexandria, VA: Association for Supervision and Curriculum. Author.

Ehman, L. H., & Glenn, A. D. (1991). Interactive technology in social studies. In J. P. Shaver (Ed.), *Handbook of research on social studies teaching and learning* (pp. 513–522). Upper Saddle River, NJ: Merrill/Prentice Hall.

Ehren, B. J. (1994). New directions for meeting the academic needs of adolescents with language learning disabilities. In G. P. Wallach & K. G. Butler (Eds.), *Language learning disabilities in school-age children and adolescents* (pp. 393–417). Upper Saddle River, NJ: Merrill/Prentice Hall.

Eisler, R. M., Miller, P. M., & Hersen, M. (1973). Components of assertive behavior. *Journal of Clinical Psychology, 29,* 295–299.

Eisner, E. W. (1985). *The educational imagination.* New York: Macmillan.

Ekwall, E. E., & Shanker, J. L. (1985). *Teaching reading in the elementary school* (2nd ed.). Upper Saddle River, NJ: Merrill/Prentice Hall.

Ekwall, E. E., & Shanker, J. L. (1988). *Diagnosis and remediation of the disabled reader.* Boston: Allyn & Bacon.

Ekwall, E. E., & Shanker, J. L. (1993). *Locating and correcting reading difficulties* (6th ed.). Upper Saddle River, NJ: Merrill/Prentice Hall.

Elias, M. (1995, September 19). Can do ways give hope to young pessimists. *USA Today,* p. 6D.

Elium, M. D., & McCarver, R. B. (1980). *Group vs. individual training on a self-help skill with the profoundly retarded.* (ERIC Document Reproduction Service No. ED 223 060).

Elliott, D., & McKenney, M. (1998). Four inclusion models that work. *Teaching Exceptional Children, 30*(4), 54-58.

Ellis, E. (1992). *LINCS: A starter strategy for vocabulary learning.* Lawrence, KS: Edge Enterprises.

Ellis, E.S. (1996) Reading strategy instruction. In D.D. Deshler, E.S. Ellis, & B.K. Lenz (Eds.), *Teaching adolescents with learning disabilities: Strategies and methods* (2nd ed., pp. 63-121). Denver: Love Publishing Co.

Ellis, E. S., Deshler, D. D., Lenz, B. K., Schumaker, J. B., & Clark, F. L. (1991). An instructional model for teaching learning strategies. *Focus on Exceptional Children, 23*(6), 1-24.

Ellis, E. S., & Sabornie, E. J. (1986). *Teaching learning strategies to learning-disabled students in postsecondary settings.* Unpublished manuscript, University of South Carolina, Columbia.

Emmer, E. T., Evertson, C.M., Sanford, J.P., Clements, B.S., & Worsham, M.E. (1984). *Classroom management for secondary teachers.* Upper Saddle River, NJ: Prentice Hall.

Engelmann, S., Becker, W.C., Hanner, S., & Johnson, G. (1980, 1989). *Corrective reading program.* Chicago: Science Research Associates.

Engelmann, S., & Bruner, E. (1974, 1975, 1988). *DISTAR reading.* Chicago: Science Research Associates.

Engelmann, S., & Carnine, D. (1981). *Corrective mathematics.* Chicago: Science Research Associates.

Englehard, J. B. (1991). Yes, Virginia, whole language includes reading, decoding and spelling. *VCLD Newsletter, 3*(1), 3-5.

Englert, C. S. (1983). Measuring special education teacher effectiveness. *Exceptional Children, 50,* 247-254.

Englert, C. S. (1984). Effective direct instruction practices in special education setting. *Remedial and Special Education, 5,* 38-47.

Englert, C. S., & Mariage, T. V. (1991). Shared understandings: Structuring the writing experience through dialogue. *Journal of Learning Disabilities, 24,* 330-342.

Englert, C. S. & Tarrant, K. L., & Mariage, T. V. (1992). Defining and redefining instructional practice in special education: Perspectives on good teaching. *Teacher Education and Special Education, 15,* 62-86.

Ensign, A. (1994). *Art is for everyone.* Lansing, MI: PAM Assistance Centre. (ERIC Document Reproduction Service No. ED 346 082).

Ensign, A. S. (1992). *Low-tech solutions: A place to begin.* Lansing, MI: PAM Assistance Centre. (ERIC Document Reproduction Service No. ED 342 183).

Epstein, M. H., & Cullinan, D. (1983). Academic performance of behaviorally disordered and learning-disabled pupils. *Journal of Special Education, 17,* 303-308.

Epstein, M. H., & Cullinan, D. (1987). Effective social skills curricula for behaviorally disordered students. *The Pointer, 31*(2), 21-24.

Epstein, M. H, Patton, J. R., Polloway, E. A., & Foley, R. (1992). Educational services for students with behavior disorders: A review of individualized education programs. *Teacher Education and Special Education, 15,* 41-48.

Epstein, M. H., Polloway, E. A., Foley, R. M., & Patton, J. R. (1993). Homework: A comparison of teachers, and parents, perceptions of the problems experienced by students identified as having behavioral disorders, learning disabilities, and no disabilities. *Remedial and Special Education, 14*(5), 40-50.

Epstein, M. H., Polloway, E. A., & Patton, J. R., & Foley, R. (1989). Mild retardation: Student characteristics and services. *Education and Training in Mental Retardation, 24,* 7-16.

ERIC/OSEP (1997). School-wide behavioral management systems: A promising practice for safer schools. *Research Connections in Special Education, 1*(1), 1-5.

Esler, W. K., Midgett, J., & Bird, R. C. (1977). Elementary science materials and the exceptional child. *Science Education, 61,* 181-184.

Eurich, G. (1996). Modeling respect in the classroom. *Intervention in School and Clinic, 31,* 119-120.

Evans, E. D., & Richardson, R. C. (1995). Corporal punishment: What teachers should know. *Teaching Exceptional Children, 27*(2), 33-36.

Evans, R. W. (1989). The future of issue-centered education. *The Social Studies, 80,* 176-177.

Evans, S. S., Evans, W. H., & Mercer, C. D. (1986). *Assessment for instruction.* Boston: Allyn & Bacon.

Evertson, C. M., Emmer, E. T., Clements, B. S., Sanford, J. P. & Worsham, M. E. (1984). *Classroom management for elementary teachers.* Upper Saddle River, NJ: Prentice Hall.

Eylon, B. S., & Linn, M. C. (1988). Learning and instruction: An examination of four research perspectives in science education. *Review of Educational Research, 58,* 251–301.

Fad, K., & Riddle, M. (1995). *Inclusion notes for busy teachers.* Longmont, CO: Sopris West.

Fad, K. M., & Gilliam, J. E. (1996). *Putting it all together for student success.* Longmont, CO: Sopris West.

Fad, K., Patton, J. R., & Polloway, E. A. (1998). *Behavioral intervention planning.* Austin, TX: Pro-Ed.

Fad, K., Patton, J. R., & Polloway, E. A. (2000). *Behavioral intervention planning* (2nd ed.). Austin, TX: Pro-Ed.

Fad, K. S., & Ryser, G. R. (1993). Social/behavioral variables related to success in general education. *Remedial and Special Education, 14*(1), 25–35.

Farris, P. J. (1991). Views and other views: Handwriting instruction should not become extinct. *Language Arts, 68,* 312–314.

Felton, R. G., & Allen, R. F. (1990). Using visual materials as historical sources. *The Social Studies, 81,* 84–87.

Ferguson, D. L. (1994). Magic for teacher work groups: Tricks for colleague communication. *Teaching Exceptional Children, 27,* 42–47.

Fernald, G. M. (1943). *Remedial techniques in basic school subjects.* New York: McGraw-Hill.

Ferster, C. B., Culbertson, S., & Boren, M. C. P. (1975). *Behavior principles* (2nd ed.). Upper Saddle River, NJ: Prentice Hall.

Fey, M. (1986). *Language intervention with young children.* San Diego, CA: College-Hill Press.

Fey, M., Warr-Leeper, G., Webber, S., & Disher, L. (1988). Repairing children's repairs: Evaluation and facilitation of children's clarification requests and responses. *Topics in Language Disorders, 8,* 63–64.

Fiedler, J. F., & Knight, R. R. (1986). Congruence between assessed needs and IEP goals of identified behaviorally disabled students. *Behavioral Disorders, 12,* 22–27.

Fiechtl, B., Rule, S., & Innocenti, M. S. (1989). It's time to get ready for school. *Teaching Exceptional Children, 21*(2), 63–65.

Field, S., & Hoffman, A. (1992). *Steps to self determination (field-test version).* Detroit: Wayne State University, College of Education, Developmental Disabilities Institute.

Field, S., & Hoffman, A. (1994). Development of a model for self-determination. *Career Development for Exceptional Individuals, 17,* 159–169.

Fink, W. T., & Sandall, S. R. (1980). A comparison of one-to-one and small group instructional strategies with developmentally disabled preschoolers. *Mental Retardation, 18,* 73–84.

Finson, K. D., & Ormsbee, C. K. (1998). Rubrics and their use in inclusive science. *Intervention in School and Clinic, 34*(2), 79–88.

Fitzgerald, E. (1966). *Straight language for the deaf.* Washington, DC: Volta Bureau.

Fitzgerald, J. (1951). *The teaching of spelling.* Milwaukee: Bruce.

Fitzgerald, M., Kay, P., Tefft, K., & Colburn, T. (1994). *Authentic assessment for all students: An analysis of IEPs and portfolios.* Unpublished manuscript, University of Vermont.

Fleck, R. M. (1995). Easing into elementary school. *Principal, 74,* 25–27.

Fletcher, J. M., Foorman, B. R., Francis, D. J., & Schatschneider, C. (June, 1998). Prevention of reading failure. *The Virginia Branch (of the Orton Society) Newsletter,* 3–5.

Fletcher, T. V., Bos, C. S., & Johnson, L. M. (1999). Accommodating English language learners with language and learning disabilities in bilingual education classes. *Learning Disabilities Research & Practice, 14,* 80–91.

Fogarty, R. (1995). *Designs for cooperative interactions.* Palatine, IL: Skylight.

Ford, M. E. (1985). The concept of competence: Themes and variations. In H. A. Marlow & R. B. Weinberg (Eds.), *Competence development: Theory and practice in special populations* (pp. 3–38). Springfield, IL: Charles C. Thomas.

Forest, M., & Lusthaus, E. (1989). Promoting educational equality for all students: Circles and maps. In S. Stainback, W. Stainback, & M. Forest (Eds.), *Educating all students in the mainstream of regular education* (pp. 43–58). Baltimore: Paul H. Brookes.

Forness, S. R. (1985). Effects of public policy at the state level: California's impact on MR, LD, and ED. *Remedial and Special Education, 6*(3), 36–43.

Forness, S. R., Kavale, K. A., MacMillan, D. L., Asarnow, J. R., & Duncan, B. B. (1996). Early detection and prevention of emotional or behavioral disorders: Developmental aspects of systems of care. *Behavioral Disorders, 21,* 226–240.

Forness, S. R., & Knitzer, J. (1990). *A new proposed definition and terminology to replace "serious emotional disturbance" in Education of the Handicapped Act.* Unpublished paper, National Mental Health and Special Education Coalition.

Forness, S. R., Serna, L. A., Kavale, K. A., Nielsen, E. (in press). Mental health and Head Start: Teaching adaptive skills. *Education and Treatment of Children.*

Foster, S. L., & Richey, W. L. (1979). Issues in the assessment of social competence in children. *Journal of Applied Behavior Analysis, 12,* 625-638.

Fowler, G. L. (1982). Developing comprehension skills in primary students through the use of story frames. *The Reading Teacher, 36*(2), 176-180.

Fowler, G. L., & Davis, M. (1986). The story frame approach: A tool for improving reading comprehension for EMR children. *Teaching Exceptional Children, 17,* 296-298.

Franca, V. M., Kerr, M. M., Reitz, A. L., & Lambert, D. (1990). Peer tutoring among behaviorally disordered students: Academic and social benefits to tutor and tutee. *Education and Treatment of Children, 13,* 109-128.

Freeman, S. (1992). *Literature notes for "Alexander and the terrible, horrible, no good, very bad day".* Torrence, CA: Frank Schaffer.

Freides, D., & Messina, C. A. (1986). Memory improvement via motor encoding in learning disabled children. *Journal of Learning Disabilities, 19,* 113-115.

Friebel, A. C., & Gingrich, C. K. (1972). *Math applications kit.* Chicago: Science Research Associates.

Friedman, M. (1994). Systems, philosophy, curriculum integration, and units of joy: Cultivating a new paradigm for an information intensive world. *Middle School Journal, 25,* 11-14.

Fritz, M. T. (1990). A comparison of social interactions using friendship awareness activity. *Education and Training in Mental Retardation, 25,* 352-359.

Fuchs, D., Fernstrom, P., Scott, S., Fuchs, L., & Vandermeer, L. (1994). Classroom ecological inventory: A process for mainstreaming *Teaching Exceptional Children, 26*(3), 11-15.

Fuchs, D., & Fuchs, L. S. (1987). *Mainstream assistance teams to accommodate difficult-to-teach students in general education.* Nashville, TN: George Peabody College for Teachers. ED 292 277.

Fuchs, D., & Fuchs, L. (1994). Inclusive schools movement and the radicalization of special education. *Exceptional Children, 60,* 294-309.

Fuchs, L., Deno, S., & Mirkin, P. (1984). The effects of frequent curriculum-based measurement and evaluation on pedagogy, student achievement, and student awareness of learning. *American Educational Research Journal, 21,* 449-460.

Fuchs, L., Fuchs, D., Hamlett, C., & Hasselbring, T. (1987). Using computers with curriculum-based monitoring: Effects on teacher efficiency and satisfaction. *Journal of Special Education Technology, 8*(4), 14-27.

Fuchs, L. S., & Deno, S. L. (1994). Must instructionally useful performance assessment be based in the curriculum? *Exceptional Children, 61,* 15-24.

Fuchs, L. S., & Fuchs, D. (1987). Effects of systematic formative evaluation: A meta-analysis. *Exceptional Children, 53,* 199-208.

Furnham, A. (1987). Social skills training with adolescents and young adults. In C. R. Hollin & P. Trower (Eds.), *Handbook of social skills: Applications across the life span* (vol. 1, pp. 33-57). New York: Pergamon Press.

Gall, M. D. (1981). *Handbook for evaluating and selecting curriculum materials.* Boston: Allyn & Bacon.

Garard, J. E., & Weinstock, G. (1981). *Language proficiency test.* Novato, CA: Academic Therapy Publications.

Garcia, E. E. (1988). Attributes of effective school for language minority students. *Education and Urban Society, 20,* 387-398.

Garcia, G. E. (1994). Ethnography and classroom communication: Taking an "emic" perspective. In K. G. Butler (Ed.), *Best practices I: The classroom as an assessment arena* (pp. 3-15). Gaithersburg, MD: Aspen.

Garcia, S. B., & Malkin, D. H. (1997). Toward defining programs and services for culturally and linguistically diverse learners in special education. In K. L. Friberg (Ed.), *Education Exceptional Children* (9th ed.) (pp. 113-119). Guilford, CT: Dushkin/McGraw-Hill.

Gardner, E. F., Rudman, H. C., Karlsen, B., & Merwin, J. C. (1982). *Stanford Achievement Test.* San Antonio, TX: Psychological Corporation.

Gardner, J. E., & Edyburn, D. L. (1993). Teaching applications with exceptional children. In J. D. Linsey (Ed.), *Computers and Exceptional Individuals* (2nd ed., pp. 273-310). Austin, TX: Pro-Ed.

Garrison, B. (1994). Ronni Cohen reinvents the classroom. *University of Delaware Messenger, 3*(3), 12.

Gartland, D. (1994). Content area reading: Lessons from the specialists. *LD Forum, 19*(3), 19-22.

Gast, D. L., & Nelson, C. M. (1977). Legal and ethical considerations for the use of timeout procedures in special education settings. *Journal of Special Education, 11,* 457-467.

Gates, A. I., & Russell, D. (1940). *Gates-Russell Spelling Diagnostic Test.* New York: Columbia University Press.

Gearheart, B. R., Weishahn, M. W., & Gearheart, D. (1995). *The exceptional student in the regular classroom* (4th ed.). Upper Saddle River, NJ: Merrill/Prentice Hall.

Gebhard, J. G. (1996). *Teaching English as a Foreign or Second Language.* Ann Arbor, MI: University of Michigan Press.

Geller, E. S. (1991). If only more would actively care. *Journal of Applied Behavior Analyses, 24,* 607–612.

Geller, E. S. (1994a). The human element in integrated environmental management. In J. Cairns, T. V. Crawford, & H. Salwasser (Eds.), *Implementing integrated environmental management* (pp. 5–26). Blacksburg, VA: Virginia Tech.

Geller, E. S. (1994b). Ten principles for achieving a total safety culture. *Professional Safety, 39*(9), 18–24

George, N. L., & Lewis, T. J. (1991). EASE: Exit assistance for special educators—Helping students make the transition. *Teaching Exceptional Children, 23*(2), 34–39.

Gerber, A. (1993). *Language-related learning disabilities: Their nature and treatment.* Baltimore, MD: Paul H. Brookes.

Gerber, M. M. (1985). The Department of Education's sixth annual report to Congress on PL 94-142: Is Congress getting the full story? *Exceptional Children, 51,* 209–224.

Gerber, M. M. (1988). Cognitive-behavioral training in the curriculum: Time, slow learners, and basic skills. In E. L. Meyer, G. A. Vergason, & R. J. Whelan (Eds.), *Effective instructional strategies for exceptional children* (pp. 45–64). Denver, CO: Love.

Gersten, R., Baker, S. K., Moses, S U. (1998). *Teaching English-language learners with learning difficulties.* Reston, VA: The Council for Exceptional Children.

Gersten, R., & Dimino, J. (1990). Reading instruction for at-risk students: Implications of current research. *Oregon School Study Council Bulletin, 33,* 3–24.

Gersten, R., & Dimino, J. (1993). Visions and revisions: A special education perspective on the whole language controversy. *Remedial and Special Education, 14*(4), 5–13.

Gersten, R., Woodward, J., & Darsch, C. (1987). Direct instruction: A research-based approach to curriculum design and teaching. *Exceptional Children, 33,* 17–31.

Giangreco, M. F., Cloninger, C. J., & Iverson, V. S. (1993). I've counted Jon: Transformational experiences of teacher educating students with disabilities. *Exceptional Children, 59,* 359–372.

Gibb, G. S., & Dyches, T. T. (2000). *Guide to writing quality individualized education programs: What's best for students with disabilities?* Boston: Allyn & Bacon.

Gillingham A., & Stillman, B. *Remedial teaching for children with specific disability in reading, spelling, and penmanship.* Cambridge, MA: Educators Publishing Service.

Ginsburg, H. P., & Mathews, S. C. (1984). *Diagnostic Test of Arithmetic Strategies.* Austin, TX: Pro-Ed.

Glass, E. W., & Glass, G. G. (1978). *Glass analysis for decoding only.* New York: Easier to Learn.

Glisan, E. M. (1984). *Record keeping for individualized junior-senior high school special education programs.* Freeport, IL: Peekan.

Goddard, Y. L., & Heron, T. E. (1998). Please, teacher, help me learn to spell better. *Teaching Exceptional Children, 30,* 38–43.

Goetz, L., Lee, M., Johnston, S., & Gaylord-Ross, R. (1991). Employment of persons with dual sensory impairments: Strategies for inclusion. *Journal of The Association for Persons with Severe Handicaps, 16,* 131–139.

Goldstein, A. P., Sprafkin, R. P., Gershaw, N. J., & Klein, P. (1980). *Skillstreaming the adolescent: A structured learning approach to teaching prosocial skills.* Champaign, IL: Research Press.

Goldsworthy, C. (1982). *Multilevel Informal Language Inventory.* Upper Saddle River, NJ: Merrill/Prentice Hall.

Good, T. L. (1983). Classroom research: A decade of progress. *Educational Psychologist, 18,* 127–144.

Good, T. L., & Brophy, J. E. (1995). *Contempory educational psychology.* Reading MA: Addison-Wesley Publishing.

Goodman, K. (1991). Whole language: What makes it whole? In B. M. Power and R. Hubbard (Eds.), *Literacy in process* (pp. 88–95). Portsmouth, NH: Heinemann.

Gordon, J. M., Vaughn, S., & Schumm, J. S. (1993). Spelling interventions: A review of literature and implications for instruction with students with learning disabilities. *Learning Disabilities Research and Practice, 8,* 175–181.

Gould, B. W. (1991). Curricular strategies for written expression. In A. M. Bain, L. L. Bailet, & L. C. Moats (Eds.), *Written language disorders: Theory into practice* (pp. 129-164). Austin, TX: Pro-Ed.

Graden, J., Thurlow, M. L., & Ysseldyke, J. E. (1982). *Academic engaged time and its relationship to learning: A review of the literature* (Monograph No. 17). Minneapolis: University of Minnesota, Institute for Research on Learning Disabilities.

Graham, S. (1983). The effects of self-instructional procedures on LD students, handwriting performance. *Learning Disability Quarterly, 6,* 231-234.

Graham, S. (1992). Helping students with LD progress as writers. *Intervention in School and Clinic, 27,* 134-144.

Graham, S. (1999). Handwriting and spelling instruction for students with learning disabilities: A review. *Learning Disability Quarterly, 22,* 78-98.

Graham, S., Harris, K. R., & Loynachin, C. (1994) The spelling for writing list. *Journal of Learning Disabilities, 27,* 210-214.

Graham, S., Harris, K., MacArthur, C. A., & Schwartz, S. (1991). Writing and writing instruction for students with learning disabilities: Review of a research program. *Learning Disability Quarterly, 14,* 89-114.

Graham, S., Harris, K., & Sawyer, R. (1987). Composition instruction with learning-disabled students. *Focus on Exceptional Children, 20*(4), 1-11.

Graham, S. (1999). Handwriting and spelling instruction for students with learning disabilities: A review. *Learning Disability Quarterly.*

Graham, S., & Johnson, L. A. (1989). Teaching reading to learning-disabled students: A review of research supported procedures. *Focus on Exceptional Children, 21,* 1-12.

Graham, S., & Miller, L. (1979). Spelling research and practice: A unified approach. *Focus on Exceptional Children, 12*(2), 1-16.

Graham, S., & Miller, L. (1980). Handwriting research and practice: A unified approach. *Focus on Exceptional Children, 13*(2), 1-16.

Graham, S., & Voth, V. P. (1990). Spelling instruction: Making modifications for students with learning disabilities. *Academic Therapy, 25,* 447-457.

Grant, R. (1993). Strategic training for using text headings to improve students, processing of content. *Journal of Reading, 36,* 482-488.

Graves, D. H. (1985). All children can write. *Learning Disabilities Focus, 1*(1), 36-43.

Graves, D. H. (1994). *A fresh new look at writing.* Portsmouth, NH: Heineman.

Graves, A., & Hauge, R. (1993). Using cues and prompts to improve story writing. *Teaching Exceptional Children, 25,* 38-40.

Green, R. L. (1994). Speech time is all the time. *Teaching Exceptional Children, 27*(1), 60-61.

Greene, G. (1994). Research into practice: The magic of mnemonics. *LD Forum, 19*(3), 34-37.

Greene, J. F., (1998). Another chance. Help for older students with limited literacy. *American Federation of Teachers,* 74-79.

Greenland, R., & Polloway, E. A. (1994). Handwriting and students with disabilities: Overcoming first impressions. (ERIC Document Reproduction Service No. ED 378 754).

Gregory, G. P. (1979). Using the newspaper in the mainstreamed classroom. *Social Education, 43,* 140-143.

Gregory, R. P., Hackney, C., & Gregory, N. M. (1982). Corrective reading programme: An evaluation. *British Journal of Educational Psychology, 52,* 33-50.

Gresham, F. M. (1982). Misguided mainstreaming. The case for social skills training with handicapped children. *Exceptional Children, 48,* 422-433.

Gresham, F. M. (1983). Social skills assessment as a component of mainstreaming placement decisions. *Exceptional Children, 49,* 331-386.

Gresham, F M., & Elliott, S. N. (1990). *Social skills rating system.* Circle Pines, MN: American Guidance Service.

Grossen, B., & Carnine, D. (1993). Phonics instruction: Comparing research and practice. *Teaching Exceptional Children, 25*(2), 22-25.

Guerin, G. R., & Maier, A. S. (1983). *Informal assessment in education.* Palo Alto, CA: Mayfield.

Guillaume, A. M., Yopp, R. H., & Yopp, H. K. (1996). Accessible science. *The Journal of Educational Issues of Language Minority Students, 17,* 67-85.

Guttman, M. (1995, October 29). Doctors and parents are focusing on whether popular drugs "unquestionably helpful to some children" are overprescribed. *USA WEEKEND* [On-line]. Available America Online.

Gurganus, S., Janas, M., & Schmitt, L. (1995). Science instruction: What special education teachers need to know and what roles they need to play. *Teaching Exceptional Children, 27*(4), 7-9.

Hagood, B. F. (1997). Reading and writing with help from story grammar. *Teaching Exceptional Children, 29*(4), 10-14.

Haines, A. H. (1992). Strategies for preparing preschool children with special needs for the kindergarten mainstream. *Journal of Early Intervention, 16,* 320-333.

Hallahan, D. P., & Kauffman, J. M. (1977). Labels, categories, behaviors: ED, LD, and EMR reconsidered. *Journal of Special Education, 11,* 129-149.

Hallahan, D. P., Kauffman, J. M., & Lloyd, J. W. (1985). *Introduction to learning disabilities* (2nd ed.). Upper Saddle River, NJ: Prentice Hall.

Hallahan, D. P., Lloyd, J. W., & Stoller, L. (1982). *Improving attention with self-monitoring: A manual for teachers.* Charlottesville: University of Virginia Learning Disabilities Research Institute.

Halpern, A. S. (1993). Quality of life as a conceptual framework for evaluating transition outcomes. *Exceptional Children, 59,* 486-498.

Halpern, A. S. (1985). Transition: A look at the foundation. *Exceptional Children, 51,* 479-486.

Halpern, A. S., & Benz, M. R. (1987). A statewide examination of secondary special education for students with mild disabilities: Implications for the high school curriculum. *Exceptional Children, 54,* 122-129.

Hamilton, C., Miller, A., & Wood, P. (1987). Group books. *Teaching Exceptional Children, 19*(3), 46-47.

Hammill, D. D. (1986). Correcting handwriting deficiencies. In D. D. Hammill & N. E. Bartel (Eds.), *Teaching children with learning and behavior problems* (4th ed., pp. 154-177). Boston: Allyn & Bacon.

Hammill, D. D. (1987). Assessing students in the schools. In D. D. Hammill (Ed.). *Assessing the abilities and instructional needs of students.* (pp. 5-37). Austin, TX: Pro-Ed.

Hammill, D. D., & Bartel, N. (1990). *Teaching students with learning and behavior problems* (5th ed.). Austin, TX: Pro-Ed.

Hammill, D. D., & Bartel, N. R. (1982). *Teaching children with learning and behavior problems* (3rd ed.). Boston: Allyn & Bacon.

Hammill, D. D., Brown, V. L., Larsen, S. C., & Wiederholt, J. L. (1994). *Test of Adolescent Language-3.* Austin, TX: Pro-Ed.

Hammill, D. D., & Larsen, S. C. (1996) *The Test of Written Language-3 (TOWL-3).* Austin, TX: Pro-Ed.

Hammill, D. D., & Newcomer, P. L. (1991). *Test of language development—2: Intermediate.* Austin, TX: Pro-Ed.

Hamre-Nietupski, S., McDonald, J., & Nietupski, J. (1992). Integrating elementary students with multiple disabilities: Challenges and solutions. *Teaching Exceptional Children, 24*(3), 6-11.

Handleman, J. S., & Harris, S. L. (1983). A comparison of one-to-one versus couplet instruction with autistic children. *Behavioral Disorders, 9,* 22-26.

Hansen, M. J., & Lynch, E. W. (1995). *Early intervention: Implementing child and family services for infants and toddlers who are at risk or disabled.* Austin, TX: Pro-Ed.

Harden, L. (1987). Reading to remember. *The Reading Teacher, 40*(6), 580-581.

Hargis, C. H. (1982). Word recognition development. *Focus on Exceptional Children, 14*(9), 1-8.

Haring, N., & Liberty, K. A. (1990). Matching strategies with performance in facilitating generalization. *Focus on Exceptional Children, 22*(8), 1-16.

Harlan, J. E. (1993). *Yes we can: Overcoming obstacles to creativity.* Paper presented at the annual meeting of the American Association on Mental Retardation, Washington, DC. (ERIC Document Reproduction Service No. 360 761)

Harn, W. E., Bradshaw, M. L., & Ogletree, B. (1999). The speech-language pathologist in the schools: Changing roles. *Intervention in School and Clinic 34,* 163-169.

Harris, A. J., & Sipay, E. R. (1990). *How to increase reading ability.* New York: Longman.

Harris, K. (1990). Developing self-regulated learners: The role of practice, speech and self-instruction. *Educational Psychologist, 25,* 35-49.

Harris, K. R., & Graham, S. (1992). *Helping young writers master the craft: Strategy instruction and self-regulation in the writing process.* Cambridge, MA: Brookline Books.

Harris, K. R., Graham, S., Reid, R., McElroy, K., & Hamby, R. S. (1994). Self-monitoring of attention versus self-monitoring of performance: Replication and cross-task comparison studies. *Learning Disability Quarterly, 17,* 121-139.

Harris, W. J., & Schultz, P. N. B. (1993). *The special education resource program: Rationale and implementation.* Project Heights, IL: Waveland Press.

Hart, B., & Risley, T. R. (1975). Incidental teaching of language in preschool. *Journal of Applied Behavioral Analysis, 8,* 411-420.

Harter, S. (1982). The perceived competence scale for children. *Child Development, 52,* 87-97.

Haughton, E. (1974). Myriad counter: Or beads that aren't for worrying. *Teaching Exceptional Children, 7,* 203-209.

Hawaii Transition Project. (1987). Transition resources. Honolulu: University of Hawaii, Department of Special Education.

Hawkins, B. (1994). Leisure as an adaptive skill area. *AAMR News and Notes, 7*(1), 5-6.

Hayden, T. (1980). *One child.* New York: Avon Books.

Hayes, D. (1988). Toward students learning through the social studies text. *The Social Studies, 79,* 266-270.

Haynes, M. C., & Jenkins, J. R. (1986). Reading instruction in special education resource rooms. *American Educational Research Journal, 23,* 161-190.

Haynes, W. O., Moral, M. J., & Pindzola, R. H. (1990). *Communication disorders in the classroom.* Dubuque, IA: Kendall/Hunt Publishing.

Hazel, J. S., Schumaker, J. B., Sherman, J. A., & Sheldon-Wildgen, J. B. (1981a). ASSET: *A social skills program for adolescents.* Champaign, IL: Research Press.

Hazel, J. S., Schumaker, J. B., Sherman, J. A., & Sheldon-Wildgen, J. B. (1981b). Group social skills: A program for court-adjudicated probationary youth. *Criminal Justice & Behavior, 9,* 35-52.

Heilman, A., Blair, T., & Rupley, W. (1981). *Principles and practices of teaching reading.* Upper Saddle River, NJ: Merrill/Prentice Hall.

Heilman, A. W., Blair, T. R., & Rupley, W. H. (1986). *Principles and practices of teaching reading* (6th ed.). Upper Saddle River, NJ: Merrill/Prentice Hall.

Heimlich, J. E., & Pittelman, S. D. (1986). *Semantic mapping: Classroom applications.* Newark, DE: International Reading Association.

Heller, H. W., Spooner, F., Anderson, D., & Mimms, A. (1988). Homework: A review of special education practices in the southwest. *Teacher Education and Special Education, 11,* 43-51.

Helmke, L., Havekost, D. M., Patton, J. R., & Polloway, E. A. (1994). Life skills programming: Development of a high school science course. *Teaching Exceptional Children, 26*(2), 49-53.

Henderson, M., & Hollin, C. R. (1987). Social skills training and delinquency. In C. L. Hollin & P. Trower (Eds.), *Handbook of social skills training: Application across the life span* (vol. 1, pp. 79-101). New York: Pergamon Press.

Henk, W. A., Helfeldt, J. P., & Platt, J. M. (1986). Developing reading fluency in learning-disabled students. *Teaching Exceptional Children, 18,* 202-206.

Henley, D. R. (1990). Adapting art education for exceptional children. *School Arts, 90*(4), 18-20.

Heron, T. (1978). Punishment: A review of the literature with implications for the teacher of mainstreamed children. *Journal of Special Education, 12,* 243-252.

Heron, T. E. (1987). Response cost. In J. O. Cooper, T. E. Heron, & W. E. Heward (Eds.), *Applied behavior analysis* (pp. 454-464). Upper Saddle River, NJ: Merrill/Prentice Hall.

Heron, T. E., & Harris, K. C. (1982). *The educational consultant: Helping professionals, parents, and mainstreamed students.* Boston: Allyn & Bacon.

Hess, L. J., & Fairchild, J. L. (1988). Model, analyse, practise (MAP): A language therapy model for learning-disabled adolescents. *Child Language Teaching and Therapy, 4,* 325-338.

Hess, R., Miller, A., Reese, J., & Robinson, G. A. (1987). *Grading-credit-diploma: Accommodation practices for students with mild disabilities.* (ERIC Document Reproduction Service No. 294 403).

Heukerott, P. B. (1987). "Little books" for content areas vocabulary. *The Reading Teacher, 40,* 489.

Hildebrandt, C. (1998). Creativity in music and early childhood. *Young Children, 53*(6), 68-74.

Hoffman, A., & Field, S. (1995). Promoting self-determination through effective curriculum development. *Intervention in School and Clinic, 30*(3), 134-142.

Hofmeister, A., & Thorkildsen, R. (1993). Interactive videodisc and exceptional individuals. In J. D. Lindsey (Ed.), *Computers and exceptional Individuals* (2nd ed., pp. 87-107). Austin, TX: Pro-Ed.

Hollingsworth, P. M., & Reutzel, D. R. (1988). Whole language and LD children. *Academic Therapy, 23,* 477-488.

Holmes, M., & Croll, P. (1989). Time spent on homework and academic achievement. *Educational Research, 31,* 36-45.

Homme, L. (1969). *How to use contingency contracting in the classroom.* Champaign, IL: Research Press.

Hong, Z, & Aiex, N. K. (1999). Oral language development across the curriculum, K-12. [WWW document]. URL *http://www.indiana/edu/~eric_rec/ieo/digest/d107.html*

Hoover, J. J. (1989). Implementing a study skills program in the classroom. *Academic Therapy, 24,* 471-476.

Hoover, J. J. (1990a). Curriculum adaptations: A five-step process for classroom implementation. *Academic Therapy, 25,* 407-416.

Hoover, J. J. (1990b). *Using study skills and learning strategies in the classroom: A teacher's handbook.* Boulder, CO: Hamilton.

Hoover, J. J. (1991). *Classroom applications of cognitive learning styles.* Boulder, CO: Hamilton.

Hoover, J. J., & Patton, J. R. (1997). *Teaching students with learning problems to use study skills.* Austin, TX: Pro-Ed.

Hoover, J. J. (in press). Teaching students to use study skills. In D. D. Hammill & N. R. Bartel (Eds.), *Teaching students with learning and behavior problems* (pp. 347–380). Austin, TX: Pro-Ed.

Hoover, J. J., & Collier, C. (1992). Sociocultural considerations in teaching study strategies. *Intervention in School and Clinic, 27,* 228–232.

Hoover J. J, & Patton, J. R. (1995). *Teaching students with learning problems to use study skills: A teacher's guide.* Austin, TX: Pro-Ed.

Hoover, J. J., & Patton, J. R. (1997). *Curriculum adaptations for students with learning and behavior problems: Principles and practices.* Austin: Pro-Ed.

Hoover, J. J., & Rabideau, D. K. (1995). Teaching study skills through semantic webs. *Intervention in School and Clinic, 30,* 292–296.

Horn, E. (1954). *Teaching spelling.* Washington, DC: American Educational Research Association.

Hoskins, B. (1994). Language and literacy: Participating in the conversation. In K. G. Butler (Ed.), *Best practices* II: *The classroom as an intervention context* (pp. 201–217). Gaithersburg, MD: Aspen Publication.

Houk, C., & McKenzie, R. G. (1985). *ASSIST: Aides serving students: An individual system of training.* Bowling Green: Western Kentucky University College of Education.

Howe, E., Joseph, A., & Victor, E. (1971). *A source book for elementary science.* New York: Harcourt Brace Jovanovich.

Howell, K. W., Kaplan, J. S., & O'Connell, C. Y. (1979). *Evaluating exceptional children: A task analysis approach.* Upper Saddle River, NJ: Merrill/Prentice Hall.

Howell, K. W., & Morehead, M. K. (1987). *Curriculum-based evaluation in special and remedial education.* Upper Saddle River, NJ: Merrill/Prentice Hall.

Howell, K. W., Rueda, R., & Rutherford, R. B. (1983). A procedure for teaching self-recording to moderately retarded students. *Psychology in the Schools, 20,* 202–209.

Hresko, W. P., Reid, D. K., & Hammill, D. D. (1982). *Prueba del Desarrollo Inicial del Lenguaje.* Austin, TX: Pro-Ed.

Hresko, W. P., Reid, D. K., & Hammill, D. D. (1991). *Test of early language development.* Austin, TX: Pro-Ed.

Hughes, C. A., Korinek, L., & Gorman, J. (1991). Self-management for students with mental retardation in public school settings: A review of research. *Education and Training in Mental Retardation, 26,* 271–291.

Hughes, C. A., Ruhl, K. L., & Misra, A. (1989). Self-management with behaviorally disordered students in school settings: A promise unfulfilled? *Behavioral Disorders, 14,* 250–262.

Hunt, P. (1995, summer). *Collaboration: What does it take? What's working: Transition in Minnesota,* p. 1. Minneapolis: University of Minnesota Institute on Community Integration.

Hurst, J. B. (1986). A skills-in-living perspective rather than trivial pursuit. *The Social Studies, 77*(2), 69–73.

Hymes, D. (1971). Competence and performance in linguistic theory. In R. Huxley & E. Ingram (Eds.), *Language acquisition: Models and methods* (pp. 3–24). New York: Academic Press.

Idol, L. (1989). The resource/consulting teacher: An integrated model of service delivery. *Remedial and Special Education, 10*(6), 41–48.

Idol, L. (1993). *Special educator's consultation handbook* (2nd ed.). Austin, TX: Pro-Ed.

Idol, L. (1997). *Reading success: A specialized literacy program for learners with challenging reading needs.* Austin, TX: Pro-Ed.

Idol, L., Nevin, A., & Paolucci-Whitcomb, P. (1986). *Models of curriculum-based assessment.* Austin, TX: Pro-Ed.

Idol, L., Nevin, A., & Paolucci-Whitcomb, P. (1994). *Collaborative consultation* (2nd ed.). Austin, TX: Pro-Ed.

Idol, L., & West, J. F. (1991). Educational collaboration: A catalyst for effective schooling. *Intervention in School and Clinic, 27,* 70–78.

Idol, L., & West, J. F. (1992). *Effective instruction of difficult-to-teach students: An inservice and preservice professional development program for classroom, remedial, and special education teachers.* Austin, TX: Pro-Ed.

Institute of Research in Learning (1995). *Workshop on pedagogues for diversity in secondary schools.* Lawrence, KS: Author.

Isaacson, S. L. (1987). Effective instruction in written language. *Focus on Exceptional Children, 19*(6), 1–12.

Isaacson, S. L. (1989). Role of secretary vs. author in resolving the conflict in writing instruction. *Learning Disability Quarterly, 12,* 200-217.

Israel, L. (1984). Word knowledge and word retrieval: Phonological and semantic strategies. In G. Wallace & K. Butler (Eds.), *Language learning disabilities in school-age children* (pp. 230-250). Baltimore, MD: Williams & Wilkins.

Jackson, N. F., Jackson, D. A., & Monroe, C. (1983). *Program guide: Getting along with others.* Champaign, IL: Research Press.

Jacobson, W. J., & Bergman, A. B. (1991). *Science for children: A book for teachers* (3rd ed.). Upper Saddle River, NJ: Prentice Hall.

James, S., & Pedrazzini, L. (1975). *Simple lattice approach to mathematics.* Upper Saddle River, NJ: Prentice Hall Learning Systems.

Jamison, P. J., & Shevitz, L. A. (1985). RATE: A reason to read. *Teaching Exceptional Children, 18*(1), 46-50.

Jarolimek, J. (1981). The social studies: An overview. In H. D. Mehlinger & O. I. Davis (Eds.), *The social studies: Eightieth yearbook of the National Society for the Study of Education* (pp. 3-18). Chicago: University of Chicago Press.

Jastak, S. R., & Wilkinson, G. S. (1984). *The Wide Range Achievement Test—Revised.* Wilmington, DE: Jastak Associates.

Jayanthi, M., Bursuck, W., Epstein, M. H., & Polloway, E. A. (1997). Strategies for successful homework. *Teaching Exceptional Children, 30*(1), 4-7.

Jayanthi, M., Bursuck, W., Havekost, D. M., Epstein, M. H., & Polloway, E. A. (1994). School district testing policies and students with disabilities: A national survey. *School Psychology Review, 23,* 694-703.

Jayanthi, M., Nelson, J. S., Sawyer, V., Bursuck, W., & Epstein, M. H. (1994). *Homework communication problems among parents, general education and special education teachers: An exploratory study.* Manuscript submitted for publication.

Jayanthi, M., Sawyer, V., Nelson, J. S., Bursuck, W. D., & Epstein, M. H. (1995). Recommendations for homework-communication problems: From parents, classroom teachers, and special education teachers. *Remedial and Special Education, 16,* 212-225.

Jenkins, J. R., Leigh, J., & Patton, J. (1996). *State certification standards for teachers of students with learning disabilities: An update.* Manuscript submitted for publication.

Jenkins, J. R., Pious, C. G., & Jewell, M. (1990). Special education and the regular education initiative:

Basic assumptions. *Exceptional Children, 56,* 479-491.

Jenkins, J. R., Stein, M. L., & Osborn, J. R. (1981). What next after decoding? Instruction and research in reading comprehension. *Exceptional Education Quarterly, 2*(1), 27-39.

Jerger, M. A. (1996). Phoneme awareness and the role of the educator. *Intervention in School and Clinic, 32,* 5-13.

Johnson, D. A., & Rising, G. R. (1972). *Guidelines for teaching mathematics.* Belmont, CA: Wadsworth.

Johnson, D. W., & Johnson, R. T. (1990). What is cooperative learning? In M. Brubacher, R. Payne, & K. Rickett (Eds.), *Perspectives on small group learning* (pp. 5-30). Oakville, ONT: Rubicon.

Johnson, D. W., & Johnson, R. T. (1989a). Cooperative learning in mathematics education. In P. R. Trafton & A. P. Shulte (Eds.), *New directions for elementary school mathematics* (1989 yearbook, pp. 234-245). Reston, VA: National Council of Teachers of Mathematics.

Johnson, D. W., & Johnson, R. T. (1989b). Using cooperative learning in math. In N. Davidson (Ed.), *Cooperative learning in mathematics* (pp. 103-125). Menlo Park, CA: Addison-Wesley.

Johnson, D. W., Johnson, R. T., & Holubec, E. J. (1986). *Circles of learning: Cooperation in the classroom.* Edina, MN: Interaction Book.

Johnson, D. W., Johnson, R. T., & Holubec, E. J. (1994). *The new circles of learning.* Alexandria, VA: Association for Supervision and Curriculum Development.

Johnston, E. B., & Johnston, A. V. (1990). *Communication Abilities Diagnostic Test.* Chicago: Riverside.

Johnston, J. R. (1983). Discussion: Part I: What is language intervention? The role of theory. In J. Miller, D. E. Yoder, & R. Schiefelbusch (Eds.), *Contemporary issues in language intervention.* Rockville, MD: ASHA.

Johnston, R. C. (1994). Policy details who paddles students and with what. *Education Week, 14(11),* p. 5.

Jones, B. F., Palincsar, A. S., Ogle, D. S., & Carr, E. G. (1987). *Strategic teaching and learning: Cognitive instruction in the content areas.* Washington, DC: Association of Supervision and Curriculum Development.

Jones, M. M., & Carlier, L. L. (1995). Creating inclusionary opportunities for learners with multiple disabilities: A team-teaching approach. *Teaching Exceptional Children, 27*(3), 23-27.

Jones, R. M., & Steinbrink, J. E. (1991). Home teams: Cooperative learning in elementary science. *School Science and Mathematics, 91,* 139-143.

Joyce, B., & Weis, M. (1980). *Models of teaching.* Upper Saddle River, NJ: Prentice Hall.

Kagan, S. (1990). A structural approach to cooperative learning. *Educational Leadership, 47*(4), 12-15.

Kagan, S. (1992). *Cooperative learning resources for teachers* (7th ed.). San Juan Capistrano, CA: Resources for Teachers.

Kaluger, G., & Kolson, C. J. (1969). *Reading and learning disabilities.* Upper Saddle River, NJ: Merrill/Prentice Hall.

Kamps, D. M., & Tankersly, M. (1996). Prevention of behavioral and conduct disorders: Trends and research issues. *Behavioral Disorders, 22,* 41-48.

Kangas, K. A., & Lloyd, L. L. (1998). Augmentative and alternative communication. In G. H. Shames, E. Wiig, & W. A. Secord (Eds.), *Human communication disorders* (5th ed.) (pp. 510-551). Boston: Allyn & Bacon.

Kataoka, J. C., & Lock, R. (1995). Whales and hermit crabs: Integrated programming and science. *Teaching Exceptional Children, 27*(4), 17-21.

Kataoka, J. C., & Patton, J. R. (1989). Teaching exceptional learners: An integrated approach. *Science and Children, 16,* 52-58.

Kauffman, J. M. (1989). The regular education initiative as Reagan-Bush education policy: A trickle-down theory of education of the hard-to-teach. *The Journal of Special Education, 23,* 256-278.

Kauffman, J. M., & Hallahan, D. P. *inclusion.* Austin, TX: Pro-Ed.

Kauffman, J. M., & Payne, J. S. (1975). *Mental retardation: Introduction and personal perspectives.* Upper Saddle River, NJ: Merrill/Prentice Hall.

Kauffman, J. M., Pullen, P. L., & Akers, E. (1988). Classroom management: Teacher-child-peer relationships. In E. L. Meyen, G. A. Vergason, & R. J. Whelan (Eds.), *Effective instructional strategies for exceptional children* (pp. 32-44). Denver, CO: Love.

Kaufman, A. S., & Kaufman, N. L. (1985). *Kaufman Test of Educational Achievement.* Circle Pines, MN: American Guidance Service.

Kavale, K. A., & Forness, S. R. (1987). The far side of heterogeneity: A critical analysis of empirical subtyping research in learning disabilities. *Journal of Learning Disabilities, 20,* 374-382.

Kayser, H. (1995). Intervention with children from linguistically and culturally diverse backgrounds. In M. E. Fey, J. Windsor, & S. F. Warren (Eds.), *Language intervention preschool through the elementary years.* Baltimore: Paul H. Brookes.

Kazdin, A. E., & Bootzin, R. R. (1972). The token economy: An evaluative review. *Journal of Applied Behavior Analysis, 5,* 343-372.

Kazdin, A. E., & Erickson, L. M. (1975). Developing responsiveness to instructions in severely and profoundly retarded residents. *Journal of Behavior Therapy and Experimental Psychiatry, 6,* 17-21.

Kazdin, A. E., & Polster, R. (1973). Intermittent token reinforcement and response maintenance in extinction. *Behavior Therapy, 4,* 386-391.

Kelley, S., Serna, L. A., & Noonan, M. J. (1992). *Preparing elementary students for the mainstream: A study of the generalization of social skills across environments.* Unpublished manuscript.

Kelly, E. J. (1979). *Elementary school social studies instruction: A basic approach.* Denver, CO: Love.

Kelner, L. B. (1993). *Creative classroom: A guide for using creative drama in the classroom,* PreK-6. Portsmouth, NH: Heinemann.

Kerr, M. M., Nelson, C. M., & Lambert, D. L. (1987). *Helping adolescents with learning and behavior problems.* Upper Saddle River, NJ: Merrill/Prentice Hall.

Khilnani, S., & Culhane, D. (1995). Linking sculpture to core subjects. *Teaching Exceptional Children, 27* (4), 68-70.

Kiburtz, C. S., Miller, S. R., & Morrow, L. W. (1984). Structured learning using self-monitoring to promote maintenance and generalization of social skills across settings for a behaviorally disordered adolescent. *Behavior Disorders, 4,* 47-55.

Kinder, D., & Bursuck, W. (1992). The search for a unified social studies curriculum: Does history really repeat itself? In D. Carnine & E. J. Kameenui (Eds.), *Higher order thinking: Designing curriculum for mainstreamed students* (pp. 23-37). Austin, TX: Pro-Ed.

Kinder, D., & Bursuck, W. (1993). History strategy instruction: Problem-solution-effect analysis, timeline, and vocabulary instruction. *Exceptional Children, 59,* 324-335.

Kinder, D., & Bursuck, W., & Epstein, M. (1992). An evaluation of history textbooks. *Journal of Special Education, 25,* 472-491.

King, E. W. (1980). *Teaching ethnic awareness: Methods and materials for the elementary school.* Santa Monica, CA: Goodyear.

Kirk, S., Kirk, W., & Minskoff, E. (1986). *Phonic remedial reading lessons.* Novato, CA: Academic Therapy.

Kirk, S. A., & Johnson, G. O. (1951). *Educating the retarded child.* Cambridge, MA: Houghton Mifflin.

Kirk, S. A., Kliebhan, J. M., & Lerner, J. (1978). *Teaching reading to slow and disabled learners.* Boston: Houghton Mifflin.

Kirk, S. A., & Monroe, M. (1940). *Teaching reading to slow-learning children.* Boston: Houghton Mifflin.

Klein, H. B., & Moses, N. (1999). *Intervention planning for children with communication disorders.* Boston: Allyn & Bacon.

Kline, S. (1987). Dear diary . . . I couldn't teach without you! *Instructor, 96,* 80–81.

Knackendoffel, E. A., Robinson, S. M., Deshler, D. D., & Schumaker, J. B. (1992). *Collaborative problem solving: A step-by-step guide to creating educational solutions.* Lawrence, KS: Edge Enterprises.

Knapczyk, D. (1991). Effects of modeling in promoting generalization of student question asking and question answering. *Learning Disabilities Research & Practice, 6,* 75–82.

Knowles, M. (1990). *The adult learner: A neglected species* (4th ed.). Houston, TX: Gulf.

Kohn, A. (1993). *Punished by rewards: The trouble with gold stars, incentive plans, A's, praise, and other bribes.* Boston: Houghton Mifflin Company.

Kolstoe, O. P. (1976). *Teaching educable mentally retarded children* (2nd ed.). New York: Holt, Rinehart & Winston.

Kolstoe, O. P., & Frey, R. M. (1965). *A high school work-study program for mentally subnormal students.* Carbondale: Southern Illinois University Press.

Kosiewicz, M. M., Hallahan, D. P., Lloyd, J., & Graves, A. W. (1982). Effects of self-instruction and self-correction procedures on handwriting performance. *Learning Disability Quarterly, 5,* 71–78.

Kotting, D. (1987). Round robin vocabulary. *The Reading Teacher, 40,* 711–712.

Kounin, J. (1970). *Discipline and group management in classrooms.* New York: Holt, Rinehart & Winston.

Kovarsky, D. (1992). Ethnography and language assessment: Toward the contextualized description and interpretation of communicative behavior. *Best Practices in School Speech-Language Pathology, 2,* 115–122.

Kroegel, M. (1999). *Making the grade: A case study of assessment and grading practices in an elementary inclusive classroom.* Unpublished doctoral dissertation, Virginia Tech.

Krueger, K., & Fox, H. (1984). *Techniques for teacher-aide communication.* Paper presented at in-service training workshop, Albuquerque Public Schools Special Education Department, Albuquerque, New Mexico.

Kyle, W. C. (1984). Curriculum development projects of the 1960s. In D. Holdzkom & P. B. Lutz (Eds.), *Research within reach: Science education* (pp. 3–24). Washington, DC: National Science Teachers Association.

Kyle, W. C., Bonnstetter, R. J. McClosky, S., & Fults, B. A. (1985). Science through discovery: Students love it. *Science and Children, 23*(2), 39–41.

Lahey, M. (1988). *Language disorders and language development.* New York: Macmillan.

Lake, J. C. (1987). Calling all letters. *The Reading Teacher, 40,* 815.

Lambert, N., Nihira, K., & Leland, H. (1993). AAMR adaptive behavior scale—school (2nd ed.). Austin, TX: Pro-Ed.

Lambie, R. A. (1980). A systematic approach for changing materials, instruction, and assignments to meet individual needs. *Focus on Exceptional Children, 12*(1), 1–12.

Landers, M. F. (1984). Helping the LD child with homework: Ten tips. *Academic Therapy, 20,* 209–215.

Langone, J. (1998). Managing inclusive instructional settings: Technology, cooperative planning, and team-based organization. *Focus on Exceptional Children, 30*(8), 1–15.

Langone, J. (1990). *Teaching students with mild and moderate learning problems.* Boston: Allyn & Bacon.

Larsen, S. C., & Hammill, D. D. (1976). *Test of Written Spelling.* Austin, TX: Pro-Ed.

Larsen, S. C., & Hammill, D. D. (1989). *Test of Legible Handwriting.* Austin, TX: Pro-Ed.

Larson, V. L. & McKinley, N. (1995). *Language disorders in older students: Preadolescents and adolescents.* Eau Claire, WI: Thinking Publications.

Larson, V. L., & McKinley, N. L. (1987). *Communication assessment and intervention strategies for adolescents.* Eau Claire, WI: Thinking Publications.

Lasky, E., & Cox, L. (1983). Auditory processing and language interactions: Evaluation and intervention strategies. In E. Lasky & J. Katz (Eds.), *Central auditory processing disorders: Problems of speech, language, and learning* (pp. 243–268). Austin, TX: Pro-Ed.

Lasley, T. J., & Walker, R. (1986). Time on-task: How teachers can use class time more effectively. *National Association of Secondary School Principals Bulletin, 70,* 59–64.

Laughlin, M. K., & Kardaleff, P. P. (1991). *Literature-based social studies: Children's books and activities to enrich the K-5 curriculum.* Phoenix, AZ: Oryx Press.

Lawton, M. (1999). Co-teaching: Are two heads better than one in an inclusion classroom? *Harvard Education Letter, 15*(2), 1-4.

Lazzari, A. M. (1991). *The transition sourcebook: A practical guide for early intervention programs.* Tucson, AZ: Communication Skill Builders.

Learning Disabilities Association (1999a). *Fact sheet: Spoken language problems.* [WWW document]. *http://www.ldanatl.org/factsheet/Spoken.html*

Learning Disabilities Association of America (1999b). *Speech & language milestone chart.* [WWW document]. *http://www.ldonline.org_indepth/speech-language/lda-milestones.html*

Leavell, A., & Ioannides, A. (1993). Using character development to improve story writing. *Teaching Exceptional Children, 25*(4), 41-45.

Leitner, R. K., & Bishop, K. (Ed.). (1989). *Competency-based training for job coaches: A self-guided study course for trainers in supported employment.* San Francisco: University of San Francisco, California Supported Employment Training Project.

Lenz, B. K., Bulgren, J. A., Schumaker, J. B., Deshler, D. D., & Boudah, D. A. (1994). *The unit organizer routine.* Lawrence, KS: Edge Enterprises, Inc

Lenz, B. K., Marrs, R. W., Schumaker, J. B., & Deshler, D. D. (1993). *The lesson organizer routine.* Lawrence, KS: Edge Enterprises, Inc.

Lenz, B. K., Schumaker, J. B., Deshler, D. D., & Bulgren, J. A. (1998). *The course organizer routine.* Lawrence, KS: Edge Enterprises, Inc.

Lerner, J. W. (1996). *Learning disabilities: Theories, diagnosis, and teaching strategies.* Boston: Houghton Mifflin.

Lettau, J. H. (1975). *3-R math readiness.* Upper Saddle River, NJ: Prentice Hall Learning Systems.

Leverentz, F., & Garman, D. (1987). What was that you said? *Instructor, 96,* 66-77.

Levine, M. D. (1990). *Keeping ahead in school.* Cambridge, MA: Educators Publishing Service.

Levy, N. R. (1996). Teaching analytical writing: Help for general education middle school teachers. *Intervention in School and Clinic, 32,* 95-103.

Lewis, R. B., & Doorlag, D. H. (1998). *Teaching special students in the mainstream.* Upper Saddle River, NJ: Merrill/Prentice Hall.

Lewis, R. B., & Doorlag, D. H. (1999). *Teaching special students in general education classrooms* (5th ed.). Upper Saddle River, NJ: Merrill/Prentice Hall.

Liberman, R. P., King, L. W., DeRisi, W. J., & McCann, M. (1975). Personal effectiveness: *Guiding people to assert themselves and improve their social skills.* Champaign, IL: Research Press.

Libet, J. M., & Lewinsohn, P. M. (1973). Concept of social skill with special reference to the behavior of depressed persons. *Journal of Consulting and Clinical Psychology, 40,* 304-312.

Lindamood, C., & Lindamood, P. (1998a). *Lindamood auditory conceptualization test.* Austin, TX: Pro-Ed.

Lindamood, C., & Lindamood, P. (1998b). *The Lindamood program for reading, spelling, and speech.* Austin, TX: Pro-Ed.

Lindsey, J. D. (2000). *Technology end exceptional individuals.* Austin: Pro-Ed.

Lindsley, O. R. (1964). Direct measurement and prosthesis of retarded behavior. *Journal of Education, 147,* 62-81.

Livermore, S. (1996). A flagged town and a long winding road: Art for Learning disabled students. *School Arts, 95*(9), 16-18.

Lloyd, J. W., Forness, S. R., & Kavale, K. A. (1998). Some methods are more effective than others. *Intervention in School and Clinic, 33,* 195-200.

Lloyd, J. W., Landrum, T., & Hallahan, D. P. (1991). Self-monitoring applications for classroom intervention. In Stoner, G., Shinn, M. R., & Walker, H. M. (Eds.), *Interventions for achievement and behavior problems* (pp. 201-213). Washington, DC: National Association of School Psychologists.

Locke, E. T., & Abbey, D. E. (1989). A unique equation: Learning strategies and generalization = success. *Academic Therapy, 24,* 569-575.

Loeb, D. F. (1997). Diagnostic and descriptive assessment. In L. McCormick, D. F. Loeb, & R. L. Schiefelbusch (Eds.), *Supporting children with communication disorders in inclusive settings: School-based language intervention* (pp. 179-222). Boston: Allyn & Bacon.

Logging in. (1994, November 16). *Education Week, 14*(11), 2.

A long way to go. (1995, November/December). *Teacher Magazine, 17.*

Lorenz, L., & Yockell, E. (1979). Using the neurological impress method with learning-disabled readers. *Journal of Learning Disabilities, 12,* 67-69.

Lovano-Kerr, J., & Savage, S. L. (1976). Survey of art programs and art experiences for the mentally retarded in Indiana. *Education and Training of the Mentally Retarded, 11,* 200-211.

Lovejoy, M. C., & Routh, D. K. (1988). Behavior-disordered children's social skills: Increased by training, but not sustained or reciprocated. *Child & Family Behavior Therapy, 10,* 15-27.

Lovitt, T. C. (1975). Applied behavior analysis and learning disabilities: Part 2. *Journal of Learning Disabilities, 8,* 504-518.

Lovitt, T. C., Fister, S., & Kemp, K. (1988, October). *Translating research on effective instruction into secondary classrooms.* Presentation at CLD 10th Annual Conference on Learning Disabilities, Louisville, KY.

Lovitt, T. C., & Horton, S. V. (1991). Adapting textbooks for mildly handicapped adolescents. In G. Stoner, M. R. Shinn, & H. M. Walker (Eds.), *Interventions for achievement and behavior problems* (pp. 439-471). Silver Spring, MD: National Association of School Psychologists.

Luckasson, R., et al. (1992). *Mental retardation: Definition, classification, and systems of support* (9th ed.). Washington, DC: American Association of Mental Retardation.

Lynch, E. M., & Jones, S. D. (1989). Process and product: A review of the research on LD children's writing skills. *Learning Disability Quarterly, 12,* 74-86.

Lyon, G. R. (1995, May). *Research in learning disabilities supported by the National Institute of Child Health Human Development.* Presentation to Subcommittee on Disability Policy, Committee on Labor Human Resources, United States Senate. Unpublished manuscript.

MacArthur, C., Schwartz, S., & Graham, S. (1991). Effects of a reciprocal peer revision strategy in special education classrooms. *Learning Disabilities Research and Practice, 6,* 201-210.

MacArthur, C. A., Graham, D., & Skarvold, J. (1986). *Learning-disabled students, composing with three methods: Handwriting, dictation, and word processing* (Research report #109). College Park: University of Maryland, Institute for the Study of Exceptional Children and Youth.

Macciomei, N. R. (1995). Loss and grief awareness: A Class Book project. *Teaching Exceptional Children, 28*(2), 72-73.

Machart, N. C. (1987). Creating an opportunity for student-teacher reading conferences. *The Reading Teacher, 40,* 488-489.

MacMillan, D. L., Forness, S., & Trumbull, J. (1973). The role of punishment in the classroom. *Exceptional Children, 40,* 85-96.

Maguire, J. (1985). *Creative storytelling: Choosing, inventing, and sharing tales for children.* New York: McGraw-Hill.

Maker, C. J., & Nielson, A. B. (1996). *Curriculum development and teaching strategies for gifted learners* (2nd ed.). Austin, TX: Pro-Ed.

Male, M. (1991). Cooperative learning and computers: Maximizing instructional power with minimal equipment. *ConnSENSL Bulletin, 8*(1), 12-13.

Mandlebaum, L. H., Lightbourne, L., & VandenBrock, J. (1994). Teaching with literature. *Intervention in School and Clinic, 29,* 134-150.

Mandlebaum, L. H., & Wilson, R. (1989). Teaching listening skills in the special education classroom. *Academic Therapy, 24*(4), 449-459.

Mann, P., Suiter, P., & McClung, R. (1979). *Handbook in diagnostic-prescriptive teaching.* Boston: Allyn & Bacon.

Manning, M. L. (1986). Responding to renewed emphasis on handwriting. *The Clearing House, 59,* 211-213.

Manning, M. L., & Lucking, R. (1991). The what, why, and how of cooperative learning. *The Social Studies, 80,* 173-175.

Mannix, D. (1987). *Oral language activities for special children.* West Nyack, NY: The Center for Applied Research in Education.

Markwardt, F. C. (1989). *Peabody Individual Achievement Test—Revised.* Circle Pines, MN: American Guidance Service.

Maroney, S. A., & Searcy, S. (1996b). Real teachers don't plan that way. *Exceptionality, 6,* 197-200.

Marshall, O. W., & Tomcala, M. J. (1981, August). *Effects of different genres of music on stress levels.* Paper presented at the 89th annual meeting of the American Psychological Association, Los Angeles, CA. (ERIC Document Reproduction Service No. 255 883)

Marston, D., Deno, S. L., Kim, D., Diment, K., & Rogers, D. (1995). Comparison of reading intervention approaches for students with mild disabilities. *Exceptional Children, 62,* 20-37.

Martin, B. (1983). *Brown bear, brown bear, what do you see?* New York: Scholastic.

Martin, E. W. (1986). Some thoughts on transition: A current appraisal. In L. G. Perlman & G. F. Austin (Eds.), *The transition to work and independence for youth with disabilities* (pp. 107–117). Alexandria, VA: National Rehabilitation Association.

Martin, G., & Pear, J. (1992). *Behavior modification: What it is and how to do it* (4th ed.). Upper Saddle River, NJ: Prentice Hall.

Martin, J. E., & Huber-Marshall L. (1995). ChoiceMaker: A comprehensive self-determination transition program. *Intervention in School and Clinic, 30*(3), 147–156.

Massialas, B. G. (1989). The inevitability of issue-centered discourse in the classroom. *The Social Studies, 80,* 173–175.

Masters, L. F., & Mori, A. A. (1986). *Teaching secondary students with mild learning and behavior problems.* Rockville, MD: Aspen.

Masters, L. F., Mori, B. A., & Mori, A. A. (1999) *Teaching secondary students with mild learning and behavior problems* (3rd ed.). Austin, TX: Pro-Ed.

Mastropieri, M. A., & Scruggs, T. E. (1989). Reconstructive elaborations: Strategies for adapting content area information. *Academic Therapy, 24,* 394–397.

Mastropieri, M. A., & Scruggs, T. E. (1993). *A practical guide for teaching science to students with special needs in inclusive settings.* Austin, TX: Pro-Ed.

Mastropieri, M. A., & Scruggs, T. E. (1994). *Effective instruction for special education* (2nd ed.). Austin, TX: Pro-Ed.

Mastropieri, M. A., & Scruggs, T. E. (1994). Text-based vs. hands-on science curriculum: Implications for students with disabilities. *Remedial and Special Education, 15,* 72–85.

Mastropieri, M. A., & Scruggs, T. E. (1995). Teaching science to students with disabilities in general education settings. *Teaching Exceptional Children, 27*(4), 10–13.

Mastropieri, M. A., & Scruggs, T. E., (1997). Best practices in promoting reading comprehension in students with learning disabilities. *Remedial and Special Education, 18,* 197–213.

Mather, N. (1992). Whole language reading instruction for students with learning disabilities: Caught in the cross fire. *Learning Disabilities Research & Practice, 7,* 87–95.

Matson, J. L., DiLorenzo, T. M., & Esveldt-Dawson, K. (1981). Independence training as a method of enhancing self-help skills acquisition of the mentally retarded. *Behavior Research and Therapy, 19,* 399–405.

McBride, J. W., & Forgnone, C. (1985). Emphasis of instruction provided LD, EH, and EMR students in categorical and cross-categorical programming. *Journal of Research and Development in Education, 18*(4), 50–54.

McCarl, J. J., Svobodny, L., & Beare, P. L. (1991). Self-recording in a classroom for students with mild to moderate mental handicaps: Effects on productivity and on-task behavior. *Education and Training in Mental Retardation, 26,* 79–88.

McClure, A. A. (1985). Predictable books: Another way to teach reading to learning disabled children. *Teaching Exceptional Children 17,* 267–273.

McCombs, B. L., & Marzano, R. J. (1990). Putting the self in self-regulated learning: The self in integrating will and skill. *Educational Psychologist, 25,* 51–70.

McConnell, M. E., Hilvitz, P. B., & Cox, C. J. (1998). Functional assessment: A systematic process for assessment and intervention in general and special education classrooms. *Intervention in School and Clinic, 34,* 10–20.

McConnell, S. (1987). Entrapment effects and the generalization and maintenance of social skills training for elementary school students with behavioral disorders. *Behavioral Disorders 12,* 252–263.

McCord, J., & Haynes, W. (1988). Discourse errors in students with learning disabilities and their normally achieving peers: Molar versus molecular views. *Journal of Learning Disabilities, 21,* 237–243.

McCormick, L. (1997a). Ecological assessment and planning. In L. McCormick, D. F. Loeb, & R. L. Schiefelbusch (Eds.), *Supporting children with communication disorders in inclusive settings: School-based language intervention* (pp. 223–256). Boston: Allyn & Bacon.

McCormick, L. (1997b). Language intervention and support. In L. McCormick, D. F. Loeb, & R. L. Schiefelbusch (Eds.), *Supporting children with communication disorders in inclusive settings: School-based language intervention* (pp. 257–306). Boston: Allyn & Bacon.

McCormick, L., & Kawate, J. (1982). Kindergarten survival skills: New directions for preschool special education. *Education and Training of the Mentally Retarded, 17,* 247–252.

McEvoy, M. A., Shores, R. E., Wehby, J. H., Johnson, S. M., & Fox, J. J. (1990). Special education teachers, implementation of procedures to promote social interactions among children in integrated settings. *Education and Training in Mental Retardation, 25*(3), 267-275.

McFall, R. M., & Dodge, K. A. (1982). Self-management and interpersonal skills learning. In P. Karoly & F. H. Kanfer (Eds.), *Self-management and behavior change: From theory to practice.* New York: Pergamon Press.

McGinnis, E., Goldstein, A. P., Sprafkin, R. P., & Gershaw, N. J. (1984). *Skillstreaming the elementary school child: A guide for teaching prosocial skills.* Champaign, IL: Research Press.

McGowan, T., & Guzzetti, B. (1991). Promoting social studies understanding through literature-based instruction. *The Social Studies, 82,* 16-21.

McKay, B., & Sullivan, J. (1990, April 23-27). *Effective collaboration: The student assistance team model.* Paper presented at the 68th Annual Convention of the Council for Exceptional Children, Toronto, Canada. (ERIC Document Reproduction Service NO. ED 322 695.)

McKenzie, R. G. (1991a). Content area instruction by secondary learning disabilities in teachers: A national survey. *Learning Disability Quarterly, 14,* 115-122.

McKenzie, R. G. (1991b). Developing study skills through cooperative learning activities. *Intervention, 26,* 227-229.

McKenzie, R. G. (1991c). The form and substance of secondary resource models: Content area vs. skills instruction. *Journal of Learning Disabilities, 24,* 467-470.

McKenzie, R. G., & Houk, C. S. (1993). Across the great divide: Transition from elementary to secondary settings for students with mild disabilities. *Teaching Exceptional Children, 25*(2), 16-20.

McLaughlin, T. F., Krappman, V. F., & Welsh, J. M. (1985). The effects of self-recording for on-task behavior of behaviorally disordered special education students. *Remedial and Special Education, 6*(4), 42-45.

McLaughlin, T. F., & Skinner, C. H. (1996). Improving academic performance through self-management: Cover, copy and compare. *Intervention in School and Clinic, 32,* 113-118.

McLoughlin, J. A., & Lewis, R. B. (1994). *Assessing special students: Strategies and procedures.* Upper Saddle River, NJ: Merrill/Prentice Hall.

McNaughton, D., Hughes, C. A., & Clark, K. (1994). Spelling instruction for students with learning disabilities: Implications for research and practice. *Learning Disability Quarterly, 17,* 169-185.

McNinch, G. H. (1981). A method for teaching sight words to disabled readers. *The Reading Teacher, 34,* 269-272.

McNutt, G. (1984). A holistic approach to language arts instruction in the resource room. *Learning Disability Quarterly, 7,* 315-320.

McNutt, G., & Mandlebaum, L. H. (1980). General assessment competencies for special education teachers. *Exceptional Education Quarterly, 1*(3), 21-29.

McTighe, J., & Lyman, F. G., Jr. (1988). Cueing thinking in the classroom: The promise of theory-embedded tools. *Educational Leadership, 47*(7), 18-24.

Medina, V. (1982). *Issues regarding the use of interpreters and translators in a school setting.* (ERIC Document Reproduction Services No. ED 329 454)

Meehan, K. A., & Hodell, S. (1986). Measuring the impact of vocational assessment activities upon program decisions. *Career Development for Exceptional Individuals, 9,* 106-112.

Meichenbaum, D. (1983). Teaching thinking: A cognitive-behavioral approach. In *Interdisciplinary voices in learning disabilities and remedial education* (pp. 127-155). Austin, TX: Pro-Ed.

Memory, D. M., & McGowan, T. M. (1985). Using multi-level textbooks in social studies classes. *The Social Studies, 76,* 174-179.

Memory, D. M., & Uhlhorn, K. W. (1991). Multiple textbooks at different readability levels in the science classroom. *School Science and Mathematics, 91,* 64-72.

Mercer, C. D. (1979). *Students with learning disabilities.* Columbus, OH: Merrill.

Mercer, C. D., & Mercer, A. R. (1996). *Teaching students with learning problems* (3rd ed.). Upper Saddle River, NJ: Merrill/Prentice Hall.

Merritt, D. D., & Culatta, B. (1998) *Language intervention in the classroom.* San Diego: Singular Publishing.

Meyen, E. L., & Lehr, D. H. (1980). Evolving practices in assessment and intervention for mildly handicapped adolescents: The case for intensive instruction. *Exceptional Education Quarterly, 1*(2), 19-26.

Meyen, E. L., Vergason, G. A., & Whelan, R. J. (Eds.), (1983). *Promising practices for exceptional children: Curriculum implications.* Denver, CO: Love.

Meyer, L. A. (1984). Long-term academic effects of the direct instruction project Follow-Through. *The Elementary School Journal, 84,* 380-394.

Michael, A. (1989). *The transition from language theory to therapy: Test of two instructional methods.* Unpublished doctoral dissertation. Vanderbilt University. Nashville, TN.

Michaels, K. (1988). Caution: Second wave reform taking place. *Educational Leadership, 45*(5), 3.

Miles, D. D., & Forcht, J. P. (1995). Mathematics strategies for secondary students with learning disabilities or mathematics deficiencies: A cognitive approach. *Intervention in School and Clinic, 31,* 91-96.

Miller, S. D., & Brand, M. (1983). Music in other cultures in the classroom. *The Social Studies, 74,* 62-64.

Miller, Susan P., Butler, F. M., & Lee Kit-hung. (1998). Validated practices for teaching mathematics to students with learning disabilities: A review of literature. *Focus on Exceptional Children, 30,* 1-16.

Mira, M. P., Tucker, B. F., & Tyler, J. S. (1992). *Traumatic brain injury in children and adolecents: A sourcebook for teachers and other school personnel.* Austin, TX: Pro-Ed.

Modolfsky, P. B. (1983). Teaching students to determine the central story problem: A practical application of schema theory. *The Reading Teacher, 36,* 740-745.

Montague, M., & Graves, A. (1993). Improving students, story writing. *Teaching Exceptional Children, 25*(4), 36-40.

Montague, M., & Leavell, A. G. (1994). Improving the narrative writing of students with learning disabilities. *Remedial and Special Education, 15,* 21-33.

Montague, M., & Warger, C. (1997). Helping students with attention deficit hyperactivity disorder succeed in the classroom. *Focus on Exceptional Children, 30*(4), 1-16.

Moody, S. W., Vaughn, S., & Schumm, J. S., (1997). Instructional grouping for reading: Teachers, views. *Remedial and Special Education, 18,* 347-356.

Moore, J. E., & Camilli, T. (1991). *Exploring science through literature.* Monterey, CA: Evan-Moor.

Moos, R. (1976). *The human context: Environmental determinants of behavior.* New York: Wiley.

Moran, M. R. (1983). Analytical evaluation of formal written language skills as a diagnostic procedure. *Diagnostique, 8,* 17-31.

Morgan, D. L., & Guilford, A. M. (1984). *Adolescent Language Screening Test.* Austin, TX: Pro-Ed.

Morgan, K. B. (1995). Creative phonics: A meaning-oriented reading program. *Intervention in School and Clinic, 30,* 287-291.

Morocco, C., & Neuman, S. (1987). *Teachers, children, and the magical writing machine.* Newton, MA: Education Development Center.

Morris, L. (1991). *Creative movement activities for students with disabilities.* Paper presented at the annual Florida Council of Exceptional Children conference. Daytona, FL.

Moses, B. (1983). Individual differences in problem solving. *Arithmetic Teacher, 30*(4), 10-14.

Mullins, J., Joseph, F., Turner, C., Zawadski, R., & Saltzman, L. (1972). A handwriting model for children with learning disabilities. *Journal of Learning Disabilities, 5,* 306-311.

Munk, D. D., Bruckert, J., Call, D. T., Stoehrmann, T., & Radant, E. (1998). Strategies for enhancing the performance of students with LD in inclusive science classes. *Intervention in School and Clinic, 34*(2), 73-78.

Munson, S. M. (1987). Regular education teacher modifications for mainstreamed mildly handicapped students. *Journal of Special Education, 20,* 489-502.

Myers, P. I. (1987). *Assessing the oral language development and intervention needs of students.* Austin, TX: Pro-Ed.

Nakashima, J. C., & Patton, J. R. (1989). An integrated approach to teaching exceptional learners. *Science and Children, 27,* 48-50.

National Coalition of Advocates for Students. (1985). *Barriers to excellence: Our imperative for educational reform.* Washington, DC: U.S. Department of Education.

National Commission on Excellence in Education. (1983). *A nation at risk.* Washington, DC: U.S. Department of Education.

National Council for the Social Studies. (1994). *Curriculum standards for social studies: Expectations of excellence.* Washington, DC: Author.

National Council of Supervisors of Mathematics. (1977). Position paper on basic mathematical skills. *The Arithmetic Teacher, 25,* 19-22.

National Council of Teachers of Mathematics (1991). *Professional standards for teaching mathematics.* Reston, VA: Author.

National Council of Teachers of Mathematics. (1980). *An agenda for action: Recommendations for school mathematics of the 1980s.* Reston, VA: Author.

National Council of Teachers of Mathematics. (1989). *Curriculum and evaluation standards for school mathematics.* Reston, VA: Author.

National Joint Committee on Learning Disabilities. (1990). *Learning disabilities: Issues on definition.* Unpublished manuscript.

National Research Council. (1996). *National science education standards.* Washington, DC: National Academy Press.

Neel, R. S., Meadows, N., Levine, P., & Edgar, E. B. (1988). What happens after special education: A statewide follow-up study of secondary students who have behavioral disorders. *Behavioral Disorders, 13,* 209–216.

Nelson, C. M., & Rutherford, R. B. (1983). Time-out revisited: Guidelines for its use in special education. *Exceptional Education Quarterly, 3*(4), 56–67.

Nelson, N. W. (1998). *Childhood language disorders in context: Infancy through adolescence.* Boston: Allyn & Bacon.

Nelson, J. S., Epstein, M. H., Bursuck, W. D., Jayanthi, M., & Sawyer, V. (1998). The preferences of middle school students for homework adaptations made by general education teachers. *Learning Disabilities Research & Practice, 13,* 109–117.

Nelson, J. R., Smith, D. J., Young, R. K., & Dodd, J. M. (1991). A review of self-management outcome research conducted with students who exhibit behavioral disorders. *Behavioral Disorders, 16,* 169–179.

Nelson, J. R., Crabtree, M., Marchand-Martella, N., & Martella, R. (1998). Teaching good behavior in the whole school. *Teaching Exceptional Children, 30*(4), 4–9.

Nelson, N. W. (1989). Curriculum-based language assessment and intervention. *Language Speech, and Hearing Services in School, 20,* 170–183.

Nelson, N. W. (1993). *Childhood language disorders in context: Infancy through adolescence.* Upper Saddle River, NJ: Merrill/Prentice Hall.

Nelson, R. O., Lipinski, D. P., & Boykin, R. A. (1978). The effects of self-recorders, training and the obtrusiveness of the self-recording device on the accuracy and reactivity of self-monitoring. *Behavior Therapy, 9,* 200–208.

Nelson, N. W. (1993). *Childhood language disorders in context: Infancy through adolescence.* Upper Saddle River, NJ: Merrill/Prentice Hall.

Neville, D. D., & Hoffman, R. R. (1981). The effect of personalized stories on the cloze comprehension of seventh grade retarded readers. *Journal of Reading, 24,* 475–478.

Nevin, A., Thousand, J., Paolucci-Whitcomb, P., & Villa, R. (1990). Collaborative consultation: Empowering public school personnel to provide heterogeneous schooling for all or, Who rang that bell? *Journal of Educational and Psychological Consultation, 1,* 41–67.

Newcomer, P. L. (1990). *Diagnostic Achievement Battery-2.* Austin, TX: Pro-Ed.

Newcomer, P. L. & Hammill, D. D. (1991). *Test of Language Development—Primary.* Austin, TX: Pro-Ed.

Newcomer, P. L., & Hammill, D. D. (1991). *Test of Language Development—Intermediate.* Austin, TX: Pro-Ed.

Nezu, A., & D'Zurilla, T. J. (1981). Effects of problem definition and formulation of decision making in the social problem-solving process. *Behavior Therapy, 12,* 100–106.

Nibbelink, W. H., & Witzenberg, H. G. (1981). A comparison of two methods for teaching younger children to tell time. *School Science and Mathematics, 81,* 429–435.

Nickell, P., & Kennedy, M. (1987). How to do it: Global perspectives through children's games. *Social Education, 51*(3), 1–8.

Nihira, K., Foster, R., Shellhaas, M., & Leland, H. (1974). *AAMD Adaptive behavior scale manual.* Washington, DC: American Association of Mental Deficiency.

Nolan, K., & Polloway, E. A. (1993). *The use of reconstructive elaborations: Applications in science instruction.* ERIC Document Reproduction Service (No. ED 350 770).

Nolet, V., & Tindal, G. (1993). Special education in content area classes: Development of a model and practical procedures. *Remedial and Special Education, 14*(1), 36–48.

Norris, J., & Hoffman, P. (1993). *Whole language intervention for school-aged children.* San Diego, CA: Singular.

Norton, D. E. (1985). *The effective teaching of language arts* (2nd ed.). Upper Saddle River, NJ: Merrill/Prentice Hall.

Notari-Syverson, A., & Losardo, A. (1996). Curriculum-based assessment. In K. Cole, P. Dale, & D. Thal (Eds.), *Advances in assessment of communication and language.* Baltimore, MD: Paul H. Brookes.

Nowacek, E. J. (1991). Cooperative learning. *VCLD Journal, 2*(1), 3–4.

Nowak, F. (1981). *Musart.* Paper presented at the Utica Department of Education, Seminar in Resource Teaching, Utica, NY.

O'Leary, K. D., & Drabman, R. (1971). Token reinforcement programs in the classrooms: A review. *Psychological Bulletin, 75,* 379–398.

Oak Ridge Associated Universities. (1978). *Solar energy.* Oak Ridge, TN: U.S. Department of Energy.

Oberlin, L. (1982). How to teach children to hate mathematics. *School Science & Mathematics, 82,* 261.

Ochoa, A. S., & Shuster, S. K. (1980). *Social studies in the mainstreamed classroom, K-6.* Boulder, CO: Social Science Education Consortium.

Oi, A. K. (1988). *Art and special education.* Unpublished master's paper, University of Hawaii.

Okolo, C. M. (1993). Computers and individuals with mild disabilities. In J. D. Lindsey (Ed.), *Computers and exceptional individuals* (2nd ed., pp. 111-114).

Oliva, P. F., & Henson, K. T. (1980). What are the essential generic teaching competencies? *Theory into Practice, 19,* 117-121.

Oliver, P. R. (1983). Effects of teaching different tasks in group versus individual training formats with severely handicapped individuals. *Journal of the Association for Persons with Severe Handicaps, 8,* 79-91.

Oliver, P. R., & Scott, T. L. (1981). Group versus individual training in establishing generalization of language skills with severely handicapped individuals. *Mental Retardation, 19,* 285-289.

Olson, L. (1994, June 15). Writing still needs work, report finds. *Education Week, 13*(38), 1, 10.

Olson, L. (1995, February 8). Student's best writing needs work, study shows. *Education Week,* 5.

O'Neil, J. (1994, June). Rewriting the book on literature. *Curriculum Update,* 5.

O'Neill, B. (1994). The invention of the school discipline lists: A concocted story of myths about public education passed down. *The School Administrator, 51*(11), 8-11.

Orelove, F. P. (1982). Acquisition of incidental learning in moderately and severely handicapped adults. *Education and Training of the Mentally Retarded, 17,* 131-136.

Orkwis, R., & McLane, K. (1998). *A curriculum every student can use: Design principles for student access.* ERIC/OSEP Topical Brief, Reston, VA: Council for Exceptional Children.

Orton, J. L. (1964). *A guide to teaching phonics.* Winston-Salem, NC: Orton Reading Center.

Osborn, R., Curlin, L., & Hill, G. (1979). Revision of the NCSS social studies curriculum guidelines. *Social Education, 43,* 261-273.

Osborne, A. G., & Dimattia, P. (1994). The IDEA's least restrictive environment mandate: Legal implications. *Exceptional Children, 61,* 6-14.

O'Shea, D. J., Williams, A. L., & Sattler, R. O. (1999). Collaboration across special education and general education: Preservice teachers, views. *Journal of Teacher Education, 50*(2), 147-157.

Owens, R. E. (1999). *Language disorders* (3rd ed.). Boston: Allyn & Bacon.

Owens, R. E. (1995). *Language disorders* (2nd ed.) Boston: Allyn & Bacon.

Oyama, E. (1986). *Curricular integration through a basal reading series.* Unpublished master's paper. Honolulu: University of Hawaii.

Palincsar, A. S. (1986). Metacognitive strategy instruction. *Exceptional Children, 53,* 118-124.

Palincsar, A. S., Brown, A., & Campione, A. (1994). Models and practices of dynamic assessment. In G. P. Wallach & K. G. Butler (Eds.), *Language learning disabilities in school-age children and adolescents.* New York: Merrill/Macmillan.

Paris, S. G., & Newman, R. S. (1990). Developmental aspects of self-regulated learning. *Educational Psychologist, 25,* 87-105.

Parks, B. J. (1976). Career development—How early? *Elementary School Journal, 76,* 468-474.

Parmer, R., Cawley, J. F., & Miller, J. H. (1994). Differences in mathematics performance between students with learning disabilities and students with mental retardation. *Exceptional Children, 60,* 549-563.

Partin, R. L. (1998). *The Prentice Hall directory of online social studies resources: 1000 of the most valuable social studies web sites, electronic mailing lists and newsgroups.* Paramus, NJ: Prentice Hall.

Pascale, L. (1993). *Multi-arts resource guide.* Boston: Very Special Arts Massachusetts. (ERIC Document Reproduction Service No. 370 330).

Passe, J., & Beattie, J. (1994). Social studies instruction for students with mild disabilities: A progress report. *Remedial and Special Education, 15,* 227-233.

Patton, J. R. (1988). Science. In G. Robinson, J. R. Patton, E. A. Polloway, & L. R. Sargent (Eds.), *Best practices in mental disabilities* (vol. 2, pp. 325-349). Des Moines, IA: Iowa Department of Education, Bureau of Special Education.

Patton, J. R. (1993). Individualization for science and social studies. In J. Wood (Ed.), *Mainstreaming: A practical approach for teachers* (2nd ed., pp. 366-413). Upper Saddle River, NJ: Merrill/ Prentice Hall.

Patton, J. R. (1994). Practical recommendations for using homework with students with learning disabilities. *Journal of Learning Disabilities, 27,* 570-578.

Patton, J. R. (1995). Teaching science to students with special needs. *Teaching Exceptional Children, 27* (4), 4-6.

Patton, J. R., Blackbourn, J. M., & Fad, K. (1996). *Exceptional individuals in focus* (2nd ed.). Upper Saddle River, NJ: Merrill/Prentice Hall.

Patton, J. R., & Browder, P. (1988). Transitions into the future. In B. Ludlow, R. Luckasson, & A. Turnbull (Eds.), *Transitions to adult life for persons with mental retardation: Principles and practices* (pp. 293-311). Baltimore: Paul H. Brookes.

Patton, J. R., Cronin, M. E., Bassett, D., & Koppel, A. E. (1997). Preparing students with learning disabilities for the real math demands of adulthood: A life skills orientation to mathematics instruction. *Journal of Learning Disabilities, 30,* 178-187.

Patton, J. R., Cronin, M. E., & Wood, S. (1999). *Infusing real-life topics into existing curricula at the elementary, middle, and high school levels: Recommended procedures and instructional examples.* Austin, TX: Pro-Ed.

Patton, J. R., & Dunn, C. (1996). *Transition from school to young adulthood for students with special needs: Basic concepts and recommended practices.* Unpublished manuscript.

Patton, J. R., & Dunn, C. (1998) *Transition from school to young adulthood: Basic concepts and recommended practices.* Austin, TX: Pro-Ed.

Patton, J. R., Polloway, E. A., & Cronin, M. E. (1986). *Science education for students with mild disabilities: A status report.* (ERIC Document Reproduction Service No. ED 370 329).

Patton, J. R., Polloway, E. A., & Cronin, M. E. (1987). Social studies instruction for handicapped students: A review of current practices. *The Social Studies, 71,* 131-135.

Patton, J. R., Polloway, E. A., & Cronin, M. E. (1994). *Science education for students with mild disabilities: A status report.* Austin, TX: Learning for Living (ERIC Document Reproduction Service No. ED 370 329).

Patton, J. R., Polloway, E. A., & Smith, T. E. C. (2000). Educating students with mild mental retardation. In M. L. Wehmeyer & J. R. Patton (Eds), *Mental retardation and the 21st century.* Austin, TX: Pro-Ed.

Patton, J. R., Polloway, E. A., Smith, T. E. C., Clark, G., Edgar, E., & Lee, S. (1996). Individuals with mild retardation: Postsecondary outcomes and implications for educational policy. *Education and Training in Mental Retardation and Developmental Disabilities, 31,* 75-85.

Paul, R. (1995). *Language disorders from infancy through adolescence.* St. Louis, MO: Mosby.

Paulson, F. L., Paulson, P. R., & Mayer, C. A. (1991). What makes a portfolio a portfolio? *Educational Leadership, 48*(5), 60-63.

Payne, J. S. (1972). Teaching teachers and teaching mind readers. *Phi Delta Kappan, 53,* 375-376.

Pearson, V. L. (1987). Vocabulary building: Old word retirement. *Teaching Exceptional Children, 19*(2), 77.

Peck, C. A. (1989). Assessment of social communicative competence: Evaluating environments. *Seminars in Speech and Language, 10,* 1-15.

Peterson, D. L. (1972). *Functional mathematics for the mentally retarded.* Upper Saddle River, NJ: Merrill/Prentice Hall.

Pfeuffer-Guay, D. M. (1993a). Cross-site analysis of teaching practices: Visual art education with students experiencing disabilities. *Studies in Art Education, 34,* 222-232.

Pfeuffer-Guay, D. M. (1993b). Normalization in art with extra challenged students: A problem-solving framework. *Art Education, 46*(1), 58-63.

Pfiffner, L., & Barkley, R. (1990). Educational placement and classroom management. In R. Barkley (Ed.), *Attention deficit hyperactivity disorder: A handbook for diagnosis and treatment* (pp. 498-539). New York: Guilford.

Phelps-Gunn, T., & Phelps-Terasaki, D. (1982). *Written language instruction: Theory and remediation.* Rockville, MD: Aspen Systems.

Phelps-Terasaki, D., & Phelps, T. (1980). *Teaching written expression: The Phelps sentence guide program.* Novato, CA: Academic Therapy Publications.

Phelps-Terasaki, D., & Phelps-Gunn, T. (1988). *Teaching competence in written language: A systematic program for developing writing skills.* Austin, TX: Pro-Ed.

Phillips, E. L. (1978). *The social skills basis of psychopathology: Alternative to abnormal psychology and psychiatry.* New York: Grune & Stratton.

Phillips, E. L. (1985). Social skills: History and prospect. In L. L'Abate & M. A. Milan (Eds.), *Handbook of social skills: Training and research.* New York: Wiley.

Phillips, E. L., Phillips, E. A., Fixsen, D. L., & Wolf, M. M. (1974). *The teaching-family handbook.* Lawrence, KS: Beach Center on Families and Disability.

Pickett, A. L. (1989). *A training program to prepare teachers to supervise and work more effectively with paraprofessional personnel.* New York: City University of New York, National Resource Center for Paraprofessionals.

Pickett, A. L., Faison, K., & Formanek, J. (1993). *A core curriculum and training program to prepare paraeducators to work in inclusive classrooms serving school age students with disabilities.* New York: City University of New York.

Pickett, A. L., & Gerlach, K. (Eds.), (1997). *Supervising paraeducators in school settings.* Austin: Pro-Ed.

Platt, J. M., & Janeczko, D. (1991). Adapting art instruction for students with disabilities. *Teaching Exceptional Children, 24*(1), 10-12.

Polirstok, S. R. (1986). Training problematic adolescents as peer tutors: Benefits for the tutor and the school at large. Techniques: *Journal for Remedial Education and Counseling, 2,* 204-210.

Polloway, C. H., & Polloway, E. A. (1978). Expanding reading skills through syllabication. *Academic Therapy, 13,* 455-462.

Polloway, E. A., Bursuck, W. D., & Epstein, M. H. (in press). Homework for students with learning disabilities: Policies, practices, and problems. *Reading and Writing Quarterly.*

Polloway, E. A., Bursuck, W., Jayanthi, M., & Epstein, M. H. (1996). Treatment acceptability: Determining appropriate interventions within inclusive classrooms. *Intervention in School and Clinic, 31,* 133-144.

Polloway, E. A., Cronin, M. E., & Patton, J. R. (1986). The efficacy of group instruction vs. one-to-one instruction: A review. *Remedial and Special Education, 7*(1), 22-30.

Polloway, E. A., Epstein, M. H., Bursuck, W., Jayanthi, M. & Cumblad, C. (1994). A national survey of classroom homework practices with students with disabilities. *Journal of Learning Disabilities 27,* 500-509. (Reprinted in *Homework,* Pro-Ed, 1995).

Polloway, E. A., Epstein, M. H., Bursuck, W., Roderique, T., McConeghey, J., & Jayanthi, M. (1993). A national survey of classroom grading policies. *Remedial and Special Education, 15,* 162-170.

Polloway, E. A., Epstein, M. H., Polloway, C., Patton, J. R., & Ball, D. W. (1986). Corrective reading program: An analysis of effectiveness with learning disabled and mentally retarded students. *Remedial and Special Education, 7*(4), 41-47.

Polloway, E. A., Patton, J. R., & Cohen, S. B. (1983). Written language for mildly handicapped students. In E. L. Meyen, G. A. Vergason, & R. J. Whelan (Eds.), *Promising practices for exceptional children: Cur-* *riculum implications* (pp. 285-320). Denver, CO: Love.

Polloway, E. A., Patton, J. R., Epstein, M. H., & Smith, T. E. C. (1989). Comprehensive curriculum for students with mild handicaps. *Focus on Exceptional Children, 21*(8), 1-12.

Polloway, E. A., Patton, J. R., Smith, T. E. C., & Buck, G. H. (1997). Mental retardation and learning disabilities: Conceptual and applied issues. *Journal of Learning Disabilities, 30,* 297-308, 345.

Polloway, E. A., Patton, J. R., Smith, J. D., & Roderique, T. W. (1992). Issues in program design for elementary students with mild retardation: Emphasis on curriculum development. *Education and Training in Mental Retardation, 26,* 142-150.

Polloway, E. A., & Polloway, C. H. (1979). Auctions: Vitalizing the token economy. *Journal for Special Educators, 15,* 121-123.

Polloway, E. A., & Polloway, C. H. (1981). Survival words for disabled readers. *Academic Therapy, 16,* 443-448.

Polloway, E. A., & Smith, J. D. (1988). Current status of the mild mental retardation construct: Identification, placement, and programs. In M. C. Wang, M. C. Reynolds, & H. J. Walberg (Eds.), *The handbook of special education: Research and practice* (pp. 7-22). Oxford, England: Pergamon Press.

Polloway, E. A., Smith, J. P., Patton, J. R., & Smith, T. E. C. (1996). Historic changes in mental retardation and developmental disabilities. *Education and Training in Mental Retardation and Developmental Disabilities, 31,* 3-12.

Polloway, E. A., & Smith, T. E. C. (1999). *Language instruction for students with disabilities* (2nd ed., rev.). Denver, CO: Love Publishing.

Poteet, J., Choate, J. S. & Stewart, S. C. (1993). Perform assessment and special education: Practices and prospects. *Focus on Exceptional Children, 26*(1), 1-20.

Pottenger, F. M., & Young, D. B. (1992). *Foundational approaches in science teaching (FAST I Program).* Honolulu: Curriculum Research and Development Group, University of Hawaii. (ERIC Document Reproduction Service No. ED 365 549).

Potter, M. L., & Wamre, H. M. (1990). Curriculum-based measurement and developmental reading models: Opportunities for cross-validation. *Exceptional Children, 57,* 16-23.

Potter, S. (1978). Social studies for students with reading difficulties. *The Social Studies, 69,* 56-64.

Prater, M. A., Joy, R., Chilman, B., Temple, J., & Miller, S. R. (1991). Self-monitoring of on-task behavior by adolescents with learning disabilities. *Learning Disability Quarterly, 14,* 164-177.

Premack, D. (1959). Toward empirical behavior laws: I. Positive reinforcement. *Psychological Review, 66,* 219-233.

Prescott, G. A., Balow, I. H., Hogan, T. P., & Farr, R. (1984). *Metropolitan Achievement Tests.* San Antonio, TX: Psychological Corporation.

Pressley, M., & Rankin, J. (1994). More about whole language methods of reading instruction for students at risk for early reading failure. *Learning Disabilities Research & Practice, 9,* 157-168.

Price, M., Ness, J., & Stitt, M. (1982). Beyond the three R's: Science and social studies instruction for the mildly handicapped. In T. L. Miller & E. E. Davis (Eds.), *The mildly handicapped student* (pp. 367-370). New York: Grune & Stratton.

Prutting, C. A., & Kirchner, D. M. (1987). A clinical appraisal of the pragmatic aspects of language. *Journal of Speech and Hearing Disorders, 52,* 105-119.

Putnam, M. L., & Wesson, C. L. (1990). The teacher's role in teaching content-area information. *LD Focus, 16*(1), 55-60.

Quay, H. C., & Peterson, D. R. (1967). *Manual for the behavior problem checklist.* Champaign, IL: University of Illinois, Children's Research Center.

Raborn, D. T. (1988). *The effects of language of instruction and review-preview-review on science achievement for bilingual Hispanic handicapped students.* Unpublished dissertation. The University of New Mexico.

Raborn, D. T. & Daniel, M. J. (1999). Oobleck: A scientific encounter of the Special Education kind. *Teaching Exceptional Children, 31*(6), 32-40.

Rakes, T. A., & Choate, J. S. (1990). *Science and health: Detecting and correcting special needs.* Boston: Allyn & Bacon.

Ranieri, L., Ford, A., Vincent, L., & Brown, L. (1984). 1:1 versus 1:3 instruction of severely multihandicapped students. *Remedial and Special Education, 5*(5), 23-28.

Reed, V. A. (1986). *An introduction to children with language disorders.* New York: Macmillan.

Reed, V. A. (1994). *An introduction to children with language disorders* (2nd ed.). Upper Saddle River, NJ: Merrill/Prentice Hall.

Reeve, R. E. (1990). ADHD: Facts and fallacies. *Intervention in School and Clinic, 26,* 71-78.

Reeves, C. K. (1989). Designing a mainstreamed environment. In J. W. Wood (Ed.), *Mainstreaming: A practical approach for teachers.* Upper Saddle River, NJ: Merrill/Prentice Hall.

Reid, D. K., Baker, G., Lasell, C., & Easton, S. (1993). Teaching reading comprehension to special needs learners: What matters? *Intervention in School and Clinic, 28,* 198-215.

Reid, D. K., & Kuykendall, M. (1996). In D. K. Reid, W. P. Hresko, & H. L. Swanson. (Eds.), *Cognitive approaches to learning disabilities,* (3rd. ed.). Austin, TX: Pro-Ed.

Reid, R., Schmidt, T., Harris, K., & Graham, S. (1997). Cognitive strategy instruction: Developing self-regulated learners. *Reclaiming Children and Youth, 6,* 97-102.

Reisman, F. K., & Kauffman, S. H. (1980). Teaching mathematics to children with special needs. Upper Saddle River, NJ: Merrill/Prentice Hall.

Renzulli, J. S. (1994). *Schools for talent development: A practical plan for total school improvement.* Mansfield Center, CT: Creative Learning Press.

Renzulli, J. S., & Reis, S. M. (1985). *The school-wide enrichment model: A comprehensive plan for educational excellence.* Mansfield Center, CT: Creative Learning Press.

Repp, A. C. (1983). *Teaching the mentally retarded.* Upper Saddle River, NJ: Prentice Hall.

Repp, A. C., Felce, D., & Barton, L. E. (1991). The effects of initial interval size on the efficacy of DRO schedules of reinforcement. *Exceptional Children, 57,* 417-424.

Reynolds, K. E. (1978). Science space. *California Science Teachers Journal, 8*(4), 8-9.

Reynolds, M. C., Wang, M. C., & Walberg, H. J. (1987). The necessary restructuring of regular and special education. *Exceptional Children, 53,* 391-398.

Rice, M. L., Sell, M. A., & Hadley, P. A. (1990). The social interactive coding system (SICS): An on-line clinically relevant descriptive tool. *Language, Speech, and Hearing Services in Schools, 21,* 2-14.

Richard, G. J., & Hanner, M. A. (1985). *Language Processing Test.* East Moline, IL: LinguiSystem.

Richardson, J., Harris, A., & Sparks, O. (1979). *Life science.* Morristown, NJ: Silver Burdett.

Rights, M. (1981). *Beastly neighbors: All about wild things in the city, or why earwigs make good mothers.* Boston: Little, Brown.

Rincover, A., & Koegel, R. L. (1977). Classroom treatment of autistic children: II. Individualized instruction in a group. *Journal of Abnormal Child Psychology, 5,* 113-126.

Robinson, S. M., Braxdale, C. T., & Colson, S. E. (1985). Preparing dysfunctional learners to enter junior high school: A transition curriculum. *Focus on Exceptional Children, 18*(4), 1-10.

Roe, B. D., Stoodt, B. D., & Burns, P. C. (1995). *Secondary school reading instruction: The content areas* (5th ed.). Boston: Houghton Mifflin.

Roff, J. E. (1972). The academic and social competence of school children vulnerable to schizophrenia and other behavior pathologies. *Journal of Abnormal Psychology, 80,* 225-243.

Rojewski, J. W., Pollard, R. R., & Meers, G. D. (1990). Grading mainstreamed special needs students: Determining practices and attitudes of secondary vocational educators using a qualitative approach. *Remedial and Special Education, 12*(1), 7-28.

Rooney, K. (1988). *Learning strategies.* Richmond, VA: Learning Resource Center.

Rooney, K. (1989). *Independent strategies for effective study.* Richmond, VA: Educational Enterprises.

Rooney, K., Polloway, E. A., & Hallahan, D. P. (1985). The use of self-monitoring procedures with low-IQ learning disabled students. *Journal of Learning Disabilities, 18,* 384-390.

Rose, T. L. (1988). Current disciplinary practices with handicapped students: Suspensions and expulsions. *Exceptional Children, 55,* 230-239.

Rose, T. L. (1989). Corporal punishment with mildly handicapped students: Five years later. *Remedial and Special Education, 10*(4), 43-51.

Rosenberg, M. S. (1989). The effects of daily homework assignments on the acquisition of basic skills by students with learning disabilities. *Journal of Learning Disabilities, 22,* 314-323.

Rosenshine, B., & Stevens, R. (1986). Teaching functions. In M. C. Wittrock (Ed.), *Handbook of research on teaching* (3rd ed., pp. 376-391). Upper Saddle River, NJ: Merrill/Prentice Hall.

Rossman, M. (1985). Why kids fail to learn science and what to do about it. *Learning, 12,* 77-80.

Roy, P. A. (1990). *Cooperative learning: Students learn together.* Richfield, MN: Patricia Roy.

Rubin, D. L. (1994). Divergence and convergence between oral and written communication. In K. G. Butler (Ed.), *Best practices I: The classroom as an assessment arena* (pp. 56-73). Gaithersburg, MD: Aspen Publications.

Rucker, G. & Dilley, C. (1981). *Heath mathematics.* Lexington, MA: Allyn & Bacon.

Rucker, W. E., Dilley, C., & Lowry, D. W. (1987). *Heath mathematics: Teacher's edition.* Lexington, MA: D. C. Heath.

Ruder, K., Bunce, B., & Ruder, C. (1984). Language intervention in a preschool classroom setting. In L. McCormick & R. Schiefelbusch (Eds.), *Early language intervention* (pp. 267-298). Upper Saddle, NJ: Merrill/Prentice Hall.

Ruedy, L. R. (1983). Handwriting instruction: It can be part of the high school curriculum. *Academic Therapy, 18,* 421-429.

Ruef, M. B., Higgins, C., Glaeser, B.J.C., & Patrode, M. (1998). Positive behavioral support: Strategies for teachers. *Intervention in School and Clinic, 34,* 21-32.

Runge, A., Walker, J., & Shea, T. (1975). A passport to positive parent-teacher communications. *Teaching Exceptional Children, 7*(3), 91-92.

Salend, S. J. (1990). *Effective mainstreaming.* Upper Saddle River, NJ: Merrill/Prentice Hall.

Salend, S. (1994). *Effective mainstreaming: Creating inclusive classrooms* (2nd ed.). Upper Saddle River, NJ: Merrill/Prentice Hall.

Salend, J. S. (1998). *Effective mainstreaming: Creating inclusive classrooms* (3rd ed.). Upper Saddle River, NJ: Merrill/Prentice Hall.

Salend, S. J., Esquirel, L., & Pine, P. B. (1984). Regular and special education teachers' estimates of use of aversive consequences. *Behavioral Disorders, 9,* 89-94.

Salend, S. J., & Schliff, J. (1989). An examination of the homework practices of teachers of students with learning disabilities. *Journal of Learning Disabilities, 22,* 621-623.

Salend, S. J., & Viglianti, D. (1982). Preparing secondary students for the mainstream. *Teaching Exceptional Children, 14*(4), 137-140.

Salvia, J., & Hughes, C. (1990). *Curriculum-based assessment: Testing what is taught.* Upper Saddle River, NJ: Merrill/Prentice Hall.

Sakvuam H, & Ysseldyke, J. E. (1998). *Assessment in special and remedial education.* Boston: Houghton Mifflin.

Samuels, S. J. (1979). The method of repeated readings. *The Reading Teacher, 32,* 403-408.

Sanger, D., Maag, J. W., & Shapera, N. R. (1994). Language problems among students with emotional and behavioral disorders. *Intervention in School and Clinic, 30,* 103-105.

Sargent, L. R. (1991). *Social skills for school and community: Systematic instruction for children and youth with cognitive delays.* Reston, VA: Division on Mental Retardation and Developmental Disabilities, Council for Exceptional Children.

Sasaki J., & Serna, L. A. (1995). FAST science: Teaching science to adolescents with mild disabilities. *Teaching Exceptional Children, 27*(4), 14-16.

Saul, W., & Newman, A. R. (1986). *Science fare: An illustrated guide and catalog of toys, books, and activities for kids.* New York: Harper & Row.

Savage, J. F., & Mooney, J. F. (1979). *Teaching reading to children with special needs.* Boston: Allyn & Bacon.

Savage, T. V., & Armstrong, D. G. (1996). *Effective teaching in elementary social studies* (3rd ed.). Upper Saddle River, NJ: Merrill/Prentice Hall.

Saver, K., & Downes, B. (1991). PIT crew: A model for teacher collaboration in an elementary school. *Intervention, 27,* 116-122.

Scarmadalia, M., & Bereiter, C. (1986). Research on written composition. In M. C. Wittrock (Ed.), *Handbook of research on teaching* (3rd ed., pp. 778-803). Upper Saddle River, NJ: Merrill/Prentice Hall.

Schewel, R. H. (1989). Semantic mapping: A study skills strategy. *Academic Therapy, 24,* 439-447.

Schewel, R. H., & Waddell, J. G. (1986). Metacognitive skills: Practical strategies. *Academic Therapy, 22,* 19-25.

Schilit, J., & Caldwell, M. L. (1980). A word list of essential career/vocational words for mentally retarded students. *Education and Training of the Mentally Retarded, 15,* 113-117.

Schloss, P., Alper, S., & Jayne, D. (1994). Self-determination for persons with disabilities: Choice, risk, and dignity. *Exceptional Children, 60,* 215-225.

Schminke, C., & Dumas, E. (1981). *Math activities for child involvement.* Boston: Allyn & Bacon.

Schneider, D. O., & Brown, M. J. (1980). Helping students study and comprehend their social studies textbooks. *Social Education, 44,* 105-112.

Schniedewind, N., & Salend, S. (1987). Cooperative learning works. *Teaching Exceptional Children, 19,* 22-25.

Schoeller, K. (1995, Summer). Coordinating success: PACER's Project Youth. *What's working: Transition in Minnesota* Minneapolis MN: State of Minnesota.

Schoenbrodt, L., Kumin, L., & Sloan, J.M. (1997). Learning disabilities existing concomitantly with communication disorders. *Journal of Learning Disabilities, 30,* 261-281.

Schubert, W. H. (1993). Curriculum reform. In G. Cawelti (Ed.), *ASCD 1993 yearbook: Challenges and achievements of American education* (pp. 80-115). Alexandria, VA: Association for Supervision and Curriculum Development.

Schulz, E. (1994, October 5). Beyond behaviorism. *Education Week, 14*(5), 19-21, 24.

Schulz, J. B., Carpenter, C. D., & Turnbull, A. P. (1991). *Mainstreaming exceptional students: A guide for classroom teachers* (3rd ed.). Boston: Allyn & Bacon.

Schumaker, J. B., Deshler, D. D., Alley, G. R., & Denton P. H. (1982). Multipass: A learning strategy for improving comprehension. *Learning Disability Quarterly, 5,* 295-304.

Schumaker, J. B., Deshler, D. D., & Denton, P. (1984). *The learning strategies curriculum: The paraphrasing strategy.* Lawrence, KS: University of Kansas.

Schumaker, J. B., Deshler, D. D., Nolan, S., Clark, F. L., Alley, G. R., & Warner, M. M. (1981). *Error monitoring: A learning strategy for improving academic performance of LD adolescents* (Research Report No. 32). Lawrence: University of Kansas, Institute for Research on Learning Disabilities.

Schumaker, J. B., & Hazel, J. S. (1984). Social skill assessment and training for the learning disabled: Who's on first and what's on second? Part I. *Journal of Learning Disabilities, 17,* 422-430.

Schumaker, J. B., Hazel, J. S., & Pederson, C. S. (1989). *Social skills for daily living.* Circle Pines, MN: American Guidance Service.

Schumaker, J. B., Hazel, J. S., Sherman, J. A., & Sheldon-Wildgen, J. B. (1982). Social skill performances of learning disabled, non-learning disabled, and delinquent adolescents. *Learning Disability Quarterly, 5,* 358-397.

Schumaker, J. B., Pederson, C. S., Hazel, J. S., & Meyen, E. L. (1983). Social skills curricula for mildly handicapped adolescents: A review. *Focus on Exceptional Children, 4,* 1-16.

Schumm, J. S., & Magnum, C. T. (1991). FLIP: A framework for textbook thinking. *Journal of Reading, 35,* 120-124.

Schumm, J. S., & Strickler, K. (1991). Guidelines for adapting content area textbooks: Keeping teachers and students content. *Intervention, 27,* 79-84.

Scott, S. S. (1991). College writing labs: Are they meeting the needs of students with LD? *Intervention, 26,* 170-174.

Scruggs, T. E., & Mastropieri, M. A. (1989). Reconstructive elaborations: A model for content area learning. *American Educational Research Journal, 26,* 311-327.

Scruggs, T. E., & Mastropieri, M. A. (1993). Current approaches to science education: Implications for mainstream instruction to students with disabilities. *Remedial and Special Education, 14,* 15-24.

Scruggs, T. E., & Mastropieri, M. A., Bakken, J. P., & Brigham, F. J. (1993). Reading vs. doing: The relative effectiveness of textbook-based and inquiry-oriented approaches to science education. *Journal of Special Education, 27,* 1-15.

Scruggs, T. E., Mastropieri, M. A., & Wolfe, S. (1994–1995). Scientific reasoning of students with mild retardation: Investigating preconceptions and conceptional changes. *Exceptionality, 5,* 223-244.

Searcy, S., & Maroney, S. A. (1996). Lesson planning practices of special education teachers. *Exceptionality, 6,* 175-185.

Sedlak, R. A., & Fitzmaurice, A. M. (1981). Teaching arithmetic. In J. M. Kauffman & D. P. Hallahan (Eds.), *Handbook of special education* (pp. 475-490). Upper Saddle River, NJ: Prentice Hall.

Semel, E. M., Wiig, E. H., & Secord, W. (1987). *Clinical evaluation of language fundamentals—revised.* San Antonio, TX: The Psychological Corporation.

Sendak, M. (1962). *Chicken soup with rice.* New York: Harper & Row.

Serna, L. A., & Lau-Smith, J. A. (1994-1995). *Learning with PURPOSE: Instruction manuals for teaching self-determination skills to students who are at risk for failure.* Unpublished manuals, Honolulu: University of Hawaii.

Serna, L. A., Forness, S. R., & Nielsen, M. E. (1998). Intervention versus affirmation: Proposed solutions to the problem of disproportionate minority representation in special education. *Journal of Special Education, 32,* 48-51.

Serna, L. A., & Lau-Smith, J. A. (1995). Learning with PURPOSE: Self-determination skills for students who are at risk for school and community failure. *Intervention in School and Clinic, 30*(3), 142-146.

Serna, L. A., Nielsen, M. E., & Forness, S. R. (1997). Systematic early detection and self-determination approach for mental health intervention Head Start. Grant funded by Department of Health and Administration for Children and Families. *CDFA:* 93.600.

Serna, L. A., Nielsen, M. E., Lambros, K., & Forness, S. R. (in press). The use of self-determination curriculum to impact the behavior of young children with behavior problems. *Behavior Disorders.*

Shames, G. J., Wiig, E., & Secord, W. A. (1998). *Human communication disorders: An introduction* (5th ed.). Boston: Allyn & Bacon.

Shannon, T., & Polloway, E. A. (1993). Promoting error monitoring in middle school students with learning disabilities. *Intervention in School and Clinic, 28,* 160-164.

Shaywitz, S., & Shaywitz, B. (1997). *The science of reading: Implications for children and adults with learning disabilities.* 13th Annual Learning Disorders Conference, Harvard Graduate School of Education.

Shea, T. M., & Bauer, A. M. (1987). *Teaching children and youth with behavior disorders.* Upper Saddle River, NJ: Prentice Hall.

Shepherd, G. D., & Ragan, W. B. (1982). *Modern elementary curriculum* (6th ed.). New York: Holt, Rinehart & Winston.

Sherwin, J. S. (1964). *Four problems in teaching English: A critique of research.* Scranton, PA: International Textbook.

Shields, J. D., Green, R., Cooper, B. A. B., & Ditton, P. (1995). The impact of adults, communication clarity versus communication deviance on adolescents with learning disabilities. *Journal of Learning Disabilities, 28,* 372-384.

Shore, K. (1986). *The special education handbook.* New York: Teachers College Press.

Shulman, B. (1986). *Test of pragmatic skills—Revised.* Tucson, AZ: Communication Skill Builders.

Shymansky, J. A. (1989). About ESS, SCIS, and SAPA. *Science and Children,* 33-35.

Sideridis, G. D., & Chandler, J. P. (1996). Comparison of attitudes of teachers of physical and musical education toward inclusion of children with disabilities. *Psychological Reports, 78,* 768-771.

Silbert, J., Carnine, D., & Stein, M. (1990). *Direct instruction mathematics* (2nd ed.). Upper Saddle River, NJ: Merrill/Prentice Hall.

Silvaroli, N. J. (1990). *Classroom Reading Inventory.* Dubuque, IA: Wm. C. Brown.

Simmons, D. C., Gunn, B., Smith, S. B., & Kameenui, E. J. (1994). Phonological awareness: Applications of instructional design. *LD Forum, 19*(2), 7-10.

Simmons, D. C., & Kameenui, E. J. (1996). A focus on curriculum design: When children fail. *Focus on Exceptional Children, 28* (7), 1-16.

Simon, C. S. (1979). *Communicative competence: A functional-pragmatic approach to language therapy.* Tempe, AZ: Communi-Cog Publications.

Simon, C. S. (1985a). Functional flexibility: Developing communicative competence in speaker and listener roles. In C. S. Simon (Ed.), *Communication skills and classroom success* (pp. 135-178). San Diego, CA: College-Hill Press.

Simon, C. S. (1985b). The language-learning disabled student: Description and therapy implications. In C. S. Simon (Ed.), *Communication skills and classroom success* (pp. 1-56). San Diego, CA: College-Hill Press.

Simon, C. S. (1987a). *Classroom communication screening procedures for early adolescents.* Tempe, AZ: Communi-Cog Publications.

Simon, C. S. (1987b). Out of the broom closet and into the classroom: The emerging SLP. *Journal of Childhood Communication Disorders, 11,* 41-66.

Simpson, R. (1998). Behavior modification for children and adolescents with exceptionalities. *Intervention in School and Clinic, 33,* 219-226.

Sindelar, P. T., Smith, M. A., Harriman, N. E., Hall, R. L., & Wilson, R. J. (1986). Teacher effectiveness in special education programs. *Journal of Special Education, 20,* 195-207.

Sink, D. M. (1975). Teach-write/Write-teach. *Elementary English, 52,* 175-177.

Skiba, R., & Raison, J. (1990). Relationship between the use of timeout and academic achievement. *Exceptional Children, 57,* 36-45.

Skinner, B. F. (1971). *Beyond freedom and dignity.* New York: Knopf.

Slavin, R. E. (1980). Cooperative learning. *Review of Educational Research, 50,* 315-342.

Slavin, R. E. (1983). *Cooperative learning.* New York: Longman.

Slavin, R. E. (1987). Cooperative learning and individualized instruction. *Arithmetic Teacher, 35,* 14-16.

Slavin, R. E., (1987). *What research says to the teacher on cooperative learning: Student teams* (2nd ed.). Washington, DC: National Education Association

Slavin, R. E. (1989). Student team learning in mathematics. In N. Davidson (Ed.), *Cooperative learning in mathematics: A handbook for teachers* (pp. 69-102). Menlo Park, CA: Addison-Wesley.

Slavin, R. E., Madden, N. A., & Leavey, M. (1984). Effects of cooperative learning and individualized instruction on mainstreamed students. *Exceptional Children, 50,* 434-443.

Slingerland, B. H. (1962). *Screening tests for identifying children with specific language disability.* Cambridge, MA: Educators Publishing Services.

Slosson, R. L. (1983). *Slosson Intelligence Test for Children and Adults.* East Aurora, NY: Slosson Educational Publications.

Smith, C. L. (1986). *Classroom survival skills: Requisites to mainstreaming.* Unpublished master's thesis, University of Hawaii at Manoa, Honolulu, HI.

Smith, F. (1979). *Reading without nonsense.* New York: Teachers College Press.

Smith, F. (1988). *Understanding reading: A psycholinguistic analysis of reading and learning to read* (4th ed.) New York: Holt, Rinehart, & Winston.

Smith, G. J., Edelen-Smith, P. J., & Stodden, R. A. (1995). How to avoid the seven pitfalls of systematic planning: A school and community plan for transition. *Teaching Exceptional Children, 27,* 42-47.

Smith, J. D., Polloway, E. A., & West, K. G. (1979). Corporal punishment and its implications for exceptional children. *Exceptional Children, 45,* 264-268.

Smith, J. E., & Payne, J. S. (1980). *Teaching exceptional adolescents.* Upper Saddle River, NJ: Merrill/Prentice Hall.

Smith, L. J., & Smith, D. L. (1990). *Social studies: Detecting and correcting special needs.* Boston: Allyn & Bacon.

Smith, S. W. (1990a). Comparison of IEPs of students with behavioral disorders and learning disabilities. *Journal of Special Education, 24,* 85-99.

Smith, S. W. (1990b). Individualized education programs (IEPs) in special education: From intent to acquiescence. *Exceptional Children, 57,* 6-14.

Smith, T. E. C., Polloway, E. A., & Beirne-Smith, M. (1995). *Written language instruction for students with disabilities.* Denver: Love.

Smith, T. E. C., Polloway, E. A., Patton, J. R., & Dowdy, C. A. (1999). *Teaching students with special needs in inclusive settings.* (2nd ed.) Boston: Allyn & Bacon.

Smith, T. E. C., Price, B. J., & Marsh, G. E. (1986). *Mildly handicapped children and adults.* St. Paul, MN: West.

Smith, W. D. (1978). Minimal competencies: A position paper. *The Arithmetic Teacher, 26*(3), 25-26.

Smull, M. W. (1994). Moving toward a system of support. *AAMR News & Notes, 7*(5), 3-5.

Snow, C., Midkiff-Borunda, S., Small, A., & Proctor, A. (1984). Therapy as social interaction: Analyzing the contexts for language remediation. *Topics in Language Disorders, 7*(2), 32-44.

Soderlund, J., Bursuck, B., Polloway, E. A., & Foley, R. A. (1995). A comparison of the homework problems of secondary school students with behavior disorders and nondisabled peers. *Journal of Emotional and Behavioral Disorders, 3,* 150-155.

Sosniak, L. A., & Ethington, C. A. (1994). When teaching problem solving proceeds successfully in U.S. eighth-grade classrooms. In I. Westbury, C. A. Ethington, L. A. Sosniak, & D. P. Baker (Eds.), *In search of more effective mathematics education* (pp. 33-60). Norwood, NJ: Ablex.

Sparrow, S. S., Balla, D. A., & Cicchetti, D. V. (1984). *Vineland Adaptive Behavior Scales.* Circle Pines, MN: American Guidance Service.

Speech Communication Association (1996). *Speaking, listening, and medial literacy standards for K through 12 education.* Annandale, VA: Clark Publishing.

Spekman, J. J. (1981). Dyadic verbal communication abilities of learning disabled and normally achieving fourth- and fifth-grade boys. *Learning Disability Quarterly, 4,* 139-151.

Spencer, I. (1992). *Recent approaches to art instruction in special education: A review of the literature.* (ERIC Document Reproduction Service No. 349 724)

Spivack, G., & Shure, M. B. (1974). *Social adjustment of young children: A cognitive approach to solving real-life problems.* San Francisco: Jossey-Bass.

Spivack, G., Spotts, J., & Haines, P. (1966). *Devereux adolescent behavior rating scale.* Devon, PA: Devereux Foundation.

Squires, D. A., Huitt, W. G., & Segars, J. K. (1983). *Effective schools and classrooms: A research-based perspective.* Alexandria, VA: Association for Supervision and Curriculum Development.

Staats, A. W. (1971). *Child learning, intelligence, and personality.* New York: Harper & Row.

Staats, A. W. (1975). *Social behaviorism.* Homewood, IL: Dorsey Press.

Stainback, W. C., Payne, J. S., Stainback, S. B., & Payne, R. A. (1973). *Establishing a token economy in the classroom.* Upper Saddle River, NJ: Merrill/Prentice Hall.

Stebbins, L. B., St. Pierre, R. G., Proper, E. C., Anderson, R. B., & Cerva, T. R. (1977). *Education as experimentation: A planned variation model* (vol. 4A). Cambridge, MA: Abt Associates.

Steinbrink, J. E., & Jones, R. M. (1991). Focused test review items: Improving textbook-test alignment in social studies. *The Social Studies, 82,* 72-76.

Stephens, T. M. (1970). *Directive teaching of children with learning and behavioral problems.* Upper Saddle River, NJ: Merrill/Prentice Hall.

Sternberg, L., & Sedlak, R. (1978). Mathematical programming for problem adolescents. In D. Sabatino & A. Mauser (Eds.), *Intervention strategies for specialized secondary education.* Boston: Allyn & Bacon.

Stevens, D. D., & Englert, C. S. (1993). Making writing strategies work. *Teaching Exceptional Children, 26*(1), 34-39.

Stevens, R., & Rosenshine, B. (1981). Advances in research on teaching. *Exceptional Education Quarterly, 2*(1), 1-9.

Stodden, R. A. (1998). School-to-work transition: Overview of disability legislation. In F. R. Rusch & J. G. Chadsey (Eds.), *Beyond high school: Transition from school to work.* Belmont, CA: Wadsworth.

Stokes, T. F., & Baer, D. M., (1977). An implicit technology of generalization. *Journal of Applied Behavior Analysis, 10,* 349-367.

Stone, C. A. (1998). The metaphor of scaffolding: Its utility for the field of learning disabilities. *Journal of Learning Disabilities, 31,* 344-364.

Strong, W. (1973). *Sentence combining: A composing book.* New York: Random House.

Strong, W. (1983). *Sentence combining: A composing book* (2nd ed.). New York: Random House.

Strichart, S. S., Iannuzzi, P., & Mangrum, C. (1998). *Teaching study skills and strategies to students with learning disabilities, attention deficit disorders, or special needs.* Upper Saddle River NJ: Prentice Hall.

Sund, R., Tillery, B., & Trowbridge, L. (1970). *Elementary science discovery lessons: The earth sciences.* Boston: Allyn & Bacon.

Swanson, P. N., & de la Paz, S. (1998). Teaching effective comprehension strategies to students with learning and reading disabilities. *Intervention in School and Clinic, 33,* 209-218.

Swicegood, P. (1994). Portfolio-based assessment practices. *Intervention in School and Clinic, 30,* 6-16.

Talbott, E., Lloyd, J. W., & Tankersley, M. (1994). Effects of reading comprehension interventions for students with learning disabilities. *Learning Disability Quarterly, 17,* 223-232.

Tamura, E. H., & Harstad, J. R. (1987). Freewriting in the social studies classroom. *Social Education, 51,* 256-259.

Taylor, F., Artuso, A. A., Hewett, F. M., Johnson, A., Kramer, G., & Clark, K. (1972). *Individualized reading instruction: Games and activities.* Denver, CO: Love.

Terwilliger, J. S. (1977). Assigning grades—Philosophical issues and practical recommendations. *Journal of Research and Development in Education, 10*(3), 21–39.

Teters, P., Gabel, D., & Geary, P. (1984). Elementary teachers, perspectives on improving science education. *Science and Children, 22*(3), 41–43.

Thistle, L. (1987). Make a story come alive: Dramatize. *Arts and Activities, 101*(5), 24–28.

Thomas, C. C., Englert, C. S., & Gregg, S. (1987). An analysis of errors and strategies in the expository writing of learning-disabled students. *Remedial and Special Education, 8*(1), 21–30.

Thomas, P. J., & Carmack, F. F. (1997). Speech: Language: The foundation of learning. In J. S. Choate (Ed.), *Successful inclusive teaching* (2nd ed.) (pp. 148–153). Boston: Allyn & Bacon.

Thompson, K. L., & Taymans, J. M. (1994). Development of a Reading Strategies Program: Bridging the gaps among decoding, literature, and thinking skills. *Intervention in School and Clinic, 30,* 17–27.

Thorkildsen, R., Fodor-Davis, J., & Morgan, D. (1989). Evaluation of a videodisc training program. *Journal of Special Education Technology, 10*(2), 86–97.

Thorne, M. T. (1978). Payment for reading: The use of the corrective reading scheme with junior maladjusted boys. *Remedial Education, 13*(2), 87–90.

Thorp, E. K. (1997). Increasing opportunities for partnership with culturally and linguistically diverse families. *Intervention in School and Clinic, 32,* 261–269.

Thousand, J., & Villa, R. (1990a). Sharing expertise and responsibilities through teaching teams. In W. Stainback & S. Stainback (Eds.), *Support networks for inclusive schooling: Interdependent integrated education* (pp. 151–166). Baltimore: Brookes.

Thousand, J. S., & Villa, R. A. (1990b). Strategies for educating learners with severe disabilities within their local home schools and communities. *Focus on Exceptional Children, 23*(3), 1–24.

Thousand, J. S., & Villa, R. A. (1991). A futuristic view of the REI: A response to Jenkins, Pious, and Jewell. *Exceptional Children, 57,* 556–562.

Thurber, D. N. (1987). *D'Nealian handwriting* (rev. ed.). Glenview, IL: Scott, Foresman.

Tikunoff, W. J. (1982). *An emerging description of successful bilingual instruction: An executive summary of Part I of SBIF descriptive study.* Washington, DC: National Institute of Education.

Tikunoff, W. J. (1987). Mediation of instruction to obtain equality of effectiveness. In S. H. Fradd & W. J. Tikunoff (Eds.), *Bilingual education and bilingual special education: A guide for administrators.* Austin, TX: Pro-Ed.

Tindal, G. A., & Marston, D. B. (1990). *Classroom-based assessment: Evaluating instructional outcomes.* Upper Saddle River, NJ: Merrill/Prentice Hall.

Tindall, S. K. (1985). *Adaptation of a basic math text for special learners.* Unpublished master's paper, University of Hawaii.

Torgeson, J., & Bryant, B. (1994). *Phonological awareness training for reading.* Austin, TX: Pro-Ed.

Torgesen, J. K. (1982). The learning-disabled child as an inactive learner: Educational implications. *Topics in Learning and Learning Disabilities, 2*(1), 45–51.

Treiman, R., Caesar, M., & Zukowski, A. (1994). What types of linguistic information do children use in spelling? The case of flaps. *Child Development, 65,* 1318–1337.

Truch, S. (1998). *Phonological processing, reading and the Lindamood Phoneme Sequencing Program: A review of related research.* Austin, TX: Pro-Ed.

Tucker, J. (1985). Curriculum-based assessment: An introduction. *Exceptional Children, 52,* 199–204.

Turla, P. A., & Hawkins, K. L. (1983). *Time management made easy.* New York: Dutton.

Turnbull, A. P., & Schulz, J. B. (1979). *Mainstreaming handicapped students: A guide for the classroom teacher.* Boston: Allyn & Bacon.

Turnbull, H. R., & Turnbull, A. P. (1998). *Free appropriate public education: The law and children with disabilties* (5th ed.). Denver: Love Publishing Company.

Turner, T. N. (1976). Making the social studies textbook a more effective tool for less able readers. *Social Education, 40,* 38–41.

Turner, T. N., & Oaks, T. (1997). Stories on the spot: Introducing students to impromptu storytelling. *Childhood Education, 73,* 154–157.

Tyler, J. S., & Mira, M. P. (1999). *Traumatic brain injury in children and adolescents: A sourcebook for teachers and other school personnel* (2nd ed.). Austin, TX: Pro-Ed.

United States Department of Education. (1986). *The reading report card.* Washington, DC: Author.

United States Department of Education. (1990). *Twelfth annual report to Congress on the imple-*

mentation of the Education for All Handicapped Children Act. Washington, DC: Author.

United States Department of Education. (1991). *New application for assistance under the research in education of Individuals with Disabilities Program.* Washington, DC: Author.

United States Department of Education. (1994). *Sixteenth annual report to Congress on the implementation of the Individuals with Disabilities Education Act.* Washington, DC: Author.

United States Department of Education. (1995). *Seventeenth annual report to Congress on the implementation of the Individuals with Disabilities Education Act.* Washington, DC: Author.

United States Department of Education. (1998). *Twentieth annual report to Congress on the implementation of the Individual with Disabilities Education Act.* Washington, DC: Author.

Vacc, N. (1987). Word processor versus handwriting: A comparative study of writing samples produced by mildly mentally handicapped students. *Exceptional Children, 54,* 156–165.

Valdes, K. A., Williamson, C. L., & Wagner, M. M. (1990). *The national longitudinal transition study of special education students* (vol. 1). Menlo Park, CA: SRI International.

Valeri, M., & McKelvey, J. (1985). *Wiggle your waggles away: A movement handbook for preschool teachers.* Hyattsville, MD: Krieg-Taylor Lithograph.

Vallecorsa, A. L., & deBettencourt, L. U. (1992). Teaching composition skills to learning-disabled adolescents using a process-oriented strategy. *Journal of Developmental and Physical Disabilities, 4,* 277–296.

Vasa, S. F., Steckelberg, A. L., & Sundermeier, C.A. (1989). *Supervision strategies for special educators in working with instructional professionals.* (ERIC Document Reproduction Service No. 312 830).

Vaughn, S., Moody, S. W., & Schumm, J. S., (1998). Broken promises: Reading instruction in the resource room. *Exceptional Children, 64,* 211–225.

Vergason, G. A. (1983). Curriculum content. In E. L. Meyen, G. A. Vergason, & R. J. Whelan (Eds.), *Promising practices for exceptional children: Curriculum implications.* Denver, CO: Love.

Viadero, D. Who's minding the books? (1995, March). *Teacher Magazine, 19.*

Villa, R. A., Thousand, J. S., Nevin, A. I., & Malgeri, C. (1996) Instilling collaboration for inclusive schooling as a way of doing business in public schools. *Remedial and Special Education, 17*(3), 169–181.

Vinograd-Bausell, C. R., Bausell, R. B., Proctor, W., & Chandler, B. (1986). Impact of unsupervised parent tutors on word recognition skills. *Journal of Special Education, 20,* 83–90.

Voltz, D. L. (1998). Associate editor's exchange: Cultural diversity and special education teacher preparation: Critical issues confronting the field. *Teacher Education and Special Education, 21,* 63–70.

Vygotsky, L. S. (1962). *Thought and language.* Cambridge, MA: MIT Press.

Wagener, E. H. (1977). Drama: Key to history for the visually impaired child. *Education of the Visually Handicapped, 9,* 45–47.

Wagner, M., Blackorby, J., Cameto, R., Hebbeler, K., & Newman, L. (1993). *The transition experiences of young people with disabilities: A summary of findings from the National Longitudinal Transition Study of special education students.* Menlo Park, CA: SRI International.

Wagner, M., Newman, L., D'Amico, R., Jay, E. D., Butler-Nalin, P., Marder, C., & Cox, R. (1991). *Youth with disabilities: How are they doing?* The first comprehensive report from the National Longitudinal Transition Study of special education students. Menlo Park, CA: SRI International.

Walberg, H. J. (1986). What works in a nation still at risk. *Educational Leadership, 44(1),* 7–10.

Walker, H. M. (1983). Applications of response cost in school settings: Outcomes, issues, and recommendations. *Exceptional Education Quarterly, 3*(4), 47–55.

Walker, H. M., McConnell, S., Holmes, D., Todis, B., Walker, J., & Golden, N. (1983). *The Walker social skills curriculum: The ACCEPTS program.* Austin, TX: Pro-Ed.

Walker, J. E., & Shea, T. M. (1988). *Behavior management: A practical approach for educators* (4th ed.). Upper Saddle River, NJ: Merrill/Prentice Hall.

Wallace, G., Cohen, S. B., & Polloway, E. A. (1987). *Language arts: Teaching exceptional students.* Austin, TX: Pro-Ed.

Wallace, G., & Hammill, D. D. (1994). *Comprehensive receptive and Expressive vocabulary test.* Austin, TX: Pro-Ed.

Wallace, G., & Kauffman, J. M. (1986). *Teaching children with learning and behavior problems* (2nd ed.). Upper Saddle River, NJ: Merrill/Prentice Hall.

Wallace, G., Larsen, S. C., & Elksnin, L. (1992). *Educational assessment of learning problems: Testing for teaching.* Boston: Allyn & Bacon.

Wallace, G., & McLoughlin, J. A. (1988). *Learning disabilities: Concepts and characteristics* (3rd ed.). Upper Saddle River, NJ: Merrill/Prentice Hall.

Wallach, G. (1994). Magic buries Celtics: Looking for broader interpretations of language learning and literacy. In K. G. Butler (Ed.), *Best practices II: The classroom as an intervention context* (pp. 137-154). Gaithersburg, MD: Aspen.

Wallach, G. P., & Miller, L. (1988). *Language intervention and academic success.* Boston: College Hill/Little, Brown.

Walsh, B. F., & Lamberts, F. (1979). Errorless discrimination and picture fading as techniques for teaching sight words to TMR students. *American Journal of Mental Deficiency, 83,* 473-479.

Wang, M. C., Reynolds, M. C., & Walberg, H. J. (1986). Rethinking special education. *Educational Leadership, 44*(1), 26-32.

Ward, M. J. (1988). The many facets of self-determination. *National Information Center for Children and Youth with Handicaps: Transition Summary, 5,* 2-3.

Watson, D. L. Tharp, R. G. (1993). *Self-directed behavior: Self-modification for personal adjustment.* Pacific Grove, CA; Books/Cole.

Watterman, B. B. (1994). Assessing children for the presence of disability. *NICHY News Digest, 4,* 277-296.

Webber, J., & Scheuerman, B. (1991). Managing problem behavior: Accentuate the positive—eliminate the negative. *Teaching Exceptional Children, 24,* 13-19.

Wehman, P. (1995). *Individual transition plans: The teacher's curriculum guide for helping youth with special needs.* Austin, TX: Pro-Ed.

Wehman, P., Renzaglia, A., & Bates, P. (1985). *Functional living skills for moderately and severely handicapped individuals.* Austin, TX: Pro-Ed.

Wehmeyer, M. (1992). Self-determination as an educational outcome. *Impact, 6*(4), 16-17, 26.

Wehmeyer, M. L. (1995). A career education approach: Self-determination for youth with mild cognitive disabilities. *Intervention in School and Clinic, 30*(3), 157-163.

Wehmeyer, M.L., Morningstar, M., & Husted, D. (1999). Family involvement in transition planning and implementation. (Pro-Ed Series on Transition). Austin, TX: Pro-Ed.

Weinstein, R. S., & Mayer, B. (1986). Learning strategies. In M. C. Wittrock (Ed.), *Handbook of research in teaching* (3rd ed.). Upper Saddle River, NJ: Merrill/Prentice Hall.

Weintraub, N., & Graham, S. (1998). Writing legibly and quickly: A study of children's ability to adjust their handwriting to meet common classroom demands. *Learning Disabilities Research and Practice, 13,* 146-152.

Weisenfeld, R. B. (1986). The IEPs of Down syndrome children: A content analysis. *Education and Training of the Mentally Retarded. 21,* 211-219.

Weitzman, D. (1975). *My backyard history book.* Boston: Little, Brown.

Welch, M., & Jensen, J. B. (1990). Write, P.L.E.A.S.E.: A video-assisted strategic intervention to improve written expression of inefficient learners. *Remedial and Special Education, 12*(1), 37-47.

Welch, M., & Link, D. P. (1991). The instructional priority system: A method for assessing the educational environment. *Intervention, 27,* 91-96.

Wells, C. (1996). *Literacies lost: When students move from progressive middle school to a traditional high school.* New York: Teachers College Press.

Wepman, J. M. (1973). *Auditory Discrimination Test.* Palm Springs, CA: Language Research Associates.

Wesson, C., King, R., & Deno, S. (1984). Facilitating the efficiency of ongoing curriculum-based measurement. *Teacher Education and Special Education, 9,* 166-172.

Wesson, C., Otis-Wilborn, A., Hasbrouck, J., & Tindal, G. (1989). Linking assessment, curriculum, and instruction of oral and written language. *Focus on Exceptional Children, 22,* 1-12.

West, G. K. (1986). *Parenting without guilt.* Springfield, IL: Charles C. Thomas.

West, G. K. (1994, November 10). Discipline that works: Part one. *The News and Daily Advance* (pp. 13-14).

West, G. K., & Polloway, E. A., (1996). Murphy's laws of higher education. *Psycholllogical Bulletin, 4,* 17-18.

West, J. F., Idol, L., & Cannon, G. (1989). *Collaboration in the schools: An inservice or preservice curriculum for teachers, support staff, and administrators.* Austin, TX: Pro-Ed.

Westby, C. E., & Costlow, L. (1994). Implementing whole language in a special education class. In K. G. Butler (Ed.), *Best practices II: The classroom as an intervention context* (pp. 39-54). Gaithersburg, MD: Aspen Press.

Westling, D. L., Ferrell, K., & Swenson, K. (1982). Intra-classroom comparison of two arrangements for teaching profoundly mentally retarded children. *American Journal of Mental Deficiency, 86,* 601-608.

Wheeler, J. J. (1998). Reducing challenging behaviors in learners with developmental disabilities through the modification of instructional practices. In A. Hilton & R. Ringlaben (Eds.), *Best and promising practices in developmental disabilities.* (pp. 263–272). Austin, TX: Pro-Ed.

Wiebe, J. H. (1993). The software domain. In J. D. Lindsey (Ed.), *Computers and exceptional individuals* (2nd ed., pp. 45–64). Austin, TX: Pro-Ed.

Wiederholt, J. L., & Bryant, B. (1986). *Gray Oral Reading Test—Revised.* Austin, TX: Pro-Ed.

Wiederholt, J. L., Hammill, D. D., & Brown, V. L. (1983). *The resource teacher: A guide to effective practices* (2nd ed.). Austin, TX: Pro-Ed.

Wiederholt, J. L., Hammill, D. D., & Brown, V. L. (1993). *The resource program: Organization and implementation.* Austin, TX: Pro-Ed.

Wiederholt, J. L., & McNutt, G. (1979). Assessment and instructional planning: A conceptual framework. In D. Cullinan & M. H. Epstein (Eds.), *Special education for adolescents: Issues and perspectives* (pp. 63–87). Upper Saddle River, NJ: Merrill/ Prentice Hall.

Wiedmeyer, D., & Lehman, J. (1991). House plan: Approach to collaborative teaching and consultation. *Teaching Exceptional Children, 23*(3), 6–10.

Wiener, H. (1981). *The writing room.* New York: Oxford University Press.

Wiig, E. H. (1982). *The "Let's Talk" Inventory for Adolescents.* Upper Saddle River, NJ: Merrill/ Prentice Hall.

Wiig, E. H., & Secord, W. (1992). *Test of word knowledge.* San Antonio, TX: The Psychological Corporation.

Wiig, E. H., & Semel, E. (1984). *Language assessment and intervention for the learning disabled* (2nd ed.). Upper Saddle River, NJ: Merrill/ Prentice Hall.

Wilkening, P. (1993). *Recreation and leisure time as part of the transition program for individuals with disabilities.* (Technical Assistance Packet #4). Gainesville, FL: University of Florida, Project Retain/Florida Network.

Will, M. (1984). *OSERS programming for the transition of youth with disabilities: Bridges from school to working life.* Washington, DC: Office of Special Education and Rehabilitative Services.

Will, M. (1986). Educating children with learning problems: A shared responsibility. *Exceptional Children, 52,* 411–415.

Williams, R. M., & Rooney, K. J. (1986). *A handbook of cognitive behavior modification procedures for teachers.* Charlottesville: University of Virginia Institute for Research on Learning Disabilities.

Willis, S. (1994, October). Making schools more inclusive: Teaching children with disabilities in regular classrooms. *ASCD Curriculum Update,* pp. 1–3.

Willis, S. (1995, May). Making integrated curriculum a reality. *Education Updated 37*(4), 4.

Wilson, C. R. (1983). Teaching reading comprehension by connecting the known to the new. *The Reading Teacher, 36,* 382–390.

Wilson, M. (1992). Measuring levels of mathematical understanding. In T. A. Romberg (Ed.), *Mathematics assessment and evaluation: Imperatives for mathematics education* (pp. 213–241). Albany, NY: State University of New York Press.

Winzer, M. A., & Mazurek, L. (1998). *Special education in multicultural contexts.* Upper Saddle River, NJ: Merrill/Prentice Hall.

Wisconsin Department of Public Instruction (1989). *Strategic learning in the content areas.* Madison, WI: Wisconsin Department of Public Instruction.

Wolery, M. (1989). Transitions in early childhood special education: Issues and procedures. *Focus on Exceptional Children, 22*(2), 1–16.

Wolpe, J. (1958). *Psychotherapy by reciprocal inhibition.* Palo Alto, CA: Stanford University Press.

Wong, B. Y. L. (1982). Understanding learning-disabled students' reading problems: Contributions from cognitive psychology. *Topics in Learning and Learning Disabilities, 1*(4), 43–50.

Wong, K. L. H., Kauffman, J. M., & Lloyd, J. W. (1991). Choices for integration: Selecting teachers for mainstreamed students with emotional or behavioral disorders. *Intervention, 27,* 108–115.

Wood, J. W (1992). *Adapting instruction for mainstreamed and at-risk students* (2nd ed.). Upper Saddle River, NJ: Merrill/Prentice Hall.

Wood, J. W. (1993). *Mainstreaming: A practical approach for teachers* (2nd ed.). Upper Saddle River, NJ: Merrill/Prentice Hall.

Wood, J. W., & Miederhoff, J. W. (1989). Bridging the gap. *Teaching Exceptional Children, 21*(2), 66–68.

Wood, R. W., Webster, L., Gullickson, A., & Walker, J. (1987). Comparing handwriting legibility with three teaching methods for sex and grade differences. *Reading Improvement, 24,* 24–30.

Woodcock, R. W. (1986). *Woodcock Reading Mastery Test: Revised.* Circle Pines, MN: American Guidance Service.

Woodcock, R. W. (1991). *Woodcock Language Proficiency Battery–Revised.* Chicago: Riverside Publishing.

Woodward, A., Elliott, D. L., & Nagel, K. C. (1986). Beyond textbooks in elementary social studies. *Social Education, 50,* 50-53.

Woodward, J., & Noell, J. (1992). Science instruction at the secondary level: Implications for students with learning disabilities. In D. Carnine & E. J. Kameenui (Eds.), *Higher-order thinking: Designing curriculum for mainstreamed students* (pp. 39-58). Austin, TX: Pro-Ed.

Workman, E. A., & Katz, A. M. (1995). *Teaching behavioral self-control to students.* Austin, TX: Pro-Ed.

Worrall, R. S. (1990). Detecting health fraud in the field of learning disabilities. *Journal of Learning Disabilities, 23,* 207-212.

Wulpe, W. W. (1968). A form constancy technique for spelling proficiency. In J. I. Arena (Ed.), *Building spelling skills in dyslexic children.* San Rafael, CA: Academic Therapy.

Yager, R. E. (1989). A rationale for using personal relevance as a science curriculum focus in schools. *School Science and Mathematics, 89,* 144-156.

York, J., Doyle, M. B., & Kronberg, R. (1992). A curriculum development process for inclusive classrooms. *Focus on Exceptional Children, 25*(4), 1-16.

Young, K. R., West, R. P., Li, L., & Peterson, L. (1997). Teaching self-management skills to students with learning and behavior problems. *Reclaiming Children and Youth, 6,* 90-96.

Ysseldyke, J. E., & Christenson, S. L. (1986). *The Instructional Environment Scale.* Austin, TX: Pro-Ed.

Ysseldyke, J. E., & Christenson, S. L. (1987). Evaluating students, instructional environments. *Remedial and Special Education, 8*(3), 17-24.

Zachman, L., Huisingh, R., Barrett, M., Orman, J., & Bragden, C. (1989). *The Word Test—Adolescent.* East Moline, IL: LinguiSystems.

Zentall, S. (1983). Learning environments: A review of physical and temporal factors. *Exceptional Education Quarterly, 4*(2), 90-109.

Zigmond, N. (1990). Rethinking secondary school programs for students with learning disabilities. *Focus on Exceptional Children, 23*(1), 1-12.

Zigmond, N., Levin, E., & Laurie, T. (1985). Managing the mainstream: An analysis for teacher attitudes and student performance in mainstream high school programs. *Journal of Learning Disabilities, 18,* 535-541.

Zigmond, N., & Miller, S. (1991). *Improving high school programs for students with learning disabilities: A matter of substance as well as form.* Unpublished manuscript, University of Pittsburgh.

Zigmond, N., & Sansone, J. (1986). Designing a program for the learning-disabled adolescent. *Remedial and Special Education, 7*(5), 13-17.

Zigmond, N., Vallecorsa, A., & Leinhardt, G. (1980). Reading instruction for students with learning disabilities. *Topics in Language Disorders, 1*(1), 89-98.

Zimmerman, B. J. (1986). Development of self-regulated learning: Which are the key subprocesses? *Contemporary Educational Psychology, 16,* 307-313.

Zurkowski, J. K., Kelly, P. S., & Griswold, D. E. (1998). Discipline and IDEA 1997: Instituting a new balance. *Intervention in School and Clinic, 34,* 3-9.

Author Index

Subject Index